Global Passages

Sources in World History

VOLUME I: TO 1500

Roger Schlesinger
Washington State University

Fritz Blackwell
Washington State University

Kathryn Meyer
Washington State University

Mary Watrous-Schlesinger
Washington State University

HOUGHTON MIFFLIN COMPANY   Boston   New York

In Memory of Donna (1937–2002)

Editor-in-Chief: Jean Woy
Senior Sponsoring Editor: Nancy Blaine
Development Editor: Julie Dunn
Senior Project Editor: Ylang Nguyen
Editorial Assistant: Wendy Thayer
Associate Production/Design Coordinator: Christine Gervais
Senior Marketing Manager: Sandra McGuire
Senior Manufacturing Coordinator: Marie Barnes

Photo Credits:
p. 153, top; p. 158, bottom; p. 160, top: Mary Watrous-Schlesinger.
p. 158, top; p. 160, bottom: Roger Schlesinger.

Printed in the U.S.A.
Library of Congress Catalog Card Number: 2001131550
ISBN: 0-618-06795-7
123456789-EB-06 05 04 03 02

Contents

Preface   *viii*

Part I: *Foundations of Civilization*   *1*

CHAPTER 1 Myths of Creation and Stories of Floods   *3*

Two Sources for Egyptian Creation Myths
Coffin Text Spell 1130 and
The Shabaka Stone   *5*

The Babylonian Flood Story
The Epic of Gilgamesh   *9*

The Hebrew Creation and Flood Stories
Genesis 1–2   *12*

The Hindu Hymn of Origins
The Rig Veda   *18*

Fragments from China
Ch'u Tz'u (Questions of Heaven), Huai-nan
Tzu (The Grand and Illustrious Explication of
Master Huai-nan, or the History of the Great
Light), San Wu li chi (Records of Cycles in
Threes and Fives), and Wu yun li-nien chi
(Chronicle of the Five Cycles of Time)   *19*

The Inca Flood Story
The Huarochirí Manuscript   *22*

Three Creation Stories from Africa
Oral Traditions from the Bambara,
the Wapangwa, and the Fang   *24*

An Aboriginal Tale from Australia
Yhi Brings Life to the World   *29*

A Cherokee Myth of Creation
UGVWIYUHI: How the World
Was Made   *31*

CHAPTER 2 Heroes and Heroines   *34*

The Birth and Boyhood of Sargon I
The Legend of Sargon of Akkad   *35*

Romulus and Remus Found the City of Rome
LIVY: History of Rome, Book I   *37*

*Boudicca Leads a Revolt of British Tribes
Against the Romans*
CASSIUS DIO: Roman History,
Book 62   *41*

The Shakti of Kannaki
ILANGO ADIGAL: Shilappadikaram
(The Jeweled Anklet)   *45*

The Hero Twins Devise the Harvest Ritual
Popol Vuh   *53*

*A Hawaiian Runner Defeats Death
and Pleases the King*
Legends of the South Seas   *60*

CHAPTER 3 Earliest Journeys   *65*

An Egyptian in Eastern Palestine
The Tale of Sinuhe   *65*

The Journeys of Abraham
Genesis 12:1–13:18   *72*

Jason and the Voyage of the Argo
APOLLONIUS RHODIUS:
The Argonautica   *75*

A Chou Emperor Travels Around the World
The Travels of Emperor Mu   *78*

Native American Myth of the Southwest
How the Pueblo People Came to
the Middle Place   *81*

Kwasi Benefo Travels to the Land of the Dead
Journey to Asamando   *86*

Part II: *Classical Civilizations,*
800 B.C.E.–800 C.E.   91

CHAPTER 4   Europe,
800 B.C.E.–800 C.E.   93

A Greek Statesman Praises Athens (430 B.C.E.)
THUCYDIDES: "The Funeral Oration of
Pericles," The Peloponnesian Wars   94

*A Roman Biographer Admires a Theban General
(c. 34 B.C.E.)*
CORNELIUS NEPOS: "The Life of
Epaminondas," On Famous Men   99

*A Roman Satirist Derides Greeks in Rome
(c. 112–116 C.E.)*
JUVENAL: Satire III   103

*A Greek Historian Extols the Virtues of
the Romans (second century B.C.E.)*
POLYBIUS: The Histories, Book VI   107

A Greek Poet Exalts Rome (second century B.C.E.)
MELINNO: Hymn to Rome   110

A Roman General Describes Britain (54 B.C.E.)
JULIUS CAESAR: The Gallic War,
Book V   111

*Chinese Travelers Describe the Roman
Empire (25–220 C.E.)*
FAN YEH: The Hou-han-shu   113

*A Roman Historian Examines the Tribes
of Germany (98 C.E.)*
TACITUS: Germania   116

*A Roman Historian Describes the Huns
(late fourth century)*
AMMIANUS MARCELLINUS: A History in
Thirty-One Books   121

CHAPTER 5   The Ancient Near East,
800 B.C.E.–800 C.E.   124

Two Views of Moab (mid-ninth century B.C.E.)
King Mesha of Moab Inscribes His
Accomplishments on the Moabite Stone
and The Hebrews Describe the Moabite War,
2 Kings 3:4–27   126

*An Assyrian King Boasts About His Achievements
(860–824 B.C.E.)*
The Monolith Inscription of
Shalmaneser III   129

*A Hebrew Prophet Celebrates the Fall of Nineveh
(seventh century B.C.E.)*
Nahum 2:12–3:17   135

*A Greek Historian Examines Persian Customs
(fifth century B.C.E.)*
HERODOTUS: The Histories, Book I   136

*A Greek Soldier Admires a Persian Prince
(late fifth century B.C.E.)*
XENOPHON: Anabasis, Book I   139

*A Han Ambassador Reports on Bactria
and Its Neighbors (138–126 B.C.E.)*
SSU-MA CH'IEN: Shi Chi, The Diplomatic
Report of Chang Ch'ien   143

*An Iberian Pilgrim Observes Christian Customs
in Jerusalem (fourth century C.E.)*
The Travels of Egeria   147

CHAPTER 6   The Americas,
800 B.C.E.–800 C.E.   151

*Olmec Priest In Serpent's Mouth (about 800 B.C.E.)
and Jaguar Toy (700 B.C.E.)*   152

*Chavín Pot (200 B.C.E.) and Chavín Zoomorphic
Heads (200 B.C.E.)*   154

*Quetzalcoatl Heads at Teotihuacan (500 C.E.)
and Quetzalcoatl Temple at Chichen Itza
(500 C.E.)*   157

*Jaguar Mural from Teotihuacan (before 800 C.E.)
and Two-Headed Jaguar Sculpture from Uxmal
(800 C.E.)*   159

CHAPTER 7   Africa,
800 B.C.E.–800 C.E.   161

*A Greek Historian Describes Egypt
(fifth century B.C.E.)*
HERODOTUS: The Histories, Book II   162

*A Kushite Writer Describes the Accession of
King Aspalta (593 B.C.E.)*
The Annals of Nubian Kings   166

Greek Interpretations of African Faces
(third century B.C.E.*)*
   Three Pieces of Jewelry from Greece   *170*

A Carthaginian Law Concerning Sacrifices
(fourth or fifth century B.C.E.*)*
   The Corpus Inscriptionum Semiticarum,
   Volume I, no. 165   *172*

A Greek Philosopher Discusses the Constitution
of Carthage (fourth century B.C.E.*)*
   ARISTOTLE: Politics, Book II   *174*

Two European Views of Africans
   Greek Kantharos (Athens, sixth century
   B.C.E.) and Roman Rhyton (Apuleia,
   fourth century B.C.E.)   *177*

A Roman Intellectual Describes Africa
(first century C.E.*)*
   PLINY THE ELDER: Natural History,
   Book V   *178*

Three Inscriptions from Aksum Relate the Deeds
of King Ezana (c. 350 C.E.*)*
   The Ethiopian Royal Chronicles   *180*

A Byzantine Historian Observes the Moors
and the Vandals (sixth century C.E.*)*
   PROCOPIUS: History of the Wars,
   Book IV   *183*

CHAPTER **8**   South and
               Southwest Asia,
               800 B.C.E.–800 C.E.   *186*

A Greek Diplomat Describes Life in Pataliputra
(c.320–297 B.C.E.*)*
   MEGASTHENES: Indika, Fragment 27   *187*

An Indian Epic Describes a Determined Wife
(c. 200 B.C.E.*)*
   The Story of Savitri, The Mahabharata   *189*

An Egyptian-Greek Merchant Describes
Commercial Sea Routes
   Periplus Maris Erythraei
   (c.30–230 C.E.)   *199*

A Buddhist Monk Observes India (399–414 C.E.*)*
   The Travels of Fa-Hien   *204*

CHAPTER **9**   East and Southeast Asia,
               800 B.C.E.–800 C.E.   *209*

Two Chinese Prose Essays Depict Women's
Relationships with Men (Han Dynasty, probably
first century B.C.E.*)*
   LIU HSIANG: The Mother of Mencius
   and FENG YEN: Letter to His
   Brother-in-Law   *209*

A Chinese Scholar Laments the Lack of Morality
in Political Appointments (c.100–150 C.E.*)*
   WANG FU: Essay on Social Relations   *213*

Chinese Historians Record Accounts of Travelers
to Japan (third to seventh centuries C.E.*)*
   Accounts of the Eastern Barbarians and
   CH'EN SHOU: The Japanese   *216*

Chinese Ambassadors Report on the
Malay Peninsula (c. 600 C.E.*)*   *223*

Chinese Buddhists Recount Their Travels
into India (518–521 C.E.*)*
   The Mission of Sung-yun and Hwei-sang
   to Obtain Buddhist Books in the West   *226*

Japanese Poems Portray the Human Condition
(eighth century C.E.*)*
   Manyoshu or Collection of
   Myriad Leaves   *229*

Part III: *Expanding Civilizations,*
           800–1500   *235*

CHAPTER **10**   Europe,
                800–1500   *237*

A Muslim Envoy Describes a Viking Funeral (922)
   AHMED IBN FADLAN: Yakut Ibn Abdallah's
   Geographical Lexicon   *238*

A Moorish Magistrate Describes Regulations for
the Markets of Seville (early twelfth century)
   IBN 'ABDUN: Hisba Manual   *242*

A Syrian Prince Delineates the Character
of the Franks (twelfth century)
   USAMAH IBN-MUNQIDH: Memoirs   *246*

*Two Christian Clergymen Recount the Story of
a Jewish Girl's Desire to Convert to Christianity
(early thirteenth century)*
CAESARIUS OF HEISTERBACH: Dialogus
de miraculis and THOMAS OF CANTIMPRÉ:
Bonum universale de apibus   *251*

A Spanish Physician Offers Advice (1315)
PETER FARGAROLA: Letter to
His Sons   *254*

*A Castilian Noblewoman Recounts Her
Adventures (1370s)*
LEONOR LÓPEZ DE CÓRDOBA:
Memorias   *258*

CHAPTER 11 Africa,
800–1500   *264*

*A Persian Gulf Sailor Recounts his Adventures
on the East African Coast (922)*
Buzurg Ibn Shahriyar of Ramhormuz:
Kitab al-Ajaib al-Hind   *265*

*A Muslim Trader Describes His Experiences in
East Africa (tenth century)*
Al-Mas'udi: Muruj al-Dhahab wa
Ma'adin al-Jawhar   *268*

A Spanish Muslim Describes Ghana (1067)
AL BAKRI: Roads and Kingdoms   *271*

*A Muslim Depiction of Mansa Musa's Travels
in Mali and Egypt (1340s)*
IBN FADL ALL'H AL-'UMARI: Pathway
of Vision in the Realms of the
Metropolises   *273*

*Two African Accounts Depict Kano
(late fourteenth century) and Kanem (tenth century)*
The Kano Chronicle and Yakut: Quoting
From The Lost Work of Al Muhallabi   *279*

*A Portuguese Explorer Portrays Life in Africa
(1497–1499)*
VASCO DA GAMA: A Journal of the First
Voyage of Vasco da Gama   *281*

*A Portuguese Priest Describes Ethiopia (1520)
and Axum (sixteenth century)*
FRANCISCO ALVARES: A True Relation of
the Lands of the Prester John   *285*

CHAPTER 12 South and Southwest
Asia, 800–1500   *290*

*A Muslim Scholar from Central Asia Studies
Hindu Society (1017)*
ALBERUNI: Alberuni's India   *291*

A Persian Poet Praises India (1318)
AMIR KHUSRAU: Praises of India   *296*

A Dominican Friar Observes Hindu Society (c.1330)
FRIAR JORDANUS: The Wonders of
the East   *300*

*A Muslim Pilgrim Depicts Society in Bengal
(1346–1347)*
IBN BATTUTA: The Travels of
Ibn Battuta   *305*

*Chinese Sailors Describe the Nicobar Islands
and Sri Lanka (1414)*
Stone Tablet Erected by Cheng Ho, FEI-HSIN:
Description of the Starry Raft, and MA HUAN:
Cheng Ho's Naval Expeditions   *308*

*A Portuguese Explorer Describes Calecut
(1497–1499)*
VASCO DA GAMA: A Journal of the
First Voyage   *312*

CHAPTER 13 East and Southeast
Asia, 800–1500   *318*

*A Japanese Monk Describes His Pilgrimage
to China (838–847)*
ENNIN: The Record of a Pilgrimage to
China in Search of the Law   *318*

Arab Writers Describe Zabag (851, 916)
SULAIMAN and ABU ZAID HASAN   *323*

*Two Japanese Women Depict Their Social World
(tenth to eleventh century)*
MURASAKI SHIKIBU: Diary and SARASHINA:
As I Crossed a Bridge of Dreams   *325*

*A Rabbi Observes Jewish Communities in East Asia
(1160–1173)*
RABBI BENJAMIN: The Travels of Rabbi
Benjamin of Tudela   *334*

A Chinese Scholar Offers Advice to Women (1178)
YÜAN TSAI: Family and Property in Sung China   *337*

A Friar Recounts His Journey to the Mongols (1245)
FRIAR GIOVANNI DA PIAN DEL CARPINI: The Journey of Friar Giovanni da Pian del Carpini   *340*

A Spanish Ambassador Describes the Mongol Court (1403–1406)
RUY GONZALEZ DE CLAVIJO: The Narrative of the Embassy of Ruy Gonzalez de Clavijo to the Court of Timur   *344*

Chinese Travelers Describe Malacca (1451, 1436)
MA-HUAN: Ying-Yai Sheng-Lan (1451) and FEI-HSIN: Hsing-Ch'a Sheng-Lan (1436)   *348*

CHAPTER **14** The Americas, 800–1500   *352*

A Norse Epic Recounts Early Voyages in the North Atlantic (late twelfth century)
The Vinland Sagas   *353*

An Italian Explorer Describes the "New World" (1504)
AMERIGO VESPUCCI: Letters From a New World   *360*

An Italian Voyager Describes South American Natives (1519–1522)
ANTONIO PIGAFETTA: The First Voyage Around the World   *364*

An Italian Traveler Observes Native Society in Hispaniola (1541–1556)
GIROLAMO BENZONI: History of the New World   *371*

A Spanish Clergyman Assess Mayan Culture (c. 1566)
FRAY DIEGO DE LANDA: Relacíon de las Cosas de Yucatan   *376*

Web Resources   *383*
List of Sources   *387*

Preface

A graduate student's remark provided the conceptual framework for this project. A few years ago, one of the authors of this book had a student from the People's Republic of China as a teaching assistant. One day he showed her a memo written by a university administrator. The professor was interested in the content, but the Chinese student focused on a grammatical mistake the administrator had overlooked. When the professor commented on the student's sharp eye, she responded, "Perhaps when you learn a language as a foreigner, you look more carefully at it than a native does." The same notion, we believe, is true of observers who describe a given society's culture. Foreigners or travelers are more likely to take careful notice of customs, manners, and rituals than native inhabitants, who often tend to take them for granted.

We decided students and instructors needed a primary source reader for World Civilizations courses that focused on foreigners' accounts of societies and cultures. We included all parts of the world from ancient times to the present. The sources in *Global Passages* emphasize daily life—marriage and funeral customs, food, social and religious rituals and ceremonies—rather than the behavior or policies of political elites. Frankly, we believe that the daily lives and customs of a people reveal their society's collective beliefs and values more clearly and accurately than any discussion of elite political behavior. Moreover, most of the selections in this reader serve a second function: they describe some facet of a society and illuminate and exemplify the values and beliefs of the observer.

Not all of the selections in *Global Passages,* however, were written by foreigners or travelers. We have included natives' observations as well because they serve to illustrate the different ways that foreigners, travelers, and "insiders" might

view the same or similar cultural phenomena. These writers also had a variety of motivations: entertainment, social commentary, rebuttal of criticism, and justification of their socioeconomic systems. When reading both types of accounts, students should keep in mind the authors' motivations, backgrounds, and prejudices.

While most of the readings in this collection are non-fiction, in a few cases we have incorporated literary materials that are especially effective in conveying cultural values or perspectives. In addition to literary materials and narrative accounts, *Global Passages* includes illustrations. We have used these sources especially for societies that have left no written sources, or whose writings were strictly political in nature (e.g., Mayan, Andean, and early sub-Saharan African), as illustrations provide the best evidence of social values and belief systems.

ORGANIZATION

The two volumes of *Global Passages* are divided into three chronological sections. Only Part I of Volume I, "Foundations of Civilization," departs somewhat from this organizational principle. Focusing on the religious and philosophical beliefs of peoples at early stages of their development, the myths, legends, and travel accounts in Part I illustrate time periods ranging from the twenty-first century B.C.E. to the twentieth century C.E. Parts II and III of Volume I, however, adhere to specific chronological divisions: "Classical Civilizations, 800 B.C.E.–800 C.E.," and "Expanding Civilizations, 800–1550." In Part II, selections describe well-established civilizations that instituted distinct patterns of life that prevailed for at least a millennium, and in many cases, longer. In Part III, selections document changes that civilizations experienced primarily in response to increasing intercultural contacts, especially overland ones. The theme of contact is continued in Volume II, which opens with "The Early Modern World, 1500–1800." In Part I, sources reveal that maritime exploration laid the foundation for the global civilization in which we live today—by 1800 the peoples of the earth had a thorough knowledge of the size of the planet, its major bodies of water and land masses, and its diverse inhabitants. Part II of Volume II, "On the Eve of Modernity, 1800–1918," illustrates the rapid increase in contact among the earth's peoples that followed; and Part III, "Toward the Contemporary World, 1918 to the Present," brings even previously isolated areas into a mutually dependent global network. Finally, each of the chronological sections in both volumes has been further subdivided by region. These are Africa, the Americas and Oceania, East and Southeast Asia, South and Southwest Asia, and Europe.

LEARNING AIDS

In addition to the selections themselves, *Global Passages* includes a number of learning aids. There is an introduction to each Part, Chapter, and selection in these volumes as well as suggested discussion questions for each selection and an annotated list of relevant websites for further investigation at the end of each volume. Our introductions to the individual selections vary in length according to the nature and complexity of each source. We have tried to provide enough context to facilitate understanding but also to avoid furnishing the very ideas that classroom discussion and debate should themselves elicit. Some selections include bracketed editorial definitions or explanations, our own footnotes (indicated by symbols, for example, *, †), or footnotes from the original edited source (indicated by number). The date cited for any selection is that of its actual composition; when that cannot be ascertained, we have used the date of the publication of the work from which the selection was taken. Although limited by the need to include selections in the English language, we

have chosen narratives from a variety of fields, languages, and periods of time. Unless specifically noted, we have not attempted to modernize spelling, syntax, or punctuation.

ACKNOWLEDGMENTS

Any work of such a broad scope usually necessitates expert advice. *Global Passages* is no exception. Among our colleagues in the Department of History at Washington State University, we thank Lydia Gerber, Candice Goucher, Thomas Kennedy, John Kicza, Thomas Pesek, Robert Staab, Heather Streets, Orlan Svingen, Marina Tolmacheva, Richard Williams, and Baodi Zhou. From Washington State University's Department of Anthropology we thank Peter Mehringer, and formerly from the Libraries we thank Mary Jane Engh. From Houghton Mifflin we thank Peter Atwood (for encouragement at an early stage), Nancy Blaine, Julie Dunn, and Ylang Nguyen. Finally, we thank the following reviewers for their helpful comments and suggestions: Deborah D. Buffton, University of Wisconsin-LaCrosse; Timothy Coates, College of Charleston; Joan L. Coffey, Sam Houston State University; Anna Dronzek, University of Minnesota-Morris; Bruce Garver, University of Nebraska-Omaha; Mary Halavais, Sonoma State University; William V. Hudon, Bloomsburg University; David M. Kalivas, Middlesex Community College; Joy Kammerling, Eastern Illinois University; Donald L. Layton, Indiana State University; Matthew Lenoe, Assumption College; Mark W. McLeod, University of Delaware; Robert J. Rowland, Jr., Loyola University; Peter von Sivers, University of Utah; Anthony J. Steinhoff, University of Tennessee-Chattanooga; and Alexander Zukas, National University.

AFRICA

Locale ▪ Traveler/Reading ▪ Number

Aksum, Ethiopian Royal Chronicles, 11
Ashanti, Journey to Asamando, 15
Axum, Francisco Alvares, 10
Cairo, Ibn Fadl All'h al-'Umari, 2
Carthage, Aristotle and The Corpus Inscriptionum Semiticarum, 1
Congo River, Oral Traditions from the Bambara, the Wapangwa, and the Fang, 16
Elephantine, Herodotus, 5
Ghana, Al Bakri, 7
Heliopolis, Coffin Text Spell 1130, 3
Kanem, Al Muhallabi, 13
Lake Chad, Kano Chronicle, 14
Malindi, Vasco de Gama, 17
Mauritania, Procopius, 6
Memphis, Shabaka Stone, 4
Meröe, Annals of Nubian Kings, 9
Napata, Annals of Nubian Kings, 8
Niger River, Pliny the Elder, Oral Traditions from the Bambara, the Wapangwa, and the Fang, 12
Zambezi River, Oral Traditions from the Bambara, the Wapangwa, and the Fang, 19
Zanzibar, Al-Mas'udi, 18

AMERICAS AND OCEANIA

Locale ▪ Traveler/Reading ▪ Number

Anasazi, How the Pueblo People Came to the Middle Place, 2
Australia, Yhi Brings Life to the World, 16
Cape Santa Maria, Antonio Pigafetta, 17
Chavin de Húantar, Chavín Pot and Zoomorphic Heads, 15
Chichen Itza, Quetzalcoatl Temple, 11
Guatemala and Yucatan Peninsula, *Popol Vuh*, 10
Hawaiian Islands, Hawaiian Runner Defeats Death and Pleases the King, 4
Hispaniola, Girolamo Benzoni, 12
Huaricoto, Huarochirí Manuscript, 14
Izamal, Fray Diego de Landa, 7
Jalisco, Jaguar Toy, 8
L 'Anse aux Meadows, Vinland Sagas, 1
La Venta, Olmec Priest in Serpent's Mouth, 6
Orinoco River, Amerigo Vespucci, 13
Southeastern U.S., How the World Was Made, 3
Teotihuacan, Quetzalcoatl Heads and Jaguar Mural, 5
Uxmal, Two-Headed Jaguar Sculpture, 9

EAST/SOUTHEAST ASIA

Locale ▪ Traveler/Reading ▪ Number

Anyang, Liu Hsiang and Feng Yen, 5
China, Emperor Mu, 10
Hangzhou, Yüan Tsai, 12
Karakorum, Friar Giovanni da Pian del Carpini, 1
Khmer Kingdom, Abbé Renaudot, 13
Jiangxi, Yüan Tsai, 11
Kyoto, Murasaki Shikibu and Sarashina Nikki, 7
Kyushu, Accounts of the Eastern Barbarians and Ch'en Shou, 6
Luoyang, Wang Fu, 4
Malacca Islands, Ma-Huan and Fei-Hsin, 14
Nara, Manyoshu, 8
Seng-Chih, Ambassador's Report on Malay Peninsula, 15
Tibet, San Wu li chi and Wu yun li-nien chi, 9
Wei River, Huai-nan Tzu, 2
Yellow River, Ch'u Tz'u, 3

SOUTH/SOUTHWEST ASIA

Locale ▪ Traveler/Reading ▪ Number

Akkad, Legend of Sargon of Akkad, 15
Bactria, Shi Chi, 5
Basra, Buzurg Ibn Shahiyar of Ramhormuz, 16
Calah (modern Nimrud), Shalmaneser III, 2
Calicut, Vasco da Gama, 24
Ceylon (Sri Lanka), Rabbi Benjamin of Tudela and Cheng Ho, 26
Cunaxa, Xenophon, 13
Damascus, Usamah Ibn-Munqidh, 7
Delhi, Amir Khusrau, 19
Harran, Travels of Abraham, 3
Jerusalem, Egeria, 11
Kabul, Alberuni, 17
Kingdom of Judah, Genesis, 12
Kurukshetra, Mahabharata, 20
Madurai, Ilango Adigal, 25
Malabar Coast, Friar Jordanus, 23
Mesopotamia, Epic of Gilgamesh, 10
Moab, Moabite Stone and 2 Kings, 9
Nepal to Pataliputra, The Travels of Fa-hien, 21
Nineveh, Nahum and Shalmaneser's Inscription, 8
Panjab, Rig Veda, 18
Pataliputra, Megasthenes, 22
Samarkand, Ruy Gonzalez de Clavijo, 4
Sardis, Xenophon, 1
Susa, Herodotus, 14
Syria, Tale of Sinuhe, 6

EUROPE

Locale ▪ Traveler/Reading ▪ Number

Antioch, Fan Yeh, 15
Apuleia, Roman Rhyton, 10
Athens, Thucydides and Greek Kantharos, 13
Bosporus, Apollonius Rhodius, 14
British Isles, Cassius Dio, 2
Cologne and the Rhine River, Tacitus, 6
Kurgan, Sung-yun and Hwei-sang, 1
Louvain, Caesarius of Heisterbach and Thomas of Cantimpré, 5
Region of the Huns, Ammianus Marcellinus, 11
Rome, Juvenal, Polybius, Melinno, and Livy, 9
Seville, Ibn 'Abdun and Leonor López de Córdoba, 8
Southeastern Coastal Britain, Julius Caesar, 4
Thebes, Cornelius Nepos, 12
Toulouse, Peter Fargarola, 7
Vologda, Ibn Fadlan, 3

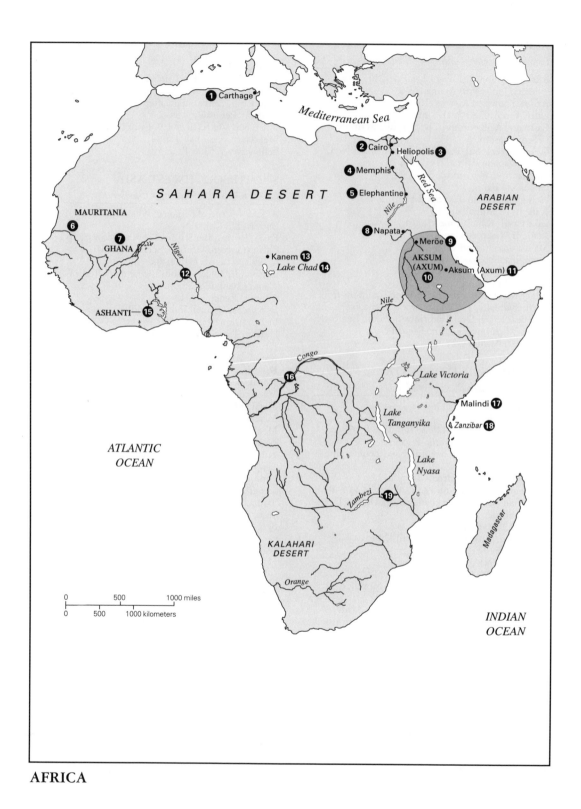

1 Carthage

Mediterranean Sea

2 Cairo • Heliopolis 3

4 Memphis

5 Elephantine

SAHARA DESERT

Nile

Red Sea

ARABIAN DESERT

MAURITANIA

6

7

GHANA

Niger

8 Napata •

Meröe 9

AKSUM (AXUM)
10 Aksum (Axum) 11

Kanem 13

Lake Chad 14

12

ASHANTI— 15

Nile

Congo

Lake Victoria

16

Lake Tanganyika

Malindi 17

Zanzibar 18

ATLANTIC OCEAN

Lake Nyasa

Zambezi 19

Madagascar

0   500   1000 miles
0   500   1000 kilometers

KALAHARI DESERT

Orange

INDIAN OCEAN

AFRICA

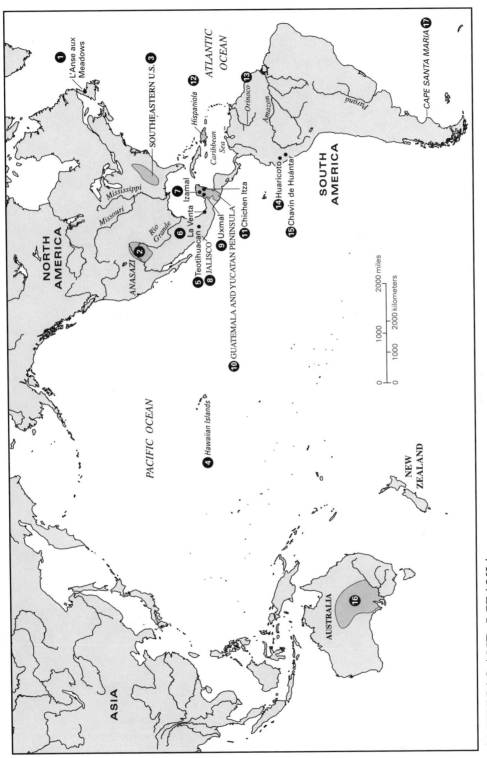

AMERICAS AND OCEANIA

NORTH AMERICA

SOUTH AMERICA

ASIA

AUSTRALIA

NEW ZEALAND

PACIFIC OCEAN

ATLANTIC OCEAN

Caribbean Sea

1 L'Anse aux Meadows

2 ANASAZI

3 SOUTHEASTERN U.S.

4 Hawaiian Islands

5 Teotihuacan

6 La Venta

7 Izamal

8 JALISCO

9 Uxmal

10 GUATEMALA AND YUCATAN PENINSULA

11 Chichen Itza

12 Hispaniola

13 Orinoco

14 Huaricoto

15 Chavin de Huántar

16 (Australia)

17 CAPE SANTA MARIA

Mississippi

Missouri

Rio Grande

Amazon

Orinoco

Paraná

2000 miles

2000 kilometers

1000

1000

0

0

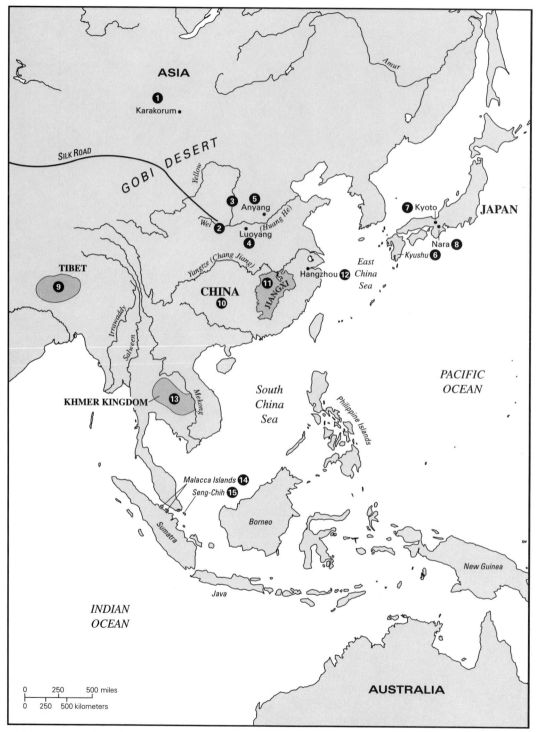

ASIA

Karakorum •

SILK ROAD

GOBI DESERT

Yellow

Wei

3
②
⑤ Anyang
④ Luoyang
(Huang He)

Amur

⑦ Kyoto

JAPAN

Nara ⑧
Kyushu ⑥

TIBET

⑨

Yangtze (Chang Jiang)

CHINA

⑩

⑪
JIANGXI

Hangzhou ⑫

East China Sea

PACIFIC OCEAN

Irrawaddy

Salween

KHMER KINGDOM

⑬

Mekong

South China Sea

Philippine Islands

INDIAN OCEAN

Malacca Islands ⑭
Seng-Chih ⑮

Sumatra

Borneo

Java

New Guinea

AUSTRALIA

0   250   500 miles
0   250   500 kilometers

EAST/SOUTHEAST ASIA

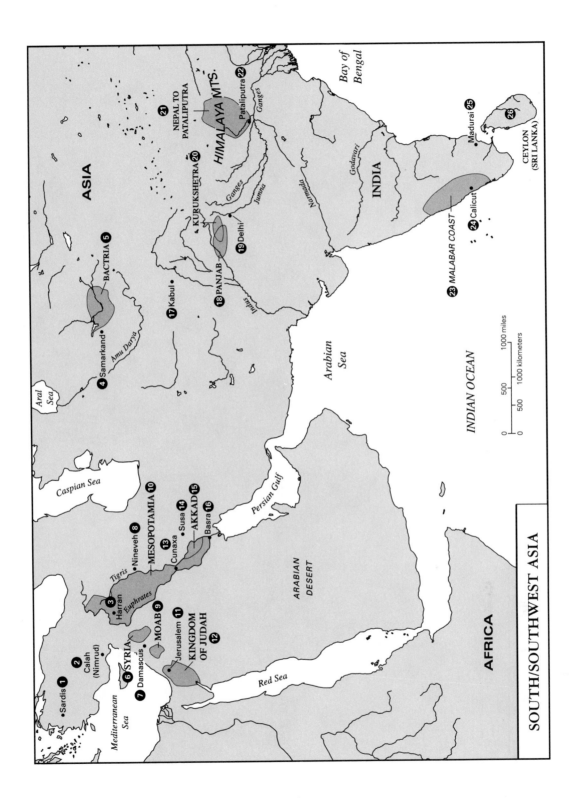

SOUTH/SOUTHWEST ASIA

ASIA

INDIA

AFRICA

Bay of Bengal

Aral Sea

Caspian Sea

Mediterranean Sea

Red Sea

Arabian Sea

INDIAN OCEAN

Persian Gulf

ARABIAN DESERT

CEYLON (SRI LANKA)

HIMALAYA MTS.

Tigris

Euphrates

Amu Darya

Ganges

Jumna

Indus

Narmada

Godavari

1 •Sardis
2 Calah (Nimrud)•
3 •Harran
5 BACTRIA
4 •Samarkand
6 SYRIA
7 •Damascus
8 •Nineveh
9 •MOAB
10 MESOPOTAMIA
11 •Jerusalem
12 KINGDOM OF JUDAH
13 •Cunaxa
14 •Susa
15 AKKAD
16 •Basra
17 •Kabul
18 PANJAB
19 •Delhi
20 KURUKSHETRA
21 NEPAL TO PATALIPUTRA
22 •Pataliputra
23 MALABAR COAST
24 •Calicut
25 •Madurai
26

1000 miles
1000 kilometers
500
500
0
0

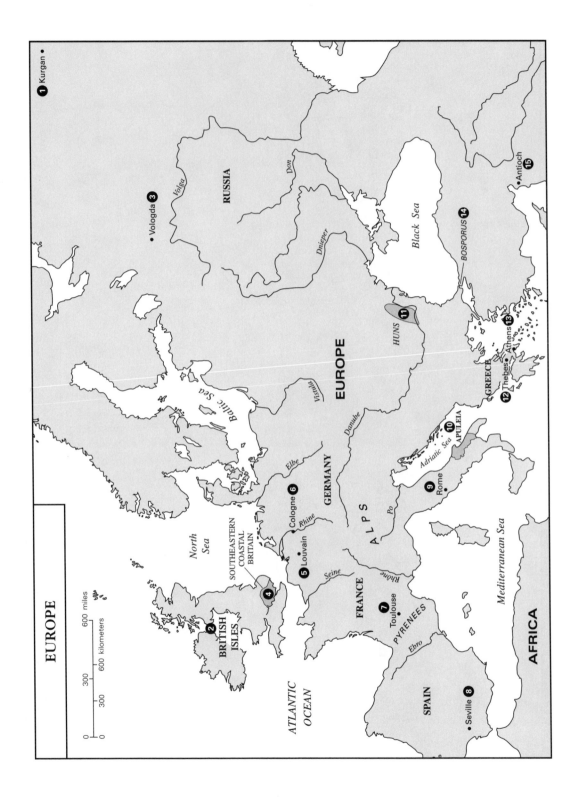

EUROPE

1 Kurgan
2 BRITISH ISLES
3 Vologda
4 SOUTHEASTERN COASTAL BRITAIN
5 Louvain
6 Cologne
7 Toulouse
8 Seville
9 Rome
10 APULEIA
11 HUNS
12 Thebes
13 Athens
14 BOSPORUS
15 Antioch

RUSSIA
GERMANY
FRANCE
SPAIN
GREECE
EUROPE
AFRICA

ATLANTIC OCEAN
North Sea
Baltic Sea
Black Sea
Adriatic Sea
Mediterranean Sea

ALPS
PYRENEES

Volga
Don
Dnieper
Vistula
Elbe
Rhine
Danube
Seine
Rhône
Po
Ebro

0   300   600 miles
0   300   600 kilometers

Part I

Foundations of Civilization

Part I of this volume presents writings that express the religious and philosophical beliefs of different peoples. "Travelers' accounts," which are the focus of *Global Passages,* either do not exist for this very early time period or are frustratingly brief and uninformative. Many of the writings in Part I are oral traditions that were recorded many years—often centuries—after they were first told. It is clear that some inhabitants of the world's earliest civilizations, especially traders and soldiers, did visit foreign lands, but either most ancient travelers did not record their experiences or such writings have not survived antiquity. Nevertheless, there was significant exchange of material objects between various cultures, and there is abundant written confirmation of travel and foreign conquest. For example, Genesis 12 relates the journey of Abraham and his wife Sara to Egypt, possibly as early as 1800 B.C.E., but it tells practically nothing of Egypt at that time.

Readers will immediately notice that the myths of origin, the flood stories, and the tales of heroes and heroines and their journeys in Part I share a number of common characteristics and themes, which may indicate widespread exchange of ideas and beliefs. Similarly, the vast differences between some of these stories may be evidence of lack of interaction between peoples. These accounts explain how the world and human beings came into existence, how humanity interacts with gods and other natural forces, and how society's institutions originated. One theme is the description of "irreconcilable opposites" (heaven and earth, darkness and light) and, at the same time, events totally outside the common range of perception and reason (a "time" in which heaven and earth were not yet separated, and darkness and light intermingled). A second theme is the origin of human beings. In some of these accounts, humans are placed on the earth by a divine power or powers, in others they ascended from the depths of the earth (as in "How the Pueblo People Came to the Middle Place"), and in still others humans are said to be fashioned from the dust of the ground (as in Genesis). In American creation stories, animals exhibit human behavior and often play tricks on humans. In all cases, however, humans enjoy a conspicuous place in creation. Indeed, in most creation narratives, the final or culminating act is the creation of human beings.

In addition to the creation of the material world and the human beings who inhabit it, these narratives sometimes center around conflicts. They describe conflicts between gods (for example, the Hero Twins), between gods and humans (the Hebrew flood story), between groups of peoples (the story of Boudicca), and between individuals (Romulus and Remus). These conflicts may be ideological or physical, but they are important because they explain the way the world was organized at the time the myth was alive. These myths also illuminate cultural differences in different parts of the world. For example, in the stories from Europe, the Middle East, and the Americas, gods are normally portrayed as having human characteristics and emotions. In the Asian accounts, on the other hand, the gods are not as clearly defined and remain more mysterious and abstract.

These early narratives clearly express a people's values and beliefs at the most basic level. Despite the lack of "travelers' accounts" in this time period, it is still possible to get a sense of the ideas that these people did or did not exchange and that often had profound and lasting effects on their civilizations.

1

Myths of Creation and Stories of Floods

Creation myths and flood stories are much more than attempts to explain the origins of the natural world and threats to its existence. These myths grapple with extraordinarily complex questions: How is Something created from Nothing? How does Order proceed from Chaos? How does One produce Many? How does the Unmanifest become Manifest? Flood stories likewise pose universal questions: What is the relationship between human beings and the divine? Does any kind of human behavior justify its extinction by divine forces? To which group—gods or human beings—does the earth belong? In whose hands should the fate of the world rest?

Three broad patterns of thought and belief—or combinations of these patterns—can be distinguished in creation myths. First, there is creation from nothing or from a vague substance-less material often called chaos. In the beginning, nothing recognizable as matter exists. This is expressed in the Bambara account of creation, in which emanations of sound (represented by the word *Yo*) from a void create the universe and all living things. The Vedic concept of latency is similar. For example, the Hindu Hymn of Origins speaks of an "undifferentiated depth" and primal darkness, "enwrapped in voidness."

Second, there is creation through natural and/or spontaneous processes. In this model, the world or something else already exists, and no attempt is made to explain how it came into being. Over time, this something proceeds to divide, expand, rise, reproduce, or awaken. Only later do divine beings appear. This pattern is particularly pronounced in the Australian myth of Yhi, the sun goddess. In the beginning the world lies sleeping, quiet, and dark. The gods and goddesses exist, as do the "bare bones" of the earth and the seeds of most plant and animal life. They need only to be awakened by Yhi, and creation takes place. Often plants, animals, and insects play important roles in this type of creation stories as well, such as in the myth of the Wapangwa, which features a cosmic tree, ants, and various beings that are produced, more or less spontaneously, from the atmosphere. Similarly, in the Cherokee myth, a large number of animals exist prior to creation—so many, in fact, that the realm where they live (beyond the stone arch of the sky, which is situated over a vast body of water) becomes overcrowded. For this reason, insects, birds, and fish—in that order—take steps to create the earth.

Finally, there is creation by a preexisting powerful creator god or a group of deities, frequently depicted as family members. These creator gods sometimes employ natural or unusual reproductive means to create the world; however, often a creator can simply will the world into existence by thought or speech. A well-known example, of course, is the Hebrew myth of Genesis, in which God creates the world from a formless and lightless void by using speech, translated from the original Hebrew as *logos* in Greek and *word* in English. God's existence is not explained. Likewise, the

Fang, from West Africa, believe that the god Nzame created the world out of absolutely nothing, and in Memphis, the Egyptians believed that Ptah existed before all other things. Like the Hebrews, the Fang and Egyptians made no attempt to explain how their creator gods came into being.

Many creation myths involve a combination of two or more of these patterns. A particularly common pairing is the emergence of a single creator deity (or a divine couple or family) from nothing, chaos, or preexisting matter—often visualized as water. In the earliest creation myths of China, a misty nothingness, chaos, exists at first; out of it come Yin and Yang, who produce the elements, the seasons, the lands and the waters, the heavenly objects, and so on. The Egyptian creation story from Heliopolis (parts of which are found in Coffin Text Spell 1130) actually combines all three patterns: the cosmos begins as a primeval ocean, out of which a mound of earth slowly forms. The sun god eventually appears and begins to reproduce through onanism; his children form the earth, the atmosphere, the heavens, and eventually all other living things.

One important theme in many of these myths is conflict: men versus women, the old versus the young, animals versus humans, and, of course, good versus evil. There are great wars in the creation myths of many ancient societies; one example in this chapter can be found in the myths of the Wapangwa, who live in Tazania. In fact, life is often the result of death. In the Chinese story of P'an Ku, each part of the giant's dying body transforms into a vital part of the universe: the wind, clouds, thunder, fields, rocks, rain, and even people.

Perhaps the greatest conflict of all, however, is that of the god(s) versus human beings. Nowhere is the conflict more violent and destructive than in stories of catastrophic floods, which are common throughout the world. In most stories, human beings somehow provoke the anger of the gods—often personifications of natural forces like wind, water, and rain—who then decide to destroy them. Such is the case in the Babylonian and Hebrew flood stories, although the human protagonists and their actions vary somewhat. This is not the case, however, in the story of the Inca flood, in which the world—which seems to have a consciousness of its own—simply decides to end itself and the oceans begin to rise. In all, however, wise individuals (human beings in the Eastern Hemisphere and animals in the Western) manage to foil the plans of the gods (sometimes with the help of a divine friend) by building boats or finding refuge on the highest mountains. Thus, both humanity and the animal kingdom achieve a kind of victory over divine will—an undeniably powerful and hopeful image. Although it is tempting to view the similarities of these flood stories as "proof" of one great cataclysmic event at some point in the distant past, this is probably not the case. Rather, it seems more likely that most ancient cultures were concerned with natural disasters, especially floods.

The study of creation myths and flood stories illuminates the mentality of peoples in the early stages of cultural development. Not surprisingly, nature and natural processes of growth, reproduction, death, and destruction are the focus of many of these stories. Myths are also important because their similarities can explain and exemplify the network of cultural connections that bound peoples from different societies together—especially in regions that were geographically contiguous. It should not surprise readers that there are striking similarities in the creation myths and flood stories of the Mesopotamians, Egyptians, and Hebrews. Many of these connections were merely the by-product of incidental contacts resulting from commerce, war, and migration. Other connections, such as those between Greek and Roman myths, were the deliberate result of government policy, which regarded religion and a common cultural heritage as an essential ingredient in a well-ordered and cohesive state. Sometimes, however, similarities in myths did not result from such cultural contact. Rather, they inform us about the nature of human consciousness and imagination. The striking similarities between the Mayan and Egyptian precreation oceans, or between the Aboriginal Great Spirit and the Greco-Roman idea of Theos, can only be coincidental. Some ideas, it seems, must be innate to the human condition.

Two Sources for Egyptian Creation Myths

Coffin Text Spell 1130 and *The Shabaka Stone*

Although many modern summaries of Egyptian creation myths are available to students of ancient Egyptian religion, unfortunately no single narrative creation myth has survived from antiquity—if, indeed, one ever existed. Instead, scholars have pieced together creation stories from fragments and references to creation from an assortment of hymns, prayers, spells, rituals, religious instructions, and art. The Egyptians may very well have assumed that since everyone knew the stories of creation, there was no need to write them down. Similarly, there is no Egyptian law code such as the Code of Hammurabi in Mesopotamia. The pharaoh's will was law and the goddess of justice, Ma'at, resided in him; thus no written code was necessary.

Many different versions of creation emerge from the vast body of Egyptian religious writings, but two predominate: one from Iwnw, which the Greeks called Heliopolis, and one from Memphis. In the first version, the cosmos existed as a primeval ocean. The sun (called Atum, Aten, Re, Ra, or Aton, depending on the place and the time period, and/or the translator), appeared on the surface of the water and produced, through masturbation, two children. Shu was the god of dry air, and Tefnut was the goddess of moist air. These two deities married and produced two children of their own, the sky god Nut and the earth god Geb. Shu and Tefnut, the atmosphere, stand on Geb, the earth, and hold up Nut, the sky. Geb and Nut, in turn, gave birth to many more gods and goddesses. Other deities arose from the sweat of Atum, and human beings were created from the tears shed by his eye, which had an intellect of its own and could assume a separate existence. In Memphis, however, the Egyptians worshipped Ptah as the creator of the universe. They believed that Ptah existed before all other things and did not explain how Ptah came into being. He created the cosmos from a void, simply by thinking of the universe. He then spoke the word and the universe appeared. Shortly thereafter he created all the living things in the universe: plants, animals, human beings, and gods.

The first selection contains elements of the creation tradition from Heliopolis. It belongs to a collection of spells called the Coffin Texts, which were written on coffins to guide the deceased on the long journey to the afterlife. Such spells first began to appear in the last part of the Old Kingdom (2700–2200 B.C.E.) but appear most commonly during the Middle Kingdom (2040–1800 B.C.E.). The spells are both repetitive and varied; they assume knowledge of religious beliefs that are not explicitly stated anywhere else, and they reflect differences in local traditions. Spell 1130 comes from the coffin of Gewa, the chief physician of the monarch Djhutilhotep. The first half takes the form of a declaration made by the sun god in his role as Creator. In the second half of the first selection, Gewa assumes the power of the god in order to journey safely to the afterlife. In the original text, the two halves are distinguished by the use of first black and then red ink.

The second selection illustrates beliefs from Memphis. The excerpt comes from an eighth-century B.C.E. reproduction of a worm-eaten papyrus or leather text from the Old Kingdom. Originally inscribed on black granite and located in the temple of Ptah at Memphis, it was commissioned by Shabaka, a Kushite king who ruled Egypt during the twenty-fifth dynasty. This text is called either the Shabaka Stone or the Memphite Theology. Scholars disagree over its original purpose: some believe it was part of a dramatic play; others believe it was part of a religious treatise.

COFFIN TEXT SPELL 1130

"Proceed in peace!
I shall repeat to you four good deeds
that my own heart made for me
within the serpent's coils, for love of stilling
    evil.
I did four good deeds within the portals of the
    horizon:
I made the four winds that every man might
    breathe in his place.
This is one deed thereof.
I made the great inundation, that the wretched
    should have power over it like the great.
This is one deed thereof.
I made every man like his fellow:
I did not ordain them to do evil, but, it was
    their own hearts which destroyed that which
    I pronounced.
This one deed thereof.
I made that their hearts should refrain from
    ignoring the west,

for love of making offerings to the gods of the
    nomes.
This is one deed thereof.
I created the gods from my sweat.
Man is from the tears of my eye.[1]

I shine, and am seen every day
in this authority of the Lord to the Limit.
I made the night for the Weary-hearted.[2]
I will sail aright in my bark;
I am the lord of the waters, crossing heaven.
I do not suffer for any of my limbs.
Utterance together with Magic[3]
are felling for me that evil being.
I shall see the horizon and dwell within it.
I shall judge the wretch from the powerful,

---

[1]A word play between "man" (*rmt*) and "tears" (*rmjjt*) which evokes the tearfulness of the human condition.
[2]The Weary-hearted one is Osiris, the god of the dead. He and the creator, the "lord of life" are the two poles of divinity.
[3]Two personifications of the god's creative power, who combat the personification of chaos ("that evil being").

and do likewise against the evildoers.
Life is mine; I am its lord.
The sceptre shall not be taken from my hand.
I have placed millions of years
between me and that Weary-hearted one,
   the son of Geb;
then I shall dwell with him in one place.
Mounds will be towns.
Towns will be mounds.
Mansion will destroy mansion."[4]

I AM THE LORD OF FIRE WHO LIVES ON TRUTH,
THE LORD OF ETERNITY, MAKER OF JOY,
   AGAINST WHOM THE OTHERWORLDLY
   SERPENTS HAVE NOT REBELLED.
I AM THE GOD IN HIS SHRINE, THE LORD OF
   SLAUGHTER, WHO CALMS THE STORM,
WHO DRIVES OFF THE SERPENTS, THE MANY-
   NAMED WHO COMES FORTH FROM HIS
   SHRINE,

THE LORD OF WINDS WHO FORETELLS THE
   NORTHWIND,
MANY-NAMED IN THE MOUTH OF THE
   ENNEAD,
LORD OF THE HORIZON, CREATOR OF LIGHT,
WHO ILLUMINES HEAVEN WITH HIS OWN
   BEAUTY.
I AM HE! MAKE WAY FOR ME
SO THAT I SHALL SEE NIU AND AMEN.
FOR I AM A BLESSED SPIRIT, EQUIPPED WITH
   OTHERWORLDLY KNOWLEDGE;
I SHALL PASS BY THE FEARFUL ONES—
<THEY CANNOT SPEAK (THE SPELL)> WHICH IS
   ON THE END OF THE BOOK-ROLL;
THEY CANNOT SPEAK FOR FEAR OF HIM
   WHOSE NAME IS CONCEALED, WHO IS
   WITHIN MY BODY.
I KNOW HIM; I AM NOT IGNORANT OF HIM.
I AM EQUIPPED, EXCELLENT IN OPENING
   PORTALS.

As for any man who knows this spell,
he shall be like Re in the east of heaven,
like Osiris within the Netherworld;
he descends into the entourage of fire,
without there being a flame being against him,
   for all time and eternity!

---

[4]The life of the created world is alluded to as the period the creator god, the lord of life, spends apart from Osiris, the son of the earth god, Geb. At the end of the world the two gods will reunite.

THE SHABAKA STONE

There took shape in the heart, there took shape on the tongue the form of Atum. For the very great one is Ptah, who gave life to all the gods and their *ka*s[*] through this heart and through this tongue, in which Horus had taken shape as Ptah, in which Thoth[†] had taken shape as Ptah.

   Thus heart and tongue rule over all the limbs in accordance with the teaching that it (the heart, *or:* he, Ptah) is in every body and it (the tongue, *or:* he, Ptah) is in every mouth of all gods, all men, all cattle, all creeping things, whatever lives, thinking whatever it (*or:* he) wishes and commanding whatever it (*or:* he) wishes.

   His (Ptah's) Ennead[‡] is before him as teeth and lips. They are the semen and the hands of Atum. For the Ennead of Atum came into being

---

[*]The Egyptians believed that the soul of a human being had three primary parts. The *ka* was essentially the life force.
[†]Thoth was the god of writing and wisdom. He was usually depicted as an ibis.

[‡]An ennead is a group of nine Egyptian divinities. Every locality had its own ennead. For example, at Heliopolis, Re, his wife, their children, and grandchildren formed one ennead; at Memphis, Ptah and his divine family formed another.

through his semen and his fingers. But the Ennead is the teeth and lips in this mouth which pronounced the name of every thing, from which Shu and Tefnut came forth, and which gave birth to the Ennead.*

Sight, hearing, breathing—they report to the heart, and it makes every understanding come forth. As to the tongue, it repeats what the heart has devised. Thus all the gods were born and his Ennead was completed. For every word of the god came about through what the heart devised and the tongue commanded.

Thus all the faculties were made and all the qualities determined, they that make all foods and all provisions, through this word. Thus justice is done to him who does what is loved, and punishment to him who does what is hated. Thus life is given to the peaceful, death is given to the criminal. Thus all labor, all crafts are made, the action of the hands, the motion of the legs, the movements of all the limbs, according

---

*This paragraph amounts to an unsubtle repudiation of the cosmology of Heliopolis, asserting that Ptah's creation of the gods through the power of his speech is superior to Atum's creation of the gods through onanism. The conflict of religious ideas was a significant component of political rivalries between the two cities of Memphis and Heliopolis.

to this command which is devised by the heart and comes forth on the tongue and creates the performance of every thing.

Thus it is said of Ptah: "He who made all and created the gods." And he is Ta-tenen, who gave birth to the gods, and from whom every thing came forth, foods, provisions, divine offerings, all good things. Thus it is recognized and understood that he is the mightiest of the gods. Thus Ptah was satisfied after he had made all things and all divine words.

He gave birth to the gods,
He made the towns,
He established the nomes,
He placed the gods in their shrines,
He settled their offerings,
He established their shrines,
He made their bodies according to their
    wishes.
Thus the gods entered into their bodies,
Of every wood, every stone, every clay,
Every thing that grows upon him
In which they came to be.
Thus were gathered to him all the gods and
    their *ka*s,
Content, united with the Lord of the Two
    Lands.

REVIEW QUESTIONS

1. What unique and identifiable elements of Egyptian cosmology can be found in these two selections?
2. How do elements of creation found on the Shabaka Stone compare and contrast to elements of creation in the Coffin Text Spell?
3. In Coffin Text Spell 1130, what seems to be the main theme of the sun god's speech to the deceased?
4. What religious purposes are evident in the excerpt from the Shabaka Stone? What nonreligious purposes might this poem have served?

The Babylonian Flood Story

The Epic of Gilgamesh

Located between the Euphrates and Tigris Rivers, ancient Mesopotamia was subject to frequent and often disastrous floods. A deposit of nearly eight feet of sediment in one area is evidence as to just how destructive these floods sometimes were. It is therefore likely that the Sumero-Babylonian flood epic is loosely based on one or more actual events.

The most complete version of the flood is found in *The Epic of Gilgamesh,* a collection of adventures and mythological tales of a semilegendary, semidivine king named Gilgamesh, who was the fifth ruler of the first dynasty of Uruk (c. 2700 B.C.E.). Woven together in Babylon in approximately 2000 B.C.E., these stories focus on Gilgamesh's ultimately fruitless search for the secret of immortality. At one point in his quest, Gilgamesh descended into the Netherworld to seek out a man to whom the gods had given eternal life. His name was Ut-napishtim (Ziusudra in earlier Sumerian versions of the flood story), and he explained to Gilgamesh the reasons for his unusual gift.

The following flood story is from one of twelve tablets that were discovered in the ruins of Nineveh during the nineteenth century. There are earlier Sumerian versions of the flood story, and other versions and fragments of *The Epic of Gilgamesh* exist as well; so it is clear to scholars that the flood story was not an original part of the epic, but was tacked on at a later date. It bears striking similarities to the Hebrew story of Noah and the Ark, as well as to the Greek story of Deucalion and Pyrrha. The spread of the flood story to other civilizations, however, should not be viewed as proof of some universal catastrophic deluge in the third millennium; rather, it should be viewed as evidence of the degree of contact between peoples in the ancient Near East and Mediterranean worlds and the impact of their ideas upon one another.

Ut-napishtim spoke to him, to Gilgamesh,
 [saying]

Let me reveal to you a closely guarded matter,
 Gilgamesh,
And let me tell you the secret of the gods.
Shuruppak is a city that you yourself know,
Situated on the bank of the Euphrates.
That city was already old when the gods
 within it
Decided that the great gods should make
 a flood.
There was Anu their father,
Warrior Ellil their counsellor,
Ninurta was their chamberlain,

Ennugi their canal-controller.
Far-sighted Ea swore the oath of secrecy with
 them,
So he repeated their speech to a reed hut,[*]
"Reed hut, reed hut, brick wall, brick wall,
Listen, reed hut, and pay attention, brick wall:
 This is the message:
Man of Shuruppak, son of Ubara-Tutu,
Dismantle your house, build a boat.
Leave possessions, search out living things.

———

[*]Ea was the god of water and wisdom, and "friend of mankind." Since he had sworn to the other gods that he would not tell any human being about their planned flood, he kept his promise by speaking to the reed hut, knowing, of course, that Ut-napishtim would overhear him.

Reject chattels and save lives!
Put aboard the seed of all living things, into
　　the boat.
The boat that you are to build
Shall have her dimensions in proportion,
Her width and length shall be in harmony,
Roof her like the Apsu."*
I realized and spoke to my master Ea,
"I have paid attention to the words that you
　　spoke in this way,
My master, and I shall act upon them.
But how can I explain myself to the city, the
　　men and the elders?"
Ea made his voice heard and spoke,
He said to me, his servant,
"You shall speak to them thus:
"I think that Ellil† has rejected me,
And so I cannot stay in your city,
And I cannot set foot on Ellil's land again.
I must go down to the Apsu and stay with my
　　master Ea.
Then he will shower abundance upon you,
A wealth of fowl, a treasure of fish.
　　. . .‡ prosperity a harvest
In the morning cakes/"darkness",§
In the evening a rain of wheat/"heaviness" he
　　will shower upon you."‖
When the first light of dawn appeared
The country gathered about me.
The carpenter brought his axe,
The reed-worker brought his stone . . .

Children carried the bitumen,
The poor fetched what was needed

On the fifth day I laid down her form.
One acre was her circumference, ten poles each
　　the height of her walls,
Her top edge was likewise ten poles all round.
I laid down her structure, drew it out,
Gave her six decks,
Divided her into seven.
Her middle I divided into nine,
Drove the water pegs into her middle.
I saw to the paddles and put down what was
　　needed . . .

The launching was very difficult;
Launching rollers had to be fetched from above
　　to below.
Two-thirds of it stood clear of the water line
I loaded her with everything there was,
Loaded her with all the silver,
Loaded her with all the gold
Loaded her with all the seed of living things,
　　all of them.
I put on board the boat all my kith and kin.
Put on board cattle from open country, wild
　　beasts from open country, all kinds of
　　craftsmen.
Shamash# had fixed the hour: . . .

"Enter into the boat and shut your door!"
That hour arrived . . .
In the morning cakes/"darkness", in the
　　evening a rain of wheat/"heaviness" showered
　　down.

I saw the shape of the storm,
The storm was terrifying to see.
I went aboard the boat and closed the door.
To seal the boat I handed over the floating
　　palace with her cargo to Puzur-Amurru the
　　boatman.
When the first light of dawn appeared,
A black cloud came up from the base of the sky.
Adad kept rumbling inside it.
Shullat and Hanish were marching ahead,
Marched as chamberlains over mountain and
　　country

---

*"Apsu" is a reference to the sweet, fresh waters beneath the
earth, the abode of Ea and a group of gods called the Seven
Sages. The meaning here is that the roof of the boat should
be extremely large.
†Ellil is a Babylonian name for Enlil. He was the god of
wind and agriculture, as well as the elected head of the assembly of gods.
‡These ellipsis points indicate a missing or unreadable section of the original text. Other ellipses in the text (unless
otherwise indicated) are marks of modern editing.
§This is a cruel pun. The word for cake (*kukku*) is nearly
identical to the word for darkness (*kukkû*). Instead of a rain
of cakes, darkness will descend.
‖Another pun. The word for wheat (*kibtu*) is very similar to
the word for heaviness (*kibittu*).

#Shamash was the sun god, the patron deity of the cities of
Sippar and Larsa.

Erakal* pulled out the mooring poles,
Ninurta† marched on and made the weir(s)
 overflow.
The Anunnaki had to carry torches,
They lit up the land with their brightness,
The calm before the Storm-god came over the
 sky,
Everything light turned to darkness.

On the first day the tempest rose up
Blew swiftly and brought the flood-weapon
Like a battle force the destructive *kašušu*-
 weapon passed over the people
No man could see his fellow,
Nor could people be distinguished from the
 sky.
Even the gods were afraid of the flood-weapon.
They withdrew; they went up to the heaven of
 Anu.‡
The gods cowered, like dogs crouched by an
 outside wall . . .

The gods, humbled, sat there weeping.
Their lips were closed and covered with scab.
For six days and seven nights
The wind blew, flood and tempest
 overwhelmed the land;
When the seventh day arrived the tempest,
 flood and onslaught
Which had struggled like a woman in labor,
 blew themselves out.
The sea became calm, the *imhullu*-wind grew
 quiet, the flood held back.
I looked at the weather; silence reigned,
For all mankind had returned to clay.
The flood-plain was flat as a roof.
I opened a porthole and light fell on my
 cheeks.
I bent down, then sat. I wept.
My tears ran down my cheeks.

---

*Erakal is another name for Nergal, the god of the Under-
world.
†Ninurta was a warrior god, the son of Ellil.
‡The Mesopotamians did not believe in "heaven" as a place
where the dead went. Instead, heaven was simply a place
where the gods lived. There were three heavens, ranked hi-
erarchically. The topmost heaven was the abode of Anu.

I looked for banks, for limits to the sea.
Areas of land were emerging everywhere
The boat had come to rest on Mount Nimush.
The mountain Nimush held the boat fast and
 did not let it budge.
The first and second day the mountain Nimush
 held the boat fast and did not let it budge.
The third and fourth day the mountain
 Nimush held the boat fast and did not let it
 budge.
The fifth and sixth day the mountain Nimush
 held the boat fast and did not let it budge.
When the seventh day arrived,
I put out and released a dove.
The dove went; it came back,
For no perching place was visible to it, and it
 turned round.
I put out and released a swallow.
The swallow went; it came back,
For no perching place was visible to it, and it
 turned round.
I put out and released a raven.
The raven went, and saw the waters receding.
And it ate, preened, lifted its tail and did not
 turn round.
Then I put everything out to the four winds,
 and I made a sacrifice,
Set out a *surqinnu*-offering upon the mountain
 peak,
Arranged the jars seven and seven;
Into the bottom of them I poured essences of
 reeds, pine, and myrtle
The gods smelt the fragrance,
The gods smelt the pleasant fragrance,
The gods like flies gathered over the
 sacrifice. . . .

Let other gods come to the *surqinnu*-offering
But let Ellil not come to the *surqinnu*-offering,
Because he did not consult before imposing the
 flood,
And consigned my people to destruction!"
As soon as Ellil arrived
He saw the boat. Ellil was furious,
Filled with anger at the Igigi gods.
"What sort of life survived? No man should
 have lived through the destruction!"

Ninurta made his voice heard and spoke,
He said to the warrior Ellil,
"Who other than Ea would have done such
     a thing?
For Ea can do everything!"
Ea made his voice heard and spoke,
He said to the warrior Ellil,
"You are the sage of the gods, warrior,
So how, O how, could you fail to consult, and
     impose the flood?
Punish the sinner for his sin, punish the
     criminal for his crime,
But ease off, let work not cease; be patient, let
     not . . .*
Instead of your imposing a flood, let a lion
     come up and diminish the people.
Instead of your imposing a flood, let a wolf
     come up and diminish the people.
Instead of your imposing a flood, let famine be
     imposed and [lessen] the land.

Instead of your imposing a flood, let Erra rise
     up and savage the people.
I did not disclose the secret of the great gods,
I just showed Atrahasis a dream, and thus he
     heard the secret of the gods."
Now the advice that prevailed was his advice.
Ellil came up into the boat,
And seized my hand and led me up.
He led up my woman and made her kneel
     down at my side.
He touched our foreheads, stood between us,
     blessed us:
"Until now Ut-napishtim was mortal,
But henceforth Ut-napishtim and his woman
     shall be as we gods are.
Ut-napishtim shall dwell far off at the mouth
     of the rivers."†
They took me and made me dwell far off, at the
     mouth of the rivers.

_____

†The "mouth of the rivers" probably refers to Dilmun (modern Bahrain). The Mesopotamians believed that the Tigris and Euphrates Rivers flowed beneath the Persian Gulf, surfacing on the islands of Bahrain and Failake, which explained their mysterious supplies of fresh water.

_____

*Again, the ellipses indicate missing or illegible text on the original tablet.

REVIEW QUESTIONS

1. Who helped Ut-napishtim build his boat? Why? What was their reward?
2. What is the relationship of human beings to the gods, as described in the story of the flood?
3. What is the myth's primary meaning? What message was it meant to convey to readers and listeners?
4. What does this myth say, in general, about the religious outlook of the Mesopotamians?

The Hebrew Creation and Flood Stories

Genesis 1–2

The Hebrew version of the creation of the world and its subsequent destruction by flood is found in the book of Genesis, the first book of the Hebrew Scriptures and part of the Torah or the Law. The books of the Torah are also called the Pentateuch. These books tell the history of the Jews from the Creation through the death of Moses, and they contain the Ten Commandments and the basic laws of Judaism.

For many centuries, the first five books of the Hebrew Scriptures were attributed to Moses as the sole author. Modern textual analysis, however, has revealed a variety of writing styles (including five different names for God), a lack of sequence, and a great many repetitions and variations in the narrative. Thus these books were no doubt written by several authors and at different times. Anachronistic historical references help date the writing of different passages. For example, in Genesis 11:31 the Hebrew patriarch Abraham is described as he leaves "Ur of the Chaldaeans" to go to Canaan circa 1800 B.C.E.; but the city of Ur could only have been identified as Chaldaean between 612 and 539, the period of the short-lived Chaldaean Empire. Thus, the existing version of the Torah could not have been written any earlier than the late seventh century B.C.E. Earlier writings probably existed but were not preserved after Hebrew priests in this time period combined them into one sacred and comprehensive religious text.

The following translation has identified two sources of the creation story in the book of Genesis: a "priestly" source and a "Yahwist" source. The priestly version was written most recently, sometime after 539 B.C.E. The Yahwist version, which follows the priestly version, is much older, probably dating ultimately to a very early oral tradition. Note the repetition in the second story of creation, as well as the lack of direct chronology from one to the other.

THE FIRST ACCOUNT OF THE CREATION

1 In the beginning God created the heavens and the earth. Now the earth was a formless void, there was darkness over the deep, and God's spirit hovered over the water.

God said, "Let there be light," and there was light. God saw that light was good, and God divided light from darkness. God called light "day," and darkness he called "night." Evening came and morning came: the first day.

God said, "Let there be a vault[1] in the waters to divide the waters in two." And so it was. God made the vault, and it divided the waters above the vault from the waters under the vault. God called the vault "heaven." Evening came and morning came: the second day.

God said, "Let the waters under heaven come together into a single mass, and let dry land appear." And so it was. God called the dry land

"earth" and the mass of waters "seas," and God saw that it was good.

God said, "Let the earth produce vegetation: seed-bearing plants, and fruit trees bearing fruit with their seed inside, on the earth." And so it was. The earth produced vegetation: plants bearing seed in their several kinds, and trees bearing fruit with their seed inside in their several kinds. God saw that it was good. Evening came and morning came: the third day.

God said, "Let there be lights in the vault of heaven to divide day from night, and let them indicate festivals, days and years. Let them be lights in the vault of heaven to shine on the earth." And so it was. God made the two great lights[2]: the greater light to govern the day, the smaller light to govern the night, and the stars. God set them in the vault of heaven to shine on the earth, to govern the day and the night

---

[1]For the ancient Semites, the "arch," or "vault" of the sky was a solid dome holding the upper waters in check.

[2]Their names are omitted deliberately: the sun and the moon were worshiped by neighboring peoples, and here they are treated as no more than lamps to light the earth and regulate the calendar.

and to divide light from darkness. God saw that it was good. Evening came and morning came: the fourth day.

God said, "Let the waters teem with living creatures, and let birds fly above the earth within the vault of heaven." And so it was. God created great sea-serpents and every kind of living creature with which the waters teem, and every kind of winged creature. God saw that it was good. God blessed them, saying, "Be fruitful, multiply, and fill the waters of the seas; and let the birds multiply upon the earth." Evening came and morning came: the fifth day.

God said, "Let the earth produce every kind of living creature: cattle, reptiles, and every kind of wild beast." And so it was. God made every kind of wild beast, every kind of cattle, and every kind of land reptile. God saw that it was good.

God said, "Let us* make man in our own image, in the likeness of ourselves, and let them† be masters of the fish of the sea, the birds of heaven, the cattle, all the wild beasts and all the reptiles that crawl upon the earth."

God created man in the image of himself,
in the image of God he created him,
male and female he created them.

God blessed them, saying to them, "Be fruitful, multiply, fill the earth and conquer it. Be masters of the fish of the sea, the birds of heaven and all living animals on the earth." God said, "See, I give you all the seed-bearing plants that are upon the whole earth, and all the trees with seed-bearing fruit; this shall be your food. To all wild beasts, all birds of heaven and all living reptiles on the earth I give all the foliage of plants for food." And so it was. God saw all he had made, and indeed it was very good. Evening came and morning came: the sixth day.

2   Thus heaven and earth were completed with all their array. On the seventh day God completed the work he had been doing. He rested on the seventh day after all the work he had been doing. God blessed the seventh day and made it holy, because on that day he had rested after all his work of creating.

Such were the origins of heavens and earth when they were created.

THE SECOND ACCOUNT OF THE CREATION

At the time when Yahweh God made earth and heaven there was as yet no wild bush on the earth nor had any wild plant yet sprung up, for Yahweh God had not sent rain on the earth, nor was there any man to till the soil. However, a flood was rising from the earth and watering all the surface of the soil. Yahweh God fashioned man of dust from the soil. Then he breathed into his nostrils a breath of life, and thus man became a living being.

Yahweh God planted a garden in Eden which is in the east, and there he put the man he had fashioned. Yahweh God caused to spring up from the soil every kind of tree, enticing to look at and good to eat, with the tree of life and the tree of the knowledge of good and evil in the middle of the garden. A river flowed from Eden to water the garden, and from there it divided to make four streams. The first is named the Pishon,‡ and this encircles the whole land of Havilah where there is gold. The gold of this land is pure; bdellium[3] and onyx stone are found there. The second river is named the Gihon, and this encircles the whole land of Cush.§ The third river is named the Tigris, and this flows to the east of Ashur. The fourth river is the Euphrates. Yahweh God took the man and settled him in the garden of Eden to cultivate and take care of it. Then Yahweh God gave the man this admonition, "You may eat indeed of all the trees in the garden. Nevertheless of the tree of the knowl-

---

*A common name for God was "Elohim," which is actually plural. "Us" might also refer to God and his attendants, the "heavenly host" (angels).
†Likewise, the Hebrew word for man or mankind, "Adam," was plural.

‡The locations of the Pishon and Gihon Rivers are unknown.
[3]An aromatic resin.
§This is not the Cush located on the Nile River south of Egypt.

edge of good and evil you are not to eat, for on the day you eat of it you shall most surely die."

Yahweh God said, "It is not good that the man should be alone. I will make him a helpmate." So from the soil Yahweh God fashioned all the wild beasts and all the birds of heaven. These he brought to the man to see what he would call them; each one was to bear the name the man would give it. The man gave names to all the cattle, all the birds of heaven and all the wild beasts. But no helpmate suitable for man was found for him. So Yahweh God made the man fall into a deep sleep. And while he slept, he took one of his ribs and enclosed it in flesh. Yahweh God built the rib he had taken from the man into a woman, and brought her to the man. The man exclaimed:

> "This at last is bone from my bones,
> and flesh from my flesh!
> This is to be called woman,
> for this was taken from man."[4]

This is why a man leaves his father and mother and joins himself to his wife, and they become one body.

Now both of them were naked, the man and his wife, but they felt no shame in front of each other. . . .

THE CORRUPTION OF MANKIND

Yahweh saw that the wickedness of man was great on the earth, and that the thoughts in his heart fashioned nothing but wickedness all day long. Yahweh regretted having made man on the earth, and his heart grieved. "I will rid the earth's face of man, my own creation," Yahweh said, "and of animals also, reptiles too, and the birds of heaven; for I regret having made them." But Noah had found favor with Yahweh.

This is the story of Noah:

Noah was a good man, a man of integrity among his contemporaries, and he walked with

God. Noah became the father of three sons, Shem, Ham and Japheth. The earth grew corrupt in God's sight, and filled with violence. God contemplated the earth: it was corrupt, for corrupt were the ways of all flesh on earth.

PREPARATIONS FOR THE FLOOD

God said to Noah, "The end has come for all things of flesh; I have decided this, because the earth is full of violence of man's making, and I will efface them from the earth. Make yourself an ark out of resinous wood. Make it with reeds and line it with pitch inside and out. This is how to make it: the length of the ark is to be three hundred cubits, its breadth fifty cubits, and its height thirty cubits. Make a roof for the ark . . . put the door of the ark high up in the side, and make a first, second and third deck.

"For my part I mean to bring a flood, and send the waters over the earth, to destroy all flesh on it, every living creature under heaven; everything on earth shall perish. But I will establish my Covenant with you, and you must go on board the ark, yourself, your sons, your wife, and your sons' wives along with you. From all living creatures, from all flesh, you must take two of each kind aboard the ark, to save their lives with yours; they must be a male and a female. Of every kind of bird, of every kind of animal and of every kind of reptile on the ground, two must go with you so that their lives may be saved. For your part provide yourself with eatables of all kinds, and lay in a store of them, to serve as food for yourself and them." Noah did this; he did all that God had ordered him.

7   Yahweh said to Noah, "Go aboard the ark, you and all your household, for you alone among this generation do I see as a good man in my judgment. Of all the clean animals you must take seven of each kind, both male and female; of the unclean animals you must take two, a male and its female (and of the birds of heaven also, seven of each kind, both male and female), to propagate their kind over the whole earth. For in seven days' time I mean to make it rain on the earth for forty days and nights, and I will rid

---

[4]In Hebrew a play on the words *ishshah* (woman) and *ish* (man).

the earth of every living thing that I made." Noah did all that Yahweh ordered.

Noah was six hundred years old when the flood of waters appeared on the earth.

Noah with his sons, his wife, and his sons' wives boarded the ark to escape the waters of the flood. (Of the clean animals and the animals that are not clean, of the birds and all that crawls on the ground, two of each kind boarded the ark with Noah, a male and a female, according to the order God gave Noah.) Seven days later the waters of the flood appeared on the earth.

In the six hundredth year of Noah's life, in the second month, and on the seventeenth day of that month, that very day all the springs of the great deep broke through, and the sluices of heaven opened. It rained on the earth for forty days and forty nights.

That very day Noah and his sons Shem, Ham and Japheth boarded the ark, with Noah's wife and the three wives of his sons, and with them wild beasts of every kind, cattle of every kind, reptiles of every kind that crawls on the earth, birds of every kind, all that flies, everything with wings. One pair of all that is flesh and has the breath of life boarded the ark with Noah; and so there went in a male and a female of every creature that is flesh, just as God had ordered him.

And Yahweh closed the door behind Noah.

THE FLOOD

The flood lasted forty days on the earth. The waters swelled, lifting the ark until it was raised above the earth. The waters rose and swelled greatly on the earth, and the ark sailed on the waters. The waters rose more and more on the earth so that all the highest mountains under the whole of heaven were submerged. The waters rose fifteen cubits higher, submerging the mountains. And so all things of flesh perished that moved on the earth, birds, cattle, wild beasts, everything that swarms on the earth, and every man. Everything with the breath of life in its nostrils died, everything on dry land. Yahweh destroyed every living thing on the face of the earth, man and animals, reptiles, and the birds of heaven.

He rid the earth of them, so that only Noah was left, and those with him in the ark. The waters rose on the earth for a hundred and fifty days.

THE FLOOD SUBSIDES

8   But God had Noah in mind, and all the wild beasts and all the cattle that were with him in the ark. God sent a wind across the earth and the waters subsided. The springs of the deep and the sluices of heaven were stopped. Rain ceased to fall from heaven; the waters gradually ebbed from the earth. After a hundred and fifty days the waters fell, and in the seventh month, on the seventeenth day of that month, the ark came to rest on the mountains of Ararat. The waters gradually fell until the tenth month when, on the first day of the tenth month, the mountain peaks appeared.

At the end of forty days Noah opened the porthole he had made in the ark and he sent out the raven. This went off, and flew back and forth until the waters dried up from the earth. Then he sent out the dove, to see whether the waters were receding from the surface of the earth. The dove, finding nowhere to perch, returned to him in the ark, for there was water over the whole surface of the earth; putting out his hand he took hold of it and brought it back into the ark with him. After waiting seven more days, again he sent out the dove from the ark. In the evening, the dove came back to him and there it was with a new olive branch in its beak. So Noah realized that the waters were receding from the earth. After waiting seven more days he sent out the dove, and now it returned to him no more.

It was in the six hundred and first year of Noah's life, in the first month and on the first of the month, that the water dried up from the earth. Noah lifted back the hatch of the ark and looked out. The surface of the ground was dry!

In the second month and on the twenty-seventh day of the month the earth was dry.

THEY DISEMBARK

Then God said to Noah, "Come out of the ark, you yourself, your wife, your sons, and your sons' wives with you. As for all the animals with you, all things of flesh, whether birds or animals or reptiles that crawl on the earth, bring them out with you. Let them swarm on the earth; let them be fruitful and multiply on the earth." So Noah went out with his sons, his wife, and his sons' wives. And all the wild beasts, all the cattle, all the birds and all the reptiles that crawl on the earth went out from the ark, one kind after another.

Noah built an altar for Yahweh, and choosing from all the clean animals and all the clean birds he offered burnt offerings on the altar. Yahweh smelled the appeasing fragrance and said to himself, "Never again will I curse the earth because of man, because his heart contrives evil from his infancy. Never again will I strike down every living thing as I have done.

"As long as earth lasts,
sowing and reaping,
cold and heat,
summer and winter,
day and night
shall cease no more."

THE NEW WORLD ORDER

9   God blessed Noah and his sons, saying to them, "Be fruitful, multiply and fill the earth. Be the terror and the dread of all the wild beasts and all the birds of heaven, of everything that crawls on the ground and all the fish of the sea; they are handed over to you. Every living and crawling thing shall provide food for you, no less than the foliage of plants. I give you everything, with this exception: you must not eat flesh with life, that is to say blood, in it. I will demand an account of your lifeblood. I will de-

mand an account from every beast and from man. I will demand an account of every man's life from his fellow men.

"He who sheds man's blood,
shall have his blood shed by man,
for in the image of God
man was made.

"As for you, be fruitful, multiply, teem over the earth and be lord of it."

God spoke to Noah and his sons, "See, I establish my Covenant with you, and with your descendants after you; also with every living creature to be found with you, birds, cattle and every wild beast with you: everything that came out of the ark, everything that lives on the earth. I establish my Covenant with you: no thing of flesh shall be swept away again by the waters of the flood. There shall be no flood to destroy the earth again."

God said, "Here is the sign of the Covenant I make between myself and you and every living creature with you for all generations: I set my bow in the clouds and it shall be a sign of the Covenant between me and the earth. When I gather the clouds over the earth and the bow appears in the clouds, I will recall the Covenant between myself and you and every living creature of every kind. And so the waters shall never again become a flood to destroy all things of flesh. When the bow is in the clouds I shall see it and call to mind the lasting Covenant between God and every living creature of every kind that is found on the earth."

God said to Noah, "This is the sign of the Covenant I have established between myself and every living thing that is found on the earth."

REVIEW QUESTIONS

1. In your opinion, what is the single most important element of the Hebrew creation story? Why?
2. Compare the two Hebrew versions of the creation in Genesis. Is this scholarly separation a valid one? Why or why not?
3. Compare the Hebrew creation myth to Ptah's creation of the world in Egypt. What is

the agent of creation in both stories? How does this type of creation enhance the prestige and power of these two gods?

4. Compare the Hebrew flood story to the Babylonian flood story. How do you account for the similarities? Which is likely derived from the other, and why?

The Hindu Hymn of Origins

The Rig Veda

The Rig Veda, from which this hymn comes, was written around 1000 B.C.E. and is the oldest text in any Indo-European language. It existed as oral tradition, passed from father to son, for millennia. Like the religious texts known as the Upanishads, this hymn is interrogative in tone rather than dogmatic. Unlike many other religious hymns, it is not one of praise to a deity, but one of philosophical inquiry and speculation. In essence, it says that beyond the many, beyond duality, is the One, which cannot be "known," for knowing necessitates duality—subject and object.

In this translation Professor Jeanine Miller uses the terms *Unmanifest* and *Manifest* for words that others have translated "Nonbeing" and "Being," or "Nonexistent" and "Existent." She captures the spirit of the hymn, and of Hinduism in general, by explaining that Being is an emergence from latency. The point is that the categories of Being and Nonbeing (the literal meanings of the Sanskrit words), although opposites, are not absolute and that beyond all opposites and categories is the One—"undifferentiated" (verse III)—from which all differentiations (existence) emerge. Being is a potential in the latency of Nonbeing, and the One, God (He—verse VII), is both the origin and the cause.

The Unmanifest was not then, or the Manifest;
spatial depths or heaven beyond were not.
What encompassed, where, who nurtured it?
What ocean, profound, unfathomable, pervaded?

Death was not then or immortality.
Neither night's nor day's confine existed.
Undisturbed, self-moved, pulsated the One
    alone.
And beyond that, other than that, was naught.

Darkness there was; at first hidden in darkness
this all was undifferentiated depth.
Enwrapped in voidness, that which flame-
    power
kindled to existence emerged.

Desire, primordial seed of mind, in the
    beginning, arose in That.
Seers, searching in their heart's wisdom,
discovered the kinship of the created with the
    uncreate.

Their vision's rays stretched afar.
There was indeed a below, there was indeed an
    above.
Seed-bearers there were, mighty powers there
    were;
energy below, will above.

Who knows the truth, who can here proclaim
whence this birth, whence this projection?
The gods appeared later in this world's creation.
Who then knows how it all came into being?

REVIEW QUESTIONS

1. What do you think is the most important element of this hymn? Why?
2. What basic philosophical differences do you see between this creation account and others?
3. What does this hymn tell you about early Hindu thought?

Fragments from China

Ch'u Tz'u *(Questions of Heaven),* Huai-nan Tzu *(The Grand and Illustrious Explication of Master Huai-nan,* or the *History of the Great Light),* San Wu li chi *(Records of Cycles in Threes and Fives),* and Wu yun li-nien chi *(Chronicle of the Five Cycles of Time)*

In contrast to the Mesopotamians and Hebrews the early Chinese did not produce great epic literature that included well-elaborated mythological beliefs, particularly concerning their ideas of creation—or, if they did, it has not survived. Existing information is fragmentary and incomplete, partly because of state censorship and persecution of Confucian intellectuals during the Q'in (Ch'in) dynasty. In particular, the infamous "burning books decree" during the reign of Emperor Shi Huang Ti (221–210 B.C.E.) resulted in the destruction of countless classic texts. After censorship was lifted in the following century, Han scholars painstakingly labored to locate or reconstitute lost works. The degree of their success is still controversial today.

Chinese religious beliefs were also affected by the development of Confucian thought, the popular spread of Taoism, and the introduction of Buddhism to China. Confucius and his followers believed in Heaven (T'ien) and continued to worship the ancestors, but Confucian philosophy had very little concern for preserving traditional Chinese myths. The Taoists tended to reshape religious practices and ideas, and the Buddhists brought new beliefs into China from India. In addition, as the various kingdoms and principalities of China coalesced into a powerful empire, the mythological world evolved until it featured a hierarchical organization that resembled the structure of the Chinese government. Despite the influence of the political system on religious beliefs in China, however, it is important to remember that early imperial China did not impose religious beliefs on its subjects.

The following five short excerpts reflect changes in Chinese cosmological belief over a period of some seven hundred years, from the fourth century B.C.E. to the third century C.E. Taoist ideas become increasingly well articulated with each selection, culminating in the creation of the Earth from the dying body of P'an Ku, a giant who was neither fully divine nor fully human.

The first selection, entitled "Questions of Heaven," comes from a fourth-century B.C.E. work called the *Ch'u Tz'u,* or *The Songs of Ch'u,* Ch'u being a state in the Yangtze River Valley. The existing text was compiled by a scholar named Wang Yi (89–158 C.E.) during the Han dynasty. The universe is described indirectly; readers must infer that the world was formed from a "formless expanse." The second and third excerpts are taken from the *Huai-nan Tzu,* a compilation of twenty-one chapters on metaphysics, politics, and behavior that were collected and reworked in 139 C.E. under the patronage of Liu An, a member of the imperial family. The text gets its name from the patron's title, King of Huai-nan. Both the second and third selections elaborate upon the concept of dualistic deities mentioned in "Questions of Heaven," and they also take creation a step further, progressing from the creation of celestial bodies to the creation of living beings on earth.

Finally, the fourth and fifth selections recount the myth of P'an Ku (also Pangu or Pan Gu). The fourth comes from the *San Wu li chi (Records of Cycles in Threes and Fives)* and the fifth from the *Wu yun li-nien chi (Chronicle of the Five Cycles of Time).* Both were written in the third century C.E., during the period of the Three Kingdoms (220–589). Only fragments of these two works have survived, and they are quoted by later authors. Even though the story of P'an Ku is the most recent of those presented here, it is the most widely accepted creation myth in China. It may have originated in Tibet, where the author of both excerpts, Hsu Cheng, lived for a time. The fourth and fifth texts, because of their anthropogenic emphasis, differ dramatically from the three selections that precede them.

CH'U TZ'U

At the beginning of remote antiquity, who was there to pass down the tale of what happened? And before the upper and lower worlds were formed, how could they be explored? Since darkness and light were hidden and closed, who could fathom them? In the formless expanse when there were only images, how could anyone know what they were? When were brightness and gloom created? Yin and Yang commingled three times; what was their original form and how were they transformed? The round sphere and its ninefold gates, who planned and measured them? Whose achievement was this? Who first created them? How are Dipper's Ladle and the Cord fastened, and how were the poles of the sky linked? Why do the eight pillars lean to the southeast and why is there a fault? Where are the ends of the Nine Skies situated and where do they join up? Their corners and edges are so many that who knows what they number? How do the heavens coordinate their twelve divisions? How are the sun and moon connected? How are the serried stars arranged?

HUAI-NAN TZU, FRAGMENT 1

Long ago, before Heaven and earth existed, there were only images but no forms, and all was dark and obscure, a vast desolation, a misty expanse, and nothing knew where its own portals were. There were two gods born out of chaos who wove the skies and designed the earth. So profound were they that no one knew their lowest deeps, and so exalted were they that no one knew where they came to rest. Then they divided into Yin and Yang and separated into the Eight Poles. The hard and the soft formed, and the myriad living things took shape. The dense cloudy vapor became insects, and the pure vapor became humans.

HUAI-NAN TZU, FRAGMENT 2

Before Heaven and earth had formed, there was a shapeless, dark expanse, a gaping mass; thus it was called the Great Glory. The Way [Tao] first came from vacant space, vacant space gave birth to the cosmos, the cosmos gave birth to the Breath, and the Breath had its limits. The limpid light [Yang] rose mistily and became the sky, the heavy turbidness congealed and became earth. Because rare limpidity easily condensed but heavy turbidity congealed with difficulty, the sky was the first to form, and earth settled into shape later. The double essence of sky and earth became Yin and Yang, the complex essence of Yin and Yang became the four seasons, the diffuse essence of the four seasons became the ten thousand things in nature. The hot Breath of concentrated Yang gave birth to fire, the essence of the fiery Breath became the sun, and the cold Breath of concentrated Yin became water, the essence of watery Breath became the moon. The excess from sun and moon became the stars. The sky received the sun, moon, and stars, and the earth received rivers and rain water, and dust and silt. . . .

Heaven is round; earth is square.

SAN WU LI CHI

Heaven and earth were in chaos like a chicken's egg, and P'an Ku was born in the middle of it. In eighteen thousand years Heaven and earth opened and unfolded. The limpid that was Yang became the heavens, the turbid that was Yin became the earth. P'an Ku lived within them, and in one day he went through nine transformations, becoming more divine than Heaven and wiser than earth. Each day the heavens rose ten feet higher, each day the earth grew ten feet thicker, and each day P'an Ku grew ten feet taller. And so it was that in eighteen thousand years the heavens reached their fullest height, earth reached its lowest depth, and P'an Ku became fully grown. Afterward, there were the Three Sovereign Divinities. Numbers began with one, were established with three, perfected by five, multiplied with seven, and fixed with nine. That is why Heaven is ninety thousand leagues from earth.

In many versions of the preceding myth, P'an Ku broke open the egg of creation with an axe. The light parts of the egg, the heavens (the Yang), rose and the heavy part of the egg, the earth (the Yin), sank. All the while, P'an

Ku had to stand between them to prevent them from colliding. Day after day, year after year, P'an Ku stood on the earth and held up the heavens. Each day he grew ten feet taller, and it was this growth that moved heaven and earth farther and farther away from each other. Finally, when a great distance separated the heavens from the earth, P'an Ku became tired. So he sat down, went to sleep, and died.

WU YUN LI-NIEN CHI

When the firstborn, P'an Ku, was approaching death, his body was transformed. His breath became the wind and clouds; his voice became peals of thunder. His left eye became the sun; his right eye became the moon. His four limbs and five extremities became the four cardinal points and the five peaks. His blood and semen became water and rivers. His muscles and veins became the earth's arteries; his flesh became fields and land. His hair and beard became the stars; his bodily hair became plants and trees. His teeth and bones became metal and rock; his vital marrow became pearls and jade. His sweat and bodily fluids became streaming rain. All the mites on his body were touched by the wind and were turned into the black-haired people.

REVIEW QUESTIONS

1. What similar elements of creation can be found in all five selections? What elements of Taoism can you find in each?
2. How are the "Questions of Heaven" answered by the succeeding four selections? Are any questions left unanswered? If so, which ones?
3. How do the creation myths of early China compare to other creation myths you have read? Which non-Chinese mythological character does P'an Ku resemble most, and why?

The Inca Flood Story

The Huarochirí Manuscript

The origins of the following excerpt from the Huarochirí Manuscript are similar to those of the *Popol Vuh* and other accounts of the native peoples of the Americas found in the two volumes of *Passages.* The preconquest natives of the Andes Mountains did not record this myth for several reasons, only one of which was that they had no writing system. This flood story was part of their oral tradition, from the "beginning of times." In much the same manner as among the Maya and Aztecs of Meso-America, Spanish priests recorded the religious beliefs of the Andean peoples during the last half of the sixteenth century. In this case, the story was written in Quechua, the language of the

Inca, much later translated into Spanish, and finally translated into the English that appears here.

The terrain and the geological factors of the Andes are particularly important to understanding the origins of a "flood story" involving people and animals several thousand feet above sea level. First, the mountain range is a relatively new one and very active with earthquakes and volcanic eruptions. These phenomena have occurred throughout the history of the peoples who have resided in the region. Such events, which continue today, include heavy rains that can cause enormous floods in the thousands of valleys that run from these steep mountains into the sea. Finally, compounding the problem was the occasional tsunami that struck these river valleys, caused by the gigantic undersea movement of continental shelves. Any combination of these events could have led to the following story about how the world flooded.

The excerpt reveals much about the strong connections between humans, animals, and the environment. Andean natives depended upon the llama as their draft animal; they also used its wool for clothing, its meat and milk for food, and its dung for heating. Consequently, the llama, as indicated in the following story, had many supernatural powers. The mountain that becomes the island of safety during the flood, Villca Coto, was revered by the Inca court in Cuzco and may be the mountain that is located northwest of the city of San Damián, near Huanre and Sucro. Today this mountain is about 5,000 feet high (2,300 meters). As with other flood stories, life depended upon cooperation and understanding, in this story between men and animals, ultimately resulting in the salvation of those life forms.

WHAT HAPPENED TO THE INDIANS IN ANCIENT TIMES WHEN THE OCEAN OVERFLOWED

Now we'll return to what is said of very early people.

The story goes like this.

In ancient times, this world wanted to come to an end.

A llama buck, aware that the ocean was about to overflow, was behaving like somebody who's deep in sadness. Even though its <crossed out:> [father] owner let it rest in a patch of excellent pasture, it cried and said, "In, in," and wouldn't eat.

The llama's <crossed out:> [father] owner got really angry, and he threw the cob from some maize he had just eaten at the llama.

"Eat, dog! This is some fine grass I'm letting you rest in!" he said.

Then that llama began speaking like a human being.

"You simpleton, whatever could you be thinking about! Soon, in five days, the ocean will overflow. It's a certainty. And the whole world will come to an end," it said.

The man got good and scared. "What's going to happen to us? Where can we go to save ourselves?" he said.

The llama replied, "Let's go to Villca Coto mountain.
<margin, in Spanish:> [This is a mountain that is between Huanri and Surco.]
There we'll be saved. Take along five days' food for yourself."

So the man went out from there in a great hurry, and himself carried both the llama buck and its load.

When they arrived at Villca Coto mountain, all sorts of animals had already filled it up: pumas, foxes, guanacos, condors, all kinds of animals in great numbers.

And as soon as that man had arrived there, the ocean overflowed.

They stayed there huddling tightly together.

The waters covered all those mountains and it was only Villca Coto mountain, or rather its very peak, that was not covered by the water.

Water soaked the fox's tail.

That's how it turned black.

Five days later, the waters descended and began to dry up.

The drying waters caused the ocean to retreat all the way down again and exterminate all the people.

Afterward, that man began to multiply once more.

That's the reason there are people until today.

Regarding this story, we Christians believe it refers to the time of the Flood.

But they believe it was Villca Coto mountain that saved them.

REVIEW QUESTIONS

1. Why do you think the llama warned the man that the ocean was going to overflow?
2. How many human beings took refuge on the mountain of Villca Coto? Why do you suppose there were many more animals? How do you account for the difference?
3. How does the Andean story of the flood compare to others in this chapter, particularly the flood stories of the Hebrews and Babylonians? What are the most important similarities and differences?
4. What feature of this flood story surprised you the most? Why?

Three Creation Stories from Africa

Oral Traditions from the Bambara, the Wapangwa, and the Fang

The following three creation myths testify to the great religious variety of the African continent. Each myth represents a different type of creation story. In the first, from the Bambara in Mali, absolutely nothing exists before creation, not even space or time. Sound is the agent of creation. In the second, from the Wapangwa in Tanzania, the world is created naturally through spontaneous processes, in this case plant growth and insect excretion. Both exist prior to creation. Finally, from the Fang in West Africa, the world is formed by a pre-existing powerful deity, who is the creator.

The Bambara live in Mali, on the Niger River. Like many other peoples in western Africa, they have produced a compellingly rich and psychologically complex creation mythology. In the Bambara story of creation, the world originally emerged from, and eventually will dissolve back into, the root sound "Yo"— which can be compared to the "Om" in Hindu culture. Similarly, the Dogon (who live upstream from the Bambara) believe that creation was facilitated by the utterance of a series of divine words. The neighboring Yoruba also believe in the power of a divine word, in this case "Hòò," but they also believe in a pantheon of deities that typify important archetypes of human nature, somewhat analogous to the Greek pantheon. In contrast, however, most African gods exist to serve mankind (and frequently seek humanity), not vice versa.

The Wapangwa live on the northeast shore of Lake Mawali in Tanzania. Their creation myth centers around a "tree of life," an upside-down tree inhabited by ants, whose excrement eventually becomes the earth itself. There are parallels to this inverted tree in several other places and eras in world history. For example, the Hindu scriptures, the Upanishads, describe a Tree of Eternity (Brahman, pure spirit) that has its roots in heaven and its branches in the earth. In Renaissance Europe, Dante envisioned a similar upside-down tree in his visionary ascent through Purgatory—an inverted version of the Tree of Knowledge, with its roots in the Garden of Eden.

Finally, the Fang from Gabon, north of the Congo River in West Africa, believe that the world was made by the god Nzame, "an uncreated creator," who is transcendent and immanent, a "beingless being"—by definition existing both prior to and beyond creation. Nzame also has male and female incarnations, Mebere and Nkwa. Nzame creates the earth by blowing on the waters; it is his spirit and his will that animate all living things. This type of creation story, of course, has interesting parallels in the Judeo-Christian tradition.

BAMBARA CREATION STORY

In the beginning there was nothing but the emptiness of the void (*fu*). . . .

The entire universe began from a single point of sound, the root sound of creation, Yo. Yo is the first sound, but it is also the silence at the core of creation. . . .

Emanations from this void, through the root sound Yo, created the structure of the heavens, of the earth, and of all living and nonliving things. . . .

"Yo comes from itself, is known by itself, departs out of itself, from the nothingness that is itself." All is Yo. . . .

Out of the void, the vibrations of Yo gave rise to *gla gla zo,* the highest state of consciousness. *Gla gla zo* ultimately manifested itself in the creation of human consciousness. . . .

For those who know, therefore, there is silence at the core of the universe, from it all things continually spring forth. In the face of the noise of the material, social universe, the elders strive to return to the primal silence.

WAPANGWA CREATION STORY

The sky was large, white, and very clear. It was empty; there were no stars and no moon; only a tree stood in the air and there was wind. This tree fed on the atmosphere, and ants lived on it.

Wind, tree ants, and atmosphere were controlled by the power of the Word. But the Word was not something that could be seen. It was a force that enabled one thing to create another. . . .

The Wind, it seems, was annoyed with the tree, which stood in its way, so it blew until a branch snapped, carrying away with it the colony of white ants. When the branch finally came to rest, the ants ate all the leaves except one large one upon which they left their excrement. This excrement grew into a large heap and eventually into a mountain that approached the top of the tree of origin. Now in contact again with the primordial tree, the ants had more food to consume and waste to eliminate, from which they fashioned a huge object, the earth, with mountains and valleys, all of which touched the top of the tree of origin.

One day the Word sent a terrible wind, and white frost appeared on the earth. Soon a warm wind followed, and the ice melted into water. The waters swelled and drowned the ants, and in the end flooded the whole earth, until no spot remained dry. In those days the earth was as large as it is now, and it was a desert of water. . . .

One day the atmosphere brought forth beings that moved about in the air—they spoke and cried and sang. They settled on the earth and each created his own sound. Birds, animals, and men—each had his own cry.

There was little food. The animals wanted to eat the tree of origin, but men forbade them to do it. But when men saw that the animals did not obey, they called them into a valley and began a great war, attacking each other with sticks and stones. It was a terrible war. The wind blew powerfully and the water roared. Many died before the war was finally over. Some animals remained men's prisoners, others escaped to the forest. But the animals of the forest began to attack men and to eat them. So all evil came into the world—murder and eating one another. . . .

The very earth began to tremble and bits of it broke loose. Some of the pieces began to glow with heat as they whirled through the air. These were the sun, the moon, and the stars. The sun glowed most, because it broke off with fire. The moon and stars broke off without fire, but later they began to shine also through the light of the sun. For the sun's rays shone through them, as they are only thin, transparent disks.

When the war came to an end, many new things were created that still exist today: the gods, rain, thunder, and lightning. . . .

In times of war men used to pray to the wind, trees, and other things for help. In those days men had more gods than today. Many people then prayed to thunder. When the war ended, a sheep was born with a long tail and a long pointed horn. It was so happy about the end of the war that it became mad. It started to jump and play and it hurled itself into the air. It floated along in the air and caught fire in the atmosphere. Since that time it causes thunder and lightning when heavy rain falls. It is said that this sheep finally killed the Word and thus became the God of the world. It ruled over everything: earth, moon, stars, sun, and rain, and was the god of thunder and lightning. . . .

When human beings ask about the conflict between themselves and animals, a god replies.

"You men kept a sheep, you made war, and your sheep became mad—it flew through the air and it killed the Word, from which all things that adorn the world have sprung. Well, I am the younger brother of the Word. And I tell you, you were great, but because of the things you have done you shall be reduced, you shall be small until in the end your height shall not even be half of your present stature. And in the end your entire world shall be consumed with fire." . . .

So in the end, the Word returns the world to its source.

FANG CREATION STORY

At the beginning of things, when there was nothing, neither man, nor animals, nor plants, nor heaven, nor earth. But God *was* and he was called Nzame. The three who are Nzame, we call them Nzame, Mebere, and Nkwa. At the beginning Nzame made the heaven and the earth and he reserved the heaven for himself. Then he blew onto the earth, and earth and water were created, each on its side. . . .

Nzame made everything: heaven, earth, sun, moon, stars, animals, plants—everything. When he had finished everything that we see today, he called Mebere and Nkwa and showed them his work.

"This is my work. Is it good?"

They replied, "Yes, you have done well."

"Does anything remain to be done?"

Mebere and Nkwa answered him, "We see many animals, but we do not see their chief; we see many plants, but we do not see their master."

As masters for all these things, they appointed the elephant, because he had wisdom; the leopard, because he had power and cunning; and the monkey, because he had malice and suppleness.

But Nzame wanted to do even better, and working together, he, Mebere, and Nkwa created a being almost like themselves. One gave him force, the second sway, and the third beauty. Then the three of them said:

"Take the earth. You are henceforth the master of all that exists. Like us you have life, all things belong to you, you are the master."

Nzame, Mebere, and Nkwa returned to the heights to their dwelling place, and the new creature remained below alone, and everything obeyed him. But among all the animals the elephant remained the first, the leopard the second, and the monkey the third, because it was they whom Mebere and Nkwa had first chosen.

Nzame, Mebere, and Nkwa called the first man Fam, which means "power."

Proud of his sway, his power, and his beauty, because he surpassed in these three qualities the elephant, the leopard, and the monkey, proud of

being able to defeat all the animals, this first man grew wicked; he became arrogant and did not want to worship Nzame. He scorned him:

> Yeye, O, layeye,
> God on high, man on the earth,
> Yeye, O, layeye,
> God is God,
> Man is man,
> Everyone in his house, everyone for himself!

God heard the song. "Who sings?" he asked.

"Look for him," cried Fam.

"Who sings?"

"Yeye, O, layeye!"

"Who sings?"

"Eh! It is me!" cried Fam.

Furious, God called Nzalan, the thunder. "Nzalan, come!" Nzalan came running with great noise: boom, boom, boom! The fire of heaven fell on the forest. The plantations burned like vast torches. Foo, foo, foo!—everything in flames. The earth was then, as today, covered with forests. The trees burned, the plants, the bananas, the cassava, even the pistachio nuts, everything dried up; animals, birds, fishes, all were destroyed, everything was dead. But when God had created the first man, he had told him, "You will never die." And what God gives he does not take away. The first man was burned, but none knows what became of him. He is alive, yes, but where? . . .

But God looked at the earth, all black, without anything, and idle; he felt ashamed and wanted to do better. Nzame, Mebere, and Nkwa took counsel, and they did as follows: over the black earth covered with coal they put a new layer of earth; a tree grew, grew bigger and bigger, and when one of its seeds fell down a new tree was born; when a leaf severed itself, it grew and grew and began to walk. It was an animal, an elephant, a leopard, an antelope, a tortoise—all of them. When a leaf fell into the water it swam; it was a fish, a sardine, a crab, an oyster—all of them. The earth became again what it had been and what it still is today. The proof that this is the truth is this: when one digs up the earth in certain places, one finds a hard black stone that breaks; throw it in the fire and it burns. . . .

But Nzame, Mebere, and Nkwa took counsel again; they needed a chief to command all the animals. "We shall make a man like Fam," said Nzame, "the same legs and arms, but we shall turn his head and he shall see death."

This was the second man and the father of all. Nzame called him Sekume, but did not want to leave him alone, and said, "Make yourself a woman from a tree."

Sekume made himself a woman, and she walked, and he called her Mbongwe.

When Nzame made Sekume and Mbongwe, he made them in two parts—an outer part called Gnoul, the body, and the other that lives in the body, called Nsissim.

Nsissim is what produces the soul; Nsissim is the soul—it is the same thing. It is Nsissim who makes Gnoul live. Nsissim goes away when man dies, but Nsissim does not die. Do you know where he lives? He lives in the eye. The little shining point you see in the middle, that is Nsissim.

Stars above
Fire below
Coal in the hearth
The soul in the eye
Cloud smoke and death.

Sekume and Mbongwe lived happily on earth and had many children. But Fam, the first man, was imprisoned by God under the earth. With a large stone God blocked the entrance. But the malicious Fam tunneled through the earth for a long time, and one day, at last, he was outside! Who had taken his place? The new man. Fam was furious with him. Now he hides in the forest, waiting to kill the couple, or under the water, waiting to capsize their boats.

Remain silent,
Fam is listening,
to bring misfortune;
remain silent.

REVIEW QUESTIONS

1. On which of the following does the Bambara creation myth focus: how the world was created, why it was created, or who created it? Speculate as to the significance of this focus.
2. After the creation of the world by ants living on the Tree of Origin, the tree continues to play an important role in Wapangwa mythology. What happens—both directly and indirectly—because of the existence of the tree? Why?
3. Explain the relationship of Nzame to Mebere and Nkwa. What is their role in the Fang story of creation?
4. Can you identify any common themes that might tie these three myths together? Explain.
5. Specifically, what does each of these African myths have in common with other creation stories in this chapter?

An Aboriginal Tale from Australia

Yhi Brings Life to the World

The practical nature of the Australian Aborigines, many of whom depended on a relatively harsh environment for their existence, is apparent in their myths. Their strong connection to nature is reflected in their view of the universe, which was expressed through totems—symbols of objects, plants, or animals that represent individuals and groups and that serve as affiliations with particular aspects of nature or nature deities.

Beliefs about the structure of the universe were remarkably similar throughout Aboriginal Australia. In most creation myths, creation takes place during a time period called "Dreamtime," the "Time Before" or the "Time of Creation." There is no formless void or watery chaos prior to creation; instead the universe already exists in Dreamtime, though not in its present state. Thus the Aborigines believed that the universe was made from preexisting material; it seemed clear to them that something could not be made out of nothing. Consequently, in nearly all Aboriginal creation myths, the universe is well defined at the outset. Three primary planes usually exist: (1) the earth, a flat, circular disc; (2) the heavens, usually depicted as a dome that stretches from horizon to horizon; and (3) the underworld, a poorly defined place that is located below the earth.

At the beginning of a typical creation myth, the earth is portrayed as a featureless plain; subsequently, supernatural beings (who also had prior existence) awake and create human beings, animals, plants, and other aspects of nature. In the following myth, many of these aspects, too, have prior existence; they are created by the sun goddess Yhi out of other materials, like soil or water or seeds, or they are merely awakened by her touch. Once their work of creating or awakening the world is finished, the gods and goddesses either disappear into the heavens or the underworld, or they change into animals or into natural features of the earth: hills, rivers, and so on. Thus they are not gone; they are present in the natural environment of the Aborigines. In addition to these spirits or deities, all nature is sustained by the Great Spirit, Baiame.

The text of the following myth is not ancient in the conventional sense; the words were not written down for the first time hundreds or thousands of years ago. The story, however, is ancient in the oral tradition of the Aborigines. Note in particular the joyous tone to the story and the absence of any sense of dualism: everything in nature is part of one unifying whole, life and the universe are essentially good, and darkness is not equated with any kind of evil or negativity.

In the beginning the world lay quiet, in utter darkness. There was no vegetation, no living or moving thing on the bare bones of the mountains. No wind blew across the peaks. There was no sound to break the silence.

The world was not dead. It was asleep, waiting

for the soft touch of life and light. Undead things lay asleep in icy caverns in the mountains. Somewhere in the immensity of space Yhi stirred in her sleep, waiting for the whisper of Baiame, the Great Spirit, to come to her.

Then the whisper came, the whisper that woke the world. Sleep fell away from the goddess like a garment falling to her feet. Her eyes opened and the darkness was dispelled by their shining. There were coruscations of light in her body. The endless night fled. The Nullarbor Plain was bathed in a radiance that revealed its sterile wastes.

Yhi floated down to earth and began a pilgrimage that took her far to the west, to the east, to north, and south. Where her feet rested on the ground, there the earth leaped in ecstasy. Grass, shrubs, trees, and flowers sprang from it, lifting themselves towards the radiant source of light. Yhi's tracks crossed and recrossed until the whole earth was clothed with vegetation.

Her first joyous task completed, Yhi, the sun goddess, rested on the Nullarbor Plain, looked around her, and knew that the Great Spirit was pleased with the result of her labour.

"The work of creation is well begun," Baiame said, "but it has only begun. The world is full of beauty, but it needs dancing life to fulfil its destiny. Take your light into the caverns of earth and see what will happen."

Yhi rose and made her way into the gloomy spaces beneath the surface. There were no seeds there to spring to life at her touch. Harsh shadows lurked behind the light. Evil spirits shouted, "No, no, no," until the caverns vibrated with voices that boomed and echoed in the darkness. The shadows softened. Twinkling points of light sparkled in an opal mist. Dim forms stirred restlessly.

"Sleep, sleep, sleep," the evil spirits wailed, but the shapes had been waiting for the caressing warmth of the sun goddess. Filmy wings opened, bodies raised themselves on long legs, metallic colours began to glow. Soon Yhi was surrounded by myriads of insects, creeping, flying, swarming from every dark corner. She retreated slowly. They followed her out into the

world, into the sunshine, into the embrace of the waiting grass and leaves and flowers. The evil chanting died away and was lost in a confusion of vain echoes. There was work for the insects to do in the world, and time for play, and time to adore the goddess.

"Caves in the mountains, the eternal ice," whispered Baiame. Yhi sped up the hill slopes, gilding their tops, shining on the snow. She disappeared into the caverns, chilled by the black ice that hung from the roofs and walls, ice that lay hard and unyielding, frozen lakes in icebound darkness.

Light is a hard thing, and a gentle thing. It can be fierce and relentless, it can be penetrating, it can be warm and soothing. Icicles dripped clear water. Death came to life in the water. There came a moving film over the ice. It grew deeper. Blocks of ice floated to the surface, diminished, lost their identity in the rejoicing of unimprisoned water. Vague shapes wavered and swam to the top—shapes which resolved themselves into fish, snakes, reptiles. The lake overflowed, leaped through the doorways of caves, rushed down the mountain sides, gave water to the thirsty plants, and sought the distant sea. From the river the reptiles scrambled ashore to find a new home in grass and rocks, while fish played in the leaping waters and were glad.

"There are yet more caves in the mountains," whispered Baiame.

There was a feeling of expectancy. Yhi entered the caves again, but found no stubborn blocks of ice to test her strength. She went into cave after cave and was met by a torrent of life, of feather and fur and naked skin. Birds and animals gathered round her, singing in their own voices, racing down the slopes, choosing homes for themselves, drinking in a new world of light, colour, sound, and movement.

"It is good. My world is alive," Baiame said.

Yhi took his hand and called in a golden voice to all the things she had brought to life.

"This is the land of Baiame. It is yours for ever, to enjoy. Baiame is the Great Spirit. He will guard you and listen to your requests. I have nearly finished my work, so you must listen to my words.

"I shall send you the seasons of summer and winter—summer with warmth which ripens fruit ready for eating, winter for sleeping while the cold winds sweep through the world and blow away the refuse of summer. These are changes that I shall send you. There are other changes that will happen to you, the creatures of my love.

"Soon I shall leave you and live far above in the sky. When you die your bodies will remain here, but your spirits will come to live with me."

She rose from the earth and dwindled to a ball of light in the sky, and sank slowly behind the western hills. All living things sorrowed, and their hearts were filled with fear, for with the departure of Yhi darkness rushed back into the world.

Long hours passed, and sorrow was soothed by sleep. Suddenly there was a twittering of birds, for the wakeful ones had seen a glimmer of light in the east. It grew stronger and more birds joined in until there came a full-throated chorus as Yhi appeared in splendour and flooded the plains with her morning light.

One by one the birds and animals woke up, as they have done every morning since that first dawn. After the first shock of darkness they knew that day would succeed night, that there would always be a new sunrise and sunset, giving hours of daylight for work and play, and night for sleeping.

The river spirit and the lake spirit grieve most of all when Yhi sinks to rest. They long for her warmth and light. They mount up into the sky, striving with all their might to reach the sun goddess. Yhi smiles on them and they dissolve into drops of water which fall back upon the earth as rain and dew, freshening the grass and the flowers and bringing new life.

One last deed remained to be done, because the dark hours of night were frightening for some of the creatures. Yhi sent the Morning Star to herald her coming each day. Then, feeling sorry for the star in her loneliness, she gave her Bahloo, the Moon, for her husband. A sigh of satisfaction arose from the earth when the white moon sailed majestically across the sky, giving birth to myriads of stars, making a new glory in the heavens.

REVIEW QUESTIONS

1. What was the role of the Great Spirit, Baiame, in the creation of the Aboriginal World? Who do you think was more important, Baiame or Yhi? Who do you think was more powerful?
2. How are the living things of the world reminded of Yhi's creations each day?
3. How does "Yhi Brings Life to the World" compare to other stories of creation you have read in this volume? Which are the most similar and which are the most different? Why?

A Cherokee Myth of Creation

UGVWIYUHI, *How the World Was Made*

For hundreds of years the Cherokee nation thrived in the southern Appalachian Mountains before the Spanish and French explorers ventured into their world in the late sixteenth century. The Cherokee adopted many cultural attributes from the southern Iroquois (who inhabited the mountains to their north) and built their towns around the earthen mounds left by the eastern Mounds Builders of the ninth century C.E. Like many other peoples in the Americas, they had not developed a writing system but kept the memory of their history and religious beliefs alive by a rich tradition of storytelling.

In the twentieth century, the Cherokee realized that their stories must be saved. When, in the 1830s, the U.S. government forced the Cherokee to migrate into the Oklahoma Territory, many of their elders died. Nevertheless, a small group of survivors clung jealously to the faithful retelling of their beliefs. Until the 1940s, U.S. government policy aimed to "Americanize" these and other native groups. In the 1950s and 1960s, however, a heightened awareness of the civil rights of minority peoples created an environment in which the Cherokee could appreciate their collective identity and share their rich heritage. The result was the collection and publication of their myths and legends. This excerpt of the creation myth of the Cherokee Nation is one of those important stories, saved by recent scholarship.

HOW THE WORLD WAS MADE

The earth is a great island floating in a sea of water, and suspended at each of the four cardinal points by a cord hanging down from the sky vault, which is of solid rock. When the world grows old and worn out, the people will die and the cords will break and let the earth sink down into the ocean, and all will be water again. The Indians are afraid of this.

When all was water, the animals were above in Galunlati, beyond the arch; but it was very much crowded, and they were wanting more room. They wondered what was below the water, and at last Dayunisi "Beaver's Grandchild," the little Water-beetle, offered to go and see if it could learn. It darted in every direction over the surface of the water, but could find no firm place to rest. Then it dived to the bottom and came up with some soft mud, which began to grow and spread on every side until it became the island which we call the earth. It was afterward fastened to the sky with four cords, but no one remembers who did this.

At first the earth was flat and very soft and wet. The animals were anxious to get down, and sent out different birds to see if it was yet dry, but they found no place to alight and came back again to Galunlati. At last it seemed to be time,

and they sent out the Buzzard and told him to go and make ready for them. This was the Great Buzzard, the father of all the buzzards we see now. He flew all over the earth, low down near the ground, and it was still soft. When he reached the Cherokee country, he was very tired, and his wings began to flap and strike the ground, and wherever they struck the earth there was a valley, and where they turned up again there was a mountain. When the animals above saw this, they were afraid that the whole world would be mountains, so they called him back, but the Cherokee country remains full of mountains to this day.

When the earth was dry and the animals came down, it was still dark, so they got the Sun and set it in a track to go every day across the island from east to west, just overhead. It was too hot this way and Tsiskagili, the Red Crawfish, had his shell scorched a bright red, so that his meat was spoiled; and the Cherokee do not eat it. The conjurers put the sun another handbreadth higher in the air, but it was still too hot. They raised it another time, and another, until it was seven handbreadths high and just under the sky arch. Then it was right, and they left it so. That is why the conjurers call the highest place Gulkwagine Digalunlatiyun, "the seventh height," because it is seven hand-breadths above the earth. Every day the sun goes along under this arch, and returns at night on the upper side to the starting place.

There is another world under this, and it is like ours in everything, animals, plants, and people, save that the seasons are different. The streams that come down from the mountains are the trails by which we reach this underworld, and the springs at their heads are the doorways by which we enter it, but to do this one must fast and go to water and have one of the underground people for a guide. We know that the seasons in the underworld are different from ours, because the water in the springs is always warmer in winter and cooler in summer than the outer air.

When the animals and plants were first made, we do not know by whom, they were told to watch and keep awake for seven nights, just as young men now fast and keep awake when they pray to their medicine. They tried to do this, and nearly all were awake through the first night, but the next night several dropped off to sleep, and the third night others were asleep, and then others, until, on the seventh night, of all the animals only the owl, the panther, and one or two more were still awake. To these were given the power to see and go about in the dark, and to make prey of the birds and animals which must sleep at night. Of the trees only the cedar, the pine, the spruce, the holly, and the laurel were awake to the end, and to them it was given to be always green and to be greatest for medicine, but to the others it was said: "Because you have not endured to the end you shall lose your hair every winter."

Men came after the animals and plants. At first there were only a brother and sister until he struck her with a fish and told her to multiply, and so it was. In seven days a child was born to her, and thereafter every seven days another, and they increased very fast until there was danger that the world could not keep them. Then it was made that a woman should have only one child in a year, and it has been so ever since.

REVIEW QUESTIONS

1. What characteristics of Cherokee culture are revealed by this myth?
2. Compare and contrast the role of animals in this selection with that in the *Popol Vuh.*
3. What other creation myth in this chapter is most like the one offered here? The least like the one offered here? Explain your choices.

2

Heroes and Heroines

The heroes revered by the members of any group or culture give us important insights into that particular society. In the mythical, legendary, and historical tales of heroes and heroines, their actions and ideals reveal the values and aspirations of the group from which they came. A quick look at the heroes of the present day—extraordinarily wealthy athletes, pop stars, and corporate executives—will quickly reveal what is most admired and thus valued in modern society. The culture heroes of the past, however, were charged with more serious tasks than entertaining fans, amusing an audience, or amassing great wealth. Instead, they effected or blocked the will of divine beings, founded cities and empires, exhibited great courage and strength in the face of overwhelming opposition, showed initiative and originality, served as moral examples to guide future generations, and sacrificed themselves for the greater good.

Not surprisingly, the heroes and heroines in this chapter came from widely different backgrounds and experiences, not to mention widely different parts of the globe. Some were mortal, some not; some were male, some female. Some were virtuous; others, like Boudicca, who led an army of Britons against the Romans, flouted tradition. Some were motivated by altruism and the desire to serve the divine; others simply aspired to become the stuff of legend. For example, Sargon of Akkad quite deliberately publicized and promoted his own exploits to justify and ensure the success of his reign. Similarly, the legendary Roman twins Romulus and Remus set out to honor themselves by building and then ruling a city on the site where the famous she-wolf rescued them from the waters of the Tiber River.

These heroes and heroines nearly always exhibited great courage, cleverness, or strength—or combinations thereof—though often at the cost of their lives. Kannaki, the heroine of *The Jeweled Anklet,* bravely bowed to the Fire God's will and inflicted punishment upon the people who unjustly caused her husband's death. She paid for her courage with her life, however, as did Boudicca, who dared to defy the might of Rome. Some heroes demonstrated bravery less conspicuously, such as the Hawaiian runner, Eleio. Knowing that he risked angering the king, he temporarily abandoned his royal errand to help a spirit woman regain possession of her body. And some heroes set off to do battle with enemies somewhat reluctantly—or perhaps nonchalantly—such as the Hero Twins of Maya mythology. Unlikely heroes at the onset, they eventually sacrificed themselves repeatedly in order to overthrow the lords of the underworld.

One thing many heroes frequently share is an unusual, if not miraculous, birth story. Sargon and Romulus and Remus were all abandoned and left to die as infants, only to experience remarkable rescues. The mother of the Hero Twins was impregnated by the skull of their long dead father. Love often features prominently in the stories of heroes and heroines, though the stories frequently focus on the separation of the lovers. Nowhere is this more pain-filled than in the tale of Kovalan and Kannaki, and death is the ultimate barrier to their happiness. Many of the heroes achieved success only after long journeys or lives of arduous work fraught with obstacles, perils, and tests of courage and strength.

The similarities in many of these stories are sometimes mere coincidence, but often they are the direct result of intercultural contacts. Exciting adventures and heroic deeds are perhaps the most popular of all oral tales. They have been told in front of countless fires, in every age, to every kind of audience; and they have provided examples of courage, bravery, perseverance, and strength for travelers and voyagers since human beings first developed speech and imagination.

The Birth and Boyhood of Sargon I

The Legend of Sargon of Akkad

In the last part of the twenty-fourth century B.C.E., a man by the name of Sargon apparently rose from humble beginnings to found the first empire in Mesopotamia. As the king of Akkad (also called Agade), his empire at its height included all of Mesopotamia and even some lands to the west. Sargon's empire was the first of its kind in Mesopotamia; prior to his conquests the region was divided into independent city-states that were frequently at war with each other. Following the establishment of the Akkadian Empire in approximately 2350 B.C.E., Mesopotamia experienced a period of economic prosperity and cultural growth that lasted until the empire's collapse in about 2160 B.C.E. Sargon's example inspired empire building by later kings, including Ur-Nammu of Ur and Hammurabi of Babylon.

The following two short descriptions of Sargon's life are very different. The first reading, an inscription describing his birth and childhood, dates to the reign of Sargon or shortly afterward, but its accuracy is questionable. According to other legends, he began his career in politics as the cupbearer to the king of Kish, whom he eventually overthrew. The second reading is a type of historical record called a chronology. Unlike history, which incorporates analysis and evaluation into the text, a chronology is a simple recitation of events.

THE LEGEND OF SARGON OF AGADE, INSCRIPTION

1. Sargon, the mighty king, king of Agade am I,
2. My mother was lowly; my father I did not know;[1]
3. The brother of my father dwelt in the mountain.
4. My city is Azupiranu, which is situated on the bank of the Euphrates.
5. My lowly mother conceived me, in secret she brought me forth.
6. She placed me in a basket of reeds, she closed my entrance with bitumen,
7. She cast me upon the river, which did not overflow me.
8. The river carried me, it brought me to Akki, the irrigator.

---

[1] Another tablet reads "a father I had not."

9. Akki, the irrigator, in the goodness of his heart lifted me out,
10. Akki, the irrigator, as his own son . . . . . . brought me up;
11. Akki, the irrigator, as his gardener appointed me.
12. When I was a gardener the goddess Ishtar* loved me,
13. And for four years I ruled the kingdom.
14. The black-headed[2] peoples I ruled, I governed;
15. Mighty mountains with axes of bronze I destroyed (?).
16. I ascended the upper mountains;
17. I burst through the lower mountains.

18. The country of the sea I besieged three times;
19. Dilmun[3] I captured (?).
20. Unto the great Dur-ilu I went up, I . . . .
21. . . . . I altered . . . .
22. Whatsoever king shall be exalted after me,
23. . . . .
24. Let him rule, let him govern the black-headed peoples;
25. Mighty mountains with axes of bronze let him destroy;
26. Let him ascend the upper mountains,
27. Let him break through the lower mountains;
28. The country of the sea let him besiege three times;
29. Dilmun let him capture;
30. To great Dur-ilu let him go up.

---

*Ishtar, the daughter of Anu, was considered the "Queen of Heaven." She was essentially a fertility goddess and was considered to have a voracious sexual appetite. The earlier Sumerians had worshipped her under the name Inanna or Innini.

[2]A name for the Semitic peoples of Babylonia.

---

[3]An island in the Persian Gulf.

THE LEGEND OF SARGON OF AGADE, CHRONOLOGY

Sargon, king of Agade, overseer of Ishtar, king of Kish, appointed priest of Anu, king of the country, great *ensi** of Enlil: he defeated Uruk and tore down its wall; in the battle with the inhabitants of Uruk he was victorious. Lugalzag-gisi, king of Uruk, he captured in the battle, and brought by a halter to the gate of Enlil. Sargon, king of Agade, was victorious in the battle with the inhabitants of Ur: he conquered the town and tore down its wall. He defeated E-Ninmar and tore down its wall and conquered its entire territory from Lagash to the sea; then he washed his weapons in the sea. In the battle with the inhabitants of Umma he was victorious, he conquered the town and tore down its wall. Enlil did not let anyone oppose Sargon, the king of the country. Enlil gave him the land from the Upper Sea to the Lower Sea.

---

*An *ensi* was the governor or agent of a city that was controlled by the king of another city. In this list of his titles, Sargon claimed to be the direct agent of the god Enlil. In other words, Sargon was not subservient to any man on earth; moreover, he ruled on behalf of the gods.

REVIEW QUESTIONS

1. What are the primary differences between the two readings? How do they differ in both tone and purpose?
2. Why do you suppose it was important to Sargon or to his people to emphasize his lower-class parentage and early career as a gardener?
3. Why might the inhabitants of ancient Mesopotamia have preferred living in a large state ruled by a monarch to living in independent city-states?

Romulus and Remus Found the City of Rome

LIVY, *History of Rome, Book I*

Livy (Titus Livius) was a Roman historian who lived from 59 B.C.E. to 17 C.E. His only work was a monumental history of Rome, *Ab urbe condita libri* (*Books from the Foundation of the City*). Forty-five of its original 142 books still survive. Livy's primary theme was the rise of Rome from obscurity to greatness—which he believed was its destiny from the beginning.

At the time Livy was writing, the Roman Empire was undergoing a transition from republic to empire. Its first emperor, Augustus Caesar, had assumed power in 30 B.C.E. and was slowly moving the state toward autocracy. As part of this program, the emperor sponsored writers like the historian Livy, as well as poets, artists, and architects, whose task it was to make Rome appear noble, powerful, and superior to all neighbors. Readers at the time would not have failed to apply these qualities to Rome's emperor as well, for it was common knowledge that the imperial family, the Julians, claimed descent not only from Romulus, but from his ancestor Aeneas and two divinities, Venus and Mars. Thus Livy and other early imperial writers not only created a "golden age" of literature, they played an important role in enabling the Roman populace to accept—with few complaints—both its new emperor and its loss of political involvement in government.

The following excerpt is from Book I of Livy's history. It tells the mythical story of the foundation of Rome in 753 B.C.E., a date that was eventually used as the first year in the Roman calendar. (Their dating system sometimes used numerical years appended with the letters *a.u.c.—ab urbe condita—*"from the founding of the city.") Created by the Romans in response to contact with the Greeks, the story of Romulus and Remus is an artificial and deliberate amalgamation of several stories circulating in Italy by the fourth and fifth centuries. By that time Latin tradition was focusing on seven mythical kings of Rome, the first of whom was named Romulus and the last of whom was overthrown circa 510 B.C.E. If lengthy reigns were attributed to each king, Rome's foundation could only be traced back to somewhere around 750 B.C.E. When the Romans came into contact with the Greek colonies in southern Italy, however, they learned that the Greek myths ascribed the foundation of Rome to a Trojan prince, Aeneas, who had fled from the Greek victory over Troy in 1184 B.C.E. To resolve the discrepancy between the dates, the Romans chose to designate Aeneas as the first king of a neighboring town, Alba Longa; then they added twelve more Latin kings and attributed the founding of Rome itself to Romulus. In the fifth century B.C.E., the story was further complicated when the Greeks invented an eponymous founder of Rome named Rhomos. Because of rivalries between the Greeks and Romans—and perhaps also because of the prevalence of twins in Greco-Roman myths— the Romans transformed Rhomos into Romulus's twin brother Remus and rejected him as a legitimate founder of the city.

Despite its "factual" unreliability, the myth of Romulus and Remus is valuable to students of history because it explains a great deal about Rome in the fourth century B.C.E. Particularly important themes in this regard are Rome's relationships with its neighbors, its propensity for violence, the importance of correct religious observance, the relationship between men and women, and the inherent rightness of Rome's very existence.

Proca . . . begat Numitor and Amulius; to Numitor, the elder, he bequeathed the ancient realm of the Silvian family. Yet violence proved more potent than a father's wishes or respect for seniority. Amulius drove out his brother and ruled in his stead. Adding crime to crime, he destroyed Numitor's male issue; and Rhea Silvia, his brother's daughter, he appointed a Vestal* under pretence of honouring her, and by consigning her to perpetual virginity, deprived her of the hope of children.

IV. But the Fates were resolved, as I suppose, upon the founding of this great City,† and the beginning of the mightiest of empires, next after that of Heaven. The Vestal was ravished, and having given birth to twin sons, named Mars as the father of her doubtful offspring, whether actually so believing, or because it seemed less wrong if a god were the author of her fault. But neither gods nor men protected the mother herself or her babes from the king's cruelty; the priestess he ordered to be manacled and cast into prison, the children to be committed to the river. It happened by singular good fortune that the Tiber having spread beyond its banks into stagnant pools afforded nowhere any access to the regular channel of the river, and the men who brought the twins were led to hope that being infants they might be drowned, no matter how sluggish the stream. So they made shift to discharge the king's command, by exposing the babes at the nearest point of the overflow, where the fig-tree Ruminalis—formerly, they say, called Romularis—now stands. In those days this was a wild and uninhabited region. The story persists that when the floating basket in which the children had been exposed was left high and dry by the receding water, a she-wolf, coming down out of the surrounding hills to slake her thirst, turned her steps towards the cry of the infants, and with her teats gave them suck so gently, that the keeper of the royal flock found her licking them with her tongue. Tradition assigns to this man the name of Faustulus, and adds that he carried the twins to his hut and gave them to his wife Larentia to rear. Some think that Larentia,‡ having been free with her favours, had got the name of "she-wolf" among the shepherds, and that this gave rise to this marvellous story. The boys, thus born and reared, had no sooner attained to youth than they began—yet without neglecting the farmstead or the flocks—to range the glades of the mountains for game. Having in this way gained both strength and resolution, they would now not only face wild beasts, but would attack robbers laden with their spoils, and divide up what they took from them among the shepherds, with whom they shared their toils and pranks, while their band of young men grew larger every day. . . .

The twins' activities result in the capture of Remus, who is charged with raiding and pillaging royal lands. Faustulus, who had suspected that his adopted sons were of royal birth for a long time, is now forced to reveal the twins' identities to Romulus, who subsequently kills Amulius and releases Remus. The brothers restore their grandfather, Numitor, to the throne.

The Alban state being thus made over to Numitor, Romulus and Remus were seized with

---

*The Vestal Virgins were important priestesses in Rome, which had not been founded at this point in the story. They were required to be celibate for their thirty-year terms of office.
†Rome.

‡The Latin word *lupa* (wolf) was a slang word for prostitute.

the desire to found a city in the region where they had been exposed and brought up. And in fact the population of Albans and Latins was too large; besides, there were the shepherds. . . . These considerations were interrupted by the curse of their grandsires, the greed of kingly power, and by a shameful quarrel which grew out of it, upon an occasion innocent enough. Since the brothers were twins, and respect for their age could not determine between them, it was agreed that the gods who had those places in their protection should choose by augury[*] who should give the new city its name, who should govern it when built. Romulus took the Palatine for his augural quarter, Remus the Aventine.[†] VII. Remus is said to have been the first to receive an augury, from the flight of six vultures. The omen had been already reported when twice that number appeared to Romulus. Thereupon each was saluted king by his own followers, the one party laying claim to the honour from priority, the other from the number of the birds. They then engaged in a battle of words and, angry taunts leading to bloodshed, Remus was struck down in the affray. The commoner story is that Remus leaped over the new walls in mockery of his brother,[‡] whereupon Romulus in great anger slew him, and in menacing wise added these words withal, "So, perish whoever else shall leap over my walls!" Thus Romulus acquired sole power, and the city, thus founded, was called by its founder's name. . . .

Romulus begins to build his city, building strong walls and appointing a Senate of one hundred men who will become the ancestors of the patrician class in Rome. He also offers asylum to anyone who will settle in Rome, which attracts nearby shepherds and

fugitives—a "miscellaneous rabble"—all of whom are men.

IX. Rome was now strong enough to hold her own in war with any of the adjacent states; but owing to the want of women a single generation was likely to see the end of her greatness, since she had neither prospect of posterity at home nor the right of intermarriage with her neighbours. So, on the advice of the senate, Romulus sent envoys round among all the neighbouring nations to solicit for the new people an alliance and the privilege of intermarrying. Cities, they argued, as well as all other things, take their rise from the lowliest beginnings. As time goes on, those which are aided by their own worth and by the favour of Heaven achieve great power and renown. They said they were well assured that Rome's origin had been blessed with the favour of Heaven, and that worth would not be lacking; their neighbours should not be reluctant to mingle their stock and their blood with the Romans, who were as truly men as they were. Nowhere did the embassy obtain a friendly hearing. In fact men spurned, at the same time that they feared, both for themselves and their descendants, that great power which was then growing up in their midst; and the envoys were frequently asked, on being dismissed, if they had opened a sanctuary for women as well as for men, for in that way only would they obtain suitable wives. This was a bitter insult to the young Romans, and the matter seemed certain to end in violence. Expressly to afford a fitting time and place for this, Romulus, concealing his resentment, made ready solemn games in honour of the equestrian Neptune, which he called Consualia.[§] He then bade proclaim the spectacle to the surrounding peoples, and his subjects

---

[*]A method of foretelling the future by observing the flight of birds.

[†]The Palantine and Aventine are two of the seven hills of Rome.

[‡]By leaping over the new walls—the sacred pomerium, or boundary of the city—Remus not only mocked his brother, but he committed sacrilege, a serious religious offense against the gods.

[§]The Consualia, a festival to the granary god Consus (whose name comes from the verb *condere*,, "to store"), was celebrated on August 21. As part of the rituals of this day, the Romans threw the entrails of sacrificed animals into waters that Neptune protected. They also decorated horses and asses with garlands. As a result, later Romans misidentified Consus as the god Neptunus Equester.

prepared to celebrate it with all the resources within their knowledge and power, that they might cause the occasion to be noised abroad and eagerly expected. Many people—for they were also eager to see the new city—gathered for the festival, especially those who lived nearest, the inhabitants of Caenina, Crustumium, and Antemnae. The Sabines, too, came with all their people, including their children and wives. They were hospitably entertained in every house, and when they had looked at the site of the City, its walls, and its numerous buildings, they marvelled that Rome had so rapidly grown great. When the time came for the show, and people's thoughts and eyes were busy with it, the preconcerted attack began. At a given signal the young Romans darted this way and that, to seize and carry off the maidens. In most cases these were taken by the men in whose path they chanced to be. Some, of exceptional beauty, had been marked out for the chief senators, and were carried off to their houses by plebeians to whom the office had been entrusted. One, who far excelled the rest in mien and loveliness, was seized, the story relates, by the gang of a certain Thalassius. Being repeatedly asked for whom they were bearing her off, they kept shouting that no one should touch her, for they were taking her to Thalassius,* and this was the origin of the wedding-cry. The sports broke up in a panic, and the parents of the maidens fled sorrowing. They charged the Romans with the crime of violating hospitality, and invoked the gods to whose solemn games they had come, deceived in violation of religion and honour. The stolen maidens were no more hopeful of their plight, nor less indignant. But Romulus himself went amongst them and explained that the pride of their parents had caused this deed, when they had refused their neighbours the right to intermarry; nevertheless the daughters should be wedded and become co-partners in all the possessions of the Romans, in their citizenship and,

*Thalassius is the Roman name for the Greek god of marriage, Hymenaeus. It was tradition for guests at Roman and Greek weddings to shout the god's name or use it in songs.

dearest privilege of all to the human race, in their children; only let them moderate their anger, and give their hearts to those to whom fortune had given their persons. A sense of injury had often given place to affection, and they would find their husbands the kinder for this reason, that every man would earnestly endeavour not only to be a good husband, but also to console his wife for the home and parents she had lost. His arguments were seconded by the wooing of the men, who excused their act on the score of passion and love, the most moving of all pleas to a woman's heart. . . .

The parents of the kidnapped daughters rush back to their respective city-states, urging them to declare war on Rome. Several conflicts ensue, culminating in a great battle between the Romans and the Sabines. When it looks as though the Romans have the advantage, the brides intervene.

XIII. Then the Sabine women, whose wrong had given rise to the war, with loosened hair and torn garments, their woman's timidity lost in a sense of their misfortune, dared to go amongst the flying missiles, and rushing in from the side, to part the hostile forces and disarm them of their anger, beseeching their fathers on this side, on that their husbands, that fathers-in-law and sons-in-law should not stain themselves with impious bloodshed, nor pollute with parricide the suppliants' children, grandsons to one party and sons to the other. "If you regret," they continued, "the relationship that unites you, if you regret the marriage-tie, turn your anger against us; we are the cause of war, the cause of wounds, and even death to both our husbands and our parents. It will be better for us to perish than to live, lacking either of you, as widows or as orphans." It was a touching plea, not only to the rank and file, but to their leaders as well. A stillness fell on them, and a sudden hush. Then the leaders came forward to make a truce, and not only did they agree on peace, but they made one people out of the two.

REVIEW QUESTIONS

1. What does this myth have to do with Roman religion? What examples can you find that demonstrate religious belief or practice?
2. How did Livy characterize the first inhabitants and citizens of Rome? How is this important for the way later Romans might have viewed themselves and their city?
3. Do Romulus and Remus deserve to be labeled heroes? Why or why not?
4. What does this story say about the role of women in Roman society?
5. Does this story work as imperial propaganda? Explain.

Boudicca Leads a Revolt of British Tribes Against the Romans

CASSIUS DIO, *Roman History, Book 62*

Cassius Dio (c. 164–229 C.E.) was the author of an eighty-book history of Rome from its origins in 753 B.C.E. to 229 C.E. A member of a prominent political family in Nicaea (modern Isnik, Turkey), he was a member of the Senate, held several magistracies, and was appointed to high administrative positions in the provinces of Africa, Dalmatia, and Upper Pannonia. In 229 he was coconsul with the twenty-year-old emperor, Severus Alexander. He retired later that same year, possibly for health reasons, and nothing further is known of him. His history ends with a brief description of his own retirement, and it is presumed that he died soon afterward.

The tumultuous times through which Dio lived shaped his view of his own era, as well as that of earlier periods. He was a teenager when the last of the "good emperors," Marcus Aurelius, died in 180. Thus Dio's political career did not begin until the twelve-year reign of Commodus, and it continued through the chaotic period that followed Commodus's assassination, the reestablishment of imperial power by the general Lucius Septimius Severus, and its subsequent decline under young Severan heirs, whose female guardians often ruled Rome on behalf of their sons. Dio and many of his senatorial colleagues despised the increasing autocracy and tyranny of Commodus and Severus, but they chafed under the administration of women like Julia Maesa, the grandmother of Elagabalus, and Julia Mamaea, the mother of Alexander Severus. Above all, these senators longed for a return to the values of an earlier era: when Rome was a republic, when the senatorial class dominated all things military and political, and when women did not meddle in public affairs. Dio, whose cultural background was Greek, very likely felt the loss of republican freedoms and liberties even more keenly than most.

Dio's views can be seen quite clearly in the following call to victory, which he placed in the mouth of the British warrior queen, Boudicca (also Boadicea and Buduica). Queen of the Iceni, Boudicca was the widow of a Roman client king, Prasutagus, who had willed his kingdom jointly to his wife and daughters, naming the emperor Nero as coruler as well. Imperial agents, however, saw the situation as an opportunity to take advantage of the Iceni. They imposed harsh taxes, confiscated the estates of prominent nobles, whipped Boudicca, and raped her daughters. In 61 c.e., Boudicca led an alliance of the Iceni and their neighbors, the Trinovantes, in a rebellion against Rome. While the British governor, Suetonius Paulinus, was absent, Boudicca and her army successfully sacked several Roman cities, including Londinum, but Suetonius returned and the Romans crushed the British revolt. Boudicca committed suicide.

While this sort of child's play* was going on at Rome, a terrible disaster occurred in Britain. Two cities were sacked, eighty thousand of the Romans and of their allies perished, and the island was lost to Rome. Moreover, all this ruin was brought upon the Romans by a woman, a fact which in itself caused them the greatest shame. Indeed, Heaven gave them indications of the catastrophe beforehand. For at night there was heard to issue from the senate-house foreign jargon mingled with laughter, and from the theatre outcries and lamentations, though no mortal man had uttered the words or the groans; houses were seen under the water in the river Thames, and the ocean between the island and Gaul once grew blood-red at flood tide.

An excuse for the war was found in the confiscation of the sums of money that Claudius[†] had given to the foremost Britons; for these sums, as Decianus Catus, the procurator of the island, maintained, were to be paid back. This was one reason for the uprising; another was found in the fact that Seneca,[‡] in the hope of receiving a good rate of interest, had lent to the islanders 40,000,000 sesterces that they did not want, and had afterwards called in this loan all at once and had resorted to severe measures in

exacting it. But the person who was chiefly instrumental in rousing the natives and persuading them to fight the Romans, the person who was thought worthy to be their leader and who directed the conduct of the entire war, was Boudicca, a Briton woman of the royal family and possessed of greater intelligence than often belongs to women. This woman assembled her army, to the number of some 120,000, and then ascended a tribunal which had been constructed of earth in the Roman fashion. In stature she was very tall, in appearance most terrifying, in the glance of her eye most fierce, and her voice was harsh; a great mass of the tawniest hair fell to her hips; around her neck was a large golden necklace; and she wore a tunic of divers colours over which a thick mantle was fastened with a brooch. This was her invariable attire. She now grasped a spear to aid her in terrifying all beholders and spoke as follows:

"You have learned by actual experience how different freedom is from slavery. Hence, although some among you may previously, through ignorance of which was better, have been deceived by the alluring promises of the Romans, yet now that you have tried both, you have learned how great a mistake you made in preferring an imported despotism to your ancestral mode of life, and you have come to realize how much better is poverty with no master than wealth with slavery. For what treatment is there of the most shameful or grievous sort that we have not suffered ever since these men made their appearance in Britain? Have we not been robbed entirely of most of our possessions, and those the greatest, while for those that remain

---

*The "child's play" to which Dio sarcastically referred was the behavior of Rome's young ruler, Nero (emperor from 54 to 68). Only sixteen at his accession, he detested anything related to governing and was inordinately fond of art, music, drama, chariot racing, and Greek-style athletic competitions.

[†]The emperor Claudius (10 B.C.E.–54 C.E.), Nero's predecessor and adoptive father.

[‡]Annaeus Seneca (c. 4 B.C.E.–65 C.E.), a Stoic philosopher who was Nero's tutor and chief political advisor.

we pay taxes? Besides pasturing and tilling for them all our other possessions, do we not pay a yearly tribute for our very bodies? How much better it would be to have been sold to masters once for all than, possessing empty titles of freedom, to have to ransom ourselves every year! How much better to have been slain and to have perished than to go about with a tax on our heads! Yet why do I mention death? For even dying is not free of cost with them; nay, you know what fees we deposit even for our dead. Among the rest of mankind death frees even those who are in slavery to others; only in the case of the Romans do the very dead remain alive for their profit. Why is it that, though none of us has any money (how, indeed, could we, or where could we get it?), we are stripped and despoiled like a murderer's victims? And why should the Romans be expected to display moderation as time goes on, when they have behaved toward us in this fashion at the very outset, when all men show consideration even for the beasts they have newly captured?

"But, to speak the plain truth, it is we who have made ourselves responsible for all these evils, in that we allowed them to set foot on the island in the first place instead of expelling them at once as we did their famous Julius Caesar,—yes, and in that we did not deal with them while they were still far away as we dealt with Augustus and with Gaius Caligula and make even the attempt to sail hither a formidable thing. As a consequence, although we inhabit so large an island, or rather a continent, one might say, that is encircled by the sea, and although we possess a veritable world of our own and are so separated by the ocean from all the rest of mankind that we have been believed to dwell on a different earth and under a different sky, and that some of the outside world, aye, even their wisest men, have not hitherto known for a certainty even by what name we are called, we have, notwithstanding all this, been despised and trampled underfoot by men who know nothing else than how to secure gain. However, even at this late day, though we have not done so before, let us, my countrymen and friends and kinsmen,—for

I consider you all kinsmen, seeing that you inhabit a single island and are called by one common name,—let us, I say, do our duty while we still remember what freedom is, that we may leave to our children not only its appellation but also its reality. For, if we utterly forget the happy state in which we were born and bred, what, pray, will they do, reared in bondage?

"All this I say, not with the purpose of inspiring you with a hatred of present conditions,—that hatred you already have,—nor with fear for the future,—that fear you already have,—but of commending you because you now of your own accord choose the requisite course of action, and of thanking you for so readily co-operating with me and with each other. Have no fear whatever of the Romans; for they are superior to us neither in numbers nor in bravery. And here is the proof: they have protected themselves with helmets and breastplates and greaves and yet further provided themselves with palisades and walls and trenches to make sure of suffering no harm by an incursion of their enemies. For they are influenced by their fears when they adopt this kind of fighting in preference to the plan we follow of rough and ready action. Indeed, we enjoy such a surplus of bravery, that we regard our tents as safer than their walls and our shields as affording greater protection than their whole suits of mail. As a consequence, we when victorious capture them, and when overpowered elude them; and if we ever choose to retreat anywhere, we conceal ourselves in swamps and mountains so inaccessible that we can be neither discovered nor taken. Our opponents, however, can neither pursue anybody, by reason of their heavy armour, nor yet flee; and if they ever do slip away from us, they take refuge in certain appointed spots, where they shut themselves up as in a trap. But these are not the only respects in which they are vastly inferior to us: there is also the fact that they cannot bear up under hunger, thirst, cold, or heat, as we can. They require shade and covering, they require kneaded bread and wine and oil, and if any of these things fails them, they perish; for us, on the other hand, any grass or root serves as bread, the juice of any plant as oil, any water as wine, any tree as a house. Furthermore, this region is familiar to us and is our ally, but to them it is unknown and hostile. As for the rivers, we swim them naked, whereas they do not get across them easily even with boats. Let us, therefore, go against them trusting boldly to good fortune. Let us show them that they are hares and foxes trying to rule over dogs and wolves."

When she had finished speaking, she employed a species of divination, letting a hare escape from the fold of her dress; and since it ran on what they considered the auspicious side, the whole multitude shouted with pleasure, and Boudicca, raising her hand toward heaven, said: "I thank thee; Andraste,* and call upon thee as woman speaking to woman; for I rule over no burden-bearing Egyptians as did Nitocris,† nor over trafficking Assyrians as did Semiramis‡ (for we have by now gained thus much learning from the Romans!), much less over the Romans themselves as did Messalina§ once and afterwards Agrippina‖ and now Nero (who, though in name a man, is in fact a woman, as is proved by his singing, lyre-playing and beautification of his person); nay, those over whom I rule are Britons, men that know not how to till the soil or ply a trade, but are thoroughly versed in the art of war and hold all things in common, even children and wives, so that the latter possess the same valour as the men. As the queen, then, of such men and of such women, I supplicate and pray thee for victory, preservation of life, and liberty against men insolent, unjust, insatiable,

impious,—if, indeed, we ought to term those people men who bathe in warm water, eat artificial dainties, drink unmixed wine, anoint themselves with myrrh, sleep on soft couches with boys for bedfellows,—boys past their prime at that,—and are slaves to a lyre-player and a poor one too. Wherefore may this Mistress Domitia-Nero# reign no longer over me or over you men; let the wench sing and lord it over Romans, for they surely deserve to be the slaves of such a woman after having submitted to her so long. But for us, Mistress, be thou alone ever our leader."

Having finished an appeal to her people of this general tenor, Boudicca led her army against the Romans; for these chanced to be without a leader, inasmuch as Paulinus, their commander, had gone on an expedition to Mona, an island near Britain. This enabled her to sack and plunder two Roman cities, and, as I have said, to wreak indescribable slaughter. Those who were taken captive by the Britons were subjected to every known form of outrage. The worst and most bestial atrocity committed by their captors was the following. They hung up naked the noblest and most distinguished women and then cut off their breasts and sewed them to their mouths, in order to make the victims appear to be eating them; afterwards they impaled the women on sharp skewers run lengthwise through the entire body. All this they did to the accompaniment of sacrifices, banquets and wanton behaviour, not only in all their other sacred places, but particularly in the grove of Andate. This was their name for Victory, and they regarded her with most exceptional reverence. . . .

The British governor, Suetonius Paulinus, then returned from Mona and led the Roman army against Boudicca's forces.

Boudicca, at the head of an army of about 230,000 men, rode in a chariot herself and as-

---

*The Icenian name for the British goddess of victory.

†A legendary sixth-dynasty queen of Egypt, Nitocris avenged herself—at the cost of her own life—on a group of Egyptian nobles who had murdered her brother in order to make her queen, circa 2200 B.C.E.

‡The Greek name of Samnmu-ramat, the mother of Adadnirari III of Assyria. In 805 B.C.E., she participated in her son's campaign against Commagene.

§The third wife of Claudius, Messalina (c. 20–48 C.E.) was forced to commit suicide after an unsuccessful attempt to overthrow her husband.

‖The mother of Nero and fourth wife of Claudius, Agrippina (14–59 C.E.) successfully schemed to place her son on the throne, briefly involved herself in affairs of state, and was murdered at Nero's order for her efforts.

#Domitia is the feminized version of one of Nero's preaccession names, Lucius Domitius Ahenobarbus.

signed the others to their several stations. Paulinus could not extend his line the whole length of hers, for, even if the men had been drawn up only one deep, they would not have reached far enough, so inferior were they in numbers; nor, on the other hand, did he dare join battle in a single compact force, for fear of being surrounded and cut to pieces. He therefore separated his army into three divisions, in order to fight at several points at one and the same time, and he made each of the divisions so strong that it could not easily be broken through. . . .

They contended for a long time, both parties being animated by the same zeal and daring. But finally, late in the day, the Romans prevailed; and they slew many in battle beside the wagons and the forest, and captured many alive. Nevertheless, not a few made their escape and were preparing to fight again. In the meantime, however, Boudicca fell sick and died.* The Britons mourned her deeply and gave her a costly burial; but, feeling that now at last they were really defeated, they scattered to their homes. So much for affairs in Britain.

———
*Actually, Boudicca poisoned herself.

REVIEW QUESTIONS

1. In his opening remarks, Dio comments that losses in Britain were especially shameful because "all this ruin was brought upon the Romans by a woman." Does the depiction of Boudicca that follows his remark reinforce or undermine his statement? Explain.
2. What can you learn about British customs and beliefs from this excerpt of Dio's *Roman History*? How reliable do you think this information is? Why?
3. How does Boudicca's speech characterize the Romans? Do you think this portrayal was primarily Boudicca's view or Dio's? Explain.
4. Look up the definition of *hero, heroine, heroism,* and *heroic.* Is success a prerequisite for heroism? Was Boudicca a heroine? A success? Explain your answer.

The Shakti of Kannaki

ILANGO ADIGAL, *Shilappadikaram (The Jeweled Anklet)*

The Dravidian languages are spoken almost entirely in the four southernmost states of India. A minor related language is found in an area of the Indus River (in what is now Pakistan), which has contributed to speculation that the Dravidian speakers of south India, especially the Tamils, may well be the descendants of the ancient Indus (or Harappan) civilization.

Tamil literature has a rich heritage that is likely as old as Sanskrit. One of the most important works is the *Shilappadikaram,* or *The Jeweled Anklet,* which has been dated from 171 C.E. to as late as the fifth century. The story in a simpler form had most likely been around for centuries before it was developed into a written "epic." Rather than an epic, the work might better be described as a novel in verse (although the translation from which the following selection is taken is mostly in prose). The work is attributed to a Jain prince,

Ilango Adigal, brother of a Hindu king. The story shows people of both religions, along with Buddhists, living peacefully together. It is a morality story, with some Jain doctrine and principles included.

Unlike the famous Greek and Sanskrit epics, the central figures are of the merchant class, not the aristocracy. Furthermore, the setting is urban. In a sense it is a love story, albeit a tragic one. The two most notable features are the metaphorical use of nature imagery (e.g., "Kovalan and Kannaki lay entwined like two black serpents on their couch") and the demonstration of three basic Indian religio-philosophical principles: dharma (duty), karma (behavior and its consequences), and shakti (the mystic cosmic power embedded in a virtuous woman). The anklet is itself both a symbol and a catalyst. When Kovalan, the young husband, and Kannaki, the wife, are together, her anklets are together; when the anklets are separated, so are the lovers. The anklet is instrumental in a breach in their marriage and in Kovalan's death.

The first separation—of the anklets and the couple—involves Kovalan's infatuation with a young courtesan (who, near the end of the book, renounces her profession for a religious life). Kannaki dutifully takes him back when he returns full of remorse. They move from their home city of Puhar to Madurai, an important city with a great temple complex even today. It is a difficult move for Kannaki, leaving her parents and hometown, but as a good wife she follows her husband. The anklet plays a central role in Kovalan's karma— past behavior in this and previous lives—which catches up with him.

The following excerpt begins as Kovalan takes one of Kannaki's anklets to exchange it, as he tells her, for money. Through a quick series of turns, Kovalan is accused of having stolen the anklet from the queen, and he is killed. By allowing this injustice to happen, the king has failed in his dharma (duty). Kannaki literally becomes the instrument of karma, through her womanly virtue (shakti) exacting terrible retribution upon the king and his city, which becomes "purified by fire" after the king and queen fall dead (she with the remark, "Never can a woman survive her husband's death"). Kannaki's action should not be misunderstood as a means of her own vengeance: She tells the dying queen, "I have orders {from "the god of Fire"} to destroy this city." Only evildoers are destroyed; good people, children, and cows are spared. Kannaki, too, cannot outlive her husband; she is apotheosized, or deified.

THE SITE OF AGONY

. . . Kôvalan said:

"You left your old parents, your friends, your attendants, your nurse, and all your retinue, and kept at your service only your modesty, your faith, your virtue, and your loyalty. You came with me and relieved me of remorse. Precious as a golden liana,* girl with the fragrant plaits! You

---
*A woody climbing tropical vine.

are the incarnation of faithfulness, the beacon of the world, the tender bud of chastity, the store of all virtues. I must now go to the town, taking with me one of the gold circlets that grace your charming ankles. Having exchanged it for money, I shall soon return. Till then do not let your courage fail."

After kissing the long black hair he loved, heartbroken to leave her all alone, and holding back the tears that filled his eyes, he walked heavily away. As a stranger to those parts, he could not know that the humped bull that stood before him as he passed the meeting place of the cowherds was a fearful omen.

Passing through the street of the courtesans, he reached the bazaar. There he saw a goldsmith in court dress, who was walking along, tweezers in hand, followed by a hundred jewelers all famous for their craftsmanship. Kôvalan thought this must be the goldsmith of the Pândya monarch. So he approached him and inquired:

"Could you estimate the value of an ankle bracelet worthy of the consort of the great king who protects us?"

The goldsmith had the face of Death's dread messenger. He answered with obsequious politeness:

"I am a novice in this great art: I know only how to make diadems and a few royal ornaments." Kôvalan opened the packet containing the precious anklet. The perfidious goldsmith examined the fine workmanship of the chiseling in pure gold and the rare rubies and diamonds. After a pause he said: "This circlet can be purchased only by the great queen herself. I am going to the palace, and shall speak to the victorious king. You may wait with the anklet near my humble home till I return."

Kôvalan sat down in a small shrine that stood near the villain's cottage. When he saw him waiting in the narrow temple, the hardhearted thief thought: Before anyone discovers that it was I who stole the [queen's] anklet, I shall accuse this foreigner before the king. He then walked on.

The great queen, resentful of the king's interest in Madurai's pretty dancers, who sing songs of all sorts and show in their movements their understanding of music, was disguising her jealousy under the mask of a friendly quarrel. Pretending a sudden headache, she left the royal presence. Later, when ministers and counselors had gone, the king entered the inner apartment where the great queen lay surrounded by maids with long alluring eyes.

The goldsmith met the king near the innermost door, where guards had been posted. He bowed low, praising the monarch in a hundred ways. Then he said:

"The man who stole an anklet from this palace has been found. He apparently did not use heavy tools or crowbars, but just the power of magic words, with which he put to sleep the soldiers who were guarding the doors. He then quietly took away the handsomest ankle bracelet in the palace. He is now hiding near my humble house, fearing the guards that patrol the city."

Now it befell that this was the moment when the actions of Kôvalan's past lives had become ripe like a mature crop in the fields. The king, who wears the garland of margosa leaves, did not call for any inquiry. He simply summoned some town guards and ordered:

"Should you find, in the hands of a most clever thief, an ankle ornament resembling a wreath of flowers, which belongs to my consort, put the man to death and bring me the bracelet."

When he heard the royal order, the infamous goldsmith, with mirth in his heart, thought: I've brought it off! He led the guards to Kôvalan, whom a merciless fate had thrown into his net, and told him:

"On orders from the king, whose army has won all battles, these officers have come with me to look at your piece of jewelry." He pointed out to them the details of the ankle bracelet's design. But they protested:

"The appearance of this good man is surely not that of a thief. We cannot put him to death."

The astute goldsmith smiled contemptuously. He explained to these simple men that the people whose shameful trade is theft have invented eight ways to deceive their innocent victims: these are spells, bewitching, drugs, omens, and magic, as well as place, time, and devices.

"If you let yourselves become intoxicated by the drugs this man dares use, you expose yourselves to the anger of our great king.

"The thief who utters magic spells becomes invisible, like a child of the gods. When he calls for the help of celestial genii, he can carry away his stolen objects unseen. Stupefying his victims with his drugs, he renders them incapable of the slightest movement. Unless omens are good, a real thief abstains from any activity even when he sees before him objects of great value ready to fall into his hands. When he makes use of enchantments, he can despoil the king of the gods himself of the wreath that adorns his chest. If he has chosen in advance the place of his rapine, no one can see him there. When he has set the time, the gods themselves could not stop him from seizing the object he wants. If he uses his implements to steal things of great value, no one can find him out. If you should read in the thieves' sacred book, you would see that their art requires arduous study, and that it has almost no limits.

"It happened once that a clever thief, disguised as an ambassador, had stood a whole day before the door of the palace. At night he changed himself into a young woman, and, entering unnoticed, hid in the shadow cast by a lamp. He seized the rare diamond necklace, bright as the sun, that shone round the neck of the sleeping crown prince. Waking up, the prince felt that his necklace was not on his shoulders. He drew his sword, but the thief was able to grasp it and keep the prince from striking a blow. When he tired of this, the prince tried fighting with his hands, but the thief, expert in his profession, ran away, leaving the prince alone and fighting against a stone pillar studded with precious gems. There is no thief on earth equal to this villain. If one of you has a better one, then he may bring him to me."

A young hangman who had been listening to the criminal goldsmith's words, spear in hand, said:

"In the season of rains, during a dark night when my village was fast asleep, a thief came armed with a ploughshare like those used in the fields. Dressed in black, searching for jewels, he seemed fiercer than a tiger. I drew my sword but he tore it away from me and vanished, never to be found. The deeds of thieves are amazing. If we do not obey the king, we shall surely be in trouble. Brave soldiers, let's do our duty."

Thereupon one of these drunkards hurled his sword at Kôvalan. It pierced his body. Blood gushing from the wound fell upon the Earth,

mother of men, and she shuddered with grief. Defeated by his fate, Kôvalan fell; and the virtuous scepter of the Pândyas was bent.

Coda

And since the champion of justice
failed to safeguard Kannaki's beloved
    spouse,
the upright scepter of the Pândya kings
became forever bent.
All these events had been foreseen,
for actions, be they good or evil,
bear their inexorable fruits.
This is the reason that wise men
make all their actions
accord with the great moral laws. . . .

Kannaki . . . asked:

"Will you not speak to me, my friend? Tell me. My husband has not yet returned, and my heart feels oppressed. My breath is as hot as that from a blacksmith's bellows. Have you not brought some news from the city? Long may you live, my friend.

"Though the sun is still high, I am trembling. Why has my beloved not come back? My heart is becoming heavy with fear. Since you see that I am worried by his absence, please distract me with some gossip from town. May the gods bless you, friend.

"Shall I beg your help? My lord has not yet returned. I fear he may be in danger. My mind is bewildered; I feel anxious. Are you hiding something from me? Pray speak to me, my friend. Tell me what people who live in your city, strangers to me, have said."

At last the cowgirl spoke:

"They abused him. They said he was a thief, come secretly to steal a wonderful ankle bracelet from the royal palace. They accused him, calling him a robber, mysterious in his behavior. And the royal soldiers, those who wear noisy anklets, put him to death."

On hearing this, Kannaki leaped up in her anger, then collapsed to the ground. It seemed as if the moon had risen in the sky; then fallen, shrouded with clouds. She wept, and her eyes became still redder. She clamored, "Where are you, beloved husband?" and fell in a swoon. When she came back to her senses, she lamented:

"And must I die of sorrow, like the wretched women who take fearful oaths upon the pyres of their beloved husbands? For I have lost the man who dearly loved me, by the fault of a king his own subjects must despise.

"Must I die of despair, like the lonely women who carry their grief from pilgrimage to pilgrimage, and bathe in holy rivers, after the death of husbands who wore fragrant flower-garlands on their broad chests?

"Must I die, an embodiment of meaningless virtue, through the fatal error of a ruler who bears the scepter of injustice? Must I languish in loneliness, like the forlorn women who, after their tender husbands have vanished in the funeral pyre's smoke, remain, half alive, in abject widowhood?

"Must I, with broken heart, suffer an endless agony, because in tragic error the scepter of a Pândya king has gone astray from the path of right?

"Look at me! Hearken to my words, you honest cowgirls here assembled! It was with just foreboding that you danced the dance of love. Now hearken to my words! Listen to me, cowherds' daughters!

"Sun god, whose rays are flames! You, the eternal witness of all the deeds committed on the sea-encircled earth, speak! Could my husband be called a thief?"

A voice was heard, coming from the sky:

"He was never a thief! Woman of the carplike eyes, this city shall be purified by fire!"

THE MURMURS OF THE CITY

The Sun had given its verdict. The woman with the bright armlets stood up. Holding in her hand her remaining ankle bracelet, mate to the one she had given to Kôvalan, Kannaki went to the city, and walked through it, crying:

"Virtuous women who live in this city ruled by a nefarious monarch, listen to me! Today I underwent unspeakable agony. What must nowise

happen has happened. Never shall I accept this iniquitous injustice. Was my husband a thief? No, he was killed to avoid paying him the price of my ankle bracelet. Can there be a more flagrant denial of justice? Should I ever see the body of the man who dearly loved me, I shall not hear from him the words I need to hear, saying he is not at fault. Is that justice? He can no longer protect me, so why don't you come and accuse me too of some invented crime? Do you hear me?"

The people of the rich city of Madurai were dismayed at the sight of this distracted woman. In their stupefaction, they exclaimed:

"The just and virtuous scepter of our king has been forever bent. A crime that nothing can undo has been committed against this innocent woman. What shall this lead us to? Tarnished is the honor of Tennavan, the king of kings, who inherited an infallible spear and a stainless white parasol. What are we to think? The parasol of our victorious king was protecting the land, keeping us cool under its shade; and now the fierce rays of the sun may devour us. What are we to expect?

"A new and mighty goddess has appeared to us. In her hand she carries an ankle bracelet made of gold. Is this a portent from heaven? From the desperate woman's eyes, red and running with black collyrium, tears are flowing. She seems possessed by a genie. What must we think?"

Thus bewildered, the people of Madurai gathered around her, showing their good will and attempting to console her. Everywhere indignant words could be heard. In the midst of this disorder, someone showed Kannaki the body of her dear husband. The lianalike woman saw him; he could not see her.

The Sun was unable to bear this sight. Suddenly it extinguished its rays, hiding behind the hills. The veil of night covered the earth. In the evening dusk Kannaki, resembling a frail reed in bloom, lamented, and the whole city resounded with her cries. That very morning, between two kisses, she had received from her husband a flower wreath he was wearing, and with it she had adorned her tresses. Now on the evening of the same day she looked down at him lying in a pool of blood that had flowed from his open wound.

He could not even see her grief. She cried out in anger and despair:

"O witness of my grief, you cannot console me. Is it right that your body, fairer than pure gold, lie unwashed here in the dust? Will people not say that it was my ill luck that led a just king to a mistake that was the fruit of his ignorance? Is it just that in the red glow of the twilight your handsome chest, framed with a flower wreath, lies thrown down on the bare earth, while I remain alone, helpless and abandoned to despair? Shall people not be led to say that it was my own predestination that compelled the innocent Pândya to such an injustice when the whole world could easily see that he had committed an error?

"Is there no woman here? Is there no real woman, or only the sort of woman who would allow such an injustice to be done to her lawful husband? Are there such women here?

"Is there no man in this land? Is there no honest man, or only the sort of man who nourishes and protects only the sons of his own blood?

"Is there no god? Is there no god in this country? Can there be a god in a land where the sword of the king is used for the murder of innocent strangers? Is there no god, no god?"

Thus lamenting, Kannaki clasped her husband's chest that Fortune had so dearly cherished. Suddenly Kôvalan arose and exclaimed, "Your moonlike face appears tarnished." With affectionate hands he wiped away the tears that burned her eyes. The lovely woman fell to the ground, weeping and moaning. With bracelet-laden hands she grasped the feet of her beloved husband. But he departed, rising into the air. Surrounded by hosts of angels, he shed his mortal frame and disappeared. His voice could still be heard, fading away:

"Beloved! Stay there, stay! Remain peacefully in life!"

She thought: Is this an illusion of my demented mind? What else could all this be? Is some spirit eager to deceive me? Where can I discover the truth? I shall not search for my husband before he is avenged. I shall meet this inhuman king and ask for his justice against himself.

She stood up, and then she remembered her vision. Tears fell from her long carp-shaped eyes. She stiffened, and recalled her anger. Wiping away her burning tears, she ran to the majestic gate of the royal palace.

THE CALL FOR JUSTICE

The Pândya queen spoke:

"Alas! I saw, in a dream, a scepter bent, a fallen parasol. The bell at the gate moved of itself and rang loudly. Alas! I also saw . . . I saw the eight directions of space wavering, the night devouring the sun. Alas! I also saw . . . I saw the rainbow shining in the night, a glittering star falling by day. Alas!"

The Omens

"The scepter of justice and the white parasol fallen to the hard ground, the bell ringing alone at the gate of a victorious king's palace, my heart trembling with fear, the rainbow in the night, the star falling by day, the directions of space vacillating—all these are portents of a fearful danger at hand. I must inform the king."

Adorned with resplendent jewels, she went to the king's apartments, followed by maids who carried her mirror and her various trifles. With her went her hunchbacks, dwarfs, deaf-mutes, and buffoons, carrying silks, betel, cosmetics, pastes, garlands, feather-fans, and incense. The ladies in waiting, with flowers in their hair, sang her praise:

"May the consort of the Pândya, who protects the vast universe, live many happy days."

Thus the great queen, followed by her guards and maids singing her praises and bowing before her feet, went to King Tennavan, on whose chest Fortune rests. He was seated on the lion throne. She told him her sinister dream.

At the same moment cries were heard:

"Hoy, doorkeeper! Hoy, watchman! Hoy, palace guards of an irresponsible ruler whose vile heart lightly casts aside the kingly duty of rendering justice! Go! Tell how a woman, a widow, carrying a single ankle bracelet from a pair that once joyfully rang together, waits at the gate. Go! Announce me!"

The watchman bowed before the king and said:

"Long live the ruler of Korkai! Long live Tennavan, lord of the southern mountains, whose fair name calumny and scandal have never touched!

"A woman is waiting at the gate. She is not Korravai, the victorious goddess who carries in her hand a glorious spear and stands upon the neck of a defeated buffalo losing its blood through its fresh wounds. She is not Anangu, youngest of the seven virgins, for whom Shiva once danced; and she is not Kâlî, who dwells in the darkest forests inhabited by ghosts and imps. Neither is she the goddess who pierced the chest of the mighty Dâruka. She seems filled with a mad fury, suffused with rage. She has lost someone dear to her, and stands at the gate clasping an ankle bracelet of gold in her hands."

The king said:

"Let her come in. Bring her to me." The gate-keeper let the woman enter, and brought her to the king. When she drew near the monarch, he said: "Woman, your face is soiled from weeping. Who are you, young woman? What brings you before us?"

Kannaki answered sharply:

"Inconsiderate king! I have much to say. I was born in Puhâr, that well-known capital, the names of whose kings remain unsullied. One of them, Shibi, in ancient times sacrificed his own life to save a dove, in the presence of all the gods. Another, Manunîtikanda, when a cow with weeping eyes rang the palace bell in search of justice for her calf, crushed under a chariot wheel, sacrificed his own son, guilty of the act, under the same wheel. There in Puhâr a man named Kôvalan was born. He was the son of a wealthy merchant, Mâshâttuvan. His family is known, and his name untarnished. Led by fate, O king, he entered your city, with ringing anklets, expecting to earn a living. When he tried to sell my ankle bracelet, he was murdered. I am his wife. My name is Kannaki."

The king answered:

"Divine woman, there is no injustice in putting a robber to death. Do you not know that that is the duty of a king?"

The beautiful girl said:

"King of Korkai, you went astray from the path of duty. Remember that my ankle bracelet was filled with precious stones."

"Woman," the king answered, "what you have said is pertinent. For ours was filled, not with gems, but with pearls. Let it be brought." The ankle bracelet was brought and placed before the king. Kannaki seized it and broke it open. A gem sprang up into the king's face. When he saw the stone, he faltered. He felt his parasol fallen, his scepter bent. He said: "Is it right for a king to act upon the word of a miserable goldsmith? I am the thief. For the first time I have failed in my duty as protector of the southern kingdom. No way is left open to me save to give up my life." And having spoken, the king swooned. The great queen fell near him. Trembling, she lamented:

"Never can a woman survive her husband's death." And, placing the feet of her lord on her head, the unfortunate queen fainted away.

Kannaki said:

"Today we have seen evidence of the sage's warning: *The Divine Law appears in the form of death before the man who fails in his duty.* Consort of a victorious king who committed a deed both cruel and unjust! I too am guilty of great sins. Be witness to the cruel deed I perform."

Coda

The poet speaks:

With terror I saw Kannaki, tears streaming from her blood-red eyes, holding in her hand her remaining ankle bracelet, her body lifeless, her undone hair resembling a dark forest.

I saw the sovereign of Kudal become a corpse. I must be guilty of great crimes to be witness to such fearful events.

The lord of the Vaigai saw Kannaki's body, soiled with dust, her black disheveled hair, her tears, and the solitary ankle bracelet in her fair hand. Overwhelmed with sorrow, he listened to the words Kannaki had said in her rage. He could not bear to remain alive, and fell dead.

THE MALEDICTION

Kannaki then spoke to the dying Pândya queen:

"Wife of a great monarch! I too am a victim

of fate. I have never wished to cause pain. But it is said that he who has wronged another in the morning must, before darkness falls, repay his debt.

"A woman with abundant hair one day asked and obtained that at midday her kitchen and the oven's fire should take human form to testify to her purity.

"Once, as a joke, her friends told a virtuous and naïve widow, whose pubis showed some stripes, that her husband was a sand effigy modeled on the bank of the Kâverî. The faithful woman stayed near the image. The rising tide, which had surrounded her, stayed aloof, not daring to approach.

"A daughter of the famous king, Karikâla, once jumped into the sea that had carried away her husband Vanjikkôn, calling to him, 'Lord with shoulders like mountains!' The god of the Sea himself brought back her husband to her. Clasping him like a liana, she led him to their home.

"Another good woman changed herself into stone and remained in a garden near the shore gazing at the approaching ships. She recovered her human shape only on the day when her husband returned home.

"When the son of a co-wife fell into a well, a woman threw in her own son and succeeded in saving both.

"Because a stranger had glanced at her with lustful eyes, a chaste woman changed her moon-like face into that of a monkey. Only when her husband returned did this flowerlike woman, who treasured her body more than a jewel, take back her human face.

"There was also a girl, fair and lovely as a statue of gold. She heard her mother say to her father, 'Women's settlements unsettle all things. Once, as a joke, I told my maid, "When I have a daughter, and when you, maid with pretty bangles, have a son, my daughter shall be your son's bride." The maid kept this in her memory, and today she asked me for the girl. I am at my wits' end, not knowing what to say. How unfortunate

I am!' When she overheard this, the girl like a golden statue put on a silk dress, tied her hair, and came to the maid's son. She knelt before him and placed his foot upon her head.

"It was in Puhâr, the city from which I come, that they all lived, these noble women with fragrant braids. If these stories are true, and if I am faithful, I cannot allow your city to survive. I must destroy it, together with its king. You shall soon see the meaning of my words."

Kannaki then left the king's palace, shouting:

"Men and women of Madurai, city of the four temples! And you, gods of heaven! Listen to me! I curse this town whose ruler put to death the man I dearly loved. The blame is not mine."

Suddenly, with her own hands, she twisted and tore her left breast from her body. Then she walked three times round the city, repeating her curse at each gate. In her despair she threw away her lovely breast, which fell in the dirt of the street. Then before her there appeared the god of Fire in the shape of a priest. His body was all blue and encircled with tongues of flames. His hair was as red as the evening sky, his milk-white teeth shone brightly. He said:

"Faithful woman! I have orders to destroy this city on the very day you suffered such great wrong. Is there someone that should be spared?"

Kannaki bade him:

"Spare Brahmins, good men, cows, truthful women, cripples, old men, children. Destroy evildoers."

And the city of Mandurai, capital of the Pândyas, whose chariots are invincible, was immediately hidden in flames and smoke.

Coda

When the glorious Pândya, his dancers and
    his palace,
his soldiers holding shining bows, even
his elephants, were all burnt down to ashes,
destroyed by the flames of virtue,
the wretched town's immortals went away,
for they are blameless.

REVIEW QUESTIONS

1. How do you see the position of women as wives?
2. How would you describe the feminine power of shakti?
3. In what ways does this work reflect a fierceness in regard to justice?
4. In your opinion, does the king deserve his fate? Why or why not? What about the queen?
5. How would you describe Kannaki's character? To what degree does she seem to be strong? To what degree does she seem to be acting independently?

The Hero Twins Devise the Harvest Ritual

Popol Vuh

The story in this selection focuses on the Hero Twins, Hunahpu and Xbalanque. Mischievous and unruly as boys, they are selfish, dishonest, and lazy even as young men. By the end of the story, however, they come to realize the value of personal sacrifice, an integral principle of the Maya and, indeed, all Central American religion.

The following selection opens with the birth of the Hero Twins. Their father and his brother, One Hunahpu and Seven Hunahpu, had been sacrificed by One Death and Seven Death, the principal dieties of Xibalba (the underworld) for daring to make too much noise above ground while playing the ball game. The severed head of One Hunahpu was placed in a calabash tree, from where the skull impregnated the twins' mother, Blood Woman, by spitting into her hand. Her miraculous pregnancy, however, displeased her father, Blood Gatherer. Using trickery she faked her death and fled to the home of One and Seven Hunahpu's mother, Xmucane, referred to in this selection as "the grandmother."

As the story recounts, the grandmother had hidden the ball game equipment of her sons in the rafters of her home. The Hero Twins managed to recover it and began playing the game again. The ball game, of course, was essential for the welfare of the people, since the blood sacrifices made after the game fed the sun god and guaranteed that he would have enough energy to continue his journey across the sky each day. The noise of the ball game, however, offended the gods of Xibalba again, who summoned Hunahpu and Xbalanque to the underworld to answer for their crime, just like their father and uncle before them. Understanding the seriousness of their obligation, the Twins (who would sacrifice their lives repeatedly for the greater good) not only faced the challenge ahead of them, but also found a way to reassure the grandmother during their absence. In doing so, they created a harvest ritual that the Quiche people still observe today. The ears of corn (maize) planted in the house were not to be used as food or seed, but to serve as a reminder that the corn was alive even if it was dried up. When the corn dried at harvest, it would be a sign of the Hero Twins' deaths; but when it sprouted again in the spring, it would be a sign that the Twins were alive again.

And this is their birth; we shall tell of it here.

Then it came to the day of their birth, and the maiden named Blood Woman gave birth. The grandmother was not present when they were born; they were born suddenly. Two of them were born, named Hunahpu and Xbalanque. They were born in the mountains, and then they came into the house. Since they weren't sleeping:

"Throw them out of here! They're really loud-mouths!"* said the grandmother.

After that, when they put them on an ant-hill, they slept soundly there. And when they removed them from there, they put them in brambles next.

And this is what One Monkey and One Artisan[†] wanted: that they should die on the anthill and die in the brambles. One Monkey and One Artisan wanted this because they were rowdyish and flushed with jealousy. They didn't allow their younger brothers in the house at first, as if they didn't even know them, but even so they flourished in the mountains.

And One Monkey and One Artisan were great flautists and singers, and as they grew up they went through great suffering and pain. It had cost them suffering to become great knowers. Through it all they became flautists, singers, and writers, carvers. They did everything well. They simply knew it when they were born, they simply had genius. And they were the successors of their fathers who had gone to Xibalba, their dead fathers.

Hunahpu and Xbalanque now plot the downfall of their elder brothers.

Since One Monkey and One Artisan were great knowers, in their hearts they already realized everything when their younger brothers came into being, but they didn't reveal their insight because of their jealousy. The anger in their hearts came down on their own heads; no great harm was done. They were decoyed by Hunahpu and Xbalanque, who merely went out shooting every day. These two got no love from the grandmother, or from One Monkey and One Artisan. They weren't given their meals; the meals had been prepared and One Monkey and One Artisan had already eaten them before they got there. . . .

"We'll just turn their very being around with our words. So be it, since they have caused us great suffering. They wished that we might die and disappear—we, their younger brothers. Just as they wished us to be slaves here, so we shall defeat them there. We shall simply make a sign of it," they said to one another.

And then they went there beneath a tree, the kind named yellowwood, together with the elder brothers. When they got there they started shooting. There were countless birds up in the tree, chittering, and the elder brothers were amazed when they saw the birds. And not one of these birds fell down beneath the tree:

"Those birds of ours don't fall down; just go throw them down," they told their elder brothers.

"Very well," they replied.

And then they climbed up the tree, and the tree began to grow, its trunk got thicker.

After that, they wanted to get down, but now One Monkey and One Artisan couldn't make it

---

*This was the grandmother's way of complaining that the babies cried all the time.
[†]One Monkey and One Artisan were the older half-brothers of the Hero Twins. Their mother had been the wife of One Hunahpu.

down from the tree. So they said, from up in the tree:

"How can we grab hold? You, our younger brothers, take pity on us! Now this tree looks frightening to us, dear younger brothers," they said from up in the tree. Then Hunahpu and Xbalanque told them:

"Undo your pants, tie them around your hips, with the long end trailing like a tail behind you, and then you'll be better able to move," they were told by their younger brothers.

"All right," they said.

And then they left the ends of their loincloths trailing, and all at once these became tails. Now they looked like mere monkeys.

After that they went along in the trees of the mountains, small and great. They went through the forests, now howling, now keeping quiet in the branches of trees.

Such was the defeat of One Monkey and One Artisan by Hunahpu and Xbalanque. They did it by means of their genius alone. . . .

And now they began to act out their self-revelation before their grandmother and mother. First they made a garden:

"We'll just do some gardening, our dear grandmother and mother," they said. "Don't worry. We're here, we're your grandchildren, we're the successors of our elder brothers," said Hunahpu and Xbalanque.

And then they took up their axe, their mattock, their hoe; each of them went off with a blowgun on his shoulder. They left the house having instructed their grandmother to give them their food:

"At midday bring our food, dear grandmother," they said.

"Very well, my dear grandchildren," said their grandmother.

After that, they went to their gardening. They simply stuck their mattock in the ground, and the mattock simply cultivated the ground.

And it wasn't only the mattock that cultivated, but also the axe. In the same way, they stuck it in the trunk of a tree; in the same way,

it cut into the tree by itself, felling, scattering, felling all the trees and bushes, now leveling, mowing down the trees.

Just the one axe did it, and the mattock, breaking up thick masses, countless stalks and brambles. Just one mattock was doing it, breaking up countless things, just clearing off whole mountains, small and great.

And then they gave instructions to that creature named the mourning dove. They sat up on a big stump, and Hunahpu and Xbalanque said:

"Just watch for our grandmother, bringing our food. Cry out right away when she comes, and then we'll grab the mattock and axe."

"Very well," said the mourning dove.

This is because all they're doing is shooting; they're not really doing any gardening.

And as soon as the dove cries out they come running, one of them grabbing the mattock and the other grabbing the hoe, and they're tying up their hair.

One of them deliberately rubs dirt on his hands; he dirties his face as well, so he's just like a real gardener.

And as for the other one, he deliberately dumps wood chips on his head, so he's like a real woodcutter.

Once their grandmother has seen them they eat, but they aren't really doing their gardening; she brings their food for nothing. And when they get home:

"We're really ready for bed, our dear grandmother," they say when they arrive. Deliberately they massage, they stretch their legs, their arms in front of their grandmother.

And when they went on the second day and arrived at the garden, it had all grown up high again. Every tree and bush, every stalk and bramble had put itself back together again when they arrived.

"Who's been picking us clean?" they said.

And these are the ones who are doing it, all the animals, small and great: puma, jaguar, deer, rabbit, fox, coyote, peccary, coati, small birds, great birds. They are the ones who did it; they did it in just one night.

After that, they started the garden all over again. Just as before, the ground worked itself, along with the woodcutting.

And then they shared their thoughts, there on the cleared and broken ground:

"We'll simply have to keep watch over our garden. Then, whatever may be happening here, we'll find out about it," they said when they shared their thoughts. And when they arrived at the house:

"How could we get picked clean, our dear grandmother? Our garden was tall thickets and groves all over again when we got there awhile ago, our dear grandmother," they said to their grandmother and mother. "So we'll go keep watch, because what's happening to us is no good," they said.

After that, they wound everything up, and then they went back to the clearing.

And there they took cover, and when they were well hidden there, all the animals gathered together, each one sat on its haunches, all the animals, small and great.

And this was the middle of the night when they came. They all spoke when they came. This is what they said:

"Arise, conjoin, you trees!
Arise, conjoin, you bushes!"

they said. Then they made a great stir beneath the trees and bushes, then they came nearer, and then they showed their faces.

The first of these were the puma and jaguar. The boys tried to grab them, but they did not give themselves up. When the deer and rabbit came near they only got them by the tail, which just broke off: the deer left its tail in their hands. When they grabbed the tail of the deer, along with the tail of the rabbit, the tails were shortened. But the fox, coyote, and peccary, coati did not give themselves up. All the animals went by in front of Hunahpu and Xbalanque.

So now there was fire in their hearts, because they didn't catch them. And one more came, the last one now, jumping as he came, then they cut him off. In their net they caught the rat.

And then they grabbed him and squeezed him behind the head. They tried to choke him; they burned his tail over a fire. Ever since the rat's tail got caught, there's been no hair on his tail, and his eyes have been the way they are since the boys tried to choke him, Hunahpu and Xbalanque.

"I will not die by your hand! Gardening is not your job, but there is something that is," said the rat.

"Where is what is ours? Go ahead and name it," the boys told the rat.

"Will you let me go then? My word is in my belly, and after I name it for you, you'll give me my morsel of food," said the rat.

"We'll give you your food, so name it," he was told.

"Very well. It's something that belonged to your fathers, named One Hunahpu and Seven Hunahpu, who died in Xibalba. What remains is their gaming equipment. They left it up under the roof of the house: their kilts, their arm guards, their rubber ball. But your grandmother doesn't take these down in front of you, because this is how your fathers died."

"You know the truth, don't you!" the boys told the rat.

There was great joy in their hearts when they got word of the rubber ball. When the rat had named it they gave the rat his food, and this is his food: corn kernels, squash seeds, chili, beans, pataxte, cacao. These are his.

"If anything of yours is stored or gets wasted, then gnaw away," the rat was told by Hunahpu and Xbalanque.

"Very well, boys. But what will your grandmother say if she sees me?" he said.

"Don't be fainthearted. We're here. We know what our grandmother needs to be told. We'll set you up under the corner of the roof right away. When that's taken care of you'll go straight to where the things were left, and we'll look up there under the roof, but it's our stew we'll be looking at," they told the rat when they gave him his instructions.

Hunahpu and Xbalanque made their plans overnight and arrived right at noon, and it wasn't obvious that they had a rat with them when they arrived. One of them went right inside the house when he reached it, while the other went to the corner of the house, quickly setting up the rat. And then they asked their grandmother for their meal:

"Just grind something for our stew, we want chili sauce, our dear grandmother," they said.

After that, she ground chili for their stew. A bowl of broth was set out in front of them, but they were just fooling their grandmother and mother. They had emptied the water jar:

"We're really parched! Bring us a drink," they told their grandmother.

"Yes," she said, then she went, and they kept on eating. They weren't really hungry; they just put on false appearances.

And then they saw the rat reflected in their chili sauce: here was the rat loosening the ball that had been left in the peak of the roof. When they saw him in the chili sauce they sent a mosquito, that creature the mosquito, similar to a gnat. He went to the water, then he punctured the side of the grandmother's jar. The water just gushed out from the side of the jar. She tried, but she could not stop up the side of her jar.

"What has our grandmother done? We're choking for lack of water, our parched throats will do us in," they told their mother, then they sent her there.

After that, the rat cut the ball loose. It dropped from beneath the roof, along with the yokes, arm guards, kilts. These were taken away then; they went to hide them on the road, the road to the ball court.

After that, they went to join their grandmother at the water, and their grandmother and mother were unable to stop up the side of the jar, either one of them.

After that, the boys arrived, each with his blowgun. When they arrived at the water:

"What have you done? We got weary at heart, so we came," they said.

"Look at the side of my jar! It cannot be stopped," said their grandmother, and they quickly stopped it up.

And they came back together, the two of them ahead of their grandmother.

In this way, the matter of the rubber ball was arranged.

Happy now, they went to play ball at the court. So they played ball at a distance, all by themselves. They swept out the court of their fathers.

And then it came into the hearing of the lords of Xibalba:

"Who's begun a game again up there, over our heads? Don't they have any shame, stomping around this way? Didn't One and Seven Hunahpu die trying to magnify themselves in front of us? So, you must deliver another summons," they said as before, One and Seven Death, all the lords.

"They are hereby summoned," they told their messengers. "You are to say, on reaching them:

"'They must come,' say the lords. 'We would play ball with them here. In seven days we'll have a game,' say the lords,' you will say when you arrive," the messengers were told. . . .

"From Xibalba comes the messenger of One and Seven Death:

"'In seven days they are to come here. We'll play ball. Their gaming equipment must come along: rubber ball, yokes, arm guards, kilts. This will make for some excitement here,' say the lords,' is the word that came from them,'" says your grandmother. So your grandmother says you must come. Truly your grandmother cries, she calls out to you to come."

"Isn't it the truth!" the boys said in their thoughts. When they heard it they left at once and got to their grandmother, but they went there only to give their grandmother instructions:

"We're on our way, dear grandmother. We're just giving you instructions. So here is the sign of our word. We'll leave it with you. Each of us will plant an ear of corn. We'll plant them in the center of our house. When the corn dries up, this will be a sign of our death:

'Perhaps they died,' you'll say, when it dries up. And when the sprouting comes:

'Perhaps they live,' you'll say, our dear grandmother and mother. From now on, this is the sign of our word. We're leaving it with you," they said, then they left.

Hunahpu planted one and Xbalanque planted another. They were planted right there in the house; neither in the mountains nor where the earth is damp, but where the earth is dry, in the middle of the inside of their house. They left them planted there, then went off, each with his own blowgun.

The Twins go down to Xibalba, where the lords of the underworld test them. Each test is progressively more difficult than the last, but they survive. Darkness does not defeat them, nor knives, cold, jaguars, or fire. In the house of Bats, the Twins face a setback, however, when Hunahpu's head is stolen by a snatch-bat. Cleverly, they substitute it with a pumpkin, which enables Hunahpu to help his brother defeat the gods in the ball game and to win his head back.

And here it is: the epitaph, the death of Hunahpu and Xbalanque.

Here it is: now we shall name their epitaph, their death. They did whatever they were instructed to do, going through all the dangers, the troubles that were made for them, but they did not die from the tests of Xibalba, nor were they defeated by all the voracious animals that inhabit Xibalba. . . .

After that, messengers came to get the boys, the messengers of One and Seven Death:

"'They must come. We'll go with the boys, to see the treat we've cooked up for them,' say the lords, you boys," they were told.

"Very well," they replied. They went running and arrived at the mouth of the oven.

And there they tried to force them into a game:

"Here, let's jump over our drink four times, clear across, one of us after the other, boys," they were told by One Death.

"You'll never put that one over on us. Don't we know what our death is, you lords? Watch!" they said, then they faced each other. They grabbed each other by the arms and went head first into the oven.

And there they died, together, and now all the Xibalbans were happy, raising their shouts, raising their cheers:

"We've really beaten them! They didn't give up easily," they said.

After that they summoned Xulu and Pacam, who kept their word: the bones went just where the boys had wanted them. Once the Xibalbans had done the divination, the bones were ground and spilled in the river, but they didn't go far— they just sank to the bottom of the water. They became handsome boys; they looked just the same as before when they reappeared.

And on the fifth day they reappeared. They were seen in the water by the people. The two of them looked like channel catfish when their faces were seen by Xibalba. And having germinated in the waters, they appeared the day after that as two vagabonds, with rags before and rags behind, and rags all over too. They seemed unrefined when they were examined by Xibalba; they acted differently now. . . .

They performed many miracles now. They would set fire to a house, as if they were really burning it, and suddenly bring it back again. Now Xibalba was full of admiration.

Next they would sacrifice themselves, one of them dying for the other, stretched out as if in death. First they would kill themselves, but then they would suddenly look alive again. The Xibalbans could only admire what they did. Everything they did now was already the groundwork for their defeat of Xibalba.

And they came to the lords. Feigning great humility, they bowed their heads all the way to the ground when they arrived. They brought themselves low, doubled over, flattened out, down to the rags, to the tatters. They really looked like vagabonds when they arrived. . . .

So then they began their songs and dances, and then all the Xibalbans arrived, the spectators crowded the floor, and they danced everything: they danced the Weasel, they danced the Poorwill, they danced the Armadillo. Then the lord said to them:

"Sacrifice my dog, then bring him back to life again," they were told.

"Yes," they said.

When they sacrificed the dog
    he then came back to life.
And that dog was really happy
    when he came back to life.
Back and forth he wagged his tail
    when he came back to life.

And the lord said to them:

"Well, you have yet to set my home on fire," they were told next, so then they set fire to the home of the lord. The house was packed with all the lords, but they were not burned. They quickly fixed it back again, lest the house of One Death be consumed all at once, and all the lords were amazed, and they went on dancing this way. They were overjoyed.

And then they were asked by the lord:

"You have yet to kill a person! Make a sacrifice without death!" they were told.

"Very well," they said.

And then they took hold of a human sacrifice.

And they held up a human heart on high.

And they showed its roundness to the lords.

And now One and Seven Death admired it, and now that person was brought right back to life. His heart was overjoyed when he came back to life, and the lords were amazed:

"Sacrifice yet again, even do it to yourselves! Let's see it! At heart, that's the dance we really want from you," the lords said now.

"Very well, lord," they replied, and then they sacrificed themselves.

And this is the sacrifice of Hunahpu by Xbalanque. One by one his legs, his arms were spread wide. His head came off, rolled far away outside. His heart, dug out, was smothered in a leaf, and all the Xibalbans went crazy at the sight.

So now, only one of them was dancing there: Xbalanque.

"Get up!" he said, and Hunahpu came back to life. The two of them were overjoyed at this— and likewise the lords rejoiced, as if they were doing it themselves. One and Seven Death were as glad at heart as if they themselves were actually doing the dance.

And then the hearts of the lords were filled with longing, with yearning for the dance of Hunahpu and Xbalanque, so then came these words from One and Seven Death:

"Do it to us! Sacrifice us!" they said. "Sacrifice both of us!" said One and Seven Death to Hunahpu and Xbalanque.

"Very well. You ought to come back to life. After all, aren't you Death? And aren't we making you happy, along with the vassals of your domain?" they told the lords.

And this one was the first to be sacrificed: the lord at the very top, the one whose name is One Death, the ruler of Xibalba.

And with One Death dead, the next to be taken was Seven Death. They did not come back to life.

And then the Xibalbans were getting up to leave, those who had seen the lords die. They underwent heart sacrifice there, and the heart sacrifice was performed on the two lords only for the purpose of destroying them.

As soon as they had killed the one lord without bringing him back to life, the other lord had been meek and tearful before the dancers. He didn't consent, he didn't accept it:

"Take pity on me!" he said when he realized. All their vassals took the road to the great canyon, in one single mass they filled up the deep abyss. So they piled up there and gathered together, countless ants, tumbling down into the canyon, as if they were being herded there. And when they arrived, they all bent low in surrender, they arrived meek and tearful.

Such was the defeat of the rulers of Xibalba. The boys accomplished it only through wonders, only through self-transformation. . . .

And this is their grandmother, crying and calling out in front of the corn ears they left planted. Corn plants grew, then dried up.

And this was when they were burned in the oven; then the corn plants grew again.

And this was when their grandmother burned something, she burned copal before the corn as a memorial to them. There was happiness in their grandmother's heart the second time the corn plants sprouted. Then the ears were deified by their grandmother, and she gave them names: Middle of the House, Middle of the Harvest, Living Corn, Earthen Floor became their names.

And she named the ears Middle of the House, Middle of the Harvest, because they had planted them right in the middle of the inside of their home.

And she further named them Earthen Floor, Living Corn, since the corn ears had been placed up above an earthen floor.

And she also named them Living Corn, because the corn plants had grown again. So they were named by Xmucane. They had been left behind, planted by Hunahpu and Xbalanque, simply as a way for their grandmother to remember them.

And the first to die, a long time before, had been their fathers. One Hunahpu and Seven Hunahpu. And they saw the face of their father again, there in Xibalba. Their father spoke to them again when they had defeated Xibalba.

REVIEW QUESTIONS

1. Why do you think the grandmother and the stepbrothers treated the Hero Twins so badly when they were small?
2. What was the role of animals in this myth? What was the role of women?
3. Which of the Twins' behaviors and activities do you consider heroic? Why?
4. How do the Twins compare to other heroes in this chapter? Which other heroes do they most resemble? Why?

A Hawaiian Runner Defeats Death and Pleases the King

Legends of the South Seas

Hawaii, a group of islands in the Pacific lying north of the equator, was settled by Polynesians approximately 1,800 years ago. Long before the Phoenicians, the Vikings, and other famous seafaring peoples, the ancestors of the Hawaiians had set out from Polynesia, crossing one of the largest and emptiest stretches of water in the world. The Polynesians, in turn, had originated in Southeast Asia, migrating into the South Pacific circa 1500 B.C.E. Thus, Hawaiian myths are naturally related to those of Polynesia and, to a lesser extent, Southeast Asia; but the Hawaiians also developed unique stories that explained their new environment and their adaptation to it. The story in this selection blends traditional Polynesian values with "newer" Hawaiian customs. Like other such oral traditions that were first collected and published by "interested amateurs," it was first recorded by a judge, Abraham Fornander, who died in Hawaii in 1887.

First and most obviously, this selection describes how the Hawaiian kings originally came to wear the *ahu ula,* the striking cape of scarlet feathers of the mamo bird. Captain James Cook, the first known European to sail to Hawaii (1778), noted the Pacific Islanders' exceptional fondness for red feathers, which he said were "as valuable as jewels in Europe." Anything red was understandably treasured on islands that, before the arrival of the Europeans (with their dyed fabrics and flags), was almost completely dominated by the colors blue, green, and white. Red flowers might wither away, but feathers lasted. Because of their rare beauty and their endurance, the *ahu ula* were symbols of the divine power of kings. It is not surprising, therefore, that their origin was linked to the supernatural.

Heroism is also a primary theme of this selection. Although Polynesian and Hawaiian heroes had obligations to their families and chief, their primary obligation was to themselves, to proving their physical prowess or to fulfilling their desire for victory. Thus Eleio felt free to deviate from his mission for the chief, and he was compelled to race with the spirit woman. Kanikaniaula, too, was a hero in the sense that she was the instigating agent of her own resurrection. Finally, her people behaved heroically because they adhered to traditional Hawaiian custom with regard to the exchange of gifts. Nothing—goods, services, or honors—was ever given without equal compensation. Thus Eleio returned with a bride for the king and the first *ahu ula,* as well as the kava for which he was sent in the first place.

AHU ULA: THE FIRST FEATHER CLOAK

Kakaalaneo, the high chief of his land Maui, had runners in his service at Lahaina who would take his messages across the land as straight as birds. Swift men, these kukini. Up the mountain; over the rocks; down the cliffs; through the streams, through the bush; straight, direct. The ariki valued them, rewarded them well with food and garments. Among our people it was said: "Send a kukini of the chief to Hana and he will be back before a fish in the umu is ready to be turned over."

Eleio was the swiftest runner Kakaalaneo had. He could run round Maui three times in a day. If he was sent to Hana on the far side of the land the people said, "He will be back before a fish is cooked on one side." He was therefore sent away for kava when the meal was to be cooked, he chewed the kava on his homeward journey.* Yet

---

*Kava is a Polynesian shrub that belongs to the pepper family. Its roots can be made into a narcotic beverage. Since the first step in its preparation was chewing, Eleio was merely shortening the time in which it would be ready to drink.

if Eleio was delayed, then his chief, who expected much, was angry, threatened death.

Eleio was a skilled kahuna also; his family were kahuna, he was well instructed in their arts. He knew the chants that heal. Also, he could see spirit-people. He could make a person's spirit go back into the dead body, so long as the rotting had not started. These things about Eleio were known in all the land. The spirit-people knew them also.

When Eleio was going to Hana by the north side of this land a spirit-woman used to run after him. Three times this wailua pursued Eleio; she wanted him to return her to her body. She frightened him, that spirit-person, but his sister Pohaku helped him. Pohaku turned round and lifted up her skirt, showed her bottom to the spirit-woman, made her run away for shame. Afterwards Eleio went to Hana by the south side of the land.

One day Kakaalaneo sent Eleio to Hana for the kava that grows in that place. The people said: "Eleio will be back before the meal is ready for the chief." Eleio left, ran swiftly, ran direct.

Soon after leaving Olowalu, as he was climbing up Aalaloloa, he saw ahead of him a beautiful woman. This woman went as fast as he did. Eleio hastened, but the woman kept always ahead of him: whatever he did she kept her distance. His pride was gnawing him. She led him over the rocks and mountains, down the cliffs, through the streams and through the bush, until they-two came to the cave of Hanamanuloa at Kahikinui, beyond Kaupo. Then he caught her; that person let him catch her at the entrance of a puoa which stood in that place. He seized her as she was entering that tower of bamboo where corpses of chiefly persons are laid to rot.

Eleio snatched her garment at the entrance; she turned to him, cried, "Let me live. I am not human, I am spirit. Inside here is my house." Said Eleio, "I know already that you are a wailua. No human person could run more quickly than I, Eleio." The wailua said to him, "Let us-two be friends. Over there in that house which you can see live my parents and my relatives. Go and ask them for a pig, for tapa cloth,* some fine mats, and the feather cloak. Tell them you have seen me and say that I told them to give these things to you. The ahu ula for which you will ask them is not yet finished. It is only so-wide, but it will measure two tall men in width when it is finished. There are enough feathers and fibre for the netting there to finish it, these things are in the house. Tell them to finish it for you." Then the wailua vanished, that woman disappeared.

Eleio went into the puoa and climbed to the platform. The body of the girl was there, the rotting had not yet started. He left that place, ran to the house to which that wailua had pointed. A woman wailing. It was this circumstance that caused delay:

"I here am a stranger, but I had a travelling companion who led me to that puoa, then disappeared."

The woman stopped her wailing, called to her husband, told him what was said. Eleio asked them, "Does this house belong to you?" "It does."

Then Eleio said: "My message is to you. My travelling companion who was running with me owns a hog the length of a tall man, a pile of fine Paiula tapa-cloth, and a pile of fine mats. She also has a feather cloak which is not yet finished. You are to finish this cloak with the things that are here to finish it, and all these belongings you are to give to me. She has told me to ask you for them."

Then Eleio described that spirit-person, and the woman and the man knew that their daughter who was dead had adopted this kukini as her brother, by giving him her precious things. In their own thoughts, therefore, they-two looked upon him as their son, and they said that they would kill the pig and make a feast. Said Eleio: "Wait. Are all these people here your friends?" "They are our relatives. They are the uncles, aunts and cousins of the wailua who has adopted you." "Will they do what you ask them to do?" "They will."

Therefore Eleio told the relatives to build a large lanai, to be covered entirely with ferns and ginger, maile and 'ie'ie. All these sweet-scented plants were to be used in that arbour. "At one end of the lanai you are to build an altar." All the people came to their work, the men and women and the young. That lanai was soon completed.

Then Eleio told them, "Cook the pig." He ordered them also to bring red and white fish, black and white fowls, and bananas both lele and maoli, and to place all these things on the altar. "All the men and women then must remain in their houses, to assist the prayers. The children, the pigs, the fowls and dogs are all to be kept silent. Take the children inside. Put the animals in dark places. Those men who have to work are to be mindful of the gods."

Then that kukini sped away, he ran to Hana and pulled up two bushes of the kava of Kaeleku, that plant for which his high chief Kakaalaneo had sent him on his errand. He returned to the place before the pig was cooked. Next kava was made, and when all the preparations for the feast were complete, Eleio went away some distance from the people, he went to be alone. Then the

---

*A strong fabric made from the inner bark of the paper mulberry tree.

people understood the intention of Eleio, they knew that he was going to perform the kapuku and restore the wailua of that young woman to her body.

Eleio went apart, he made his invocations. All the people were quiet in their houses to assist the prayers. Then Eleio caught the spirit again and took it to the puoa, climbed to the platform of the corpse. He placed that spirit against the insteps of the feet, pressed hard, he spoke his chants. The spirit was going in, returning to its former place; but when it came to the knees it would not go any further, because the rotting in the stomach had begun. The wailua did not want to touch that mess. Eleio spoke his potent chants, he called upon his gods and pushed the spirit up the legs beyond the knees. At the thigh-bones, that spirit stopped, refused. Therefore Eleio worked at his chants; he got the spirit past the stomach to the throat. It stopped again, refused.

Here were the relatives around, the father, mother, uncles and male cousins. They gathered on the platform with Eleio, spoke their prayers as well. After much work Eleio got the spirit past the neck, then the girl gave a sort of crow. This made all persons hopeful. Eleio worked, worked at his chants, he got the spirit down the arms, past the elbows and wrists. It struggled to be put through these places, then it gave in— was back in the body. That girl was alive, sat up.

They took her to the ceremonies of purification, cleaned away the stomach. Then that girl was taken to the lanai where the offerings were laid. These things were presented to the gods, who took what they required of them. Could not be seen, that part of offerings. Then all the people feasted on the food, as guests of the gods.

After the feast the tapa cloths and fine mats, the feather cloak as well—these things were brought out and displayed to Eleio. Said the father: "Take the woman you have made alive again. Have her for your wife and remain here with us. You will be our son, loved by us as she is."

But Eleio said, "No, I will take her into my care, but as for a wife she is worthy of a higher one than I. Give her to me and I will take her to Kakaalaneo." Said the father: "She is yours to do with as you wish. You made her live. But know that you have parents here, and that this house is yours."

Then Eleio told them to finish the cloak. All those who could do feather-work sat down to this task; that wondrous cloak was soon completed, full to its size. When the cloak was finished, they told him that the name of the girl was Kanikaniaula. They-two then set out together for Lahaina, carrying with them the cloak, and the remainder of the kava of Kaeleku for the chief. Their going was slow on this journey, for Kanikaniaula had only the strength of a woman, not of a spirit. Said Eleio, "I am late returning. There is danger. My chief commands my death."

They arrived at Launiupoko. Said Eleio: "You wait here in the bushes while I go on alone. If by sunset I have not returned, then I am dead. You are to return to your people. But if I am not dead, I shall return here soon."

He came on to Makila, near Lahaina, saw some people heating an umu to cook food. They were the high-chief's servants. When they saw Eleio they began to tie him up and roast him alive, as Kakaalaneo had ordered them. But he put those people off with this word: "Let me die at the feet of my master." Thus Eleio successfully passed those servants of Kakaalaneo, passed the oven that was heated for him.

He arrived before his chief. "How is it that you are not yet killed, as I ordered? How did you get past my servants?"

Said Eleio: "The slave wished to die at the feet of his chief, if he must die. But sir, this would be a great loss to you, for I have brought with me that which will make your name known to the generations." Then Eleio took his bundle off his back, unrolled the mats and tapa, showed his chief the cloak of scarlet feathers. It was the first ahu ula seen by the people of this land. All were amazed, the chief was greatly pleased. The kava which Eleio brought was used that evening in the offerings of Kakaalaneo to the gods.

Then Eleio told the rest of it. Said the high-chief, "Bring this woman." Kanikaniaula was brought from her hiding place. The chief desired her; took her for wife. Thus the highest chiefs of this land Maui trace their descent from Kakaalaneo and Kanikaniaula, and they wear that sacred cloak on ceremonial occasions.

REVIEW QUESTIONS

1. Why did Eleio run away from the first spirit woman he met? Why did he pursue the second?
2. Compare and contrast the roles of men and women in early Hawaii. How do these roles compare to those of other civilizations you have studied?
3. Which qualities does Eleio possess that qualify him as a hero in the broader sense of the word? In the Polynesian sense?
4. As a hero, how does Eleio compare to other heroes and heroines in this chapter? Explain.

3

Earliest Journeys

It is important to note that, although accounts of actual journeys are extremely rare in the earliest stages of global civilizations, there was nevertheless a good deal of travel both within and between regions. The fact that the record of many of these early journeys survives today only in myths is revealing. It indicates that people traveled from their homes to other places, sometimes permanently, and also that the experience of the journey has remained an important part of their cultural identity and memory.

Mythical and legendary journeys sometimes depict travel to actual places, such as the voyage of Jason and the Argonauts through the "Clashing Rocks" of the strait of the Bosporus. Often, however, they take their heroes to or from imaginary places. Kwasi Benefo, for example, traveled to the "Land of the Dead" (Asamondo) to ensure that his four deceased wives were safe and comfortable. The Pueblos, on the other hand, originated in the underworld and sought a home in the real world.

An important element of many myths that focus on travel is the idea of the hero and the quest. Some were searching for very specific items, such as the Golden Fleece, which was the object of Jason's desire. Others, like Kwasi Benefo, were hoping to find peace of mind. Another type of quest is the search for a new home. The Pueblos, of course, had this goal in mind, as did both Sinuhe and Abraham—both of whom were also fleeing dangerous political and/or economic conditions. In contrast, the Emperor Mu's quest was almost entirely subjective. He wanted to make his name known throughout the world, and enjoy himself in the process.

These myths reveal that, even in the absence of traditional historical sources, travel is an integral part of the human experience. In addition to the objectives already noted, the journey has value as a process as well as merely a means to an end. With few exceptions, the individuals who made these journeys grew and developed as human beings, learning important new lessons about life.

An Egyptian in Eastern Palestine

The Tale of Sinuhe

The Tale of Sinuhe was one of the most popular pieces of Egyptian literature ever written. It may be pure fiction, or it may be loosely based on the life of an actual court official. Either way, it is a valuable historical document because it contains a great deal of information about Egypt and the neighboring region to the east, Canaan, before the arrival of the Hebrews. It is also a fine example of the literature of the Middle Kingdom, a period that—in terms of general cultural achievement—is seen as never quite equaling the previous era, the Old Kingdom, or the next one, the New Kingdom, the period of imperial expansion. The Middle Kingdom, however, was a great literary age in Egypt, during which an immense amount of poetry, fiction, and religious writings was composed. *The Tale of Sinuhe* is one of the best-known pieces of Middle Kingdom literature—both then and now. It was a favorite of the ancient Egyptians, and it was reproduced on papyrus for hundreds of years after it was originally composed.

The story opens with the death of King Amenemhet I (whose name after death is changed to Sehetepibre). Sinuhe, a court official and noble of high rank, is on assignment with the king's son and coregent, Sesostris, somewhere in Libya following a successful military expedition. After messengers bring news of the elder king's death to camp, Sinuhe accidentally learns that the dead king's sons are plotting to steal the throne from their older brother, Sesostris. For reasons that are never completely explained, Sinuhe panics and flees to the East. The selection below is the story of his escape from Egypt, his long exile in "Upper Retenu" (Canaan or Aram), and his ultimate return to Egypt.

The Prince, Count, Governor of the domains of the sovereign in the lands of the Asiatics, true and beloved Friend of the King, the Attendant Sinuhe, says:

I was an attendant who attended his lord, a servant of the royal harem, waiting on the Princess, the highly praised Royal Wife of King Sesostris in Khenemsut, the daughter of King Amenemhet in Kanefru, Nefru, the revered.[1]

Year 30, third month of the inundation, day 7: the god ascended to his horizon. The King of Upper and Lower Egypt, *Sehetepibre,* flew to heaven and united with the sun-disk, the divine body merging with its maker. Then the residence was hushed; hearts grieved; the great portals were shut;   the courtiers were head-on-knee; the people moaned.

His majesty, however, had despatched an army to the land of the Tjemeh, with his eldest son as its commander, the good god Sesostris. He had been sent to smite the foreign lands and to punish those of Tjehenu.[2]   Now he was

returning, bringing captives of the Tjehenu and cattle of all kinds beyond number. The officials of the palace sent to the western border to let the king's son know the event that had occurred at the court. The messengers met him on the road, reaching him at night. Not a moment did he delay. The falcon flew with his attendants, without letting his army know it.

But the royal sons who had been with him on this expedition had also been sent for.   One of them was summoned while I was standing (there). I heard his voice, as he spoke, while I was in the near distance. My heart fluttered, my arms spread out, a trembling befell all my limbs. I removed myself in leaps, to seek a hiding place. I put   myself between two bushes, so as to leave the road to its traveler.

I set out southward. I did not plan to go to the residence. I believed there would be turmoil and did not expect to survive it. I crossed Maaty near Sycamore; I reached Isle-of-Snefru. I spent the day there at the edge   of the cultivation. Departing at dawn I encountered a man who stood on the road. He saluted me while I was afraid of him. At dinner time I reached "Cattle-Quay." I crossed in a barge without a rudder, by the force of the westwind. I passed to the east of the quarry,   at the height of "Mistress of the Red Mountain." Then I made

---

[1]Sinuhe was specifically in the service of Princess Neiru, the wife of Sesostris I, the latter being co-regent at the time of his father's death. Khenemsut and Kanefru are the names of the pyramids of Sesostris I and Amenemnet I.

[2]Tjemeh and Tjehenu designated two distinct Libyan peoples who merged in the course of time. In this story the terms are used interchangeably.

my way northward. I reached the "Walls of the Ruler," which were made to repel the Asiatics and to crush the Sand-farers. I crouched in a bush for fear of being seen by the guard on duty upon the wall.

I set out   at night. At dawn I reached Peten. I halted at "Isle-of-Kem-Wer." An attack of thirst overtook me; I was parched, my throat burned. I said, "This is the taste of death." I raised my heart and collected myself when I heard the lowing sound of cattle   and saw Asiatics. One of their leaders, who had been in Egypt, recognized me. He gave me water and boiled milk for me. I went with him to his trible. What they did for me was good.

Land gave me to land. I traveled to Byblos; I returned to Qedem. I spent   a year and a half there. Then Ammunenshi, the ruler of Upper Retenu, took me to him, saying to me: "You will be happy with me; you will hear the language of Egypt." He said this because he knew my character and had heard of my skill, Egyptians who were with him having borne witness for me. He said to me: "Why   have you come here? Has something happened at the residence?" I said to him: "King Sehetepibre departed to the horizon, and one did not know the circumstances." But I spoke in half-truths: "When I returned from the expedition to the land of the Tjemeh, it was reported to me and my heart grew faint. It carried   me away on the path of flight, though I had not been talked about; no one had spat in my face; I had not heard a reproach; my name had not been heard in the mouth of the herald. I do not know what brought me to this country; it is as if planned by god. As if a Delta-man saw himself in Yebu, a marsh-man in Nubia."

Then he said to me: "How then is that land without that excellent god, fear of whom was throughout   the lands like Sakhmet in a year of plague?" I said to him in reply: "Of course his son has entered into the palace, having taken his father's heritage.

He is a god without peer,
No other comes before him;

He is lord of knowledge, wise planner,
   skilled leader,
One goes and comes by   his will

He was the smiter of foreign lands,
While his father stayed in the palace,
He reported to him on commands carried
   out.

He is a champion who acts with his arm,
A fighter who has no equal,
When seen engaged in archery,
When joining the melee.

Horn-curber who makes hands turn weak,
His foes   can not close ranks;
Keen-sighted he smashes foreheads,
None can withstand his presence.

Wide-striding he smites the fleeing,
No retreat for him who turns him his back;
Steadfast in time of attack,
He makes turn back and turns not his back.

Stouthearted when he sees the mass,
He lets not slackness fill his heart;
Eager at the sight of combat,
Joyful when he works his bow.

Clasping his shield he treads under foot,
No second blow needed to kill;
None can escape his arrow,
None turn aside his bow.

The Bowmen flee before him,
As before the might of the goddess;
As he fights he plans the goal,
Unconcerned about all else.

Lord of grace, rich in kindness,
He has conquered through affection;
His city loves him more than itself,
Acclaims him more than its own god.

Men outdo women in hailing him,
Now that he is king;
Victor while yet in the egg,
Set to be ruler since his birth.

Augmenter of those born with him,
He is unique, god-given;
Happy the land that he rules!

Enlarger of frontiers,
He will conquer southern lands,
While ignoring northern lands,
Though made to smite Asiatics and tread on
    Sand-farers!

"Send to him! Let him know your name as one who inquires while being far from his majesty. He will not fail to do   good to a land that will be loyal to him."

He said to me: "Well then, Egypt is happy knowing that he is strong. But you are here. You shall stay with me. What I shall do for you is good."

He set me at the head of his children. He married me to his eldest daughter. He let me choose for myself of his land,   of the best that was his, on his border with another land. It was a good land called Yaa. Figs were in it and grapes. It had more wine than water. Abundant was its honey, plentiful its oil. All kinds of fruit were on its trees. Barley was there and emmer, and no end of cattle of all kinds.

Much also came to me because of the love of me; for he had made me chief of a tribe in the best part of his land. Loaves were made for me daily, and wine as daily fare, cooked meat, roast fowl, as well as desert game.   For they snared for me and laid it before me, in addition to the catch of my hounds. Many sweets were made for me, and milk dishes of all kinds.

I passed many years, my children becoming strong men, each a master of his tribe. The envoy who came north or went south to the residence   stayed with me. I let everyone stay with me. I gave water to the thirsty; I showed the way to him who had strayed; I rescued him who had been robbed. When Asiatics conspired to attack the Rulers of Hill-Countries, I opposed their movements. For this ruler of   Retenu made me carry out numerous missions as commander of his troops. Every hill tribe against which I marched I vanquished, so that it was driven from the pasture of its wells. I plundered its cattle, carried off its families, seized their food, and killed people   by my strong arm, by my bow, by my movements and my skillful plans. I

won his heart and he loved me, for he recognized my valor. He set me at the head of his children, for he saw the strength of my arms.

There came a hero of Retenu,
To challenge me   in my tent.
A champion was he without peer,
He had subdued it all.
He said he would fight with me,
He planned to plunder me,
He meant to seize my cattle
At the behest of his tribe.

The ruler conferred with me and I said: "I do not know him; I am not his ally,   that I could walk about in his camp. Have I ever opened his back rooms or climbed over his fence? It is envy, because he sees me doing your commissions. I am indeed like a stray bull in a strange herd, whom the bull of the herd charges,   whom the longhorn attacks. Is an inferior beloved when he becomes a superior? No Asiatic makes friends with a Delta-man. And what would make papyrus cleave to the mountain? If a bull loves combat, should a champion bull retreat for fear of being equaled? If he wishes to fight, let him declare his wish. Is there a god who does not know what he has ordained, and a man who knows how it will be?"

At night I strung my bow, sorted my arrows, practiced with my dagger, polished my weapons. When it dawned Retenu came.   It had assembled its tribes; it had gathered its neighboring peoples; it was intent on this combat.

He came toward me while I waited, having placed myself near him. Every heart burned for me; the women jabbered. All hearts ached for me thinking: "Is there another champion who could fight him?" He <raised> his battle-axe and shield,   while his armful of missiles fell toward me. When I had made his weapons attack me, I let his arrows pass me by without effect, one following the other. Then, when he charged me, I shot him, my arrow sticking in his neck. He screamed; he fell on his nose;   slew him with his axe. I raised my war cry over his back, while every Asiatic shouted. I gave praise to Mont, while his people mourned him. The ruler Ammunenshi took me in his arms.

Then I carried off his goods; I plundered his cattle. What he had meant to do   to me I did to him. I took what was in his tent; I stripped his camp. Thus I became great, wealthy in goods, rich in herds. It was the god who acted, so as to show mercy to one with whom he had been angry, whom he had made stray abroad. For today his heart is appeased.

> A. fugitive fled (150) his surroundings—
>   I am famed at home.
> A laggard lagged from hunger—
>   I give bread to my neighbor.
> A man left his land in nakedness—
>   I have bright clothes, fine linen.
> A man ran for lack of one to send—
>   I am   rich in servants.
> My house is fine, my dwelling spacious—
>   My thoughts are at the palace!

Whichever god decreed this flight, have mercy, bring me home! Surely you will let me see the place in which my heart dwells! What is more important than that my corpse be buried in the land   in which I was born! Come to my aid! What if the happy event should occur![3] May god pity me! May he act so as to make happy the end of one whom he punished! May his heart ache for one whom he forced to live abroad! If he is truly appeased today, may he hearken to the prayer of one far away! May he return one whom he made roam the earth to the place from which he carried him off!

May Egypt's king have mercy on me, that I may live by his mercy! May I greet the mistress of the land who is in the palace! May I hear the commands of her children! Would that my body were young again! For old age has come; feebleness has overtaken me. My eyes are heavy, my arms weak;   my legs fail to follow. The heart is weary; death is near. May I be conducted to the city of eternity! May I serve the Mistress of

All! May she speak well of me to her children; may she spend eternity above me![4]

Now when the majesty of King Kheperkare was told of the condition in which I was, his majesty sent word   to me with royal gifts, in order to gladden the heart of this servant like that of a foreign ruler. And the royal children who were in his palace sent me their messages. Copy of the decree brought to this servant concerning his return to Egypt:

Horus: Living in Births; the Two Ladies: Living in Births; the King of Upper and Lower Egypt: *Kheperkare;* the Son of Re: *Sesostris,* who lives forever. Royal decree to the Attendant Sinuhe:

This decree of the King if brought to you to let you know: That you circled the foreign countries, going from Qedem to Retenu, land giving you to land, was the counsel of your own heart. What had you done that one should act against you? You had not cursed, so that your speech would be reproved. You had not spoken against the counsel of the nobles, that your words should have been rejected. This matter—it carried away your heart. It was not in my heart against you. This your heaven in the palace lives and prospers to this day.[5] Her head is adorned with the kingship of the land; her children are in the palace. You will store riches which they give you; you will live on their bounty. Come back to Egypt! See the residence in which you lived! Kiss the ground at the great portals, mingle with the courtiers! For today   you have begun to age. You have lost a man's strength. Think of the day of burial, the passing into reveredness.

A night is made for you with ointments and wrappings from the hand of Tait. A funeral procession is made for you on the day of burial; the mummy case is of gold, its head of lapis lazuli. The sky is above you as you lie in the hearse, oxen drawing you, musicians going before you. The dance of   the *mww*-dancers is done at

---

[3]I.e., "what if death should occur while I am still abroad?"

[4]"Mistress of All" could be either the queen or the goddess Nut.
[5]The queen is meant.

the door of your tomb; the offering-list is read to you; sacrifice is made before your offering-stone. Your tomb-pillars, made of white stone, are among (those of) the royal children. You shall not die abroad! Not shall Asiatics inter you. You shall not be wrapped in the skin of a ram to serve as your coffin. Too long a roaming of the earth! Think of your corpse, come back!

This decree reached me while I was standing in the midst of my tribe. When it had been read to me, I threw myself on my belly. Having touched the soil, I spread it on my chest. I strode around my camp shouting: "What compares with this which is done to a servant whom his heart led astray to alien lands? Truly good is the kindness that saves me from death! Your *ka* will grant me to reach my end, my body being at home!"

Copy of the reply to this decree:

The servant of the Palace, Sinuhe,   says: In very good peace! Regarding the matter of this flight which this servant did in his ignorance. It is your *ka,* O good god, lord of the Two Lands, which Re loves and which Mont lord of Thebes favors; and Amun lord of Thrones-of-the-Two-Lands, and Sobk-Re lord of Sumenu, and Horus, Hathor, Atum with his Ennead, and Sopdu-Neferbau-Semseru the Eastern Horus, and the Lady of Yemet—may she enfold your head—and the conclave upon the flood, and Min-Horus of the hill-countries, and Wereret lady of   Punt, Nut, Haroeris-Re, and all the gods of Egypt and the isles of the sea—may they give life and joy to your nostrils, may they endue you with their bounty, may they give you eternity without limit, infinity without bounds! May the fear of you resound in lowlands and highlands, for you have subdued all that the sun encircles! This is the prayer of this servant for his lord who saves from the West.

The lord of knowledge who knows people knew   in the majesty of the palace that this servant was afraid to say it. It is like a thing too great to repeat. The great god, the peer of Re, knows the heart of one who has served him willingly. This servant is in the hand of one who thinks about him. He is placed under his care.

Your Majesty is the conquering Horus; your arms vanquish all lands. May then your Majesty command to have brought to you the prince of Meki from Qedem,   the mountain chiefs from Keshu, and the prince of Menus from the lands of the Fenkhu. They are rulers of renown who have grown up in the love of you. I do not mention Retenu—it belongs to you like your hounds.

Lo, this flight which the servant made—I did not plan it. It was not in my heart; I did not devise it. I do not know what removed me from my place. It was like   dream. As if a Delta-man saw himself in Yebu, a marsh-man in Nubia. I was not afraid; no one ran after me. I had not heard a reproach; my name was not heard in the mouth of the herald. Yet my flesh crept, my feet hurried, my heart drove me; the god who had willed this flight   dragged me away. Nor am I a haughty man. He who knows his land respects men. Re has set the fear of you throughout the land, the dread of you in every foreign country. Whether I am at the residence, whether I am in this place, it is you who covers this horizon.   The sun rises at your pleasure. The water in the river is drunk when you wish. The air of heaven is breathed at your bidding. This servant will hand over   to the brood which this servant begot in this place. This servant has been sent for! Your Majesty will do as he wishes! One lives by the breath which you give. As Re, Horus, and Hathor love your august nose, may Mont lord of Thebes wish it to live forever!

I was allowed to spend one more day in Yaa, handing over my possessions to my children, my eldest son taking charge of my tribe;   all my possessions became his—my serfs, my herds, my fruit, my fruit trees. This servant departed southward. I halted at Horusways. The commander in charge of the garrison sent a message to the residence to let it be known. Then his majesty sent a trusted overseer of the royal domains with whom were loaded ships,   bearing royal gifts for the Asiatics who had come with me to escort me to Horusways. I called each one by his name, while every butler was at his task. When I had started and set sail, there was kneading and straining beside me, until I reached the city of Itj-tawy.

When it dawned, very early, they came to summon me. Ten men came and ten men went to usher me into the palace. My forehead touched the ground between the sphinxes,   and the royal children stood in the gateway to meet me. The courtiers who usher through the forecourt set me on the way to the audience-hall. I found his majesty on the great throne in a kiosk of gold. Streched out on my belly, I did not know myself before him, while this god greeted me pleasantly. I was like a man seized by darkness.   My *ba* was gone, my limbs trembled; my heart was not in my body, I did not know life from death.

His majesty said to one of the courtiers: "Lift him up, let him speak to me." Then his majesty said: "Now you have come, after having roamed foreign lands. Flight has taken its toll of you. You have aged, have reached old age. It is no small matter that your corpse will be interred without being escorted by Bowmen. But don't act thus, don't act thus, speechless   though your name was called!" Fearful of punishment I answered with the answer of a frightened man: "What has my lord said to me, that I might answer it? It is not disrespect to the god! It is the terror which is in my body, like that which caused the fateful flight! Here I am before you. Life is yours. May your Majesty do as he wishes!"

Then the royal daughters were brought in, and his majesty said to the queen: "Here is Sinuhe,   come as an Asiatic, a product of nomads!" She uttered a very great cry, and the royal daughters shrieked all together. They said to his majesty: "Is it really he, O king, our lord?" Said his majesty: "It is really he!" Now having brought with them their necklaces, rattles, and sistra, they held them out to his majesty:[6]

Your hands   upon the radiance, eternal king,
   Jewels of heaven's mistress!

The Gold gives life to your nostrils,
The Lady of Stars enfolds you!

Southcrown fared north, northcrown south,
Joined, united by your majesty's word.
While the Cobra decks your brow,
You deliver the poor from harm.
Peace to you from Re, Lord of Lands!
Hail to you and the Mistress of All!

Slacken your bow, lay down your arrow,
Give breath to him who gasps for breath!
Give us our good gift on this good day,
Grant us the son of northwind, Bowman
   born in Egypt!

He made the flight in fear of you,
He left the land in dread of you!
A face that sees you shall not pale,
Eyes that see you shall not fear!

His majesty said: "He shall not fear, he shall not   dread!" He shall be a Companion among the nobles. He shall be among the courtiers. Proceed to the robing-room to wait on him!"

I left the audience-hall, the royal daughters giving me their hands.

We went through the great portals, and I was put in the house of a prince. In it were luxuries: a bathroom and mirrors. In it were riches from the treasury; clothes of royal linen, myrrh, and the choice perfume of the king and of his favorite courtiers were in every   room. Every servant was at his task. Years were removed from my body. I was shaved; my hair was combed. Thus was my squalor returned to the foreign land, my dress to the Sand-farers. I was clothed in fine linen; I was anointed with fine oil. I slept on a bed. I had returned the sand to those who dwell in it   the tree-oil to those who grease themselves with it.

I was given a house and garden that had belonged to a courtier. Many craftsmen rebuilt it, and all its woodwork was made anew. Meals were brought to me from the palace three times, four times a day, apart from what the royal children gave without a moment's pause.   A stone

---

[6]The princesses hold out the emblems sacred to Hathor and perform a ceremonial dance and a song in which they beg a full pardon for Sinuhe.

pyramid was built for me in the midst of the pyramids. The masons who build tombs constructed it. A master draughtsman designed in it. A master sculptor carved in it. The overseers of construction in the necropolis busied themselves with it. All the equipment that is placed in   a tomb-shaft was supplied. Mortuary priests were given me. A funerary domain was made for me. It had fields and a garden in the right place, as is done for a Companion of the first rank. My statue was overlaid with gold, its skirt with electrum. It was his majesty who ordered it made. There is no commoner for whom the like has been done. I was in   the favor of the king, until the day of landing[7] came.

Colophon: It is done from beginning to end as it was found in writing.

---

[7]The day of death. Through its beginning and its ending, the story is given the form of the tomb-autobiography in which the narrator looks back on his completed life.

REVIEW QUESTIONS

1. How did Ammunenshi, the king of Upper Retenu, treat Sinuhe? Why do you suppose the king treated him this way?
2. Describe Sinuhe's life in Upper Retenu. Do you think he was happy there? Why or why not?
3. Why did Sinuhe return to Egypt? What did his return cost him in personal terms? How did it benefit him?
4. Why do you think this story was so well liked by the ancient Egyptians?
5. Despite its popularity as "historical fiction" in ancient Egypt, modern scholars regard *The Tale of Sinuhe* as a piece of royal propaganda. What elements of this story support their opinion?

The Journeys of Abraham

Genesis 12:1–13:18

Abraham, from whom both present-day Jews and Muslims trace their descent, supposedly made three major journeys in his life. First, he traveled from Ur, a city in the lower Euphrates Valley, to Haran, a city on the Middle Euphrates, in northwest Mesopotamia. There he and his family prospered for an indeterminate period. When Abraham's father died (allegedly at the age of 205), the patron god of the family, Yahweh, commanded Abraham to undertake a second journey—to leave Haran and travel southwest to Canaan, where Yahweh promised Abraham he would prosper and grow famous. In Canaan, however, a famine prompted him to make a third journey, this time to Egypt and back, where fertile and productive fields along the Nile River produced a surplus of grain during most years. Only after his return to Canaan did Yahweh's promise to Abraham come true.

It is difficult to ascertain dates for the three journeys of Abraham. This section of Abraham's story contains no historical references, not even the name of the Egyptian king who took Abraham's wife Sara into his household. Scholars have argued in favor of dates ranging from 2200 to 1450 B.C.E., but several circumstances indicate 1750 to 1550 as the most reasonable period. Primarily, 1700 coincides with the fall of Ur—and indeed, all of Sumer—which had experienced severe environmental, economic, and political problems from 2000 to 1800. These difficulties were compounded by invaders, the Amorites and the Elamites, who made war on not only the Sumerians, but on each other as well. Ultimately the Amorites prevailed, establishing their capital at Babylon circa 1750; but for nearly 300 years, conditions in lower Mesopotamia were so chaotic that a number of groups may have decided to move on to greener and more peaceful pastures. Pastoral peoples may have been especially inclined to leave, particularly the Habiru—seminomadic tribes that lived on the fringes of civilization from Mesopotamia to Egypt. Northwest Mesopotamia proved to be no more stable than the south, however. By 1600, the Mitanni and Kharri invaded from the north, forcing the inhabitants to leave their homes on the Middle Euphrates, where Haran was a major city. This time these groups moved to the southwest, to Palestine, Canaan, and Syria. Thus, the Hebrew migration to Canaan was part of a great movement of peoples that included many others: the Moabites, Ammonites, Edomites, and Aramaeans, to name a few.

The text uses the earliest forms of their names for its protagonist and his wife: Abram for Abraham, and Sarai for Sara. It is entirely possible that the names Abram and Abraham—which mean patriarch ("exalted father") in Babylonian and Canaanite, respectively—refer not to a single individual, but to a series of individuals. Likewise, Sarai (which means "contentious" or "bitter waters") and Sara (which means "princess") also might be the names of more than one person. Thus, it is possible that the primary authors of this text, the Yahwists, telescoped events that took place over several centuries into the lifespan of a single, legendary figure. By the time it was written in its present form, nearly one thousand years later, oral versions of the story had changed and mutated (see the Hebrew Creation Story, Chapter 1). Since the goal of the Yahwist authors was to emphasize the singular power and existence of one almighty God, Abraham emerged as more than a simple patriarch; he was the founder and leader of a great religious movement. His God was both abstract and personal, required no priests or temples, and justified the conquest and subjugation of the polytheistic and "idolatrous" Canaanites. Taking strength and courage from Yahweh's support, Abraham's descendants, who believed they were the chosen people of God, eventually became as numerous as "the stars in the sky" and "the sand on the sea shore."

Terah took his son Abram, his grandson Lot the son of Haran, and his daughter-in-law the wife of Abram, and made them leave Ur of the Chaldaeans to go to the land of Canaan. But on arrival in Haran they settled here.

Terah's life lasted two hundred and five years; [t]hen he died at Haran.

Yahweh said to Abram, "Leave your country, your family and your father's house, for the land I will show you. I will make you a great nation; I will bless you and make your name so famous that it will be used as a blessing.

"I will bless those who bless you:
I will curse those who slight you
All the tribes of the earth
shall bless themselves by you."

So Abram went as Yahweh told him, and Lot went with him. Abram was seventy-five years old when he left Haran. Abram took his wife Sarai, his nephew Lot, all the possessions they had amassed and the people they had acquired in Haran. They set off for the land of Canaan,* and arrived there.

Abram passed through the land as far as Shechem's holy place, the Oak of Moreh.† At that time the Canaanites were in the land. Yahweh appeared to Abram and said, "It is to your descendants that I will give this land." So Abram built there an altar for Yahweh who had appeared to him. From there he moved on to the mountainous district east of Bethel, where he pitched his tent, with Bethel to the west and Ai to the east.‡ There he built an altar to Yahweh and invoked the name of Yahweh. Then Abram made his way stage by stage to the Negeb.§

When famine came to the land Abram went down into Egypt to stay there for the time, since the land was hard pressed by the famine. On the threshold of Egypt he said to his wife Sarai, "Listen! I know you are a beautiful woman. When the Egyptians see you they will say, 'That is his wife,' and they will kill me but spare you. Tell them you are my sister,‖ so that they may treat me well because of you and spare my life out of regard for you." When Abram arrived in Egypt the Egyptians did indeed see that the woman was very beautiful. When Pharaoh's officials saw her they sang her praises to Pharaoh and the woman was taken into Pharaoh's palace. He treated Abram well because of her, and he received flocks, oxen, donkeys, men and women slaves, she-donkeys and camels. But Yahweh inflicted severe plagues on Pharaoh and his household because of Abram's wife Sarai. So Pharaoh summoned Abram and said, "What is this you have done to me? Why did you not tell me she was your wife? Why did you say, 'She is my sister,' so that I took her for my wife? Now, here is your wife. Take her and go!" Pharaoh committed him to men who escorted him back to the frontier with his wife and all he possessed.

From Egypt Abram returned to the Negeb with his wife and all he possessed, and Lot with him. Abram was a very rich man, with livestock, silver and gold. By stages he went from the Negeb to Bethel, where he had first pitched his tent, between Bethel and Ai, at the place where he had formerly erected the altar. Here Abram invoked the name of Yahweh.

Lot, who was traveling with Abram, had flocks and cattle of his own, tents too. The land was not sufficient to accommodate them both at once, for they had too many possessions to be able to live together. Dispute broke out between the herdsmen of Abram's livestock and those of Lot's. (The Canaanites and the Perizzites# were then living in the land.) Accordingly Abram said to Lot. "Let there be no dispute between me and you, nor between my herdsmen and yours, for we are brothers. Is not the whole land open before you? Part company with me: if you take the left, I will go right; if you take the right, I will go left."

Looking around, Lot saw all the Jordan plain, irrigated everywhere—this was before Yahweh destroyed Sodom and Gomorrah—like the garden of Yahweh or the land of Egypt, as far as Zoar.[1] So Lot chose all the Jordan plain for himself and moved off eastward. Thus they parted company: Abram settled in the land of Canaan; Lot settled among the towns of the plain, pitch-

---

*The region between the Jordan River and the Mediterranean Sea, roughly southern Phoenicia.

†Shechem was a town near Mt. Gerizim, east of the Jordan River. It is now a Palestinian settlement. The Oak of Moreh refers either to the forest or to the plain of Moreh, depending on the translation of the world *elon*. A *moreh* was a teacher or oracle. Many believe the Oak of Moreh was the spot where Abraham sat when Yahweh first revealed the lands promised to him.

‡The locations of the Canaanite cities Bethel and Ai are unknown, though some scholars believe they were located approximately 10 miles north of Jerusalem. Bethel lay west of Ai.

§A desert that lay to the south of Judah.

‖Not a complete falsehood, for Sara was Abraham's half-sister. He also used this deception with Abimelech, the king of Gerar. See Gen. 20:12.

#Literally, "village dwellers." Apparently the Perizzites were either Canaanites or related to them.

[1]At the end of the Dead Sea.

ing his tents on the outskirts of Sodom. Now the people of Sodom were vicious men, great sinners against Yahweh.

Yahweh said to Abram after Lot had parted company with him, "Look all around from where you are toward the north and the south, toward the east and the west. All the land within sight I will give to you and your descendants for ever. I will make your descendants like the dust on the ground: when men succeed in counting the specks of dust on the ground, then they will be able to count your descendants! Come, travel through the length and breadth of the land, for I mean to give it to you.". . .

REVIEW QUESTIONS

1. Why did Abraham tell the Egyptian pharaoh that Sara was his sister? What happened as a result?
2. What did Abraham find when he and Sara returned to Canaan? How did he and his nephew Lot resolve their territorial conflicts?
3. How would you characterize Abraham's god, Yahweh, as portrayed in this story?

Jason and the Voyage of the Argo

APOLLONIUS RHODIUS, *The Argonautica*

The story of Jason and the Argonauts is one of the oldest mythical stories in the ancient Greek world—so old, in fact, that Homer mentioned it in the *Iliad* (originally an oral epic, perhaps dating to the twelfth century B.C.E.). Like *The Tale of Sinuhe,* the story of Jason's journey to find the Golden Fleece was extremely popular. But instead of faithfully reproducing the original tale like the Egyptians did, the Greeks and Romans used it as the basis for other compositions. For example, a number of Greek playwrights used the myth as inspiration for drama. Euripides' *Medea* is the most famous example, but Sophocles and Aeschylus also wrote about Jason's exploits. Similarly, the Roman poet Pindar centered the *Fourth Pythian Ode* on Jason. The most complete version of the entire myth, however, was written in the third century B.C.E. by Apollonius Rhodius.

Apollonius of Rhodes was not actually from Rhodes. He was born in Alexandria, sometime between 296 and 260 B.C.E. In this period, Alexandria was the Ptolemaic capital of Egypt, and its rulers—Macedonians descended from the half-brother of Alexander the Great—were great patrons of art and literature. Alexandria was the home of both the Library and the Museum, centers of scholarship that enjoyed royal patronage and supported scholars and students from all over the Mediterranean. At different times in his life, Apollonius was both. As a young man he was the pupil of Callimachus, the Librarian. Apollonius wrote the *Argonautica* while apparently still in his teens; but when he recited it in public for the first time, it was denounced and its author ridiculed. Undaunted, Apollonius moved to Rhodes, where he gave a second public recitation of his epic, this time to thunderous applause. He subsequently made his move to Rhodes a permanent one, appending the name *Rhodius* (of Rhodes) to his name. He returned to Alexandria only in his old age to assume the post of Librarian. The date of his death is not known.

Much like the ancient Alexandrians, most modern scholars do not hail the *Argonautica* as a high-quality example of epic poetry. Nevertheless, its attention to detail makes it the fullest existing account of the myth of Jason and the Argonauts. It describes in detail how Pelius, who had usurped the throne of Thessaly, sent Jason, the young but rightful king, on a quest for the famous Golden Fleece—in hopes that he would never return, of course. The journey of the Argo and its crew, the Argonauts, may be the archetype of right-of-passage myths in which a young man must suffer terrible ordeals in order to claim a birthright. Like other heroes, Jason and his men successfully completed their mission, though only with the help of two women: the goddess Athena, who wanted to punish Pelias for failing to honor her, and the Colchian princess Medea, who fell in love with Jason, married him, and then betrayed her father, the king. With Medea's help, Jason also took revenge upon Pelias and became king of Thessaly. The two did not live happily ever after, however. After two children and many years, Jason divorced Medea to marry a Corinthian princess. Spurned, Medea took her revenge on Jason by killing their children and driving him to suicide.

The following short selection describes the passage of the Argo through the strait of the Bosporus, a particularly difficult spot called the Symplegades Rocks, or the "Clashing Rocks." When any ship tried to pass through them, the rocks rushed together and crushed the ship. Pinning their hopes on a blind seer named Phineus, however, the Argonauts attempted to trick the rocks, but were not able to navigate successfully through them until the goddess Athene came to their rescue. Thereafter, the rocks remained in one place, fulfilling a prophecy that they would never move again once humans sailed safely between them. It is likely that this story has distant origins in the opening of maritime trade between the Black Sea and the Mediterranean, which could only be accomplished by sailing through the forbidding straits of the Bosporus.

Argo's departure did not escape Athene's eye. She promptly took her stand on a cloud which, though light, could bear her formidable weight, and swept down to the sea, filled with concern for the oarsmen in the ship. There comes a moment to the patient traveller (and there are many such that wander far afield) when the road ahead of him is clear and the distance so foreshortened that he has a vision of his home, he sees his way to it over land and sea, and in his fancy travels there and back so quickly that it seems to stand before his eager eyes. Such was Athene's speed she darted down to set foot on the inhospitable coast of Thynia.*

In due course they found themselves entering the narrowest part of the winding straits. Rugged cliffs hemmed them in on either side, and *Argo* as she advanced began to feel a swirling undercurrent. They moved ahead in fear, for now the clash of the colliding Rocks and the thunder of surf on the shores fell ceaselessly on their ears.

———

*An Island off the southern shore of the Black Sea.

Euphemus* seized the dove and climbed on to the prow, while the oarsmen, at Tiphys'† orders, made a special effort, hoping by their own strength of arm to drive *Argo* through the Rocks forthwith. They rounded a bend and saw a thing that no one after them has seen—the Rocks were moving apart. Their hearts sank; but now Euphemus launched the dove on her flight and the eyes of all were raised to watch her as she passed between the Rocks.

Once more the Rocks met face to face with a resounding crash, flinging a great cloud of spray into the air. The sea gave a terrific roar and the broad sky rang again. Caverns underneath the crags bellowed as the sea came surging in. A great wave broke against the cliffs and the white foam swept high above them. *Argo* was spun round as the flood reached her.

But the dove got through, unscathed but for the tips of her tail-feathers, which were nipped off by the Rocks. The oarsmen gave a cry of triumph and Tiphys shouted at them to row with all their might, for the Rocks were opening again. So they rowed on full of dread, till the backwash, overtaking them, thrust *Argo* in between the Rocks. Then the fears of all were turned to panic. Sheer destruction hung above their heads.

They had already reached a point where they could see the vast sea opening out on either side,

when they were suddenly faced by a tremendous billow arched like an overhanging rock. They bent their heads down at the sight, for it seemed about to fall and overwhelm the ship. But Tiphys just in time checked her as she plunged forward, and the great wave slid under her keel. Indeed it raised her stern so high in the air that she was carried clear of the Rocks. Euphemus ran along shouting to all his friends to put their backs into their rowing, and with answering shouts they struck the water. Yet for every foot that *Argo* made she lost two, though the oars bent like curved bows as the men put out their strength.

But now another overhanging wave came rushing down on them, and when *Argo* had shot end-on like a rolling-pin through the hollow lap of this terrific sea, she found herself held back by the swirling tide just in the place where the Rocks met. To right and left they shook and rumbled; but *Argo* could not budge.

This was the moment when Athene intervened. Holding on to the hard rock with her left hand, she pushed the ship through with the other; and *Argo* clove the air like a winged arrow, though even so the Rocks, clashing in their accustomed way, sheared off the tip of the mascot on the stern. When the men had thus got through unhurt, Athene soared up to Olympus. But the Rocks were now rooted for ever in one spot close to one another. It had been decided by the happy gods that this should be their fate when a human being had seen them and sailed through. The Argonauts, freed from the cold grip of panic, breathed again when they saw the sky once more and the vast ocean stretching out ahead. They felt that they had come through Hell alive.

---

*Euphemus was one of the Argonauts, a son of the sea god Poseidon. According to myth, he had the chance to become the founding father of Cyrene (a city on the coast of North Africa), but he let the opportunity slip through his fingers.
†Tiphys was the helmsman for the *Argo*. He was supposedly endowed with superhuman skills.

REVIEW QUESTIONS

1. What method did the Argonauts use to pass through the Clashing Rocks? Did it work? Why or why not?
2. The Argonauts were unable to navigate the rocks without the intervention of a divine agency. What does this tell you about the religious beliefs of the Greeks?
3. What do you think of the literary quality of this selection? Do you agree with the ancient Alexandrians or the Rhodians? Explain.

A Chou Emperor Travels Around the World

The Travels of Emperor Mu

Like the *Tale of Sinuhe,* the *Travels of Emperor Mu* may be historical, fictional, or a perplexing combination of both. According to ancient Chinese tradition, the story was discovered during the reign of the Han emperor Wu-Ti (140–87 B.C.E.), in the tomb of Ling-wang, the son of Hui-ch'eng-wang, a ruler of Wei circa 245 B.C.E. It and other books found in the tomb are called the "Bamboo Books" and the "Bamboo Annals" because their pages were made of strips of bamboo that had been covered with sheets of fine white silk and inscribed with black ink. Each page was 2.3 feet long and contained forty characters. The books were not in good condition when they were found; many pages had been either "destroyed or disarranged," according to their editor, Hsün Hsü. Their contents exist today only because Wu-ti ordered Hsün Hsü to copy and re-edit the bamboo books.

*mythic
Tales of
exploration/
travel*

This selection is a partial account of the adventures of King Mu, the fifth emperor of the Chou dynasty. According to Hsün Hsü, Mu ruled for 55 years, from 1001 to 945 B.C.E. Mu may very well have ruled the Chin state in that period, but his adventures resemble myth more than history. According to Hsün Hsü, quoting a commentary on the *Classic of Spring and Autumn,* Mu wished to mark "the countries under the sky with the wheels of his chariot and the hoofs of his horses." So, with his horses Tao-li and Luh-erh, his driver Tsao Fu, and six divisions of soldiers, Mu set out to travel to the four corners of the world.

On the day *mou-yin,*[1] Emperor Mu started out for the north by crossing the river Chang. Two days later the company reached . . . where the emperor was entertained at a banquet by the people of this country upon a hill . . . the emperor himself did not alight from his chariot. The company then proceeded forward until they arrived at the foot of the Hsing Mountain [in Hopei].

On the day *kuei-wei* it snowed, and the emperor went out hunting on the western ranges of the mountain. Crossing the valley of the moun-

tain he followed a course north to the southern bank of the Ho-t'o River. The emperor proceeded north and . . . arrived at the domain of the Ch'uan-jung (a northern barbarous tribe) and was entertained by the people on the southern bank of the Tang River. He was very pleased. . . . The north wind blew on the day *kêng-yin* and snow fell. The emperor ordered his followers to stop and rest, because the weather was cold.

On *chia-wu,* the emperor proceeded to the west and soon crossed the hills of the Yü Gate or Pass,[2] at the frontier. On the day *chi-hai* the company arrived at the plains of Yen-chu and Yu-chih. On the day *hsin-ch'ou,* the emperor marched on to the west and reached the king-

---

[1]The Chinese have a special way of counting the years. There are ten characters known as the ten stems of heaven and another twelve characters known as the twelve branches of earth. The combinations of these two sets of characters give names to the sixty years of the Chinese cycle. The days are named and counted the same way. This system has actually been in use since the Yin Dynasty, 1766?–1112? B.C.E.

[2]Through the mountains northwest of Tai-chou, Shansi Province.

dom of Pëng-jen. The people of this country were the descendants of Ho-tsung (the god of the Yellow River). Po Hsü, the duke of P'êng-en, proceeded to Chih-shih to welcome the royal guest, offering as presents ten leopards' skins and twenty-six good horses. Duke Ching accepted the presents by the emperor's command.

On the day *kuei-yu* the company camped in the neighborhood of the Ch'i Lake. The emperor went fishing in the river and paid a visit to the country of Chih-shih. The next day the emperor went hunting and captured a white fox and a black *lo* [a kind of fox] with which he made sacrifice to the God of the River. Two days later a banquet was spread by the river and the emperor reviewed his company, which was composed of six divisions of soldiers. On the day *mou-yin* the emperor made his way to the west, marching on as far as the Yang-yu Mountains, where in ancient days Wu Yi, the God of the River, had established his family, the house of Ho-tsung.[3] A member of this house welcomed the emperor . . . offering as presents a piece of silk fabric and a *pi*[4]

On the auspicious day *mou-wu* the emperor robed himself appropriately in the ceremonial costume, the cap, the gown, the handkerchief, the girdle and the *fou*,[5] with ornamental hangings on both sides. And, holding a *pi* in his hands, he took his stand . . . facing the south. Tseng Chu was the assistant at the ceremony. When the officials had arranged the sacrific[i]al animals in their proper order, the emperor presented the *pi* to the God of the River. Po Yao received it from him, turned to the west and submerged the present in the river. After performing this he knelt before the Son of Heaven and touched his head to the earth many times. Tseng Chu then submerged the sacrificial animals . . . the ox, the horse, the pig and the sheep. Then the God of the River appeared from

the water, and, bearing good tidings from God, he addressed the emperor by name, saying, "Mu Man, be thou forever on the throne and may thy rule be wise and prosperous!" To the south the emperor bowed many times.

"Mu Man," continued the God of the River, "let me show thee the precious articles of the Ch'un Mountain and the beautiful palaces of K'un-lun.[6] Proceed, then, to the K'un-lun Mountain, and behold the precious articles of the Ch'un Mountain."

The voice dropped low and died away. . . .

On the day *ting-ssŭ* the emperor ascended the . . . mountain on the southwest. It was the domain of Mu Hua, where big trees and large bushes spread wide, and wild animals were abundant. It was a good place for hunting.

On the day *mou-wu,* Chu Yü, of the people of Shou Yü, offered as presents one hundred measures of wine. After the entertainment the emperor advanced and halted at the ridge of the K'un-lun by the southern bank of the Red River. . . . On the auspicious day *hsin-yu* the emperor ascended the K'un-lun Mountain and visited the palaces of the Yellow Emperor.[7] And, in order to identify the burial place of the God of the Clouds for future generations, he heaped up earth upon his grave. . . . The emperor marched on to the north and halted at Chu-tse, or the Pearl Pond, to fish in the running stream. It is said that the marshes of the Pearl Pond were thirty *li* square, and that in them grew all kinds of reeds and rushes. . . . On the day *ting-mao,* in the last month of the summer, the emperor ascended the Ch'un Mountain on the north, from where he could see the wilderness stretching in all four directions. . . .

It is said that the Ch'un Mountain was the richest mountain in the world, a store of precious

---

[3]This god has a man's face and rides on two dragons; he lives in the Stream of Ts'ung-chi, which is 300 feet deep.

[4]An ancient jade badge of office, made round with a hole.

[5]A tablet, about three feet long, made of ivory, precious stones, wood or bamboo that was held before the breast by courtiers at audience, even as late as the Ming Dynasty, 1368–1644.

[6]This mountain, the center of Chinese mythology, was where all the gods assembled; it is also the name of a range in Chinese Turkestan where there are four plains from which flow seventy springs.

[7]The so-called Father of the Chinese race, who is supposed to have ruled the empire in peace for a hundred years beginning 2697 B.C.

stones and valuable jades. It was a place where the most flourishing crops grew and the trees were tall and the bushes beautiful. The emperor gathered some species of these excellent crops so that he might cultivate them in the central kingdom when he returned. It is also said that the emperor rested at the foot of the mountain for five days and amused himself with music. Ch'i then presented to the emperor many beautiful women. Among them, Lady T'ing and Lady Lieh soon became his favorite concubines. It is said that the country of the Red Bird was famous for its beautiful women and valuable jade.

On the day *chi-mao* the emperor marched on to the north, driving forward without taking any rest, until he crossed the Yang River and on the next day arrived at the domain of Ts'ao Nu. . . . On the day *jen-wu* the emperor rode to the north and turned eastward on the way back, arriving at the Black River on the day *chia-shen*. The people of the wild west call the river Hunglu. It rained for seven days and the emperor stopped to wait for the soldiers of the six divisions. Here he conferred on Ch'ang-kung, a member of the Long-armed People, the right to rule over the western portion of the Black River. . . . On *kuei-ch'ou* the emperor rode westward arriving at Bitter Mountain. The name of the wild west was Garden of Prosperity. The emperor stopped for hunting and here he tasted the bitter herb. On the day *ting-hsü* the emperor marched to the westward and on *chi-wei* the company stayed for the night to the west of Yellow Rat Mountain. . . . They proceeded westward until on *kuei-hai* they arrived, at the domain of the Royal Mother of the West.[8]

On the auspicious day *chia-tzu* the emperor, carrying a white *kuei*[9] and a black *pi*, paid a visit to the Royal Mother of the West. To her he offered as presents one hundred pieces of embroidered silk and three hundred pieces of *wu* fabric. After bowing many times, the Royal Mother accepted the presents.

On the next day the emperor invited the Royal Mother to a banquet on Emerald Pond. During the occasion she sang extempore:

"Hills and mountains come in view
As fleecy clouds ascend the sky.
Far and wide, divided by waters and mountain ranges
Our countries separately lie.
Should long life preserve thee,
Come again."

To this the emperor responded:

"When I to east return
To millions bringing order and peace;
When they enjoy prosperity and ease
To thee shall I return;
From this day count three years
To this country again I shall come."

The emperor then rode on the Hsi Mountains and on the rocks engraved a record of his visit. He planted a memorial tree of sophora and named the place the Mountain of the Royal Mother of the West.

From here the emperor took his way back to the east. . . . On the day *ting-wei* the emperor took a drink at Hot Mountain and the next day went out fowling. The following day, he drank at the bank of the Ju River and gave orders for the six divisions of soldiers to gather together.

In this region there were forests, marshy swamps and ponds full of water, and there were also smooth plains and high plateaus where birds scattered their feathers. Now the six divisions of soldiers had concentrated in this region where it is said the emperor stayed for three months. The emperor gave a big banquet to the ministers of state, the royal princes, the big feudal lords, the officials and all the companies of the seven regiments in Yu-ch'in, a higher plain in this wide region. . . . The soldiers started out

---

[8]Semi-devil, semi-goddess, or, it has even been suggested, the Queen of Sheba.
[9]A small stone scepter given to nobles as a sign of rank—the size varying with the rank—that is held in both hands during levees.

on horseback on their expedition with their hounds before them. The hunting was carried on for fully nine days and they captured all the birds and animals in this region, the number of victims being countless. On the plain Yu-ch'in they presented all they had obtained. The good furs and the beautiful feathers were carefully selected and carried home in their carriages. The emperor had for himself one hundred carriages full. . . .

The emperor hurried on eastward, crossing the desert on the south . . . he was thirsty and water could not be obtained in the desert, so Kao Pên-jung, a member of the seven regiments, stabbed the left horse of his chariot in the neck and presented a drink of pure blood to his royal master. The emperor was very much pleased and gave him a piece of ornamental jade, which the soldier received by kneeling down and touching his head to the ground.

The emperor then proceeded southward and reached the end of the Piled Stone Mountain Range, where he found cypresses growing abundantly.

REVIEW QUESTIONS

1. What do you think was the purpose of Emperor Mu's journey? What evidence supports your opinion?
2. How did Mu pass his time as he was traveling from place to place? What was his favorite pursuit?
3. How did Mu react to foreign rulers he encountered? How did they react to him?
4. How did the various regions that Mu visited differ from each other? Based on your knowledge of Asian geography, do any of them resemble actual places? Is it important that they do? Why or why not?

Native American Myth of the Southwest

How the Pueblo People Came to the Middle Place

The various groups of Pueblo Indians who inhabit the American Southwest share many nearly identical religious myths. One of the most widespread is the story of how the people journeyed from their earliest home in the dark underworld to the Middle Place, the land of sunlight, clear air, and brilliant colors. There, Spider Woman, the earth goddess and grandmother of all things, showed them maize (corn) and counseled them to travel south toward Turtle Mountain, which was to be their new home. Instead of following her advice, however, the people quarreled and set off in the wrong direction. After a number of disastrous encounters, particularly with the Comanches and wild animals, they finally resolved to follow Spider Woman's advice.

This selection, the Tewa version of the myth, describes two journeys: the passage of the people from darkness to light, and their exploration of the lands of the Southwest.

In the beginning, the whole world was dark. The people lived underground, in the blackness. These people did not know that their world was dark all around them, because they had never seen the light. They had not been taught the difference between the black world underground and the blue sky world.

After a long time in darkness, the people began to get restless. Some of them said to one another, "Is this all the world there is? Will there never be another world?"

"There must be more of a world somewhere."

Then Mole came to visit them, digging his way along through the darkness with his little paws and sharp-pointed nails. The old men of the people asked Mole, "Is there more of a world than this, friend? You travel around, going far and fast underground. What have you found out? Is there more of a world somewhere?"

Mole answered, "It is true that I travel, and that I go far and fast in the darkness. Sometimes I go up, and sometimes I go down. When I go up, the world *feels* different. I think there is a new kind of air there, when I go up. I can not see the difference because I am blind and my eyes can not see the daylight as yours could. Maybe if some of you went up there and looked around, you could see whether there is another world above or whether all there is is here below."

"How should we travel?" the old men asked him then. "How shall we know where to go, or how to recognize that place when we reach it?"

"Follow along behind me," Mole replied. "I can tell you when we come out in that different world, because I will feel the change."

Then the people formed themselves into a line behind Mole, and he began to dig his way upward. He went up in a straight line and a slanting line and then a straight line again. As Mole clawed away the earth, the people took it from his little paw-hands and passed it back along their line, from one person to the next, to get it out of their way. That is why the tunnel that Mole dug upward for the people was closed behind them. That is why they could never find their way back to their old dark world.

When at last Mole stopped digging and the people came out in their new world, the light shone all around them and washed over them like a blessing. The people were blinded by the light, like Mole. Then the people became frightened. They hid their eyes with their hands, so that sight would not be burned out of their heads. Some of the people said, "This is as bad as the darkness. We can see nothing here, either."

Others said, "Let us go back. If we are to be blind anyhow, we will be safer in the world that we have always known. We can't see where we are in the darkness, but after all, we are used to that."

While all the people were standing there, arguing about what was best to be done, they heard a little small voice of a woman speak to them.

"Be patient, my children," the small voice said, "and I will help you."

The oldest man of the people asked her, "Who are you, my mother?"

Then she answered him, "Take your hands away from your eyes, but do it slowly, slowly. Now wait a minute. Move them a little bit farther away. Now, do it again. And again."

Four times in all the people moved their hands. At last their eyes were freed and opened, and the people could see her who had been talking to them. She was the bent little old Spider Woman, the grandmother of the Earth and of all living things.

Grandmother Spider sat on the ground before the people. Standing beside her were two young men, her twin grandsons, the War Twins.* Grandmother said to the oldest men of the people:

"These twin grandsons of mine are silly. Now that you have come out in the Blue Sky World, I want you to act more wisely than they do. Look at them, the way they carry their weapons around with them. One has a bow and the other has a spear, and they both have throwing sticks. Those twin boys go around ready for war all the

---

*The War Twins are gods of war and hunting. Not really twins, but brothers, they were responsible for creating some of the natural landscape. In this version of the myth they are unusually mischievous.

time. That is foolish, for people always to be fighting one another.

"I want you people always to remember this, and to stop whenever you are tempted to quarrel with one another. Never make yourselves weapons, because if you do you will be tempted to use them. And if you ever give in to that temptation, and do hurt to one another, then you will learn what sorrow is. To be happy, you must never hurt anyone in any way."

Then Grandmother Spider pointed with her lips and chin—away in the distance she pointed—and she said to the oldest man of all the people, "What do you see there, my child?"

And he answered her. "We see something green and growing, our Grandmother."

"That is right," said Grandmother Spider, "you see well. The name of that green growing thing is CORN, and it is food for all my people. You will have to learn to plant it and to care for it. You will have to weed it and hoe it and water it. You will have to work hard for the corn, but if you work right, with good hearts and love for each other within them, the corn will take care of you always."

And the oldest men of the people asked her, "Where shall we plant our corn fields, Grandmother?"

Grandmother Spider looked around her, and the people looked all around them, too. She asked them, "What do you see, my grandchildren?"

And the old men of the people answered her, "We see a red mountain in the east, Grandmother."

Grandmother Spider told him, "That is the Red Eastern Mountain [the Sangre de Cristo Range], and the snow on its slopes is stained red with the blood of the people who have died fighting the wild Indians who live on the east side of the mountains. Keep away from those mountains, my children, or the Comanches will kill you too. Now the daylight is going, and soon it will be night. Look again, quickly. What do you see over there?"

"There is a white mountain to the north, Grandmother."

Spider Woman said to them, "The name of that mountain is Mountain Standing [Taos Mountain]. If you go north of Mountain Standing, you will be cold, my grandchildren. The corn you plant beyond there will freeze in the ground, and it will never grow for you. So your home is not so far away, in that direction. Now, look again. What do you see over there, grandchildren?"

And the oldest man of all the old men of the people answered her, "We see a black mountain in the west, Grandmother."

Then Spider Woman said, "That is Black Mountain West [Mount Taylor]. Behind it is the Place Where the Sun Lies Down and Dies. If you go too far in that direction, your corn will wilt and droop in the darkness, and will never grow and ripen. Keep away from the west, my children, or you will be back in the world of night." Then she said to them, "Now, look again. What do you see in that direction?"

And they looked again, very quickly, almost glancing from the sides of their eyes, and the youngest one of all the old men of the people said, "We see something golden and gleaming, far away to the south of us, Grandmother. It is too far away for us to be sure what it is. We can not see clearly enough."

Then she answered, "That is the Mountain of the South, the Turtle Mountain [Sandia Mountain], and when you reach it, you will know that you have reached your home."

So the old men of the people asked her, "What means that word, turtle, our Grandmother?"

And in a voice that was growing tired and tiny. Grandmother Spider answered them, "When you find the signs of your two friends again—when you find Mole again and me again—then you will have found the turtle and his mountain that he carries on his back." And Grandmother Spider's voice faded as the daylight faded, and she and her twin grandsons were gone.

The people huddled together all that long night—the first night they had ever known, and the longest they would ever know—and waited for the daylight to return, half afraid and half hopeful that it would. They looked above them and saw the stars—hundreds and hundreds and hundreds of stars—white against the blackness like sparks that had scattered off the sun, and they watched as the stars walked across the sky. Some of the people noticed that certain stars were brighter than others, and they began to name them over to themselves, like naming new-born children.

When morning came, the stars faded and vanished. The people, standing there in full daylight, began to quarrel. Some wanted to go one way, some another. They all wanted to go straight to the mountains they could see most clearly, in the east, in spite of Grandmother Spider's warning. Those mountains looked closer to them than the Turtle Mountain she had told them was to be their home. They still couldn't see that mountain plainly. They couldn't quite make out its shape, or decide what a turtle looked like.

At last the people decided to travel to the Red Mountains of the East. There the Comanches surprised them, and before the people could defend themselves, many of them were killed. The white snow on the mountains was dyed red with their blood. Wherever you looked you saw still bodies lying. Wherever you listened you heard the last moans of the dying. That is why the mountains are called the Mountains of Blood— Los Sangres.

Now, today, in the east of the summer sky, you can see a feathered war bonnet. One Comanche man dropped it and forgot it and left it, on his way home, he was so loaded with the people's scalps.

Again the people quarreled among themselves, for some of them wanted to go south and others north. Some of these last people picked up sharp-pointed stones, like knives and spear heads, and hit their brothers with them. Then they ran away, to the north. When they came to the cold slope of Taos Mountain, a white bear came down its side, and breathed its cold breath on them. Some of those people fell down dead. Those who were left alive ran away, as fast as they could, sorrowing. The bear went back up the side of Taos Mountain, and on up into the sky. You can see him there in winter, early in the night.

Again the people began to quarrel among

themselves about which way they should go. Some made themselves spears and spear throwers; they hurled the spears at their brothers and pierced them. And the men who were pierced fell down and died.

The others, weeping, ran away to the west, where the War Twins were standing. The twins shook their own weapons at the people, and threatened them, saying, "Go away, you foolish people, for this is the Place Where the Sun Lies Down and Dies. This is where every living thing must die. You can not stay here and live."

The frightened people ran away, while the young men stood and laughed at them. Then the young men turned their backs, and went back up the Black Mountain, into the sky. You can see them there in the springtime, about the middle of the night.

And again the frightened people quarreled, and some of them said, "At least let us go back to the place where we met our grandmother, the Spider. If she is still there, perhaps she can tell us what to do."

But the others said, "Where shall we find her? We have looked everywhere."

"We can go back to the place where we came out," said the old men of the people. The others were too tired to argue any more. They said, "Let us go back."

So the people turned sorrowfully away from the laughing War Twins in the western sky, and started traveling back. Their feet were tired; their sandals were worn out. They traveled back over the black lava beds (near Grants, New Mexico), and the knife-edged stones cut their feet. The people left a trail of bloody footprints behind them. You can see the red marks on the sharp black lava today.

But when the weary people came to the place where they came out, which was the Place of the Middle of the World, they could not find their grandmother again. When night came, they looked into the sky above their heads, and learned why they could not find her. For Grandmother Spider sat there in her star web, shaking her head and crying little star tears because her people were so foolish. Some of the people cried, too, and they ran away, up into the sky, to join their grandmother. The white road along which they ran is the Milky Way. On beyond it, in the summer, you can see the Spider's web. It is always there, so she can come back to her house whenever she wants to.

Now there were only two of all the people left, a man and a woman. They were very tired. Because there was nowhere else left for them to go, they turned and journeyed south. Their road was hard. They traveled through the desert, parallel to the course of the Rio Grande, and it was dusty and sandy. At last the woman stopped and looked around her.

"There are green trees over there to our right," she said.

The man looked at the dry world all around them, and he replied, "Let us go over there and look at them. At least we can sit down in the shade and be cool."

So they crossed the heavy sand of the Jornado del Muerto [Dead Man's Road], and they came to the line of green trees. There was another line, of blue water, shining beyond the trees. It was the Rio Grande.

The woman said to her husband, "Indeed, this is a very beautiful place. Let us sit down here and rest, for the world feels as if it would be good to us."

After the man had rested a while, and felt stronger, he looked around him. He said to the woman, "Look! There is a golden mountain over there, shining and gleaming, across the valley to the south. I wonder what it is?"

The woman warned him, "Keep away from it. Stay away from it forever. You know what happened to our people who went up into the other mountains."

So the man sat still on the river bank beside her, but he sat facing the golden mountain.

Presently the woman looked down at the sand beside her.

"Look!" she said to her husband. "Something is crawling along the sand. I wonder what that little thing is, moving so slowly, slowly?"

Then the man, in his turn, warned her. "Leave it alone. You know what happened to the people who went near the dangerous animal, on the Mountain of the North."

The woman obeyed her husband, and did not touch the little crawling thing, but still she watched it. Presently her husband began to watch it, too, as it moved slowly along the sand before them.

The man said to his wife, "Look what a strange track this thing leaves in the sand. We have seen tracks like that before, somewhere, haven't we? They looked like the mole's tracks, don't they?"

The woman studied the little animal, and then she said to her husband, "Look. Only look. Its back is as hard as a stone, but it has a design carved and painted on it. Look! That design is Grandmother Spider's web!"

Together the man and the woman watched the little crawling thing. Together they said to each other, "Look! It is shaped like the Shining Golden Mountain!"

They looked again at the far away golden gleam of the mountain, which seemed to draw closer to them as they gazed. They looked down again at the little turtle, crawling along the sand. They looked at each other, and they smiled. They had found their friends Mole and Spider again, and their friend had shown the man and woman their home, as Grandmother Spider had promised he would.

You can read this, the end of the story, in the autumn stars. Look right directly above you for the man and woman, and the turtle who guided them home to the Middle Land, the land between the Rio Grande and the Sandia Mountain, the land that the Tewa Indians call their home.

REVIEW QUESTIONS

1. What is the role of animals in this myth? How does it compare to other Native American myths in Part I?

2. What is the role of the War Twins?
3. To what extent can this story also be considered a creation story? Explain.
4. What is the moral of this story?

Kwasi Benefo Travels to the Land of the Dead

Journey to Asamando

Journeys in myth and legend sometimes involve travel to actual places, but often they take their heros to more unearthly realms. Such is the case in this story of an African hero, an Ashanti farmer named Kwasi Benefo. Grieving and bereft, he traveled to Asamando, the underground land of the dead that is the mirror image of the world of the living. As in this world, death in Asamando takes place for each successive generation. As long as the names of departed souls can be remembered and spoken by the living, those who have died—especially parents and ancestors, but also spouses, children, and friends—are still alive in Asamando. And as long as they have life in the afterlife, these spirits can be involved in the lives of the living, by appearing to them in dreams or in states of deep meditation. Belief in Asamando is emotionally satisfying and practical. Although death in the real world is almost always beyond the powers of human beings to control, death in the afterlife can be postponed through the love and compassion of the living.

The Ashanti (also Assante) can trace their religious beliefs to the thirteenth century C.E. or even earlier. Descended from the Akans, who formed many small but powerful states in West Africa in the Middle Ages, the Ashanti can be found today in northern and central Ghana. In the seventeenth century, they built a small empire that included most of modern Togo, Ghana, and the Ivory Coast. Using wealth from plentiful deposits of gold (it could even be panned from alluvial soils), they purchased large numbers of slaves (both from neighboring African peoples and from the Portuguese), mined even more gold, and cleared much of the forested lands in southern West Africa for use as cropland. A thriving agriculture soon developed, based on indigenous crops like rice and plantain and enriched by American crops like maize (corn) and cassava. The Ashanti became prosperous farmers with a stable economy and thriving culture. European attempts to dominate them from the fifteenth to the nineteenth centuries did not result in significant numbers of white settlers, nor did they present a serious threat to Ashanti beliefs.

JOURNEY TO ASAMANDO, LAND OF THE DEAD

Among the Ashanti, a young man was living there. His name was Kwasi Benefo. His fields flourished, he had many cattle. He lacked only a wife to bear children for him, to care for his household, and, when the time should come, to mourn his death. Kwasi Benefo went looking. In his village he found a young woman who greatly pleased him. They married. They were content with each other. But soon the young woman faded, and death took her. Kwasi Benefo grieved. He bought her an amoasie, a piece of silk-cotton cloth to cover her genitals, and beads to go around her waist, and in these things she was buried.

Kwasi Benefo could not forget her. He looked for her in his house, but she was not there. His heart was not with living anymore. His brothers spoke to him, his uncle spoke to him, his friends spoke to him, saying: "Kwasi, put it from your mind. This is the way it is in the world. Find yourself another wife." At last Kwasi Benefo comforted himself. He went to another village. He found a young woman there and made arrangements. He brought her home. Again he became contented with living. The woman had a good character. She took good care of the household. She tried in every way to please her husband. Kwasi Benefo said, "Yes, living is worthwhile." But after she had been pregnant for some time, the young woman became ill. She grew gaunt. Death took her. Kwasi Benefo, his heart hurt him. His wife was dressed in her amoasie, she was buried. Kwasi Benefo could not be consoled. He sat in his house. He would not come out. People said to him: "People have died before. Arise, come out of the house. Mingle with your friends as you used to do." But Kwasi Benefo did not desire life anymore. He remained in his house.

The family of the young woman who had died heard about Kwasi Benefo's grief. They said: "He is suffering too much. This man loved our daughter. Let us give him another wife." They sent messengers to Kwasi Benefo, and they brought him to their village. They said to him: "One must grieve, yes, but you cannot give your life to it. We have another daughter, she will make a good wife for you. Take her. This way you will not be alone. What is past is past, one cannot go there anymore. What a man has loved is in his heart, it does not go away. Yet the dead live with the dead, and the living with the living."

Kwasi Benefo pondered on it. He said, "Now, how can I take another wife when the one who

has died calls to me?" They answered: "Yes, that is the way a person feels. But in time it will be different." Kwasi Benefo went home. He resumed working in his fields. And after some months he returned to the village where his wife's family lived. He said, "The daughter you spoke of, I have been thinking of her." They said: "Yes, our daughter will make a good wife. She has a good character. She will do well for you." They talked, they made arrangements. At last Kwasi Benefo arose, and with his new wife he returned to his house. They went on living. The young woman conceived, and a boy child was born. There was a celebration in the village. People danced and sang. Kwasi Benefo gave out gifts. He said: "My life is good. When has it ever been so good?"

One day Kwasi Benefo was working in his fields. Some women of the village came crying that a tree had fallen. Kwasi Benefo ceased his hoeing, saying, "Who cries over a falling tree?" Then darkness covered his spirit. He said, "Is there something left unspoken?" They said: "Your wife was coming back from the river. She sat beneath the tree to rest. A spirit of the woods weakened the roots and the tree fell on her." Kwasi Benefo ran to the village. He went to his house. His wife lay upon her mat without life in her body. Kwasi Benefo cried out. He threw himself on the ground and lay there as if life had departed from him also. He heard nothing, felt nothing. People said, "Kwasi Benefo is dead." The medicine men came. They said: "No, he is not dead. He lingers between here and there." They worked on Kwasi Benefo. They revived him. He stood up. He made the arrangements that were necessary. There was a wake, and the next day his wife was buried in her amoasie. After that, Kwasi Benefo brooded. He thought: "Evil is working against me. Each of my wives has died. I do not want another wife, yet if I did, what family would trust me with its daughter?" What was in Kwasi Benefo's thoughts was also in the minds of other people. They said, "It is not good to be a wife of Kwasi Benefo."

Kwasi Benefo said: "Of what value are my fields and my cattle? They are nothing to me."

He took his boy child and left the village. He abandoned his house, he abandoned his farm. He carried his son to the place where his wife's family lived and left him there. He went out into the bush. He walked for many days, not caring where he was. He arrived at a distant village, but he departed from it at once and went deeper into the bush country. At last, at a wild place, he stopped. He said, "This place, far from people, I will stay here." He built a crude house. He gathered roots and seeds to eat. He made traps for small game. Thus he lived. His clothing turned to rags, and he began to wear the skins of animals. In time he almost forgot that his name was Kwasi Benefo, and that he had once been a prosperous farmer. His life was wretched, but he did not care. This is the way it was with Kwasi Benefo.

A year passed, then another. Little by little the desire for life came back to Kwasi Benefo. Once again he began to farm. He burned the brush and planted corn. He built a new house. He travelled to a distant village and acquired cloth, and he clothed himself. His farm began to prosper. He acquired cattle. And once again he yearned to have a woman to care for his house and bear children. Thus he sought once more a wife. He married again. Things were going well for Kwasi Benefo until this wife, his fourth, became sick and died.

This time Kwasi said, "How can I go on living?" He abandoned his farm, his house and his cattle and journeyed back to the village where he was born. People were surprised because they had thought of him as dead. His family and his friends gathered to celebrate his return, but Kwasi Benefo said: "No, there is to be no celebration. I have come back only to die in my own village and be buried here near the graves of my ancestors." He settled again in his old house, which was now open to the weather and falling down. But he made no effort to repair anything, nor did he go out to his fields, which were grown up with brush. He lived on this way, thinking of all his wives, tormented by the thought that when his time came to die there

would be no one to mourn his death and sing praise songs for him.

One night as he lay sleepless the thought came to him that he should go to Asamando, the Land of the Dead, and see the four young women who had shared his life. He arose. He went out of his house and departed from his village. He went to the forest place called Nsamandow, where the dead were buried. He reached it, he went on. There were no paths to follow. There was no light. All was darkness. He passed through the forest and came to a place of dim light. No one was living there. There were no sounds in the air. No voices of man, no birds, no animals broke the stillness. Kwasi Benefo went on, until he came at last to a river. He tried to ford the river, but he could not do it, for the water was too deep and it was running too fast. He thought, "Here my journey comes to an end."

But at this moment he felt the splash of water on his face. Sitting on the far bank was an old woman with a brass pan at her side. The pan was full of women's loincloths and beads. By this sign Kwasi Benefo knew her to be Amokye, the person who welcomed the souls of dead women to Asamando, and took from each of them her amoasie and beads. This was the reason why women prepared for burial were dressed as they were, so that each could give her amoasie and beads to Amokye at the river crossing. Amokye said to Kwasi Benefo, "Why are you here?" And he answered: "I have come to see my wives. I cannot live any longer, because every woman that stays in my house, death takes her. I cannot sleep, I cannot eat, I want nothing that the living world has for the living." Amokye said to him: "Oh, you must be Kwasi Benefo. Yes, I have heard of you. Many persons who came through here have spoken of your misfortune. But you are not a soul, you are a living man, therefore you cannot cross." Kwasi Benefo said, "Then I will remain here until I die and become a soul."

Amokye, the guardian at the river, took compassion on Kwasi Benefo. She said, "Because of your suffering I will let you come across." She caused the water to run slowly. She caused it to become shallow. She said: "Go that way. There you will find them. But they are like the air, you will not be able to see them, though they will know you have come." Kwasi Benefo crossed the river, and he went on. Now he was in Asamando. He came to a house, he entered. Outside the house he heard the sounds of village activities. He heard people calling to one another. He heard hoeing in the fields, the clearing of brush, and grain being pounded in mortars.

A bucket of water appeared, and washcloths suddenly came into view before him. He washed off the dust of his journey. Outside the house, now, he heard his wives singing a song of welcome. The bucket and washcloths disappeared, and in their place he saw a gourd dish of food and a jug of water. While he ate, the voices of his wives went on singing Kwasi's praises. They told of what a kind husband he had been in the land of the living, and spoke of his gentleness. When he was through eating, the dish and the jug disappeared, and then there was a sleeping mat for Kwasi. His wives invited him to rest. He lay down on the mat. His wives sang again,

and in their song they told Kwasi to continue living until his natural death, when his soul would come to Asamando unencumbered by a body. When this time arrived, they said, they would be waiting for him. Meanwhile, they said, Kwasi should marry again, and this time his wife would not die.

Hearing these sweet words from the women he loved, Kwasi Benefo fell into a deep sleep. When at last he awoke he was no longer in Asamando, but in the forest. He arose. He made his way back to his house in the village. He called on his friends to come and help him build a new house. When that was done, he sent messengers to the people who belonged to his fraternal society, saying that on such and such a day there would be a clearing of his fields. The men gathered on that day. They cleared and burned his fields, they began the hoeing. Kwasi Benefo planted. His crops grew and he cultivated. Again he mingled among people. In time he found a wife. They had children. They lived on. That is the story of Kwasi Benefo. The old people told it that way.

REVIEW QUESTIONS

1. Describe, in general, the Ashanti attitude toward death as it is portrayed in this myth. Would you say the Ashanti fear death or not? Why?
2. What does this selection tell you about the relationship between men and women in Ashanti society?
3. Why did Kwasi Benefo decide to travel to Asamando? What did he hope to accomplish? Did he succeed? Why or why not?
4. A hero on a quest often has to cross a "threshold," a symbolic or actual barrier of some kind. What was Kwasi Benefo's threshold? How did he cross it?

Part II

Classical Civilizations, 800 B.C.E.–800 C.E.

Part II begins in approximately 800 B.C.E. Although civilization was firmly established in a number of locations around the globe—and had been for more than two millennia—the next one thousand years witnessed the rise and development of "classical civilizations." These civilizations attained standards of excellence in all areas of human endeavor against which future cultures were measured. Standards were established in such varied fields as literature, art and architecture, government and law, and religion and philosophy. Indeed, to label something as a "classic" (a classic automobile, classical music, etc.) is always an expression of high praise and approval.

Today, elements of ancient civilizations are still identifiable in their modern descendants. Four of the most important literary genres are represented in Part II, including biography and history as distinct forms of prose (for example, Cornelius Nepos's *Life of Epaminondas,* Herodotus's *Histories,* and a number of works by Chinese dynastic historians), as well as drama and poetry (for example, selections from *Manyoshu,* or *The Collection of Myriad Leaves*).

Several good examples of classical art are provided in this section. In Chapter 6 on the Americas, many of the illustrations are classical Meso-American expressions of religious and cultural concepts. A millennium and a half later, the Aztecs would easily recognize and understand the motifs and specific characteristics of their ancestors' art. Moreover, even today tourists in Mexico City perceive the cultural significance and main outlines of the ancient iconography that features prominently in contemporary art, advertising, and interior decoration. The uniqueness of ancient Roman artistic endeavor, in this case architecture, was immediately obvious to several Chinese envoys to the eastern Roman Empire; and the two vases included in Chapter 7 are instantly recognizable as the products of Greek and Roman artisans even though the subject matter is African. Greco-Roman aesthetic principles, of course, continue to dominate standards of both elite and popular culture in the West.

Another enduring legacy of the classical world is the establishment of systems of government and law on which many modern states depend. Elements of democratic Athens, described by Pericles in Chapter 4, were deliberately incorporated into many modern governments (just as Athenian architecture was the model for many of the monuments and buildings in Washington, D.C., as well as other world capitals). Monarchy, at the other end of the political spectrum, has also been a widespread form of government for millennia. In fact, many selections in Part II testify to the authority of kings and the variety of their powers. Even more powerful than kings, rulers of vast empires established centralized governments and attempted to win or compel the allegience of linguistically and culturally diverse peoples who lived within their borders. Even a modern world leader might recognize and appreciate (or abhor) the strategies, objectives, and tactics of men like Shalmaneser III of Assyria, Ezana of Aksum, or even Julius Caesar.

A fourth foundational characteristic of classical civilizations is the creation and advancement of culturally distinct philosophical perspectives, which often (but not always) include religious beliefs. Each culture responded to its particular environment and historical circumstances in a unique manner. One of the most important intellectual tasks confronting all classical civilizations was to explain their universe. In the case of Polybius, this endeavor went beyond mere attempts to understand the principles underlying the structure of the natural world; he probed into more sophisticated questions: how had the Romans risen to a position of dominance in the Mediterranean, and why did they deserve to rule others? Just as Rome sought hegemony in the Mediterrranean, China also considered itself worthy of the respect and obedience of its neighbors. In fact, so confident was the "Middle Kingdom" that it sent envoys to other parts of the world to acquaint them with China's existence and excellence—and to gather information and, where possible, tribute. Finally, classical civilizations valued the acquisition of knowledge of all kinds, both material and spiritual. Buddhist scholars such as Fâ-hien and Sung-yun, as well as the Christian pilgrim Egeria, traveled long distances to seek religious texts and to absorb the holiness of sacred sites.

By 800 C.E. a number of significant changes had occurred in many parts of the world. The Roman Empire in the West had disappeared, succeeded in Europe by the empire of the Germanic chieftan Charlemagne. The eastern provinces of Rome (referred to after 500 C.E. as the Byzantine Empire) had been greatly reduced in territory and influence by the onslaught of the Arabs, who had begun, in the previous century, to build a series of empires that would eventually stretch from Spain across northern Africa to the Ganges River. In Meso-America, 800 C.E. is the traditional date for the beginnings of the "Time of Troubles," when overpopulation, environmental problems, and conflicts between cities began the decline of Mayan civilization. Finally, any definition of the end of an era on a global scale must admit some exceptions. In this case, the most outstanding one is China, where peace and security reigned under the wise and benevolent rule of the Tang emperors.

4

Europe, 800 B.C.E.–800 C.E.

Between 800 B.C.E. and 800 C.E., Europe can be described as roughly consisting of two contrasting regions: the sophisticated and often urban world of southern Europe, which was inhabited and dominated primarily by the Greeks and Romans; and the unsophisticated and mostly rural world of northern Europe, which was inhabited by peoples like the Celts, Gauls, and Germans—and for a time by the Huns, Asian nomads who invaded eastern and central Europe in the fourth and fifth centuries C.E. Over time, the north was increasingly dominated by the south, particularly after the first century C.E., when imperial Rome began pursuing an active program of Romanization in its provinces, especially Spain, Gaul, and Britain. The Romans built cities in their own well-ordered style, introduced Greco-Roman religious ideas, and encouraged subject peoples to speak Latin and to emulate Roman civilization in as many ways as possible. Throughout this period contacts between different European regions were increasingly common as traders, soldiers, colonists, slaves, and eventually Christian missionaries crossed back and forth. Even in areas outside the Roman sphere of influence, such as Germany, reciprocal cultural influences were not uncommon.

Greek and Roman views of both themselves and others provide useful insights into the varied cultures of Europeans in this time period. Both were sharply aware of the differences between the groups that inhabited southern and northern Europe. Not only were the "civilized" peoples clearly aware of their own superiority to the "uncivilized," but they were often convinced of their own superiority to each other as well. Thus Roman writers like Julius Caesar, Tacitus, and Ammianus Marcellinus condescendingly described, or even vilified, admirable traits in the Germans and the Huns; and the Greek statesman Pericles spoke confidently, perhaps even arrogantly, about the superiority of Athens to Sparta. Juvenal's vitriolic condemnation of Greeks living in Rome was by no means an isolated attack. There is ample precedent for anti-Greek sentiment in the writings of earlier Roman authors, especially comedic playwrights, who liked to portray the Greeks as greasy and dishonest, but none approached the intensity of Juvenal's invective.

On the other hand, many Romans admired Greek culture and vice versa. The Roman biographer Cornelius Nepos believed that the ethical behavior and military skill of one of his subjects, the Greek general Epaminondas, should serve as an example for Romans to emulate. The Greek poet Melinno wrote a panegyric that leaves no doubt that she very much appreciated and understood the benefits of Roman imperialism. Likewise, the Greek historian Polybius spent many years of his life laboring to explain and justify Roman culture and expansion to the Greeks.

Unfortunately, there are no true outside views of the Greeks and Romans—a few northern views of southern Europe exist, but they were filtered through the lens of the Greco-Roman worldview. For example, the historian, Dio Cassius, recreated the speech of the British heroine and warrior queen, Boudicca (see Chapter 2), but followed it with the story of her humiliating defeat by the superior army of the Romans. Consequently, there is no way of knowing the actual opinions of this non-Roman or any others whose perspectives are occasionally included in Roman literature. Surprisingly, however, several Chinese travelers visited the Roman Empire, at least the eastern provinces, and their experiences are recorded in a series of dynastic histories of China. Their views of the Roman Empire as an exotic foreign locale provide an important counterpoint to the other selections in this chapter.

A Greek Statesman Praises Athens (430 B.C.E.)

THUCYDIDES, *"The Funeral Oration of Pericles," The Peloponnesian Wars*

Pericles (490–429 B.C.E.) was an Athenian statesman whose legislation is generally credited with bringing Athenian democracy to its peak. At the time he gave this speech, probably in early 430, he was serving as *strategos,* one of ten generals who were elected by the male citizens of Athens.

The speech survives today because a Greek historian was present in the audience. Thucydides (c. 450–400 B.C.E.), the author of *The Peloponnesian Wars,* did not reproduce it verbatim, nor did he record the exact wording of this or any other speech that he included in his history, but he attempted to catch the mood of the speaker and the intent of what he said. Thucydides frankly confided to his readers that it was hard to remember exactly what different speakers said. "I have therefore put into the mouths of each speaker the views that, in my opinion, they would have been most likely to express, as the particular occasion demanded, while keeping as nearly as I could to the general purport of what was actually said." This practice was common in the ancient Mediterranean world.

The "Funeral Oration of Pericles" is one of the most famous descriptions of ancient Athens ever written. It is a complicated and sophisticated speech, with meanings on several levels. First, it is a tribute to Athenian soldiers killed in the first year of the Peloponnesian War, which was fought between Athens and Sparta between 431 and 404 B.C.E. Second, because it is a comparison between the two states, it serves as an effective example of wartime propaganda. Finally, it is a celebration of the greatness of Athenian civilization, with particular emphasis on the benefits that democratic government conferred upon the city.

In the same winter the Athenians, following their annual custom, gave a public funeral for those who had been the first to die in the war. These funerals are held in the following way: two days before the ceremony the bones of the fallen are brought and put in a tent which has been erected, and people make whatever offerings they wish to their own dead. Then there is a funeral procession in which coffins of cypress wood are carried on wagons. There is one coffin for each tribe, which contains the bones of members of that tribe. One empty bier is decorated and carried in the procession: this is for the missing, whose bodies could not be recovered. Everyone who wishes to, both citizens and foreigners, can join in the procession, and the women who are related to the dead are there to make their laments at the tomb. The bones are laid in the public burial-place, which is in the most beautiful quarter outside the city walls. Here the Athenians always bury those who have fallen in war. The only exception is those who died at Marathon,* who, because their achievement was considered absolutely outstanding, were buried on the battlefield itself.

When the bones have been laid in the earth, a man chosen by the city for his intellectual gifts and for his general reputation makes an appropriate speech in praise of the dead, and after the speech all depart. This is the procedure at these burials, and all through the war, when the time came to do so, the Athenians followed this ancient custom. Now, at the burial of those who were the first to fall in the war Pericles, the son of Xanthippus, was chosen to make the speech. When the moment arrived, he came forward from the tomb and, standing on a high platform, so that he might be heard by as many people as possible in the crowd, he spoke as follows:

"Many of those who have spoken here in the past have praised the institution of this speech at the close of our ceremony. It seemed to them a mark of honour to our soldiers who have fallen in war that a speech should be made over them. I do not agree. These men have shown themselves valiant in action, and it would be enough, I think, for their glories to be proclaimed in action, as you have just seen it done at this funeral organized by the state. Our belief in the courage and manliness of so many should not be hazarded on the goodness or badness of one man's speech. Then it is not easy to speak with a proper sense of balance, when a man's listeners find it difficult to believe in the truth of what one is saying. The man who knows the facts and loves the dead may well think that an oration

tells less than what he knows and what he would like to hear: others who do not know so much may feel envy for the dead, and think the orator over-praises them, when he speaks of exploits that are beyond their own capacities. Praise of other people is tolerable only up to a certain point, the point where one still believes that one could do oneself some of the things one is hearing about. Once you get beyond this point, you will find people becoming jealous and incredulous. However, the fact is that this institution was set up and approved by our forefathers, and it is my duty to follow the tradition and do my best to meet the wishes and the expectations of every one of you.

"I shall begin by speaking about our ancestors, since it is only right and proper on such an occasion to pay them the honour of recalling what they did. In this land of ours there have always been the same people living from generation to generation up till now, and they, by their courage and their virtues, have handed it on to us, a free country. They certainly deserve our praise. Even more so do our fathers deserve it. For to the inheritance they had received they added all the empire we have now, and it was not without blood and toil that they handed it down to us of the present generation. And then we ourselves, assembled here to-day, who are mostly in the prime of life, have, in most directions, added to the power of our empire and have organized our State in such a way that it is perfectly well able to look after itself both in peace and in war.

"I have no wish to make a long speech on subjects familiar to you all: so I shall say nothing about the warlike deeds by which we acquired our power or the battles in which we or our fathers gallantly resisted our enemies, Greek or foreign. What I want to do is, in the first place, to discuss the spirit in which we faced our trials and also our constitution and the way of life which has made us great. After that I shall speak in praise of the dead, believing that this kind of speech is not inappropriate to the present occasion, and that this whole assembly, of citizens and foreigners, may listen to it with advantage.

---

*Marathon was the first battle of the Persian Wars. It was fought 26 miles from Athens in 490 B.C.E. Although the Athenians and their allies were outnumbered two to one, they managed to win a stunning victory.

"Let me say that our system of government does not copy the institutions of our neighbours. It is more the case of our being a model to others, than of our imitating anyone else. Our constitution is called a democracy because power is in the hands not of a minority but of the whole people. When it is a question of settling private disputes, everyone is equal before the law; when it is a question of putting one person before another in positions of public responsibility, what counts is not membership of a particular class, but the actual ability which the man possesses. No one, so long as he has it in him to be of service to the state, is kept in political obscurity because of poverty. And, just as our political life is free and open, so is our day-to-day life in our relations with each other. We do not get into a state with our next-door neighbour if he enjoys himself in his own way, nor do we give him the kind of black looks which, though they do no real harm, still do hurt people's feelings. We are free and tolerant in our private lives; but in public affairs we keep to the law. This is because it commands our deep respect.

"We give our obedience to those whom we put in positions of authority, and we obey the laws themselves, especially those which are for the protection of the oppressed, and those unwritten laws which it is an acknowledged shame to break.

"And here is another point. When our work is over, we are in a position to enjoy all kinds of recreation for our spirits. There are various kinds of contests and sacrifices regularly throughout the year; in our own homes we find a beauty and a good taste which delight us every day and which drive away our cares. Then the greatness of our city brings it about that all the good things from all over the world flow in to us, so that to us it seems just as natural to enjoy foreign goods as our own local products.

"Then there is a great difference between us and our opponents, in our attitude towards military security. Here are some examples: Our city is open to the world, and we have no periodical deportations in order to prevent people observing or finding out secrets which might be of military advantage to the enemy. This is because we rely, not on secret weapons, but on our own real courage and loyalty. There is a difference, too, in our educational systems. The Spartans, from their earliest boyhood, are submitted to the most laborious training in courage; we pass our lives without all these restrictions, and yet are just as ready to face the same dangers as they are. Here is a proof of this: When the Spartans invade our land, they do not come by themselves, but bring all their allies with them; whereas we, when we launch an attack abroad, do the job by ourselves, and, though fighting on foreign soil, do not often fail to defeat opponents who are fighting for their own hearths and homes. As a matter of fact none of our enemies has ever yet been confronted with our total strength, because we have to divide our attention between our navy and the many missions on which our troops are sent on land. Yet, if our enemies engage a detachment of our forces and defeat it, they give themselves credit for having thrown back our entire army; or, if they lose, they claim that they were beaten by us in full strength. There are certain advantages, I think, in our way of meeting danger voluntarily, with an easy mind, instead of with a laborious training, with natural rather than with state-induced courage. We do not have to spend our time practising to meet sufferings which are still in the future; and when they are actually upon us we show ourselves just as brave as these others who are always in strict training. This is one point in which, I think, our city deserves to be admired. There are also others:

"Our love of what is beautiful does not lead to extravagance; our love of the things of the mind does not make us soft. We regard wealth as something to be properly used, rather than as something to boast about. As for poverty, no one need be ashamed to admit it: the real shame is in not taking practical measures to escape from it. Here each individual is interested not only in his own affairs but in the affairs of the state as well: even those who are mostly occupied with their own business are extremely well-informed on general politics—this is a peculiarity of ours:

we do not say that a man who takes no interest in politics is a man who minds his own business; we say that he has no business here at all. We Athenians, in our own persons, take our decisions on policy or submit them to proper discussions: for we do not think that there is an incompatibility between words and deeds; the worst thing is to rush into action before the consequences have been properly debated. And this is another point where we differ from other people. We are capable at the same time of taking risks and of estimating them beforehand. Others are brave out of ignorance; and, when they stop to think, they begin to fear. But the man who can most truly be accounted brave is he who best knows the meaning of what is sweet in life and of what is terrible, and then goes out undeterred to meet what is to come.

"Again, in questions of general good feeling there is a great contrast between us and most other people. We make friends by doing good to others, not by receiving good from them. This makes our friendship all the more reliable, since we want to keep alive the gratitude of those who are in our debt by showing continued goodwill to them: whereas the feelings of one who owes us something lack the same enthusiasm, since he knows that, when he repays our kindness, it will be more like paying back a debt than giving something spontaneously. We are unique in this. When we do kindnesses to others, we do not do them out of any calculations of profit or loss: we do them without afterthought, relying on our free liberality. Taking everything together then, I declare that our city is an education to Greece, and I declare that in my opinion each single one of our citizens, in all the manifold aspects of life, is able to show himself the righful lord and owner of his own person, and do this, moreover, with exceptional grace and exceptional versatility. And to show that this is no empty boasting for the present occasion, but real tangible fact, you have only to consider the power which our city possesses and which has been won by those very qualities which I have mentioned. Athens, alone of the states we know, comes to her testing time in a greatness that

surpasses what was imagined of her. In her case, and in her case alone, no invading enemy is ashamed at being defeated, and no subject can complain of being governed by people unfit for their responsibilities. Mighty indeed are the marks and monuments of our empire which we have left. Future ages will wonder at us, as the present age wonders at us now. We do not need the praises of a Homer, or of anyone else whose words may delight us for the moment, but whose estimation of facts will fall short of what is really true. For our adventurous spirit has forced an entry into every sea and into every land; and everywhere we have left behind us everlasting memorials of good done to our friends or suffering inflicted on our enemies.

"This, then, is the kind of city for which these men, who could not bear the thought of losing her, nobly fought and nobly died. It is only natural that every one of us who survive them should be willing to undergo hardships in her service. And it was for this reason that I have spoken at such length about our city, because I wanted to make it clear that for us there is more at stake than there is for others who lack our advantages; also I wanted my words of praise for the dead to be set in the bright light of evidence. And now the most important of these words has been spoken. I have sung the praises of our city; but it was the courage and gallantry of these men, and of people like them, which made her splendid. Nor would you find it true in the case of many of the Greeks, as it is true of them, that no words can do more than justice to their deeds.

"To me it seems that the consummation which has overtaken these men shows us the meaning of manliness in its first revelation and in its final proof. Some of them, no doubt, had their faults; but what we ought to remember first is their gallant conduct against the enemy in defence of their native land. They have blotted out evil with good, and done more service to the commonwealth than they ever did harm in their private lives. No one of these men weakened because he wanted to go on enjoying his wealth: no one put off the awful day in the hope that he might live to escape his poverty and grow rich. More to be desired than such things, they chose to check the enemy's pride. This, to them, was a risk most glorious, and they accepted it, willing to strike down the enemy and relinquish everything else. As for success or failure, they left that in the doubtful hands of Hope, and when the reality of battle was before their faces, they put their trust in their own selves. In the fighting, they thought it more honourable to stand their ground and suffer death than to give in and save their lives. So they fled from the reproaches of men, abiding with life and limb the brunt of battle; and, in a small moment of time, the climax of their lives, a culmination of glory, not of fear, were swept away from us.

"So and such they were, these men—worthy of their city. We who remain behind may hope to be spared their fate, but must resolve to keep the same daring spirit against the foe. It is not simply a question of estimating the advantages in theory. I could tell you a long story (and you know it as well as I do) about what is to be gained by beating the enemy back. What I would prefer is that you should fix your eyes every day on the greatness of Athens as she really is, and should fall in love with her. When you realize her greatness, then reflect that what made her great was men with a spirit of adventure, men who knew their duty, men who were ashamed to fall below a certain standard. If they ever failed in an enterprise, they made up their minds that at any rate the city should not find their courage lacking to her, and they gave to her the best contribution that they could. They gave her their lives, to her and to all of us, and for their own selves they won praises that never grow old, the most splendid of sepulchres— not the sepulchre in which their bodies are laid, but where their glory remains eternal in men's minds, always there on the right occasion to stir others to speech or to action. For famous men have the whole earth as their memorial: it is not only the inscriptions on their graves in their own country that mark them out; no, in foreign lands also, not in any visible form but in peo-

ple's hearts, their memory abides and grows. It is for you to try to be like them. Make up your minds that happiness depends on being free, and freedom depends on being courageous. Let there be no relaxation in face of the perils of the war. The people who have most excuse for despising death are not the wretched and unfortunate, who have no hope of doing well for themselves, but those who run the risk of a complete reversal in their lives, and who would feel the difference most intensely, if things went wrong for them. Any intelligent man would find a humiliation caused by his own slackness more painful to bear than death, when death comes to him unperceived, in battle, and in the confidence of his patriotism.

"For these reasons I shall not commiserate with those parents of the dead, who are present here. Instead I shall try to comfort them. They are well aware that they have grown up in a world where there are many changes and chances. But this is good fortune—for men to end their lives with honour, as these have done, and for you honourably to lament them: their life was set to a measure where death and happiness went hand in hand. I know that it is difficult to convince you of this. When you see other people happy you will often be reminded of what used to make you happy too. One does not feel sad at not having some good thing which is outside one's experience: real grief is felt at the loss of something which one is used to. All the same, those of you who are of the right age must bear up and take comfort in the thought of having more children. In your own homes these new children will prevent you from brooding over those who are no more, and they will be a help to the city, too, both in filling the empty places, and in assuring her security. For it is impossible for a man to put forward fair and honest views about our affairs if he has not, like everyone else, children whose lives may be at stake. As for those of you who are now too old to have children, I would ask you to count as gain the greater part of your life, in which you have been happy, and remember that what remains is not long, and let your hearts be lifted up at the thought of the fair fame of the dead. One's sense of honour is the only thing that does not grow old, and the last pleasure, when one is worn out with age, is not, as the poet said, making money, but having the respect of one's fellow men.

"As for those of you here who are sons or brothers of the dead, I can see a hard struggle in front of you. Everyone always speaks well of the dead, and, even if you rise to the greatest heights of heroism, it will be a hard thing for you to get the reputation of having come near, let alone equalled, their standard. When one is alive, one is always liable to the jealousy of one's competitors, but when one is out of the way, the honour one receives is sincere and unchallenged.

"Perhaps I should say a word or two on the duties of women to those among you who are now widowed. I can say all I have to say in a short word of advice. Your great glory is not to be inferior to what God* has made you, and the greatest glory of a woman is to be least talked about by men, whether they are praising you or criticizing you. I have now, as the law demanded, said what I had to say. For the time being our offerings to the dead have been made, and for the future their children will be supported at the public expense by the city, until they come of age. This is the crown and prize which she offers, both to the dead and to their children, for the ordeals which they have faced. Where the rewards of valour are the greatest, there you will find also the best and bravest spirits among the people. And now, when you have mourned for your dear ones, you must depart."

---

*The use of *God* in this translation does not refer to the Judeo-Christian God, but to *theos,* a word often used by the Greeks to refer to an unidentifiable deity or force or to denote things that human beings were not able to understand.

REVIEW QUESTIONS

1. How does Sparta compare to Athens in Pericles' funeral oration? What evidence supports your opinion?
2. How accurate do you think Pericles' description of Athens is? Would he have had any reason to stretch the truth a bit? Explain.
3. Can you tell, by his writing style and the things he emphasized in Pericles' speech, that Thucydides was an Athenian officer in the Peloponnesian War? Why or why not?
4. What does Pericles' speech tell you about the lives of women in fifth-century Athens?

A Roman Biographer Admires a Theban General (c. 34 B.C.E.)

CORNELIUS NEPOS, *"The Life of Epaminondas," On Famous Men*

Nowhere in the Mediterranean world did Greek cultural ideals and accomplishments inspire more admiration and imitation than in Rome, especially in the last days of the Republic and the early years of the Empire. Educated Romans studied Greek literature and philosophy, Roman artists copied Greek sculpture, Roman architects used Greek buildings as models, and Roman moralists pointed to famous Greeks as examples of noble character and ethical behavior.

The following selection is an excellent example of the Roman love of all things Greek, an attitude called phil-Hellenism. Its author, Cornelius Nepos (c. 99–24 B.C.E.), was the first Roman biographer to write in Latin, not Greek. Born in Cisalpine Gaul (northern Italy), he moved to Rome sometime before 65 and quickly became a member of a literary circle that included the famous orator and writer Cicero and the poet Catullus. Like them, Nepos was a professional writer—and a prolific one, too. In addition to biography, he also wrote a three-volume history of the world (*Chronica*), a five-book collection of anecdotes (*Exempla*), a book on geography, letters to his friend Cicero, and some erotic poetry that was apparently so bad that it was never published. His most famous and popular work, *De Viris Illustribus (On Famous Men)*, was a sixteen-volume collection of four hundred biographies of mostly Roman and Greek political and military figures. It was published sometime before 34 B.C.E. and was popular enough that Nepos produced a revised and expanded version of it a few years later. Unfortunately, only one section, "On Eminent Foreign Leaders," is extant.

Nepos's biography of Epaminondas exemplifies the phil-Hellenism of both its author and his audience, who found much to admire about the life of this Greek general and statesman from Thebes. Most famous as the commander who defeated the Spartans at the battle of Leuctra in 371 and again at Mantineia in 362, Epaminondas (c. 418–362) also made important tactical innovations in the use of the phalanx. His character and personality were admired both by his contemporaries and by later generations, and he seems to have possessed all the qualities that the Greeks cherished most: eloquence, honesty, courage, and selflessness. It should be noted, however, that Nepos tended to be eulogistic and uncritical, for which reason he has been called "an intellectual pygmy" by at least one modern historian. Historical objectivity, however, was not Nepos's goal. Instead, he sought to entertain and to inspire; and he deliberately wrote for the general public rather than for scholars. Thus his biographies reflect widely held Roman attitudes and opinions of prominent Greek historical figures and the culture that produced them.

1. Epaminondas, the Theban, son of Polymnis. Before writing about this man, I think I ought to warn my readers not to judge the customs of other nations by their own, and not to consider conduct which in their opinion is undignified as so regarded by other peoples. We know, for example, that according to our ideas music is unsuited to a personage of importance, while dancing is even numbered among the vices; but with the Greeks all such accomplishments were regarded as becoming and even praiseworthy. Since, then, I wish to portray the life and habits of Epaminondas, it seems to me that I ought to omit nothing which contributes to that end. Therefore I shall speak first of his family, then of the subjects which he studied and his teachers, next of his character, his natural qualities, and anything else that is worthy of record. Finally, I shall give an account of his exploits, which many writers consider more important than mental excellence.

2. Well, then, he was born of the father whom I have mentioned; his family was an honourable one, but had been in moderate circumstances for

some time; yet in spite of that he received as good an education as any Theban. Thus he was taught to play the lyre, and to sing with an instrumental accompaniment, by Dionysius, who in the musical world was equal in reputation to Damon or Lamprus, whose names are known everywhere. He learned to play the pipes from Olympiodorus and to dance from Calliphron. In philosophy he had as his master Lysis of Tarentum, the Pythagorean, and to him he was so attached that in his youth he was more intimate with that grave and austere old man than with any of the young people of his own age; and he would not allow his teacher to leave him until he so far surpassed his fellow-students in learning, that it could readily be understood that in a similar way he would surpass all men in all other accomplishments. Now these last, according to our views, are trivial, or rather, contemptible; but in Greece, especially in bygone days, they were highly esteemed.

As soon as Epaminondas attained military age and began to interest himself in physical exercise, he aimed less at great strength than at agility; for he thought that the former was necessary for athletes, but that the latter would be helpful in warfare. Accordingly, he trained himself thoroughly in running and wrestling, but in the latter only to the extent of being able, while still standing, to seize his opponent and contend with him. But it was to the use of arms that he devoted his greatest efforts.

3. To the bodily strength that he thus acquired there were added still greater mental gifts; for he was temperate, prudent, serious, and skilful in taking advantage of opportunities; practised in war, of great personal courage and of high spirit; such a lover of the truth that he never lied even in jest. Furthermore, he was self-controlled, kindly, and forbearing to a surprising degree, putting up with wrongs, not only from the people, but even from his friends; he was most particular in keeping secrets, a quality which is sometimes no less valuable than eloquence, and he was a good listener; for he thought that to be the easiest way of acquiring

information. Therefore, whenever he was in a gathering where there was an argument about affairs of state or philosophical discussion, he never left until the conversation was ended.

He found it so easy to endure narrow means that from his public services he gained nothing but glory, and he declined to use the wealth of his friends for his own necessities. In aiding others, on the contrary, he made such use of their trust in him that one might suppose that he and his friends shared all their possessions in common. For if anyone of his fellow-citizens had been taken by the enemy, or if a friend's daughter was of marriageable age but could not be wedded because of lack of means, he took counsel of his friends and fixed the amount of the contribution which each was to make, adapting the sum to the contributor's means. And having made up the necessary amount, before taking the money he presented the one who was in need to the contributors, in order that the man who received help might know how much he owed each one.

4. His integrity was tested by Diomedon, of Cyzicus, who, at the request of King Artaxerxes, had undertaken to bribe Epaminondas. Diomedon came to Thebes with a great amount of gold, and with five talents won the support of a young man named Micythus, to whom Epaminondas was greatly attached at that time. Micythus went to Epaminondas and explained the reason for Diomedon's coming. But the great man dealt with the Persian face to face, saying: "There is no need of money; for if what the king wishes is to the interest of the Thebans, I am ready to do it free of charge; but if the contrary is true, he has not gold and silver enough; for I would not take all the riches in the world in exchange for my love of country. As for you, who do not know me, I am not surprised that you have tried to tempt me and believed me to be a man like yourself, and I forgive you; but leave here at once, so that you may not corrupt others, since you have failed with me. And you, Micythus, give this man back his money; and if you do not do so immediately, I shall hand you over to the magistrates." When

Diomedon asked that he might go away in safety and be allowed to take the money that he had brought with him, Epaminondas replied: "I will grant your request, not, however, for your sake, but for my own; for I fear that if your money should be taken from you, someone might say that the sum which I had refused when it was offered as a gift had come into my hands through confiscation."

Epaminondas then asked the Persian where he wished to be taken, and when Diomedon named Athens, he gave him an escort, to secure his safe arrival. And he was not even satisfied with that, but through Chabrias, the Athenian, . . . he saved Diomedon from being molested before he embarked. Of Epaminondas' integrity this will be sufficient proof. . . .

7. That he was patient and submitted to the injustice of his fellow-citizens because he thought it impious to show anger towards his country, appears from the following evidence. The Thebans because of jealousy had refused to make him commander of their army and had chosen a leader without experience in warfare. When the man's blunder had resulted in making that large force of soldiers fearful of their safety, since they were shut up in a narrow defile and blackaded by the enemy, they came to feel the need of Epaminondas' carefulness; and he was present, as it happened, serving as a soldier without a commission. When they appealed to him for help, he entirely overlooked the slight that he had suffered, freed the army from siege, and led it home in safety. And this he did not once, but very often. Conspicuous among these was the time when he led the army to the Peloponnesus against the Lacedaemonians [Spartans] and had two colleagues, one of whom was Pelopidas, a man of courage and energy.

All these generals had become, through the charges of their opponents, objects of suspicion, and for that reason their command had been taken from them and other leaders had been appointed in their place. Epaminondas refused to obey the people's decree, persuaded his colleagues to follow his example, and continued the war which he had begun; for he knew that unless he did so, the entire army would be lost, owing to the incapacity of the generals and their ignorance of warfare. There was a law at Thebes which punished with death anyone who had retained a command beyond the time provided by that law. Since Epaminondas realized that the law in question had been passed for the safety of his country, he did not wish it to contribute to the ruin of the state; consequently, he retained his command for four months longer than the time fixed by the people.

8. After they returned home, his colleagues were brought to trial for their disobedience. Epaminondas allowed them to throw the entire responsibility upon him and to urge in their defence that it was due to him that they had disobeyed the law. That plea freed them from danger, and no one thought that Epaminondas would put in an appearance, since he had nothing to say in his defence. But he came into court, denied none of the charges of his opponents, admitted everything that his colleagues had said, and did not refuse to submit to the penalty named in the law. He made only one request of the judges, namely, that they should enter the following record of his sentence.

"Epaminondas was condemned to death by the Thebans because at Leuctra he compelled them to vanquish the Lacedaemonians, whom before he took command no Boeotian had dared to face in battle, and because in a single contest he not only saved Thebes from destruction, but also secured freedom for all Greece and so changed the situation of the contending parties that the Thebans attacked the Lacedaemonians, while the Lacedaemonians were satisfied with being able to save themselves; and he did not bring the war to an end until by the restoration of Messene he placed Sparta in a state of siege."

When he had said this, there was laughter and merriment throughout the assembly and no juror ventured to vote for his condemnation. Thus from a capital charge he gained the greatest glory.

9. Finally, when commander at Mantinea, in the heat of battle he charged the enemy too boldly. He was recognized by the Lacedaemoni-

ans, and since they believed that the death of that one man would ensure the safety of their country, they all directed their attack at him alone and kept on until, after great bloodshed and the loss of many men, they saw Epaminondas himself fall valiantly fighting, struck down by a lance hurled from afar. By his death the Boeotians were checked for a time, but they did not leave the field until they had completely defeated the enemy. But Epaminondas, realizing that he had received a mortal wound, and at the same time that if he drew out the head of the lance, which was separated from the shaft and fixed in his body, he would at once die, retained it until news came that the Boeotians were victorious. As soon as he heard that, he cried: "I have lived long enough since I die unconquered." Then he drew out the iron and at once breathed his last.

10. Epaminondas never took a wife. Because of this he was criticized by Pelopidas, who had a son of evil reputation; for his friend said that the great Theban did a wrong to his country in not leaving children. Epaminondas replied; "Take heed that you do not do her a greater wrong in leaving such a son as yours. And besides, I cannot lack offspring; for I leave as my daughter the battle of Leuctra, which is certain, not merely to survive me, but even to be immortal." . . .

Enough will have been said of this great man's virtues and of his life, if I add this one thing, which nobody will deny. Before the birth of Epaminondas, and after his death, Thebes was subject constantly to the hegemony of others; but, on the contrary, so long as he was at the head of the state, she was the leading city of all Greece. This fact shows that one man was worth more than the entire body of citizens.

REVIEW QUESTIONS

1. In the first paragraph, Nepos warned his readers "not to judge the customs of other nations by their own." What aspects of the life of Epaminondas did Nepos think Roman readers would find distasteful? Explain.
2. Which of Epaminondas's many noble qualities do you think Nepos most admired? Why?
3. Which of Epaminondas's qualities do you find most interesting or attractive? Why?
4. If you read between the lines, can you find any flaws in Epaminondas's character or behavior? What were they, and why might Nepos have chosen to overlook them?

A Roman Satirist Derides Greeks in Rome (c. 112–116 C.E.)

JUVENAL, *Satire III*

Unlike Cornelius Nepos, many Romans had distinctly unfavorable opinions of the Greeks, especially in the centuries following Rome's formal annexation of Greece in 27 B.C.E. By the second century C.E., many Romans despised the Greeks, especially those who lived in Rome itself. By then, Rome was a cosmopolitan city where many nationalities lived and many languages were spoken, and one of the most visible and flourishing minorities was a large and successful population of well-educated and ambitious Greeks. Many were prosperous doctors, teachers, merchants, and artisans. Moreover, in the previous century, a few Greek freedmen had achieved powerful positions in government because of their employment as imperial secretaries and agents by the first emperor, Augustus, and his successors. Thus the Greeks were frequently the targets of jealous and disgruntled attacks from Romans whose power and prestige the Greeks had supplanted. It was all too common for Roman authors to portray the Greeks as dirty, dishonest, immoral, and greedy, particularly in mime, street theater, and comedic plays. Thus it should come as no surprise to find a venomous attack on the Greeks in one of the sixteen satires by Decimus Iunius Iuvenalis, better known as Juvenal.

Historians can only speculate on the reasons for Juvenal's bitterness, since practically nothing is known about the life of this popular and famous writer. He was probably born circa 55, either in Rome or in a hill town near present-day Monte Cassino. As a young man he may have seen military service (or have spent time in exile) in Britain, Egypt, or both, because his writing shows fairly extensive knowledge of both regions. He might also have belonged to the Roman elite, whose members keenly felt their loss of political power and declining prestige. At any rate, he was intensely Roman and hated any degeneration from the old Roman standard of manliness and virtue. He could only see the evil effects of Greek influence, and they blinded him to its humanizing value. Since his work was extremely popular, clearly he was not alone in his sentiments. References to his works, however, disappeared from literary discussions after 138, the year in which Antoninus Pius became emperor, perhaps because Juvenal's biting criticisms of aristocratic life were a little too accurate and the objects of his ridicule too easy to identify.

This selection is taken from *Satire III,* a description of Rome that paints the discomforts and dangers of the city in vivid and negative detail. It was probably published in the second decade of the second century, and it is an excellent example of Juvenal's early body of work, which often descends to angry and very personal ranting. His later writing tends to be more sophisticated and emotionally detached. For centuries, traditionally minded literary critics have appreciated Juvenal for his moral outrage and grimly acerbic sense of humor; his satires, in fact, have been credited with giving shape and definition to the genre. Many modern scholars, however, feel that it is also important to call attention to his bigotry, misogyny, xenophobia, and homophobia.

"Now let me turn to that race which goes down so well
With our millionaires, but remains *my* special pet aversion,
And not mince my words. I cannot, citizens, stomach
A Greek-struck Rome. Yet what fraction of these sweepings
Derives, in fact, from Greece? For years now Syrian
Orontes* has poured its sewerage into our native Tiber—

*Here Juvenal was referring to the eastern half of the Roman Empire. This area was culturally Greek, at least superficially, and had been since the fourth-century B.C.E. conquests of Alexander the Great.

Its lingo and manners, its flutes, its outlandish
   harps
With their transverse strings, its native
   tambourines,
And the whores who hang out round the race-
   course. (That's where to go if you fancy a
   foreign piece in one of those saucy toques.)
Our beloved Founder* should see how his
   homespun rustics
Behave today, with their dinner-pumps—
   trechedipna†
They call them—not to mention their *niceteria*
(Decorations to you) hung round their *ceromatic*
   (that's mud-caked) wrestlers' necks. Here's
   one from Sicyon,
Another from Macedonia, two from Aegean
   islands—
Andros, say, or Samos—two more from Caria,
All of them lighting out for the City's classiest
   districts
And burrowing into great houses, with a long-
   term plan
For taking them over. Quick wit, unlimited
   nerve, a gift
Of the gab that outsmarts a professional public
   speaker—
These are their characteristics. What do you
   take
That fellow's profession to be? He has brought
   a whole bundle
Of personalities with him—schoolmaster,
   rhetorician,
Surveyor, artist, masseur, diviner, tightrope-
   walker,
Magician or quack, your versatile hungry
   Greekling
Is all by turns. Tell him to fly—he's airborne.
The inventor of wings was no Moor or Slav,
   remember,

Or Thracian, but born in the very heart of
   Athens.‡
   "When such men as these wear the purple,
   when some creature
Blown into Rome along with the figs and
   damsons
Precedes me at dinner-parties, or for the wit-
   nessing
Of manumissions and wills—*me,* who drew my
   first breath
On these Roman hills, and was nourished on
   Sabine olives!—
Things have reached a pretty pass. What's
   more, their talent
For flattery is unmatched. They praise the
   conversation
Of their dimmest friends; the ugly they call
   handsome,
So that your scrag-necked weakling finds him-
   self compared
To Hercules holding the giant Antaeus aloft
Way off the earth. They go into ecstasies over
Some shrill and scrannel voice that sounds like
   a hen
When the cock gets at her. We can make the
   same compliments, but
It's they who convince. On the stage they
   remain supreme
In female parts, courtesan, matron or slave-girl,
With no concealing cloak: you'd swear it was a
   genuine
Woman you saw, and not a masked performer.§
Look there, beneath that belly: no bulge, all
   smooth, a neat
Nothingness—even a hint of the Great Divide.
   Yet back home
These queens and dames pass unnoticed.
   Greece is a nation

---

*A reference to Augustus Caesar, the first emperor of Rome, who frequently affected the dress and manners of the common Roman man.
†A type of Greek footware, probably slippers, that was disdained by the sandal-wearing Romans.

---

‡According to myth, Daedalus fashioned two pairs of wax wings so that he and his son, Icarus, could escape imprisonment by the minotaur on Crete. Icarus, however, flew too close to the sun, melted his wax wings, and plunged to his death. Daedalus flew safely to Sicily. Juvenal was probably implying that the Greeks were stupid, or selfish, or both.
§Men played all roles, both male and female, in Greek and Roman plays.

Of actors. Laugh, and they split their sides. At
  the sight
Of a friend's tears, they weep too—though
  quite unmoved.
If you ask for a fire in winter, the Greek puts
  on his cloak;
If you say "I'm hot", *he* starts sweating. So you
  see
We are not on an equal footing: he has the
  great advantage
Of being able on all occasions, night and day,
To take his cue, his mask, from others. He's
  always ready
To throw up his hands and applaud when a
  friend delivers
A really resounding belch, or pisses right on
  the mark,
With a splendid drumming sound from the
  upturned golden basin.
    "Besides, he holds nothing sacred, not a soul
  is safe
From his randy urges, the lady of the house,
  her
Virgin daughter, her daughter's still unbearded
Husband-to-be,* her hitherto virtuous son—
And if none of these are to hand, he'll cheer-
  fully lay

His best friend's grandmother. (Anything to
  ferret
Domestic secrets out, and get a hold over
  people.)
    "And while we are on the subject of Greeks,
  let us consider
Academics and their vices—not the gymna-
  sium crowd
But big philosophical wheels, like that Stoic
  greybeard
Who narked on his friend and pupil, and got
  him liquidated.†
He was brought up in Tarsus, by the banks of
  that river
Where Bellerophon fell to earth from the
  Gorgon's flying nag.
No room for honest Romans when Rome's
  ruled by a junta
Of Greek-born secret agents, who—like all
  their race—
Never share friends or patrons. One small dose
  of venom
(Half Greek, half personal) dropped in that
  ready ear
And I'm out, shown the back-door, my years of
  obsequious
Service all gone for nothing. Where can a
  hanger-on
Be ditched with less fuss than in Rome?

---

*Referring to a man as unbearded simply indicated a teenage boy who was too young to grow a man's beard. The Romans married young, and it was the custom for boys to begin shaving only after their beards had become reasonably thick. This phrase—as well as the one following ("hitherto virtuous son")—also refers to the well-known and common practices of homosexuality and bisexuality in Greece.

---

†The Stoic philosopher from Tarsus was Publius Egnatius Celer. His victim was Barea Soranus. A detailed account of the incident can be found in Tacitus's *Annals* (16.23.33).

REVIEW QUESTIONS

1. What was Juvenal's chief complaint against Greeks living in Rome? Why did this bother him so much?
2. Reading between the lines, what positive attributes of the Greeks can you discover in this excerpt?
3. What information about the author's background and prejudices did you learn in this selection? In general, why do you think Juvenal hated the Greeks?

A Greek Historian Extols the Virtues of the Romans (second century B.C.E.)

POLYBIUS, *The Histories, Book VI*

Polybius (c. 201–120 B.C.E.) was a Greek historian who sought to explain the greatness of Rome to the Greeks and to reconcile them to Roman domination. Surprisingly, he developed his favorable view of the Romans while a hostage in Rome after its war with Perseus of Macedonia. In 169, Polybius had commanded a unit of Greek cavalry that was sent to offer aid to the Roman army, but his assistance was politely refused. After the Romans won, they brought charges against 1,000 leading Greeks, including Polybius, for not having supported the Roman cause strongly enough. They were subsequently detained as hostages, without trial, in towns across Italy. Polybius, however, was allowed to serve his "captivity" in Rome, where he remained for many years. He became a close friend of the politically prominent Scipio family, accompanied the general Publius Cornelius Scipio Africanus Minor on several military campaigns, witnessed Rome's destruction of Carthage in 146, and helped Rome establish colonies in Greece after the fall of Corinth (also 146). His experiences and observations convinced him that mastery of the Mediterranean world was passing to Rome and that it would be folly for the Greeks to oppose Rome's ongoing and inevitable expansion. Astonishingly, the Greeks did not resent Polybius for this; instead, they paid tribute to him by erecting statues in his honor all over Greece. Their inscriptions thank him for being "the ally of the Romans" and making them "cease from their anger against Greece."

The subject of Polybius's writing was very specifically the events of the Second and Third Punic Wars (218–146 B.C.E.), during which Rome made itself into the dominant power in much of the Mediterranean. His chief focus was politics, but he was careful to include any topic that explained how and why Rome rose to power. Thus Polybius examined not only the political and military institutions of Rome, but also its social classes, religions, customs, and economic foundation. He called this approach "pragmatic history," the value of which, he believed, was to teach by example.

The following selection is an excellent example of Polybius's historical style. It explains Roman funeral customs, relates a famous historical legend, compares Roman and Carthaginian values, and briefly discusses Roman religion. Each topic is explored with regard to one question: how did it strengthen the Roman state? This particular excerpt is from the sixth of forty books that constituted Polybius's *Histories*. Only the first five are extant in their original form. Most of the remaining books have been partially reconstructed using the works of other ancient historians who quoted Polybius.

53. Whenever any illustrious man dies, he is carried at his funeral into the forum to the so-called rostra,* sometimes conspicuous in an upright posture and more rarely reclined. Here with all the people standing round, a grown-up son, if he has left one who happens to be present, or if not some other relative mounts the rostra and discourses on the virtues and successful achievements of the dead. As a consequence the multitude and not only those who had a part in these achievements, but those also who had none, when the facts are recalled to their minds and brought before their eyes, are moved to such sympathy that the loss seems to be not confined to the mourners, but a public one affecting the whole people. Next after the interment and the performance of the usual ceremonies, they place the image of the departed in the most conspicuous position in the house, enclosed in a wooden shrine. This image is a mask reproducing with remarkable fidelity both the features and complexion of the deceased. On the occasion of public sacrifices they display these images, and decorate them with much care, and when any distinguished member of the family dies they take them to the funeral, putting them on men who seem to them to bear the closest resemblance to the original in stature and carriage. These representatives wear togas, with a purple border if the deceased was a consul or praetor, whole purple if he was a censor, and embroidered with gold if he had celebrated a triumph† or achieved anything similar. They all ride in chariots preceded by the fasces,‡ axes, and other insignia by which the different magistrates are wont to be accompanied according to the respective dignity of the offices of state held by each during his life; and when they arrive at the rostra they all seat themselves in a row on ivory chairs. There could not easily be a more ennobling spectacle for a young man who aspires to fame and virtue. For who would not be inspired by the sight of the images of men renowned for their excellence, all together and as if alive and breathing? What spectacle could be more glorious than this?   54. Besides, he who makes the oration over the man about to be buried, when he has finished speaking of him recounts the successes and exploits of the rest whose images are present, beginning from the most ancient. By this means, by this constant renewal of the good report of brave men, the celebrity of those who performed noble deeds is rendered immortal, while at the same time the fame of those who did good service to their country becomes known to the people and a heritage for future generations. But the most important result is that young men are thus inspired to endure every suffering for the public welfare in the hope of winning the glory that attends on brave men. What I say is confirmed by the facts. For many Romans have voluntarily engaged in single combat in order to decide a battle, not a few have faced certain death, some in war to save the lives of the rest, and others in peace to save the republic. Some even when in office have put their own sons to death contrary to every law or custom, setting a higher value on the interest of their country than on the ties of nature that bound them to their nearest and dearest.

Many such stories about many men are related in Roman history, but one told of a certain person will suffice for the present as an example and as a confirmation of what I say.   55. It is narrated that when Horatius Cocles was engaged in combat with two of the enemy at the far end of the bridge over the Tiber that lies in the front of the town, he saw large reinforcements coming up to help the enemy, and fearing lest they should force the passage and get into the town, he turned round and called to those behind him to retire and cut the bridge with all speed. His order was obeyed, and while they were cutting the bridge, he stood to his ground receiving

---

*The speaker's platform in the Roman forum was decorated by *rostra,* the prows (or beaks) of ships captured by the Romans in battle. The word (in its plural form) became a name for the platform itself (in the singular).

†The victory procession of a Roman general—the ultimate accolade a military man could receive.

‡The fasces were bundles of rods wrapped around a single-headed axe and tied together with strips of red leather. They symbolized magisterial authority in Rome.

many wounds, and arrested the attack of the enemy who were less astonished at his physical strength than at his endurance and courage. The bridge once cut, the enemy were prevented from attacking; and Cocles, plunging into the river in full armour as he was, deliberately sacrificed his life,[1] regarding the safety of his country and the glory which in future would attach to his name as of more importance than his present existence and the years of life which remained to him. Such, if I am not wrong, is the eager emulation of achieving noble deeds engendered in the Roman youth by their institutions.

56. Again, the laws and customs relating to the acquisition of wealth are better in Rome than at Carthage. At Carthage nothing which results in profit is regarded as disgraceful; at Rome nothing is considered more so than to accept bribes and seek gain from improper channels. For no less strong than their approval of money-making by respectable means is their condemnation of unscrupulous gain from forbidden sources. A proof of this is that at Carthage candidates for office practise open bribery, whereas at Rome death is the penalty for it. Therefore as the rewards offered to merit are the opposite in the two cases, it is natural that the steps taken to gain them should also be dissimilar.

But the quality in which the Roman commonwealth is most distinctly superior is in my opinion the nature of their religious convictions. I believe that it is the very thing which

among other peoples is an object of reproach, I mean superstition, which maintains the cohesion of the Roman State. These matters are clothed in such pomp and introduced to such an extent into their public and private life that nothing could exceed it, a fact which will surprise many. My own opinion at least is that they have adopted this course for the sake of the common people. It is a course which perhaps would not have been necessary had it been possible to form a state composed of wise men, but as every multitude is fickle, full of lawless desires, unreasoned passion, and violent anger, the multitude must be held in by invisible terrors and suchlike pageantry. For this reason I think, not that the ancients acted rashly and at haphazard in introducing among the people notions concerning the gods and beliefs in the terrors of hell, but that the moderns are most rash and foolish in banishing such beliefs. The consequence is that among the Greeks, apart from other things, members of the government, if they are entrusted with no more than a talent, though they have ten copyists and as many seals and twice as many witnesses, cannot keep their faith; whereas among the Romans those who as magistrates and legates are dealing with large sums of money maintain correct conduct just because they have pledged their faith by oath. Whereas elsewhere it is a rare thing to find a man who keeps his hands off public money, and whose record is clean in this respect, among the Romans one rarely comes across a man who has been detected in such conduct. . . .

---

[1]According to Livy, Horatius swam across and was saved.

REVIEW QUESTIONS

1. What did Polybius think was the primary function of Roman funerals?
2. How does the story of Horatius Cocles illustrate Roman values?
3. Why did Polybius think Rome was a more virtuous state than Carthage?
4. Why did Polybius believe that religion was "the very thing" that maintained the "cohesion of the Roman State?"

A Greek Poet Exalts Rome (second century B.C.E.)

MELINNO, *Hymn to Rome*

Very little is known about the woman who wrote the following poem, not even when she lived or where. Melinno wrote in Greek, not Latin, and she may have come from Lesbos, where there was a tradition of female poets (going back to Sappho in the seventh century B.C.E.), but this is speculation. Some scholars believe that the dialect in which the poem was written suggests that her home was on the mainland. Because Melinno referred to Rome as having "sovereign strength" and steering "the cities of people," scholars know that the poem was written no earlier than the second century B.C.E., when Rome began to build its empire in the Mediterranean. Her failure to mention an emperor probably indicates that the poem was written in the Republic, and her lavish praise suggests that it was a time of prosperity and growth. Because the next century was frequently plagued by economic crisis and civil war, it is not likely that the setting for the *Hymn* was the first century B.C.E. Thus Melinno may have been a contemporary of Polybius and, like him, profoundly impressed by Rome's initial rise to power.

Although few Greek women wrote professionally—and even fewer of their writings survive—there appears to have been a small group of women, especially from Ionia (the western coast of Asia Minor and the islands nearby), who were fairly well known for their poetry. Sappho, of course, is the best known of these women, but there were others. Their names were sometimes recorded on lists of winners of the poetry contests that were an important part of many Greek religious festivals and ceremonies. Only a few of their poems survive, often in mere fragments. The best known of these women are Anyte of Tegea, who wrote at least eighteen funerary epigrams (some for animals) and Nossis of Locri, the author of twelve known epigrams. Both women lived in the third century B.C.E.

Melinno's *Hymn to Rome* is a type of writing called a panegyric, which is characterized by extravagant praise. Like nearly all Greek poetry, a panegyric was delivered publicly, often in a theatrical declamation. Melinno's poem is unique; its content differs substantially from that of poems written by other Greek female poets, who focused primarily on religion, love, or nature. It is impossible to know whether panegyric was Melinno's specialty, however. None of her other work—if, indeed, she wrote anything else—has survived antiquity.

Hail, Roma, daughter of Ares,*
gold-banded warrior queen,
who dwells on earth in sacred Olympos
ever indestructible.

To you alone, Eldest, has Fate
given royal glory of unbreakable rule,
that with sovereign strength
you might lead the way.

Under your yoke of strong straps,
breasts of earth and white-capped sea

———
*The Greek god of war (Mars to the Romans).

are bound together: without stumbling
you steer the cities of peoples.

The greatest span of time—making all things
    fall
and molding life now in one way, now in
    another—
for you alone does not change the wind
filling the sails of rule.

Indeed, out of all, you alone bear
the strongest men, great spearwielders,
making a crop of men spring up
like the rich corn crops of Demeter.*

———

*The Greek goddess of grain (Ceres to the Romans).

REVIEW QUESTIONS

1. Melinno personified Rome as female, but as a warrior. How does this support and/or contradict what you know about Roman society?
2. Why did Melinno believe that passage of time, which makes "all things fall," would not diminish the Roman Empire?
3. In your opinion, is this poem an effective piece of propaganda? Why or why not?

A Roman General Describes Britain (54 b.c.e.)

Julius Caesar, *The Gallic War, Book V*

Gaius Julius Caesar (100–44 b.c.e.) was one of the most famous figures in Roman history. Statesman, general, and ultimately dictator, he was also the author of two histories, *The Gallic War* and *The Civil War.* Both describe events in which Caesar played the leading role. His motives for writing were two-fold: first, he genuinely seems to have wanted to provide the "raw material" of history by accurately recording events he personally witnessed; second, he wanted to make sure that his view of these events would endure through time.

The political climate of Rome in the middle of the first century was characterized by factionalism and frequent violence. Supporters of continued aristocratic dominance of the state, the *optimates,* struggled to limit the increasing influence of more liberal politicians, who advocated democratic reforms to the constitution of the Roman Republic. The situation provided many chances for opportunists and demagogues—like Caesar and others—to build their own personal power to previously unprecedented levels. On top of this, military expertise and experience were necessary requirements for a Roman political career. A man could not run for political office without a background of military service, and he could not hope to attain or maintain political prestige without a history of impressive and successful commands.

By Caesar's time it was common for the Senate to extend the power (*imperium*) of consuls for a year or more after their one-year terms of office concluded, sending them as generals into the provinces and beyond.

Thus, after Caesar's term as consul for 59 expired, he secured for himself a five-year command of Cisalpine Gaul (northern Italy) and Illyricum (roughly modern Serbia, Croatia, and Slovenia). In 58, the Senate increased Caesar's territories to include Transalpine Gaul (modern France), a region not yet annexed to Rome, and in 55, his command was extended for another five years. Caesar's brilliant leadership in Gaul earned him the respect and enduring loyalty of his troops; his regular reports home (essentially, the chapters that constitute *The Gallic War*) increased his already phenomenal popularity in Rome, and, of course, his military activities resulted in the subjugation and annexation of the entire region.

The following selection describes the Britons, whom Caesar encountered during two brief "raids" into Britain in 55 and in 54. Ancient seafarers had known about the islands of Britannia for many centuries, and the northern Gauls had close economic and political contacts with the Britons, who shared similar customs and religious beliefs. This connection afforded Caesar a plausible excuse to invade Britain. He claimed that the Britons were providing support to the Gauls, and he aimed to sever their links. Caesar never intended to conquer Britain, but he did pique Rome's interest in it. Following his expeditions, contacts between Britain and Rome increased substantially. Conquest and formal annexation to the Roman Empire took place in 43 C.E.

The inland part of Britain is inhabited by tribes declared in their own tradition to be indigenous to the island, the maritime part* by tribes that migrated at an earlier time from Belgium to seek booty by invasion. Nearly all of these latter are called after the names of the states from which they sprang when they went to Britain; and after the invasion they abode there and began to till the fields. The population is innumerable; the farm-buildings are found very close together, being very like those of the Gauls; and there is great store of cattle. They use either bronze, or gold coins, or instead of coined money tallies of iron, of a certain standard of weight. In the midland districts of Britain tin is produced, in the maritime iron, but of that there is only a small supply; the bronze they use is imported. There is timber of every kind, as in Gaul, save

beech and pine. They account it wrong to eat of hare, fowl, and goose; but these they keep for pastime or pleasure. The climate is more temperate than in Gaul, the cold seasons more moderate.

The natural shape of the island is triangular, and one side lies opposite to Gaul. Of this side one angle, which is in Kent (where almost all the ships from Gaul come in to land), faces the east, the lower angle faces south. This side stretches about five hundred miles. The second side bears towards Spain and the west, in which direction lies Ireland, smaller by one half, as it is thought, than Britain; the sea-passage is of equal length to that from Gaul to Britain. Here in mid-channel is an island called Man; in addition, several smaller islands are supposed to lie close to land, as touching which some have written that in midwinter night there lasts for thirty whole days. We could discover nothing about this by inquiries; but by exact water mea-

---

*Caesar used the term *maritime part* to refer to the coastal and lowland areas of Britain.

Bloody! (handwritten)

household (handwritten)

surements,[1] we observed that the nights were shorter than on the Continent. The length of this side, according to the belief of the natives, is seven hundred miles. The third side bears northwards, and has no land confronting it; the angle, however, of that side faces on the whole towards Germany. The side is supposed to be eight hundred miles long. Thus the whole island is two thousand miles in circumference.

Of all the Britons the inhabitants of Kent, an entirely maritime district, are by far the most civilised, differing but little from the Gallic manner of life. Of the inlanders most do not sow corn,[*] but live on milk and flesh and clothe themselves in skins. All the Britons, indeed, dye themselves with woad,[†] which produces a blue

---

[1] *I.e.* measurements made with a water-clock, *clepsydra.*
[*] A reference to grain in general, not to be confused with maize, a crop that grew only in the Americas before the European voyages of exploration (beginning in 1492).
[†] A European plant grown very specifically for the dye that could be extracted from its leaves.

colour, and makes their appearance in battle more terrible. They wear long hair, and shave every part of the body save the head and the upper lip. Groups of ten or twelve men have wives together in common, and particularly brothers along with brothers, and fathers with sons; but the children born of the unions are reckoned to belong to the particular house to which the maiden was first conducted.

The horsemen and charioteers of the enemy engaged in fierce conflict with our cavalry on the march, with the result, however, that our troops proved their superiority in all respects, and drove them into the woods and highlands; but, pursuing too eagerly after slaying several of the enemy, they lost some of their own number. After an interval, however, when our troops were off their guard and engaged in entrenching the camp, the enemy suddenly dashed out from the woods, and charging the detachments on outpost duty in advance of the camp, they fought fiercely.

REVIEW QUESTIONS

1. How did the tribes who inhabited "maritime parts" of Britain differ from the "inlanders"?
2. Which tribe did Caesar consider to be the most "civilized"? What criteria did he use to assess this tribe's level of civilization?
3. Which British customs did Caesar find most admirable? Why? Which did he find most distasteful? Why?
4. Do you think Caesar's description of Britain is objective or biased? Explain.

Chinese Travelers Describe the Roman Empire (25–220 C.E.)

FAN YEH, *The Hou-han-shu*

Chinese dynastic histories contain a number of references to a "country on the western part of the sea," called Ta-ts'in (also Li-chien or Li-kin, and eventually Fu-lin). Historians are divided over whether the "Western Sea" was the Mediterranean Sea, the Black Sea, the Persian Gulf, or even the Euphrates

River at flood stage. Thus they are also unsure whether Ta-ts'in was the Chinese name for the greater Roman Empire, or simply for the eastern edge of the empire—specifically Syria, Egypt, and Asia Minor. Geographic details seem to point to Rome and Italy, but many of the descriptions of western life—like the manufacture of storax (a vanilla-scented balsam), the architectural use of glass and precious stones, travel by caravan, and the threat of wild animal attacks on the roads—suggest that Ta-ts'in was actually one of the eastern Roman provinces. Thus the capital city described was most likely Antioch rather than Rome, for to Chinese travelers Antioch (called An-tu in later Chinese histories) may have looked like an imperial, rather than a regional, capital. Some details, however, do not support this theory. For example, the description of rulers as "men of merit" rather than hereditary kings sounds far more Roman than Syrian, although the Chinese ambassadors may have mistaken Roman provincial governors, who were appointed by the emperors, for monarchs.

Much of this confusion is due to the way in which Chinese dynastic histories were written 1,500 years ago. Most were heavily dependent on earlier histories, and much information was simply copied into newer versions. Thus many of these histories were updated compilations of ancient works. As a regular feature, most included a section called "Traditions Regarding Western Countries," in which reports of the original travelers to the West were told and retold. Specific travelers' names were seldom mentioned, nor were definite dates for their travels. Every few hundred years new information from additional journeys to Ta-ts'in was incorporated into the existing historical record. Earlier material was often copied verbatim into a new history, or the old material was shortened and updated. It is also fairly clear that some of the information was based on hearsay rather than eye-witness accounts.

The Chinese travelers who went to Ta-ts'in seem to have been ambassadors, sent for the purpose of establishing and maintaining formal diplomatic relations with the West. They always focused on the exchange of gifts or tribute, which was fundamental to Chinese relations with foreign nations. Moreover, the *Hou-han-shu* clearly states that the king of Ta-ts'in, An-tun, sent an embassy to China in return. This "king" was probably the emperor Antoninus Pius (r. 138–161). A later history, the *Liang-shu* (written in 629 about events between 502 and 556), also mentions the visit of a merchant (named Ts'in-lun) from Ta-ts'in to China, though few details are given. In the ancient world there was clear, and occasionally direct, contact between Rome and China, for purposes of both trade and diplomacy.

The country of Ta-Ts'in is also called Li-chien (Li-kin) and, as being situated on the western part of the sea, Hai-hsi-kuo [*i.e,* "country of the western part of the sea"]. Its territory amounts to several thousand li;* it contains over four hundred cities, and of dependent states there are several times ten. The defences of cities are made of stone. The postal stations and mile-stones on the roads are covered with plaster. There are pine and cypress trees and all kinds of other trees and plants. The people are much bent on agriculture, and practice the planting of trees and the rearing of silk-worms. They cut the

---

*One *li* was equal to a Greek *stade* or Roman *stadium,* a measure of approximately 125 paces or 600 feet.

hair of their heads, wear embroidered clothing, and drive in small carriages covered with white canopies; when going in or out they beat drums, and hoist flags, banners, and pennants. The precincts of the walled city in which they live measure over a hundred li in circumference. In the city there are five palaces, ten li distant from each other. In the palace buildings they use crystal* to make pillars; vessels used in taking meals are also so made. The king goes to one palace a day to hear cases. After five days he has completed his round. As a rule, they let a man with a bag follow the king's carriage. Those who have some matter to submit, throw a petition into the bag. When the king arrives at the palace, he examines into the rights and wrongs of the matter. The official documents are under the control of thirty-six chiang (generals?) who conjointly discuss government affairs. Their kings are not permanent rulers, but they appoint men of merit. When a severe calamity visits the country, or untimely rain-storms, the king is deposed and replaced by another. The one relieved from his duties submits to his degradation without a murmur. The inhabitants of that country are tall and well-proportioned, somewhat like the Chinese, whence they are called Ta-ts'in. The country contains much gold, silver, and rare precious stones, especially the "jewel that shines at night," "the moonshine pearl," the hsieh-chi-hsi,† corals, amber, glass, langkan [a kind of coral], chu-tan [cinnabar?], green jadestone [ching-pi], gold-embroidered rugs and thin silk-cloth of various colours. They make gold-coloured cloth and asbestos cloth. They further have "fine cloth," also called Shui-yang-ts'ui [*i.e.,* down of the water-sheep‡]; it is made from the cocoons of wild silk-worms. They collect all

kinds of fragrant substances, the juice of which they boil into su-ho (storax). All the rare gems of other foreign countries come from there. They make coins of gold and silver. Ten units of silver are worth one of gold. They traffic by sea with An-hsi [Parthia] and T'ien-chu [India], the profit of which trade is ten-fold. They are honest in their transactions, and there are no double prices. Cereals are always cheap. The budget is based on a well-filled treasury. When the embassies of neighbouring countries come to their frontier, they are driven by post to the capital, and, on arrival, are presented with golden money. Their kings always desired to send embassies to China, but the An-hsi [Parthians] wished to carry on trade with them in Chinese silks, and it is for this reason that they were cut off from communication. This lasted till the ninth year of the Yen-hsi period during the emperor Huan-ti's reign [A.D. 166] when the king of Ta-ts'in, An-tun, sent an embassy who, from the frontier of Jih-nan [Annam] offered ivory, rhinoceros horns, and tortoise shell. From that time dates the [direct] intercourse with this country. The list of their tribute contained no jewels whatever, which fact throws doubt on the tradition. It is said by some that in the west of this country there is the Jo-shui ["weak water"] and the Liu-sha ["flying sands, desert"] near the residence of the Hsi-wang-mu ["mother of the western king"], where the sun sets. The [Ch'ien]-han-shu says: "From T'iao-chih west, going over 200 days, one is near the place where the sun sets"; this does not agree with the present book. Former embassies from China all returned from Wu-i; there were none who came as far as T'iao-chih. It is further said that, coming from the land-road of An-hsi [Parthia], you make a round at sea and, taking a northern turn, come out from the western part of the sea, whence you proceed to Ta-ts'in. The country is densely populated; every ten li [of a road] are marked by a t'ing; thirty li by a chih [resting-place]. One is not alarmed by robbers, but the road becomes unsafe by fierce tigers and lions who will attack passengers, and unless these be travelling in caravans of a hundred men or more, or be protected

---

*Probably a reference to glass, which the Romans used extensively.
†Literally, "chicken-frightening rhinoceros." This has been described in Chinese sources as a white gem that frightened chickens if placed on a pile of rice in the middle of a flock.
‡Probably cotton, but referred to as the "down water-sheep," which were described in later Chinese descriptions of the West. These "animals" sprouted from the ground and died if the connections from their navels to the ground were severed.

by military equipment, they may be devoured by those beasts. They also say there is a flying bridge* [fei-chiao] of several hundred li, by which one may cross to the countries north of the sea. The articles made of rare precious stones produced in this country are sham curiosities and mostly not genuine,† whence they are not [here] mentioned.

*Possibly a reference to the Hellespont, which Alexander crossed in 334 B.C.E. using a bridge of boats.

†Another reference to glass.

REVIEW QUESTIONS

1. What aspects of Ta-ts'in most impressed Chinese visitors? What particularly surprised them? Why?
2. Much like the Romans, the Chinese in this time period were noted for their attitudes of superiority. What in this selection supports this assumption? Does anything contradict it?
3. What does this selection tell you about Chinese values? About Roman values?

A Roman Historian Examines the Tribes of Germany (98 C.E.)

TACITUS, *Germania*

Publius Cornelius Tacitus (c. 56–120 C.E.) served as a Roman official during the reigns of the Flavian emperors. Best known for two major historical works, *The Histories* and *The Annals,* his writing career began in 98 with the publication of a biography of his dead father-in-law, Agricola, a former governor of Britain. Later the same year, Tacitus wrote the *Germania*. Like many other educated Romans, Tacitus believed that the earlier Republic had been superior in nearly all regards to his own period, the early Empire. He understood the necessity of one-man rule and praised those few emperors who served the state unselfishly, but his overall view of his own society was marked by disillusionment and cynicism.

Though not the major theme of the *Germania,* Tacitus's negative view of Roman government and society can sometimes be seen in the following selection. Nevertheless, it is not primarily a critique on Roman morals, as some claim; instead it is a study of German customs in general and a description of the various tribes individually. Since the Germans did not write about themselves, it is also a major source of information about Germany in this time period.

Before the nineteenth century, "Germany" did not refer to a cohesive state or nation. Instead, it was primarily a geographical and cultural term. In fact, in the late second century C.E. there were actually two regions that the Romans called *Germania.* First there was the vast territory north of the Danube and east of the Rhine River. Within this somewhat vaguely defined area lived a wide variety of "free Germans"—tribally organized peoples at various stages of cultural development. Some were seminomadic, while others had settled into more sedentary agricultural lifestyles, and very few had attained levels of prosperity comparable to the vast majority of Romanized Gauls to the west. The second region that the Romans called *Germania* was the western half of the Rhineland, where Augustus had established two small provinces, intending to use their capitals, Colonia Agrippensis (Cologne) and Moguntiacum (Mainz), as staging areas for the Roman conquest of German territories to the east. These provinces flourished, thanks in part to government military spending, but Augustus's dream of adding further German territories to the Roman Empire was never realized.

In the peoples of Germany there has been given to the world a race untainted by intermarriage with other races, a peculiar people and pure, like no one but themselves; whence it comes that their physique, in spite of their vast numbers, is identical: fierce blue eyes, red hair, tall frames, powerful only spasmodically, and impatient at the same time of labour and hard work, and by no means habituated to bearing thirst and heat; to cold and hunger, thanks to the climate and the soil, they are accustomed.

There are some varieties in the appearance of the country, but broadly it is a land of bristling forests and unhealthy marshes; the rainfall is heavier on the side of Gaul; the winds are higher on the side of Noricum and Pannonia.

It is fertile in cereals, but unkindly to fruit-bearing trees; it is rich in flocks and herds, but for the most part they are undersized. Even the cattle lack natural beauty and majestic brows. The pride of the people is rather in the number of their beasts, which constitute the only wealth they welcome.

The gods have denied them gold and silver, whether in mercy or in wrath I find it hard to say; not that I would assert that Germany has no veins bearing gold or silver: for who has explored there? At any rate, they are not affected, like their neighbours, by the use and possession of such things. One may see among them silver vases, given as gifts to their commanders and chieftains, but treated as of no more value than earthenware. Although the border tribes for purposes of traffic treat gold and silver as precious metals, and recognise and collect certain coins of our money, the tribes of the interior practise barter in the simpler and older fashion. The coinage which appeals to them is the old and long-familiar: the denarii with milled edges, showing the two-horsed chariot. They prefer silver to gold: not that they have any feeling in the matter, but because a number of silver pieces is easier to use for people whose purchases consist of cheap objects of general utility.

Even iron is not plentiful among them, as may be gathered from the style of their weapons. Few have swords or the longer kind of lance: they carry short spears, in their language "frameae," with a narrow and small iron head, so sharp and so handy in use that they fight with the same weapon, as circumstances demand, both at close quarters and at a distance. The mounted man is content with a shield and framea: the infantry launch showers of missiles in addition, each man a volley, and hurl these to great distances, for they wear no outer clothing, or at most a light cloak.

There is no bravery of apparel among them: their shields only are picked out with choice colours. Few have breast-plates: scarcely one or two at most have metal or hide helmets. The horses are conspicuous neither for beauty nor speed; but then neither are they trained like our horses to run in shifting circles: they ride them forwards only or to the right, with but one turn from the straight, dressing the line so closely as they wheel that no one is left behind. On a broad view there is more strength in their infantry, and accordingly cavalry and infantry fight in one body, the swift-footed infantryman, whom they pick out of the whole body of warriors and place in front of the line, being well-adapted and suitable for cavalry battles. The number of these men is fixed—one hundred from each canton: and among themselves this, "the Hundred," is the precise name they use; what was once a number only has become a title and a distinction. The battle-line itself is arranged in wedges: to retire, provided you press on again, they treat as a question of tactics, not of cowardice: they carry off their dead and wounded even in drawn battles. To have abandoned one's shield is the height of disgrace; the man so disgraced cannot be present at religious rites, nor attend a council: many survivors of war have ended their infamy with a noose.

They take their kings on the ground of birth, their generals on the basis of courage: the authority of their kings is not unlimited or arbitrary; their generals control them by example rather than command, and by means of the admiration which attends upon energy and a conspicuous place in front of the line. But anything beyond this—capital punishment, imprisonment, even a blow—is permitted only to the priests, and then not as a penalty or under the general's orders, but as an inspiration from the god whom they suppose to accompany them on campaign: certain totems, in fact, and emblems are fetched from groves and carried into battle. The strongest incentive to courage lies in this, that neither chance nor casual grouping makes the squadron or the wedge, but family and kinship: close at hand, too, are their dearest, whence is heard the wailing voice of woman and the child's cry: here are the witnesses who are in each man's eyes most precious; here the praise he covets most: they take their wounds to mother and wife, who do not shrink from counting the hurts and demanding a sight of them: they minister to the combatants food and exhortation.

Tradition relates that some lost or losing battles have been restored by the women, by the incessance of their prayers and by the baring of their breasts; for so is it brought home to the men that the slavery, which they dread much more keenly on their women's account, is close at hand: it follows that the loyalty of those tribes is more effectually guaranteed from whom, among other hostages, maids of high birth have been exacted. . . .

It is the custom in their states to bestow upon the chief unasked and man by man some portion of one's cattle or crops: it is accepted as a compliment, but also serves his needs. The chiefs appreciate still more the gifts of neighbouring tribes, which are sent not merely by individuals but by the community—selected horses, heavy armour, bosses and bracelets: by this time we have taught them to accept money also.

It is well known that none of the German tribes live in cities, that even individually they do not permit houses to touch each other: they live separated and scattered, according as spring-water, meadow, or grove appeals to each man: they lay out their villages not, after our fashion, with buildings contiguous and connected; every one keeps a clear space round his house, whether it be a precaution against the chances of fire, or just ignorance of building. They have not even learned to use quarrystone or tiles: the timber they use for all purposes is unshaped, and stops short of all ornament or attraction: certain buildings are smeared with a stucco bright and glittering enough to be a substitute for paint and frescoes. They are in the habit also of opening pits in the earth and piling dung in quantities on the roof, as a refuge from the winter or a root-house, because such places mitigate the rigour of frost, and if an enemy come, he lays waste the open; but the hidden and buried houses are either missed outright or escape detection just because they require a search.

For clothing all wear a cloak, fastened with a clasp, or, in its absence, a thorn: they spend whole days on the hearth round the fire with no other covering. The richest men are distinguished by the wearing of under-clothes; not loose, like those of Parthians and Sarmatians, but drawn tight, throwing each limb into relief.*

They wear also the skins of wild beasts, the tribes adjoining the river-bank in casual fashion, the further tribes with more attention, since they cannot depend on traders for clothing. The beasts for this purpose are selected, and the hides so taken are chequered with the pied skins of the creatures native to the outer ocean and its unknown waters.

The women have the same dress as the men, except that very often trailing linen garments, striped with purple, are in use for women: the upper part of this costume does not widen into sleeves: their arms and shoulders are therefore bare, as is the adjoining portion of the breast.

None the less the marriage tie with them is strict: you will find nothing in their character to praise more highly. They are almost the only barbarians who are content with a wife apiece: the very few exceptions have nothing to do with passion, but consist of those with whom polygamous marriage is eagerly sought for the sake of their high birth.

As for dower, it is not the wife who brings it to the husband, but the husband to the wife. The parents and relations are present to approve these gifts—gifts not devised for ministering to female fads, nor for the adornment of the person of the bride, but oxen, a horse and bridle, a shield and spear or sword; it is to share these things that the wife is taken by the husband, and she herself, in turn, brings some piece of armour to her husband. Here is the gist of the bond between them, here in their eyes its mysterious sacrament, the divinity which hedges it. That the wife may not imagine herself released from the practice of heroism, released from the chances of war, she is thus warned by the very rites with which her marriage begins that she comes to share hard work and peril; that her fate will be the same as his in peace and in panic, her risks the same. This is the moral of the yoked oxen, of the bridled horse, of the exchange of

arms; so must she live and so must she die. The things she takes she is to hand over inviolate to her children, fit to be taken by her daughters-in-law and passed on again to her grandchildren.

So their life is one of fenced-in chastity. There is no arena with its seductions, no dinner-tables with their provocations to corrupt them. Of the exchange of secret letters men and women alike are innocent; adulteries are very few for the number of the people. Punishment is prompt and is the husband's prerogative: her hair close-cropped, stripped of her clothes, her husband drives her from his house in presence of his relatives and pursues her with blows through the length of the village. For prostituted chastity there is no pardon; beauty nor youth nor wealth will find her a husband. No one laughs at vice there; no one calls seduction, suffered or wrought, the spirit of the age. Better still are those tribes where only maids marry, and where a woman makes an end, once for all, with the hopes and vows of a wife; so they take one husband only, just as one body and one life, in order that there may be no second thoughts, no belated fancies: in order that their desire may be not for the man, but for marriage; to limit the number of their children, to make away with any of the later children is held abominable, and good habits have more force with them than good laws elsewhere.

There then they are, the children, in every house, filling out amid nakedness and squalor into that girth of limb and frame which is to our people a marvel. Its own mother suckles each at her breast; they are not passed on to nursemaids and wet-nurses.

Nor can master be recognised from servant by any flummery[1] in their respective bringing-up: they live in the company of the same cattle and on the same mud floor till years separate the free-born and character claims her own.

The virginity of youth is late treasured and puberty therefore inexhaustible; nor for the girls

---

*Tacitus is describing pants or trousers, which were not worn by men in the Mediterranean regions of Europe.

[1]Tacitus means that the children are all brought up without distinction, and without cosseting and pampering for the better born.

is there any hot-house forcing; they pass their youth in the same way as the boys: their stature is as tall; when they reach the same strength they are mated, and the children reproduce the vigour of the parents. Sisters' children mean as much to their uncle as to their father: some tribes regard this blood-tie as even closer and more sacred than that between son and father, and in taking hostages make it the basis of their demand, as though they thus secure loyalty more surely and have a wider hold on the family.

However, so far as heirship and succession are concerned, each man's children are his heirs, and there is no will; if there be no children, the nearest degrees of relationship for the holding of property are brothers, paternal uncles, and uncles maternal: the more relations a man has and the larger the number of his connections by marriage, the more influence has he in his age; it does not pay to have no ties.*

It is incumbent to take up a father's feuds or a kinsman's not less than his friendships; but such feuds do not continue unappeasable: even homicide is atoned for by a fixed number of cattle and sheep, and the whole family thereby receives satisfaction, to the public advantage; for feuds are more dangerous among a free people.

No race indulges more lavishly in hospitality and entertainment: to close the door against any human being is a crime. Every one according to his property receives at a well-spread board: should it fail, he who had been your host points out your place of entertainment and goes with you. You go next door, without an invitation, but it makes no difference; you are received with the same courtesy. Stranger or acquaintance, no one distinguishes them where the right of hospitality is concerned. It is customary to speed the parting guest with anything he fancies. There is the same readiness in turn to ask of him: gifts are their delight, but they neither count upon what they have given, nor are bound by what they have received.

---

*Tacitus is referring here to the Roman custom of currying favor with old and childless people, both male and female, in hopes of securing a bequest.

On waking from sleep, which they generally prolong into the day, they wash, usually in warm water, since winter bulks so large in their lives: after washing they take a meal, seated apart, each at his own table: then, arms in hand, they proceed to business, or, just as often, to revelry. To out-drink the day and night is a reproach to no man: brawls are frequent; naturally, among heavy drinkers: they seldom terminate with abuse, more often in wounds and bloodshed; nevertheless the mutual reconciliation of enemies, the forming of family alliances, the appointment of chiefs, the question even of war or peace, are usually debated at these banquets; as though at no other time were the mind more open to obvious, or better warmed to larger, thoughts. The people are without craft or cunning, and expose in the freedom of revelry the heart's previous secrets; so every mind is bared to nakedness: on the next day the matter is handled afresh; so the principle of each debating season is justified: deliberation comes when they are incapable of pretence, but decision when they are secure from illusion.

For drink they use the liquid distilled from barley or wheat, after fermentation has given it a certain resemblance to wine. The tribes nearest the river also buy wine. Their diet is simple: wild fruit, fresh venison, curdled milk. They banish hunger without sauce or ceremony, but there is not the same temperance in facing thirst: if you humour their drunkenness by supplying as much as they crave, they will be vanquished through their vices as easily as on the battlefield. . . .

Land is taken up by a village as a whole, in quantity according to the number of the cultivators: they then distribute it among themselves on the basis of rank, such distribution being made easy by the extent of domain occupied. They change the arable land yearly, and there is still land to spare, for they do not strain the fertility and resources of the soil by tasking them, through the planting of vineyards, the setting apart of water-meadows, the irrigation of vegetable gardens. Grain is the only harvest required of the land; accordingly the year itself is not divided into as many parts as with us: winter, spring, summer have a meaning and name; of autumn the name alike and bounties are unknown.

In burial there is no ostentation: the single observance is to burn the bodies of their notables with special kinds of wood. They build a pyre, but do not load it with palls or spices: to each man his armour; to the fire of some his horse also is added. The tomb is a mound of turf: the difficult and tedious tribute of a monument they reject as too heavy on the dead. Weeping and wailing they put away quickly: sorrow and sadness linger. Lamentation becomes women: men must remember.

REVIEW QUESTIONS

1. What did Tacitus particularly admire about German society? Why? What did he find distasteful? Why?
2. How did Germany's "border tribes" (meaning those living closest to the Romans) compare to "tribes of the interior"? Which did Tacitus think had superior values? Explain.
3. What was the role of women and children in German warfare? What was their effect on fighting men? On the outcome of battle?
4. How does Tacitus's description of the Germans compare with Caesar's description of the Britons?
5. Tacitus used the word *barbarians* to describe peoples who did not live within the parameters of Greco-Roman ideas of civilization. Which of the groups described in this chapter seem most "barbaric," the Britons or the Germans?
6. There are several subtle—and not-so-subtle—criticisms of Roman society in Tacitus's description of the Germans. What are they, and how well do they serve the author's purpose?

A Roman Historian Describes the Huns (late fourth century)

AMMIANUS MARCELLINUS, *A History in Thirty-One Books*

Ammianus Marcellinus (c. 330–395) has been called the last great Roman historian. He was born in the Greek-speaking city of Antioch, and as a young man he began a career in the Roman army that lasted for many years. His assignments placed him in a good position to witness the turbulent history of the fourth century: he accompanied no less than three emperors—Constantius II, Julian, and Jovian—on campaign. Eventually Ammianus retired to the city of Rome, where he wrote, in Latin, a history of the Roman Empire from the accession of Nerva to the death of Valens (96–378). He intended it to be a continuation of the work of Tacitus. Unfortunately, however, there are gaps in his narration. Like other writings of the age, not all of Ammianus's history has survived: only the last eighteen of its thirty-one books are extant. Given the paucity of sources in the late empire, what remains is extremely valuable, of course. His style is clear and comprehensive, though often very blunt. His extremely unflattering description of the Huns, excerpted for this selection, is not typical of his usual objective and fair treatment of non-Romans.

The age in which Ammianus lived was one of immense change for the Roman Empire. In 285, the general and emperor Diocletian had ended half a century of chronic civil war and economic chaos by seizing power and reforming the operation of the state. Dispensing with the Senate (much the same way that Augustus had eliminated the republican assemblies three centuries earlier), Diocletian took all power into his own hands, declaring the title of the emperor to be *dominus* (lord) instead of *princeps* (first citizen). The severe policies he then implemented managed to slow the decline of Rome, but it was by then a case of too little, too late. By the 300s, Rome's territorial holdings had shrunk considerably—a disaster for an empire that was dependent on military expansion for its economic health. Among the worst problems were population decline, urban deterioration, shrinking tax revenues, and military insufficiencies—especially in the West. Internecine squabbles among the sons of Diocletian's eventual successor, Constantine, added to Rome's woes. Then, in 372, the nomadic Huns began moving west from central Asia, crushing or compelling alliances with various nations standing in the way and prompting others to flee toward the safety of the empire. The result was a wave of migration that displaced vast numbers of peoples and transformed Europe.

The people of the Huns, but little known from ancient records, dwelling beyond the Maeotic Sea near the ice-bound ocean, exceed every degree of savagery.   2. Since there the cheeks of the children are deeply furrowed with the steel from their very birth, in order that the growth of hair, when it appears at the proper time, may be checked by the wrinkled scars, they grow old without beards and without any beauty, like eunuchs. They all have compact, strong limbs and thick necks, and are so monstrously ugly and misshapen, that one might take them for two-legged beasts or for the stumps, rough-hewn into images, that are used in putting sides to bridges.[1]   3. But although they have the form of men, however ugly, they are so hardy in their mode of life that they have no need of fire nor of savory food, but eat the roots of wild plants and the half-raw flesh of any kind of animal whatever, which they put between their thighs and the backs of their horses, and thus warm it a little.   4. They are never protected by any building, but they avoid these like tombs, which are set apart from everyday use. For not even a hut thatched with reed can be found among them. But roaming at large amid the mountains and woods, they learn from the cradle to endure cold, hunger, and thirst. When away from their homes they never enter a house unless compelled by extreme necessity; for they think they are not safe when staying under a roof.   5. They dress in linen cloth or in the skins of field-mice sewn together, and they wear the same clothing indoors and out. But when they have once put their necks into a faded tunic, it is not taken off or changed until by long wear and tear it has been reduced to rags and fallen from them bit by bit.   6. They cover their heads with round caps and protect their hairy legs with goatskins; their shoes are formed upon no lasts, and so prevent their walking with free step. For this reason they are not at all adapted to battles on foot, but they are almost glued to their horses, which are hardy, it is true, but ugly, and sometimes they sit them woman-fashion and thus perform their ordinary tasks. From their horses by day or

------

[1] Used for adorning the parapets of bridges.

night every one of that nation buys and sells, eats and drinks, and bowed over the narrow neck of the animal relaxes into a sleep so deep as to be accompanied by many dreams.   7. And when deliberation is called for about weighty matters, they all consult for a common object in that fashion [on horseback]. They are subject to no royal restraint, but they are content with the disorderly government of their important men, and led by them they force their way through every obstacle.   8. They also sometimes fight when provoked, and then they enter the battle drawn up in wedge-shaped masses, while their medley of voices makes a savage noise. And as they are lightly equipped for swift motion, and unexpected in action, they purposely divide suddenly into scattered bands and attack, rushing about in disorder here and there, dealing terrific slaughter; and because of their extraordinary rapidity of movement they are never seen to attack a rampart or pillage an enemy's camp. 9. And on this account you would not hesitate to call them the most terrible of all warriors, because they fight from a distance with missiles having sharp bone, instead of their usual [metal] points, joined to the shafts with wonderful skill; then they gallop over the intervening spaces and fight hand to hand with swords, regardless of their own lives; and while the enemy are guarding against wounds from the sabre-thrusts, they throw strips of cloth plaited into nooses over their opponents and so entangle them that they fetter their limbs and take from them the power of riding or walking.   10. No one in their country ever plows a field or touches a plow-handle. They are all without fixed abode, without hearth, or law, or settled mode of life, and keep roaming from place to place, like fugitives, accompanied by the wagons in which they live; in wagons their wives weave for them their hideous garments, in wagons they cohabit with their husbands, bear children, and rear them to the age of puberty. None of their offspring, when asked, can tell you where he comes from, since he was conceived in one place, born far from there, and brought up still farther away. 11. In truces they are faithless and unreliable, strongly inclined to sway to the motion of every breeze of new hope that presents itself, and sacrificing every feeling to the mad impulse of the moment. Like unreasoning beasts, they are utterly ignorant of the difference between right and wrong; they are deceitful and ambiguous in speech, never bound by any reverence for religion or for superstition. They burn with an infinite thirst for gold, and they are so fickle and prone to anger, that they often quarrel with their allies without provocation, more than once on the same day, and make friends with them again without a mediator.

12. This race of untamed men, without encumbrances, aflame with an inhuman desire for plundering others' property, made their violent way amid the rapine and slaughter of the neighbouring peoples as far as the Halani, once known as the Massagetae.

REVIEW QUESTIONS

1. Like Tacitus, Ammianus referred to non-Romans like the Huns as "barbarians." What in this selection substantiates this opinion? What does not?
2. What, if anything, can you find in this selection to admire about the Huns? Why is this a difficult task?
3. Compare Ammianus's attitude toward the Huns with Tacitus's view of the Germans. What are the major differences between the accounts of these two men?

5

The Ancient Near East, 800 B.C.E.–800 C.E.

In the second millennium B.C.E., many small states thrived in the ancient Near East. Small empires occasionally rose and fell, but they tended to be the exception rather than the rule. Between 800 B.C.E. and 800 C.E., however, the ancient Near East was dominated by a series of extremely large empires: first the Assyrians, then the Persians, Macedonians, and Romans. Small states (such as Moab, Judah, Israel, and Edom) were seldom able to maintain their independence except in brief periods when their large neighbors were not strong.

Whether a state was large or small, maintaining hegemony over the territory it controlled was one of its primary concerns. This required the creation of a centralized government, the building of communication networks, and the use of state-generated propaganda. Two inscriptions in this chapter particularly testify to this aim. The Moabite Stone and the Monolith of Shalmaneser III of Assyria are permanent records of the accomplishments of individual rulers, and by association, their states. These monuments, one a *stela* and the other an obelisk, were designed to impress and intimidate the viewer—indeed, generations of viewers. The stones are important primary sources for the history of the ancient Near East, but they need to be evaluated with the purposes of their authors in mind. Likewise, there is a considerable element of political propaganda in the two selections from the Hebrew Scriptures. The book of 2 Kings, which recounts a battle between Moab and Israel in the ninth century B.C.E., advertises the superiority of the kingdom of Israel and its god Yahweh, as does the poem in the book of Nahum.

These four accounts, all of which were written by natives of the Near East, also illustrate a common theme in the writing of this region and this time period: hatred. It is impossible not to notice the obvious enmity with which certain groups regarded each other. The long list of atrocities committed by the armies of Shalmaneser, which he described with obvious pride and satisfaction, are a chilling testament to centuries of hatred and malice. Equally significant evidence of deep-seated hostility and resentment is Nahum's fiercely jubilant contemplation of the fall of the Assyrian capital, Nineveh.

More tolerant views of civilizations of the ancient Near East can be seen in the accounts of outsiders, such as the Greeks, Romans, and Chinese. Particularly surprising is the lack of hostility of two Greek authors, Herodotus and Xenophon, toward the Persians. Although they were the enemies of the Greeks, the celebrated historian Herodotus praised many of the Persians' customs in the first chapter of his book, *The Histories,* an examination of Persia's attempt to add Greece to its empire (490–479). At the end of the fifth century, Xenophon carried this attitude even further: There is no trace of even mild bitterness or dislike in his discussion of the Persian prince,

Cyrus the Younger, despite the fact that it was imperial policy to exacerbate rivalries between the continually warring Greek city-states. In fact, Xenophon's passage on Cyrus is nothing less than a panegyric—its extravagant praise of the prince is so overblown as to be almost unbelievable. Another appreciative account of the ancient Near East can be found in the travel account of Egeria, a pilgrim from the western half of the Roman Empire. Focusing entirely upon religious beliefs and practices she encountered on her journey to Jerusalem, she seems to have been oblivious to all else: the customs and dress of the people, the workings of the provincial governments, or even the hardships of travel in the fourth century C.E. Although Christian customs in the East were obviously very different from what she was accustomed to—and extreme by comparison—she did not criticize; she only observed and reported.

This relative objectivity may have been the result of Greco-Roman attitudes toward the craft of history itself, which Herodotus and Xenophon consciously exercised, and which might have influenced Egeria as well. History—the interpretation and analysis of past human activity—was a common literary form in the West, but it was almost nonexistent in the Near East. The only exception is the scripture of the ancient Hebrews, which contains a great deal of very valuable historical information but which cannot be considered secular history because of its single-minded religious focus. Like the Greeks and Romans, the Chinese were also intent upon accurately chronicling both their own and others' history; the Chinese selection in this chapter illustrates their fascination with the past. Several centuries after two diplomatic missions to Bactria and the eastern Roman Empire, Chinese historians considered the ambassadors' reports so important that they were included, almost verbatim, in dynastic histories of China.

Modern references to ancient Mesopotamia, Asia Minor, and the eastern coast of the Mediterranean—the areas today occupied by the states of Iran, Iraq, Turkey, Syria, Lebanon, Israel, and Jordan—tend to use the term *Middle East.* Historians and students of ancient history, however, almost always refer to the area as the "Near East." Neither is entirely satisfactory, since both take their meaning from the region's geographical proximity to other areas. *Middle East* defines this area by the position it occupies between the western democracies and the East, especially China and the former Soviet Union. *Near East* refers to the area very specifically in terms of its location to the east of the ancient Mediterranean, nearer to the Greco-Roman world than China, the *Far East.* In the modern world, use of the two terms designates two broad historical eras. Regardless of terminology, the area is extremely important as the point of intersection between East and West, where the mix of peoples, customs, and trade goods proved to be a catalyst for new ideas and philosophies. It is no surprise, therefore, that the area gave birth to three major world religions, as well as to political and ideological problems that continue to affect the world today.

Two Views of Moab (mid–ninth century B.C.E.)

King Mesha of Moab Inscribes His Accomplishments on the Moabite Stone
The Hebrews Describe the Moabite War, 2 Kings 3:4–27

Moab was the name of an ancient state in eastern Palestine that lay east of the Jordan River and the Dead Sea. Its people were Semites, as were their neighbors, the Hebrews, who had separated into two nations, Israel and Judah, after the death of King Solomon in 931. This split made it difficult for either state to do much more than retain control of its own territories. Judah, south of Israel, was particularly interested in maintaining its precarious hold on Edom (which lay immediately south of Moab), and Israel struggled to retain domination of parts of Moab, especially Medeba. All four states were culturally similar. They spoke and wrote different dialects of the same language (Hebrew and Moabite, for example, are nearly indistinguishable), engaged in nearly identical economic and agricultural pursuits, and shared similar religious rituals and beliefs—although apparently only the Judeans worshiped a single god, Yahweh. Relatively minor religious and territorial differences led to frequent conflicts—as well as occasional peaceful interaction—among the four groups. For instance, the Hebrew kings Saul and David fought against Moabite armies, and Hebrew prophets often spoke against the dangers of Moabite and Edomite religious beliefs. It is also important to remember that the Edomites claimed descent from Jacob's brother Esau, that the Moabites claimed descent from Abraham's nephew Lot, and that Ruth, the great-grandmother of King David, was a Moabite who married a Hebrew.

The following two selections offer different perspectives of a ninth-century conflict over the territory of Medeba, possession of which was disputed between kings Mesha of Moab and Jehoram of Israel. Jehoram received aid from his ally, Jehoshaphat of Judah, and consequently, from Edom as well. The first selection comes from the Moabite Stone, a black basalt stele found in 1868 on the east side of the Jordan River in the ruins of Dibon (Dhibon, a city in modern Jordan). Shortly afterward, it was broken into pieces and sold to antiquities collectors, but approximately two-thirds of the fragments have been relocated and used to reconstruct the monument to much of its original appearance. Many such ancient stelae have been found in the Middle East. Nearly all were erected by kings and attest to their great deeds (especially in war) and accomplishments (especially the building of cities). The Moabite Stone, however, is unique because it is one of the oldest examples of ancient Hebrew writing. Not only is the text important linguistically, it is one of the few sources for the history of Moab that was not authored by its enemies, the Hebrews. The second selection, from the second book of Kings, provides additional information—as well as several direct contradictions—to the Moabite story.

THE MOABITE STONE

I, Mesha, son of Chemosh[yat], king of Moab, the Dibonite (my father reigned over Moab for thirty years and I reigned after my father)—I made this high place for Chemosh* in Karhoh [. . .] because he saved me from all the kings and caused me to triumph over all who opposed me.

Omri,† king of Israel, oppressed Moab for many years, because Chemosh was angry with his land.

When his son succeeded him, he too said, "I shall oppress Moab." In my days he spoke this way, but I triumphed over him and his house, and Israel was utterly destroyed forever. Omri took possession of the entire land of Medeba‡, and [Israel] lived there during his days and half the days of his son—forty years; but Chemosh restored it in my days. I built Baal-meon, making a cistern in it, and I built Kiryathaim. The men of Gad§ had lived in the land of Ataroth since ancient times, and the king of Israel had built Ataroth‖ for them; but I fought against the city and captured it, slaying all the people of the city for the satisfaction of Chemosh and Moab. I brought back from there the altar-hearth of its beloved [god], dragging it before Chemosh in Kerioth, and I settled men of Sharon and men of Maharith# there. Then Chemosh said to me, "Go capture Nebo** from Israel!"

So I went by night and fought against it from the break of dawn until noon. I captured it and slew them all—seven thousand men, boys, women, girls, and maidservants—for I had devoted it to Ashtar-Chemosh.†† I took from there the utensils of Yahweh, dragging them before Chemosh. The king of Israel had built Jahaz, and he lived there while he was fighting against me. But Chemosh drove him out before me.

I took from Moab two hundred men, all its poor citizens, and exalted them in Jahaz; I took possession of it in order to annex it to Dibon. It was I who built Karhoh, both the forest wall and the summit wall; it was I who built its gates and I who built its towers; it was I who built the palace and I who made both the reservoirs for water inside the town. There were no cisterns inside the town at Karhoh, so I said to the people, "Each of you make a cistern for himself and his house!" Also it was I who cut beams for Karhoh using Israelite captives. It was I who built Aroer; it was I who made the highway in the Arnon; and it was I who built the high-place temple, for it had been torn down. It was I who built Bezer—for it was in ruins.

[. . .] the men of Dibon armed for battle, for all Dibon is (my) bodyguard. I made one hundred [. . .] reign as kings in the towns that I annexed to the land. It was I who built [. . .] Medeba, Beth-diblathaim, and Beth-baal-meon, where I exalted the herdsmen [. . .] the sheep of the land. As for Horonaim,‡‡ [. . .] was living there [. . .] [. . .]. Then Chemosh said to me, "Go down and fight against Horonaim!" So I went down and [fought against it. I captured it, and] Chemosh restored it in my days [. . .] [. . .].

---

*The chief god of Moab.
†Omri was actually the dynastic name of the Israelite royal family, to which Ahab and his successor, Jehoram, belonged.
‡A city built by the tribe of Reuben, just south of Mount Nebo.
§One of the twelve tribes of Israel.
‖A name for three different towns in ancient Palestine. This particular Ataroth was probably located east of the Jordan River and belonged to the tribe of Gad.
#Sharon is a coastal plain between Jaffa and Mount Carmel, occupied through much of Hebrew history by either the Phoenicians or the Philistines. The location of Maharith is not known.
**An alternate name for Mount Pisgah, famous as the burial place of Moses.

††Ashtar was probably a variant of Astarte (Ishtar), a goddess worshipped by the Phoenicians, Mesopotamians, and many other peoples in the ancient Near East. The combination of the two names most likely indicates that in Moab Ashtar was the consort of Chemosh. Moreover, Mesha carefully explained that he had slain the entire population of Nebo (and earlier, Ataroth) because he had "devoted" it to Ashtar-Chemosh. This slaughter was *herem,* the "ban," an instrument of religious warfare. In exchange for victory, Chemosh required this ritual massacre; thus, Mesha was religiously bound to obey. The Hebrews also believed in *herem;* examples can be found in Joshua 6:17–21 and 1 Samuel 15:1–23.
‡‡An Edomite city.

THE HEBREW BIBLE

Mesha king of Moab was a sheep breeder and used to pay the king of Israel a hundred thousand lambs and the wool of a hundred thousand rams in tribute. But when Ahab died, the king of Moab rebelled against the king of Israel.

At once King Jehoram went out of Samaria and mustered all Israel. After this he sent word to the king of Judah, "The king of Moab has rebelled against me. Will you join with me fighting Moab?" "I will," he replied. "I am as ready as you, my men as your men, my horses as your horses," and added "which way are we to attack?" "Through the wilderness of Edom," the other answered.

So they set out, the king of Israel, the king of Judah and the king of Edom. They followed a devious route for seven days, until there was no water left for the troops or for the beasts in their baggage train. "Alas!" the king of Israel exclaimed, "Yahweh has summoned us three kings, only to put us into the power of Moab." But the king of Judah said, "Is there no prophet of Yahweh here for us to consult Yahweh through him?" One of the king of Israel's servants answered, "Elisha son of Shaphat is here, who used to pour water on the hands of Elijah."* "The word of Yahweh is with him," the king of Judah said. So they went to him, the king of Israel, the king of Judah and the king of Edom. But Elisha said to the king of Israel, "What business have you with me? Go to the prophets of your father and your mother." "No," the king of Israel an-

swered, "Yahweh has summoned us three kings, only to put us into the power of Moab." Elisha replied, "As Yahweh Sabaoth lives, whom I serve, if I did not respect Jehoshaphat king of Judah, I should not take any notice of you, or so much as look at you. Now bring me someone who can play the lyre."[1] And as the musician played, the hand of Yahweh was laid on him and he said "Yahweh says this, 'Dig ditch on ditch in this wadi,' for Yahweh says, 'You shall see neither wind nor rain, but his wadi shall be filled with water, and you and your troops and your baggage animals shall drink.' But this is only a little thing in the sight of Yahweh, for he will put Moab itself into your power. You shall storm every fortified town, fell every sound tree, block every water spring, ruin all the best fields with stones." Next morning at the time when the oblation was being offered, water came from the direction of Edom, and the country was filled with it.

When the Moabites learned that the kings had come up to fight against them, all who were of age to bear arms were called up; they took up position on the frontier. In the morning when they got up, the sun was shining on the water; and in the distance the Moabites saw the water as red as blood.[2] "This is blood!" they said. "The kings must have fought among themselves and killed one another. So now for the booty, Moab!"

But when they reached the Israelite camp, the Israelites launched their attack and the Moabites fled before them, and as they advanced they cut the Moabites to pieces. They laid the towns in ruins, and each man threw a stone into all the best fields to fill them up, and they blocked every water spring and felled every sound tree. In the end, there was only Kir-hareseth left, which the slingers surrounded and battered. When the king of Moab saw that the battle had turned against him, he mustered seven hundred swords-

---

*Elijah was a famous prophet and outspoken critic of King Ahab, who had allowed the worship of Baal in Israel. In a contest with the priests of Baal on Mount Carmel, Elijah had won the Israelites back to the worship of Yahweh. The prophet had not died, as readers unfamiliar with his story might infer from this story. Instead, the Hebrews believed that Elijah had been taken directly to heaven (not an afterlife for all, but the place where Yahweh and his angels resided) in a chariot of fire. His lieutenant, Elisha, had succeeded him as prophet.

---

[1]To stimulate a prophetic ecstasy.
[2]Perhaps owing to the red sand of Edom in the wadi el Hesa.

men in the hope of breaking a way out and going to the king of Aram,* but he failed. Then he

_____
*Aram was a state immediately north of Moab.

took his eldest son who was to succeed him and offered him as a sacrifice on the city wall. There was bitter indignation against the Israelites, who then withdrew, retiring to their own country.

REVIEW QUESTIONS

1. What role in this conflict was played by Chemosh, the god of Moab, and by Yahweh, the god of the Hebrews? What similarities and differences between the two gods do you observe?
2. Who won the conflict, Moab or Israel? Why do you think the circumstances of the victory are described so differently by the two sources?
3. How do the purpose and message of Mesha's inscription and the passage from 2 Kings compare? What are the most important similarities and differences?
4. Which version of this incident do you think is more accurate? Why?

An Assyrian King Boasts About His Achievements (860–824 B.C.E.)

The Monolith Inscription of Shalmaneser III

Assyria was the first state in the ancient Near East to build a large empire that extended well beyond the borders of Mesopotamia, eventually stretching from Egypt to Medea. In the ninth century, however, it had just begun to expand outside its original territory, a narrow strip of land on each side of the Tigris River in northwest Mesopotamia (now part of modern Iraq). For much of its early history, Assyria had been dominated by its neighbors, especially the Sumerians, Babylonians, and Hittites, but in the tenth century, a series of strong kings managed to rid Assyria of foreign domination. In the following century, expansion began with a vengeance. The Assyrians quickly gained a reputation for unmatched military prowess and ferocity, as well as for their tyrannical subjugation of conquered peoples. Not surprisingly, rebellions were not only frequent, but they were also put down with great brutality.

Thus, the thirty-five-year reign of Shalmaneser III (c. 858–823) was a constant series of campaigns against various small states that the Assyrians were trying to either conquer or control. His armies penetrated to Lake Van and Tarsus in Asia Minor, and they were able to subdue or to force tribute from Damascus, Israel, and Hittite and Phoenician cities on the northeastern Mediterranean coast. Equally important, Shalmaneser gained control of important trade routes linking Mesopotamia with the Mediterranean Sea. Near the end of his reign, however, his oldest son Assur-danin-pal led the capital, Nineveh, in a revolt against his father. The ensuing two-year civil war was finally crushed by a younger brother, Samas-Rimmon (or Samsi-Hadad). Shalmaneser died soon afterwards in 824 B.C.E.

The record of Shalmaneser's reign is engraved on an obelisk of black marble that he erected at Calah (modern Nimrud). Discovered in 1840, the monument is five feet in height and engraved on all four sides. In addition to the long inscription, which is written in cuneiform, the obelisk is covered with pictures showing princes of many nations, including Jehu of Israel, bringing tribute to the king of Assyria.

Ashur,[*] the great lord, the king of all the great gods; Anu, the king of the Igigi and Anunnaki,[†] the lord of lands; Bel, the father of the gods, the decider of fates, who fixes the boundaries of heaven and earth; Ea, the wise, the king of the deep, the patron of the arts; Nanir of heaven and earth, the majestic; Shamash, the judge of the (four) quarters of the world, who leads mankind aright; Ishtar, the mistress of contest and battle, whose pleasure is (in) war; the great gods, who love my sovereignty, have enlarged my lordship, might and rule; my important name, my exalted fame in the presence of (?) the lords they have firmly established for me. Shalmaneser, the king of all people, the prince, the priest of Ashur, the powerful king, King of Assyria, the king of the whole of the four quarters of the world; the sun of all people, who holds dominion over all countries; the king, chosen of the gods, the beloved of Bel, the viceroy of Ashur, the watchful, the lofty prince, who discovers roads and difficult (ways); who treads the tops of the mountains (and) all the mountain forests, who receives the tribute and presents of all regions, who opens up roads above and below; before his powerful battle attack the regions (i.e., the world) become alarmed and the foundations of the countries tremble at the power of his bravery; the manly, the powerful, who under the protection of Ashur and Shamash, the gods, his helpers, marches and

among the princes of the four quarters of the world has no rival; the king of countries, the strong (one), who marches over steep roads, traverses mountains and seas; the son of Ashurnaçirpal, governor of Bel, priest of Ashur, whose priesthood was pleasing to the gods, and to whose feet they subjected all countries; the brilliant descendant of Tukulti-Ninib, who subjugated all his foes and ovewhelmed them like a cyclone.

At the time when Ashur, the great lord, in the fidelity of his heart, with his clear eyes recognized me, and called me to the rule of Assyria, a powerful weapon, bringing destruction to the insubordinate, he intrusted to me all countries, and with a lofty crown he adorned my lordship, . . . he gave me stern orders to subjugate and to subdue the enemies of Ashur.

At the time, at the beginning of my rule, in the first year of my reign, (as) with pomp I took my seat upon the royal throne, I assembled my chariots (and) forces, I entered into the pass of Simesi. To the city Aridi, the stronghold of Ninni, I approached. I besieged and captured the city. I slew many of his warriors. I carried off his spoil. A pyramid of heads in front of his city I erected. Their young men (and) women I burned in a bonfire. While I was quartered in the city Aridi, I received the tribute of the Hargeans, the Harmaseans, the Simeseans, the Simereans, the Sirisheans, the Ulmaneans, horses trained to the yoke, oxen, sheep, wine.

I departed from Aridi. Steep roads, difficult mountains, which, like the point of an iron dagger, raised their peaks to the skies, with axes of bronze (and) copper I battered down. Chariots (and) forces I brought through.

I advanced to Hupushkia. Hupushkia, together with one hundred neighbouring cities, I

---

[*]The chief god of Assyria, also called Assur. The earliest capital city, Ashur (or Assur), was named for him. By Shalmaneser's time, however, Nineveh was the administrative center.

[†]Igigi was a Mesopotamian term for the great gods in general. It was often used together or interchangeably with Anunnaki, which referred specifically to the fifty children of Anu, the god of the sky and ruler of all the gods.

burned with fire. Kakia, King of Nairi, and the rest of his forces, became afraid before the brilliancy of my weapons and betook themselves to the mighty mountains. I ascended the mountains after them. A great battle I fought in the mountains (and) I accomplished their overthrow. Chariots, forces, horses trained to the yoke, from the mountains I brought back. The fear of the splendour of Ashur, my lord, overwhelmed them; they came down (and) seized my feet. Taxes and tribute I placed on them.

From Hupushkia I departed. To Sugunia, the stronghold of Aramu of the land of Urartu, I advanced; the city I besieged, I captured. I slew many of their warriors. I carried off his spoil. A pyramid of heads in front of his city I erected. Fourteen of his neighbouring cities I burned with fire.

From Sugunia I departed. To the sea of the land of Nairi I descended. I washed my weapons in the sea. I offered sacrifices to my gods. At that time, I made a life-size image of myself; the glory of Ashur, the lord, the prince, my lord, and the might of my power I wrote upon it and I set it up above the sea. On my return from the sea, I received the tribute of Asu of Guzana, horses, oxen, sheep, wine, two double-humped dromedaries; to my city Ashur I brought (them).

In the month Iyyar,* on the 13th day I departed from Nineveh, I crossed the Tigris (and) passed over the mountains Hasamu (and) Dihnunu. To the city Lalate, of Ahuni, the son of Adini, I advanced. The fear of the splendour of Ashur, my lord, overwhelmed them. They went up to the [mountains]. The city I destroyed, devastated (and) burned with fire.

From Lalate I departed. To the city of Kira(?)qa, of Ahuni, the son of Adini, I advanced. Ahuni, the son of Adini, trusted to the mass of his forces, and [to offer] engagement and battle [he advanced against me]. Under the protection of Ashur and the great gods I fought

with him (and) accomplished his overthrow. I shut him up in his city.

From Kira(?)qa I departed. To the city Burmarana, of Ahuni, the son of Adini, [I went. The city] I besieged and captured. Three hundred of their fighting men I brought low with my weapons. A pyramid of heads in front of his city I erected. . . . I received the tribute of Hapini, of the city Til-abna, of Gauni, of the city Saru . . . Giri-Ramman, . . . silver, gold, oxen, sheep, wine.

From Burmarana I departed. In ships of lambskins I crossed the Euphrates. I received the tribute of Katazilu, of the land of Qummuhu, silver, gold, oxen, sheep, wine.

To the land of [Paqarru]hbuni, the cities of Ahuni, the son of Adini, on the other side of the Euphrates, I advanced. The overthrow of the land I accomplished, his cities I brought to destruction, (and) with the overthrow of his warriors I filled the broad plain. One thousand three hundred of his fighting men I brought low with (my) weapons.

From Paqarruhbuni I departed. To the cities of Mutalli of Gamgumu I advanced. I received the tribute of Mutalli, of Gamgumu, silver, gold, oxen, sheep, wine, and his daughter with her large dowry.

From Gamgumu I departed. To Lutibu, the stronghold of Hanu of Samala, I advanced. Hanu of Samala, Sapalulme, the Patinian, Ahuni, the son of Adini, Sangara of Carchemish, trusted to each other's help, and they joined forces. They advanced to make battle, and they attacked me. With the splendid forces of Nergal,† who goes before me, with the powerful weapons which Ashur, the lord, presented, I fought with them, accomplished their overthrow (and) I brought low their fighting men with (my) weapons. Like the god Ramman‡ I rained destruction upon them. I cast them into the ditches. With the corpses of their warriors I filled the broad plain. With their blood I dyed the mountain like wool. Many chariots, horses trained to the yoke

*Assyrian months corresponded to Babylonian signs of the Zodiac. The month of Iyyar was the approximate month of Taurus.

†The Mesopotamian god of death.
‡The Assyrian god of storms.

I took away from him. I erected a pyramid of heads in front of his city. I destroyed, devastated (and) burned his cities with fire. . . .

To Dabigu, to Sazabu, the stronghold of Sangara of Carchemish, I advanced. The city I besieged, I captured. Their numerous fighting men I killed, (and) their spoil I carried off. The neighbouring cities I destroyed, devastated (and) burned with fire. The kings of the land . . . to their extent, before the brilliancy of my powerful weapons and my raging battle, became terrified and seized my feet . . . from the land of Patina three talents* of gold, one hundred talents of silver, three hundred talents of copper, three hundred talents of iron, one thousand vessels of copper, one thousand (pieces) of variegated cloth, linen, his daughter with her large dowry, twenty talents of purple cloth, five hundred oxen, five thousand sheep, I received from him. One talent of silver, two talents of purple cloth, . . . hundred beams of cedar as tribute I laid upon him. Yearly in my city Asshur I received it.

As for Hayanu, son of Gabbaru, at the foot of Mount Hamanu, ten talents of silver, ninety talents of copper, thirty talents of iron, three hundred (pieces) of variegated cloth, linen, three hundred oxen, three thousand sheep, two hundred beams of cedar, two . . . of cedar, his daughter, with her dowry, I received from him. Ten mana† of silver, one hundred beams of cedar, one hundred . . . of cedar as tribute I laid upon him. Yearly I received (it).

As for Aramu, son of Agusi, ten mana of gold, six talents of silver, five hundred oxen, five thousand sheep, I received from him. As for Sangara, of Carchemish, three talents of gold, seventy talents of silver, thirty talents of copper, one hundred talents of iron, twenty talents of purple

cloth, five hundred weapons, his daughter with (her) dowry and one hundred daughters of his nobles, five hundred oxen, five thousand sheep, I received from him. Sixty mana of gold, one talent of silver, two talents of purple cloth, I laid upon him. Yearly I received (it) from him. From Katazilu, of Qummuhu, twenty mana of silver, three hundred beams of cedar, yearly I received.

In the eponymy of Ashurbelkain, in the month Tammuz, on the 13th day, I departed from Nineveh. The river Tigris I crossed and I passed over the mountains Hasamu (and) Dihnunu. At the city Til-barsip, the stronghold of Ahuni, the son of Adini, I arrived. Ahuni, the son of Adini, before the brilliancy of my mighty weapons and my raging battle, in order to save his life, crossed the Euphrates during its high water, and passed over to other lands. By the command of Ashur, the great lord, my lord, Tilbarsip, Aligu . . . Shaguka as my royal city I seized. The men of Assyria I settled within (it). Palaces for my royal residence I built in its midst. . . .

To the land of Enzite the land of Ishua I descended. My hands captured Enzite to its whole extent. Their cities I destroyed, devastated (and) burned with fire. Their spoil, their possessions and property without number, I carried off. I made a large image of my royalty. The majesty of Ashur, the great lord, my lord, and the might of my power I wrote (described) thereon. In Saluria, at the foot of Mount Kirequ I set it up.

I departed from Enzite (and) crossed the river Arzania. I advanced to Suhme, Uashtal, its stronghold, I captured. Suhme, to its whole extent, I destroyed, devastated (and) burned with fire. Sua, the lord of their cities, I took with my hand.

From Suhme I departed. To the land of Dayaeni I descended. Dayaeni, to its whole extent, I captured. Their cities I destroyed, devastated and burned with fire. Their spoil, possessions, large property, I took away.

I departed from Dayaeni. To Arzashku, the royal city of Arramu, of Urartu, I advanced. Arramu, of Urartu, before the brilliancy of my mighty weapons, and my raging battle, became

---

*An extremely large unit of both weight and value in ancient Mesopotamia. Its size and worth varied according to location and time period. A talent was approximately 58–67 pounds.

†A large unit of weight and value, usually called a mina, which varied in size and worth. There were often 60 shekels in a mana. A shekel was approximately equivalent to half an ounce of gold or one month's wages for an average worker.

afraid. He abandoned his city and went up to the mountains of Adduri. I climbed the mountains after him and brought about a hard battle in the mountains. Three thousand four hundred of his fighting men I brought low with (my) weapons. Like Ramman I rained destruction upon them. With their blood, like wool, I dyed the mountain. His camp equipment I took away from him. His chariots, riding horses, horses, bulls, calves, his property, spoil, his large possessions, from the mountain I brought back. Arramu, in order to save his life, climbed the difficult mountains. In the strength of my manhood, like a wild bull, I trampled his land (and) his cities I turned into ruins. Arzashku, together with its neighbouring cities, I destroyed [devastated and burned with fire]. Pyramids of heads in front of his city-gate I erected. Some in the midst [of the pyramids I walled in]. Others round about the pyramids I impaled on stakes. . . .

From the sea I departed. To the land of Gilzani I advanced. Asau, King of Gilzani, with his brothers (and) his sons came forth against me. . . . Horses trained to the yoke, oxen, sheep, wine, seven two-humped dromedaries, I received from him. A large image of my royalty I made. The excellence of Ashur, the great lord, my lord, and the might of my power, which I had exercised in Nairi, I wrote (described) thereon (and) in his city, within his temple, I set (it) up.

From Gilzani I departed. To Shilaya, the stronghold of Kaki, King of Hupushkia, I advanced. I besieged (and) captured the city (and) killed many of their fighting men. Three thousand prisoners, their oxen, their sheep, horses, bulls, calves, without number, I carried off (and) brought to my city Asshur. In the passes of Enzite I entered. In the passes of Kirruru, above Arbela, I came out.

As for Ahuni, the son of Adini, who since the time of the kings, my fathers, had exercised authority and power, in the beginning of my sovereignty, in the eponymy of the year of my name, I departed from Nineveh. Til-bursip, his stronghold, I besieged. With my warriors I surrounded (it) and joined battle within it. I cut down its parks and rained the destruction of javelins upon it. Before the brilliancy of my weapons, the splendour of my lordship, he became afraid, he deserted his city (and) to save his life he crossed the Euphrates. In (my) second year, in the eponymy of Ashurbanauçur, I followed after him. The peak of the mountain Shitamrat, on the bank of the Euphrates, which hung suspended from the skies like a cloud, he had made his stronghold. By the command of Ashur, the great lord, my lord, and Nergal, who goes before me, I advanced to Shitamrat, into whose midst among the kings my fathers, no one had approached. In three days the warrior had control of the mountain, his strong heart was for war, he climbed the mountain on foot, (and) destroyed (it). Ahuni trusted to the mass of his forces and came forth against me. He formed a line of battle. The weapons of Ashur, my lord, I directed against them, and their overthrow I accomplished. I cut off the heads of his contestants and with the blood of his fighting men I dyed the mountain. Many of his (men) fled helter-skelter to the rocks of the mountains A hard battle in his city I brought about. The fear of the splendour of Ashur, my lord, overwhelmed them, they came down and seized my feet. Ahuni with his forces, chariots, riding horses, the large property of their palace, whose weight was not taken, I brought back before me, caused to cross the river Tigris, brought to my city Asshur, and reckoned them with the people of my land.

In that year I went to Mazamua. Into the pass of Bunaislu I entered. I advanced to the cities Nikdime (and) Nikdera. Before the brilliancy of my powerful weapons and my raging battle they became afraid. In ships of wickerwork they put to sea. In ships (rafts) of lamb-skins I followed them. I forced a hard battle on the sea (and) accomplished their overthrow. I dyed the sea with their blood like wool.

In the eponymy of Dan-Ashur, in the month Iyyar, on the 14th day, I departed from Nineveh. I crossed the Tigris and to the cities of Giammu on the river Balich I advanced. They were afraid of the terror of my lordship (and) the brilliancy of my powerful weapons, and with their own weapons they killed Giammu, their lord. The cities Kitlala and Tilshaturahi I entered. I brought my gods into his palaces, and I made a festival in his palaces. I opened his store-house, inspected his treasure, carried off his property and possessions, and brought (them) to my city Asshur.

I departed from Kitlala (and) advanced to Kar-Shalmaneser. In ships of lamb-skins, for the second time, I crossed the Euphrates during its high water. The tribute of the kings beyond the Euphrates, (viz.) Sangar of Carchemish, Kundashpi of Qummuhu, Arame, son of Gusi, Lalli of Melitu, Hayani, son of Gabari, Kalparuda of Patinu, Kalparuda of Gamgumu, silver, gold, copper, vessels of copper, in the city of Ashuruttiraçbat, beyond the Euphrates, on the Sagur, which the Hatti call Pitru, I received.

I departed from the Euphrates (and) advanced to Halman. They avoided battle (and) seized my feet. Silver, gold, their tribute, I received. Sacrifices to Ramman of Halman I offered.

From Halman I departed (and) to the cities of Irhuleni of Hamath I advanced. Adenu, Barga, Argana, his royal city, I captured. His spoil, possessions, the property of his palaces, I brought forth (and) his palaces I set on fire.

I departed from Argana (and) advanced to Qarqara. Qarqara, his royal city, I destroyed, devastated (and) burned with fire. One thousand two hundred chariots, one thousand two hundred riding-horses, twenty thousand soldiers of Benhadad of Damascus; seven hundred chariots, seven hundred riding-horses, ten thousand soldiers of Irhuleni of Hamath; ten thousand soldiers of Ahab, of Israel; five hundred soldiers of the Guians; one thousand soldiers of the Egyptians; ten chariots, ten thousand soldiers of the Irqanateans; two hundred soldiers of Matinubale of Arvad; two hundred soldiers of the Usanatians; thirty chariots, ten thousand soldiers of Aduni-balu of the Shianians; one thousand camels of Gindubu, the Arbean . . . ten thousand soldiers of Basa, son of Ruhubi, the Amanean; these twelve (?) kings came to his aid. To make war and battle they came against me. With the splendid forces which Ashur, the lord, had given, with the powerful weapons, which Nergal, who goes before me, had presented, I fought with them. From Qarqara to Gilzan I accomplished their overthrow. Fourteen thousand soldiers, their fighting men, I brought low with (my) weapons. Like Ramman I rained destruction upon them (and) I scattered their corpses. I filled the ruins with their numerous soldiers; with my weapons I made their blood to flow down the ravines of the district. The plain was too small for their complete overthrow; the broad stretch was used for their graves. With their bodies I damned the Orontes. In that battle, their chariots, their riding-horses, their horses trained to the yoke, I took away from them.

REVIEW QUESTIONS

1. How would you characterize the nature of Shalmaneser's most important (according to him) accomplishments? From this can you make any generalizations about the values of Assyrian culture?
2. What do you think is the purpose of deliberately repetitive patterns in the inscription of Shalmaneser?
3. How does this inscription compare to the Moabite Stone?
4. Modern apologists for the ancient Assyrian Empire claim that its reputation for violence and brutality is greatly exaggerated, primarily because its enemies wrote much of its history. They also speculate that the Assyrians themselves may have inflated stories of their cruelty. What do you think of this argument?

A Hebrew Prophet Celebrates the Fall of Nineveh (seventh century B.C.E.)

Nahum 2:12–3:17

Nahum was one of the so-called minor prophets of the ancient Hebrews. Nothing is known of Nahum himself except that he was an Alkoshite, but the location of these people is uncertain. In the Old Testament book of poetry that bears his name, he reveled in the destruction of Nineveh, the capital of Assyria, which fell to a military alliance of the Chaldeans and Medes in 612 B.C.E. Some scholars are convinced that the book of Nahum is an actual account of the fall of the city; others, however, believe that Nahum wrote the verses as prophecy, foretelling the destruction of Nineveh.

THE LION OF ASSYRIA THREATENED

Where is the lions' den,*
the cave of the lion's whelps?
When the lion made his foray the lioness
    stayed behind,
the lion's cubs too; and no one molested them.
The lion clawed enough for his whelps,
and tore up prey for his lionesses;
he filled his caves with his spoil,
and his dens with the prey.
I am here! Look to yourself!—It is Yahweh
    Sabaoth† who speaks.
I mean to send your chariots up in smoke;
the sword shall devour your lion's whelps.
I will wipe the earth clean of your plunder,
the voice of your envoys shall be heard no
    more.

NINEVEH THREATENED FOR ITS CRIMES

Woe to the city soaked in blood,
full of lies,

stuffed with booty,
whose plunderings know no end!
The crack of the whip!
The rumble of wheels!
Galloping horse,
jolting chariot,
charging cavalry,
flash of swords,
gleam of spears . . .
a mass of wounded,
hosts of dead,
countless corpses;
they stumble over the dead.
So much for all the whore's debauchery,
for that wonderful beauty, for that cunning
    witch
who enslaved nations by her debauchery
and tribes by her spells.
I am here! Look to yourself! It is Yahweh
    Sabaoth who speaks.
I mean to lift your skirts as high as your face
and show your nakedness to nations,
your shame to kingdoms.
I am going to pelt you with filth,
shame you, make you a public show.
And all who look on you
will turn their backs on you and say,
"Nineveh is a ruin."
Could anyone pity her?
Where can I find anyone to comfort her?

---

*The lion was the royal symbol of Assyria.
†The Hebrews had many different names for God, depending on the situation. Yahweh Sabaoth can be translated as "Yahweh the Warrior."

THE LESSON OF THEBES

Are you mightier than No-amon*
who had her throne beside the river,
who had the sea for outer wall,
the waters for rampart?
Her strength was Ethiopia,
Egypt too; she had no boundaries.
Men of Put and the Libyans were her auxil-
    iaries.
And yet she was forced into exile,
she went into captivity;
her little ones, too, were dashed to pieces
at every crossroad;
lots were drawn for her nobles,
all her great men were loaded with chains.
You too will be encircled,
you will be overwhelmed;
you too will have to search
for a refuge from the enemy.

NINEVEH'S PREPARATIONS USELESS

Your fortresses are all fig trees
laden with early-ripening figs:
shake, and they fall
into any mouth that wants to eat them.
Look at your people:
your inhabitants are women.
The gates of your country
stand wide open to the foe;
fire has burned up your locking beams.†
Draw water for the siege,
strengthen your bulwarks,
tread the mud, tread down the clay,
set your hand to the brick mold.
There the fire will burn you up,
the sword will cut you down.

---

*The Egyptian city of Thebes, the "city of Amon." The As-
syrians sacked Thebes in 663 during their conquest of Egypt.

†Locking beams were used to bar and lock large doors, especially the gates to cities.

REVIEW QUESTIONS

1. What values and attitudes of Assyrian culture can you discern from this poem? How
   do the Assyrians compare to the Hebrews?
2. How would you characterize the tone of this excerpt from the book of Nahum?
3. In whose voice did Nahum speak? Why do you think he chose this avenue of expression?

A Greek Historian Examines Persian Customs (fifth century B.C.E.)

HERODOTUS, *The Histories, Book I*

The Greek historian Herodotus (c. 484–425 B.C.E.), called the "Father of History," was born in Halicarnassus in Asia Minor, which was at that time a part
of the Persian Empire. His great work, *The Histories* ("Researches" or "Inquiries" in Greek), is considered the first truly analytical history in the Western world. Although it is generally considered a history of the Persian Wars
(490–479), six of its nine books trace the rise of Persia, a multiethnic empire

that stretched from the Nile to the Indus Rivers. In his quest to answer the question "Why did the Greeks and Persians go to war?" Herodotus spent approximately seventeen years traveling through Greece, the Middle East, Africa, and the Mediterranean. Everywhere he collected research materials, interviewed Greeks and non-Greeks who had participated in events related to the war, and observed firsthand the customs, religions, and histories of places he visited.

In the following selection, Herodotus described Persian society based on his own observations. He was a careful observer, but not perfect. For example, he mistook the Persian sun god, Mithras, for a female goddess of love named Mitra. However, a particular strength of Herodotus's examination of Persian customs is its surprising objectivity, especially considering that the Greeks had been forced to expel Persian invasion forces from Greece not once, but twice. Despite his apparent admiration for many Persian customs, it is important to note that Herodotus retained his Greek identity throughout his writing, examining nearly everything he saw against the model of Greek civilization.

The following are certain Persian customs which I can describe from personal knowledge. The erection of statues, temples, and altars is not an accepted practice amongst them, and anyone who does such a thing is considered a fool, because, presumably, the Persian religion is not anthropomorphic like the Greek. Zeus,* in their system, is the whole circle of the heavens, and they sacrifice to him from the tops of mountains. They also worship the sun, moon, and earth, fire, water, and winds, which are their only original deities: it was later that they learned from the Assyrians and Arabians the cult of Uranian Aphrodite.† The Assyrian name for Aphrodite is Mylitta, the Arabian Alilat, the Persian Mitra.‡

As for ceremonial, when they offer sacrifice to the deities I mentioned, they erect no altar and kindle no fire; the libation, the flute-music, the garlands, the sprinkled meal—all those things, familiar to us, they have no use for; but before a ceremony a man sticks a spray of leaves, usually myrtle leaves, into his headdress, takes his victim to some open place and invokes the deity to whom he wishes to sacrifice. The actual worshipper is not permitted to pray for any personal or private blessing, but only for the king and for the general good of the community, of which he is himself a part. When he has cut up the animal and cooked it, he makes a little heap of the softest green-stuff he can find, preferably clover, and lays all the meat upon it. This done, a Magus§ (a member of this caste is always present at sacrifices) utters an incantation over it in a form of words which is supposed to recount the Birth of the Gods. Then after a short interval the worshipper removes the flesh and does what he pleases with it.

Of all days in the year a Persian most distinguishes his birthday, and celebrates it with a dinner of special magnificence. A rich Persian on his birthday will have an ox or a horse or a camel or a donkey baked whole in the oven and served up at table, and the poor some smaller

---

*This may refer to a pre-Persian Indo-European sky or storm god, Dyaus, of whom Zeus was probably a variant. Or, it may be a reference to the Zoroastrian god of light and goodness, Ahura Mazda.
†The worship of Aphrodite can be traced to Astarte, a Mesopotamian goddess. In Plato's *Symposium,* Socrates suggested that the goddess of passion and beauty existed in two guises: the common, earthly Aphrodite, and the Uranian, or heavenly, Aphrodite. In her Uranian embodiment, she represented the desires of the soul rather than the body.
‡An erroneous reference to the god Mithras, who was not a female deity named Mitra. In fact, the worship of Mithras was limited to men.

---

§A Persian priest or wise man, usually, but not necessarily, Zoroastrian.

beast. The main dishes at their meals are few, but they have many sorts of dessert, the various courses being served separately. It is this custom that has made them say that the Greeks leave the table hungry, because we never have anything worth mentioning after the first course: they think that if we did, we should go on eating. They are very fond of wine, and no one is allowed to vomit or relieve himself in the presence of another person.

If an important decision is to be made, they discuss the question when they are drunk, and the following day the master of the house where the discussion was held submits their decision for reconsideration when they are sober. If they still approve it, it is adopted; if not, it is abandoned. Conversely, any decision they make when they are sober, is reconsidered afterwards when they are drunk.

When Persians meet in the streets one can always tell by their mode of greeting whether or not they are of the same rank; for they [do] not speak but kiss—their equals upon the mouth, those somewhat superior on the cheeks. A man of greatly inferior rank prostrates himself in profound reverence. After their own nation they hold their nearest neighbours most in honour, then the nearest but one—and so on, their respect decreasing as the distance grows, and the most remote being the most despised. Themselves they consider in every way superior to everyone else in the world, and allow other nations a share of good qualities decreasing according to distance, the furthest off being in their view the worst. By a similar sort of principle the Medes[*] extended their system of administration and government during the period of their dominance: the various nations governed each other, the Medes being the supreme authority and concerning themselves specially with their nearest neighbours; these in their

turn ruling *their* neighbours, who were responsible for the next, and so on.

No race is so ready to adopt foreign ways as the Persian; for instance, they wear the Median costume because they think it handsomer than their own, and their soldiers wear the Egyptian corselet. Pleasures, too, of all sorts they are quick to indulge in when they get to know about them—a notable instance is pederasty, which they learned from the Greeks. Every man has a number of wives, and a much greater number of concubines. After prowess in fighting, the chief proof of manliness is to be the father of a large family of boys. Those who have the most sons receive an annual present from the king—on the principle that there is strength in numbers. The period of a boy's education is between the ages of five and twenty, and they are taught three things only: to ride, to use the bow, and to speak the truth. Before the age of five a boy lives with the women and never sees his father, the object being to spare the father distress if the child should die in the early stages of its upbringing. In my view this is a sound practice. I admire also the custom which forbids even the king himself to put a man to death for a single offence, and any Persian under similar circumstances to punish a servant by an irreparable injury. Their way is to balance faults against services, and then, if the faults are greater and more numerous, anger may take its course. They declare that no man has ever yet killed his father or mother; in the cases where this has apparently happened, they are quite certain that inquiry would reveal that the son was either a changeling or born out of wedlock, for they insist that it is most improbable that the actual parent should be killed by his child. What they are forbidden to do, they are forbidden also to mention. They consider telling lies more disgraceful than anything else, and, next to that, owing money. There are many reasons for their horror of debt, but the chief is their conviction that a man who owes money is bound also to tell lies. Sufferers from the scab or from leprosy are isolated and forbidden the city. They say these diseases are punishments for of-

---

[*]Neighbors and former overlords of the Persians. The Greeks frequently mixed the two terms, calling the Persians Medes and vice versa. Herodotus did not make this mistake, however.

fending the sun, and they expel any stranger who catches them: many Persians drive away even white doves, as if they, too, were guilty of the same offence. They have a profound reverence for rivers: they will never pollute a river with urine or spittle, or even wash their hands in one, or allow anyone else to do so. There is one other peculiarity which one notices about them, though they themselves are unaware of it: all their names, which express magnificence or physical qualities, end in the letter S (the Dorian 'san').* Inquiry will prove this in every case without exception.

All this I am able to state definitely from personal knowledge. There is another practice, however, concerning the burial of the dead, which is not spoken of openly and is something of a mystery: it is that a male Persian is never buried until the body has been torn by a bird or

_____

*This is actually only true with regard to Greek translations of Persian names.

a dog.† I know for certain that the Magi have this custom, for they are quite open about it. The Persians in general, however, cover a body with wax and then bury it.‡ The Magi are a peculiar caste, quite different from the Egyptian priests and indeed from any other sort of person. The Egyptian priests make it an article of religion to kill no living creature except for sacrifice, but the Magi not only kill anything, except dogs and men, with their own hands but make a special point of doing so; ants, snakes, animals, birds—no matter what, they kill them indiscriminately. Well, it is an ancient custom, so let them keep it.

_____

†Herodotus was probably describing a custom he had heard about but not actually witnessed. The Zoroastrians placed their dead on elevated platforms, "towers of silence," where scavengers and carrion-eaters picked the bodies clean, and where the sun, wind, and rain then cleansed the bones further. Eventually the bleached bones were gathered and placed in specially constructed wells so as not to pollute the earth.
‡Although many Persians were Zoroastrian, many were not. Known for their tolerance and respect for other religions, they did not force their beliefs on their subject peoples.

REVIEW QUESTIONS

1. How did Persian and Greek religious rituals differ?
2. How did Persian and Greek dining customs differ?
3. What, if anything, can you infer about Greek family life from Herodotus's description of marriage and child-rearing in Persia?
3. What did Herodotus particularly admire about the Persians? Why?
4. Does it seem strange to you that Herodotus would admire anything about the Persians, who had twice invaded Greece? What does this say about Herodotus's character? The character of the Greeks in general?

A Greek Soldier Admires a Persian Prince (late fifth century B.C.E.)

XENOPHON, *Anabasis, Book I*

Cyrus the Younger was a son of the Persian king, Darius II. Still smarting from the Persian loss to the Greeks—especially the Athenians—Darius decided to support Sparta against Athens in the Peloponnesian Wars. In 408, he sent

Cyrus into Asia Minor as commander of the Persian forces and satrap (governor) of Lydia, Phrygia, and Cappadocia. Born after his father's accession in 424, Cyrus could not have been more than sixteen years old at the time, but he was surprisingly successful. His strenuous support of the Spartans both accelerated the career of their general, Lysander, and contributed to their ultimate victory. In return, Cyrus hoped that Lysander would help him overthrow his elder brother, Artaxerxes II, who inherited the Persian throne in 404. Under the pretext of attacking the Pisidians, a troublesome tribe in the Taurus Mountains, Cyrus gathered a large army. It included a substantial contingent of Spartans, as well as mercenaries from other Greek city-states. In the spring of 401, Cyrus and his troops marched, not into the Taurus Mountains, but into Babylonia, where they later met the army of Artaxerxes at the battle of Cunaxa. Cyrus was killed, and during negotiations after the battle, the Persian satrap Tissaphernes treacherously murdered the officers in command of the Spartans. Cyrus's Persian troops abandoned the rest of the Greek soldiers, who managed with great difficulty to march to the shores of the Black Sea, where there were several Greek colonies.

One of the Greek soldiers who participated in Cyrus's expedition was an Athenian student of Socrates named Xenophon (430–c. 355). A member of an elite but not noble family, he had fought in the Peloponnesian Wars; but the democratic Athenians disliked his class because, after the war, many of its members had supported the Spartan-imposed government of Thirty Tyrants. Thus, after his return from Persia Xenophon continued to serve with the Spartan army. After Sparta's crushing defeat at Leuctra in 371 (see Cornelius Nepos on the life of Epaminondas in the previous chapter), he retired from military life and devoted the rest of his life to writing. The date of his death is unknown; all that can be said is that he must have died sometime after 355, the date of his last book. In addition to the *Anabasis,* he wrote at least twelve major works, including the *Memorabilia (Recollections of Socrates), the Oeconomics,* and the *Symposium.*

Xenophon's first major work was a detailed history of Cyrus's expedition against Artaxerxes, the *Anabasis,* frequently called *The Persian Expedition.* Composed between 379 and 371, the *Anabasis* describes the march from Sardis to the Upper Tigris Valley and then north to the Black Sea. It was originally published under an assumed name, Themistogenes of Syracuse, presumably because he was exiled from Athens at the time and wanted the work to be judged for its own sake rather than for the politics of its author. Like Julius Caesar several centuries later, Xenophon told his story in the third person, which allowed him to distance himself from the action, describing events and people with relative detachment. Objectivity is completely missing, however, in his description of Cyrus the Younger. Xenophon obviously knew and liked the young prince tremendously. No man, he claimed, was more worthy of imperial power.

Of all the Persians who lived after Cyrus the Great, he [Cyrus the Younger] was the most like a king and the most deserving of an empire, as is admitted by everyone who is known to have been personally acquainted with him. In his early life, when he was still a child being brought up with his brother, and the other children, he was regarded as the best of them all in every way. All the children of Persian nobles are brought up at the Court, and there a child can pick up many lessons in good behaviour while having no chance of seeing or hearing anything bad. The boys see and hear some people being honoured by the King and others being dismissed in disgrace, and so from their childhood they learn how to command and how to obey. Here, at the Court, Cyrus was considered, first, to be the best-behaved of his contemporaries and more willing even than his inferiors to listen to those older than himself; and then he was remarkable for his fondness for horses and being able to manage them extremely well. In the soldierly arts also of archery and javelin-throwing they judged him to be most eager to learn and most willing to practise them. When he got to the age for hunting, he was most enthusiastic about it, and only too ready to take risks in his encounters with wild animals. There was one occasion, when a she-bear charged at him and he, showing no fear, got to grips with the animal and was pulled off his horse. The scars from the wounds he got then were still visible on his body, but he killed the animal in the end, and as for the first man who came to help him Cyrus made people think him very lucky indeed.

When he was sent down to the coast by his father as satrap [governor] of Lydia and Great Phrygia and Cappadocia,[*] and had been declared Commander-in-Chief of all who are bound to muster in the plain of Castolus [in Lydia], the first thing he did was to make it clear that in any league or agreement or undertaking that he made be attached the utmost importance to keeping his word. The cities which were in his command trusted him and so did the men. And the enemies he had were confident that once Cyrus had signed a treaty with them nothing would happen to them contrary to the terms of the treaty. Consequently when he was at war with Tissaphernes[†] all the cities, with the exception of the Milesians,[‡] chose to follow him rather than Tissaphernes. The Milesians were afraid of him because he refused to give up the cause of the exiled government. Indeed, he made it clear by his actions, and said openly that, once he had become their friend, he would never give them up, not even if their numbers became fewer and their prospects worse than they were.

If anyone did him a good or an evil turn, he evidently aimed at going one better. Some people used to refer to an habitual prayer of his, that he might live long enough to be able to repay with interest both those who had helped him and those who had injured him. It was quite natural then that he was the one man in our times to whom so many people were eager to hand over their money, their cities and their own persons.

No one, however, could say that he allowed criminals and evil-doers to mock his authority. On the contrary, his punishments were exceptionally severe, and along the more frequented roads one often saw people who had been blinded or had had their feet or hands cut off. The result was that in Cyrus's provinces anyone, whether Greek or native, who was doing no harm could travel without fear wherever he liked and could take with him whatever he wanted.

Of course it is well known that he treated with exceptional distinction all those who showed ability for war. In his first war, which was against the Pisidians and Mysians,[§] he marched into their country himself and made those whom he saw willing to risk their lives governors over the territory which he conquered; and afterwards he

---

[†]The Persian satrap of Sardis. He used the rivalry between Cyrus and Artaxerxes to his own advantage, denounced Cyrus, and then became his successor as satrap of Asia Minor.

[‡]Residents of the city of Miletus, an Ionian city in southwest Asia Minor. It had instigated the Ionian Revolt in 499, which eventually led to the Persian invasion of Greece and the ensuing Persian Wars. In 494 the Persians had captured the city and burned its temples.

[§]Mysia was a small state north of Lydia and south of the Propontis (Sea of Marmora). Its most important city was Pergamum.

---

[*]Lydia was a substantial kingdom in central eastern Asia Minor. Phrygia was a large but vaguely defined region to the east of Lydia. It stretched across much of central western Asia Minor. Cappadocia was located to the east of Phrygia.

gave them other honours and rewards, making it clear that the brave were going to be the most prosperous while the cowards only deserved to be their slaves. Consequently there was never any lack of people who were willing to risk their lives when they thought that Cyrus would get to know of it.

As for justice, he made it his supreme aim to see those who really wanted to live in accordance with its standards became richer than those who wanted to profit by transgressing them. It followed from this that not only were his affairs in general conducted justly, but he enjoyed the services of an army that really was an army. Generals and captains who crossed the sea to take service under him as mercenaries knew that to do Cyrus good service paid better than any monthly wage. Indeed, whenever anyone carried out effectively a job which he had assigned, he never allowed his good work to go unrewarded. Consequently it was said that Cyrus got the best officers for any kind of job.

When he saw that a man was a capable administrator, acting on just principles, improving the land under his control and making it bring in profit, he never took his post away from him, but always gave him additional responsibility. The result was that his administrators did their work cheerfully and made money confidently. Cyrus was the last person whom they kept in the dark about their possessions, since he showed no envy for those who became rich openly, but, on the contrary, tried to make use of the wealth of people who attempted to conceal what they had.

Everyone agrees that he was absolutely remarkable for doing services to those whom he made friends of and knew to be true to him and considered able to help him in doing whatever job was on hand. He thought that the reason why he needed friends was to have people to help him, and he applied exactly the same principle to others, trying to be of the utmost service to his friends whenever he knew that any of them wanted anything. I suppose that he received more presents than any other single individual, and this for a variety of reasons. But more than anyone else he shared them with his friends, always considering what each individual was like and what, to his knowledge, he needed most. When people sent him fine things to wear, either armour or beautiful dresses, they say that the remark he made about these was that he could not possibly wear all this finery on his own body, but he thought the finest thing for a man was that his friends should be well turned out. There is, no doubt, nothing surprising in the fact that he surpassed his friends in doing them great services, since he had the greater power to do so. What seems to me more admirable than this is the fact that he outdid them in ordinary consideration and in the anxiety to give pleasure. Often, when he had had a particularly good wine, he used to send jars half full of it to his friends with the message: "Cyrus has not for a long time come across a better wine than this; so he has sent some to you and wants you to finish it up to-day with those whom you love best." Often too he used to send helpings of goose and halves of loaves and such things, telling the bearer to say when he presented them: "Cyrus enjoyed this; so he wants you to taste it too." When there was a scarcity of fodder,—though he himself, because of the number of his servants and his own wise provision, was able to get hold of it,—he used to send round to his friends and tell them to give the fodder he sent to the horses they rode themselves, so that horses which carried his friends should not go hungry.

Whenever he went on an official journey, and was likely to be seen by great numbers of people, he used to call his friends to him and engage them in serious conversation, so that he might show what men he honoured. My own opinion, therefore, based on what I have heard, is that there has never been anyone, Greek or foreigner, more generally beloved. And an additional proof of this is in the fact that, although Cyrus was a subject, no one deserted him and went over to the King [Artaxerxes], except that Orontas* tried to do so; but in his case he soon found that the man whom he thought reliable was more of a friend to Cyrus than to him. On the other

----

*The Persian satrap of Armenia.

hand there were many who left the King and came over to Cyrus, when war broke out between the two, and these also were people who had been particularly favoured by the King; but they came to the conclusion that if they did well under Cyrus their services would be better rewarded than they would be by the King. What happened at the time of his death is also a strong proof not only of his own courage but of his ability to pick out accurately people who were reliable, devoted and steadfast. For when he died every one of his friends and table-companions died fighting for him, except Ariaeus, who had been posted on the left wing in command of the cavalry. When Ariaeus heard that Cyrus had fallen, he and the whole army which he led took to flight.

REVIEW QUESTIONS

1. How did Cyrus's childhood prepare him for leadership?
2. Which of Cyrus's many outstanding qualities did Xenophon most admire? Why? Which did he least admire? Why?
3. According to Xenophon's characterization of Cyrus, what in the prince's character made him particularly worthy to be a king?
4. Considering that the Persians were enemies of the Greeks, why do you think Xenophon, an Athenian by birth, admired Cyrus so greatly?

A Han Ambassador Reports on Bactria and Its Neighbors (138–126 B.C.E.)

SSU-MA CH'IEN, *Shi Chi, The Diplomatic Report of Chang Ch'ien*

The report of a Chinese envoy to the West, Chang Ch'ien, provides fairly detailed and reliable accounts of several regions in western Asia, particularly Ferghana, Sogdiana, Parthia, Bactria, Syria, and Babylonia. It survives in the *Shi Chi (Memoirs of a Historian),* by Ssu-ma Ch'ien, the "Chinese Herodotus," who established the model for historical writing in China. Explaining his method, he declared that his narrative was "no more than a systematization of the material that has been handed down to us. There is therefore no creation; only a faithful representation." In keeping with this philosophy, Ssu-ma Ch'ien first wrote a brief history of Chang Ch'ien's journey, then followed it with an exact copy of the ambassador's report to the emperor.

Chang Ch'ien was an official in the emperor's household in the second century B.C.E. Hoping to find allies in Bactria (roughly modern Afghanistan) to help him defeat the Huns, the Han emperor Wu-ti sent Chang Ch'ien on a mission beyond the western borders of China. He was almost immediately captured by the Hsiung-nu, nomadic and warlike nomads who were probably the ancestors of the Huns who invaded eastern Europe several centuries later (see Chapter 4). Pushed west by the Chinese, the Hsiung-nu seem to have settled for a time south of the Ural Mountains, an area through which the route to Bactria passed. Chang Ch'ien lived as a hostage with them for ten years before he escaped and finally made his way to Bactria. There he found a situation that was not particularly conducive to forging diplomatic relations or securing military aid against the Huns.

By the late first century B.C.E., Bactria was suffering from several centuries of conflict that included conquest by the Persian, Macedonian, and Hellenistic kings Cyrus, Alexander, and Seleuccus, respectively. The Greeks had done their best to Hellenize the area by speaking Greek, building new cities on their own western model, minting Greek-style coins, and introducing classical artistic aesthetics, but these influences did not last, other than to inject a strong element of Hellenism into Buddhist art. The weakness of the declining Seleucid Empire, however, gave the Bactrian satrap Diodotus an opportunity to declare Bactria an independent kingdom in 255. For slightly more than one hundred years, it flourished as a small empire, though it had continuing problems with its neighbors to the west and east, Parthia and the kingdoms of northwest India. In 159, nomads whom the Chinese called the Yueh-chih (Yu-chi) overran Bactria's northern neighbor, Sogdiana; in 139 they conquered Bactria. Severely weakened by constant invasion and war, Bactria was easy prey for the next group of conquerors, the Kushans. By 120, shortly after Chang Ch'ien's visit, Bactria had begun its final decline—within three generations it was no longer a recognizable historical entity.

Our first knowledge of Ta-yuan [Ferghana] dates from Chang Ch'ien, a native of Han-chung, in the south of Shensi Province. During the Ch'ien-yuan reign [140–134 B.C.] he was a *lang,* a titular officer of the imperial household. At that time the Son of Heaven made inquiries among those of the Hsiung-nu [Huns] who had surrendered and been made prisoners, and they all reported that the Hsiung-nu had overcome the king of the Yueh-chih and made a drinking vessel out of his skull. The Yueh-chih had decamped and were hiding somewhere, constantly scheming how to revenge themselves on the Hsiung-nu; but they had no ally to join with them in striking a blow.

The Chinese, wishing to declare war on the Huns to wipe them out, when they learned this, desired to establish contact with the Yueh-chih; but the road to them led through the territory of the Huns. The emperor called for volunteers. Chang Ch'ien, being a *lang,* responded to the call and enlisted in a mission to seek out the Yueh-chih. He took with him Kan Fu, a Tartar who had been a slave of the T'ang-i family, and set out from Kansu to cross the Hun territory. Almost immediately he was caught, taken prisoner, and sent to the Great Khan, who detained him, saying, "The Yueh-chih are to the north of us. How can China send ambassadors to them? If I wanted to send ambassadors to Kiangsi and Chekiang, would China be willing to submit to us?" He held Chang Ch'ien for more than ten years; he gave him a wife by whom he had a son. All this time Chang Ch'ien kept possession of the emperor's token of authority, and when in the course of time he was permitted greater freedom, he watched his opportunity and succeeded in making his escape with his men. He went in the direction of the Yueh-chih. Having marched several tens of days to the west, he arrived at Ta-yuan.* The inhabitants, having heard of the

---

*The Ta-yuan seem to have been related to the Hsiung-nu, or perhaps were a subsidiary tribe of the Huns.

wealth and fertility of China, had vainly tried to communicate with it. When, therefore, they saw Chang Ch'ien, they asked joyfully, "Where do you wish to go?" And he replied, "I was sent by the Emperor of China to the Yueh-chih and was made prisoner by the Hsiung-nu. I have now escaped them and would ask your king to have someone guide me to the country of the Yueh-chih. If I succeed in reaching that country, on my return my king will reward you with untold treasures."

The Ta-yuan believed his story and gave him safe-conduct on postal roads to K'ang-chu [Sogdiana] and they sent him on to the Yueh-chih. After the king of the Yueh-chih had been killed by the Huns, the people set up his heir as king (though one authority says it was the queen who named the successor). Since that time they had conquered Ta-hsia [Bactria] and occupied the country. It was a rich and fertile land, seldom harassed by robbers, and the people decided to enjoy this life of peace. Moreover, since they considered themselves too far away from China, they no longer wanted to revenge themselves on the Huns. After having made his way through so many tribes to find Bactria, Chang Ch'ien was unable to persuade the Yueh-chih to move against their former enemy. He remained there for a year and then started for home, skirting the Nan-shan in the hopes of going through the country of the Tanguts. But again he was caught and made a prisoner of the Huns. Thus a whole year passed; the khan died and the "left" highly honored prince attacked the rightful heir and usurped the throne, throwing the country into a state of confusion. This was the time Chang Ch'ien, accompanied by his Tartar wife and Kan Fu, the Tartar and former slave, escaped and made his way back to China.

The Emperor Wu-ti [reigned 140–87 B.C.] appointed Chang Ch'ien Imperial Chamberlain and gave Kan Fu the title of Gentleman Attending the Embassy. Chang Ch'ien was a man of strong physique, magnanimous and trustful, and popular with the foreign tribes in the south and west. The Tartar Kan Fu was an excellent bowman and, when supplies were exhausted, provided food by hunting game. When Chang Ch'ien started on his journey [138 B.C.] he had more than a hundred men in his caravan; thirteen years later, only two had lived to return [126 B.C.]. Of the countries he had visited personally, Chang Ch'ien gave this report to his emperor.

FERGHANA: is to the southwest of the Huns and due west of China at a distance of about 10,000 *li.* The people are settled and engage in agriculture; in their fields they raise rice and wheat. They have wine made of grapes and many good horses. The horses sweat blood and come from the stock of the Heavenly Horse. They have walled cities and houses; the large and small cities belonging to them, fully seventy in number, contain an aggregate population of several hundreds of thousands. Their arms consist of bows and halberds, and they can shoot arrows while on horseback. North of this country is Sogdiana; in the west are the Indo-Scythians; in the southwest is Bactria; in the northeast are the Wu-sun; and in the east Han-mi [?] and Khotan. All the rivers west of Khotan flow in a westerly direction and feed the Western Sea; all the rivers east of it flow east and feed the Salt Lake [Lop-nor]. The Salt Lake flows underground. To the south of Khotan is the source from which the Yellow River [the Ho] arises. The country contains much jade. The river flows through China; the towns of Lou-lan and Ku-shi with their city walls closely border on the Salt Lake, which is possibly 5000 *li* from Chang-an [Wu-ti's capital]. The Western Huns live to the east of the Salt Lake up to the Great Wall in Lung-hsi. They are bounded on the south by the Tanguts, who bar their road to China.

WU-SUN: may be 2000 *li* northeast of Ferghana. Its people are nomads following their herds of cattle; their customs resemble those of the Huns. Of archers they have several tens of thousands, all daring warriors. Formerly they were subject to the Huns, but they grew so strong that though they maintain nominal vassalage they refuse to attend the meetings of the court.

SOGDIANA: is to the northwest of Ferghana, possibly 2000 *li* distant. It also is a country of nomads with manners and customs very similar to those of the Yueh-chih. They have eighty or ninety thousand archers. The country is coterminous with Ferghana. It is small. In the south it is under the political influence of the Yueh-chih; in the east, under that of the Huns.

AORSI: lies to the northeast of Sogdiana perhaps at a distance of 2000 *li*. It is a nomad state and its manners and customs are in the main identical with those of Sogdiana. It has fully a hundred thousand archers. The country lies close to a great sea ["great marsh," the Sea of Azov] which has no limit, for it is the Northern Sea.

INDO-SCYTHIANS: are perhaps two or three thousand *li* to the west of Ferghana. They live to the north of the Oxus. South of them is Bactria; in the west is Parthia; in the north, Sogdiana. They are a nomad nation, following their flocks and changing their abodes. Their customs are the same as the Huns. They may have from one to two hundred thousand archers. In olden times they relied on their strength and thought lightly of the Huns; but when Mao-tun ascended the throne he attacked and defeated the Yueh-chih. Up to the time when Lau-chang, khan of the Huns, killed the king of the Yueh-chih and made a drinking vessel out of his skull, the Yueh-chih had lived between Tun-huang and Ch'i-lien, a hill southwest, but when they were beaten by the Huns, they fled to a distant country and crossed to the west of Ferghana, attacked Bactria, and conquered it. Subsequently, they established their capital north of the Oxus and made it the court of their king. The minority, who were left behind and were unable to follow the main body, took refuge among the Tanguts, who occupied the Nan-shan and were called the Small Yueh-chih.

PARTHIA: [*An-hsi*, the Chinese name, is derived from Antioch in Margiana, Merv.] This country I did not visit personally, but I learned that it may be several thousand *li* west of the Indo-Scythians. The people live in fixed abodes and are given to agriculture; their fields yield rice and wheat; and they make wine of grapes. Several hundred small and large cities belong to it. The territory is several thousand *li* square; it

is a very large country and close to the Oxus. Their traders and merchants travel in carts and boats to the neighboring countries, perhaps several thousand *li* distant. They make coins of silver; the coins resemble their king's face. Upon the death of a king the coins are changed for others on which the new king's face is represented. They paint rows of characters running sideways on stiff leather to serve them as records. West of this country is Babylonia; north is Aorsi.

SYRIA AND BABYLONIA: [Syria includes the Media of the Seloucids and possibly Egypt as well as the present Syria] are several thousand *li* west of Parthia and close to the Western Sea [Red Sea]. Babylonia is hot and damp. The inhabitants plow their fields in which they grow rice. There is a big bird with eggs the size of jars. The number of its inhabitants is very large, and they have in many places their own petty chiefs; but Parthia, while having added it to its dependencies, considers it a foreign country. They have clever jugglers. [This is the first mention of the "clever jugglers" from Syria.] Although the old people in Parthia maintain the tradition that the Jo-shui [?] and the Hsi-wang-mu [?] are in Babylonia, they have not been seen there.

BACTRIA: [which Chang Ch'ien did visit] is more than 2000 *li* to the southwest of Ferghana, on the south bank of the Oxus. The people have fixed abodes and live in walled cities and regular houses like the people of Ferghana. They have no great king or chief, but everywhere the cities and towns have their own petty chiefs. While the people are shrewd traders, their soldiers are weak and afraid to fight, so that when the Yueh-chih migrated westward, they made war on the Bactrians, who became subject to them. The population of Bactria may amount to more than a million. Their capital is called Lan-hsï, and it has markets for the sale of all kinds of merchandise. To the southeast of it is the country of India. [And then the chronicler quotes Chang Ch'ien's report verbatim] "When I was in Bactria, I saw there a stick of bamboo from Ch'iung [Ch'iung-chou in Szechuan] and some cloth from Szechuan. When I asked the inhabitants how they obtained possession of these they replied, 'The inhabitants of our country buy them in India.' India may be several thousand *li* to the southeast of Bactria. The people there have fixed abodes, and their customs are very much like those of Bactria, but the country is low, damp and hot. The people ride on elephants to fight in battle. The country is close to a great river. According to my calculation, Bactria must be 12,000 *li* distant from China and to the southwest of the latter. Now the country of India being several thousand *li* to the southeast of Bactria, and the produce of Szechuan being found there, that country cannot be far from Szechuan. Suppose we send ambassadors to Bactria through the country of the Tanguts, there is the danger that the Tanguts will object; and if we send them farther north, they will be captured by the Huns. But by going by way of Szechuan they may proceed directly and will be unmolested by robbers."

REVIEW QUESTIONS

1. Descriptions of the Hsiung-nu are curiously brief in Ssu-ma Ch'ien's history of Chang Ch'ien's mission and are missing altogether from the ambassador's reports. Why do you suppose this is so?
2. Which of Chang Ch'ien's reports appears to you to be the most accurate? Which report is the most interesting? Explain.
3. If you were Wu-ti, which of the ambassador's reports would you have found most useful? Why?
4. How does Chang Ch'ien's description of the regions of western Asia compare to Chinese descriptions of the eastern provinces of the Roman Empire in Chapter 4?

An Iberian Pilgrim Observes Christian Customs in Jerusalem (fourth century C.E.)

The Travels of Egeria

Egeria (also sometimes called Aetheria or Silvia) was a Christian traveler and writer who made a pilgrimage to the eastern Roman Empire in the fourth century C.E. She came from the western half of the empire, probably Iberia, and traveled extensively in Palestine, where she visited many sites of interest to Christians, participated in local religious services, and talked to clergy, ascetics, and guides. She seems to have traveled alone or with only a few attendants. She wrote a detailed account of her journey in the form of a long letter to a group of Christian women in her home region. Since Egeria and these women (who were probably nuns) were zealously interested in Christian beliefs and practices, she did not describe anything that was not directly concerned with religion (such as clothing, family life, or trade). Most of her work survives, and it is particularly important as one of the few extant female descriptions of the ancient world.

At the time of Egeria's visit in the fourth century, Palestine had been a Roman province for more than four hundred years. Although a few Jews remained, it was inhabited primarily by Christians. The Zealot Revolt (66–70 C.E.) and the Revolt of Bar-Kokhba (132–135) had triggered not only the Roman destruction of most of Jerusalem, but also the Jewish Diaspora—mandated by an imperial edict that ordered the dispersal of Jews from Jerusalem and a hundred-mile radius around the city. The conversion of the emperor Constantine to Christianity in 312 and its subsequent legalization in 313 led to a dramatic increase in the number of Christians in the entire empire, and even more particularly in Palestine. Because it was the land where Jesus had lived and preached, the region was deliberately developed by Roman and Byzantine emperors as a site of Christian pilgrimage. For this reason, Palestine enjoyed three centuries of relative peace and prosperity—marred only by occasional persecutions of the few remaining Jews and a brief period of Persian rule (611–628). Less than a century later, Arab armies overran Palestine and added it to their rapidly growing Islamic Empire.

Note that the Fortieth Day after Epiphany* is observed here with special magnificence. On this day they assemble in the Anastasis.† Everyone gathers, and things are done with the same solemnity as at the feast of Easter. All the presbyters preach first, then the bishop, and they interpret the passage from the Gospel about Joseph and Mary taking the Lord to the Temple, and about Simeon and the prophetess Anna, daughter of Phanuel, seeing the Lord, and what they said to him, and about the sacrifice offered by his parents.‡ When all the rest has been done in the proper way, they celebrate the sacrament and have their dismissal.

Then comes the Easter season, and this is how it is kept. In our part of the world we observe forty days before Easter, but here they keep eight weeks. It makes eight weeks because there is no fasting on the Sundays or the Saturdays (except one of them, which is a fast because it is the Easter vigil—but apart from that the people here never fast on any Saturday in the year). So the eight weeks, less eight Sundays and seven Saturdays—one being a fasting Saturday—make forty-one fast days. The local name for Lent is *Heortae* [feasts]. . . .

They have the Saturday service . . . before sunrise, so that the people here called hebdomadaries can break their fast as soon as possible. The Lenten fasting rule for these hebdomadaries (people who "keep a week") is that they may eat on a Sunday—when the dismissal is at eleven in the morning. And since their Sunday meal is the last they will have had, and they cannot eat till Saturday morning, they receive Communion early on the Saturday. So the Saturday service at the Anastasis takes place before sunrise for the sake of these people, so that they can break their fast all the sooner. But when I say that the service is early because of them, it is not that I mean that they are the only ones to receive Communion. Anyone who wishes may make his Communion in the Anastasis on Saturdays.

These are their customs of fasting in Lent. There are some who eat nothing during the whole week between their meal after the Sunday service, and the one they have after the service on Saturday in the Anastasis. They are the ones who "keep a week." And, though they eat on Saturday morning, they do not eat again in the evening, but only on the next day, Sunday, after the dismissal at eleven o'clock (or later), and then nothing more till the following Saturday, as I have described. The people known here as apotactites as a rule have only one meal a day not only during Lent, but also during the rest of the

---

*A Christian festival on January 6 that celebrates the visit of the Magi (Wise Men, probably Zoroastrian priests) to Bethlehem. In the Eastern Orthodox Church, Epiphany also commemorates the baptism of Jesus.

†Greek for "resurrection." Egeria was referring to a church on the site of Christ's tomb.

‡See Luke 2:22–40 for a more complete version of this incident.

year. Apotactites who cannot fast for a whole week in the way I have described eat a dinner half way through Thursday, those who in Lent cannot manage this eat on two days of the week, and those who cannot manage this have a meal every evening. No one lays down how much is to be done, but each person does what he can; those who keep the full rule are not praised, and those who do less are not criticized. That is how things are done here.

And this is what they eat during the Lenten season. They are not so much as to taste a crumb of bread, nor oil either, or anything which grows on trees; only water and a little gruel. . . .

I feel I should add something about the way they instruct those who are to be baptized at Easter. Names must be given in before the first day of Lent, which means that a presbyter takes down all the names before the start of the eight weeks for which Lent lasts here, as I have told you. Once the priest has all the names, on the second day of Lent at the start of the eight weeks, the bishop's chair is placed in the middle of the Great Church, the Martyrium, the presbyters sit in chairs on either side of him, and all the clergy stand. Then one by one those seeking baptism are brought up, men coming with their fathers and women with their mothers. As they come in one by one, the bishop asks their neighbours questions about them: "Is this person leading a good life? Does he respect his parents? Is he a drunkard or a boaster?" He asks about all the serious human vices. And if his inquiries show him that someone has not committed any of these misdeeds, he himself puts down his name; but if someone is guilty he is told to go away, and the bishop tells him that he is to amend his ways before he may come to the font. He asks the men and the women the same questions. But it is not too easy for a visitor to come to baptism if he has no witnesses who are acquainted with him.

Now, ladies and sisters, I want to write something which will save you from thinking all this is done without due explanation. They have here the custom that those who are preparing for baptism during the season of the Lenten fast go to be exorcized by the clergy first thing in the morning, directly after the morning dismissal in the Anastasis. As soon as that has taken place, the bishop's chair is placed in the Great Church, the Martyrium, and all those to be baptized, the men and the women, sit round him in a circle. There is a place where the fathers and mothers stand, and any of the people who want to listen (the faithful, of course) can come in and sit down, though not catechumens, who do not come in while the bishop is teaching.

His subject is God's Law; during the forty days he goes through the whole Bible, beginning with Genesis, and first relating the literal meaning of each passage, then interpreting its spiritual meaning. He also teaches them at this time all about the resurrection and the faith. And this is called *catechesis*. After five weeks' teaching they receive the Creed, whose content he explains article by article in the same way as he explained the Scriptures, first literally and then spiritually. Thus all the people in these parts are able to follow the Scriptures when they are read in church, since there has been teaching on all the Scriptures from six to nine in the morning all through Lent, three hours' catechesis a day. At ordinary services when the bishop sits and preaches, ladies and sisters, the faithful utter exclamations, but when they come and hear him explaining the catechesis, their exclamations are far louder, God is my witness; and when it is related and interpreted like this they ask questions on each point.

At nine o'clock they are dismissed from Catechesis, and the bishop is taken with singing straight to the Anastasis. So the dismissal is at nine, which makes three hours' teaching a day for seven weeks. But in the eighth, known as the Great Week, there is no time for them to have their teaching if they are to carry out all the services I have described. So when seven weeks have gone by, and only the week of Easter remains, the one which people here call the Great Week, the bishop comes early into the Great Church, the Martyrium. His chair is placed at the back of the apse, behind the altar, and one by one the candidates go up to the bishop, men with their fathers and women with their mothers, and repeat the Creed to him. When they have done so, the bishop speaks to them all as follows: "During these seven weeks you have received instruction in the whole biblical Law. You have heard about the faith, and the resurrection of the body. You have also learned all you can as catechumens of the content of the Creed. But the teaching about baptism itself is a deeper mystery, and you have not the right to hear it while you remain catechumens. Do you think it will never be explained; you will hear it all during the eight days of Easter after you have been baptized. But so long as you are catechumens you cannot be told God's deep mysteries."

REVIEW QUESTIONS

1. How would you characterize the tone of Egeria's letter? Is it objective or biased? Why do you think so?
2. What do you think of the fasting customs of the hebdomadaries and apotactites? What did Egeria think?
3. Describe the process by which people in Jerusalem became converts to Christianity. What did the bishop tell his catechumens about Easter week? Why do you think this process appealed to large numbers of converts?

6

The Americas, 800 B.C.E.–800 C.E.

In lieu of textual material, this chapter presents illustrations of artifacts and art from the earliest American civilizations. Four epochs are represented here, with two selections in each group to illustrate similarities and differences in development. These images depict items of importance to societies that originated in Meso- and Andean America, as well as the lifestyles of these regions' peoples. The mountainous areas from which these illustrations came have various topographies, and many cultures were quite isolated from each other. The groups presented here, however, traded and communicated with each other, adapting each other's resources and symbols. For example, the jaguar toy, constructed by people of Jalisco in Mexico, and the very large carving of the Olmec priest seated in the serpent's mouth, found in the coastal region of Vera Cruz, were created within a few hundred years of each other by people who were familiar with one another.

Although events were recorded in script form by the Maya of the Yucatan and Guatemalan region, writing had not spread to the other regions of the Americas before 800 C.E. The details of ceramic and stone figures, however, express the reverence the creators felt for their subjects. A recurrent theme is the connection between humans and the powerful animals with which they cohabited. In North and South America alike, zoomorphic figures could depict imaginary spirits of powerful beasts, such as the jaguar or puma, or they could represent men whose facial features had been altered to make them appear to be animal-like. The examples from the Chavín de Huántar civilization in the central Andean regions illustrate how the human face can be altered to suggest connections with animal spirits .

The images in these illustrations also testify to people's reverence for the environment. Rain gods, eagle and jaguar deities, and zoomorphic combinations of spirits were recognized and worshiped by ethnic groups as diverse as the Olmec, Teotihuacan, Toltec, and Maya. These native groups developed one of the most individualistic adaptations of nature's spirits, that of Quetzalcoatl. Because of his connection with the essence of the serpent or snake, Quetzalcoatl exercised great power on earth and in the underground regions. In addition, because he retained part of the form and all of the spirit of the quetzal bird, with its beautiful plumage and superior ability to soar above the earth, the god Quetzalcoatl provided a conduit between the earth and the sky.

Olmec Priest in Serpent's Mouth (about 800 B.C.E.)
Jaguar Toy (700 B.C.E.)

The following illustrations are of carvings and pottery toys that existed for totally different reasons. The Olmec priest sitting within the mouth of the serpent tells a religious story, whereas the figure of a jaguar on wheels probably brought joy to children, perhaps while teaching them the importance of this powerful spirit. Both figures were created within a few hundred years of each other: the first in the lowlands of the Isthmus of Tehuantepec and the second from further north in today's Mexican state of Jalisco. The various ethnic groups of the Olmec and Jalisco cultures worshiped the same gods, valued the same social principles, and participated in an economy based on trade and agricultural production.

The jaguar and the serpent figured prominently in the religious beliefs and daily lives of Meso-American people. The jaguar hunted by night for the same food by which the natives lived, and its rounded face may have seemed half-human. Thus it had a special spiritual connection with humans. The serpent's power lay in its ability to live and travel both above and below the ground; consequently, it could communicate with the spirits of the underworld. Shaman priests such as the one pictured here linked themselves to the serpent's special powers to confer with gods below the earth. Were-jaguars and were-serpents (animals with human characteristics) were also often depicted in Olmec art, and some anthropologists believe that priests altered their facial appearances by broadening their noses, extending their ears, and creating scars that made them resemble the jaguar or the serpent.

The jaguar toy was a child's possession that had both practical and religious purposes. On a practical level, the figure presented information about the owners' physical world and perhaps allowed them to begin to understand the importance of the animal to their lives. It was also a powerful and religiously significant object through which parents could convey stories of moral truths to their children.

In addition, the toy reveals an important fact about the people who made it. Not having large draft animals, the people of the Americas before 1500 did not build carts, chariots, or other vehicles. This object, however, is proof that they understood the concept of the wheel and axle. The circle and wheel figure prominently in the religious art and artifacts of all peoples in the Americas, and here is proof that they understood its application as a tool. Similar wheeled toys of dogs have been discovered in the Olmec region of Vera Cruz, indicating the exchange of ideas and technologies.

Olmec Priest in Serpent's Mouth

Jaguar Toy
*(Staatliche Museen
zu Berlin–Preussischer
Kulturbesitz Ethnologi-
sches Museum)*

REVIEW QUESTIONS

1. From the image of the toy, what characteristics of the jaguar do you see that would convey its spiritual as well as physical power? Explain.
2. What special powers do you believe the Olmec priest wished to convey by this monumental carving? Explain.
3. Given the larger-than-life size of the priest figure and his unusual posture, what points of the figure seem to be the most important? Why?
4. What symbols in modern life might serve the same purposes as do these two carvings? Explain with examples.

Chavín Pot (200 B.C.E.)
Chavín Zoomorphic Heads (200 B.C.E.)

The power of large cats is also a theme in the art and artifacts of the Chavín peoples of Andean South America. The images of the Chavín two-spouted pot and the tenoned heads that decorated important buildings bring to mind the South American cousin of the jaguar, the puma. On the pottery can be seen a representation of a stalking animal with various geometric decorations. This pattern is particularly clear in the lower end view of the vessel where the crouching animal seems to be entering a cave or dwelling. Pottery making in this region dates from about 3000 B.C.E., and the unusual double-spouted pots display the craftsmanship of workers in Chavín de Huántar in 800 B.C.E. Although some archaeologists have postulated connections with Southeast Asian cultures, most experts discount this association but find striking similarities between the depictions of peoples and animals on these vases and those of slightly later peoples in Meso-America. The tenoned heads give a distinctly human appearance to the head of the puma. By combining the characteristics of humans with those of the puma and snake, powerful shamans could divine the will of the gods and procure their favors.

REVIEW QUESTIONS

1. What would be the practical use of the double-spouted vessel pictured here?
2. Why might the maker of this object want to have the protection of the puma?
3. What similarities do you find between human characteristics and animal features in the tenoned heads? What differences?
4. How do these Andean head carvings compare with those of the Olmec?

Two Views of a Chavín Pot
(Wilfredo Loayza Loayza)

(Wilfredo Loayza Loayza)

Chavín Zoomorphic Heads
(Wilfredo Loayza Loayza)

(Wilfredo Loayza Loayza)   *(Wilfredo Loayza Loayza)*

Quetzalcoatl Heads at Teotihuacan (500 C.E.)
Quetzalcoatl Temple at Chichen Itza (500 C.E.)

In a high plateau valley about 40 miles north of Mexico City was the religious and economic center of Teotihuacan, which dominated the region by about 500 B.C.E. Its people thrived on the production and trade of obsidian tools and artwork, and the large valley surrounded by high mountains provided an ideal agricultural environment. Many of the artifacts and sculptures of Teotihuacan indicate the transfer of culture from Jalisco and Olmec people, and the culture of Teotihuacan was passed on to civilizations that arose after the city was destroyed around 700 C.E.

The religious center of the valley reveals that its inhabitants had an understanding and interest in the movements of the heavens, since the principal temples are positioned on strict north-south and east-west axes. The first of the two pictures in this section shows the Quetzalcoatl, or feathered serpent, as his image appears on the side of his large temple in Teotihuacan. The primary deities of Teotihuacan also included other powerful creatures such as the jaguar, seen in the following illustration of a mural in its own temple at Teotihuacan. According to the later traditions of the Nahuatl peoples of thirteenth-century C.E. Meso-America, Teotihuacan was the home of Quetzalcoatl, the priest who became a god and who represented the union of a serpent with the quetzal bird. In the 1500s C.E., the Aztecs knew Teotihuacan as the City of the Spirits, and they revered Quetzalcoatl as a key figure in their belief system.

Possibly at the same time as his religious importance grew in Teotihuacan, Quetzalcoatl became an important symbol in the earliest Maya religion of the Yucatan Peninsula and the Isthmus of Tehuantepec. The second illustration shows one of the earliest temples built at the vast Mayan site of Chichen Itza. The layers of the temple represent the levels of existence for all life forms, and the carvings on the blocks depict subsidiary spirits, such as the eagle and jaguar. In this northern Yucatan Peninsula region, the rain god, Chac, was also depicted on many temples, along with symbols of the ocean's spirits such as sea shells, dolphins, and turtles. Various cultures adopted and continued ancient traditions passed on to them by the Teotihuacanos and Olmecs while simultaneously adopting new religious figures to provide for their special needs.

REVIEW QUESTIONS

1. What would be the powers inherent in a god who represents the serpent and a colorful bird? Why do you think people would respect such a priest-god?
2. What characteristics of Quetzalcoatl do you believe would be of most value to peoples of Meso-America for the next seven hundred years?
3. What is similar in the art of the Olmecs, Teotihuacanos, and Maya? What is different?

Quetzalcoatl Heads at Teotihucan

Quetzalcoatl Temple at Chichen Itza

Jaguar Mural from Teotihuacan (before 800 C.E.)
Two-Headed Jaguar Sculpture from Uxmal (800 C.E.)

The Mayan people of Chichen Itza and Uxmal developed during what is called the Early Classic Era until the Post Classic Era, about 900 C.E. From the monuments and sculptures that remain, one can see how they adopted and adapted beliefs and priorities they inherited from earlier peoples, such as those at Teotihuacan. The following illustrations of the jaguar god, found in two locations approximately six-hundred miles apart, reveal part of this transition. One interpretation of the mural, in the first illustration, is that the jaguar god is a warrior that is drinking blood from a vessel offered by a human warrior. The symbols over the heads of the figures and on the jaguar's body depict various spirits of nature that are also being nurtured. The walls of the rooms where these art works were executed are of red sandstone, and the paints used were extremely bright blues, yellows, and greens.

Other recently discovered mural-filled chambers, not shown here, help us understand the importance of the Teotihuacan find. The temple ruins at Cacaxtla (east of Mexico City) were already well known when, in 1974, looters discovered hidden rooms with murals whose colors were as bright as when they were painted about 800 C.E. While these murals showed a distinct Mayan influence, the structures in which they were discovered resemble the flat-roofed buildings of Teotihuacan. Similarly, the two-headed jaguar throne from Uxmal shows that the Maya adopted Teotihuacan beliefs. This sculpture is contemporary with the murals at Cacaxtla. Such widespread artistic expressions of animal spirits reveal the connections between the Teotihuacanos, the Maya, and the later Toltec civilization of central Meso-America.

The two-headed jaguar, the second illustration, is situated at the Temple of the Magician near the center of the vast complex of temples. The two jaguar heads are joined at midabdomen to provide a royal seat upon which a priest or ruler could sit when delivering judgments. Although currently displayed at ground level, this impressive carving was probably situated at the top level of the temple to further indicate the noble person's superiority and the protection given by the spirit of the jaguar.

REVIEW QUESTIONS

1. What features of the jaguar mural make it distinct from the other images presented in this chapter? Are there any similarities with other images?
2. If you did not read the introduction to the jaguar image, how would you know that the jaguar is the central figure here?
3. What features of the large double-headed cats make them distinct from other images presented in this chapter?
4. What do these two illustrations tell you about the level of Meso-American craftsmanship in this period?

Jaguar Mural from Teothihuacan

Two-Headed Jaguar Sculpture from Uxmal

7

Africa, 800 B.C.E.–800 C.E.

The ancient history of Africa is shrouded in mystery. With the exception of records from the Nile valley, the earliest records of human society on that continent are far from trustworthy. Few of Africa's diverse inhabitants had writing, so very little is known of them in this time period, apart from the writings of outsiders and relatively meager archaeological artifacts. Only a small number of visitors ventured more than a few miles inland from the Mediterranean coast, where civilization was predominantly either Near Eastern or Greco-Roman. Herodotus and Procopius, for example, traveled fairly extensively in Africa to gain knowledge of Egypt and Mauritania, but most writers, such as Pliny the Elder, simply obtained their information from others, sometimes through interviews but often through rumors and myths. Reliable data on ancient African cultures can be obtained from archaeological treasures, but in many instances ancient artifacts are difficult, if not impossible, to find—especially those that once belonged to nomadic and seminomadic groups. Occasional views of Africans can also be found in the ruins of civilizations outside Africa; for example, portraits of Africans can frequently be found on Greek and Roman pottery. Non-African artistic renderings of Africans can also shed light on the continent's inhabitants. Two are included in this chapter.

A major exception to the lack of sources for ancient Africa is the Nile River valley, where the Egyptians established a highly literate civilization in the fourth millennium B.C.E. The Egyptians were prolific writers (see the Egyptian myths of creation, Chapter 1, and the Tale of Sinuhe, Chapter 3). The Kushites were less prolific writers, but because they used Egyptian hieroglyphic writing, some of their records have survived, many of which reveal a significant amount of Egyptian influence. For example, the inscription of Aspalta resembles many of its Egyptian counterparts, in both form and style, and is written in Egyptian hieroglyphics.

Two other literate civilizations also existed in Africa in this time period: Carthage, on the Mediterranean coast, and Aksum, on the Red Sea. Neither, however, left even a fraction of the written materials bequeathed to posterity by Egypt, possibly because of their preoccupation with trade and business rather than philosophy and literature. Nevertheless, these two civilizations have left sources worthy of study. The two included in this chapter are particularly interesting for their religious insights. The Carthaginian inscription stipulates how sacrifices should be conducted and therefore offers a rare glimpse into the Carthaginian mentality of the fourth and fifth centuries B.C.E. The three inscriptions of Ezana, an Aksumite king who converted to Christianity circa 350 C.E., illustrate the importance he placed on divine assistance in battle.

In many ways, Carthage and even northern Egypt belonged more to the Mediterranean world of the Greeks and Romans than to Africa. Aristotle, who was attempting to define the ideal government, noted a number of similarities, in fact, between the governments of Carthage and the Greek city-states, especially Sparta and Crete. Considering that Carthage was essentially Near Eastern in character and religion, it is surprising that Aristotle considered it worthy of study. On the other hand, perhaps his interest in Carthage is evidence of the many similarities shared by Mediterranean civilizations. Among these were military brotherhoods, the aristocratic domination of civic institutions, and an increasing inclusion of democratic elements in political life.

The materials in this chapter also illuminate the role of women in Africa. In no other region in the ancient world were women as prominent in political and economic life. In the inscription of Ezana, for example, the importance of women is obvious. Ezana owed his selection as king of Kush to the Kushite system of uterine descent, which the warriors clearly recognized as they elevated him to the throne. The unusual freedom of women was also noted by Herodotus, who was shocked to see Egyptian men performing "unmanly" tasks such as weaving.

A Greek Historian Describes Egypt (fifth century B.C.E.)

HERODOTUS, *The Histories, Book II*

The Greek author of the history of the Persian Wars, Herodotus (c. 484–425 B.C.E.), was nothing if not a careful and thorough historian. In what must be the longest prelude ever written for the history of a specific event, he devoted six of *The Histories'* nine books to tracing the rise of Persia to the point at which it invaded Greece. For example, in Book I (an excerpt of which appears in Chapter 5), Herodotus explained how the Persians rose to power in the ancient Near East, recounting their conquest of the Medes and the Lydians (a state in Asia Minor). In Book II, he focused on the next addition to the rapidly growing empire, Egypt, which was conquered by Cambyses, the son of Cyrus the Great. Very little of the second book has anything to do with Persia or with the Persian Wars, but Herodotus felt that the Greeks needed a thorough understanding of their enemies, the Persians, and that this would not be possible unless all parts of the empire were examined thoroughly. Thus the bulk of Book II is a lengthy digression on the geography, people, customs, and history of Egypt.

Herodotus acquired a great deal of his information on Egypt through firsthand experience. He traveled to Egypt sometime soon after 454, and he may have returned a second time as well. On one of these visits he traveled up the Nile as far as Elephantine, an island at the first cataract. He took pains to investigate the flooding of the Nile River, recognized its benefits, and labeled Egypt "the gift of the Nile," a phrase that historians and teachers today use with great regularity when discussing this topic. Herodotus implied that during his researches he talked with many Egyptians; in reality, he never learned to speak any language other than Greek. Thus much of his information came to him through interpreters, which may account for some of the inconsistencies and inaccuracies in his descriptions, not to mention his frequent confusion of Greek and Egyptian deities and religious rituals. His mistakes were honest ones, however. Never did he consciously seek to deceive his readers, nor did he disguise his clear belief that Greece was both the cultural and geographical center of his worldview. His belief that all educated Greeks should understand the world outside of Greece was indeed the very thing that made *The Histories* into a classic and a standard of world literature. The following passage is an excellent example of the Greeks' fascination with learning, as well as of their critical approach to the world around them.

About Egypt I shall have a great deal more to relate because of the number of remarkable things which the country contains, and because of the fact that more monuments which beggar description are to be found there than anywhere else in the world. That is reason enough for my dwelling on it at greater length. Not only is the Egyptian climate peculiar to that country, and the Nile different in its behaviour from other rivers elsewhere, but the Egyptians themselves in their manners and customs seem to have reversed the ordinary practices of mankind. For instance, women attend market and are employed in trade, while men stay at home and do the weaving. In weaving the normal way is to work the threads of the weft upwards, but the Egyptians work them downwards. Men in Egypt carry loads on their heads, women on their shoulders; women pass water standing up, men sitting down. To ease themselves they go indoors, but eat outside in the streets, on the theory that what is unseemly but necessary should be done in private, and what is not unseemly should be done openly. No woman holds priestly office, either in the service of goddess or god; only men are priests in both cases. Sons are under no compulsion to support their parents if they do not wish to do so, but daughters must, whether they wish it or not. Elsewhere priests grow their hair long; in Egypt they shave their heads. In other nations the relatives of the deceased in time of mourning cut their hair, but the Egyptians, who shave at all other times, mark a death by letting their hair grow both on head and chin. They live with their animals—unlike the rest of the world, who live apart from them. Other men live on wheat and barley, but any Egyptian who does so is blamed for it, their bread being made from spelt, or *Zea* as some call it. Dough they knead

with their feet, but clay with their hands—and even handle dung. They practise circumcision, while men of other nations—except those who have learnt from Egypt—leave their private parts as nature made them. Men in Egypt have two garments each, women only one. The ordinary practice at sea is to make sheets fast to ring-bolts fitted outboard; the Egyptians fit them inboard. In writing or calculating, instead of going, like the Greeks, from left to right, the Egyptians go from right to left—and obstinately maintain that theirs is the dexterous method, ours being left-handed and awkward. They have two sorts of writing, the sacred and the common. They are religious to excess, beyond any other nation in the world, and here are some of the customs which illustrate the fact; they drink from brazen cups which they scour every day—everyone, without exception. They wear linen clothes which they make a special point of continually washing. They circumcise themselves for cleanliness' sake, preferring to be clean rather than comely. The priests shave their bodies all over every other day to guard against the presence of lice, or anything else equally unpleasant, while they are about their religious duties; the priests, too, wear linen only, and shoes made from the papyrus plant—these materials, for dress and shoes, being the only ones allowed them. They bath in cold water twice a day and twice every night—and observe innumerable other ceremonies besides. Their life, however, is not by any means all hardship, for they enjoy advantages too: for instance, they are free from all personal expense, having bread made for them out of the sacred grain, and a plentiful daily supply of goose-meat and beef, with wine in addition. Fish they are forbidden to touch; and as for beans, they cannot even bear to look at them, because they imagine they are unclean (in point of fact the Egyptians never sow beans, and even if any happen to grow wild, they will not eat them, either raw or boiled). They do not have a single priest for each god, but a number, of which one is chief-priest, and when a chief-priest dies his son is appointed to succeed him. Bulls are considered the property of the god Epaphus—or Apis—and are therefore tested in the following way: a priest appointed for the purpose examines the animal, and if he finds even a single black hair upon him, pronounces him unclean; he goes over him with the greatest care, first making him stand up, then lie on his back, after which he pulls out his tongue to see if that, too, is "clean" according to the recognized marks—what those are I will explain later. He also inspects the tail to make sure the hair on it grows properly; then, if the animal passes all these tests successfully, the priest marks him by twisting round his horns a band of papyrus, which he seals with wax and stamps with his signet ring. The bull is finally taken away, and the penalty is death for anybody who sacrifices an animal which has not been marked in this manner. . . .

Pigs are considered unclean. If anyone touches a pig accidentally in passing, he will at once plunge into the river, clothes and all, to wash himself; and swineherds, though of pure Egyptian blood, are the only people in the country who never enter a temple, nor is there any intermarriage between them and the rest of the community, swineherds marrying their daughters and taking their wives only from amongst themselves. . . .

The Egyptians who live in the cultivated parts of the country, by their practice of keeping records of the past, have made themselves much the most learned of any nation of which I have had experience. I will describe some of their habits: every month for three successive days they purge themselves, for their health's sake, with emetics and clysters, in the belief that all diseases come from the food a man eats; and it is a fact—even apart from this precaution—that next to the Libyans they are the healthiest people in the world. I should put this down myself

to the absence of changes in the climate; for change, and especially change of weather, is the prime cause of disease. They eat loaves made from spelt—*cyllestes* is their word for them—and drink a wine made from barley, as they have no vines in the country. Some kinds of fish they eat raw, either dried in the sun, or salted; quails, too, they eat raw, and ducks and various small birds, after pickling them in brine; other sorts of birds and fish, apart from those which they consider sacred, they either roast or boil. When the rich give a party and the meal is finished, a man carries round amongst the guests a wooden image of a corpse in a coffin, carved and painted to look as much like the real thing as possible, and anything from eighteen inches to three foot long; he shows it to each guest in turn, and says: "Look upon this body as you drink and enjoy yourself; for you will be just like it when you are dead." . . .

There is another point in which the Egyptians resemble one section of the Greek people—the Lacedaemonians: I mean the custom of young men stepping aside to make room for their seniors when they meet them in the street, and of getting up from their seats when older men come in. But they are unlike any of the Greeks in that they do not greet one another by name in the streets, but make a low bow and drop one hand to the knee. The clothes they wear consist of a linen tunic with a fringe hanging round the legs (called in their language *calasiris*), and a white woollen garment on top of it. It is, however, contrary to religious usage to be buried in a woollen garment, or to wear wool in a temple. This custom agrees with the rites known as Orphic and Bacchic (actually Egyptian and Pythagorean); for anyone initiated into these rites is similarly debarred from burial in a garment of wool. They have a myth which explains the reason for this.

The Egyptians were also the first to assign each month and each day to a particular deity, and to foretell by the date of a man's birth his character, his fortunes, and the day of his death— a discovery which Greek poets have turned to account. The Egyptians, too, have made more use of omens and prognostics than any other nation; they keep written records of the observed results of any unusual phenomenon, so that they come to expect a similar consequence to follow a similar occurrence in the future. The art of divination is not attributed by them to any man, but only to certain gods: for instance, Heracles, Apollo, Athena, Artemis, Ares, and Zeus all have an oracle in the country, while the oracle of Leto in Buto is held in greater repute than any of them. The method of delivering the responses varies in the different shrines.

The practice of medicine they split up into separate parts, each doctor being responsible for the treatment of only one disease. There are, in consequence, innumerable doctors, some specializing in diseases of the eyes, others of the head, others of the teeth, others of the stomach, and so on; while others, again, deal with the sort of troubles which cannot be exactly localized. As regards mourning and funerals, when a distinguished man dies all the women of the household plaster their heads and faces with mud, then, leaving the body indoors, perambulate the town with the dead man's female relatives, their dresses fastened with a girdle, and beat their bared breasts. The men too, for their part, follow the same procedure, wearing a girdle and beating themselves like the women. The ceremony over, they take the body to be mummified.

Mummification is a distinct profession. The embalmers, when a body is brought to them, produce specimen models in wood, painted to resemble nature, and graded in quality; the best and most expensive kind is said to represent a being whose name I shrink from mentioning in this connexion; the next best is somewhat inferior and cheaper, while the third sort is cheapest of all. After pointing out these differences in quality, they ask which of the three is required, and the kinsmen of the dead man, having agreed upon a price, go away and leave the embalmers to their work. The most perfect process is as follows: as much as possible of the brain is extracted through the nostrils with an iron hook, and what the hook cannot reach is rinsed out with drugs; next the flank is laid open with a flint knife and the whole contents of the ab-

domen removed; the cavity is then thoroughly cleansed and washed out, first with palm wine and again with an infusion of pounded spices. After that it is filled with pure bruised myrrh, cassia, and every other aromatic substance with the exception of frankincense, and sewn up again, after which the body is placed in natrum, covered entirely over, for seventy days—never longer. When this period, which must not be exceeded, is over, the body is washed and then wrapped from head to foot in linen cut into strips and smeared on the under side with gum, which is commonly used by the Egyptians instead of glue. In this condition the body is given back to the family, who have a wooden case made, shaped like the human figure, into which it is put. The case is then sealed up and stored in a sepulchral chamber, upright against the wall. When, for reasons of expense, the second quality is called for, the treatment is different: no incision is made and the intestines are not removed, but oil of cedar is injected with a syringe into the body through the anus which is afterwards stopped up to prevent the liquid from escaping. The body is then pickled in natrum for the prescribed number of days, on the last of which the oil is drained off. The effect of it is so powerful that as it leaves the body it brings with it the stomach and intestines in a liquid state, and as the flesh, too, is dissolved by the natrum, nothing of the body is left but the bones and skin. After this treatment it is returned to the family without further fuss.

The third method, used for embalming the bodies of the poor, is simply to clear out the intestines with a purge and keep the body seventy days in natrum. It is then given back to the family to be taken away.

When the wife of a distinguished man dies, or any woman who happens to be beautiful or well known, her body is not given to the embalmers immediately, but only after the lapse of three or four days. This is a precautionary measure to prevent the embalmers from violating the corpse, a thing which is said actually to have happened in the case of a woman who had just died. The culprit was given away by one of his fellow workmen. If anyone, either an Egyptian or a foreigner, is found drowned in the river or killed by a crocodile, there is the strongest obligation upon the people of the nearest town to have the body embalmed in the most elaborate manner and buried in a consecrated burial-place; no one is allowed to touch it except the priests of the Nile—not even relatives or friends; the priests alone prepare it for burial with their own hands and place it in the tomb, as if were something more sacred than the body of a man.

REVIEW QUESTIONS

1. How did the roles of Egyptian men and women differ from the Greek roles? What did Herodotus think of these differences?
2. How did the religious customs of Egypt compare with those of the Greeks? What religious comparisons between the two cultures, if any, did Herodotus make?
3. What do you think is the most important section of this reading? Why?
4. Based on what you know from other sources, in your opinion how accurate is Herodotus's information on Egypt? Give examples.
5. Was Herodotus's account of Egyptian culture objective or biased? Explain, using examples.

A Kushite Writer Describes the Accession of King Aspalta (593 B.C.E.)

The Annals of Nubian Kings

Kush was an ancient civilization located south of the fourth cataract of the Nile River. In this society, women played an unusually prominent role, and queens occasionally ruled in their own right. Kings did not normally inherit the throne from their fathers; instead the succession passed from the king to one of his sister's sons, a system called "uterine descent." This can be seen very clearly in this selection, which describes the election and accession of King Aspalta (also Aspelta).

At the time Aspalta reigned over Kushite civilization (593–568 B.C.E.), it was going through a major change of location. Originally situated in the northeast of what is now Sudan, Kush had first arisen around 2000 B.C.E. or slightly earlier. There it was heavily influenced by Egypt, and Egyptian influences can be seen in its religion, artistic and architectural styles, and language. The Kushites worshiped most of the same gods as did the Egyptians, built small pyramids, and used a hieroglyphic system of writing almost identical to that of Egypt. The economy of Kush was based on the production of iron, agricultural products like rice and sorghum, cattle, and trade, both with Egypt and towns on the Red Sea to the east. At the height of their power, between 750 and 670, Kushite kings ruled Egypt as the twenty-fifth dynasty. When the Assyrians conquered Egypt in 670, however, the Kushite dynasty was forced back to its capital, Napata. Over the next century, the population of Kush gradually moved further and further south, eventually settling above the fifth cataract of the Nile. Finally, even the royal family moved, relocating at Meroë, about 150 miles northwest of modern Khartoum. The oldest royal inscription from Meroë bears Aspalta's name; thus he may have been the first Kushite king to rule from the new capital.

The relocation offered distinct advantages: It was farther from the influence and domination of the Assyrians and successive expansionistic empires, the terrain was more open and offered new trading opportunities in central Africa, and it was not so far south that the Kushites had to sever trading ties with Egypt and the Mediterranean. Moreover, in their new site, the Kushites developed their own gods, experimented with new building styles, and invented a unique system of writing. Nevertheless, Egypt continued to exert important (though considerably diminished) cultural influences on Kush until its conquest by King Ezana of Axum (Aksum) in 350 C.E.

THE ELECTION OF ASPELTA AS KING AND HIS ENTHRONEMENT

Behold now, the whole army of His Majesty was in the city, the name whereof is Tu-āb,[1] and the god who dwells there is Tetun,[2] the Governor of Ta-Sti [Northern Nubia] the god of Kesh [Kush], after the Hawk[3] had arrived upon his tomb.

Behold now, there were there six generals who filled the heart of the military assembly of His Majesty; and there were there six officials who were favourites of the Overseer of the Seal. And behold, there were there six Overseers of Books who were favourites of the Chief Overseer of Books; and behold, there were there six Princes and Overseers of the Seal of the House of the king. And they said unto the whole army, "Come, let us crown our Lord over us, who shall be like a young bull, which the herdsmen cannot subdue." And these soldiers meditated upon the matter most carefully, and they said, "Our Lord is standing among us, though we know him not.

But we must know who he is, and we will enter his service and we will serve him, even as the Two Lands served Horus, the son of Isis, after he had seated himself upon the throne of his father Osiris, and we will ascribe praise unto his two Uatchti serpents."[4]

And one said to his fellow among them, "No person whatsoever knows who he is except Rā himself; may the god drive away from him evil of every kind in every place wheresoever he may be." And one said to his fellow among them, "Rā[5] has set in Ānkhtet,[6] but his crown is in our midst." And one said to his fellow among them, "This is truth. It is the decree of Rā, from the time when the heavens came into being, and from the time when the crown of the king was created, and he made him to be his beloved son, because the king is the image of Rā among the living. Behold, Rā has set him in this land, wishing him to be the overlord of this land."

And one said to his fellow among them, "Has not Rā entered into the sky? His throne is empty of a Ruler. His noble deeds remain perfected by

[1]Presumably the town on the east bank of the Nile, facing Napata on the west bank.
[2]A very ancient Nubian god, whose original attributes are unknown.
[3]The "hawk" here mentioned is the king who had died recently.

[4]These are the two serpents which formed the chief ornament of the crown of the king of Egypt.
[5]The dead king is here identified with Rā, the Sun-god, and his death is compared to the setting of the god.
[6]The Land of Life, a common name of Āmenti, or the Other World.

his two hands. Rā has made him to be his beloved son because he knew him, saying, 'He made laws which were good while he was on his throne.'"

And all these soldiers meditated upon the matter most carefully, and said, "Our Lord is standing among us, though we know not who he is."

Then all the soldiers of His Majesty spoke with one voice (or, mouth) saying, "Surely there exists this god, Åmen-Rā, the Lord of the Throne of the Two Lands, Dweller in the Holy Mountain, the god of Kesh.

Come and let us go before him. Let us not do anything without his knowledge, for that thing which is done without his knowledge is not good. Come and place the matter with the god, who has been the god of the kings of Kesh since the time of Rā, for it is he who shall guide us.

The kings of Kesh are in his hands, and he gives the country to his beloved son. Let us give praises to his face, and let us smell the earth upon our bellies. Let us say before him, 'We have come before you, O Åmen, give to us a Lord over us, who shall make us to live, who shall build the temples of all the gods and goddesses of the Land of the South and the Land of the North, and who shall establish their offerings. We will do nothing without your knowledge, you shall be our leader (or, guide), and we will do nothing in the matter without your knowledge.'" And the whole army said, "This is a good saying in very truth, a million times over." Then the generals of His Majesty and the high officials of the House of the king went into the god-house of Åmen, and they found the servants of the god (i.e., priests) and the chief libationers standing round about the temple. And they said to them, "We have come before the god Åmen-Rā, the Dweller within the Holy Mountain, so that he may give us a Lord to be over us who shall make us to live, who shall build the temples of all the gods and goddesses of the Land of the South and the Land of the North, and shall establish their offerings. We will do nothing without the knowledge of this god, for he is our leader (or, guide)."

And the servants of the god and the chief libationers made an entrance into the temple, and

they performed all the rites which had to be performed, and they sprinkled water therein and censed it. And the generals of His Majesty and the princes of the House of the king made an entrance into the temple, and they placed themselves on their bellies in the presence of this god, and they said, "We have come to you, Åmen-Rā, Lord of the Throne of the Two Lands, Dweller within the Holy Mountain. Give to us a Lord to make us to live, to build the temples of the gods of the Land of the South and the Land of the North, and to establish the offering in them. The exalted estate of kingship rests wholly in your hands: grant it to your beloved son."

Then they placed the royal brethren before this god, but he did not lead out any one of them. And next, on the second occasion, when they set before this god the royal brother, the son of Åmen, born of the goddess Nut, the Lady of heaven, the son of Rā, [Åspelta], the everliving, this god Åmen-Rā, Lord of the Throne of the Two Lands, spoke, saying: "This is the King, your Lord, this is he who shall make you to live, this is he who shall build every temple of the Land of the South and the Land of the North, this is he who shall establish their offerings; for his father was Keb, the son of Rā, whose word is law, and his mother was the royal sister, royal mother, Queen of Kesh, daughter of Rā, [NENSELSA], the everliving; and her mother was the royal sister, the high-priestess of Åmen-Rā, the king of the gods of Thebes, whose word is law; and her mother was the royal sister, whose word is law; and her mother was the royal sister, whose word is law; and her mother was the royal sister, whose word is law; and her mother was the royal sister, whose word is law; and her mother was the royal sister and Queen of Kesh, whose word is law. He is your Lord."

And the generals of His Majesty and the high officials of the House of the king threw themselves down on their bellies before this god, and they made the most humble obeisance,[7] and they gave praise unto this god because of the strength

---

[7]Literally, "smelt the ground very much."

(or, dominion) which he had made for his beloved son, the king of the South and North, [Aspelta], the everliving.

And His Majesty entered into the temple to be crowned before his divine Father, Åmen-Rā, the Lord of the Throne of the Two Lands, and he found every crown of the kings of Kesh and their sceptres laid before this god. And His Majesty spake before this god, saying: "I have come, Åmen-Rā, the Lord of the Throne of the Two Lands, the Dweller within the Holy Mountain; grant to me the exalted dignity which shall remain permanent, which it was not in my heart [to aspire to], through the greatness of thy love, and grant to me the crown, through thy heart's love, and the sceptre." And this god said: "The crown of your divine brother, the King of the South and North, whose word is law, is yours, and it shall be established on your head even as the . . . is stablished on your head. His sceptre is in your grasp, and it shall overthrow for you all your enemies."

Then His Majesty placed on his head the crown of his divine brother, the King of the South and North, whose word is law, and took his sceptre in his grasp. And His Majesty placed himself on his belly before this god, and, making the most humble obeisance, said: "I have come unto you Åmen-Rā, the Lord of the Throne of the Two Lands, the Dweller within the Holy Mountain, god of olden time, whose love is

sweet, who hears him that makes a petition unto him straightaway, . . . grant to me life, stability, serenity of every kind, health, joy of heart of every kind, like Rā for ever, and a happy old age.

Grant to me the perception . . . in the time of Rā. Let not lie down. . . . Grant that the love of me shall be in the country of Kesh, and awe of me in the land of Kenset. . . . Grant that the love of me shall be. . . ." And this god said: "I have given unto you all these things, and you shall never, never have need to say, 'Would that I had them.'"

28. Then His Majesty made a coming forth (or, appearance) from the temple into the midst of his soldiers like the rising [of Rā], and his soldiers rejoiced in him and uttered loud cries of gladness. And the hearts of the high officers of the House of the king were exceedingly happy, and they ascribed praises unto His Majesty, and said: "Come in peace, O our Lord . . . like the years of Horus in the midst of thy soldiers. You rise (or, are crowned) upon the throne of Horus, like Rā, for ever."

And in this first year of the coronation of His Majesty he established festivals.

. . . and he gave to the priests of the temple of Åmen-Rā, the Lord of the Throne of the Two Lands, the Dweller within the Holy Mountain . . . one hundred vessels of beer, and forty *shu,* in all one hundred and forty vessels of beer.

REVIEW QUESTIONS

1. This selection includes a great many examples of the influence of Egypt on Kushite civilization. Which do you think is the most important? Why?
2. Who and/or what determined that Aspalta should be the next king? Why?
3. How can you tell from this inscription that women played an important role in Kushite civilization?
4. Several historians have perceived what they call a "hint of democracy" in the selection of Aspalta as king. What makes them think so? Do you agree?

Greek Interpretations of African Faces (third century B.C.E.)

Three Pieces of Jewelry from Greece

The items of jewelry in this picture reveal two things: continuing Greek fascination with Africans and Hellenistic influences in art. The heads that are the focal points of this jewelry depict the faces of individual Africans, with careful attention given to the hair. The bead necklace is of particular interest because it portrays the faces of two women, fashioned in garnet. The hair is made of gold wire that has been twisted into tiny spirals. The earrings also feature carefully detailed hair, also in gold wire, although the faces are reproduced in amber. The solid gold head, which perhaps topped a pin, is only 1.5 centimeters in size.

All three pieces of jewelry reflect Hellenistic changes in artistic style. Classical Greek ideals—especially the emphasis on the perfection of the human body—had given way to a new artistic honesty that manifested itself in realistic portraiture. The subject matter of these pieces of jewelry also reveals a new fascination with the exotic; contact with and interest in "foreign" lands was unusually high in the Hellenistic Age. By the third century B.C.E., the Greeks had explored not only the lands east to the Indus River, but also parts of northern Africa, especially along the Nile. Much of their knowledge of Africa came from trade with Egypt, which was ruled by the Ptolemies, a Macedonian dynasty descended from the half-brother of Alexander the Great. The impact of these and other Hellenistic rulers spread well beyond the borders of Alexander's short-lived empire. Today Hellenistic style is easily discerned in art, particularly in statues, coin portraits, and jewelry.

REVIEW QUESTIONS

1. Speculate as to why you think the craftsmen who made these pieces of jewelry used African features as focal points.
2. How do these images compare with those on the Greek and Roman vases in this chapter?
3. Do you think these images flatter their subjects? Why or why not?

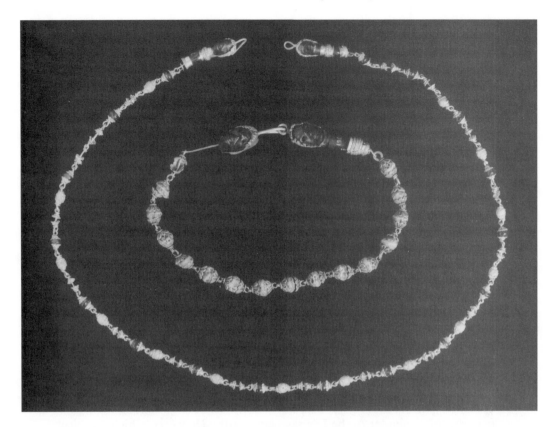

Greek Necklace, from Melos, third century B.C. Gold and garnet. L: 21.5 cm. *(Department of Greek and Roman Antiquities, TB 97, photo © Copyright The British Museum)*

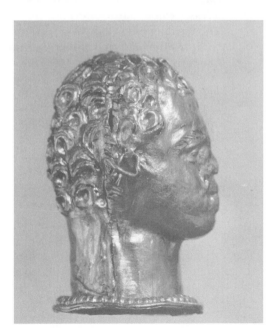

Finial in the Form of the Head of a Black. Gold with traces of black paint, ¾ × ⅜ × ½ inches, Egypt: Alexandria; Hellenistic. *(CA-7402, gift of Mathias Komor, photo by Hickey–Robertson, Houston. From the collection of The Menil Foundation)*

A Carthaginian Law Concerning Sacrifices (fourth or fifth century B.C.E.)

The Corpus Inscriptionum Semiticarum, Volume I, no. 165

The history of Carthage, one of the most famous cities of antiquity, is almost entirely dependent upon the writings of other civilizations, many of which were its enemies. Written sources from Carthage itself are extremely rare, possibly because the Carthaginians simply did not place a high priority on recording their past. It is also likely that most of their written records were destroyed when the Romans razed the city in 146 B.C.E.

Located on the northern coast of Africa in what is today northeast Tunisia, Carthage was founded by Phoenician merchants from Tyre in the late ninth or early eighth century B.C.E. Its harbor and port facilities were some of the finest in the ancient Mediterranean, and they enabled the city to amass considerable wealth and power through trade. By the sixth century, Carthage had become a capital of considerable importance, with colonies of its own on Sicily and the Balearic Islands, as well as along the southern coast of Iberia and the northwestern coast of Africa.

The following selection is one of the few surviving examples of Carthaginian writing. The inscription, which cannot be dated any earlier than the fourth or fifth century B.C.E., details the laws of sacrifice at the Temple of Baal, the chief god of the city (as well as of the Phoenicians and Canaanites). It is strikingly similar to the Levitical laws of the Hebrews, which also deal extensively with sacrificial animals and goods. For example, both use the same terms: "whole burnt-offering," the "peace-offering," and the "meal-offering." The Carthaginians, however, had no "sin-offering," and the Hebrews had no "prayer-offering." A similar inscription has also been found in Phoenicia (modern Lebanon and the Mediterranean coast of Syria). Thus the inscription from Carthage is extraordinarily important, both as a native source for Carthaginian history and as a link between the city and its ancestors and their neighbors in the ancient Near East.

Readers should be aware that ellipses in the text in this section refer to parts of the work that are missing, rather than sections that have been edited out by the author of passages.

A CARTHAGINIAN LAW CONCERNING SACRIFICES

Temple of Baal Tariff of dues, which the superintendents of dues fixed in the time of our rulers, Khalasbaal, the judge, son of Bodtanith, son of Bodeshmun, and of Khalasbaal, the judge, son of Bodeshmun, son of Khalasbaal, and their colleagues.

For an ox as a whole burnt-offering or a prayer-offering, or a whole peace-offering, the priests shall have 10 (shekels) of silver for each; and in case of a whole burnt-offering, they shall have in addition to this fee 300 shekels of flesh; and, in case of a prayer-offering, the trimmings, the joints; but the skin and the fat of the inwards and the feet and the rest of the flesh the owner of the sacrifice shall have.

For a calf whose horns are wanting, in case of one not castrated or in case of a ram as a whole burnt-offering, the priests shall have 5 shekels of silver for each; and in case of a whole burnt-offering they shall have in addition to this fee 150 shekels of flesh; and, in case of a prayer-offering, the trimmings and the joints; but the skin and the fat of the inwards and the feet and the rest of the flesh the owner of the sacrifice shall have.

In case of a ram or a goat as a whole burnt-offering, or a prayer-offering, or a whole peace-offering, the priests shall have 1 shekel of silver and 2 *zars* for each; and, in case of a prayer-offering, they shall have in addition to this fee the trimmings and the joints; but the skin and the fat of the inwards and the feet and the rest of the flesh the owner of the sacrifice shall have.

For a lamb, or a kid, or the young of a hart, as a whole burnt-offering, or a prayer-offering, or a whole peace-offering, the priests shall have ¾ (of a shekel) and . . . *zars* of silver for each; and, in case of a prayer-offering, they shall have in addition to this fee the trimmings and the joints; but the skin and the fat of the inwards and the feet and the rest of the flesh the owner of the sacrifice shall have.

For a bird, domestic or wild, as a whole peace-offering, or a sacrifice-to-avert-calamity or an oracular sacrifice, the priests shall have ¾ (of a shekel) of silver and 2 *zars* for each; but the flesh shall belong to the owner of the sacrifice.

For a bird, or sacred first-fruits, or a sacrifice of game, or a sacrifice of oil, the priests shall have 10 *gerahs* for each; but. . . .

In case of every prayer-offering that is presented before the gods, the priests shall have the trimmings and the joints; and in the case of a prayer-offering. . . .

For a cake, and for milk, and for every sacrifice which a man may offer, for a meal-offering. . . .

For every sacrifice which a man may offer who is poor in cattle, or poor in birds, the priests shall not have anything. . . .

Every freeman and every slave and every dependent[1] of the gods and all men who may sacrifice. . . , these men shall give for the sacrifice at the rate prescribed in the regulations. . . .

Every payment which is not prescribed in this table shall be made according to the regulations which the superintendents of the dues fixed in the time of Khalasbaal, son of Bodtanith, and Khalasbaal, son of Bodeshmun, and their colleagues.

Every priest who shall accept payment beyond what is prescribed in this table shall be fined. . . .

Every person who sacrifices, who shall not give . . . for the fee which. . . .

---

[1]Each temple had a number of officials connected with it besides the priests, such as carpenters, gate-keepers, slaughterers, barbers, Sodomites, and female slaves.

REVIEW QUESTIONS

1. What kinds of sacrifices did Carthaginians offer at the temple of Baal? How did payments for sacrifices vary?
2. For what reasons might this wide range of sacrifices have been available?
3. What do you think happened to the meat and other foodstuffs that were offered to Baal?
4. What can you learn about the diet of ancient Carthaginians by reading this inscription? About the class structure of ancient Carthage?
5. How did the law of sacrifices regard the poor? How did it deal with the possibility of corruption? What does this tell you about ancient Carthage in general?

A Greek Philosopher Discusses the Constitution of Carthage (fourth century B.C.E.)

ARISTOTLE, *Politics, Book II*

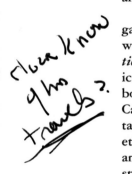

Aristotle (384–322 B.C.E.) was a philosopher, logician, moralist, biologist, and political thinker—among other things. An Ionian, he was born at Stagira, a Greek colonial town on the northwestern shore of the Aegean Sea. At seventeen he traveled to Athens and became a disciple of Plato; he studied with the philosopher for twenty years until Plato's death at age eighty-one. Between 342 and 335 he served in the employ of Philip II of Macedonia as the tutor of Philip's son Alexander the Great. Their relationship has been the subject of much speculation, for Aristotle never publicly stated his opinion of Alexander. Years later, however, he wrote against monarchy as a system of political organization, saying it was justified only if a ruler was as superior to his subjects as human beings were to beasts. In his two works that include discussions of government, *Politics* and *Nichomachean Ethics,* he conspicuously neglected to mention any example of this condition having been met. After his seven years in Macedonia, Aristotle spent the rest of his life studying the world, teaching, and writing. He was one of the most prolific writers in the ancient world.

The following selection is taken from Aristotle's *Politics.* He probably began writing it in the 340s, possibly as a series of lectures, for the work was written over several decades. Together with Plato's *Republic,* Aristotle's *Politics* and *Nichomachean Ethics* are considered the foundations of modern political science. Book II, from which this excerpt is taken, is an examination of both proposed and actual constitutions, including those of Sparta and Carthage. Examples of constitutions that seemed to work well were important to Aristotle, since he believed that the study of "practical knowledge"— ethics and politics—could enable human beings to live together peacefully and happily. Students of American history should note that when Aristotle spoke of constitutions he was not necessarily alluding to actual documents or texts. In the ancient world the word *constitution* simply meant the structure of a government, its laws, and operation. Additionally, readers should be aware that ellipses in the text in this selection refer to parts of the work that are missing, rather than sections that have been edited out by the authors of *Passages.*

By the time Aristotle had decided to write about the constitution of Carthage, the city had grown from a Phoenician colony to an independent city-state to a maritime empire with colonies of its own. In fact, by the fourth century B.C.E., Carthage was the undisputed master of the western Mediterranean. Its government, meanwhile, had also passed through several stages. Originally a dependent monarchy, by Aristotle's time it had abandoned its original aristocratic system in favor of plutocracy, and further democratic reforms awaited.

VIII.   Carthage also appears to have a good constitution, with many outstanding features as compared with those of other nations, but most nearly resembling the Spartan in some points. For these three constitutions are in a way near to one another and are widely different from the others—the Cretan, the Spartan and, thirdly, that of Carthage. Many regulations at Carthage are good; and a proof that its constitution is well regulated is that the populace willingly remain faithful to the constitutional system, and that neither civil strife has arisen in any degree worth mentioning, nor yet a tyrant.

Points in which the Carthaginian constitution resembles the Spartan are the common mess-tables of its Comradeships corresponding to the Phiditia,* and the magistracy of the Hundred and Four corresponding to the Ephors (except one point of superiority—the Ephors are drawn from any class, but the Carthaginians elect this magistracy by merit); the kings and the council of Elders correspond to the kings and Elders at Sparta, and it is another superior feature that the Carthaginian kings are not confined to the same family and that one of no particular distinction and also that if any family distinguishes itself . . . the Elders are to be chosen from these rather than by age; for as they are put in control of important matters, if they are men of no value they do great harm, and they have already injured the Spartan State.

Now most of the points in the Carthaginian system that would be criticized on the ground of their defects happen to be common to all the constitutions of which we have spoken; but the features open to criticism as judged by the principle of an aristocracy or republic are some of them departures in the direction of democracy and others in the direction of oligarchy. The reference of some matters and not of others to the popular assembly rests with the kings in consultation with the Elders in case they agree unanimously,[1] but failing that, these matters also lie with the people[2]; and when the kings introduce business in the assembly, they do not merely let the people sit and listen to the decisions that have been taken by their rulers, but the people have the sovereign decision and anybody who wishes may speak against the proposals introduced, a right that does not exist under the other constitutions. The appointment by co-optation of the Boards of Five which control many important matters, and the election by these boards of the supreme magistracy of the Hundred, and also their longer tenure of authority than that of any other officers (for they are in power after they have gone out of office and before they have actually entered upon it) are oligarchical features; their receiving no pay and not being chosen by lot and other similar regulations must be set down as aristocratic, and so must the fact that the members of the Boards are the judges in all lawsuits, instead of different suits being tried by different courts as at Sparta. But the Carthaginian system deviates from aristocracy in the direction of oligarchy most signally in respect of a certain idea that is shared by most people; they think that the rulers should be chosen not only for their merit but also for their wealth, as it is not possible for a poor man to govern well—he has not leisure for his duties. If therefore election by wealth is oligarchical and election by merit aristocratic, this will be a third system, exhibited for instance in the constitution of Carthage, for there elections are made with an eye to these two qualifications, and especially elections to the most important offices, those of the kings and of the generals. But it must be held that this divergence from aristocracy is an error on the part of a lawgiver;

---

*The *phiditia* (also called *andreia* and *syssitia*) were most common in Sparta and on Crete, but they existed in many Greek city-states as well. Basically, they were living and/or dining groups of fifteen to thirty citizen soldiers between the ages of twenty and sixty. Candidates applied for membership, and the vote usually had to be unanimous. Each member contributed fixed amounts of food and drink each month.

---

[1]*I.e.,* both parties agree to refer or not to refer.
[2]*I.e.,* even when the Kings only or the Elders only desire reference, it takes place.

for one of the most important points to keep in view from the outset is that the best citizens may be able to have leisure and may not have to engage in any unseemly occupation, not only when in office but also when living in private life. And if it is necessary to look to the question of means for the sake of leisure, it is a bad thing that the greatest offices of state, the kingship and the generalship, should be for sale. For this law makes wealth more honoured than worth, and renders the whole state avaricious; and whatever the holders of supreme power deem honourable, the opinion of the other citizens also is certain to follow them, and a state in which virtue is not held in the highest honour cannot be securely governed by an aristocracy. And it is probable that those who purchase office will learn by degrees to make a profit out of it, when they hold office for money spent; for it would be odd if a man of small means but respectable should want to make a profit but an inferior person when he has spent money to get elected should not want to. Hence the persons who should be in office are those most capable of holding office. And even if the lawgiver neglected to secure comfortable means for respectable people, it would at all events be better that he should provide for their leisure while in office.

And it might also be thought a bad thing for the same person to hold several offices, which is considered a distinction at Carthage. One man one job is the best rule for efficiency, and the lawgiver ought to see that this may be secured, and not appoint the same man to play the flute and make shoes. Hence except in a small city it is better for the state for a larger number to share in the offices and more democratic, for it is fairer to all, as we said, and also functions are performed better and more quickly when separate than when in the same hands.[3] This is clear in military and naval matters; for in both of these departments command and subordination penetrate throughout almost the whole body.[4]

But the constitution being oligarchical they best escape the dangers by being wealthy, as they constantly send out a portion of the common people to appointments in the cities; by this means they cure this defect in their system and make it stable. However, this is the achievement of fortune, whereas freedom from civil strife ought to be secured by the lawgiver; but as it is, suppose some misfortune occurs and the multitude of the subject class revolts, there is no remedy provided by the laws to restore tranquillity.

---

[3]Or "functions remaining the same, each is done better and more quickly."

[4]*I.e.,* everyone in command (except the commander-in-chief) has someone of higher rank over him.

REVIEW QUESTIONS

1. What particular aspects of Carthaginian government did Aristotle admire? What did he dislike? Explain.
2. How would you describe the government of Carthage in Aristotle's time? In whose hands were the primary decisions? What was the role of the common people?
3. What information about the constitution of Sparta can be discerned from this selection?
4. Which did Aristotle seem to prefer, the constitution of Sparta or that of Carthage? Why?

Two European Views of Africans

Greek Kantharos (Athens, sixth century B.C.E.)
Roman Rhyton (Apuleia, fourth century B.C.E.)

In the modern world, the Mediterranean Sea tends to be viewed as a body of water that divides Africa from Europe. In the ancient world, however, the Mediterranean served as a great highway that connected the two continents. In fact, the meaning of the word *Mediterranean* in Latin is "in the middle of land." In the period from 500 B.C.E. to 800 C.E., northern Africa was very much a part of the Greco-Roman world. This is evident in hundreds of examples of Africans portrayed in Greek and Roman paintings, mosaics, sculptures, and pottery.

The two drinking cups portrayed in these photographs use African natives as the primary artistic theme. The first, a high-handled cup called a *kantharos*, comes from Attica, a region around Athens, from the sixth century B.C.E. It shows the head of a man whose face is marked by either age or tattoos. The second is a footed *rhyton* from Apuleia, a region in southern Italy, from the fourth century B.C.E. It depicts a young African boy struggling with a crocodile.

Several assumptions can be made about these two cups, which are representative of hundreds that have been found in Greece and Italy. As nearly all feature markedly different portraits, it is apparent that Greek and Roman artists were in contact with many different individuals who were either African themselves or whose ancestors were. The number and variety of these vases show that interactions between the peoples who lived on the shores of the Mediterranean were more frequent and extensive than scholars once believed.

Kantharos in the Form of a Head of an Elderly Man, Greece, Attica, Athens; Archaic Period, about 500 B.C.E. Ceramic. H: 17.7 cm. *(By: the Class of Boston 00.332, © 2002 The Museum of Fine Arts, Boston; Henry Lillie Pierce Fund, 00.332.)*

Negro Youth Struggling with a Crocodile, from Apuleia, fourth century B.C.E. Terracotta. H: 22.2 cm. *(GR.58.1865. Photograph © Fitzwilliam Museum, University of Cambridge)*

REVIEW QUESTIONS

1. How does the cup from Attica differ from the vase from Apuleia? How are they alike?
2. How do these cups illustrate Greco-Roman views of Africa?
3. Do you consider the portrayal of Africans in these ancient cups to be flattering or offensive? How would you feel about them if you were an African from this time period?

A Roman Intellectual Describes Africa (first century C.E.)

PLINY THE ELDER, *Natural History, Book V*

Pliny the Elder (Gaius Plinius Secundus, 23–79 C.E.) was one of the Roman Empire's most prolific writers. He can best be described as insatiably curious about the world around him, a trait that led him to author not only his best-known work, the thirty-seven-book *Natural History,* but also a twenty-book history of the German wars, a thirty-one-book history of Rome, and numerous monographs on subjects ranging from Roman oratory to spear-throwing tactics used by the cavalry. Pliny is particularly famous for a letter to his nephew that describes the eruption of Mt. Vesuvius on August 24, 79. There his curiosity had unfortunate results: During his attempts to examine the disaster site firsthand, he inhaled high levels of noxious fumes and died a few days later.

The *Natural History* is Pliny's attempt to compile all contemporary knowledge into a single work. "Nature, which is to say Life, is my subject," he said. Thus his books cover, in detail, the animals, plants, and minerals of the ancient Mediterranean world, as well as technology, medicine, agriculture, geography, and ethnography. Although some of his information was based on his personal observations, most of it came from his extensive use of the writings of others. In fact, in his preface Pliny claimed to have consulted two thousand different written sources, many of which he cited later in the text by name. Scholars, however, maintain that Pliny severely underestimated this number.

The following selection is from Book V of the *Natural History,* which includes often fanciful, rather than accurate, descriptions of the different peoples of Africa. Pliny was not a careful scholar and he frequently garbled his information, but his uncritical and naïve use of sources was typical for this period. Nevertheless, his work is an invaluable source of information on the lifestyles of the Romans, their neighbors, and their trading partners, especially African peoples south of the Sahara.

Suetonius Paulinus, who was consul in our own times,* was the first Roman commander who actually crossed the Atlas range and advanced a distance of many miles beyond it. His report as to its remarkable altitude agrees with that of all the other authorities, but he also states that the regions at the base of the range are filled with dense and lofty forests of trees of an unknown kind, with very tall trunks remarkable for their glossy timber free from knots, and foliage like that of the cypress except for its oppressive scent, the leaves being covered with a thin downy floss, so that with the aid of art a dress-material like that obtained from the silk-worm can be made from them. The summit (the report continued) is covered with deep snowdrifts even in summer. Ten days' march brought him to this point and beyond it to the river called the Ger, across deserts covered with black dust occasionally broken by projections of rock that looked as if they had been burnt, a region rendered uninhabitable by its heat, although it was winter time when

he explored it. He states that the neighbouring forests swarm with every kind of elephant and snake, and are inhabited by a tribe called the Canarii, owing to the fact that they have their diet in common with the canine race and share with it the flesh of wild animals. . . .

In the interior circuit of Africa towards the south and beyond the Gaetulians, after an intermediate strip of desert, the first inhabitants of all are the Egyptian Libyans, and then the people called in Greek the White Ethiopians. Beyond these are the Ethiopian clans of the Nigritae, named after the river which has been mentioned, the Pharusian Gymnetes, and then bordering on the Ocean the Perorsi whom we have spoken of at the frontier of Mauretania. Eastward of all of these there are vast uninhabited regions spreading as far as the Garamantes and Augilae and the Cave-dwellers—the most reliable opinion being that of those who place two Ethiopias beyond the African desert, and especially Homer,[†] who tells us that the Ethiopians are divided into two sections, the eastward and the westward.

The river Niger has the same nature as the Nile: it produces reeds and papyrus, and the

---

*In 41 C.E., Gaius Suetonius Paulinus was made propraetor (governor) and was sent to Mauritania, a large province in northwestern Africa. Consul in 66, he was the father of Gaius Suetonius Tranquillus, the author of the *Lives of the Twelve Caesars.*

†Greek author of the *Iliad* and the *Odyssey.*

same animals, and it rises at the same seasons of the year. Its source is between the Ethiopic tribes of the Tarraelii and the Oechalicae; the town of the latter is Magium. In the middle of the desert some place the Atlas tribe, and next to them the half-animal Goat-Pans and the Blemmyae and Gamphasantes and Satyrs and Strapfoots.

The Atlas tribe have fallen below the level of human civilization, if we can believe what is said; for they do not address one another by any names, and when they behold the rising and setting sun, they utter awful curses against it as the cause of disaster to themselves and their fields, and when they are asleep they do not have dreams like the rest of mankind. The Cave-dwellers hollow out caverns, which are their dwellings; they live on the flesh of snakes, and they have no voice, but only make squeaking noises, being entirely devoid of intercourse by speech. The Garamantes do not practise marriage but live with their women promiscuously. The Augilae only worship the powers of the lower world. The Gamphasantes go naked, do not engage in battle, and hold no intercourse with any foreigner. The Blemmyae are reported to have no heads, their mouth and eyes being attached to their chests. The Satyrs have nothing of ordinary humanity about them except human shape. The form of the Goat-Pans is that which is commonly shown in pictures of them. The Strapfoots are people with feet like leather thongs, whose nature it is to crawl instead of walking. The Pharusi, originally a Persian people, are said to have accompanied Hercules on his journey to the Ladies of the West. Nothing more occurs to us to record about Africa.

REVIEW QUESTIONS

1. Pliny described various groups of people in this passage. Which of these descriptions do you find to be the most interesting and why? Least interesting and why?
2. How reliable do you think Pliny's account is? Explain.
3. In what ways do Pliny's writings reveal his own biases and prejudices?

Three Inscriptions from Aksum Relate the Deeds of King Ezana (c. 350 C.E.)

The Ethiopian Royal Chronicles

Aksum was a wealthy and ancient kingdom in the Ethiopian highlands of East Africa. Chronicles from medieval Ethiopia attribute the foundation of the kingdom to Menelek (or Ibn el-Hakim), son of the Hebrew king Solomon and the queen of Sheba (also called Saba), sometime in the second millennium B.C.E. Scholars do not know definitely when the Kingdom of Sheba declined and Aksum replaced it, or indeed whether there was a true break between the two. Aksum, however, seems to have risen to prominence around 50 C.E., at the time its capital city, also called Aksum, became an important trading center. It reached its greatest power between the 300s and the 600s, growing rich and powerful through trade out of Adule, its port on the Red Sea. The

Aksumite traders exchanged gold, ivory, and a wide variety of raw materials (such as spices and gum arabic) from Kush and central Africa with merchants from Egypt, Greece, Rome, Persia, and India. Wealth from trade allowed the kings of Aksum to build impressive granite monuments and fortresses and to expand their territory in all directions, even across the Red Sea into what is now Yemen.

The history of Aksum is known primarily from inscriptionary evidence and from occasional mention in the writings of foreign navigators and traders. Most of the inscriptions come from the reign of the most famous of the Aksumite kings, Ezana, who lived in the 300s. Ezana is particularly noteworthy for his conversion to Christianity in approximately 350 and for making Christianity the state religion of Aksum. His conquest of the Kingdom of Meroë also resulted in the decline and eventual demise of Kushite civilization. Ezana's kingdom prospered for at least two centuries after his death. Its decline began when the Persians conquered Arabia in the late 500s, which resulted in the loss of Aksum's territories across the Red Sea; and it accelerated in the 600s, when the Muslims united Arabia and Persia under one government. Subsequently, Islam spread rapidly through North and East Africa. As a result, Aksum's Christians were surrounded by non-Christians. From the 600s to the 900s, the Aksumites fought the Muslims and surrounding tribal peoples. Aksum slowly shrank in stature and territory, but its culture survived and later flourished in medieval Ethiopia.

The three stone inscriptions in this selection were set up by Ezana himself and can still be seen at Aksum today. They recount the king's conquests of various peoples, many of whom scholars cannot identify. Nevertheless, these inscriptions display Aksum at the height of its power. Of particular significance are references in the first two inscriptions to Ares, the Greek god of war, whom the Aksumites called Mahrem. The last inscription, however, speaks of the Lord of Heaven—probably the Christian God.

THE EXPEDITION AGAINST BEGA

Ezana, King of Aksum and of Himyar and of Raydan* and of Ethiopia[1] and of Saba and of Salhen and of Tseyamo and of Bega and of Kasu,† the King of Kings, the son of the invincible god, Ares.

As the peoples of the Bega had rebelled, we sent our brothers Shaiazana and Hadefan to make

war on them. And having laid down their arms [our brothers] subdued them and brought them to us with their camp-followers and 3,112 cattle and 6,224 sheep and pack animals, giving them cattle and grain to eat, and beer, wine and water to drink to the full, according to their number. They brought six tributary kings with their people, in number 4,400. They received each day 22,000 pieces of bread and wine for four months while they were bringing them to us. After giving them all kinds of food, as well as clothing, we allowed them to depart. They settled in a district called Matlia which belongs to our realm. And we commanded that food should be given to them, and we granted to the six kings 25,140 cattle.

To obtain the favour of my begetter, the

---

*Himyar was a region on the southwestern tip of the Arabian Peninsula. Raydan was the most important city in the region.

[1]The term Ethiopia seems to have been used in this inscription to refer to a region to the west of Aksum.

†Bega was the name of the territory northwest of Aksum, in the bend of the Takaze River. Kasu lay to the west of Aksum, in modern Sudan. The other regions—Saba, Salhen, and Tseyamo—cannot be accurately located.

invincible Ares, I have set up to him one statue of gold and one in silver and three in bronze.

THE EXPEDITION AGAINST THE TSARANE

Ezana, the son of Ella Amida, of the family of Halen, King of Aksum, and of Hemer [Himyar] and of Raydan, and of Sab and of Salhen, and of Tseyamo, and of Bega, and of Kasu, the son of Mahrem.

He made war on the Tsarane, whose kingdom is Afan, after they had fought us and killed a merchant caravan. And then we made war upon them; first of all we sent armies, the army of Mahaza, and the army of Dakuen, and the army of Hara, and then we ourselves followed, and we encamped at the place where the troops were assembled and we made our soldiers set out from there. And they killed, and made prisoners, and despoiled them. And we attacked Sane and Tsawante, and Gema, and Zahtan, four peoples, and we took prisoner Alita with his two children. And a slaughter took place of the men of Afan, 503 men and 202 women, in all 705. Of his camp-followers there were taken prisoner 40 men and 165 women and children, in all 205. As booty were carried off 31,957 cattle and 827 baggage animals. And [the King] returned in safety together with his people. And he set up a throne here in Shado, and committed himself to the protection of Astar and Beher and Meder. If there be anyone who would overthrow it and remove it, that person, and his land and his race, shall be overthrown and removed and be rooted out of his country. And he [the King] offered 100 cattle and 50 prisoners as a thanks-offering to Mahrem [Ares] who had begotten him.

THE EXPEDITION AGAINST NOBA

By the power of the Lord of Heaven who is mightier than everything which exists in heaven or on earth. Ezana, the son of Ella Amida, of the descent of Halen, King of Aksum and of Hemer, Raydan, Saba, Salhen, Tseyamo, Bega and Kasu, King of Kings . . . and invincible to

the enemy. By the might of the Lord of Heaven who has made me lord, who reigns as the perfect one for all eternity. . . .

By the might of the Lord of All I made war upon Noba,* for the peoples of Noba had rebelled and made a boast of it. The peoples of Noba had said: "they (*the Aksumites*) will not cross the Takaze." And they were in the habit of attacking the peoples of Mangurto and Khasa and Barya and the blacks and of making war upon the red peoples. And two or three times they had broken their solemn oaths and had killed their neighbours mercilessly, and they had stripped bare and stolen the properties of our envoys and messengers which I had sent to them to inquire into their thefts, and had stolen from them their weapons of defence.

And as I have sent warnings to them, and they would not listen to me and refused to stop their [evil] deeds and heaped insults upon me and then took to flight, I made war upon them. And I rose up in the might of the Lord of the Land, and I fought them on the Takaze, at the ford of Kemalke. Thereupon they took to flight and would not make a stand. And I followed the fugitives for twenty-three days, killing and making prisoners and capturing booty wherever I stopped. My people who marched into the country brought back prisoners and booty.

Meanwhile I burnt their towns, [both] those built of brick and those built of reeds, and [my soldiers] carried off their food, as well as copper, iron and brass; they destroyed the statues in their houses (*i.e., temples*), as well as their storehouses for food, and their cotton trees, casting them in the river Sida (*the Nile*). And there were many men who died in the water, their number being unknown to me. [The soldiers] sank their ships crowded with people, men and women, in the river. And I captured two chieftains, who had come as spies riding on female camels. . . . And I captured an Angabenawi nobleman. . . . The chieftains who died were five in number. . . .

And I came to Kasu and I fought a battle and

---

*Noba was a territory located at the confluence of the Blue Nile and Takaze Rivers.

made prisoners of its people at the junction of the rivers Sida and Takaze. And the day after I arrived I sent out the army Mahaza and the army Hara, and Damawa and Falha and Sera, to raid the country upstream of Sida, and the cities built of brick and those of reeds. The names of the cities built of brick were Alwa and Daro. And they killed and captured prisoners and cast people into the water, and they arrived safe and sound having terrified their enemies and conquered them by the might of the Lord of the Land. And after that I sent the army of Halen and the army of Laken and the army of Sabarat, and Falha and Sera, down the Sida against the towns of Noba which are made of reeds. . . . The towns of brick which the Noba had taken were Tabito and Fertoti. And my people arrived at the frontier of the red Noba and they returned safe and sound, having captured prisoners and slain the Noba and taken booty from them by the might of the Lord of Heaven. And I set up a throne in that country at the place where the rivers Sida and Takaze join, opposite the town with brick houses. . . .

The things which the Lord of Heaven has given me are: men captives, 214, women captives, 415, total captives, 629. Men slain, 602, women and children slain, 156, total slain, 700. Total of prisoners and slain, 1,387. Booty, 10,560 cattle and 51,050 sheep.

And I set up a throne here in Shado by the might of the Lord of Heaven, who has helped me and given me sovereignty.

May the Lord of Heaven make my kingdom strong! And as He has this day conquered my enemy for me may He conquer for me wherever I go. As He has this day conquered for me, and overthrown my enemy, I will rule the people with righteousness and justice, and will not oppress them. And may they preserve this throne which I have set up for the Lord of Heaven, who has made me King, and the land upon which it lies. And if there shall be anyone who shall remove it, destroy it or overthrow it, he and his kinsfolk shall be rooted out and removed from the land. I have set up this throne by the might of the Lord of Heaven.

REVIEW QUESTIONS

1. What do you think was the purpose of Ezana's expeditions against Bega and the Tsarane? What was his reason for attacking Noba? What are the similarities and differences?
2. To whom or what did Ezana attribute his success in battle? What changes do you notice in these three inscriptions, which are arranged chronologically?
3. Did Ezana's conversion to Christianity affect his dealings with his subject peoples and neighboring states? If so, how? If not, why not?

A Byzantine Historian Observes the Moors and the Vandals (sixth century C.E.)

PROCOPIUS, *History of the Wars, Book IV*

In the period commonly known as "late antiquity," the Mediterranean coast of northwest Africa (now Morocco and northern Algeria) was the Roman province of Mauritania, and it was inhabited by two African peoples, the

Berbers and the Moors. Between 427 and 432 C.E., it was overrun by a German tribe known as the Vandals. The Vandal Kingdom of North Africa, which stretched across Mauritania through Numida to eastern Libya, became one of the more stable states to emerge from the ruins of the Roman Empire in the West in the fifth century. In the sixth century, however, this area fell once again to conquering armies, this time as part of an attempt by the Byzantine emperor in the East, Justinian, to reclaim lands that had once been part of the Roman Empire. Accompanying the Byzantine army on its Mauritanian campaign in 533 was Procopius, private secretary to the general Belisarius. His eye-witness observations of the Moors and Vandals are recounted in this selection.

Born at Caesarea in Palestine toward the end of the fifth century C.E., Procopius became a lawyer, probably at Constantinople, and joined the service of Belisarius in 527. Procopius accompanied the general not just on his African campaign, but also to Persia and Italy. He recounted his observations and experiences in eight books, *The History of the Wars* (Persian, Vandal, and Gothic). Later he wrote a ponderous six-book tome entitled *The Buildings of Justinian;* and, after leaving government service, he published a candid and fascinating exposé of the imperial family, which he called *Unpublished Memoirs* (today frequently known as *The Secret History*). The date of Procopius's death is unknown, but he was still living in 560.

For of all the nations which we know that of the Vandals is the most luxurious, and that of the Moors the most hardy. For the Vandals, since the time when they gained possession of Libya, used to indulge in baths, all of them, every day, and enjoyed a table abounding in all things, the sweetest and best that the earth and sea produce. And they wore gold very generally, and clothed themselves in the Medic garments, which now they call "seric," and passed their time, thus dressed, in theatres and hippodromes and in other pleasureable pursuits, and above all else in hunting. And they had dancers and mimes and all other things to hear and see which are of a musical nature or otherwise merit attention among men. And the most of them dwelt in parks, which were well supplied with water and trees; and they had great numbers of banquets, and all manner of sexual pleasures were in great vogue among them. But the Moors live in stuffy huts both in winter and in summer and at every other time, never removing from them either because of snow or the heat of the sun or any other discomfort whatever due to nature. And they sleep on the ground, the prosperous among

them, if it should so happen, spreading a fleece under themselves. Moreover, it is not customary among them to change their clothing with the seasons, but they wear a thick cloak and a rough shirt at all times. And they have neither bread nor wine nor any other good thing, but they take grain, either wheat or barley, and, without boiling it or grinding it to flour or barley-meal, they eat it in a manner not a whit different from that of animals. . . .

A certain Moorish woman had managed somehow to crush a little corn, and making of it a very tiny cake, threw it into the hot ashes on the hearth. For thus it is the custom among the Moors to bake their loaves. And beside this hearth two children were sitting, in exceedingly great distress by reason of their hunger, the one being the son of the very woman who had thrown in the cake, and the other a nephew of Gelimer,* and they were eager to seize the cake as soon as it should seem to them to be cooked. And of the two children the Vandal got ahead of the other

---

*Gelimer was the last king of the Vandals. He was captured by Belisarius in 534.

and snatched the cake first, and, though it was still exceedingly hot and covered with ashes, hunger overpowered him, and he threw it into his mouth and was eating it, when the other seized him by the hair of the head and struck him over the temple and beat him again and thus compelled him with great violence to cast out the cake which was already in his throat. . . .

Now there are lofty mountains there, and a level space near the foothills of the mountains, where the barbarians had made preparations for the battle and arranged their fighting order as follows. They formed a circle of their camels, . . . making the front about twelve deep. And they placed the women with the children within the circle; (for among the Moors it is customary to take also a few women, with their children, to battle, and these make the stockades and huts for them and tend the horses skilfully, and have charge of the camels and the food; they also sharpen the iron weapons and take upon themselves many of the tasks in connection with the preparation for battle); and the men themselves took their stand on foot in between the legs of the camels, having shields and swords and small spears which they are accustomed to hurl like javelins. . . . Of all men the Moorish nation seems to be the most poorly equipped for war's struggle. For the most of them have no armour at all, and those who have shields to hold before themselves have only small ones which are not well made and are not able to turn aside what strikes against them. And after they have thrown those two small spears, if they do not accomplish anything, they turn of their own accord to flight. So that it is possible for you, after guarding against the first attack of the barbarians, to win the victory with no trouble at all. But as to your equipment of arms, you see, of course, how great is the difference between it and that of your opponents. And apart from this, both valour of heart and strength of body and experience in war and confidence because you have already conquered all your enemies,—all these advantages you have; but the Moors, being deprived of all these things, put their trust only in their own great throng. And it is easier for a few who are most excellently prepared to conquer a multitude of men not good at warfare than it is for the multitude to defeat them. For while the good soldier has his confidence in himself, the cowardly man generally finds that the very number of those arrayed with him produces a want of room that is full of peril. Furthermore, you are warranted in despising these camels, which cannot fight for the enemy, and when struck by our missiles will, in all probability, become the cause of considerable confusion and disorder among them. And the eagerness for battle which the enemy have acquired on account of their former success will be your ally in the fight. For daring, when it is kept commensurate with one's power, will perhaps be of some benefit even to those who make use of it, but when it exceeds one's power it leads into danger. Bearing these things in mind and despising the enemy, observe silence and order; for by taking thought for these things we shall win the victory over the disorder of the barbarians more easily and with less labour.

REVIEW QUESTIONS

1. Procopius claimed that, of all the peoples he knew, the Vandals were the most luxurious and the Moors were the hardiest. What information in this selection supports his statement?
2. Why do you think Procopius included the story of the two children and the oatcake? What did he hope to illustrate?
3. Which group did Procopius admire more, the Vandals or the Moors? Why?

8

South and Southwest Asia, 800 B.C.E.–800 C.E.

This chapter includes both native and foreign accounts of Indian society and illustrates the different approaches natives and foreigners took in their writings. In the case of native accounts, Indian literature, rather than history or social commentary, provides the best insights into the institutions, personal relationships, and religious ideology of Hindu society. In particular, this chapter includes selections that illustrate dharma, the central concept of Hindu society. It is a complex idea implying moral duty and formalized institutions such as marriage and the caste system. The word is from a verbal root that means "to hold"; thus it is the fabric that holds a society together, as ideals and institutions do in modern democracies. Dharma dictates that individuals are responsible for their own actions. The tale of Savitri illustrates the central role of dharma because she overcomes death itself—not just for herself, but also for her beloved husband, and hence the family (the central unit in Hindu society). Indeed, the family is so important that the roles of specific members of the extended family are given separate names, such as the maternal uncle and his wife, *mama* and *mami,* and the paternal uncle and his wife, *chacha* and *chachi.*

This selection reflects social ideas, especially in regard to women, whose dharmic roles as wife and mother were of utmost importance. Although individuals mattered, social responsibilities, not individual rights, were the keystone to society, for men as well as women. This led to a certain amount of stereotyping; however, in the literature the female characters were usually more distinct, admirable, likable, and stronger than their male counterparts.

The travelers' accounts, written by two Hellenistic Greeks and a Chinese Buddhist, do not discuss dharma. They contrast sharply with the native account, particularly since the Greeks and Chinese were fascinated by history. Of the three non-native accounts, that of Fâ-hien is probably the most valuable, for not only are his observations sensitive and generally accurate, but they also reflect a great curiosity. The account of Megasthenes, the Greek ambassador during the reign of Chandragupta Maurya, is also of great value. He wrote at the beginning of the first great Indian dynasty and empire, and if the later geographer Strabo had not quoted from the now-lost descriptions of Megasthenes, knowledge of these formative years in Indian history would be considerably impoverished. Finally, the notes of the anonymous ship captain show a greater knowledge of navigation in the area than is generally supposed, although detail is unfortunately lacking.

A Greek Diplomat Describes Life in Pataliputra (c. 320–297 B.C.E.)

MEGASTHENES, *Indika, Fragment 27*

When Greek intellectuals and historians began living in the newly created Hellenistic kingdoms that Alexander the Great's generals had carved out of the old Persian Empire, they felt compelled to study the natives and to learn their customs. One result of this process was the creation of systematic, well-organized ethnographies, often patronized by the ruling elite and written by experts, only a few of whom were not Greeks. These authors relied on official records and "inside knowledge." Their works combined myth, religion, geography, natural history, political history, and social customs, much like Herodotus had done centuries earlier. Hecataeus of Abdera, the earliest of these authors, wrote for Ptolemy I of Egypt; in the next generation he was followed by the Egyptian priest Manetho, whose chronology is still the basis of Egyptian history. In the Seleucid kingdom, Berossus, a priest of Baal, wrote a Babylonian history; and Megasthenes (c. 350–290 B.C.E.), whose work is excerpted here, wrote an impressive survey of the beginnings of the Mauryan Empire. This interest in other countries is without a doubt one of the most important results of Alexander's conquests. If only for a relatively brief period, the Greeks were able to consider, and wonder at, the world outside their own city-states.

Megasthenes, an Ionian Greek, was both a diplomat and a historian. He served as ambassador of Seleucus I to the court of Chandragupta Maurya (r. c. 320–297 B.C.E.) at Pataliputra (modern Patna). His four-volume account of Indian history, the *Indika,* is lost, but parts of it, including the following selection, were preserved by later writers, most notably Strabo (64 B.C.E.–25 C.E.), the celebrated Greek geographer. Megasthenes was credulous and inaccurate. For example, he erroneously believed that the ancient Indians had no writing system and practiced cannibalism. Nevertheless, the *Indika* offered the most complete account of India then known to the Greek world. The work is a fascinating mixture of observation and misunderstanding.

OF THE MANNERS
OF THE INDIANS

The Indians all live frugally, especially when in camp. They dislike a great undisciplined multitude, and consequently they observe good order. Theft is of very rare occurrence. Megasthenês says that those who were in the camp of Sandrakottos [chandragupta], wherein lay 400,000 men, found that the thefts reported on any one day did not exceed the value of two hundred drachmæ, and this among a people who have no written laws, but are ignorant of writing, and must therefore in all the business of life trust to memory. They live, nevertheless, happily enough, being simple in their manners and frugal. They never drink wine except at sacrifices.[1] Their beverage is a liquor composed from rice instead of barley, and their food is principally a rice-pottage.[2] The simplicity of their laws and their contracts is proved by the fact that they seldom

---

[1]This wine was probably Soma juice.
[2]Curry and rice, no doubt.

go to law. They have no suits about pledges or deposits, nor do they require either seals or witnesses, but make their deposits and confide in each other. Their houses and property they generally leave unguarded. These things indicate that they possess good, sober sense; but other things they do which one cannot approve: for instance, that they eat always alone, and that they have no fixed hours when meals are to be taken by all in common, but each one eats when he feels inclined. The contrary custom would be better for the ends of social and civil life.

Their favourite mode of exercising the body is by friction, applied in various ways, but especially by passing smooth ebony rollers over the skin. Their tombs are plain, and the mounds raised over the dead lowly. In contrast to the general simplicity of their style, they love finery and ornament. Their robes are worked in gold, and ornamented with precious stones, and they wear also flowered garments made of the finest muslin. Attendants walking behind hold up umbrellas over them: for they have a high regard for beauty, and avail themselves of every device to improve their looks. Truth and virtue they hold alike in esteem. Hence they accord no special privileges to the old unless they possess superior wisdom. They marry many wives, whom they buy from their parents, giving in exchange a yoke of oxen. Some they marry hoping to find in them willing helpmates; and others for pleasure and to fill their homes with children. The wives prostitute themselves unless they are compelled to be chaste. No one wears a crown at a sacrifice or libation, and they do not stab the victim, but strangle it, so that nothing mutilated, but only what is entire, may be presented to the deity.

A person convicted of bearing false witness suffers mutilation of his extremities. He who maims any one not only suffers in return the loss of the same limb, but his hand also is cut off. If he causes an artizan to lose his hand or his eye, he is put to death. The same writer says that none of the Indians employ slaves.

The care of the king's person is entrusted to women, who also are bought from their parents. The guards and the rest of the soldiery attend outside the gates. A woman who kills the king when drunk becomes the wife of his successor. The sons succeed the father. The king may not sleep during the daytime, and by night he is obliged to change his couch from time to time, with a view to defeat plots against his life.

The king leaves his palace not only in time of war, but also for the purpose of judging causes. He then remains in court for the whole day, without allowing the business to be interrupted, even though the hour arrives when he must needs attend to his person,—that is, when he is to be rubbed with cylinders of wood. He continues hearing cases while the friction, which is performed by four attendants, is still proceeding. Another purpose for which he leaves his palace is to offer sacrifice; a third is to go to the chase, for which he departs in Bacchanalian fashion. Crowds of women surround him, and outside of this circle spearmen are ranged. The road is marked off with ropes, and it is death, for man and woman alike, to pass within the ropes. Men with drums and gongs lead the procession. The king hunts in the enclosures and shoots arrows from a platform. At his side stand two or three armed women. If he hunts in the open grounds he shoots from the back of an elephant. Of the women, some are in chariots, some on horses, and some even on elephants, and they are equipped with weapons of every kind, as if they were going on a campaign.

[These customs are very strange when compared with our own, but the following are still more so;] for Megasthenês states that the tribes inhabiting the Kaukasos have intercourse with women in public, and eat the bodies of their relatives, and that there are monkeys which roll down stones, etc.

The Indians neither put out money at usury, nor know how to borrow. It is contrary to established usage for an Indian either to do or suffer a wrong, and therefore they neither make contracts, nor require securities.

REVIEW QUESTIONS

1. What subjects seem to have interested Megasthenes the most? Why do you think this was so?
2. What did Megasthenes think about the relationship between men and women?
3. What evidence is there that Megasthenes respected the natives of India? Is there evidence to suggest otherwise?

An Indian Epic Describes a Determined Wife (c. 200 B.C.E.)

The Story of Savitri, The Mahabharata

The *Mahabharata* is one of two great and highly influential Sanskrit epics (the other is the *Ramayana*). It is Indo-European, and shows similarities to the *Iliad.* Unlike the *Iliad,* however, it includes a number of insertions or side stories, and it is a huge, loosely structured work. One of the side stories is that of Savitri, a woman who saves her husband from death. This remarkable piece of epic literature shows a woman's strength in her dharma as wife; yet she has an independent spirit as well, evidenced by her insistence upon her choice of husband in spite of dire forewarnings, her resolve in regard to the three-night vow she undertakes, and her pluck in dealing with Yama, the god of death. Her strong attachment needs to be seen both as deep-seated love for her husband and as her dharmic role as Satyavat's wife (and hence daughter-in-law of the family: "joy of your family," Yama calls her when freeing her husband).

The following translation is by the noted Sanskritist J. A. B. van Buitenen, who did a remarkable job in capturing the flavor and power of the original. Because of the involved structure of the *Mahabharata,* the cast of speakers needs to be explained. Markendaya is relating the incident to King Yudhisthira, a major figure in the central narrative of the epic. Aśvapati is the king of a people known as the Madras (mud-ras; not to be confused with the modern city with the same spelling), who prays to a goddess, Savitri, for a son. She grants him a daughter (a good example of the sometimes perverse nature of ancient Indo-European gods), who is named after her. Narada is a sort of seer, a celestial busybody who warns the king of the danger in his daughter's choice of a groom, Satyavat, the son of a blind exiled king. Nevertheless, Savitri is resolute and will not renounce her choice. This sort of determination and devotion is what makes her one of the models of Hindu wifeliness.

In the land of the Madras there was a Law-spirited king steeped in the Law, brahminic, a ready refuge, true to his promises, master of his senses, a sacrificer and generous giver, competent, beloved by city folk and countrymen, a king named Aśvapati, who was intent on the well-being of all creatures. A patient man, true-spoken and in control of his senses, he was child-less, and with advancing age he became much worried; and he undertook a severe vow to beget a child. At mealtimes he restricted his food, he was continent and subdued his senses, he offered oblations a hundred thousand times with the *sāvitrī* formula, O best of kings, and forewent his meal every sixth time.

For eighteen years he lived with this life rule, and when the eighteenth year was full, Sāvitrī became contented. She showed herself to the king, O prince, arising from the *agnihotra* with much joy. And the boon-granting Goddess said to the king, "I am pleased with your continence, purity, restraint, and self-control, and with your wholehearted devotion to me, O king. Aśvapati, king of the Madras, choose whatever boon you desire, but pay heed at all times to the Law."

Aśvapati said:

I undertook this effort to obtain a child, out of desire for the Law [dharma]. May I have many sons, goddess, to prosper my lineage. If you are pleased with me, goddess, this I choose as my boon. For offspring, as the twice-born have told me, is the highest Law.

Sāvitrī said:

I knew before this of this intention of yours, O king, and I have spoken to Grandfather in your cause for sons. By the favor decreed to you on earth by the Self-existent, good man, a splendid girl shall soon be born to you. And you should make no reply at all to this, for I am pleased and say this to you on behalf of Grandfather.

Mārkaṇḍeya said:

The king acknowledged Sāvitrī's word: "So be it!" And once more he besought her: "May it happen soon." Sāvitrī disappeared, and the king went home. And he happily lived in his kingdom, ruling his subjects by the Law.

Some time went by, then the king, who was strict in his vows, planted a seed in his eldest queen who abode by the Law. The fruit waxed in the Mālava woman, who was the daughter of a king, bull of the Bharatas, as in the bright fortnight the moon waxes in the sky. When her time came, she gave birth to a lotus-eyed daughter,

and happily the king performed the rites for her. The brahmins and her father gave her the name of Sāvitrī, for she had been given by Sāvitrī when she was pleased with the oblations he had offered with the *sāvitrī*. The princess grew up like Śrī embodied, and in time the girl became adolescent. When people saw the young woman with the fine waist and broad hips, like a golden statue, they thought, "A divine maiden has come to us!" But no man chose her with the eyes of lotus petals, blazing with splendor, for her splendor kept him away.

She fasted, bathed her head, approached the Gods, offered into the fire ritually, had brahmins recite on the moon-phase day; then the divine woman took the remaining flowers, went to her great-spirited father, like Śrī incarnate, and saluted her father's feet. She first offered the leftover flowers to him, and afterward the fair-hipped woman stood at her father's side. Looking at his grownup daughter, beautiful as a Goddess, yet not asked by suitors, the king grew sorrowful.

The king said:

Daughter, the time has come to marry you off, but no one is asking me. Seek a husband for yourself with virtues that match yours. If you wish a man, tell me about him; I shall inquire and give you away. Choose whomever you want, for I have heard the brahmins recite this from the Book of the Law—listen, my pretty, as I repeat it—"A father who does not give away is reprehensible, reprehensible is the husband who does not cohabit; reprehensible is the son who does not protect his mother when her husband has died." These words you hear from me, so hurry to find a husband and act lest I become reprehensible to the deities.

Mārkaṇḍeya said:

Thus he spoke to his daughter, and he assigned old councillors to her retinue and nudged her along: "Go now!" She saluted her father's feet shyly but spiritedly, and having learned her father's orders she set out unhesitatingly. Riding on a chariot amidst the ancient councillors, she went to the lovely forests of austerities of royal seers. After saluting the feet of the estimable elders, my son, she gradually traversed all the woods.

At every ford the princess gave freely to the chief twice-born and went from place to place.

Mārkaṇḍeya said:
Meanwhile, the king of the Madras received a visit from Nārada, O Bhārata, and sat in the center of the assembly hall conversing. At that time Sāvitrī returned from her tour of all the fords and hermitages, and she entered her father's house with the councillors. Seeing her father seated with Nārada, the lovely woman lowered her head to the feet of both of them.

Nārada said:
Where has your daughter been, and from where has she returned? Why are you not marrying the young woman to a husband?

Aśvapati said:
I sent her out for that very purpose, and she has come back just now. Hear from her yourself whom she has chosen for her husband.

Mārkaṇḍeya said:
Prompted by her father with: "Speak in detail," the lovely woman obeyed and, as fate would have it, said, "In the land of the Śālvas there is a law-spirited baron and king who is famed as Dyumatsena. Later in life he became blind. An old enemy on his border, seeing his opportunity, took the wise king's realm, when he had lost his eyesight and his son was still a child. Together with his wife, whose calf was young, he departed for the forest and in the vast wilderness he performed austerities, being noble in his vows. His son Satyavat, born in the city and grown up in the forest of austerities, I have chosen in my heart as the husband who suits me."

Nārada said:
Woe! Sāvitrī has done a great wrong, king, choosing the virtuous Satyavat in her ignorance! His father speaks the truth, his mother speaks the truth, therefore the brahmins gave him the name Satyavat. When he was a child, he loved horses and fashioned them out of clay and made paintings of them; therefore he is also called Citrāśva.

The king said:
Does the prince now have splendor and wisdom, is Satyavat patient and brave, and does his father find joy in him?

Nārada said:
He is splendid as Vivasvat, wise as Bṛhaspati, brave as great Indra, patient as earth herself.

Aśvapati said:
Is Prince Satyavat generous and brahminic, is he handsome and noble, and of pleasing mien?

Nārada said:
In generosity, according to his ability, he is the equal of Rantideva Sāṃkṛti, he is brahminic and true-spoken like Śibi Auśīnara. He is noble as Yayāti, of an aspect as pleasing as the moon, and in beauty Dyumatsena's sturdy son is like one of the Aśvíns. He is self-controlled, he is kind and brave, he is true, he is the master of his senses, he is friendly, ungrudging, modest, and steady. In short, those who have grown old in austerities and character always praise him for the uprightness and fortitude that are his.

Aśvapati said:
My lord, you reply to me that he is rich in all virtues—now mention also his flaws, if indeed he has any.

Nārada said:
He has but one flaw. A year from today Satyavat's life will expire and he will abandon his body.

The king said:
Go. Sāvitrī! Go, my pretty, and choose another husband! He has one great flaw that overshadows his virtues. The venerable Nārada, who is honored by the Gods, tells me that in a year his life will run out and he will abandon his body!

Sāvitrī said:
Once does an inheritance befall, once is a daughter married off, once does a father say: "I will give her"—these three each occur but once. Long-lived or short-lived, virtuous or virtueless, I choose my husband once, and will not choose a second. Having made the decision with my mind, I am stating it with my speech, and shall accomplish it with my actions later. My mind is my authority.

Nārada said:
Best of men, your daughter Sāvitrī's mind is firmly made up. She can in no way be made to stray from this Law. No other man possesses the virtues that Satyavat has; therefore it looks correct to me for you to give your daughter away.

The king said:

The words you have spoken, my lord, are true and should not be doubted. I shall so do this, for you are my guru, my lord.

Nārada said:

May there be no impediment in the giving away of your daughter Sāvitrī. We shall finish now. Good luck to you all.

Mārkaṇḍeya said:

Having thus spoken, Nārada flew up to the sky and went to heaven. And the king had all preparations made for his daughter's marriage.

Mārkaṇḍeya said:

Wondering about the very purpose of his marrying off his daughter, the king brought together all the necessaries for the wedding. On a lucky lunar day he summoned all the brahmin elders, the sacrificial priests, and his house priest and set out with his daughter. The king betook himself to the holy wood and hermitage of Dyumatsena and approached the royal seer with his brahmins on foot. There he saw the lordly blind king seated on a cushion of *kuśa* grass by a *śāla* tree. The king paid due homage to the royal seer and presented himself in restrained words. The Law-wise king offered him the guest gift, a seat, and a cow; and he said to the king, "Why have you come?" And the other informed him fully of his intention and task regarding Satyavat.

Aśvapati said:

This is my lovely daughter, her name is Sāvitrī, royal seer. You who know the Law, take her from me according to the Law as your daughter-in-law.

Dyumatsena said:

We have lost our domain and live in the
    woods
As ascetics who strictly adhere to the Law.
How will your daughter, who does not
    deserve it.
Bear the hardships of life as a forest recluse?

Aśvapati said:

When my daughter knows as well as I do
That sorrow and happiness are and are not.

Such words do not suit a man like me—
I have come with conviction to you, O king.

Pray do not, out of friendship and affection, kill my hopes, do not deny me who have come here in a spirit of love. For in this alliance you are my peer and I am yours. Accept my girl as your daughter-in-law and Satyavat's wife.

Dyumatsena said:

Well before this have I wanted an alliance with you, but I hesitated, since I have been bereft of my kingdom. Then let this long-held wish be fulfilled for me today, for you are my wished-for guest.

Mārkaṇḍeya said:

Thereupon the two kings fetched all the brahmins who lived in the hermitage and had the wedding celebrated ceremonially. And after Aśvapati had given away his daughter with a suitable dowry, he returned to his palace most joyously. Satyavat too rejoiced at having obtained such a wife endowed with all virtues, and she was happy on having won the husband desired of her heart.

When her father had gone, she took off all her ornaments and put on bark and an ocher robe. With her attentions and virtues, her affection and restraint, and her seeing to all wants, she earned the contentment of all. Her mother-in-law she satisfied with the care of her body and with all garments and such, and her father-in-law with divine worship and control of her tongue. Likewise she contented her husband with her pleasant speech, dexterity, and even tenor, as well as her private ministrations.

As these strict people were thus living together in their hermitage and performing austerities, some time passed by, Bhārata. But Sāvitrī, lying or standing, day and night, kept thinking of the words that Nārada had spoken.

Mārkaṇḍeya said:

Then, after a stretch of many days had gone by, the time came when Satyavat was to die, O king. Sāvitrī counted every day that went by, and Nārada's words kept turning in her mind. Knowing that he was to die on the fourth day, the radiant woman undertoo[k] a three-night vow and kept standing day and night. When the king heard of this painful restraint of the bride, he felt sorry, and he rose and said soothingly to Sāvitrī, "The vow you have undertaken is too severe, daughter of a king, for standing up for three nights is exceedingly difficult."

Sāvitrī said:

Do not feel sorry, father, I shall finish the vow; for it is done with resolve, and resolve is the reason.

Dyumatsena said:

I am in no wise able to tell you to break your vow. One like me should properly tell you to finish it.

Mārkaṇḍeya said:

Having said this the great-minded Dyumatsena desisted; and Sāvitrī stood upright as though she had become wood. That last night before the day of her husband's death, bull of the Bharatas, went on by most sorrowfully for Sāvitrī, who remained standing. "Today is the day," she thought, and she made a libation into the burning fire, performed the morning rites when the sun had risen a mere four cubits. Then she saluted all the brahmin elders and her mother-in-law and father-in-law in succession, and stood subdued with folded hands. The holy ascetics, who wished Sāvitrī well, all the inmates of the hermitage, pronounced blessings for her never to be widowed. "So be it!" she mused, sunk in thought, accepting all the words of the ascetics silently. Suffering deeply, the princess waited for the time and the hour and kept thinking on Nārada's words.

Her mother-in-law and father-in-law, O best of the Bharatas, then said affectionately these words to the princess, who was standing aside:

The parents-in-law said:

You have properly accomplished the vow as it is prescribed. It is now time to eat, then do the next thing.

Sāvitrī said:

I shall eat when the sun is down and I have fulfilled my wish. This is the intention and covenant I have conceived in my heart.

Mārkaṇḍeya said:

While Sāvitrī was thus having converse regarding her meal, Satyavat put an ax over his shoulder and started for the forest. Sāvitrī said to her husband, "Please do not go alone! I shall come with you, for I cannot bear to leave you."

Satyavat said:

You have never gone into the forest before, and the path is difficult, my lovely. You are gaunt from your fast and vow—how will you manage on foot?

Sāvitrī said:

I am not weak from my fast, and I do not feel fatigue. I have set my heart on going, please don't stop me!

Satyavat said:

If you have set your heart on going, I shall do what pleases you. But first take leave of my parents, so no blame falls on me.

Mārkaṇḍeya said:

The woman of the great vows went to her mother-in-law and father-in-law and said, "My husband is going to the forest to gather fruit. I seek the lady's and my father-in-law's permission to go out with him, for I cannot bear to be separated. Your son is starting out for his parents' sake and the *agnihotra's* and he cannot be stopped. He might be stopped if he went to the forest for another reason. In close to a year I have not ventured out of the hermitage, and I am most curious to see the forest in flower."

Dyumatsena said:

From the day her father gave me Sāvitrī as a daughter-in-law I do not recall her ever having made any sort of request. Let the bride have her way then. But see to it, daughter, that you do not distract Satyavat on the way.

Mārkaṇḍeya said:

With the permission of both the glorious woman went with her husband, seemingly laughing but with burning heart. Wide-eyed she looked at the lovely and colorful woods all about, which echoed with the cries of peacocks. Gently Satyavat said to Sāvitrī, "Look at the pure currents of these streams and the beautiful flowering trees!" And the blameless woman kept watching her husband at all times, for, remembering the hermit's words at the time, she thought him already dead. She followed her husband, walking deftly, her heart cut in twain, waiting for the hour.

Mārkaṇḍeya said:

Together with his wife the gallant man gathered fruit and filled his strap with them; then he split logs of wood. While he was splitting the wood, he broke out in a sweat and the exertion gave him a headache. He went to his beloved wife and, weighed down with fatigue, said to her, "I have got a headache from the exertion, and my body and heart seem to be on fire. Sāvitrī of measured words, I feel as though I am sick. My head feels as though it is pierced with spikes. I want to sleep, my lovely, I don't have the strength to stand."

Sāvitrī came to him and embraced her husband. She sat down on the ground and put his head in her lap. Thinking on Nārada's word, the poor woman calculated the moment, hour, time of day, and the day. In a little while she saw a person in a yellow robe and a turban, a handsome man resplendent like the sun, smoothly black and red-eyed. He had a noose in his hand and looked terrifying as he stood at Satyavat's side and looked down on him. When she saw him she put down her husband's head gently and rose up at once. She folded her hands and said piteously, with trembling heart, "I know that thou art a God, for thy form is not human. Tell me, if it pleases thee, who art thou, God, and what dost thou seek here?"

Yama said:

You are a devoted wife, Sāvitrī, and possess the power of austerities. Therefore I will reply to you—know that I am Yama, good woman. The life of your husband the Prince Satyavat has run out. I shall fetter him and take him along—that is what I seek to do.

Mārkaṇḍeya said:

Having said this, the blessed lord, the King of the Ancestors proceeded to reveal his entire design exactly as a kindness to her: "This man is possessed of the Law, beautiful, and a sea of virtues. Therefore he does not deserve to be fetched by my familiars, hence I have come myself."

Thereupon Yama forcibly drew from Satyavat's body a thumb-sized person, who was fet-tered with the noose and in his power. The body gave up its spirit, its breathing stopped, its sheen faded, and it became motionless and not pleasing to watch. Having tied him, Yama set out to the south, and Sāvitrī followed sorrowfully, this stately, devoted wife, perfected by her stressful vow.

Yama said:

Go, Sāvitrī, return! Perform his obsequies. You are acquitted of all debts to your husband. You have gone as far as you can go!

Sāvitrī said:

I too must go where my husband is led, or goes by himself—that is the sempiternal Law. By the power of my austerities, my conduct toward my elders, my love for my husband, my vow; and by thy grace my course shall be unobstructed! The wise, who see the truth of the matter, say that he who walks the seven steps with one is his friend. This friendship I presuppose while I say something, listen.

> It is masters of their souls who practice
> The Law in the woods, and austerities;
> And knowing the Law they promulgate it—
> Hence the strict say the Law comes first.
>
> By the Law of the one as approved by the
>   strict
> We all proceed on the course he has set.
> I don't want a second, I don't want a third—
> Hence the strict say the Law comes first.

Yama said:

> Turn back, I am pleased with the words you
>   speak
> With vowel and consonant and fine reason.
> Now choose you a boon, excepting his life,
> I shall grant you any boon, woman sans
>   blame.

Sāvitrī said:

> My father-in-law lives a hermit's life,
> Bereft of his sight and thrown from his
>   throne.

By thy grace may the king regain his eyesight
And grow strong, ablaze like the fire or
  the sun.

Yama said:

I shall give this boon entire to you,
Just as you have said it, and so shall it be.
I see that the journey is tiring you,
Now go and return lest you get fatigued.

Sāvitrī said:

Why should I tire—I am near my husband,
For my course is sure wherever he goes;
My course will be where thou leadst, my lord,
O lord of the Gods, once more do thou listen.

With the strict a single encounter is praised
And friendship with them is higher still.
To meet a strict person is to have sure fruit;
Thence one should live in the midst of the
  strict.

Yama said:

The words that you speak are full of good
  counsel,
They are pleasing and add to the wisdom
  of sages.
Again excepting this Satyavat's life,
Choose, radiant woman, another boon!

Sāvitrī said:

My wise old father-in-law has been robbed
Of his own realm—may he regain it,
And may my guru not stray from the Law;
This I choose from you as my second boon.

Yama said:

He shall soon possess his kingdom again,
And the king shall never be lacking in Law.
Your wish is fulfilled, O child of a king,
Now go and return lest you get fatigued.

Sāvitrī said:

Thou subduest these creatures only by rule,
By the rule dost thou lead them, not by thy
  desire.
It is thus, God, that thou art famed as Yama.
Pray hear the words that I have to say.

Offering no threat to any creature by deed,
mind, or speech, kindness, and giving are the
sempiternal Law of the strict. The world is mostly
like this: people are kind just as far as they can
be, but the strict show mercy even when their
ill-wishers come.

Yama said:

The words that you speak are as satisfying
As water is to a thirsty man.
Again excepting this Satyavat's life,
Good woman, choose any boon you desire.

Sāvitrī said:

My father, the king of the land, is childless:
May he have a hundred sons, my brothers,
Who will insure that his line will last—
This boon I choose as my third from you.

Yama said:

Good woman, your father shall have a
  hundred
Of splendid sons to continue his line.
Your wish is fulfilled, O child of a king,
Return, you have come a long stretch of
  the road.

Sāvitrī said:

In my husband's presence it has not been far,
For my mind is rushing much farther still.
As thou goest thy course do thou listen again
To the ready words I shall speak to thee.

Thou art the majestic son of Vivasvat,
The wise call you therefore Vaivasvata.

The creatures please thee with Law and
control,
And that, lord, makes thee the King of the
Law.

Not even in oneself does one have so much trust
as in the strict, therefore everyone wishes to show
his love to the strict in particular. Trust, indeed,
arises from one's friendship for all creatures;
therefore people place trust in the strict particularly.

Yama said:

The words you have uttered here, beautiful
woman,
I have not but from you heard their likes
before.
I am pleased with them, therefore, excepting
his life,
Choose you a fourth boon, then you must go.

Sāvitrī said:

May be born from my womb by Satyavat,
To the two of us to continue our line,
A hundred mighty and gallant sons:
This boon I choose as my fourth from you.

Yama said:

A hundred mighty and gallant sons
Shall be born, young woman, and give you
delight.
But do not tire, O child of a king,
Return, you have gone a long stretch of
the way.

Sāvitrī said:

The strict always abide by the Law,
The strict do not tremble, nor do they
despair.
The meeting of strict with strict bears fruit,
From the strict the strict expect no danger.

With their truth do the strict give lead to
the sun,

With their penance the strict uphold the
earth.
The strict are the course of future and past,
They do not collapse in the midst of the
strict.

Knowing that this is the eternal conduct that is
practiced by the noble, the strict act in another's
cause without expecting a return from it.

No favor is fruitless among the strict.
No profit, no honor will come to naught.
As this is forever the rule of the strict,
Therefore the strict are custodians.

Yama said:

Since every time you speak so well,
So pleasing, so meaningful of the Law,
My love for you is incomparable—
Choose you a compareless boon, strict
woman!

Sāvitrī said:

You make no exception to your favor,
Pride-giver, as in the other boons!
I choose the boon that Satyavat live,
For I am as dead without my lord!

Deprived of my husband I wish no bliss,
Deprived of my husband I wish no heaven,
Deprived of my husband I wish no fortune,
Without my lord I will not live.

You have given the boon that a hundred sons
Will be born to me, yet you take my man.
I choose the boon that Satyavat live!
Your very own word shall now come true!

Mārkaṇḍeya said:
"So be it," said Yama Vaivasvata, and he loosened the nooses. Then the king of the Law said to
Sāvitrī with a joyous heart, "Look, good woman,
joy of your family, I have freed your husband.
Take him with you; he is healthy and shall succeed in his purposes. He shall attain with you to
a lifetime of four hundred years; and, after hav-

ing offered up sacrifices, he shall win fame in the world for his Law. Satyavat shall beget on you a hundred sons, and they shall all be barons and kings and have sons and grandsons. Your names shall forever be famous on earth. Your father shall have a hundred sons by your mother Mālavī, named the Mālavas, which, with their sons and grandsons, shall continue forever. They shall be your baronial brothers, the likes of the Thirty."

Having thus bestowed boons on her, the majestic King of the Law turned Sāvitrī back and went to his own house. When Yama had gone, Sāvitrī took hold of her husband and returned to the place where her husband's corpse was lying. Seeing him there on the ground, she approached her husband, embraced him, lifted his head in her lap, and sat on the ground. Satyavat returned to consciousness, and he said to Sāvitrī, looking at her lovingly again and again, as one who has returned from a journey:

Satyavat said:

Why, I have slept a long time! Why did you not wake me up? And where is that black person who dragged me from here?

Sāvitrī said:

Yes, you have slept a long time in my lap, bull among men. The blessed lord Yama, the God who subdues the creatures, is gone. You are rested now, my lord prince, and your sleep has gone. If you can, stand up, see, night has fallen.

Mārkaṇḍeya said:

Having regained consciousness, Satyavat arose as from a pleasant sleep, and looking in all directions at the woods, he said: "I went out with you, my fine-waisted woman, to gather fruit. Then as I was splitting wood I got a headache. And because of the pain in my head I was unable to stand up anymore and fell asleep in your lap. All this I remember, my lovely. I lost consciousness when I fell asleep in your embrace, then I saw a terrible darkness and an august person. Tell me, my pretty, if you know, whether it was a dream I saw, or was it real?

Sāvitrī said to him, "The night is spreading. Tomorrow I shall tell you everything as it happened, my prince. Stand up, stand up, hail to thee! You are an obedient son, so see your parents. The night has spread, and the sun is down. The rovers of the night are wandering here gleefully and making cruel noises, and the leaves are rustling from the animals that stalk the forest. Those fearfully barking jackals in the southwest are howling horribly, and they make my heart quaver."

Satyavat said:

The forest covered by dense darkness looks terrifying. You will not recognize the path and be unable to walk.

Sāvitrī said:

Here in this burned wood a dry tree is still burning and fire can be seen hither and yon, fanned by the wind. I shall bring fire from there and make it blaze high, here are these logs, don't worry. If you are unable to go—I see your head aches—and won't recognize the path in the darkness-covered forest, we'll go tomorrow morning, if you agree, when the forest is visible. We shall spend the night here, if you think so, prince sans blame.

Satyavat said:

My headache is gone and my limbs feel well. If you agree, I wish to join father and mother. I have never before returned to the hermitage out of time. Mother stops me at nightfall, and even in daytime my parents worry when I go out. Father will be looking for me with the hermitage-dwellers. I have often been reproved before by my much worried father and mother: "You have come back late!" What state will they be in over me now, I wonder! They must be very much concerned, not seeing me. These old people love me very much. Once when they were worried badly at night they told me with a flood of tears, "Without you we will not live for an hour, little son. As long as you live our life is assured, you are the crutch of two blind oldsters, the dynasty rests on you. On you depend our ancestral oblation, our fame, and our progeny." My old mother, my old father, whose crutch they say I am, what state will they be in if they don't see me tonight! I blame my sleep for causing my father and innocent mother to fear for my life. And I am in danger, and doom is upon me, for neither can I live without my father and mother! It is certain that at this very hour my father, who has only the sight of knowledge, is questioning with a perturbed mind each and every person in the hermitage. I don't mind for myself as much as for my father, my lovely, and for my mother, my very weak mother who has followed her husband. Now they will be prey to the greatest worry over me. I live if they live, I must support them, I must do what pleases them, that is what I live for.

Mārkaṇḍeya said:

Having said this the Law-spirited and devoted son, who, was obedient to his parents, lifted his arms in grief and began to weep aloud. And when Sāvitrī who walked in the Law saw her husband thus, gaunt from grief, she wiped the tears from his eyes and said, "If it is true that I have practiced austerities, if I have given, if I have offered up, then this night shall be safe for my parents-in-law and my husband. I do not recall that I have ever spoken a lie, even in jest—by that truth my parents-in-law shall live today!"

Satyavat said:

I wish to see my parents. Come, Sāvitrī, don't tarry. If I find that anything untoward has happened to mother or father, I shall not live, fair-hipped wife, I swear it by the truth! If your mind is set on the Law, or if you wish me to live, or do me a kindness, then come to the hermitage.

Mārkaṇḍeya said:

Sāvitrī thereupon stood up, and the radiant woman gathered her hair and made her husband rise, holding him by his arms. Satyavat stood and wiped his body with his hand. He looked all about him and his glance fell on the strap. Sāvitrī said, "Tomorrow you'll fetch the fruit here. But I'll take this ax of yours for safety." She hung the strap from a tree branch, took the ax, and joined her husband. The woman of the lovely thighs put her husband's arm on her left shoulder, circled his waist with her right arm, and went stepping deftly.

Satyavat said:

I am used to coming here, so I know the paths, timid girl. I can see them by the moonlight that shines between the trees. Go by the same path we came by this morning and gathered fruit, don't hesitate. And at this *palāśa* grove, the path forks. Go by the northern path and make haste. I am well, I am strong, and I want to see my parents.

Mārkaṇḍeya said:

And speaking thus he hastened on to the hermitage.

REVIEW QUESTIONS

1. What are the essential characteristics of Savitri's character?
2. How would you describe Savitri's success with Yama? Does she outwit him, or is he simply won over by her perseverance and character?
3. What is significant in the ordering of Savitri's first three requests? What is the importance of the fourth boon?
4. In this selection the Hindu concept of dharma is translated as "Law"; is that a good translation here? Just what does dharma imply?

An Egyptian-Greek Merchant Describes Commercial Sea Routes

Periplus Maris Erythraei (c. 30–230 C.E.)

Periploi (plural of *periplus*) were accounts generally kept by ships' captains. This selection was probably the work of a merchant, since it focuses on products available in various ports. He included general information about the routes down the coast of East Africa, across the Arabian Sea to central coastal India, down to Cape Comorin, and up the east coast to the mouth of the Ganges. The content and detail indicate that he wrote from personal experience, producing what was essentially a merchant's handbook for trade beyond the Red Sea (*Maris Erythraei*). It is dated from the middle of the first century C.E.

Trade began between Mesopotamia and the Indus civilization possibly as early as the latter part of the third millennium B.C.E., judging from artifacts in each area. These artifacts illustrate common themes. For example, in a scene from the Fertile Crescent, a hero bare-handedly overcomes two lions, while in a nearly identical piece of art from the Indus Valley, a bare-handed hero conquers a pair of tigers. Conversely, information about how to benefit from the monsoon was not exchanged between cultures. This information, for whatever reason, was not available to the Greeks until much later, perhaps even as late as the first millennium B.C.E., when a Greek named Hippalos was supposedly the first European to discover it. Unfortunately, the *Periplus* does not provide information about him, not even when he lived. Before Hippalos, the Greeks had unloaded their goods at a port located in what is present-day Aden, and the goods were trans-shipped to India by natives of the Arabian Peninsula. The knowledge of how to use the monsoon was crucial because it made direct contact between the Mediterranean and India possible.

There are a total of sixty-six paragraphs (sometimes called chapters) in the *Periplus*. The part concerning trade with India, from paragraph 38 on, is presented here. The detail is clear and fairly reliable for the times, although the description of the east coast of India is vague and may have come from hearsay. Although much of the information is technical, the writer included fascinating details about peoples, places and customs. A couple of items from paragraph 56 may be emphasized: money and pepper. Merchants from the Mediterranean were advised to bring lots of money because Indians had little desire or use for goods brought from Europe, whereas there was a great demand for spices, especially pepper, from India, particularly south India. Merchants are described in a Tamil poem as "arriving with gold and departing with pepper." The word *pepper* itself has a south Indian origin. From ancient times Europeans had been interested in spices and other items from India; this trade drained much of the wealth of Rome and was to be a motivation for the Age of Exploration.

38. After this region, with the coast by now curving like a horn because of the deep indentations to the east made by the bays, there next comes the seaboard of Skythia [Indus, modern Sind in present-day Pakistan], which lies directly to the north; it is very flat and through it flows the Sinthos River, mightiest of the rivers along the Erythraean Sea and emptying so great an amount of water into the sea that far off, before you reach land, its light-colored water meets you out at sea. An indication to those coming from the sea that they are already approaching land in the river's vicinity are the snakes that emerge from the depths to meet them; there is an indication as well in the places around Persis mentioned above, the snakes called *graai*. The river has seven mouths, narrow and full of shallows; none are navigable except the one in the middle. At it, on the coast, stands the port of trade of Barbarikon [unknown port at the mouth of the Indus]. There is a small islet in front of it; and behind it, inland, is the metropolis of Skythia itself, Minnagar [exact location unknown]. The throne is in the hands of Parthians, who are constantly chasing each other off it.

39. Vessels moor at Barbarikon, but all the cargoes are taken up the river to the king at the metropolis. In this port of trade there is a market for: clothing, with no adornment in good quantity, of printed fabric in limited quantity; multicolored textiles; peridot (?)*; coral; storax; frankincense; glassware; silverware; money; wine, limited quantity. As return cargo it offers: costus; bdellium; *lykion*†; nard; turquoise; lapis lazuli; Chinese pelts, cloth, and yam; indigo. Those who sail with the Indian [sc. winds] leave around July, that is, Epeiph. The crossing with these is hard going but absolutely favorable and shorter.

40. After the Sinthos River there is another bay, hidden from view, to the north. It is named Eirinon,‡ with the additional names Little and Big. Both are bodies of water with shoals and a succession of shallow eddies reaching a long way from land so that frequently, with the shore, nowhere in sight, vessels will run aground and, if caught and thrust further in, be destroyed. Beyond this bay a promontory juts out, curving from Eirinon first east and south and then west; it embraces the gulf called Barakê [Gulf of Kutch], which itself embraces seven islands. Ships around its entrance that blunder in and then pull back the short distance into open water, escape; those that get closed inside the basin of Barakê are destroyed. For not only are the waves there very big and oppressive, but the sea is choppy and turbid, with eddies and violent whirlpools. The bottom in some places has sheer drops, in others is rocky and sharp, so that the anchors lying parallel [i.e., dropped from the bows], thrust out to withstand [sc. the difficult waters], get cut loose and some even get smashed on the sea floor. An indication of these [sc. dangers] to vessels coming from the sea are the snakes, huge and black, that emerge to meet them. In the areas beyond, and around Barygaza [port on the gulf of Cambay, or Khambhat], snakes that are smaller and yellow and golden in color are met with.

41. Immediately after the gulf of Barakê is the gulf of Barygaza [gulf of Cambay] and the coast of the region of Ariakê, the beginning both of Manbanos's realm and of all of India. The part inland, which borders on Skythia, is called Abêria, the part along the coast Syrastrênê [Kathiawar peninsula]. The region, very fertile, produces grain, rice, sesame oil, ghee, cotton, and the Indian cloths made from it, those of ordinary quality. There are a great many herds of cattle, and the men are of very great size and dark skin color. The metropolis of the region is Minnagara, from which great quan-

---

*A precious stone, perhaps the yellow sapphire.
†Probably a Himalayan medicinal berry.

‡The Rann of Kutch, consisting of the Great Rann and the Little Rann, in the modern state of Gujarat (on west central coast); formerly salt-water swamps, now salt and sand flats overrun by tides during the monsoon.

tities of cloth are brought to Barygaza. In the area there are still preserved to this very day signs of Alexander's expedition, ancient shrines and the foundations of encampments and huge wells. The voyage along the coast of this region, from Barbarikon to the promontory near Astakapra across from Barygaza called Papikê, is 3000 stades.*

42. Beyond it is another gulf, on the inside of the waves, that forms an inlet directly to the north. Near the mouth is an island called Baiônês, and, at the very head, a mighty river called the Mais [the Maki, which empties into the gulf of Cambay]. Vessels whose destination is Barygaza cross the gulf, which is about 300 stades wide, leaving the island, whose highest point is visible, to the left and heading due east toward the mouth of Barygaza's river. This river is called the Lamnaios [Narmada].

43. This gulf which leads to Barygaza, since it is narrow, is hard for vessels coming from seaward to manage. For they arrive at either its right-hand side or its left-hand, and attempting it by the left-hand side is better than the other. For, on the right-hand side, at the very mouth of the gulf, there extends a rough and rock-strewn reef called Hêrônê, near the village of Kammôni. Opposite it, on the left-hand side, is the promontory in front of Astakapra called Papikê; mooring here is difficult because of the current around it and because the bottom, being rough and rocky, cuts the anchor cables. And, even if you manage the gulf itself, the very mouth of the river on which Barygaza stands is hard to find because the land is low and nothing is clearly visible even from nearby. And, even if you find the mouth, it is hard to negotiate because of the shoals in the river around it.

44. For this reason local fishermen in the king's service come out with crews [sc. of rowers] and long ships, the kind called *trappaga* and *kotymba,* to the entrance as far as Syrastrênê to meet vessels and guide them up to Barygaza.

Through the crew's efforts, they maneuver them right from the mouth of the gulf through the shoals and tow them to predetermined stopping places; they get them under way when the tide comes in and, when it goes out, bring them to anchor in certain harbors and basins. The basins are rather deep spots along the river up to Barygaza. For this lies on the river about 300 stades upstream from the mouth.

45. All over India there are large numbers of rivers with extreme ebb-and-flood tides that at the time of the new moon and the full moon last for up to three days, diminishing during the intervals. They are much more extreme in the area around Barygaza than elsewhere. Here suddenly the sea floor becomes visible, and certain parts along the coast, which a short while ago had ships sailing over them, at times become dry land, and the rivers, because of the inrush at flood tide of a whole concentrated mass of seawater, are driven headlong upstream against the natural direction of their flow for a good many stades.

46. Thus the navigating of ships in and out is dangerous for those who are inexperienced and are entering this port of trade for the first time. For, once the thrust of the flood tide is under way, restraining anchors do not stay in place. Consequently, the ships, carried along by its force and driven sideways by the swiftness of the current, run aground on the shoals and break up, while smaller craft even capsize. Even in the channels some craft, if not propped up, will tilt over on their sides during the ebb and, when the flood suddenly returns, get swamped by the first wave of the flow. So much power is generated at the inrush of the sea even during the dark of the moon, particularly if the flood arrives at night, that when the tide is just beginning to come in and the sea is still at rest, there is carried from it to people at the mouth something like the rumble of an army heard from afar, and after a short while the sea itself races over the shoals with a hiss.

47. Inland behind Barygaza there are numerous peoples: the Aratrioi, Arachusioi, Gandaraioi,

---

*300 nautical miles; the distance, however, is incorrect.

and the peoples of Proklais, in whose area Bukephalos Alexandreia is located. And beyond these is a very warlike people, the Bactrians,[*] under a king. . . . Alexander, setting out from these parts, penetrated as far as the Ganges[†] but did not get to Limyrikê [the Malabar (southeast) coast] and the south of India. Because of this, there are to be found on the market in Barygaza even today old drachmas engraved with the inscriptions, in Greek letters, of Apollodotus and Menander, rulers who came after Alexander.

48. There is in this region [sc. of Barygaza] towards the east a city called Ozênê,[‡] the former seat of the royal court, from which everything that contributes to the region's prosperity, including what contributes to trade with us, is brought down to Barygaza: onyx; agate (?); Indian garments of cotton; garments of *molochinon*[§]; and a considerable amount of cloth of ordinary quality. Through this region there is also brought down from the upper areas the nard that comes by way of Proklais (the Kattyburinê, Patropapigê, and Kabalitê), the nard that comes through the adjacent part of Skythia, and costus and bdellium.

49. In this port of trade there is a market for: wine, principally Italian but also Laodicean and Arabian; copper, tin, and lead; coral and peridot (?); all kinds of clothing with no adornment or of printed fabric; multicolored girdles, eighteen inches wide; storax; yellow sweet clover (?); raw glass; realgar; sulphide of antimony; Roman money, gold and silver, which commands an exchange at some profit against the local currency; unguent, inexpensive and in limited quantity. For the king there was imported in those times precious silverware, slave musicians, beautiful girls for concubinage, fine wine, expensive clothing with no adornment, and choice unguent. This area exports: nard; costus; bdellium; ivory;

onyx; agate (?); *lykion;* cotton cloth of all kinds; Chinese [sc. silk] cloth; *molochinon* cloth; [sc. silk] yarn; long pepper; and items brought here from the [sc. nearby] ports of trade. For those sailing to this port from Egypt, the right time to set out is around the month of July, that is Epeiph.

50. Immediately beyond Barygaza the coast runs from north to south. Thus the region is called Dachinabadês,[‖] for the word for south in their language is *dachanos.* The hinterland that lies beyond towards the east contains many barren areas, great mountains, and wild animals of all kinds—leopards, tigers, elephants, enormous serpents, hyenas, and a great many kinds of monkeys, as well as a great many populous nations up to the Ganges.

51. Of the trading centers in the region of Dachinabadês, two are the most outstanding: Paithana, twenty days' travel to the south from Barygaza; and, from Paithana, about ten days to the east, another very large city, Tagara. From these there is brought to Barygaza, by conveyance in wagons over very great roadless stretches, from Paithana large quantities of onyx, and from Tagara large quantities of cloth of ordinary quality, all kinds of cotton garments, garments of *molochinon,* and certain other merchandise from the coastal parts that finds a market locally there. The voyage as far as Limyrikê is 7000 stades in all, but most vessels continue on to the Strand.

52. The local ports [sc. of Dachinabadês], lying in a row, are Akabaru, Suppara, and the city of Kalliena; the last, in the time of the elder Saraganos,[#] was a port of trade where everything went according to law. [Sc. It is so no longer] for, after Sandanês[**] occupied it, there has been much hindrance [sc. to trade]. For the Greek ships that by chance come into these places are brought under guard to Barygaza.

53. Beyond Kalliena other local ports of trade

---

[*]Kushans, an Iranian or central Asian people with territorial power in northwest India.
[†]This is a fable. Alexander got as far as the Beas, a tributary of the Indus.
[‡]Modern Ujjain, which is north, not east.
[§]Probably another type of cotton.

[‖]The Deccan, plateau of south India.
[#]There were several south Indian kings with a variation of this name
[**]A south Indian Saka (Hun) official. The Sakas were in conflict with the Andhras (south Indians).

are: Sêmylla [near modern Bombay], Mandagora, Palaipatmai, Melizeigara, Byzantion, Toparon, Tyrannosboas. Then come the Sêsekreienai Islands [off the Malabar Coast] as they are called, the Isle of the Aigidioi, the Isle of the Kaineitoi near what is called the Peninsula, around which places there are pirates, and next White Island. Then come Naura and Tyndis, the first ports of trade of Limyrikê, and, after these, Muziris and Nelkynda, which are now the active ones.

54. Tyndis, a well-known village on the coast, is in the kingdom of Kêprobotos [modern Kerala]. Muziris, in the same kingdom, owes its prosperity to the shipping from Ariakê that comes there as well as to Greek shipping. It lies on a river 500 stades distant from Tyndis by river and sea, and from [? the river mouth] to it is 20 stades. Nelkynda is just about 500 stades from Muziris, likewise by river and sea, but it is in another kingdom, Pandiôn's. It too lies on a river, about 120 stades from the sea.

55. Another settlement lies at the very mouth of the river, Bakarê, to which vessels drop down-river from Nelkynda for the outbound voyage; they anchor in the open roads to take on their cargoes because the river has sandbanks and channels that are shoal. The kings themselves of both ports of trade dwell in the interior. Vessels coming from the open sea in the vicinity of these places get an indication that they are approaching land from the snakes that emerge to meet them; these are also black in color but shorter and with dragon-shaped head and blood-red eyes.

56. Ships in these ports of trade carry full loads because of the volume and quantity of pepper and malabathron [type of cinnamon]. They offer a market for: mainly a great amount of money; peridot (?); clothing with no adornment, in limited quantity; multicolored textiles; sulphide of antimony; coral; raw glass; copper, tin, lead; wine, in limited quantity, as much as goes to Barygaza; realgar; orpiment[*]; grain in sufficient amount for those involved

with shipping, because the [sc. local] merchants do not use it. They export pepper, grown for the most part in only one place connected with these ports of trade, that called Kottanarikê. They also export: good supplies of fine-quality pearls; ivory; Chinese [i.e., silk] cloth; Gangetic nard; malabathron, brought here from the interior; all kinds of transparent gems; diamonds; sapphires; tortoise shell, both the kind from Chrysê Island and the kind caught around the islands lying off Limyrikê itself. For those sailing here from Egypt, the right time to set out is around the month of July, that is, Epeiph.

57. The whole coastal route just described, from Kanê [an Arabian port] and Eudaimôn Arabia,[†] men formerly used to sail over in smaller vessels, following the curves of the bays. The ship captain Hippalos, by plotting the location of the ports of trade and the configuration of the sea, was the first to discover the route over open water. . . . In this locale the winds we call "etesian" blow seasonally from the direction of the ocean, and so a southwesterly makes its appearance in the Indian Sea, but it is called after the name of the one who first discovered the way across. Because of this, right up to the present, some leave directly from Kanê and some from the Promontory of Spices, and whoever are bound for Limyrikê hold out with the wind on the quarter for most of the way, but whoever are bound for Barygaza and whoever for Skythia only three days and no more, and, carried along (?) the rest of the run on their own proper course, away from the shore on the high seas, over the [? ocean] off the land, they bypass the aforementioned bays.

58. After Bakarê comes Red Mountain, as it is called, and another region extends . . . called the Seaboard, directly to the south. Its first stopping place, called Balita, is a village on the coast with a good harbor. After this comes another stopping place called Komar, where there is a little settlement and a port; in it men who wish

---

[*]Arsenic trisulfide, a yellow mineral used as a medicine and extensively as a pigment in the ancient world.

[†]Town on the coast of modern day Aden sacked by the Romans about a century previous to the writing of the *Periplus*.

to lead a holy life for the rest of their days remain there celibate; they come there and they
perform ablutions. Women, too, do the same.
For it is said that at one time the goddess remained there and performed ablutions.

59. Beyond Komar [Cape Comorin, or Kan-
niyakumari] the region extends as far as Kol-
choi,* where diving for pearls goes on; it is carried out by convicts. The region is under King
Pandiôn.

———

*Gulf between Tamil Nadu and Sri Lanka; specifically,
pearl-diving area at the mouth of the Tamraparni river.

REVIEW QUESTIONS

1. Why do you think spices were so important to Europeans?
2. What features of the document indicate that it was written "by a merchant for the use
   of merchants"?
3. What do you see as the value of the *Periplus* for ancient traders?

A Buddhist Monk Observes India (399–414 C.E.)

The Travels of Fa-Hien

Fa-hien, a native of the province of Shanxi (Shan-hsi) in northern China, fell
seriously ill as a young boy. His father, seeking the best medical care available
at the time, sent him to a Buddhist monastery. Upon his recovery, he stayed
at the monastery and became a full monk at the age of twenty. Anecdotal evidence suggests that Fa-hien devoted his life to Buddhist ideals and acted
with both wisdom and courage. These qualities undoubtedly sustained him
on his arduous journey through parts of China and central Asia (including the
Gobi Desert and the Hindu Kush) to India and then Ceylon (modern-day Sri
Lanka) in search of Buddhist texts (399–414 C.E.). He kept an account of his
travels and observations, to which he brought a strong historical interest, as
can be seen by his references to Ashoka (r.c. 268–233 B.C.E.). He returned to
China by sea and lived to an advanced old age in his monastery.

 Fa-hien's record is of great value to Indian history because his descriptions
of festivals and cities are unique. Ancient Indians seemed to have little interest in recording history or events going on around them, perhaps because of
the Hindu concept of maya (which held that the world has only relative reality) or, more likely, because they did not see themselves as "Indians" but identified themselves in terms of family, caste, and region (in that order). The
term *India* itself is not Indian, and the India that Fa-hien visited was politically fragmented. Buddhism was one of many sects, and most of the others
were what we would today call "Hindu" (also not an Indian term).

CHAPTER XXVII

Having crossed the river, and descended south for a yojana, (the travellers) came to the town of Pâtaliputtra [modern Patna], in the kingdom of Magadha, the city where king Aśoka ruled. The royal palace and halls in the midst of the city, which exist now as of old, were all made by spirits which he employed, and which piled up the stones, reared the walls and gates, and executed the elegant carving and inlaid sculpture-work,—a way which no human hands of this world could accomplish.

King Aśoka had a younger brother who had attained to be an Arhat, and resided on Gṛidhra-kûṭa hill, finding his delight in solitude and quiet. The king, who sincerely reverenced him, wished and begged him (to come and live) in his family, where he could supply all his wants. The other, however, through his delight in the stillness of the mountain, was unwilling to accept the invitation, on which the king said to him, "Only accept my invitation, and I will make a hill for you inside the city." Accordingly, he provided the materials of a feast, called to him the spirits, and announced to them, "To-morrow you will all receive my invitation; but as there are no mats for you to sit on, let each one bring (his own seat)." Next day the spirits came, each one bringing with him a great rock, (like) a wall, four or five paces square, (for a seat). When their sitting was over, the King made them form a hill with the large stones piled on one another, and also at the foot of the hill, with five large square stones, to make an apartment, which might be more than thirty cubits long, twenty cubits wide, and more than ten cubits high.

In this city there had resided a great Brahman, named Râdha-sâmi, a professor of the mahâyâna, of clear discernment and much wisdom, who understood everything, living by himself in spotless purity. The king of the country honoured and reverenced him, and served him as his teacher. If he went to inquire for and greet him, the king did not presume to sit down alongside of him; and if, in his love and reverence, he took hold of his hand, as soon as he let it go, the

Brahman made haste to pour water on it and wash it. He might be more than fifty years old, and all the kingdom looked up to him. By means of this one man, the Law of Buddha was widely made known, and the followers of other doctrines did not find it in their power to persecute the body of monks in any way.

By the side of the tope of Aśoka, there has been made a mahâyâna monastery, very grand and beautiful; there is also a hînayâna one; the two together containing six hundred or seven hundred monks. The rules of demeanour and the scholastic arrangements in them are worthy of observation.

Shamans of the highest virtue from all quarters, and students, inquirers wishing to find out truth and the grounds of it, all resort to these monasteries. There also resides in this monastery a Brahman teacher, whose name also is Mañjuśrî, whom the Shamans of greatest virtue in the kingdom, and the mahâyâna Bhikshus [monks] honour and look up to.

The cities and towns of this country are the greatest of all in the Middle Kingdom. The inhabitants are rich and prosperous, and vie with one another in the practice of benevolence and righteousness. Every year on the eighth day of the second month they celebrate a procession of images. They make a four-wheeled car, and on it erect a structure of five storeys by means of bamboos tied together. This is supported by a king-post, with poles and lances slanting from it, and is rather more than twenty cubits high, having the shape of a tope. White and silk-like cloth of hair is wrapped all round it, which is then painted in various colours. They make figures of devas, with gold, silver, and lapis lazuli grandly blended and having silken streamers and canopies hung out over them. On the four sides are niches, with a Buddha seated in each, and a Bodhisattva standing in attendance on him. There may be twenty cars, all grand and imposing, but each one different from the others. On the day mentioned, the monks and laity within the borders all come together; they have singers and skilful musicians; they pay their devotions with flowers and incense. The Brahmans come and invite the Buddhas to enter the city. These do so in order, and remain two nights in it. All through the night they keep lamps burning, have skilful music, and present offerings. This is the practice in all the other kingdoms as well. The Heads of the Vaiśya families in them establish in the cities houses for dispensing charity and medicines. All the poor and destitute in the country, orphans, widowers, and childless men, maimed people and cripples, and all who are diseased, go to those houses, and are provided with every kind of help, and doctors examine their diseases. They get the food and medicines which their cases require, and are made to feel at ease; and when they are better, they go away of themselves.

When king Aśoka destroyed the seven topes, (intending) to make eighty-four thousand, the first which he made was the great tope, more than three le [le = ⅓ mile] to the south of this city. In front of this there is a footprint of Buddha, where a vihâra has been built. The door of it faces the north, and on the south of it there is a stone pillar, fourteen or fifteen cubits in circumference, and more than thirty cubits high, on which there is an inscription, saying, "Aśoka gave the jambudvîpa to the general body of all the monks, and then redeemed it from them with money. This he did three times." North from the tope 300 or 400 paces, king Aśoka built the city of Ne-le. In it there is a stone pillar, which also is more than thirty feet high, with a lion on the top of it. On the pillar there is an inscription recording the things which led to the building of Ne-le, with the number of the year, the day, and the month.

CHAPTER XXVIII

(The travellers) went on from this to the southeast for nine yojanas, [yojana = 2½ to 9 miles] and came to a small solitary rocky hill, at the head or end of which was an apartment of stone, facing the south,—the place where Buddha sat, when Śakra, Ruler of Devas [gods], brought the deva-musician, Pañcha-(śikha), to give pleasure to him by playing on his lute. Śakra then asked Buddha about forty-two subjects, tracing (the questions) out with his finger one by one on the rock. The prints of his tracing are still there; and here also there is a monastery.

A yojana south-west from this place brought them to the village of Nâla, where Śâriputtra [a principal disciple of Buddha] was born, and to which also he returned, and attained here his pari-nirvâna. Over the spot (where his body was burned) there was built a tope, which is still in existence.

Another yojana to the west brought them to New Râjagriha,—the new city which was built by king Ajâtaśatru. There were two monasteries in it. Three hundred paces outside the west gate, king Ajâtaśatru, having obtained one portion of the relics of Buddha, built (over them) a tope, high, large, grand, and beautiful. Leaving the city by the south gate, and proceeding south four le, one enters a valley, and comes to a circular space formed by five hills, which stand all round it, and have the appearance of the suburban wall of a city. Here was the old city of king Bimbisâra; from east to west about five or six le, and from north to south seven or eight. It was here that Śâriputtra and Maudgalyâyana first saw Upasena; that the Nirgrantha made a pit of fire and poisoned the rice, and then invited Buddha (to eat with him); that king Ajâtaśatru made a black elephant intoxicated with liquor, wishing him to injure Buddha; and that at the north-east corner of the city in a (large) curving (space) Jîvaka built a vihâra in the garden of Âmbapâli, invited Buddha with his 1250 disciples to it, that he might there make his offerings to support them. (These places) are still there as of old, but inside the city all is emptiness and desolation; no man dwells in it.

CHAPTER XXIX

Entering the valley, and keeping along the mountains on the southeast, after ascending fifteen le, (the travellers) came to mount Gridhra-kûta. Three le before you reach the top, there is a cavern in the rocks, facing the south, in which Buddha sat in meditation. Thirty paces to the north-west there is another, where Ânanda was sitting in meditation, when the deva Mâra Piśuna,* having assumed the form of a large vulture, took his place in front of the cavern, and frightened the disciple. Then Buddha, by his mysterious, supernatural power, made a cleft in the rock, introduced his hand, and stroked Ânanda's shoulder, so that his fear immediately passed away. The footprints of the bird and the cleft for (Buddha's) hand are still there, and hence comes the name of "The Hill of the Vulture Cavern."

In front of the cavern there are the places where the four Buddhas sat. There are caverns also of the Arhats [adepts], one where each sat and meditated, amounting to several hundred in all. At the place where in front of his rocky apartment Buddha was walking from east to west (in meditation), and Devadatta, from among the beetling cliffs on the north of the mountain, threw a rock across, and hurt Buddha's toes, the rock is still there.

The hall where Buddha preached his Law has been destroyed, and only the foundations of the brick walls remain. On this hill the peak is beautifully green, and rises grandly up; it is the highest of all the five hills. In the New City Fâ-hien† bought incense-(sticks), flowers, oil and lamps, and hired two bhikshus, long resident (at the place), to carry them (to the peak). When he himself got to it, he made his offerings with the flowers and incense, and lighted the lamps when the darkness began to come on. He felt melancholy, but restrained his tears and said, "Here Buddha delivered the Śûrângama (Sûtra). I, Fâ-hien, was born when I could not meet with Buddha; and now I only see the footprints which he has left, and the place where he lived, and nothing more." With this, in front of the rock cavern, he chanted the Śûrângama Sûtra, remained there over the night, and then returned towards the New City.

---

*God of death and lust.
†In this recension Fâ-hien is sometimes referred to in the third person.

CHAPTER XXX

Out from the old city, after walking over 300 paces, on the west of the road, (the travellers) found the Karaṇḍa Bamboo garden, where the (old) vihâra [monastery] is still in existence, with a company of monks, who keep (the ground about it) swept and watered.

North of the vihâra two or three le there was the Śmaśânam, which name means in Chinese "the field of graves into which the dead are thrown."

As they kept along the mountain on the south, and went west for 300 paces, they found a dwelling among the rocks, named the Pippala cave, in which Buddha regularly sat in meditation after taking his (midday) meal.

Going on still to the west for five or six le, on the north of the hill, in the shade, they found the cavern called Śrataparṇa, the place where, after the nirvâna of Buddha, 500 Arhats collected the Sûtras. When they brought the Sûtras forth, three lofty seats had been prepared and grandly ornamented. Śâriputtra occupied the one on the left, and Maudgalyâyana that on the right. Of the number of five hundred one was wanting. Mahâkaśyapa was president (on the middle seat). Ânanda was then outside the door, and could not get in. At the place there was (subsequently) raised a tope, which is still existing.

Along (the sides of) the hill, there are also a very great many cells among the rocks, where the various Arhans sat and meditated. As you leave the old city on the north, and go down east for three le, there is the rock dwelling of Devadatta, and at a distance of fifty paces from it there is a large, square, black rock. Formerly there was a bhikshu who, as he walked backwards and forwards upon it, thought with himself:—"This body is impermanent, a thing of bitterness and vanity, and which cannot be looked on as pure. I am weary of this body, and troubled by it as an evil." With this he grasped a knife, and was about to kill himself. But he thought again:—"The World-honoured one laid down a prohibition against one's killing himself." Further it occurred to him:—"Yes, he did; but I now only wish to kill three poisonous thieves." Immediately with the knife he cut his throat. With the first gash into the flesh he attained the state of a Śrotâpanna; when he had gone half through, he attained to be an Anâgâmin; and when he had cut right through, he was an Arhat, and attained to pari-nirvâṇa; (and died).

REVIEW QUESTIONS

1. How would you characterize Fa-hien's attitude toward the peoples and places he visited?
2. Does Fa-hien's writing reveal his Buddhist faith? What evidence supports your opinion?
3. What features of Fa-hien's account interest you the most? Why?

9

East and Southeast Asia, 800 B.C.E.–800 C.E.

The theme of this chapter is China's cultural and political hegemony in East Asia. Chinese scholars wanted to record the history of their neighbors and preserve the history of China's supremacy in the area. They wrote the first accurate accounts of Japanese history, although many of their sources are copies of copies of original sources. One of the selections, preserved through later sources, describes an early embassy to a kingdom on the Malay Peninsula. The Chinese objective, as it has been so frequently through history, was to establish suzerainty. From the account, it would seem that the attempt was neither resisted nor unexpected. Of course, politics was not the only motivation for Chinese travel. In 518, a Buddhist pilgrim was ordered to go to India for the purpose of collecting texts. His experiences there were preserved by a later traveler, another pilgrim who also went to India to obtain Buddhist texts and who made careful notes of people and places.

Other selections give us glimpses into Chinese society. For example, an apparently frustrated scholar composed an essay lamenting the unfairness in the civil service system. Another selection demonstrates the gap between ideal and reality in regard to women. An essay praising the ideal of the mother stands in contrast to a letter of complaint about a wife. Together they show the contrast between the positions of mothers and wives.

Also included is a collection of poems showing the Chinese influence on Japanese culture. The *Manyoshu* poems were strongly influenced by Buddhism, which had come to Japan from China by way of Korea. They had a profound effect on the development of Japanese literature and thought. Even in today's technologically driven society, poetry is an integral part of Japanese life and consciousness.

Two Chinese Prose Essays Depict Women's Relationships with Men (Han Dynasty, probably first century B.C.E.)

LIU HSIANG, *The Mother of Mencius*
FENG YEN, *Letter to His Brother-in-Law*

As in many societies, the Chinese view of women was ambivalent, including both the ideal and the real. It had a strong parallel in India, where the position of mother was the ideal, and that of a wife was considerably less so. Moreover, the "three submissions" mentioned in the second-to-last paragraph are exactly as expressed in the Hindu code of Manu: As a daughter a woman is to be protected by (or subjugated to) her father, as a wife to her husband, and as a widow to her son. Similarities can be found in other societies, Western as well as Eastern.

Liu Hsiang (first century B.C.E.) was a renowned scholar, editor, and author of such works as *Biographies of Admirable Women*. In this selection, he treats the mother of the great Confucian philosopher Mencius (372–289 B.C.E.) in such an idealistic manner as to make her almost superhuman. In contrast, in Feng Yen's letter to his brother-in-law explaining his decision to divorce, an unremarkable husband draws a portrait that renders his wife almost subhuman. Although there might have been some basis for his attitude (one can assume the brother-in-law would have a general idea of the situation), it would be interesting to know the wife's side of the story. Both women represent roles, even types; neither is referred to by name.

THE MOTHER OF MENCIUS

The mother of Mencius lived in Tsou in a house near a cemetery. When Mencius was a little boy he liked to play burial rituals in the cemetery, happily building tombs and grave mounds. His mother said to herself, "This is no place to bring up my son."

She moved near the marketplace in town. Mencius then played merchant games of buying and selling. His mother again said, "This is no place to bring up my son."

So once again she moved, this time next to a school house. Mencius then played games of ancestor sacrifices and practiced the common courtesies between students and teachers. His mother said, "At last, this is the right place for my son!" There they remained.

When Mencius grew up he studied the six arts of propriety, music, archery, charioteering, writing, and mathematics. Later he became a famous Confucian scholar. Superior men commented that Mencius' mother knew the right influences for her sons. The *Book of Poetry* says, "That admirable lady, what will she do for them!"

When Mencius was young, he came home from school one day and found his mother was weaving at the loom. She asked him, "Is school out already?"

He replied, "I left because I felt like it."

His mother took her knife and cut the finished cloth on her loom. Mencius was startled and asked why. She replied, "Your neglecting your studies is very much like my cutting the cloth. The superior person studies to establish a reputation and gain wide knowledge. He is calm and poised and tries to do no wrong. If you do not study now, you will surely end up as a menial servant and will never be free from troubles. It would be just like a woman who supports herself by weaving to give it up. How long could such a person depend on her husband and son to stave off hunger? If a woman neglects her work or a man gives up the cultivation of his character, they may end up as common thieves if not slaves!"

Shaken, from then on Mencius studied hard from morning to night. He studied the philosophy of the Master and eventually became a famous Confucian scholar. Superior men observed that Mencius' mother understood the way of motherhood. The *Book of Poetry* says, "That admirable lady, what will she tell them!"

After Mencius was married, one day as he was going into his private quarters, he encountered his wife not fully dressed. Displeased, Mencius stopped going into his wife's room. She then went to his mother, begged to be sent home, and said, "I have heard that the etiquette between a man and a woman does not apply in their private room. But lately I have been too casual, and when my husband saw me improperly dressed, he was displeased. He is treating me like a stranger. It is not right for a woman to live as a guest; therefore, please send me back to my parents."

Mencius' mother called him to her and said, "It is polite to inquire before you enter a room.

You should make some loud noise to warn any-one inside, and as you enter, you should keep your eyes low so that you will not embarrass anyone. Now, you have not behaved properly, yet you are quick to blame others for their im-propriety. Isn't that going a little too far?"

Mencius apologized and took back his wife. Superior men said that his mother understood the way to be a mother-in-law.

When Mencius was living in Ch'i, he was feeling very depressed. His mother saw this and asked him, "Why are you looking so low?"

"It's nothing," he replied.

On another occasion when Mencius was not working, he leaned against the door and sighed. His mother saw him and said, "The other day I saw that you were troubled, but you answered that it was nothing. But why are you leaning against the door sighing?"

Mencius answered, "I have heard that the su-perior man judges his capabilities and then ac-cepts a position. He neither seeks illicit gains nor covets glory or high salary. If the Dukes and Princes do not listen to his advice, then he does not talk to them. If they listen to him but do not use his ideas, then he no longer frequents their courts. Today my ideas are not being used in Ch'i, so I wish to go somewhere else. But I am worried because you are getting too old to travel about the country."

His mother answered, "A woman's duties are to cook the five grains, heat the wine, look after her parents-in-law, make clothes, and that is all! Therefore, she cultivates the skills required in the women's quarters and has no ambition to manage affairs outside of the house. The *Book of Changes* says, 'In her central place, she attends to the preparation of the food.' The *Book of Poetry* says, 'It will be theirs neither to do wrong nor to do good, / Only about the spirits and the food will they have to think.' This means that a woman's duty is not to control or to take charge. Instead she must follow the 'three submissions.' When she is young, she must submit to her par-ents. After her marriage, she must submit to her husband. When she is widowed, she must sub-mit to her son. These are the rules of propriety. Now you are an adult and I am old; therefore, whether you go depends on what you consider right, whether I follow depends on the rules of propriety."

Superior men observed that Mencius' mother knew the proper course for women. The *Book of Poetry* says, "Serenely she looks and smiles, / Without any impatience she delivers her in-structions."

LETTER TO HIS BROTHER-IN-LAW

Man is a creature of emotion. Yet it is according to reason that husband and wife are joined to-gether or put asunder. According to the rules of propriety which have been set down by the Sage, a gentleman should have both a primary wife and concubines as well. Even men from poor and humble families long to possess concu-bines. I am old and approaching the end of my life, but I have never had a concubine. I will carry regret for this into my grave.

My wife is jealous and has destroyed the Way of a good family. Yet this mother of five children is still in my house. For the past five years her conduct has become worse and worse day after day. She sees white as black and wrong as right. I never err in the slightest, yet she lies about me and nags me without end. It is like falling among bandits on the road, for I constantly encounter unpredictable disasters through this woman. Those who slander us good officials seem to have no regard for the deleterious effects this has on the welfare of the country. Likewise, those who indulge their jealousy seem to have no concern for the unjust strain this puts on other people's lives.

Since antiquity it has always been considered a great disaster to have one's household be dominated by a woman. Now this disaster has befallen me. If I eat too much or too little or if I drink too much or too little, she jumps all over me like the tyrant Hsia Chieh. If I play some affectionate joke on her, she will gossip about it to everyone. She glowers with her eyes and clenches her fists tightly in anger over things which are purely the product of her imagination. I feel a severe pang in my heart, as though something is poisoning my five viscera. Anxiety cuts so deeply that I can hardly bear to go on living. My rage is so great that I often forget the calamities I might cause.

When she is at home, she is always lounging in bed. After she gave birth to my principal heir, she refused to have any more children. We have no female servants at our home who can do the work of weaving clothes and rugs. Our family is of modest means and we cannot afford a man-servant, so I have to work myself like a humble commoner. My old friends see my situation and feel very sorry for me, but this woman has not the slightest twinge of sympathy or pity.

Wu Ta, you have seen our one and only female servant. She has no hairpins or hair ornaments. She has no make-up for her face, looks haggard, and is in bad shape. My wife does not extend the slightest pity to her, nor does she try to understand her. The woman flies into a rage, jumps around, and yells at her. Her screaming is so shrill that even a sugar-peddler's concubine would be ashamed to behave in such a manner.

I should have sent this woman back long ago, but I was concerned by the fact that the children were still young and that there was no one else to do the work in our house. I feared that my children, Chiang and Pao, would end up doing servants' work. Therefore I retained her. But worry and anxiety plunge like a dagger into my heart and cause me great pain. The woman is always screaming fiercely. One can hardly bear to listen to it.

Since the servant was so mistreated, within half a year her body was covered with scabs and scars. Ever since the servant became ill, my daughter Chiang has had to hull the grain and

do the cooking, and my son Pao has had to do all sorts of dirty work. Watching my children struggle under such labor gives me distress.

Food and clothing are scattered all over the house. Winter clothes which have become frayed are not patched. Even though the rest of us are very careful to be neat, she turns the house into a mess. She does not have the manner of a good wife, nor does she possess the virtue of a good mother. I despise her overbearing aggressiveness, and I hate to see our home turned into a sty.

She relies on the power of Magistrate Cheng to get what she wants. She is always threatening people, and her barbs are numerous. It seems as if she carries a sword and lance to the door. Never will she make a concession, and it feels as if there were a hundred bows around our house. How can we ever return to a happy family life?

When the respectable members of our family try to reason with her, she flings insults at them and makes sharp retorts. She never regrets her scandalous behavior and never allows her heart to be moved. I realize that I have placed myself in a difficult position, and so I have started to plan ahead. I write you this letter lest I be remiss in keeping you informed of what is happening. I believe that I have just cause, and I am not afraid of criticism. Unless I send this wife back, my family will have no peace. Unless I send this wife back, my house will never be clean. Unless I send this wife back, good fortune will not come to my family. Unless I send this wife back, I will never again get anything accomplished. I hate myself for not having made this decision while I was still young. The decision is now made, but I am old, humiliated, and poor. I hate myself for having allowed this ulcer to grow and spread its poison. I brought a great deal of trouble on myself.

Having suffered total ruin as a result of this family catastrophe, I am abandoning the gentry life to live as a recluse. I will sever relationships with my friends and give up my career as an official. I will stay at home all the time and concentrate on working my land to supply myself with food and clothing. How can I think of success and fame?

REVIEW QUESTIONS

1. What features in Liu Hsiang's depiction of Mencius's mother strike you as unrealistic and unlikely? Why?
2. What features in Liu Hsiang's depiction of Mencius's mother strike you as realistic and likely? Why?
3. If you were the brother-in-law, how would you respond to Feng Yen's letter?
4. What do these two accounts tell you about Chinese family life? Explain.

A Chinese Scholar Laments the Lack of Morality in Political Appointments (c. 100–150 C.E.)

WANG FU, *Essay on Social Relations*

Those who held government positions were rewarded with wealth and status in Han China. Consequently, competition for government posts was intense. In this essay, Wang Fu (c. 100–150 C.E.), an acknowledged scholar without an official position, complains about the role of wealth and prestige in the awarding of government jobs. His point is that moral character, which is supposed to be the most important standard for office holding, is being ignored. Money and social influence have proved to be more important.

Although this manner of selecting bureaucrats was more prevalent throughout Chinese history than in many other cultures, Wang Fu's complaint is timeless. For example, one need only consider contemporary American politics to see how his insights continue to be valid today. Yet, if there was a more viable system, Wang Fu did not present one.

It is said, "With people, the old friends are best; with things, the new ones are best." In other words, brothers may drift apart as time goes by, but it is normal for friends to become closer with the passage of time.

Nowadays this is not so. People often seem to miss those they hardly know but forget close friends; they turn away from old friends as they seek new ones. Sometimes after several years friendships become weaker and weaker, and friendships of long standing break down. People not only discard the ancient sages' instruction to treasure old friends but also break oaths of enduring fidelity.

What are the reasons for these changes in attitude toward friendship? Careful analysis makes them clear. There are common tendencies and normal ways of operating in the world. People compete to flatter and get close to those who are wealthy and prominent; this is a common tendency. People are also quick to snub those who are poor and humble; this is a normal way of operating. If a person makes friends with the rich and prominent, he will gain the benefits of influential recommendations for advancement in office and the advantages of generous presents and other emoluments. But if he makes friends with the poor and humble, he will lose money either from giving them handouts or from unrepaid loans.

A powerful official may be as evil as the tyrant Chieh and the bandit Tao Chih, but if he rides in a magnificent carriage to summon scholars to him, they will take it as a great honor and flock to his service. How can a person avoid being drawn to those who can render him tangible benefits? A scholar may have the combined talents of Yen Hui and Pao Shang-yen, yet if he wears poor clothing when he pays visits, others will feel insulted and will look with dread upon the prospect of further calls. How can a person not avoid those who will bring him disadvantage? Therefore, those who are rich and prosperous find it easy to get along in society, while those who are poor and humble find it difficult to secure a place in the world.

The poor, if they wear fine clothes, are regarded as extravagant and ostentatious, but if they wear coarse clothing, they are taken to be in dire straits and difficulties. If they walk slowly, people say they are weak from hunger, but if they walk fast, they are accused of trying to flee from debts. If the poor do not visit others, they are regarded as arrogant, but if they come around too often, they are suspected of trying to sponge free meals. If they come empty-handed, they are taken for insincere friends, but if they bring a gift, they are regarded as degenerate. If they are confident and self-assured, they are regarded as unvirtuous. All these are the woes of being an unemployed scholar, poor and without rank.

The poor scholar, being in a humble position, has much to bear. At home he has to put up with his wife's complaints. Outside he must endure the cutting remarks of the scholar-officials. At banquets his gifts are small and considered inadequate. His own parties are simple and not up to others' standards. He is not rich enough to come to the aid of friends in need, and his power is too meager to save them, A friendship may have been long and cordial, but since the poor scholar is unable to save his friend in need, the relationship weakens. Once this occurs, the humble scholar becomes more and more aware of his own low status, while the other individual busies

himself with cultivating relationships with more useful persons and forgets his old friend.

Since friendship is founded on mutual advantage, when disadvantage arises the friendship breaks down. An oath of friendship is meaningless and eventually will be discarded. Those who communicate often become close friends because they see advantage to themselves in the relationship. A commoner will act as follows. If a person can be useful, he will draw near to him. Being close to him, he will gradually develop a feeling of love for him. Because he thinks the friend is right, he will regard him as capable, and so he will turn his heart toward him and praise him happily. A commoner will keep his distance from those whom he regards as unable to render him benefits. Because they are distant, after a time he begins to feel hatred for them. Because he hates them, he always considers them in the wrong, and so feels disgust for them. Once he feels disgust for them, his heart naturally turns away from them and he slanders them. Therefore, even if one's friendship with a wealthy and prominent man is a new one, it will become closer and closer every day; and although one's friendship with a poor and humble man is of long standing, it will tend to become weaker and more distant. These are the reasons why a poor scholar cannot compete with officials for friends.

Rulers do not understand what causes people to form friendships, and so they readily believe the words of their high officials. This is why honest scholars are always excluded from court while crafty persons always get their way. In the past when Wei Ch'i lost his power, his retainers abandoned him to serve in another place. When the general Wei Ch'ing lost imperial favor and was no longer able to shower his subordinates with rewards from the court, they left him to serve the newly powerful general Huo Ch'ü-ping. The retainers of the Chao general Lien P'o and of the Han general T'i Kung came and went, depending on whether their benefactors were in power or not. These four gentlemen were all capable and all had illustrious pasts, yet the loyalty of their subordinates wavered with the amount of power they had. How much more would this happen to those who became really poor and humble!

Only those who have the heroic virtue of the ancients will not desert their superiors and friends in such a fashion. When these people make commitments to friends, they do not abandon them their whole life long. If they love someone, their concern for him can only become greater as his situation worsens. The *Book of Poetry* says, "The virtuous man, the princely one, is uniformly correct in his deportment. His heart is as if it were tied to what is correct." Only during the cold of winter, when all other trees have lost their leaves, do people realize that the pine trees resist the cold and do not shed their needles. Likewise, it is only when difficulties are encountered that a person's virtue can be noticed. Yu Ying and Yu Jang gave their lives to retain their master's good grace. Chuan Chu and Ching K'o sacrificed their lives to render service to their masters. It is easy to die, but to die for one's master willingly when he has encountered hard times is difficult indeed. . . .

Most scholars are very shortsighted, concerned only about the present moment. If they think that a powerful man will be of use to them, they rush to his service; but if they think that someone will be of no use, they are quick to avoid him. Those who burn for rapid promotion and advancement compete with one another to get close to persons of prominence but can find no time to associate with the humble. They scrape and claw to make their way to the front but have little time to concern themselves with those who have been left behind. When the Minister Han Ankuo lost his official post, he sent some five hundred golden artifacts to the newly powerful Grand Commandant Tien Fen to seek a position. Yet not once did he give any assistance to a poor but capable scholar. Likewise the Minister Ti Fang-chin was eager to recommend Shun Yu-ch'ang, a relative of the empress, for promotion, but was unable to rec-

ommend even one humble scholar. Now, both Han An-kuo and Ti Fang-chin were good and loyal officials of the Han dynasty, and yet they still acted in such a snobbish way. How can one expect virtue from officials who are inferior to them? This is the reason that crafty, calculating individuals can worm their way up the official ladder while ordinary scholars slip ever more into obscurity. Unless the realm has a brilliant ruler, there may be no one to discern this.

Not everyone desires riches and honors; not everyone scorns poverty and humbleness. People can differ drastically in their preferences and goals. Hsü Yu refused to accept the dragon-throne, which the sage-king Yao offered to him, yet small men fight bitterly to gain a mere Magistrate's post. Mencius declined a stipend of 10,000 bushels, but there are small men who grasp after a salary of one peck. . . . Po I did not regret the need to gather wild vegetables to support himself, and Tsao Fu was content to dwell in a tree. From these cases one can see that gentlemen's intentions are varied. Therefore I say to the gentlemen of today: Although you may be rich and powerful, you must not look down upon those who are poor and humble, nor demand their submission to you.

The *Book of Poetry* says, "Virtue is light as a hair, but few are able to lift it." In this world there are four basic virtues which people are rarely able to acquire fully: reciprocity, fairness, respect, and perseverance. Reciprocity is the basis of knowledge. Fairness is the basis of righteousness. Respect is the basis of propriety. Perseverance is the basis of fidelity. When these four types of virtues are established, they form the basis for the achievement of the four kinds of good behavior, and the one who possesses them can be regarded as a true worthy. Those who do not possess these four virtues or types of good behavior—perhaps not having even one of them—are considered small men. . . .

In this world there are three things which are loathsome indeed. These may be summed up as follows: first, to express in words extremely warm affections toward others while one's heart holds nothing but cold feelings; second, to express in writing dear thoughts toward others while in fact one's thoughts are rarely with them; third, to make appointments with others while having already decided not to show up at all. If people are always suspicious of others' words, they may fear that they will dismiss the genuine sentiments of a true worthy. But if people are quick to believe what they are told, they will be often fooled. This is why those disingenuous, mediocre people are so disgusting. . . .

Alas! The gentlemen of today speak nobly but act basely. Their words are upright, but their hearts are false. Their actions do not reflect their words, and their words are out of harmony with their thoughts. In talking of antiquity they always praise the conduct of Po I, Shu Ch'i, Ch'ü Yüan, and Yen Hui; but when it comes to the present, their only concern is the scramble for official ranks and positions. In their lofty speeches they refer to virtuous and righteous persons as being worthy. But when they actually recommend people for office, they consider only such requirements as influence and prominence. If a man is just an obscure scholar, even if he possesses the virtue of Yen Hui and Ming Tzu-chien, even if he is modest and diligent, even if he has the ability of I Yin and Lu Shang, even if he is filled with the most devoted compassion for the people, he is clearly not going to be employed in this world.

REVIEW QUESTIONS

1. What specifically in Wang Fu's essay is universal, that is, relevant to most societies and in most times?
2. What features of the essay strike you as overly idealistic? As pessimistic?
3. Do you agree with his argument? Why or why not?

Chinese Historians Record Accounts of Travelers to Japan (third to seventh centuries C.E.)

Accounts of the Eastern Barbarians
CH'EN SHOU, *The Japanese*

The following accounts are from various dynastic histories written by Chinese historians between the third and seventh centuries. Although their sources of information remain unclear, scholars suggest that these authors probably relied on the accounts of travelers to the coast of the southernmost island, Kyushu. What is clear is that the Japanese kingdoms—Japan was not united—are far from being a central concern for the Chinese. The causes of this disinterest were the relative isolation of the Japanese islands (as compared to Korea, for instance) and the Chinese emphasis on the superiority of their own culture, which led them to believe that Japanese society lacked sophistication.

Japan was a relatively closed society (120 miles from mainland Asia) and had little contact with foreigners until modern times. The Japanese themselves left little documentation of their own history during this period. As a result, modern scholars have had to rely on Chinese accounts. These selections offer excellent examples of the Chinese historians' craft.

ACCOUNTS OF THE EASTERN BARBARIANS

History of the Kingdom of Wei

The people of Wa [Japan] dwell in the middle of the ocean on the mountainous islands southeast of [the prefecture of] Tai-fang. They formerly comprised more than one hundred communities. During the Han dynasty, [Wa] envoys appeared at the court; today, thirty of their communities maintain intercourse with us through envoys and scribes. . . .

The land of Wa is warm and mild. In winter as in summer the people live on raw vegetables and go about barefooted. They have [or live in] houses; father and mother, elder and younger, sleep separately. They smear their bodies with pink and scarlet, just as the Chinese use powder. They serve food on bamboo and wooden trays, helping themselves with their fingers. When a person dies, they prepare a single coffin, without an outer one. They cover the graves with earth to make a mound. When death occurs, mourning is observed for more than ten days, during which period they do not eat meat. The head mourners wail and lament, while friends sing, dance, and drink liquor. When the funeral is over, all members of the family go into the water to cleanse themselves in a bath of purification.

When they go on voyages across the sea to visit China, they always select a man who does not comb his hair, does not rid himself of fleas, lets his clothing get as dirty as it will, does not eat meat, and does not lie with women. This man behaves like a mourner and is known as the "mourning keeper." When the voyage meets with good fortune, they all lavish on him slaves and other valuables. In case there is disease or mishap, they kill him, saying that he was not scrupulous in observing the taboos. . . .

Whenever they undertake an enterprise or a journey and discussion arises, they bake bones and divine in order to tell whether fortune will be good or bad. First they announce the object of divination, using the same manner of speech as in tortoise shell divination; then they examine the cracks made by the fire and tell what is to come to pass.

In their meetings and in their deportment, there is no distinction between father and son or between men and women. They are fond of liquor. In their worship, men of importance simply clap their hands instead of kneeling or bowing. The people live long, some to one hundred and others to eighty or ninety years. Ordinarily, men of importance have four or five wives; the lesser ones, two or three. Women are not loose in morals or jealous. There is no theft, and litigation is infrequent. In case of violation of law, the light offender loses his wife and children by confiscation; as for the grave offender, the members of his household and also his kinsmen are exterminated. There are class distinctions among the people, and some men are vassals of others. Taxes are collected. There are granaries as well as markets in each province, where necessaries are exchanged under the supervision of the Wa officials. . . .

When the lowly meet men of importance on the road, they stop and withdraw to the roadside. In conveying messages to them or addressing them, they either squat or kneel, with both hands on the ground. This is the way they show respect. When responding, they say "ah," which corresponds to the affirmative "yes."

The country formerly had a man as ruler. For some seventy or eighty years after that there were disturbances and warfare. Thereupon the people agreed upon a woman for their ruler. Her name was Pimiko. She occupied herself with magic and sorcery, bewitching the people. Though mature in age, she remained unmarried. She had a younger brother who assisted her in ruling the country. After she became the ruler, there were few who saw her. She had one thousand women as attendants, but only one man. He served her food and drink and acted as a medium of communication. She resided in a palace surrounded by towers and stockades, with armed guards in a state of constant vigilance. . . .

In, the sixth month of the second year of Ching-ch'u [A.D. 238], the Queen of Wa sent the grandee Nashonmi and others to visit the prefecture [of Tai-fang], where they requested permission to proceed to the Emperor's court with tribute. The Governor, Liu Hsia, dispatched an officer to accompany the party to the capital. In answer to the Queen of Wa, an edict of the Emperor, issued in the twelfth month of the same year, said as follows: "Herein we address Pimiko, Queen of Wa, whom we now officially call a friend of Wei. The Governor of Tai-fang, Liu Hsia, has sent a messenger to accompany your vassal, Nashonmi, and his lieutenant, Tsushi Gori. They have arrived here with your tribute, consisting of four male slaves and six female slaves, together with two pieces of cloth with designs, each twenty feet in length. You live very far away across the sea; yet you have sent an embassy with tribute. Your loyalty and filial piety we appreciate exceedingly. We confer upon you, therefore, the title 'Queen of Wa Friendly to Wei,' together with the decoration of the gold seal with purple ribbon. The latter, properly encased, is to be sent to you through the Governor. We expect you, O Queen, to rule your people in peace and to endeavor to be devoted and obedient." . . .

When Pimiko passed away, a great mound was raised, more than a hundred paces in diameter. Over a hundred male and female attendants followed her to the grave. Then a king was placed on the throne, but the people would not obey him. Assassination and murder followed; more than one thousand were thus slain.

A relative of Pimiko, named Iyo, a girl of thirteen, was [then] made queen and order was restored. Cheng [the Chinese ambassador] issued a proclamation to the effect that Iyo was the ruler. Then Iyo sent a delegation of twenty under the grandee Yazaku, General of the Imperial Guard, to accompany Cheng home [to China]. The delegation visited the capital and presented thirty male and female slaves. It also offered to the court five thousand white gems and two pieces of carved jade, as well as twenty pieces of brocade with variegated designs. . . .

History of the Liu Sung Dynasty

Kō died and his brother, Bu,[1] came to the throne. Bu, signing himself King of Wa, Generalissimo Who Maintains Peace in the East Commanding with Battle-Ax All Military Affairs in the Seven Countries of Wa, Paekche, Silla, Imna, Kala, Chin-han, and Mok-han, in the second year of Sheng-ming, Shun-ti's reign [478], sent an envoy bearing a memorial which read as follows: "Our land is remote and distant; its domains lie far out in the ocean. From of old our forebears have clad themselves in armor and helmet and gone across the hills and waters, sparing no time for rest. In the east, they conquered fifty-five countries of hairy men; and in the west, they brought to their knees sixty-six countries of various barbarians. Crossing the sea to the north, they subjugated ninety-five countries. The way of government is to keep harmony and peace; thus order is established in the land. Generation after generation, without fail, our forebears have paid homage to the court. Your subject, ignorant though he is, is succeeding to the throne of his predecessors and is fervently devoted to your Sovereign Majesty. Everything he commands is at your imperial disposal. In order to go by way of Paekche, far distant though it is, we prepared ships and boats. Koguryŏ,[2] however, in defiance of law, schemed to capture them. Borders were raided, and murder was committed repeatedly. Consequently we were delayed every time and missed favorable winds. We attempted to push on, but when the way was clear, Koguryŏ was rebellious. My deceased father became indignant at the marauding foe who blocked our way to the sovereign court. Urged on by a sense of justice,

---

[1]Emperor Yūryaku, 456–479.
[2]State in North Korea.

he gathered together a million archers and was about to launch a great campaign. But because of the death of my father and brother, the plan that had been matured could not be carried out at the last moment. Mourning required the laying down of arms. Inaction does not bring victory. Now, however, we again set our armor in array and carry out the wish of our elders. The fighting men are in high mettle; civil and military officials are ready; none have fear of sword or fire.

"Your Sovereign virtue extends over heaven and earth. If through it we can crush this foe and put an end to our troubles, we shall ever continue loyally to serve [Your Majesty]. I therefore beg you to appoint me as supreme commander of the campaign, with the status of minister, and to grant to others [among my followers] ranks and titles, so that loyalty may be encouraged."

By imperial edict, Bu was made King of Wa and Generalissimo Who Maintains Peace in the East Commanding with Battle-Ax all Military Affairs in the Six Countries of Wa, Silla, Imna, Kala, Chin-han, and Mok-han.

History of the Sui Dynasty

During the twenty years of the K'ai-huang era (581–600), the King of Wa, whose family name was Ame and personal name Tarishihoko, and who bore the title of Ahakomi, sent an envoy to visit the court. The Emperor ordered the appropriate official to make inquiries about the manners and customs [of the Wa people]. The envoy reported thus: "The King of Wa deems heaven to be his elder brother and the sun, his younger. Before break of dawn he attends the court, and, sitting cross-legged, listens to appeals. Just as soon as the sun rises, he ceases these duties, saying that he hands them over to his brother." Our just Emperor said that such things were extremely senseless, and he admonished [the King of Wa] to alter [his ways].

[According to the envoy's report], the King's spouse is called Kemi. Several hundred women are kept in the inner chambers of the court. The heir apparent is known as Rikamitahori. There is no special palace. There are twelve grades of court officials. . . .

There are about 100,000 households. It is customary to punish murder, arson, and adultery with death. Thieves are made to make restitution in accordance with the value of the goods stolen. If the thief has no property with which to make payment, he is taken to be a slave. Other offenses are punished according to their nature— sometimes by banishment and sometimes by flogging. In the prosecution of offenses by the court, the knees of those who plead not guilty are pressed together by placing them between pieces of wood, or their heads are sawed with the stretched string of a strong bow. Sometimes pebbles are put in boiling water and both parties to a dispute made to pick them out. The hand of the guilty one is said to become inflamed. Sometimes a snake is kept in a jar, and the accused ordered to catch it. If he is guilty, his hand will be bitten. The people are gentle and peaceful. Litigation is infrequent and theft seldom occurs.

As for musical instruments, they have five-stringed lyres and flutes. Both men and women paint marks on their arms and spots on their faces and have their bodies tattooed. They catch fish by diving into the water. They have no written characters and understand only the use of notched sticks and knotted ropes. They revere Buddha and obtained Buddhist scriptures from Paekche. This was the first time that they came into possession of written characters. They are familiar with divination and have profound faith in shamans, both male and female. . . .

Both Silla and Paekche [Korean states] consider Wa to be a great country, replete with precious things, and they pay her homage. Envoys go back and forth from time to time.

In the third year of Ta-yeh [607], King Tarishihoko sent an envoy to the court with tribute. The envoy said: "The King has heard that to the west of the ocean a Bodhisattva of the Sovereign reveres and promotes Buddhism. For that reason he has sent an embassy to pay his respects. Accompanying the embassy are several tens of monks who have come to study Buddhism." [The envoy brought] an official message which read: "The Son of Heaven in the land where the sun rises addresses a letter to the Son of Heaven in the land where the sun sets. We hope you are in good health." When the Emperor saw this letter, he was displeased and told the official in charge of foreign affairs that this letter from the barbarians was discourteous, and that such a letter should not again be brought to his attention.

New History of the T'ang Dynasty

Japan in former times was called Wa-nu. It is 24,000 *li* distant from our capital, situated to the southeast of Silla in the middle of the ocean. It is five months' journey to cross Japan from east to west, and a three months' journey from south to north. There are no castles or stockades in that country, only high walls built by placing timbers together. The roofs are thatched with grass. There are over fifty islets there, each with a name of its own, but all under the sovereignty of Japan. A high official is stationed to have surveillance over these communities.

As for the inhabitants the women outnumber the men. The people are literate and revere the teachings of Buddha. In the government there are twelve official ranks. The family name of the King is Ame. The Japanese say that from their first ruler, known as Ame-no-minaka-nushi, to Hikonagi, there were altogether thirty-two generations of rulers, all bearing the title of *mikoto* and residing in the palace of Tsukushi. Upon the enthronement of Jimmu, son of Hikonagi, the title was changed to *tennō* and the palace was moved to the province of Yamato. . . .

In the fifth year of Chen-kuan [631], the Japanese sent an embassy to pay a visit to the court. In appreciation of this visit from such a distance, the sovereign gave orders to the official concerned not to insist on yearly tribute. . . .

At this time, Silla was being harassed by Koguryo and Paekche. Emperor Kao Tsung sent a sealed rescript to Japan ordering the King to send reinforcements to succor Silla. But after a short time, King Kōtoku died [654] and his son Ame-no-toyo-takara was enthroned. Then he also died, and his son Tenchi was enthroned. In the following year [663] an envoy came to the court accompanied by some Ainus. The Ainus also dwell on those islands. The beards of the Ainus were four feet long. They carried arrows at their necks, and without ever missing would shoot a gourd held on the head of a person standing several tens of steps away.

Then Tenchi died [671] and his son, Temmu, came to the throne. He died, and his son Sōji was enthroned.

In the first year of Hsien-heng [670] an embassy came to the court from Japan to offer congratulations upon the conquest of Koguryŏ. About this time, the Japanese who had studied Chinese came to dislike the name Wa and changed it to Nippon. According to the words of the Japanese envoy himself, that name was chosen because the country was so close to where the sun rises. Some say [on the other hand], that Nippon was a small country which had been subjugated by the Wa, and that the latter took over its name. As this envoy was not truthful, doubt still remains. Besides the envoy was boastful, and he said that the domains of his country were many thousands of square *li* and extended to the ocean on the south and on the west. In the northeast, he said, the country was bordered by mountain ranges beyond which lay the land of the hairy men.

THE JAPANESE

The Japanese live in mountainous islands located in that part of the ocean southeast of the province of Taifang.[1] They were grouped into more than one hundred countries at one time,

---

[1] Located in the northern section of modern Korea.

and some of these countries sent tribute missions to China during the Han dynasty. Now only about thirty countries on the islands maintain relations with China. . . .

Regardless of age, all male Japanese brand their faces and tattoo their bodies. Since ancient times all Japanese envoys have claimed their country's close relationship with China. The founder of their nation, said they, was a son of Shao-k'ang[2] of the Hsia dynasty who received an investiture from his father to govern K'uaichi.[3] They further stated that the ancient Japanese cut their hair short and tattooed their bodies because they believed that by doing so they would not be harmed by flood-dragons[4] that infested the area where they lived. Today the Japanese still tattoo their bodies partly because they wish to camouflage and thus protect themselves from such dangerous carnivores as the shark whenever they dive into the ocean to catch fish, oysters, and clams. For most Japanese, however, tattoos are merely decorations. The way they are tattooed is altogether different from one Japanese country to another. Sometimes the tattoos are on the left side of the body and sometimes on the right side. The size of the colored marks also varies, depending upon the rank and position of the tattooed in the society where he lives.

Judging from the known distance between China and Japan, the Japanese islands must be located east of K'uaichi.[5] The Japanese are a moral people and they have good customs. All men bind their hair into a bundle without covering it with a hat; they wear head bands made of cotton instead. Their attires are made of strips of cloth sewed together horizontally, and they are so well sewed that one can hardly notice the seams between them. The hair of a Japanese woman spreads dishevelled at its lower end but is thereafter coiled into a tail that hangs on her back. Her clothes are like a bed sheet with a hole in the center from which the head emerges.

The Japanese raise such crops as paddy rice and hemp. Their sericulture is so advanced that they know how to make the finest silk. On their islands there are no oxen, horses, tigers, leopards, or magpies.

As for weaponry, they use spears, shields, and bows and arrows. Their bows, made of wood, are longer on the upper end and lower at the bottom. They use bamboo to make arrows to which are fastened barbs made of iron or animal bones. . . .

The Japanese islands have a warm climate, and the Japanese eat their vegetables raw regardless of winter or summer. They go bare-footed in their daily routine, but they do live inside houses. Inside a house, parents and children live in separate quarters. All Japanese cover their bodies with red paint, a custom similar to that in China where people love to rub their skin with white powder. Their eating and drinking utensils are made of bamboo, and they eat with their own hands.

A dead man is laid inside a coffin without being protected by an outer vault, and the coffin is buried underneath a mound made of dirt or earth. The dead body is kept within the house for more than ten days before it is taken out for burial. During these days the chief mourner will abstain from eating meat and cry constantly, while other mourners will sing, dance, and drink wine. After the burial, all members of the family bathe themselves in water, a ritual which the Japanese call "baptism."[6]

Whenever the Japanese decide to communicate with China, they send only one person each time. Before his journey, the designated envoy is not allowed to comb his hair, clean his body from lice, change his clothes which should remain dirty, or have sexual intercourse with women. In fact, he acts as if he were undergoing a period of mourning. If nothing inauspicious occurs during this period of fasting, all people in the village will take good care of his family, livestock,

[2]Shao-k'ang was an able, enlightened king who, according to tradition, ruled China for twenty-two years in the twenty-first century B.C.
[3]Modern Chekiang province.
[4]A flood-dragon or *chiao-lung* was a mythological animal that supposedly caused flood or earthquake.
[5]Actually, they were located northeast of K'uaichi.

[6]*Lien-mu.*

and whatever valuables he might have during his absence. If on the other hand he incurs sickness or disease or suffers from violent attacks by others, they will kill him on the ground that he has not been sincere and strict with himself.

The Japanese islands produce high-quality pearls and blue jade. In their mountains can be found mercury. Among the trees are cedar, scrub oak, camphor, papaya, oak, and many others. There is also a variety of bamboos. There are other plants such as ginger, orange, pepper, and wild ginger which could be used as condiments, but the Japanese do not know how to use them. Wild animals include monkey and black pheasant.

Before a Japanese travels or undertakes any important task, he consults oracles by burning animal bones. The words of the oracle sound like an order from a superior to an inferior, and the inquirer must be explicit in his inquiry before the ritual takes place. The oracle will indicate whether the proposed undertaking is an auspicious one. The other way of conjuring oracles is by burning tortoise shells, and the diviner examines the crackings of the shell to ascertain the omens.

There are no discernible differences between father and son or men and women as far as outward conduct is concerned. All Japanese love to drink wine. Whenever a person salutes a man of noble birth, he strikes his own hands instead of kneeling and kowtowing. Some Japanese live to be one hundred years old; others live to eighty or ninety years of age.

According to the Japanese custom, a man of noble birth can have four or five wives; even a man of meagre means sometimes has two or three wives. Japanese women are not licentious by nature; they do not know such things as jealousy. The good custom of Japan is also manifested by the fact that her people do not rob or steal and that they rarely resort to lawsuits to resolve their differences. If a man commits a minor crime, his wife will be confiscated by the government, but he and all of his relatives will be put to death if his crime is that of a serious nature. There is a clear line of demarcation between the superiors and the inferiors, and each person acts and behaves in accordance with his social status. An inferior is obedient to the person socially above him. . . .

In the sixth month of the second year of Ching-ch'u (A.D. 238) the Queen of Japan sent her minister Nan-sheng-mi and others to the province of Taifang where they requested the honor of paying homage to the Son of Heaven so as to present their tribute. Liu Hsia, the governor of Taifang, dispatched officials to escort personally the Japanese envoys to the capital.[7]

In the twelfth month of the same year (A.D. 238) the Chinese emperor[8] issued an edict to the Queen of Japan which read as follows:

"By this edict I hereby confer upon you, Pei-mi-hu, the title 'Ruler of Japan: Friend of Wei.'[9] Liu Hsia, the governor of Taifang, ordered officials personally to escort your minister-envoys, Nan-sheng-mi and Niu-li, to the capital, and I wish you to know that they have safely arrived and that I have received the tribute which they presented to me on your behalf: four men, six women, and cloth of different colors totalling two bolts and two *chang* in length. The fact that you sent me tribute despite the great distance between our two countries shows clearly your loyalty and fealty as a vassal state. I cannot but feet compassionate towards you and have thus decided to confer upon you the title 'Ruler of Japan: Friend of Wei.' In a separate case you will find a golden seal with purple ribbon attached to it. This seal, to be forwarded to you by the governor of Taifang, indicates your newly acquired investiture. It is my hope that you will rule your people in a proper manner and continue your loyalty towards me without fail.

"In view of the fact that your two envoys, Nan-sheng-mi and Niu-li, have traveled a long distance to pay me tribute on your behalf, I have decided to confer on the former the title 'General of the Imperial Guards with the Propensity Towards Goodness' and the latter, 'Colonel of the Imperial Guards with the Propensity To-

---

[7]Loyang.
[8]Emperor Wei Ming-ti (r. A.D. 227–239).
[9]Wei was then the dynastic title of China's royal household.

wards Goodness.' Silver seals with blue ribbons attached to them will be awarded to these two envoys to indicate their respective positions. They will be given a farewell audience before they are sent home.

"To reward you for the tribute you sent me, I am giving you the following items: 5 bolts of crimson silk with embroidered dragons, 10 sheets of crepe woolens in red color, 50 bolts of bright crepe, 50 bolts of violet silk, 3 bolts of violet silk with embroidered scenery, 5 sheets of woolens with polka dots of various colors, 50 bolts of white silk, eight taels of gold, two knives of five feet in length, 100 bronze mirrors, fifty catties of high-quality pearls, and fifty catties of mercury. All these will be packed in cases, to be brought to you by your two envoys. Upon their arrival you shall examine these gifts to see for yourself that they are in good order. It is my hope that you will show these gifts to your countrymen so that all of them will know that being compassionate towards you, I have given you so many of my treasures."

In the first year of Cheng-shih (A.D. 240) Governor Kung Tsun sent a delegation to Japan headed by Colonel T'i Chün. The delegation brought with it the edict issued by the Chinese emperor and the official seal whereby the Japanese king would be formally proclaimed "Ruler of Japan." To the Japanese king it also brought many gifts from the Chinese emperor: gold, silk, embroideries, knives, swords, mirrors, and other valuables. Upon receiving the items described above, the Japanese king sent to the Chinese emperor a memorial to express his gratitude. . . .

REVIEW QUESTIONS

1. How do these selections demonstrate that the Chinese considered the Japanese inferior?
2. What is your opinion of the judicial system (methods of determining guilt or innocence) described here? What were its strengths? Weaknesses?
3. How would you describe the relations among China, Japan, and the Korean states of Silla and Paekche?
4. How is the last item in this selection (Ch'en Shou's *The Japanese*) different from the earlier accounts? Explain.

Chinese Ambassadors Report on the Malay Peninsula (c. 600 C.E.)

The kingdom described in the following selection was located on the Malay Peninsula, which today is home to Singapore at the tip and also to parts of Burma (Myanmar), Thailand, and Malaysia. The peninsula has had strategic historical and geographical importance for millennia, as is shown by this ambassadorial expedition of the early seventh century. China had a vested interest in knowing what was going on in nearby countries, and it exercised hegemony over them whenever it could.

The original narrative is lost, but parts were preserved in later Chinese texts. The combination of Hindu and Buddhist influences is apparent by the fourth sentence in the third paragraph: "It is the custom to worship the Buddha but greater respect is paid to the brahmans."

The kingdom of *Ch'ih-t'u,* another part of *Funan,* is situated in the South Seas. By sea one reaches it in more than a hundred days. The colour of the soil of the capital is mostly red, whence is derived the name [of the country]. Eastwards is the kingdom of *Po-lo-la,* to the west that of *P'o-lo-so,* and to the south that of *Ho-lo-tan.* Northwards it fronts on the ocean. The country is several thousand *li* in extent. The king's family name is Ch'ü-t'an, his personal name is *Li-fu-to-se.* He knows nothing of adjacent or distant countries. According to his own account, his Buddhist father abdicated so that he could preach the Word, whereupon Li-fu-to-se reigned in his stead. He has ruled for sixteen years and has three wives from among the daughters of neighbouring kings.

He resides in the city of *Seng-chih,* which has triple gates more than a hundred paces apart. On each gate are paintings of spirits in flight, *bodhisattvas* and other immortals, and they are hung with golden flowers and light bells. Several tens of women either make music or hold up golden flowers and ornaments. Four men, dressed in the manner of *chin-kang* giants on the sides of Buddhist pagodas, stand at the gate. Those stationed on the outside of the gate grasp weapons of war, those on the inside hold white cloths in the passage-way and gather flowers into white nets. All the buildings in the royal palace consist of multiple pavilions with the doors on the northern side. The king sits on a three-tiered couch, facing north and dressed in rose-coloured cloth, with a chaplet of gold flowers and necklaces of varied jewels. Four damsels attend on his right hand and on his left, and more than a hundred soldiers mount guard. To the rear of the king's couch there is a wooden shrine inlaid with gold, silver and five perfumed woods, and behind the shrine is suspended a golden light. Beside the couch two metal mirrors are set up, before which are placed metal pitchers, each with a golden incense burner before it. In front of all these is a recumbent golden ox before which hangs a jewelled canopy, with precious fans on either side. Several hundred brahmans sit in rows facing each other on

the eastern and western sides. The officials are: one *Sa-t'o-chia-lo;* two *T'o-na-ta-yu;* three *Chia-li-mi-chia* in charge of political affairs; one *Chi-lo-mo-ti* administering criminal law. Each city appoints one *Na-ya-chia* and ten *Po-ti.*

It is customary for all persons to pierce their ear lobes and cut their hair. The ceremony of prostration is not observed. The body is annointed with scented oils. It is the custom to worship the Buddha but greater respect is paid to the brahmans. Women gather their hair at the nape of the neck. Both men and women make clothes out of rose- and plain-coloured material. Although wealthy families are largely independent of authority, they affect a gold locket only by royal dispensation. For a wedding an auspicious day is selected. For five days before the chosen date the bride's family makes merry and carouses. Then the father, holding the girl's hand, delivers her to his son-in-law. On the seventh day the nuptial rites are completed and the couple considered united. After the marriage property is divided and a separate house built, but the young son must live with his father. On the death of a parent or brother [the mourner] shaves his hair and dresses in plain clothes. He roofs a chalet over the water with bamboo boughs, and piles firewood around the corpse, which is laid out inside. He burns incense, sets up a banner, blows on the conch-shell and beats a drum as an envoi; he then sets fire to the pile, after which the burnt wood finally falls into the water. Both nobility and commoners are treated in this way, but when the king has been cremated his ashes are preserved in a golden jar and deposited in a temple.

It is constantly warm in winter and summer. Rainy days are numerous, fine days few, and there is no special season for planting. [Conditions] allow [the cultivation of] padi, chi [millet], white beans and black hemp. Other products resemble those of *Chiao-chih* (Tong-king). Wine is made from sugar-cane mixed with the root of the purple gourd. The wine is yellowish red in colour, with a sweet flavour. It is also called coconut spirit.

On his accession to the throne, Yang-ti called

for men capable of opening up communications with far distant lands. In the third year of the Ta-yeh period (A.D. 607) Ch'ang-Chün, the Custodian of Military Property, and Wang Chün-cheng, a Controller of Natural Resources, were among those who requested to be sent on an embassy to *Ch'ih-t'u*. The Emperor was extremely gratified and granted to each a 100 rolls of silk, together with a suit of clothes appropriate for the season, while he sent 5,000 different sorts of gifts to the king of *Ch'ih-t'u*. In the tenth moon (November or early December) of that year Ch'ang-Chün took ship from the *Nan-hai* commandery (Canton). For twenty days and nights they sailed before a favourable wind (the northeast monsoon) and reached *Chiao-shih* (Scorched Rock) Mountain. Passing south-eastwards, they anchored at *Ling-ch'ieh-po-pa-to* Island, which faces *Lin-i* (*Campā*) on the west, and which has a temple on its summit. Then going southwards they reached *Shih-tzŭ-shih* (Lion Rock), whence there extended a chain of large and small islands. After two or three days' voyage they saw in the west the mountains of the country of *Lang-ya-hsü*. Then, continuing southwards to *Chi-lung* (Fowl Cage) Island, they reached the borders of *Ch'ih-t'u*, whose king sent the Brahman Chiu-mo-lo, with thirty ocean-going junks, to welcome them. Conches were blown and drums beaten to entertain the Sui envoys on their arrival, and a metal cable was used as a hauser for Ch'ang-Chün's vessel. It took more than a month to reach the capital.

The king sent his son, the Na-ya-chia, to welcome Ch'ang-Chün with appropriate ceremony. First he sent men to present a golden tray containing fragrant flowers, mirrors and golden forceps; two containers for aromatic oil; eight vases of scented water; and four lengths of white, folded cloth for the envoys to bathe with. On the same day at the hour of Wei (one to three p.m.), the Na-ya-chia again sent two elephants, bearing canopies of peacock feathers, to welcome the ambassadors, and a gilt-flowered, golden tray containing a decree. A hundred men and women sounded conches and drums and two Brahmans conducted the envoys to the royal palace. Ch'ang-

Chün presented his credentials in the council-chamber, where those below the King were all seated. When the proclamation had been read Ch'ang-Chün and his retinue were invited to sit while Indian music was played. When this came to an end Ch'ang-Chün and his suite returned to their dwellings, and Brahmans were sent there to offer them food. Large leaves, ten feet square, were used as platters. The Brahmans then addressed Ch'ang-Chün, saying: "We are now citizens of the Great Central States; no longer do we belong to the state of *Ch'ih-t'u*. Eat the coarse fare we provide for the sake of your great country." A few days later Ch'ang-Chün and his companions were invited to a ceremonial feast. The pageantry was similar to that on their return from the first meeting, with guards leading the way. In front of the King two divans had been erected, on which were placed leaf-platters, each fifteen feet square, containing cakes of four colours, yellow, white, purple and red, together with beef-, mutton-, fish-, turtle-, pork- and tortoise-meats of more than a hundred sorts. Then the king requested Ch'ang-Chün to mount on to the divan, while his retinue sat on the bare ground. Each took a golden goblet containing wine while maidens played music in rotation, and valuable presents were given. Subsequently the Na-ya-chia was sent to accompany Ch'ang-Chün to offer up local products as tribute, to present gold, a crown ornamented with hibiscus design and Barus camphor, to take a gold cast of a *to-lo* leaf on which was an inscription in relief, and to seal it in a golden casket. Brahmans were commanded to take fragrant flowers and, playing upon conch-shells and drums, to act as an escort.

On entering the sea the envoys saw shoals of green fish flying over the water. After voyaging over the sea for more than ten days they reached the southeastern, mountainous part of *Lin-i* and passed through a strait more than a thousand paces wide, where for a whole day's sail the air around the vessel was yellowish and fetid. This was said to be [caused by] the dung of great fish. Following the northern shore of the sea the envoys reached *Chiao-chih* (Tong-king). In the spring of the sixth year [of Ta-yeh] Ch'ang-Chün, together with the Na-ya-chia, visited the Emperor in Hung-nung, who bestowed upon Ch'ang-Chün and his suite 200 articles, and conferred upon them all the official rank of Ping-i-wei (Officer of Justice). The Na-ya-chia and his entourage were given official ranks and rewards, each in his degree.

REVIEW QUESTIONS

1. What is the importance of the brahmans' statement that they now belong to China ("the Great Central States"), rather than to the state of Ch'ih-t'u?
2. From the Chinese perspective, what is the message here?
3. What are the characteristics of family life as depicted in the selection?

Chinese Buddhists Recount their Travels into India (518–521 C.E.)

The Mission of Sung-yun and Hwei-sang to Obtain Buddhist Books in the West

Sung-yun (Song Yun) was a Buddhist from western China who was sent to "the Western World" (i.e., lands to the west of China) in search of Buddhist records from 518 to 521. He was accompanied by a monk, Hwei-sang (Huisheng). Their route was similar to that of Fa-hien a century earlier. The original account does not survive, but it was recorded by Hiuen-tsiang (Hsuan-tsang), who himself traveled to India seeking Buddhist scripture from 629 to 645.

This selection is important because it reveals several features of popular Buddhism that are not easily found in other sources: acceptance of magic, acceptance of worlds other than the human, and, of course, the unquestioned belief in rebirth (although such is only indicated in the last line of the selection). Somewhat less typical is the dismissive attitude toward non-Buddhist gods.

During the first decade of the 8th month we entered the limits of the country of Han-Pan-to (Kabhanda), and going west six days, we ascended the Tsung-ling mountains; advancing yet three days to the west, we arrived at the city of Kiueh-Yu; and after three days more, to the Puh-ho-i mountains. This spot is extremely cold. The snow accumulates both by winter and summer. In the midst of the mountain is a lake in which dwells a mischievous dragon. Formerly there was a merchant who halted at night by the side of the lake. The dragon just then happened to be very cross, and forthwith pronounced a spell and killed the merchant. The king of Pan-to, hearing of it, gave up the succession to his son, and went to the kingdom of U-chang to acquire knowledge of the spells used by the Brâhmans. After four years, having procured these secrets, he came back to his throne, and, ensconced by the lake, he enchanted the dragon, and, lo! the dragon was changed into a man, who, deeply sensible of his wickedness, approached the king. The king immediately banished him from the Tsung-ling mountains more than 1000 li [li = ⅓ mile] from the lake. The king of the present time is of the thirteenth generation (*from these events*). From this spot westward the road is one continuous ascent of the most precipitous character; for a thousand li there are overhanging crags, 10,000 fathoms high, towering up to the very heavens. Compared with this road, the ruggedness of the great pass known as the Mang-men is as nothing, and the eminences of the celebrated Hian mountains (*in Honan*) are like level country. After entering the Tsung-ling mountains, step by step, we crept upwards for four days, and then reached the highest part of the range. From this point as a centre, looking downwards, it seems just as though one was poised in mid-air. The kingdom of Han-pan-to stretches as far as the crest of these mountains. Men say that this is the middle point of heaven and earth. The people of this region use the water of the rivers for irrigating their lands; and when they were told that in the middle country (*China*) the fields were watered by the rain, they laughed and said, "How could heaven provide enough for all?" To the eastward of the capital of this country there is a rapid river (or a river, Mang-tsin) flowing to the northeast towards Sha-leh (Kashgâr) [in extreme western China]. The high lands of the Tsung-ling mountains do not produce trees or shrubs. At this time, viz., the 8th month, the air is icy cold, and the north wind carries along with it the drifting snow for a thousand li. At last, in the middle decade of the 9th month, we entered the kingdom of Poh-ho (Bolor?). The mountains here are as lofty and the gorges deep as ever. The king of the country has built a town, where he resides, for the sake of being in the mountains. The people of the country dress handsomely, only they use some leathern garments. The land is extremely cold—so much so, that the people occupy the caves of the mountains as dwelling-places, and the driving wind and snow often compel both men and beasts to

herd together. To the south of this country are the great Snowy Mountains [Himalayas], which, in the morning and evening vapours, rise up like gem-spires.

In the first decade of the 10th month we arrived at the country of the Ye-tha (Ephthalites) [Huns]. The lands of this country are abundantly watered by the mountain streams, which fertilise them, and flow in front of all the dwellings. They have no walled towns, but they keep order by means of a standing army that constantly moves here and there. These people also use felt garments. The course of the rivers is marked by the verdant shrubs. In the summer the people seek the cool of the mountains; in the winter they disperse themselves through the villages. They have no written character. Their rules of politeness are very defective. They have no knowledge at all of the movements of the heavenly bodies; and, in measuring the year, they have no intercalary month, or any long and short months; but they merely divide the year into twelve parts, and that is all. They receive tribute from all surrounding nations: on the south as far as Tieh-lo; on the north, the entire country of Lae-leh, eastward to Khotan, and west to Persia—more than forty countries in all. When they come to the court with their presents for the king, there is spread out a large carpet about forty paces square, which they surround with a sort of rug hung up as a screen. The king puts on his robes of state and takes his seat upon a gilt couch, which is supported by four golden phœnix birds. When the ambassadors of the Great Wei dynasty were presented, (*the king*), after repeated prostrations, received their letters of instruction. On entering the assembly, one man announces your name and title; then each stranger advances and retires. After the several announcements are over, they break up the assembly. This is the only rule they have; there are no instruments of music visible at all. The royal ladies of the Ye-tha country also wear state robes, which trail on the ground three feet and more; they have special train-bearers for carrying these lengthy robes. They also wear on their heads a horn, in length eight feet and more, three feet of its length being red coral. This they ornamented with all sorts of gay colours, and such is their head-dress. When the royal ladies go abroad, then they are carried; when at home, then they seat themselves on a gilded couch, which is made (*from the ivory of?*) a six-tusked white elephant, with four lions (*for supporters*). Except in this particular, the wives of the great ministers are like the royal ladies; they in like manner cover their heads, using horns, from which hang down veils all round, like precious canopies. Both the rich and poor have their distinctive modes of dress. These people are of all the four tribes of barbarians the most powerful. The majority of them do not believe in Buddha. Most of them worship false gods. They kill living creatures and eat their flesh. They use the seven precious substances, which all the neighbouring countries bring as tribute, and gems in great abundance. It is reckoned that the distance of the country of the Ye-tha from our capital is upwards of 20,000 li.

On the first decade of the 11th month we entered the confines of the country of Po-sse (Persia). This territory (*ground*) is very contracted. Seven days farther on we come to a people who dwell in the mountains and are exceedingly impoverished. Their manners are rough and ill-favoured. On seeing their king, they pay him no honour; and when the king goes out or comes in, his attendants are few. This country has a river which formerly was very shallow; but afterwards, the mountains having subsided, the course of the stream was altered and two lakes were formed. A mischievous dragon took up his residence here and caused many calamities. In the summer he rejoiced to dry up the rain, and in the winter to pile up the snow. Travellers by his influence are subjected to all sorts of inconveniences. The snow is so brilliant that it dazzles the sight; men have to cover their eyes, or they would be blinded by it; but if they pay some religious service to the dragon, they find less difficulty afterwards.

In the middle decade of the 11th month we entered the country of Shie-Mi (Sâmbî?). This country is just beyond the Tsung-ling moun-

tains. The aspect of the land is still rugged; the people are very poor; the rugged narrow road is dangerous—a traveller and his horse can hardly pass along it one at a time. From the country of Po-lu-lai (Bolor) to the country of U-chang (Udyâna) [in mountains of northern India] they use iron chains for bridges. These are suspended in the air for the purpose of crossing (over the mountain chasms). On looking downwards no bottom can be perceived; there is nothing on the side to grasp at in case of a slip, but in a moment the body is hurled down 10,000 fathoms. On this account travellers will not cross over in case of high winds.

On the first decade of the 12th month we entered the U-chang country (Udyâna). On the north this country borders on the Tsung-ling mountains; on the south it joins India. The climate is agreeably warm. The territory contains several thousand li. The people and productions are very abundant. The fertility of the soil is equal to that of the plateau of Lin-tsze in China and the climate more equable. This is the place where Pe-lo (Vessantara) gave his child as alms, and where Bôdhisattva gave his body (*to the tigress*). Though these old stories relate to things so distant, yet they are preserved among the local legends (?). The king of the country religiously observes a vegetable diet; on the great fast-days he pays adoration to Buddha, both morning and evening, with sound of drum, conch, *vîṇa* (*a sort of lute*), flute, and all kinds of wind instruments. After mid-day he devotes himself to the affairs of government. Supposing a man has committed murder, they do not suffer him to be killed; they only banish him to the desert mountains, affording him just food enough to keep him alive (lit. a bit and a sup). In investigating doubtful cases, they rely on the pure or foul effect of drastic medicines; then, after examination, the punishment is adjusted according to the circumstances. At the proper time they let the streams overflow the land, by which the soil is rendered loamy and fertile. All provisions necessary for man are very abundant, cereals of every kind (lit. of a hundred sorts) flourish, and the different fruits (lit. the five fruits) ripen in great numbers. In the evening the sound of the (convent) bells may be heard on every side, filling the air (world); the earth is covered with flowers of different hues, which succeed each other winter and summer, and are gathered by clergy and laity alike as offerings for Buddha.

The king of the country seeing Sung-Yun (*inquired respecting him, and*) on their saying that the ambassadors of the Great Wei (*dynasty*) had come, he courteously received their letters of introduction. On understanding that the Empress Dowager was devotedly attached to the law of Buddha, he immediately turned his face to the east, and, with closed hands and meditative heart, bowed his head; then, sending for a man who could interpret the Wei language, he questioned Sung Yun and said, "Are my honourable visitors men from the region of sun-rising?" Sung-Yun answered and said, "Our country is bounded on the east by the great sea; from this the sun rises according to the divine will (*the command of Tathâgata*)." The king again asked, "Does that country produce holy men?" Sung-Yun then proceeded to enlarge upon the virtues of Confucius, of the Chow and Laou (Tseu), of the Chwang (*period*), and then of the silver walls and golden palaces of Fairy Land (P'eng lai Shan), and then of the spirits, genii, and sages who dwell there; he further dilated on the divination of Kwan-lo, the medicinal art of Hwa-to, and the magical power of Tso-ts'ze; descanting on these various subjects, and properly distinguishing their several properties, he finished his address. Then the king said, "If these things are really as your worship says, then truly yours is the land of Buddha, and I ought to pray at the end of my life that I may be born in that country."

REVIEW QUESTIONS

1. Do you think Sung-yun's attitude of superiority in regard to other peoples was more reflective of his Chinese culture or of his Buddhist religion?
2. There is reference to the Bodhisattva (the Buddha in an existence earlier than that in which he achieved enlightenment) having given his body to a tigress. In the tale, the tigress is starving. What would be the point of this tale for a Buddhist?
3. Compare the observations made here to those of Fa-hien. Which strike you as being more reliable? Why?

Japanese Poems Portray the Human Condition (eighth century C.E.)

Manyoshu or *Collection of Myriad Leaves*

The *Manyoshu,* an anthology of 4,516 poems, has been called one of the world's greatest collections of poetry. Compiled in the eighth century, probably by Tachibana no Moroye, a high government official, it represents Japanese concerns about the human condition. In particular, these poems address such topics as love, loneliness, separation, and death. Perhaps the most poignant poems are those that express sorrow over the loss of a spouse. The poems also show the integral role of nature in people's lives. They reflect a strong

Buddhist sensitivity to the essential questions of life, exemplified by the Japanese fondness for cherry blossoms and autumn leaves, both of which demonstrate the beauty but also the fragility and impermanence of life.

The translations here given were made by the Japanese Classics Translation Committee under the auspices of the Nippon Gakujutsu Shinkōkai. The poet Ralph Hodgson was among those responsible for these excellent versions.

Your basket, with your pretty basket,
Your trowel, with your little trowel,
Maiden, picking herbs on this hillside,
I would ask you: Where is your home?
Will you not tell me your name?
Over the spacious Land of Yamato
It is I who reign so wide and far,
It is I who rule so wide and far.
I myself, as your lord, will tell you
Of my home and my name.
    Attributed to Emperor Yūryaku (418–479)

Upon the departure of Prince Ōtsu for the capital after his secret visit to the Shrine of Ise

To speed my brother
Parting for Yamato,
In the deep of night I stood
Till wet with the dew of dawn.

The lonely autumn mountains
Are hard to pass over
Even when two go together—
How does my brother cross them all alone!
    Princess Ōku (661–701)

In the sea of Iwami,
By the cape of Kara,
There amid the stones under sea
Grows the deep-sea *miru* weed;
There along the rocky strand
Grows the sleek sea tangle.

Like the swaying sea tangle,
Unresisting would she lie beside me—
My wife whom I love with a love

Deep as the *miru*-growing ocean.
But few are the nights
We two have lain together.

Away I have come, parting from her
Even as the creeping vines do part.
My heart aches within me;
I turn back to gaze—
But because of the yellow leaves
Of Watari Hill,
Flying and fluttering in the air,
I cannot see plainly
My wife waving her sleeve to me.
Now as the moon, sailing through the cloud-rift
Above the mountain of Yakami,
Disappears, leaving me full of regret,
So vanishes my love out of sight;
Now sinks at last the sun,
Coursing down the western sky.

I thought myself a strong man,
But the sleeves of my garment
Are wetted through with tears.

Envoys

My black steed
Galloping fast,
Away have I come,
Leaving under distant skies
The dwelling place of my love.

Oh, yellow leaves
Falling on the autumn hill,
Cease a while
To fly and flutter in the air,
That I may see my love's dwelling place!
    Kakinomoto Hitomaro (Seventh Century)

After the death of his wife

Since in Karu lived my wife,
I wished to be with her to my heart's content;

But I could not visit her constantly
Because of the many watching eyes—
Men would know of our troth,
Had I sought her too often.
So our love remained secret like a rock-pent
    pool;
I cherished her in my heart,
Looking to aftertime when we should be
    together,
And lived secure in my trust
As one riding a great ship.
Suddenly there came a messenger
Who told me she was dead—
Was gone like a yellow leaf of autumn.
Dead as the day dies with the setting sun,
Lost as the bright moon is lost behind the
    cloud,
Alas, she is no more, whose soul
Was bent to mine like bending seaweed!

When the word was brought to me
I knew not what to do nor what to say;
But restless at the mere news,
And hoping to heal my grief
Even a thousandth part,
I journeyed to Karu and searched the market
    place
Where my wife was wont to go!

There I stood and listened,
But no voice of her I heard,
Though the birds sang in the Unebi
    Mountain;
None passed by who even looked like my wife.
I could only call her name and wave my sleeve.

Envoys

In the autumn mountains
The yellow leaves are so thick.
Alas, how shall I seek my love
Who has wandered away?
I know not the mountain track.

I see the messenger come
As the yellow leaves are falling.
Oh, well I remember

How on such a day we used to meet—
My wife and I!

In the days when my wife lived,
We went out to the embankment near by—
We two, hand in hand—
To view the elm trees standing there
With their outspreading branches
Thick with spring leaves. Abundant as their
    greenery
Was my love. On her leaned my soul.
But who evades mortality?
One morning she was gone, flown like an early
    bird.
Clad in a heavenly scarf of white,
To the wide fields where the shimmering *kagerō*
    rises
She went and vanished like the setting sun.

The little babe—the keepsake
My wife has left me—
Cries and clamors.
I have nothing to give; I pick up the child
And clasp it in my arms.

In our chamber, where our two pillows lie,
Where we two used to sleep together,
Days I spend alone, broken-hearted:
Nights I pass, sighing till dawn.

Though I grieve, there is no help;
Vainly I long to see her.
Men tell me that my wife is
In the mountains of Hagai—
Thither I go,
Toiling along the stony path;
But it avails me not,
For of my wife, as she lived in this world,
I find not the faintest shadow.

Envoys

Tonight the autumn moon shines—
The moon that shone a year ago,
But my wife and I who watched it then
    together
Are divided by ever widening wastes of time.

When leaving my love behind
In the Hikite mountains—
Leaving her there in her grave,
I walk down the mountain path,
I feel not like one living.

Kakinomoto Hitomaro

Love's complaint

At wave-bright Naniwa
The sedges grow, firm-rooted—
Firm were the words you spoke,
And tender, pledging me your love,
That it would endure through all the years;
And to you I yielded my heart,
Spotless as a polished mirror.
Never, from that day, like the seaweed
That sways to and fro with the waves,
Have I faltered in my fidelity,
But have trusted in you as in a great ship.
Is it the gods who have divided us?
Is it mortal men who intervene?
You come no more, who came so often,
Nor yet arrives a messenger with your letter.
There is—alas!—nothing I can do.
Though I sorrow the black night through
And all day till the red sun sinks,
It avails me nothing. Though I pine,
I know not how to soothe my heart's pain.
Truly men call us "weak women."
Crying like an infant,
And lingering around, I must still wait,
Wait impatiently for a message from you!

An elegy on the impermanence of human life

We are helpless before time
Which ever speeds away.
And pains of a hundred kinds
Pursue us one after another.
Maidens joy in girlish pleasures,
With ship-borne gems on their wrists,
And hand in hand with their friends;
But the bloom of maidenhood,
As it cannot be stopped,

Too swiftly steals away.
When do their ample tresses
Black as a mud-snail's bowels
Turn white with the frost of age?
Whence come those wrinkles
Which furrow their rosy cheeks?
The lusty young men, warrior-like,
Bearing their sword blades at their waists,
In their hands the hunting bows,
And mounting their bay horses,
With saddles dressed with twill,
Ride about in triumph;
But can their prime of youth
Favor them for ever?
Few are the nights they keep,
When, sliding back the plank doors,
They reach their beloved ones
And sleep, arms intertwined,
Before, with staffs at their waists,
They totter along the road,
Laughed at here, and hated there.
This is the way of the world;
And, cling as I may to life,
I know no help!

Envoy

Although I wish I were thus,
Like the rocks that stay for ever,
In this world of humanity
I cannot keep old age away.

Yamanoue Okura (660–733)

A dialogue on poverty

On the night when the rain beats,
Driven by the wind,
On the night when the snowflakes mingle
With the sleety rain,
I feel so helplessly cold.
I nibble at a lump of salt,
Sip the hot, oft-diluted dregs of saké;
And coughing, snuffling,
And stroking my scanty beard,
I say in my pride,
"There's none worthy, save I!"
But I shiver still with cold.

I pull up my hempen bedclothes,
Wear what few sleeveless clothes I have,
But cold and bitter is the night!
As for those poorer than myself,
Their parents must be cold and hungry,
Their wives and children beg and cry.
Then, how do you struggle through life?

Wide as they call the heaven and earth,
For me they have shrunk quite small;
Bright though they call the sun and moon,
They never shine for me.
Is it the same with all men,
Or for me alone?
By rare chance I was born a man
And no meaner than my fellows,
But, wearing unwadded sleeveless clothes
In tatters, like weeds waving in the sea,
Hanging from my shoulders,
And under the sunken roof,
Within the leaning walls,
Here I lie on straw
Spread on bare earth,
With my parents at my pillow,
My wife and children at my feet,
All huddled in grief and tears.
No fire sends up smoke
At the cooking-place,
And in the cauldron
A spider spins its web.
With not a grain to cook,
We moan like the night thrush.
Then, "to cut," as the saying is,
"The ends of what is already too short,"
The village headman comes,
With rod in hand, to our sleeping place,
Growling for his dues.
Must it be so hopeless—
The way of this world?

Envoy

Nothing but pain and shame in this world
    of men,
But I cannot fly away,
Wanting the wings of a bird.

                          Yamanoue Okura

An elegy on the death of Furuhi

What worth to me the seven treasures,
So prized and desired by all the world?
Furuhi, born of us two,
Our love, our dear white pearl,
With dawn, with the morning star,
Frolicked about the bed with us, standing
    or sitting;
When dusk came with the evening star,
He pulled our hands, urged us to bed,
"Leave me not, father and mother,
Let me sleep between you,
Like *saki-kusa,* the three-stalked plant."
So spoke that lovely mouth.
Then we trusted, as one trusts in a great ship,
That he would grow up as time passed by,
And we should watch him, both in weal
    and woe.
But, as of a sudden sweeps the storm,
Illness caught our son.
Helpless and in grief,
I braced my sleeves with white cord,
Grasped my shining mirror,
And gazing up into the sky
I appealed to the gods of heaven;
Dropping my forehead to the ground
Madly I prayed to the gods of earth:
"It is yours to decide his fate,
To cure him or to let him die."
Nothing availed my prayers,
He languished day by day,
His voice failed each morning,
His mortal life ebbed out.
Wildly I leapt and kicked the floor,
Cried, stared up, stared down,
And beat my breast in grief,
But the child from my arms has flown;
So goes the world. . . .

Envoys

So young he will not know the way;
Here is a fee for you,
O courier from the Nether World,
Bear him on your back.
With offerings I beseech you,

Be true and lead him up
Straight along the road to heaven!

Attributed to Yamanoue Okura

On seeing a dead man while crossing the pass of
Ashigara

He lies unloosened of his white clothes,
Perhaps of his wife's weaving
From hemp within her garden fence,
And girdled threefold round
Instead of once.
Perhaps after painful service done
He turned his footsteps home,
To see his parents and his wife;
And now, on this steep and sacred pass
In the eastern land of Azuma,

Chilled in his spare, thin clothes,
His black hair fallen loose—
Telling none his province,
Telling none his home,
Here on a journey he lies dead.

From the Tanabe Sakimaro Collection

Lament for old age

When winter is gone and spring comes,
New is the year, and new the month;
But man grows old.

All things are best when new;
But perchance with man
He alone is good who is old.

Anonymous

REVIEW QUESTIONS

1. What features in these poems do you like the best? Explain.
2. Some literary critics have found the expression of separation in these poems poignant.
   Do you agree? Explain.
3. Do you find the imagery in these poems unusual? Why or why not?
4. This poetry deals with themes that are both universal and distinctly Japanese. Give
   examples from this poetry that support this assumption.

Part III

Expanding Civilizations, 800–1550

An obvious and important theme in Part III is increased contact among different civilizations of the world. Perhaps the most conspicuous example of this development was the encounter between Europeans and Americans in the "Age of Exploration." There were also other intercultural contacts during this period that have global ramifications. To cite only two obvious examples, Europeans traveled not only to the Americas but also to East and South Asia; Muslims traveled to Africa and South Asia. Moreover, there was significantly increased travel within both Asia and Europe, and at least some of these journeys are well documented. In contrast, there are very few extant narratives written by voyagers who traveled within Africa and the Americas.

The motives behind these journeys and voyages were complex and varied. Many individuals traveled to spread a particular religion or to seek knowledge about the wider world. Among those motivated by religious beliefs were Giovanni da Pian del Carpini, who traveled to promote Christianity in Asia in the thirteenth century. Others traveled to seek religious knowledge and understanding. The ninth-century Japanese scholar Ennin went to China to deepen and broaden his devotion to Buddhism. Ibn Battuta, a Muslim native of Tangier, made four pilgrimages to Mecca. His religiously motivated travel not only afforded him the opportunity to fulfill a primary obligation in Islam, but also inspired him to travel more widely and to make detailed observations of the cultures he encountered. Likewise, Rabbi Benjamin of Tudela traveled from his native Europe in the twelfth century to such far-flung destinatons as Persia, India, and China. His goal was to observe and record information about Jewish life in the places that he visited.

Religion was not the only reason for observation and contemplation of the unknown. Amerigo Vespucci traveled much like a modern-day tourist, seeking out new interesting sights and experiences. Another Italian traveler, Girolamo Benzoni, also took advantage of his American adventures to discover "new" and exotic customs, like the smoking of tobacco. Interest in "new" subjects was not limited to those who traveled long distances. An extremely important development was an increased interest in women and women's lives. In some instances a male author might offer advice to women, often of a practical nature, as the twelfth-century Chinese scholar, Yüan Tsai, did in his work on family and property in Sung China. Women also began recording their own perceptions. One of the most famous examples in world literature is *The Diary* by Lady Murasaki.

Not all writers were inspired by high ideals. Political and military domination, as well as the love of high adventure, also played crucial roles. All of these motives were especially evident in the "Age of Exploration." Spanish conquistadores became famous for their military exploits. At the same time Portugese sailor Vasco da Gama certainly was lured into the Indian Ocean by the promise of adventure in distant lands. Their activities eventually helped their sponsoring governments build overseas empires. In contrast, the state-supported expeditions of Cheng Ho (Zheng He) to India and Africa gave China no territorial gains overseas.

One of the principal objectives of governments that sought political dominion overseas was to profit from their enterprises. Even the tenth-century Norwegians who traveled to Greenland enjoyed the natural bounty that the region offered (such as salmon) and took advantage of the opportunity to trade with the native Skraelings. The most notorious commercial commodity was human beings themselves. Slavery flourished in many parts of the world, but it was particularly deleterious in Africa. The selection by the Persian Gulf sailor, Buzurg Ibn Shahriyar of Ramhormuz, offers eloquent testimony about the slave trade and provides details about this human commerce. A second important commodity that attracted the attention of traders was ivory. Unfortunately, even today, elephants are hunted for their tusks.

Contacts among peoples often expose the values and beliefs of different societies with great clarity. It is almost a commonplace to say that Europeans failed to take foreign places and peoples at face value; instead, they imposed their own standards on others. Indeed, their behavior revealed a cultural arrogance matched only by the Chinese. However, the Chinese simply wanted other peoples to recognize and accept their superiority; they built no vast political empires. The Europeans, in contrast, attempted to impose stringent economic and political control over others. In 1494, the Treaty of Tordesillas between Spain and Portugal divided the world into two spheres of influence. Magellan's voyage, reported by Antonio Pigafetta, sought to determine how the treaty applied to distant parts of the world. This arrogance, which influenced the lives of millions of people, was noticed even by European contemporaries. In a famous response to the treaty, the French king François I is alleged to have said that he wanted to see where Adam's will bequeathed the world to Spain and Portugal.

Between 800 and 1550 many of the world's societies came into contact with each other. In particular, this period witnessed a number of events that clearly delineate it from the preceding one. In Southeast Asia, there was significantly increased consolidation and trade. In Europe, more cohesive feudal armies successfully repulsed invaders (Vikings, Magyars, and Moors) from the north, east, and south. The creation of the Kievan state under Viking domination laid the foundation for the rise of Russia. In the Americas, the culture of sedentary peoples was completely reorganized: the classic empires among the Maya ended and the rise of the Toltecs began a new phase that would culminate in the development of the Aztec and Inca empires. Finally, the spread of Muslim peoples into India, Southeast Asia, western and middle China, and Africa signaled a new phase in the relationships between cultures across a vast expanse of the globe.

10

Europe, 800–1500

Feudalism and spirituality define the Middle Ages in Western civilization. Although the former, a complex socioeconomic and political system, almost defies precise definition, it provided the medieval European population with security. The leaders of the three major religious groups (Jews, Christians, and Muslims) also emphasized order and deference to authority. There was a place for everyone and everyone had a place. This sense of order (at least in theory) and the underlying tension in medieval society are reflected by the regulations of the markets of Seville. They offer precise prescriptions for proper mercantile behavior; on the other hand, they speak eloquently about the difficult relations—and even hostility—between religious groups in twelfth-century Iberia. Religious differences are also illustrated by the conversion of Catherine of Louvain. Here, some Christian clergy cooperated with Catherine's Jewish parents to dissuade her from converting to Christianity; others supported her. The account of Usamah Ibn-Munqidh also illustrates the complexity of religious passions and their relationship to other aspects of medieval life. A twelfth-century Muslim warrior, he spent more time fighting against other Muslims than Christian crusaders.

Although the feudal system and the Church gave preference to men, the lives of women do much to illustrate the principal issues and difficulties of this period. The memoirs of a Castilian noblewoman give us an outsider's view of the feudal system, especially the warlike nature of the political elite.

A different view of family life can be found in a Spanish physician's advice to his sons in college. His letter reveals the tribulations of everyday life and also demonstrates that an early-fourteenth-century father loved his children just as much as any contemporary parent. The fact that two college students traveled to southern France for their education demonstrates that medieval people were not as place-bound as historians used to believe. In fact, there was a good deal of travel throughout Europe and beyond. One traveler, Ibn Fadlan, went to Bulgaria from Baghdad to help spread the Islamic faith and to help build a fortress.

The delicate balance of order and tension that defined medieval Europe was unable to withstand a series of natural and man-made disasters in the fourteenth century. The most dramatic and destructive of these was the spread of the Black Death. Scholars are still debating how many Europeans died in the successive waves of plague following the initial outbreak in 1348 (not to mention fatalities in Asia, the Middle East, and Africa). Although European society eventually recovered from the ravages of this disastrous epidemic, it would never be the same.

A Muslim Envoy Describes a Viking Funeral (922)

Ahmed Ibn Fadlan, *Yakut Ibn Abdallah's Geographical Lexicon*

In June, 921, the caliph of Baghdad sent Ahmed Ibn Fadlan on a mission to the king of Bulgaria to instruct the king in the Islamic faith and to supervise the construction of a fortress. After traveling for almost a year, he arrived at the Bulgarian court on the Volga. Here, Ibn Fadlan encountered a people who lived primarily by trade and commerce and who had little interest in agriculture or domesticated animals. Descendants of peoples who had migrated to the region only a century before, they depended on their swords and ships to take what they needed, and on their personal valor and bravery to defend what was theirs.

Ibn Fadlan's description of a Viking funeral reflects the values of a sophisticated man who had come from one of the most developed societies in the world. He was used to homes that included indoor baths, cities that contained hospitals and libraries, and an economy that revolved around trade conducted peacefully by cultured merchants. He was quite amazed at what he saw.

I saw how the Northmen had arrived with their wares, and pitched their camp beside the Volga. Never did I see people so gigantic; they are tall as palm trees, and florid and ruddy of complexion. They wear neither camisoles nor *chaftans,* but the men among them wear a garment of rough cloth, which is thrown over one side, so that one hand remains free. Every one carries an axe, a dagger, and a sword, and without these weapons they are never seen. Their swords are broad, with wavy lines, and of Frankish make. From the tip of the finger-nails to the neck, each man of them is tattooed with pictures of trees, living beings, and other things. The women carry, fastened to their breast, a little case of iron, copper, silver, or gold, according to the wealth and resources of their husbands. Fastened to the case they wear a ring, and upon that a dagger, all attached to their breast. About their necks they wear gold and silver chains. If the husband possesses ten thousand dirhems, he has one chain made for his wife; if twenty thousand, two; and for every ten thousand, one is added. Hence it often happens that a Scandinavian woman has a large number of chains about her neck. Their most highly prized ornaments consist of small green shells, of one of the varieties which are found in [the bottoms of] ships. They make great efforts to obtain these, paying as much as a dirhem for such a shell, and stringing them as a necklace for their wives.

They are the filthiest race that God ever created. They do not wipe themselves after going to stool, nor wash themselves after a nocturnal pollution, any more than if they were wild asses.

They come from their own country, anchor their ships in the Volga, which is a great river, and build large wooden houses on its banks. In every such house there live ten or twenty, more or fewer. Each man has a couch, when he sits with the beautiful girls he has for sale. Here he is as likely as not to enjoy one of them while a friend looks on. At times several of them will be thus engaged at the same moment, each in full view of the others. Now and again a merchant will resort to a house to purchase a girl, and find her master thus embracing her, and not giving over until he has fully had his will.

Every morning a girl comes and brings a tub of water, and places it before her master. In this he proceeds to wash his face and hands, and then his hair, combing it out over the vessel. Thereupon he blows his nose, and spits into the tub, and, leaving no dirt behind, conveys it all into this water. When he has finished, the girl carries the tub to the man next him, who does the same. Thus she continues carrying the tub from one to another, till each of those who are in the house has blown his nose and spit into the tub, and washed his face and hair.

As soon as their ships have reached the anchorage, every one goes ashore, having at hand bread, meat, onions, milk, and strong drink, and betakes himself to a high, upright piece of wood, bearing the likeness of a human face; this is surrounded by smaller statues, and behind these there are still other tall pieces of wood driven into the ground. He advances to the large wooden figure, prostrates himself before it, and thus addresses it: "O my lord, I am come from a far country, bringing with me so and so many girls, and so and so many pelts of sable" [or, marten]; and when he has thus enumerated all his merchandise, he continues, "I have brought thee this present," laying before the wooden statue what he has brought, and saying: "I desire thee to bestow upon me a purchaser who has gold and silver coins, who will buy from me to my heart's content, and who will refuse none of my demands." Having so said, he departs. If his trade then goes ill, he returns and brings a second, or even a third present. If he still continues to have difficulty in obtaining what he desires, he brings a present to one of the small statues, and implores its intercession, saying: "These are the wives and daughters of our lord." Continuing thus, he goes to each statue in turn, invokes it, beseeches its intercession, and bows humbly before it. If it then chances that his trade goes swimmingly, and he disposes of all his merchandise, he reports: "My lord has fulfilled my desire; now it is my duty to repay him." Upon this, he takes a number of cattle and sheep, slaughters them, gives a portion of the meat to the poor, and carries the rest before the large statue and the smaller ones that surround it, hanging the heads of the sheep and cattle on the large piece

of wood which is planted in the earth. When night falls, dogs come and devour it all. Then he who has so placed it exclaims: "I am well pleasing to my lord; he has consumed my present."

If one of their number falls sick, they set up a tent at a distance, in which they place him, leaving bread and water at hand. Thereafter they never approach nor speak to him, nor visit him the whole time, especially if he is a poor person or a slave. If he recovers and rises from his sick bed, he returns to his own. If he dies, they cremate him; but if he is a slave they leave him as he is, till at length he becomes the food of dogs and birds of prey.

If they catch a thief or a robber, they lead him to a thick and lofty tree, fasten a strong rope round him, string him up and let him hang until he drops to pieces by the action of the wind and rain.

I was told that the least of what they do for their chiefs when they die, is to consume them with fire. When I was finally informed of the death of one of their magnates, I sought to witness what befell. First they laid him in his grave—over which a roof was erected—for the space of ten days, until they had completed the cutting and sewing of his clothes. In the case of a poor man, however, they merely build for him a boat, in which they place him, and consume it with fire. At the death of a rich man, they bring together his goods, and divide them into three parts. The first of these is for his family; the second is expended for the garments they make; and with the third they purchase strong drink, against the day when the girl resigns herself to death, and is burned with her master. To the use of wine they abandon themselves in mad fashion, drinking it day and night; and not seldom does one die with the cup in his hand.

When one of their chiefs dies, his family asks his girls and pages: "Which one of you will die with him?" Then one of them answers, "I." From the time that he utters this word, he is no longer free: should he wish to draw back, he is not permitted. For the most part, however, it is the girls that offer themselves. So, when the man of whom I spoke had died, they asked his girls,

"Who will die with him?" One of them answered, "I." She was then committed to two girls, who were to keep watch over her, accompany her wherever she went, and even, on occasion, wash her feet. The people now began to occupy themselves with the dead man—to cut out the clothes for him, and to prepare whatever else was needful. During the whole of this period, the girl gave herself over to drinking and singing, and was cheerful and gay.

When the day was now come that the dead man and the girl were to be committed to the flames, I went to the river in which his ship lay, but found that it had already been drawn ashore. Four corner-blocks of birch and other woods had been placed in position for it, while around were stationed large wooden figures in the semblance of human beings. Thereupon the ship was brought up, and placed on the timbers above mentioned. In the mean time the people began to walk to and fro, uttering words which I did not understand. The dead man, meanwhile, lay at a distance in his grave, from which they had not yet removed him. Next they brought a couch, placed it in the ship, and covered it with Greek cloth of gold, wadded and quilted, with pillows of the same material. There came an old crone, whom they call the angel of death, and spread the articles mentioned on the couch. It was she who attended to the sewing of the garments, and to all the equipment; it was she, also, who was to slay the girl. I saw her; she was dark (?), . . . thick-set, with a lowering countenance.

When they came to the grave, they removed the earth from the wooden roof, set the latter aside, and drew out the dead man in the loose wrapper in which he had died. Then I saw that he had turned quite black, by reason of the coldness of that country. Near him in the grave they had placed strong drink; fruits, and a lute; and these they now took out. Except for his color, the dead man had not changed. They now clothed him in drawers, leggings, boots, and a *kurtak* and *chaftan* of cloth of gold, with golden buttons, placing on his head a cap made of cloth of gold, trimmed with sable. Then they carried him into a tent placed in the ship, seated him on the

wadded and quilted covering, supported him with the pillows, and, bringing strong drink, fruits, and basil, placed them all beside him. Then they brought a dog, which they cut in two, and threw into the ship; laid all his weapons beside him; and led up two horses, which they chased until they were dripping with sweat, whereupon they cut them in pieces with their swords, and threw the flesh into the ship. Two oxen were then brought forward, cut in pieces, and flung into the ship. Finally they brought a cock and a hen, killed them, and threw them in also.

The girl who had devoted herself to death meanwhile walked to and fro, entering one after another of the tents which they had there. The occupant of each tent lay with her, saying, "Tell your master, 'I [the man] did this only for love of you.'"

When it was now Friday afternoon, they led the girl to an object which they had constructed, and which looked like the framework of a door. She then placed her feet on the extended hands of the men, was raised up above the framework, and uttered something in her language, whereupon they let her down. Then again they raised her, and she did as at first. Once more they let her down, and then lifted her a third time, while she did as at the previous times. They then handed her a hen, whose head she cut off and threw away; but the hen itself they cast into the ship. I inquired of the interpreter what it was that she had done. He replied: "The first time she said," 'Lo, I see here my father and mother'; the second time, 'Lo, now I see all my deceased relatives sitting'; the third time, 'Lo, there is my master, who is sitting in Paradise. Paradise is so beautiful, so green. With him are his men and boys. He calls me, so bring me to him.'" Then they led her away to the ship.

Here she took off her two bracelets, and gave them to the old woman who was called the angel of death, and who was to murder her. She also drew off her two anklets, and passed them to the two serving-maids, who were the daughters of the so-called angel of death. Then they lifted her into the ship, but did not yet admit her to the tent. Now men came up with shields and staves, and handed her a cup of strong drink. This she took, sang over it, and emptied it. "With this," so the interpreter told me, "she is taking leave of those who are dear to her." Then another cup was handed her, which she also took, and began a lengthy song. The crone admonished her to drain the cup without lingering, and to enter the tent where her master lay. By this time, as it seemed to me, the girl had become dazed [or possibly, crazed]; she made as though she would enter the tent, and had brought her head forward between the tent and the ship, when the hag seized her by the head, and dragged her in. At this moment the men began to beat upon their shields with the staves, in order to drown the noise of her outcries, which might have terrified the other girls, and deterred them from seeking death with their masters in the future. Then six men followed into the tent, and each and every one had carnal companionship with her. Then they laid her down by her master's side, while two of the men seized her by the feet, and two by the hands. The old woman known as the angel of death now knotted a rope around her neck, and handed the ends to two of the men to pull. Then with a broad-bladed dagger she smote her between the ribs, and drew the blade forth, while the two men strangled her with the rope till she died.

The next of kin to the dead man now drew near, and, taking a piece of wood, lighted it, and walked backwards toward the ship, holding the stick in one hand, with the other placed upon his buttocks (he being naked), until the wood which had been piled under the ship was ignited. Then the others came up with staves and firewood, each one carrying a stick already lighted at the upper end, and threw it all on the pyre. The pile was soon aflame, then the ship, finally the tent, the man, and the girl, and everything else in the ship. A terrible storm began to blow up, and thus intensified the flames, and gave wings to the blaze.

At my side stood one of the Northmen, and I heard him talking with the interpreter, who stood near him. I asked the interpreter what the Northman had said, and received this answer: "'You Arabs,' he said, 'must be a stupid set! You take him who is to you the most revered and beloved of men, and cast him into the ground, to be devoured by creeping things and worms. We, on the other hand, burn him in a twinkling, so that he instantly, without a moment's delay, enters into Paradise.' At this he burst out into uncontrollable laughter, and then continued: 'It is the love of the Master [God] that causes the wind to blow and snatch him away in an instant.'" And, in very truth, before an hour had passed, ship, wood, and girl had, with the man, turned to ashes.

Thereupon they heaped over the place where the ship had stood something like a rounded hill, and, erecting on the centre of it a large birchen post, wrote on it the name of the deceased, along with that of the king of the Northmen. Having done this, they left the spot.

It is the custom among the Northmen that with the king in his hall there shall be four hundred of the most valiant and trustworthy of his companions, who stand ready to die with him or to offer their life for his. Each of them has a girl to wait upon him—to wash his head, and to prepare food and drink; and, besides her, he has another who serves as his concubine. These four hundred sit below the king's high seat, which is large, and adorned with precious stones. Accompanying him on his high seat are forty girls, destined for his bed, whom he causes to sit near him. Now and again he will proceed to enjoy one of them in the presence of the above mentioned nobles of his following. The king does not descend from his high seat, and is therefore obliged, when he needs to relieve himself, to make use of a vessel. If he wishes to ride, his horse is led up to the high seat, and he mounts from there; when he is ready to alight, he rides his horse up so close that he can step immediately from it to his throne. He has a lieutenant, who leads his armies, wars with his enemies, and represents him to his subjects.

REVIEW QUESTIONS

1. What do you think Ibn Fadlan considered to be the most important difference between his own society and that which he described here?
2. Ibn Fadlan had a negative view of the people he described. What does this tell us about his values?
3. What evidence is there that the dead man's servant girl was willing to be sacrificed? Is there any evidence that she was unwilling to die?
4. In many cultures, funerals are religious ceremonies. Was this one religious? Why do you think so? If you think it was not religious, how would you describe it?

A Moorish Magistrate Describes Regulations for the Markets of Seville (early twelfth century)

IBN 'ABDUN, *Hisba Manual*

In 711 a Muslim army from North Africa crossed the Straits of Gibraltar, conquering and occupying much of the Iberian Peninsula. This conquest, the most significant encounter between Islam and Christianity on European soil, changed the course of Spanish history and that of western Europe as well. The Muslim invaders established large, culturally and economically advanced urban centers (compared to those of northern Europe) that included hospitals, libraries, civic centers, and educational institutions. Cordoba, for example, was said to have some three thouand mosques and three hundred public baths. Moreover, the Muslim conquest allowed Spanish Christians and Jews to have access to the literature of the ancient Greeks, although it was in Arabic translation. In this indirect way, much of the wisdom of Plato and Aristotle entered medieval Europe. Muslim rulers also transformed the existing Visigothic practices by establishing rules of social behavior for women and men and enacting legislation to regulate economic life and protect citizens from crime. The selection presented here offers an example of these kinds of regulations in early twelfth-century Seville.

Ibn 'Abdun, the author of these regulations, was either a judge or a market inspector. He had the power to enforce these rules and to "promote good and prevent evil." As a result of this far-ranging charge, Ibn 'Abdun had the opportunity to eliminate or reduce conflict among Muslims, Jews, and Christians. In addition to his authority in the marketplace, he was responsible for people's moral conduct, public decency, and segregation of the sexes.

Shopkeepers must be forbidden to reserve regular places for themselves in the forecourt of the great mosque or elsewhere, for this amounts to a usurpation of property rights and always gives rise to quarrels and trouble among them. Instead, whoever comes first should take his place.

The *muḥtasib* must arrange the crafts in order, putting like with like in fixed places. This is the best and most orderly way.

There must be no sellers of olive oil around the mosque, nor of dirty products, nor of anything from which an irremovable stain can be feared.

Rabbits and poultry should not be allowed around the mosque, but should have a fixed place. Partridges and slaughtered barnyard birds should only be sold with the crop plucked, so that the bad and rotten can be distinguished from the good ones. Rabbits should only be sold skinned, so that the bad ones may be seen. If they are left lying in their skins, they go bad.

Egg sellers must have bowls of water in front of them, so that bad eggs may be recognized.

Truffles should not be sold around the mosque, for this is a delicacy of the dissolute.[1]

Bread should only be sold by weight. Both the baking and the crumbs must be supervised, as it is often "dressed up." By this I mean that they take a small quantity of good dough and use it to "dress up" the front of the bread which is made with bad flour. A large loaf should not be made up out of the *poya*[2] rolls. These should be baked separately and as they are.

The glaziers must be forbidden to make fine goblets for wine; likewise the potters.

The *raṭl* weights for meat and fish and *ḥarīsa*[3] and fritters and bread should be made of iron only, with a visible seal on them. The *raṭl* weights of the shopkeepers should always be inspected, for they are bad people.

The cheese which comes from al-Madā'in[4] should not be sold, for it is the foul residue of the curds, of no value. If people saw how it is made, no one would ever eat it. Cheese should only be sold in small leather bottles, which can be washed and cleaned every day. That which is in bowls cannot be secured from worms and mold.

Mixed meats should not be sold on one stall, nor should fat and lean meat be sold on one stall. Tripe should only be sold dry on boards, for water both spoils it and increases its weight. The entrails of sheep must be taken out, so that they should not be sold with the meat and at the same price, which would be a fraud. The heads of sheep should not be skinned, except for the young. The guts must always be removed from the bodies of animals, except lambs, and should not be left there, for this too would be an occasion for fraud.

No slaughtering should take place in the market, except in the closed slaughterhouses, and the blood and refuse should be taken outside the market. Animals should be slaughtered only with a long knife. All slaughtering knives should be of this kind. No animal which is good for field work may be slaughtered, and a trustworthy and incorruptible commissioner should go to the slaughterhouse every day to make sure of this; the only exception is an animal with a defect. Nor should a female still capable of producing young be slaughtered. No animal should be sold in the market which has been brought already slaughtered, until its owner establishes that it is not stolen. The entrails should not be sold together with the meat and at the same price. A lamb weighing six *raṭls* with its offal shall not be sold at the same price as a lamb the meat of which alone is of that weight.

Fish, whether salt or fresh, shall not be washed in water for this makes it go bad. Nor should salted fish be soaked in water, for this also spoils and rots it. . . .

Left-over and rotten fish should not be sold.

Sausages and grilled rissoles should only be made with fresh meat and not with meat coming from a sick animal and bought for its cheapness.

Flour should not be mixed with the cheese used for fritters. This is fraud, and the *muḥtasib* must watch out for it.

The cream must always be pure and not mixed with cheese. The leftovers of the cooks and fryers should not be sold.

---

[1] Apparently a common view. A Spanish Arabic proverb includes the large consumption of truffles among the signs by which the dissolute may be recognized.

[2] A roll given to the baker as payment for baking bread in his oven. In modern Spanish the word denotes the money paid to the baker for this service.

[3] A dish made with meat, cracked wheat, and sour milk, regarded as a great delicacy.

[4] A term applied to the fertile islands in the lower Guadalquivir, below Seville.

Vinegar should only be bought from a trustworthy merchant, for it can be mixed with much water, which is a fraud. The vinegar maker should be ordered not to use too much water when he makes vinegar for someone, for this spoils it.

The copper pots used by the *ḥarīsa* makers, as also the spans of the fritter makers and the fryers, should be lined with tin only, since copper with oil is poisonous.

Women should be forbidden to do their washing in the gardens, for these are dens for fornication.

Grapes in large quantities should not be sold to anyone of whom it is known that he would press them to make wine. This is a matter for supervision.

Fruit must not be sold before it is ripe for this is bad, except only for grapes, which are good for pregnant women and for the sick. Large cucumbers which can be counted should not be sold by weight [?]. . . .

Wild figs may only be sold in pairs.

The seller of grapes should have baskets and nets in which to arrange them, as this is the best protection for them.

Cakes should be properly baked and should only be made wide, as thin ones are good only for the sick.

If someone assays gold or silver coins for a person, and later it emerges that there is base metal in them, the assayer must make good, for he deceived and betrayed the owner of the coins, who placed his trust in him. Swindlers when detected must be denounced in all crafts, but above all in assaying coin, for in this case the swindler can only be a person who is expert in matters of coin.

Women should not sit by the river bank in the summer if men appear there.

No barber may remain alone with a woman in his booth. He should work in the open market in a place where he can be seen and observed.

The cupper. He should only let blood into a special jar with graduation marks, so that he can see how much blood he has let. He should not let blood at his discretion, for this can lead to sickness and death.

The water wheel. Most of the holes for the spindles should be wedged, as this is best for its working.

No one may be allowed to claim knowledge of a matter in which he is not competent, especially in the craft of medicine, for this can lead to loss of life. The error of a physician is hidden by the earth. Likewise a joiner. Each should keep to his own trade and not claim any skill of which he is not an acknowledged master—especially with women, since ignorance and error are greater among them.

Only a skilled physician should sell potions and electuaries and mix drugs. These things should not be bought from the grocer or the apothecary whose only concern is to take money without knowledge; they spoil the prescriptions and kill the sick, for they mix medicines which are unknown and of contrary effect.

The sale of tame pigeons must be prohibited, for they are used only by thieves and people of no religion. The sale of cats should also be banned. Any broker who is known to be treacherous and dishonest should be excluded from the market, for he is a thief. He must be watched and not employed.

The lime stores and [other] empty places must be forbidden, because men go there to be alone with women.

Only good and trustworthy men, known as such among people, may be allowed to have dealings with women in buying and in selling. The tradespeople must watch over this carefully. The women who weave brocades must be banned from the market, for they are nothing but harlots.

On festival days men and women shall not walk on the same path when they go to cross the river. . . .

The heads of sheep, the meat of which is brought to the market, must be washed clean of blood. Otherwise, in narrow or crowded places it would not be possible to secure passersby from pollution by the blood. The ends of the stalls which protrude from the shops must be sawn off, since the meat hanging there would soil the clothes of passersby and make the way narrow.

The bakers must be ordered to wash their

pans every day and to scrape and polish their boards to prevent vermin from entering them. They must not make large loaves with the dough for *poya* rolls. These must be cooked separately and sold by weight.

Graves should be slightly lengthened and widened. I saw a corpse which was exhumed from the grave three times; graves should allow for this. I saw another which had to be forced into the grave. The first concern of the *muḥtasib* should be to demolish buildings erected in the cemetery and to watch over this for reasons I have already explained above.

Paper should be of somewhat larger format, with more glazing.

Raw bricks should be thicker and smoother.

The basins in the public baths should be covered. If they are left uncovered, they cannot be protected from pollution, yet this is a place of purity. The bath attendant, the masseur, and the barber should not walk about in the baths without a loincloth or drawers.

A Muslim must not massage a Jew or a Christian nor throw away his refuse nor clean his latrines. The Jew and the Christian are better fitted for such trades, since they are the trades of those who are vile. A Muslim should not attend to the animal of a Jew or of a Christian, nor serve him as a muleteer, nor hold his stirrup. If any Muslim is known to do this, he should be denounced.

Muslim women shall be prevented from entering their abominable churches, for the priests are evil-doers, fornicators, and sodomites. Frankish[4] women must be forbidden to enter the church except on days of religious services or festivals, for it is their habit to eat and drink and fornicate with the priests, among whom there is not one who has not two or more women with whom he sleeps. This has become a custom among them, for they have permitted what is forbidden and forbidden what is permitted. The priests should be ordered to marry, as they do in the eastern lands. If they wanted to, they would.

No women may be allowed in the house of a priest, neither an old woman nor any other, if he refuses marriage. They should be compelled to submit to circumcision, as was done to them by al-Muʿtaḍid ʿAbbād.[5] They claim to follow the rules of Jesus, may God bless and save him. Now Jesus was circumcised, and they celebrate the day of his circumcision as a festival, yet they themselves do not practice this.

The contractor[6] of the bathhouse should not sit there with the women, for this is an occasion for license and fornication. The contractor of hostelries for traders and travelers should not be a woman, for this is indeed fornication. The broker of houses shall not be a young man, but a chaste old man of known good character.

Clothes must not be cleaned with beetles. Laundry men should be forbidden to do this, as it is harmful to the clothes.

A Jew must not slaughter meat for a Muslim.[7] The Jews should be ordered to arrange their own butcher's stalls.

The qāḍi must order the people of the villages to appoint a keeper in every village to guard private property from encroachment, for the peasants regard the property of the people of the city as licit to them. No riding animal or cattle should be turned loose without a halter. In the words of the proverb, "In the keeper is the protection of the State."

The property of the people and of the Muslims must be protected at the time of the harvest and other times from any kind of injury whatsoever. When the ears of the grain begin to form, it must be forbidden to cut and sell them. This is done only to avoid paying the tithe.

The curriers and silk dyers must be ordered to ply their trades outside the city only.

The felt makers should be ordered to improve

---

[4]That is, Christians from outside Spain and from those parts of Spain not under Muslim rule.

[5]Ruler of Seville, 1040–1069. This story is not confirmed by the chroniclers.
[6]That is, the tax farmer who operates or controls the establishment.
[7]Some Muslim jurists allow Muslims to eat meat from animals killed by Jews, whose dietary code in part coincides with that of Islam. Animals killed by Christians, who have no dietary laws, are always forbidden.

their work. They make the felts slack, with little wool, and useless. The wool must be shaken free of lime.

The furriers must be advised not to use pigeons' dung to disguise worn out furs. This is a deceit which they practice.

Dyers must be forbidden to dye green with passerine or to dye light blue with brazilwood. This is fraudulent, since these dyes lose their color quickly. Some grocers use lycium leaf to make the henna green. This gives the henna a bright and fine green color. This is fraud.

A garment belonging to a sick man,[8] a Jew, or a Christian must not be sold without indicating its origin; likewise, the garment of a debauchee. Dough must not be taken from a sick man for baking his bread. Neither eggs nor chickens nor milk nor any other foodstuff should be bought from him. They should only buy and sell among themselves.

The sewer men must be forbidden to dig holes in the streets, as this harms them and causes injury to people, except when they are cleaning the entire street.

Itinerant fortune-tellers must be forbidden to

---

go from house to house, as they are thieves and fornicators.

A drunkard must not be flogged until he is sober again.

Prostitutes must be forbidden to stand bareheaded outside the houses. Decent women must not bedeck themselves to resemble them. They must be stopped from coquetry and party making among themselves, even if they have been permitted to do this [by their husbands]. Dancing girls must be forbidden to bare their heads.

No contractor, policeman, Jew, or Christian may be allowed to dress in the costume of people of position, of a jurist, or of a worthy man. They must on the contrary be abhorred and shunned and should not be greeted with the formula, "Peace be with you," for the devil has gained mastery over them and has made them forget the name of God. They are the devil's party, "and indeed the devil's party are the losers" [Qur'ān, lvii, 22]. They must have a distinguishing sign by which they are recognized to their shame. . . .

When fruit or other foodstuffs are found in the possession of thieves, they should be distributed in prisons and given to the poor. If the owner comes to claim his goods and is recognized, they should be returned to him.

[8]Probably lepers are meant.

REVIEW QUESTIONS

1. What does this selection reveal about religious tolerance in Seville?
2. What does it reveal about relations between women and men in Seville?
3. Would you feel comfortable buying something in this marketplace? Why or why not?
4. What single piece of information in this selection surprised you the most? Why?

A Syrian Prince Delineates the Character of the Franks (twelfth century)

USAMAH IBN-MUNQIDH, *Memoirs*

Few topics excite more interest among students of the Middle Ages than the Crusades. Historians, too, recognize them as one of the most important episodes in world history. The Crusades are noteworthy primarily because they clearly reveal some basic and central characteristics of European and Muslim civilizations. One of the more meaningful consequences of the eight Crusades that occurred between 1096 and 1270, for example, is the increased knowledge that both cultures gained about each other. And they had a lot to learn. Muslims at the time of the Crusades had not traveled widely in Christian Europe and usually had used Jewish intermediaries for diplomatic purposes or commercial business. For them, European civilization had little to offer. Likewise, Europeans disdained Muslims as enemies of Christianity. It is not surprising, therefore, that most contemporary Christian and Muslim accounts of each other are derogatory.

The selection offered here is an important exception. The *Memoirs* of Usamah Ibn-Munqidh (1095–1188), an Arab Syrian prince who became a high-ranking government official in Egypt and then in Damascus, offers an invaluable description of ordinary life during the time of the Crusades. Ibn-Munqidh spent more time in battle against other Muslims than against Christians, and he often traveled to Crusader lands for business or on diplomatic missions. His descriptions of Europeans are absorbing. Although many contemporary histories of this era incorporate Western eye-witness accounts, only a few include the Muslim perspective. Ibn-Munqidh shared his vast knowledge with the reader, imparting as well his personal biases. The latter helps us understand the mind of the Crusader-era Muslim, even today often considered an enemy of Western "Christendom."

AN APPRECIATION OF THE FRANKISH CHARACTER

Their lack of sense

Mysterious are the works of the Creator, the author of all things! When one comes to recount cases regarding the Franks, he cannot but glorify Allah (exalted is he!) and sanctify him, for he sees them as animals possessing the virtues of courage and fighting, but nothing else; just as animals have only the virtues of strength and carrying loads. I shall now give some instances of their doings and their curious mentality.

In the army of King Fulk, son of Fulk, was a Frankish reverend knight who had just arrived from their land in order to make the holy pilgrimage and then return home. He was of my intimate fellowship and kept such constant company with me that he began to call me "my brother." Between us were mutual bonds of amity and friendship. When he resolved to return by sea to his homeland, he said to me:

My brother, I am leaving for my country and I want thee to send with me thy son (my son, who was then fourteen years old, was at that time in my company) to our country, where he can see the knights and learn wisdom and chivalry. When he returns, he will be like a wise man.

Thus there fell upon my ears words which would never come out of the head of a sensible man; for even if my son were to be taken captive, his captivity could not bring him a worse misfortune than carrying him into the lands of the Franks. However, I said to the man:

By thy life, this has exactly been my idea. But the only thing that prevented me from carrying it out was the fact that his grandmother, my mother, is so fond of him and did not this time let him come out with me until she exacted an oath from me to the effect that I would return him to her.

Thereupon he asked, "Is thy mother still alive?" "Yes." I replied. "Well," said he, "disobey her not."

Their curious medication

A case illustrating their curious medicine is the following:

The lord of al-Munayṭirah wrote to my uncle asking him to dispatch a physician to treat certain sick persons among his people. My uncle sent him a Christian physician named Thābit. Thābit was absent but ten days when he returned. So we said to him, "How quickly hast thou healed thy patients!" He said:

They brought before me a knight in whose leg an abscess had grown; and a woman afflicted with imbecility. To the knight I applied a small poultice until the abscess opened and became well; and the woman I put on diet and made her humor wet. Then a Frankish physician came to them and said, "This man knows nothing about treating them." He then said to the knight, "Which wouldst thou prefer, living with one leg or dying with two?" The latter replied, "Living with one leg." The physician said, "Bring me a strong knight and a sharp ax." A knight came with the ax. And I was standing by. Then the physician laid the leg of the patient on a block of wood and bade the knight strike his leg with the ax and chop it off at one blow. Accordingly he struck it—while I was looking on—one blow, but the leg was not severed. He dealt another blow, upon which the marrow of the leg flowed out and the patient died on the spot. He then examined the woman and said, "This is a woman in whose head there is a devil which has possessed her. Shave off her hair." Accordingly they shaved it off and the woman began once more to eat their ordinary diet—garlic and mustard. Her imbecility took a turn for the worse. The physician then said, "The devil has penetrated through her head." He therefore took a razor, made a deep cruciform incision on it,

peeled off the skin at the middle of the incision until the bone of the skull was exposed and rubbed it with salt. The woman also expired instantly. Thereupon I asked them whether my services were needed any longer, and when they replied in the negative I returned home, having learned of their medicine what I knew not before.

I have, however, witnessed a case of their medicine which was quite different from that.

The king of the Franks had for treasurer a knight named Bernard [barnād], who (may Allah's curse be upon him!) was one of the most accursed and wicked among the Franks. A horse kicked him in the leg, which was subsequently infected and which opened in fourteen different places. Every time one of these cuts would close in one place, another would open in another place. All this happened while I was praying for his perdition. Then came to him a Frankish physician and removed from the leg all the ointments which were on it and began to wash it with very strong vinegar. By this treatment all the cuts were healed and the man became well again. He was up again like a devil.

Another case illustrating their curious medicine is the following:

In Shayzar we had an artisan named abu-al Fath, who had a boy whose neck was afflicted with scrofula. Every time a part of it would close, another part would open. This man happened to go to Antioch on business of his, accompanied by his son. A Frank noticed the boy and asked his father about him. Abu-al-Fath replied, "This is my son." The Frank said to him, "Wilt thou swear by thy religion that if I prescribe to thee a medicine which will cure thy boy, thou wilt charge nobody fees for prescribing it thyself? In that case, I shall prescribe to thee a medicine which will cure the boy." The man took the oath and the Frank said:

Take uncrushed leaves of glasswort, burn them, then soak the ashes in olive oil and sharp vinegar. Treat the scrofula with them until the spot on which it is growing is eaten up. Then take burnt lead, soak it in ghee butter [*samn*] and treat him with it. That will cure him.

The father treated the boy accordingly, and the boy was cured. The sores closed and the boy returned to his normal condition of health.

I have myself treated with this medicine many who were afflicted with such disease, and the treatment was successful in removing the cause of the complaint.

Newly arrived Franks are especially rough: One insists that Usāmah should pray eastward

Everyone who is a fresh emigrant from the Frankish lands is ruder in character than those who have become acclimatized and have held long association with the Moslems. Here is an illustration of their rude character.

Whenever I visited Jerusalem I always entered the Aqṣa Mosque, beside which stood a small mosque which the Franks had converted into a church. When I used to enter the Aqṣa Mosque, which was occupied by the Templars, who were my friends, the Templars would evacuate the little adjoining mosque so that I might pray in it. One day I entered this mosque, repeated the first formula, "Allah is great," and stood up in the act of praying, upon which one of the Franks rushed on me, got hold of me and turned my face eastward saying, "This is the way thou shouldst pray!" A group of Templars hastened to him, seized him and repelled him from me. I resumed my prayer. The same man, while the others were otherwise busy, rushed once more on me and turned my face eastward, saying, "This is the way thou shouldst pray!" The Templars again came in to him and expelled him. They apologized to me, saying, "This is a stranger who has only recently arrived from the land of the Franks and he has never before seen anyone praying except eastward." Thereupon I said to myself, "I have had enough prayer." So I

went out and have ever been surprised at the conduct of this devil of a man, at the change in the color of his face, his trembling and his sentiment at the sight of one praying towards the *qiblah.*

Another wants to show to a Moslem God as a child

I saw one of the Franks come to al-Amīr Muʿīn-al-Dīn (may Allah's mercy rest upon his soul!) when he was in the Dome of the Rock and say to him, "Dost thou want to see God as a child?" Muʿīn-al-Dīn said, "Yes." The Frank walked ahead of us until he showed us the picture of Mary with Christ (may peace be upon him!) as an infant in her lap. He then said, "This is God as a child." But Allah is exalted far above what the infidels say about him!

Franks lack jealousy in sex affairs

The Franks are void of all zeal and jealousy. One of them may be walking along with his wife. He meets another man who takes the wife by the hand and steps aside to converse with her while the husband is standing on one side waiting for his wife to conclude the conversation. If she lingers too long for him, he leaves her alone with the conversant and goes away.

Here is an illustration which I myself witnessed:

When I used to visit Nāblus, I always took lodging with a man named Muʿizz, whose home was a lodging house for the Moslems. The house had windows which opened to the road, and there stood opposite to it on the other side of the road a house belonging to a Frank who sold wine for the merchants. He would take some wine in a bottle and go around announcing it by shouting, "So and so, the merchant, has just opened a cask full of this wine. He who wants to buy some of it will find it in such and such a place." The Frank's pay for the announcement made would be the wine in that bottle. One day this Frank went home and found a man with his wife in the same bed. He asked him, "What could have made thee enter into my wife's room?" The man replied, "I was tired, so I went in to rest." "But how," asked he, "didst thou get into my bed?" The other replied, "I found a bed that was spread, so I slept in it." "But," said he, "my wife was sleeping together with thee!" The other replied, "Well, the bed is hers. How could I therefore have prevented her from using her own bed?" "By the truth of my religion," said the husband, "if thou shouldst do it again, thou and I would have a quarrel." Such was for the Frank the entire expression of his disapproval and the limit of his jealousy.

Another illustration:

We had with us a bath-keeper named Sālim, originally an inhabitant of al-Maʿarrah, who had charge of the bath of my father (may Allah's mercy rest upon his soul!). This man related the following story:

> I once opened a bath in al-Maʿarrah in order to earn my living. To this bath there came a Frankish knight. The Franks disapprove of girding a cover around one's waist while in the bath. So this Frank stretched out his arm and pulled off my cover from my waist and threw it away. He looked and saw that I had recently shaved off my pubes. So he shouted, "Sālim!" As I drew near him he stretched his hand over my pubes and said, "Sālim, good! By the truth of my religion, do the same for me." Saying this, he lay on his back and I found that in that place the hair was like his beard. So I shaved it off. Then he passed his hand over the place, and finding it smooth, he said, "Sālim, by the truth of my religion, do the same to madame," referring to his wife. He then said to a servant of his, "Tell madame to come here." Accordingly the servant went and brought her and made her enter the bath. She also lay on her back. The knight repeated, "Do what thou hast done to me." So I shaved all that hair while her husband was sitting looking at me. At last he thanked me and handed me the pay for my service.

Consider now this great contradiction! They have neither jealousy nor zeal but they have great courage, although courage is nothing but the product of zeal and of ambition to be above ill repute.

Here is a story analogous to the one related above:

> I entered the public bath in Ṣūr [Tyre] and took my place in a secluded part. One of my servants thereupon said to me, "There is with us in the bath a woman." When I went out, I sat on one of the stone benches and behold! the woman who was in the bath had come out all dressed and was standing with her father just opposite me. But I could not be sure that she was a woman. So I said to one of my companions, "By Allah, see if this is a woman," by which I meant that he should ask about her. But he went, as I was looking at him, lifted the end of her robe and looked carefully at her. Thereupon her father turned toward me and said, "This is my daughter. Her mother is dead and she has nobody to wash her hair. So I took her in with me to the bath and washed her head." I replied, "Thou hast well done! This is something for which thou shalt be rewarded [by Allah]!"

Another curious case of medication

A curious case relating to their medicine is the following, which was related to me by William of Bures, the lord of Ṭabarayyah [Tiberias], who was one of the principal chiefs among the Franks. It happened that William had accompanied al-Amīr Muʿīn-al-Dīn (may Allah's mercy rest upon his soul!) from ʿAkka to Ṭabarayyah when I was in his company too. On the way William related to us the following story in these words:

> We had in our country a highly esteemed knight who was taken ill and was on the point of death. We thereupon came to one of our great priests and said to him, "Come with us and examine so and so, the knight." "I will," he replied, and walked along with us while we were assured in ourselves that if he would

only lay his hand on him the patient would recover. When the priest saw the patient, he said, "Bring me some wax." We fetched him a little wax, which he softened and shaped like the knuckles of fingers, and he stuck one in each nostril. The knight died on the spot. We said to him, "He is dead." "Yes," he replied, "he was suffering great pain, so I closed up his nose that he might die and get relief."

REVIEW QUESTIONS

1. How would you characterize Ibn-Munqidh's attitude toward the Franks? What evidence supports your opinion?
2. What aspects of Frankish behavior impressed Ibn-Munqidh the most? The least? Why?
3. What generalizations can you draw about Frankish-Muslim relations from this account?

Two Christian Clergymen Recount the Story of a Jewish Girl's Desire to Convert to Christianity (early thirteenth century)

CAESARIUS OF HEISTERBACH, *Dialogus de miraculis*
THOMAS OF CANTIMPRÉ, *Bonum universale de apibus*

Many accounts in the Middle Ages emphasize the prejudice and intolerance shown by Christians toward Jews. The Fourth Lateran Council of 1215, for example, decreed that Jews must wear ribbons or yellow badges to distinguish themselves from Christians. In 1290, King Edward I expelled all Jews from England. In 1306, King Philip IV expelled all Jews from France; under his successors, Jews were readmitted in 1315 and expelled again in 1322. In the mid–fourteenth century, violence against Jews increased when Christians accused Jews of causing the Black Death by poisoning water wells. In Germany, more than sixty Jewish communities were destroyed by 1351. Jews were also persecuted in Spain and were expelled in 1492.

The following selection by two Christian clergymen yields a contrasting and more complex perspective on Jewish-Christian relations in the Middle Ages. In this case, a young Jewish girl, Rachel, wanted to convert to Christianity, much to her parents' dismay. The narrative tells us that some Christian officials were willing to help Rachel's parents prevent their daughter's conversion, but it also repeats stereotypes applied to Jews—that they smell and that they are greedy and stubborn. The version presented here is a conflation of two contemporary accounts.

Recently the young daughter of a certain Jew of Louvain converted to the Christian faith in the following way. A priest who was chaplain to the duke of Brabant[1] customarily entered the home of a certain Jew who was a foreigner in that same city and disputed with him concerning the Christian faith. He had a small daughter who listened intently to the disputation in accordance with the capacity of her intelligence, weighing both the priest's word and the father's response. And so she grasped the meaning through divine disposition and was brought to the Catholic faith. So great was the girl's understanding that, although not yet five years old, in the home of her Jewish parents she began to consider why there was such a difference between the name of the Jew and of the Christian; since the men of both peoples possessed the same appearance and language. She was more attached (as she said afterward) to the Christian than the Jewish name, and she was especially delighted to hear the name of the blessed Mary, which Christians customarily used both in prayer and while swearing. She used to hide bread from her parents' table under her sleeves and secretly gave it to beggar children so that she could hear them thanking her in the name of Mary. In these matters she continued from time to time in a wonderful way, but wisely hid them, so that neither of her parents could learn or hear anything about their daughter's thoughts.

It happened that in the course of time she came with several children to the home of the priest master Rayner. This priest knew her by name, and asked her, "Have you come, dearest Rachel, to become a Christian?" And she said, "I want you to teach me what it is to be a Christian." Then the priest, being a holy man and joyful in spirit, felt that this girl would have a divine future. And starting with the Creation, he began to explain Scripture to her, through which the faith of Christ, or Christ Himself, can be explained or shown. The explanation of these matters (as she reported afterward) was so complete that at the age of six and a half she comprehended by means of such great understanding of the spirit, so that rarely did the priest repeat any explanation. They studied for a year and a half in secret, in the course of meetings during which he taught the excited girl furtively and at the right time. What evidence of wonder! Rachel could never be satisfied, nor did she tire of hearing the word of God. Since both the priest and his assistant Martha, a religious[2] and prudent woman, were often tired, they would teach her in turns.

What more? Soon her parents turned their attention to their daughter, and in consultation with the other Jews agreed that the girl should be sent away from Louvain to the other side of the Rhine in order to be bound in marriage.[3] When the girl found out, she tearfully told the priest that if that very night he did not remove her, and she did not become a Christian, she would be lost and troubled forever. When the priest had heard this, he told her to come to the usual entrance early in the morning. After she had agreed, in the evening she said to her mother, "Mother, I want to sleep by myself tonight." Since she was still a little girl, her mother refused for a long time, but agreed in the end, and ordered her daughter's bed to be prepared as a pillow at her feet. The little girl slept until morning, and since she disregarded what she had promised the priest the previous night, the glorious mother of God appeared to her dressed in a robe as white as snow and offering her a shining staff, saying, "Get up, Catherine, and take the road; a great road awaits you." When she heard these things, Rachel, believing she was grasping the wand, fell out of bed and cried out. Her mother, awakened by the cry, asked why she was crying, and the girl carefully dissimulated. Rachel then got up and went to the agreed-upon spot, where she soon found the priest. He joyfully lifted her up and went to the

---

[1]Henry I (1218–35), duke of Brabant, was buried at the church of St. Peter of Louvain.

[2]Martha may have been a beguine.

[3]The center of Jewish life in the region was at Cologne in the Rhineland.

Cistercian monastery of Parc-aux-Dames, which was situated a league and a half from Louvain. He baptized her in the presence of many onlookers, giving her the name Catherine, which she had first been called by the mother of Christ, and she was baptized while wearing the holy garb of the order.

When her father and his friends heard what had happened, without delay they angrily approached the local duke, the bishop of Liège, and Pope Honorius[4] in order to give them a great deal of money so that the girl would be returned to her parents, since she had been taken away before she had reached the legal age.[5] Should she remain in her parents' home until the age of twelve, and should she remain firm in the faith, then she could rightly take a Christian name. They evilly thought that they could easily change the child's mind should she return to her parents' home. How grievous are the treacherous struggles of our times! Many great and learned men cherish the money that has been given them; which is why the priest was very concerned. He therefore tearfully invoked both Christ and his Mother, as she had been the cause of this event. Because the duke wanted to restore the Jewish daughter to her Jewish father, the priest Rayner stood firm and said, "Oh my lord, if you commit this evil deed against God and his bride, your soul will never be saved." The lord abbot Walter of Villers also approached the duke.

The Jew saw that the hope he had placed in the duke was in vain. He decided to bribe Hugh, the lord bishop of Liège. At the Jew's request, Hugh sent letters to nuns at the convent of Parc, urging that his daughter be restored to him. Finally the Jew came with his friends and relatives to the convent, where Catherine was studying in the cloister. Although she knew nothing whatsoever of their coming, she felt a great warmth, and said openly, "I don't know what it is, but

the Jewish stench oppresses me." In the meantime, as the Jews knocked on the window, the abbess spoke to the girl, "My daughter Catherine, your parents want to see you." She replied, "It is their stench I feel, although I don't see them." She refused to go out. The bishop of Liège has recently made an accusation concerning this matter, in the presence of the lord Archbishop Engelbert of Cologne[6] in his synod, and it has been decided that he should no long trouble the convent concerning the baptized girl.

At that time he submitted, but in the end he did not obey. For afterward he summoned the girl to Liège by letter under pain of excommunication in order to respond to her father's objections. She came, but under good protection. The Jewish contention was that she had been taken away as a minor and baptized by force. They said to the girl, "Catherine, we are told that you will willingly return to your father if allowed." She replied, "Who says this?" They replied, "Your father." She then said the following in a clear voice, "My father lies totally through his beard." Oh what a wonderful thing, that up to now, through the centuries, has been unheard of! The girl asked the priest to accompany her to every summons and judge. "Perhaps," she said, "the judges are persuaded by my age and moved by my sacrifice." It happened as she said. She came to Liège, and in the presence of the bishop, clerics, and magnates she confounded and moved various lawyers and judges with constant and truthful reasoning. For a great distance the voices of persons crying out with tears were heard from the church of St. Lambert of Liège. Astonished, all clearly saw and said that the wisdom of the divine spirit had remained strong in one so young. At this point, when the Jews' lawyer got up, lord Walter, abbot of Villers[7] excitedly said to him, "Master, you speak against God and your honor. You should surely know

---

[4]Hugh of Pierrepont, bishop of Liège (1220–29), and Pope Honorius III (1216–27).
[5]The age of discretion was twelve for girls and fourteen for boys.

[6]Archbishop Engelbert of Cologne, who was consecrated in 1216 and martyred on November 9, 1225, was also the subject of a biography by Caesarius of Heisterbach.
[7]Abbot Walter (1214–21) of Villers, one of the largest Cistercian monasteries.

that should you utter anything against the girl, I will go to the pope and request that you be permanently silenced in all legal proceedings." Secretly fearful, he answered the abbot, "Lord abbot, who will it harm if I am able to extort money from the Jews. I will say nothing that will injure this girl." Since he would soon receive his payment, he said to the Jew, "I dare not say any more."

Around that time, when lord Guy, abbot of Clairvaux, visited the monasteries of his order in the diocese of Liège, he conferred with the bishop, admonishing and asking him how long, in God's honor, he would continue harassing a girl already consecrated to Christ. The bishop answered him, "Good lord abbot, why is this case important to you?" The abbot replied, "It is important for two reasons: firstly because I am a Christian; and secondly because the house where she lives belongs to the line of Clairvaux." And he added, "I decree that the girl and her case should be under the pope's protection, and I appeal those letters sent by you against her." He did what he said, and sent to the prior of Parc

those letters sent by the pope against the bishop, lest the bishop try to disturb the convent because of the girl, and so that they could defend themselves with those letters.

After two years the matter came to an end by legal judgment. A deceptive snare was then prepared by the Jews, using a handsome Jewish youth for the purpose. He came to the convent where the girl lived, pretending that he wanted to be baptized. When he had represented himself in that way, he asked to speak to his cousin Catherine because of her learning. He said the following, "The word of my cousin will be more effective to me than the speech of others." Catherine perceived the youth's falsehood in coming to the Faith, and neither imprecations nor money or any obedience could persuade her to speak even a single word with the youth. When the Jews saw this, they left her alone, and the Jew returned to his vomit.

After the above, much grace flourished in the person of the most elect Catherine, who was loved by all; no one was more serene than she.

REVIEW QUESTIONS

1. Why do you think these authors wrote this account?
2. Why did Rachel want to convert to Christianity?
3. What does this selection reveal about Jewish family life in the thirteenth century?
4. Do Rachel's parents seem to be "modern" in any way? Explain.

A Spanish Physician Offers Advice (1315)

PETER FAGAROLA, *Letter to His Sons*

Europe's High Middle Ages (approximately 1000 to 1350) witnessed great artistic and intellectual accomplishments—great Gothic cathedrals and the revival known today as the twelfth-century renaissance. Until the middle of the eleventh century, the Church controlled the most important intellectual centers. Then, new institutions of higher learning appeared, the universities, which were corporate bodies of students and masters formed to protect and regulate their common interests. These associations took two forms. At the University of Bologna, for example, students ran the university. They had the power to hire or fire professors, to set lecture fees, and to fine professors who were late for class, failed to cover appropriate material, or ran overtime. Most universities south of the Alps modeled themselves on Bologna. At the University of Paris, on the other hand, the masters had the upper hand. They regulated the life of the university, set fees, and accepted students as a master might teach apprentices in a guild. In general, the University of Paris became the model for universities north of the Alps.

The student body of a medieval university differed in some important ways from its modern counterpart. First, all students were male. Many started their undergraduate studies at a younger age than students in the United States do today. There are also some distinct similarities between then and now. Many medieval students took their studies seriously and worked diligently at them. Others were distracted by the lure of "drinking, brawling, and wenching." The selection that follows is from a letter written in 1315 by a Spanish physician to his two sons, away at the university in Toulouse. It demonstrates a medieval father's interest in the well-being of his children. He offered advice about such everyday matters as food, clothing, personal hygiene, and the right amount of sleep (six hours a night). In so doing, the father, Peter Fagarola, helps us understand both student and family life in the early fourteenth century.

OF FOODS, OR HOW TO EAT

Beware of eating too much and too often especially during the night. Avoid eating raw onions in the evening except rarely, because they dull the intellect and senses generally.

Avoid all very lacteal foods such as milk and fresh cheese except very rarely. Beware of eating milk and fish, or milk and wine, at the same meal, for milk and fish or milk and wine produce leprosy.

Don't have fresh pork too often. Salt pork is all right.

Don't eat many nuts except rarely and following fish. I say the same of meat and fruit, for they are bad and difficult to digest.

Thy drink be twice or thrice or four times during a meal. Between meals drink little, for it would be better once in a while to drink too much at table than to drink away from table. Don't take wine without water, and, if it is too cold, warm it in winter. For 'tis bad to grow used to strong wine without admixture of water.

Remember about the well water of Toulouse.

Wherefore boil it, and the same with water of the Garonne, because such waters are bad.

Also, after you have risen from the table wash out your mouth with wine. This done, take one spoonful of this powdered confection:

Of meat prepared with vinegar and dried coriander similarly prepared a modicum each; of roast meat, fennel seed, flowers of white eyebright, two ounces each; of candied coriander, candied anise, scraped licorice, each one ounce and a half; of cloves, mast, cubebs, each three drams; of galingale and cardamomum each two drams; of white ginger six drams; of white loaf sugar three drams; made into a powder and put in a paste. And keep this in your room in a secret [or, *dry*] place, for it will comfort your digestion, head, vision, intellect and memory, and protect from rheum.

AS TO SLEEP

Sufficient and natural sleep is to sleep for a fourth part of a natural day or a trifle more or less. To do otherwise is to pervert nature. Too much is a sin, wherefore shun it, unless the case is urgent and necessary.

Avoid sleeping on your back except rarely, for it has many disadvantages, but sleep on your side or stomach, and first on the right side, then on the left.

Don't sleep in winter with cold feet, but first warm them at the fire or by walking about or some other method. And in summer don't sleep with bed slippers on your feet, because they generate vapors which are very bad for the brain and memory.

Don't go straight to bed on a full stomach but an hour after the meal. Also, unless some urgent necessity prevents, walk about for a bit after a meal, at least around the square, so that the food may settle in the stomach and not evaporate in the mouth of the stomach, since the vapors will rise to the head and fill it with rheum and steal away and cut short memory.

Also, avoid lying down in a rheumatic place, such as a basement or room underground.

OF AIR OR ONE'S SURROUNDINGS

Choose lodgings removed from all foul smells as of ditches or latrines and the like, since in breathing we are continually drawing in air which, if it is infected, infects us more and more forcibly than tainted food and drink do.

Likewise in winter keep your room closed from all noxious wind and have straw on the pavement lest you suffer from cold.

Furthermore, if you can have coals or chopped wood in a clay receptacle of good clay, or if you have a chimneyplace and fire in your room, it is well.

Also, be well clad and well shod, and outdoors wear pattens to keep your feet warm.

Also, don't make yourself a cap "de salsamentis,"[1] as some do, for they are harmful.

And when you see other students wearing their caps, do you do likewise, and, if need be, put on one of fur.

And at night, when you study, you should wear a nightcap over the cap and about your cheeks (or throat?).

And when you go to bed at night, have a white nightcap on your head and beneath your cheeks, and another colored one over it, for at night the head should be kept warmer than during the day.

Moreover, at the time of the great rains it is well to wear outdoors over your cap a bonnet or helmet of undressed skin, that is, a covering to keep the head from getting wet. Indeed, some persons wear a bonnet over the cap in fair weather, more especially when it is cold, so that in the presence of the great they may remove the bonnet and be excused from doffing the cap.

Also, look after your stockings and don't permit your feet to become dirty.

Also, wash the head, if you are accustomed to wash it, at least once a fortnight with hot lye and in a place sheltered from draughts on the eve of a feast day towards nightfall. Then dry your hair with a brisk massage; afterwards do it up; then put on a bonnet or cap.

Also comb your hair daily, if you will morning and evening before eating or at least afterwards, if you cannot do otherwise.

Also look out that a draught does not strike you from window or crack while you study or sleep, or indeed at any time, for it strikes men without their noticing.

Also, in summer, in order not to have fleas or to have no more of them, sweep your room daily with a broom and not sprinkle it with water, for they are generated from damp dust. But you may spray it occasionally with strong vinegar which comforts heart and brain.

If you will, walk daily somewhere morning and evening. And if the weather is cold, if you can run, run on empty stomach, or at least walk rapidly, that the natural heat may be revived. For a fire is soon extinguished unless the sticks are moved about or the bellows used. However, it is not advisable to run on a full stomach but to

---

[1]Literally, of sauces or pickles or salt fish or sausages, which seems an impossible translation. Probably we have to do with a slang phrase for some current type of head-covering.

saunter slowly in order to settle the food in the stomach.

If you cannot go outside your lodgings, either because the weather does not permit or it is raining, climb the stairs rapidly three or four times, and have in your room a big heavy stick like a sword and wield it now with one hand, now with the other, as if in a scrimmage, until you are almost winded. This is splendid exercise to warm one up and expel noxious vapors through the pores and consume other superfluities. Jumping is a similar exercise. Singing, too, exercises the chest. And if you will do this, you will have healthy limbs, a sound intellect and memory, and you will avoid rheum. The same way with playing ball. All these were invented not for sport but for exercise. Moreover, too much labor is to be avoided as a continual practice.

OF ACCIDENTS OF THE SOUL

Accidents of the soul have the greatest influence, such as anger, sadness, and love of women, fear, excessive anxiety: concerning all which I say nothing more than that you avoid all passions of the soul harmful to you and enjoy yourself happily with friends and good companions, and cultivate honesty and patience which bring the more delights to the soul, and especially if you love God with your whole heart.

FOR A COUGH

If you are troubled with a cough, beware of all cold or sour things, or salt and fried. And if cold rheum is the cause of the cough, then make a bag of camamille, salt, and calamint in equal parts mixed together, and make a pepper poultice which should be placed on top of the head or over the commissure. And a small piece of licorice should be kept in the mouth and chewed between the teeth, or a candy should be made of licorice.

Equally good is sirup of Venus' hair, sirup of hyssop, sirup of bug-loss, if they are taken with water of scabiosa, water of lily, elder water, water of betony, water of rosemary in equal parts, or wash the mouth with a tepid gargle.

Equally good are dyera yeris of Solomon, diapenidion, cold diagragant, preserved penidiarum, grains of pine, and the like.

And if the cough is accompanied by hot rheum, of which the signs are extreme heat, a burning sensation in the throat, saltiness, and great thirst, in this case take cold diagragant or diapenidion without spices with sirup of violets or sirup of pepper. And let this be taken in sips and not swallowed suddenly. And this is to be done without eating anything morning and evening. Immediately afterwards take a fine linen cloth and dip it in tepid oil of roses and apply it tepid to the commissure of the head, and this do twice daily.

And in cold rheum beware of all broth and meat puddings as much as is possible and of superfluous drink. And eat only roast meats not stewed in water, and eat any thick foodstuffs such as sweetbreads, split beans with their skins removed, and the like, cooked with meat.

Also in hot rheum one should eat barley-gruel, rice, oatmeal cooked with milk of almonds and sugar, pears and apples cooked with sugar, which are also good in case of cold rheum.

And one should drink yellow wine, clear and limpid.

Also equally beneficial in this case are cold diagragant, diapenidion without spices, sugar of violets, preserved penidiarum, and the like. And let this suffice so far as rheum is concerned.

Thus it ends. Thanks to God. Amen, Amen.

REVIEW QUESTIONS

1. How is this letter different from one that modern students might receive from their parent? How is it similar? Are the similarities or differences more important?

2. How would you characterize the father's concerns? What types of things was he worried about?
3. What do you think were the most significant obstacles to these students' enjoyment of life, based on the father's advice?
4. Does this letter change your opinion of life in the Middle Ages? If so, how? If not, why not?

A Castilian Noblewoman Recounts Her Adventures (1370s)

LEONOR LÓPEZ DE CÓRDOBA, *Memorias*

The Spanish struggle to reconquer Iberia from Muslim control eventually resulted in a complete victory in 1492. During the reconquest, however, Spanish nobles failed to present a united front to the enemy. Often they fought against each other for control of newly acquired territories. In this politically and militarily unstable environment, security came from the strength and position of one's own family and the alliances it made with other elite families in the same region. Although the values of the feudal system, with its emphasis on martial skills, favored men over women, this selection allows us to appreciate the priorities that members of this society recognized, and the dangers to which they were exposed, from a woman's point of view.

Leonor López de Córdoba (c. 1362–c. 1412), the author of this memoir, belonged to an aristocratic family that supported King Pedro I of Castile. After Pedro was killed in battle by his half-brother, Enrique de Trastámara (King Enrique II), Leonor's father, Martín, refused to recognize the new king. He continued to fight against him and encouraged King Fernando of Portugal to invade Castile and take over the government. Martín's political objectives were shattered when Enrique and Fernando negotiated a peace treaty in 1371. Indeed, Martín surrendered to Enrique with an assurance that his children and those of King Pedro, who had been under his protection, would be allowed to leave the country. Enrique did not keep his word. He had Martín executed and his family imprisoned. This selection describes some of the hardships that Leonor endured during her imprisonment and following her release in 1379.

I am the daughter of the said master who was Lord of Calatrava in the time of King Pedro. The king did my father the honor of giving him the commission of Alcántara, which is in the city of Seville. The king then made him master of Alcántara and, in the end, of Calatrava. This master, my father, was a descendant of the house of Aguilar, and the great-nephew of Don Juan Manuel, son of his niece who was the daughter of his brother. He rose to a very high estate, as can be discovered in the chronicles of Spain. And as I have said, I am the daughter of Doña Sancha Carrillo, niece and ward of King Alfonso of most illustrious memory, to whom God granted paradise, who was the father of King Pedro.

My mother died very early, and so my father

married me at seven years old to Ruy Gutierrez de Henestrosa. He was the son of Juan Fernández de Henestrosa, King Pedro's head valet, his chancellor of the royal seal, and head major-domo of Queen Blanca his wife; Juan Fernández married Doña María de Haro, mistress of Haro and the Cameros. To my husband were left many of his father's goods and several estates. He received three hundred mounted soldiers of his own, and forty strands of pearls as fat as chick-peas, and five hundred Moorish servants, and silver tableware worth two thousand marks. The jewels and gems of his house could not be written on two sheets of paper. All this came to him from his father and mother because they had no other son and heir. My father gave me twenty thousand *doblas* as a dowry; we lived in Carmona with King Pedro's daughters, my husband and I, along with my brothers-in-law, my sisters' husbands, and with one brother of mine, who was named Don Lope López de Córdoba Carrillo. My brothers-in-law were named Fernán Rodríguez de Aza, Lord of Aza and Villalobos, and Ruy García de Aza, and Lope Rodríguez de Aza. They were the sons of Alvaro Rodríguez de Aza and Doña Costanza de Villalobos.

That was how things stood when King Pedro was besieged at the castle of Montiel by his brother, King Enrique. My father went down to Andalusia to bring people to aid King Pedro, and on the way he discovered that the king was dead at the hands of his brother. Seeing this disgrace, he took the road to Carmona where the princesses were, King Pedro's daughters, who were very close relatives of my husband, and of myself through my mother. King Enrique, becoming King of Castile, came to Seville and surrounded Carmona. As it is such a strong town, it was surrounded for many months.

But by chance my father had left Carmona, and those of King Enrique's camp knew how he was gone, and that it would not remain so well protected. Twelve knights volunteered to scale the town, and they climbed the wall. They were captured, and then my father was informed of what had happened. He came to Carmona then, and ordered them to be beheaded for their au-

dacity. King Enrique observed this, and because he could not enter Carmona by force of arms to satisfy himself about this deed, he ordered the constable of Castile to discuss terms with my father.

The terms that my father put forward were two. First, King Enrique's party was to free the princesses and their treasure to leave for England, before he would surrender the town to the King. (And so it was done. He ordered certain noblemen, his kinsmen and natives of Córdoba bearing his family name, to accompany the princesses and the rest of the people who intended to leave with them.) The second condition was that my father, his children, his guard, and those in the town who had obeyed his orders would be pardoned by the king, and that they and their estates would be considered loyal. And so it was granted him, signed by the constable in the king's name. Having achieved this, my father surrendered the town to the constable in King Enrique's name, and he left there—with his children and the rest of the people—to kiss the king's hand. King Enrique ordered them to be arrested and put in the dungeon of Seville. The constable, who saw that King Enrique had not fulfilled the promise he had made in his name to this master (my father), left the court and never returned to it.

The king ordered my father to be beheaded in the Plaza de San Francisco in Seville, and his goods confiscated, as well as those of his son-in-law, guardsmen, and servants. While he was on his way to be decapitated, my father encountered Mosen Beltran de Clequin, a French knight, the knight, in fact, whom King Pedro had trusted and who had freed him when he was trapped in the castle of Montiel, but who had not fulfilled his promise, and instead surrendered him to King Enrique to be killed. As Mosen Beltran met with my father, he said to him, "Master, didn't I tell you that your travels would end in this?" And my father replied, "Better to die loyal, as I have done, than to live as you live, having been a traitor."

The rest of us remained in prison for nine years, until King Enrique died. Our husbands each had seventy pounds of iron on their feet, and my brother, Don Lope López, had a chain between the irons in which there were seventy links. He was a boy of thirteen years, the most beautiful creature in the world. My husband especially was made to go hungry. For six or seven days he neither ate nor drank because he was the cousin of the princesses, the daughters of King Pedro.

A plague came into the prison, and so my brothers and all of my brothers-in-law and thirteen knights from my father's house all died. Sancho Miñez de Villendra, my father's head valet, said to my brothers and sisters and me, "Children of my lord, pray to God that I live for your sakes, for if I do, you will never die poor." It was God's will that he died the third day without speaking. After they were dead they took them all out to the smith to have their chains taken off, like Moors.

My poor brother, Don Lope López, asked the mayor who had us in his charge to tell Gonzalo Ruíz Bolante that much charity was shown to us, and much honor, for the love of God. "Lord Mayor, it would be merciful of you to take off my irons before my soul departs, and not to take me to the smith." The mayor replied to him as if to a Moor, "If it were up to me, I would do it." At this, my brother's soul departed while he was in my arms. He was a year older than I. They took him away on a slab to the smith, like a Moor, and they buried him with my brothers and my sisters and my brothers-in-law in the church of San Francisco of Seville.

Each of my brothers-in-law used to wear a gold necklace around his throat, for they were five brothers. They put on those necklaces in Santa María de Guadalupe, and they vowed not to take them off until all five lay themselves down in Santa María. Because of their sins, one died in Seville, and another in Lisbon, and another in England, and so they died scattered. They ordered that they be buried with the gold necklaces, but the monks, after burying them, greedily removed the necklaces.

No one from the house of my father, Master Don Martín López, remained in the dungeon ex-

cept my husband and myself. At this time, the most high and illustrious King Enrique, of very sainted and illustrious memory, died; he ordered in his will that we were to be taken out of prison, and that all that was ours be returned. I stayed in the house of my lady aunt, Doña María García Carrillo, and my husband went to demand his goods. Those who held them paid him little attention, because he had no rank or means to demand their return. You already know how rights depend on one's petition being granted. So my husband disappeared, and wandered through the world for seven years, a wretch, and never discovered relative nor friend who would do him a good turn or take pity on him. After I had spent seven years in the household of my aunt, Doña María García Carrillo, they told my husband, who was in Badajoz with his uncle Lope Fernández de Padilla in the Portuguese War, that I was in good health and that my relatives had treated me very well. He mounted his mule, which was worth very little money, and the clothes he wore didn't amount to thirty *maravedis,* and he appeared at my aunt's door.

Not having known that my husband was wandering lost through the world, I requested my lady aunt, my lady mother's sister, to speak with Doña Teresa Fernández Carrillo, who was a member of the Order of Guadalajara, which my great grandparents founded; they have given an endowment to support forty wealthy women of their lineage who should join the order. I sent my aunt to petition that Doña Teresa would wish to receive me into that order, for through my sins my husband and I were lost. She, and all the order, agreed to this, for my lady mother had been brought up in their monasteries. King Pedro had taken her from there and had given her to my father in marriage because she was the sister of Gonzalo Díaz Carrillo and of Diego Carrillo, sons of Don Juan Fernández Carrillo and Doña Sancha de Rojas. Because these uncles of mine were afraid of King Pedro, who had killed and exiled many of his lineage and had demolished my grandfather's houses and given his property to others, those uncles of mine left there, in order to serve King Enrique when he was count, because of this outrage. I was born in Calatayud, in the king's house. The lady princesses, his daughters, were my godmothers, and they brought me with them to the fortress of Segovia, along with my lady mother, who died there. I was of such an age that I never knew her.

And after my husband arrived, as I said, I left the house of my lady aunt, which was in Córdoba next to San Ipólito, and my husband and I were received into some houses there, next to hers, and we came there with little rest.

For thirty days I prayed to the Virgin Saint Mary of Bethlehem. Each night on my knees I said three hundred Ave Marías, in order to reach the heart of my lady aunt so she would consent to open a postern to her houses. Two days before my praying ended, I demanded of my lady aunt she allow me to open that private entrance, so that we wouldn't walk through the street, past so many nobles that there were in Córdoba, to come eat at her table. In her mercy she responded to me and granted it, and I was greatly consoled. Another day, when I wanted to open the postern, her servants had changed her heart and she would not do it. I was so disconsolate that I lost patience, and she that had caused me the most trouble with my lady aunt died at my hands, eating her tongue.

Another day, when only one day remained to complete my prayer, a Saturday, I dreamed I was passing through San Ipólito touching the alb. I saw in the wall of the courtyard an arch, very large and very tall. I entered through it and gathered flowers from the earth, and saw a very great heaven. At this I awoke, and I was hopeful that my Virgin St. Mary would give me a home.

At this time there was a robbery in the Jewish quarter, and I took in an orphan boy who was there, so that he would be instructed in the faith. I had him baptized so that he would be instructed in the faith.

One day, coming with my lady aunt from mass at San Ipólito, I saw being distributed among the clerics of San Ipólito those grounds where I had dreamed there was the great arch. I implored my lady aunt, Doña Mencía Carrillo, to purchase that site for me, since I had been her

companion for seventeen years, and she bought it for me. She gave these grounds to me with the condition—which she indicated—that I build a chapel (erected over the houses) for the soul of King Alfonso, who built that church in the name of San Ipolito because he was born on that saint's day. These chaplains have another six or seven chapels built by Don Gonzalo Fernández, my lady aunt's husband, and Don Alfonso Fernández, lord of Aguilar, and by the children of the marshal. Then, when I had done this favor, I raised my eyes to God and to the Virgin Mary, giving them thanks.

There came to me a servant of Master Don Martín López, my lord and father, who lives with Martín Fernández, mayor of the doncels, who was there hearing mass. I sent a request with this servant to Don Martín Fernández that, as a kinsman, he thank my lady aunt for the kindness she had shown me. He was greatly pleased, and so he did it well, saying that he received her kindness to me as if it were shown to him.

Now that possession of these grounds had been given to me, I opened a door on the very place where I had seen the arch which the Virgin Mary showed me. It grieved the abbots to hand over that site to me, for I was of a great lineage, and my children would be great. They were abbots, and had no need of great knights so near them. This I heard from a reliable voice, and I told them to hope in God that it would be so. I made myself so agreeable to them that I opened the door in the place that I wanted. God helped me by giving me that beginning of a house because of the charity I performed in raising the orphan in the faith of Jesus Christ. For thirty days before this, I had gone at Matins to the image of St. Mary the Fainting, which is in the Order of San Pablo of Córdoba, barefoot and with tears and sighs, and I prayed to her the prayer that follows sixty-three times, with sixty-six Ave Marías, in reverence for the sixty-six years that she lived with bitterness in this world, so that she would give me a home, and she gave me a home, and houses better than I deserved, out of her mercy. Here begins the prayer: "Mother St. Mary, your well-taught son took on great pain for you. You saw him tormented with great tribulation; your heart fainted after his tribulation. He gave you consolation; Lady, you who know my pain, give the same to me." It was the Virgin St. Mary's will that with the help of my lady aunt, and by the labor of my hands, I built in that yard two mansions, and an orchard, and another two or three houses for servants.

In this period of time a very cruel plague came. My lady aunt did not want to leave the city; I requested of her the kindness to permit me to flee with my children so that they would not die. She was not pleased but she gave me leave. I left Córdoba and went to Santa Ella with my children. The orphan that I raised lived in Santa Ella, and he lodged me in his house. All of the neighbors of the town were delighted by my coming. They received me with warm welcome, for they had been servants of the lord my father, and so they gave me the best house there was in that place, which was that belonging to Fernando Alonso Mediabarba. Being without suspicion, my lady aunt came there with her daughters, and I withdrew to a small room. Her daughters, my cousins, never got on well with me because of all the good their mother had done me. I suffered so much bitterness from them that it cannot be written.

The plague came there, so my lady left with her people for Aguilar, and she took me with her as one of her own daughters, for she loved me greatly and said great things of me. I had sent the orphan that I raised to Ezija. The night that we arrived in Aguilar, the boy came from Ezija with two small tumors in his throat and three carbuncles on his face, and with a high fever. In that house there were Don Alonso Fernández, my cousin, and his wife and all of his household. Though all of the girls were my nieces and my friends, knowing that my servant came in such a condition, they came to me and said, "Your servant, Alonso, comes with the plague, and if Don Alonso Fernández sees it he will be furious at his being here with such an illness."

And the pain that reached my heart anyone who hears this history can well understand. I be-

came worldly wise and bitter. Thinking that through me such great sorrow had entered that house, I had Miguel de Santa Ella called to me. He had been a servant of the master, my lord and father, and I begged him to take that boy to his house. The wretched man was afraid, and he said, "Lady, how can I take him with the plague, which will kill me?" And I said to him, "Son, God would not want that." Shamed by me, he took the boy; and through my sins, thirteen persons who watched over him by night all died.

I made a prayer which I had heard, which a nun said before a crucifix. It seems that she was a great devotee of Jesus Christ, and she says that after she had heard Matins she came before a crucifix. On her knees she prayed seven thousand times "Pious Son of the Virgin, may piety conquer you." One night, when the nun was near that place, she heard that the crucifix answered her, and it said, "Pious you called me, and pious I will be for you." I found great devotion in these words. I prayed this prayer each night, begging God to free me and my children, and if he had to take someone, let it be the eldest, for he was very sick.

One night it was God's will that there was no one to watch over that sorrowful boy, for all who had until then watched over him had died. My son, who was called Juan Fernández de Henestrosa like his grandfather, and who was twelve years and four months old, came to me and said, "Lady is there no one to watch over Alonso tonight?" And I told him, "You watch over him, for the love of God." He replied to me, "Lady, now that the others have all died, do you want to kill me?" I said to him, "For my charity, God will take pity on me." And my son, so as not to disobey me, went to keep vigil. Through my sins, that night he was given the pestilence, and another day I buried him. The sick one lived after all the others had died.

Doña Teresa, the wife of my cousin Don Alonso Fernández, became very angry because my son was dying in her house at that time. She ordered that he be removed from the house on account of his illness. I was so transfixed by grief that I could not speak for the shame that those words caused me. My poor son said, "Tell my lady Doña Teresa not to cast me away, for my soul will leave now for heaven." He died that night. He was buried in Santa María la Coronada, which is in the same town. Because Doña Teresa felt very hostile to me, and I did not know why, she ordered that he not be buried within the town. When they took him to be buried, I went with him. As I went through the streets with my son, people came out, making a great hue and cry, ashamed for me. They said, "Come out, lords, and see the most unfortunate, forsaken, and accursed woman in the world!" with shouts that trespassed the heavens. Like those of that place, all who were there in that crowd were servants of the lord my father, and had been brought up by him. Although they knew that it grieved their present lords, they made a great lament with me as if I were their lady.

This same night, after I came from burying my son, they told me to return to Córdoba. I went to my lady aunt to see if she had ordered this. She said to me, "Lady niece, I cannot fail to do it, for I have promised my daughter-in-law and my daughters, for they are acting as one. In the meantime, it distresses me to have you leave, although I have granted permission. I do not know what annoyance you have caused my daughter-in-law Doña Teresa, that makes her so hostile to you."

I said to her with many tears, "Lady, if I have deserved this, may God not save me." And so I returned to my house in Córdoba.

REVIEW QUESTIONS

1. What particular values did the members of this society cherish the most? Was there a difference between men and women?
2. How would you characterize the role that Leonor played in the events described here?
3. What role did religion play in Leonor's life? In the life of this society?
4. Do you think that Leonor's conduct was admirable? Why or why not?

⫸ 11 ⫷

Africa, 800–1500

The accounts of travelers included in this chapter reveal some of the most significant events and circumstances in African history in the period from 800 to 1500. Although Christianity was practiced in Ethiopia and Axum, it had not advanced beyond that region. The spread of Islam, however, began by the early eighth century and dramatically influenced the lives of millions of people in North, West, and East Africa. Simultaneously, the demand for gold, ivory, salt, and other commodities brought international traders from Persia, India, China, and Portugal. This trade increased the wealth of African peoples and changed their cultures, and the combination of these two experiences produced a rippling effect upon the states and peoples far into the interior of the continent. To be sure, the available source material in English does not do justice to the magnitude of these changes. Great Zimbabwe and other kingdoms of South and Central Africa grew wealthy because of the activities of foreigners, but no written descriptions of these exchanges are available in English. The same is true for the lives of those people living in the interior of the continent, from Mt. Kilimanjaro to the Congo River drainage.

Although two of the selections in this chapter are of Portuguese origin, the majority are from Arabic sources and written by professionals, missionaries, and traders. As a result, most of our information about African history comes from the writings of men who were educated and belonged to prominent families. Because of their economic perspective, they were well aware of peoples' customs, lifestyles, and material culture. Their accounts differ sharply from that of the Portuguese seaman, Vasco da Gama, who paid close attention to politics and the nuances of diplomacy and competition.

In three cases, the authors of these selections traveled to other places; Africa was not their final destination. Buzurg Ibn Shahriyar traveled throughout the Mediterranean and Persian Gulf as well as to Somalia and Kenya in his slave trading business. The trader Al-Mas'udi was familiar with India and China, as well as Persia and the Swahili coast of Africa. As a result of their wide-ranging journeys, these men had a cosmopolitan and relatively sophisticated perspective on the peoples and societies they described. Consequently, they were in a good position to draw comparisons among the various peoples they met.

The caravan trade across the Sahara colored the accounts of Al-Bakri and influenced al-'Umari's description of Mansa Musa's travels. Al Bakri's narrative is almost three hundred years earlier than Mansa Musa's pilgrimage. These two accounts provide contrasting views of the Muslim world in Africa and also reveal the cosmopolitan nature of West African urban centers, which compared favorably to Cairo in Egypt. In both selections the presence or absence of wealth made great differences in personal relationships.

The record of the Portuguese in East Africa is based not on the accounts of traders but on the narratives of missionaries and explorers. Missionary descriptions of Africa vary greatly from those of the traders. Father Francisco Alvares was not interested in the material culture or even the quality of the lives of the peoples he met; he focused on the spiritual wealth of Ethiopia. Conversely, Vasco da Gama left religious issues to others in his expedition. His mission was to explore the Indian Ocean ports of Africa and ascertain the chances that Portuguese traders would find an entry to established markets. But while the wealth of trade would come to others, da Gama wanted to experience the excitement of discovery.

One selection in this chapter stands alone. Two short excerpts from the writings of a Muslim merchant named Yakut describe trading activities in the central region of Africa, east of the Niger River, and in the area around Lake Chad. These narratives present a world of trade that resembles that in other parts of West Africa, but the economy of the region that Yakut described was based only on agriculture, with neither gold nor ivory to attract other merchant travelers.

A Persian Gulf Sailor Recounts His Adventures on the East African Coast (922)

BUZURG IBN SHAHRIYAR OF RAMHORMUZ, *Kitab al-Ajaib al-Hind*

This Persian Gulf sailor probably wrote his collection of sailors' tales, known as the *Kitab al-Ajaib al-Hind,* in the middle of the tenth century. The author said that he was told this particular story by another sailor, Ismailawaih. Although this is a second-person account and so may contain some fiction, it nevertheless includes important information about the tenth-century slave trade. The area to which the Zanj king was taken after his capture is the same as that where a large number of African slaves were taken to work as agricultural laborers on the Euphrates River near the region of Basra today (see the following account by Al-Mas'udi). After a Zanj rebellion in 868, slave laborers controlled the vital region that provided ships from Baghdad access to the Persian Gulf. The revolt was suppressed by the end of the ninth century, but the subsequent decline in the region's economic growth produced the disruption that allowed the African king to escape from his Baghdad owner. The overland return to Africa he describes shows the increased camel trade between the Persian Gulf and Cairo that resulted from the disruption of shipping routes.

Ismailawaih told me, and several sailors who were with him, that in the year A.H. 310 [A.D. 922] he left Oman in his ship to go to Kanbalu. A storm drove him towards Sofala on the Zanj coast. "Seeing the coast where we were, the captain said, and realizing that we were falling among cannibal negroes and were certain to perish, we made the ritual ablutions and turned our hearts towards God, saying for each other the prayers for the dead. The canoes of the negroes surrounded us and brought us into the harbour; we cast anchor and disembarked on the land. They led us to their king. He was a young negro, handsome and well made. He asked us who we were, and where we were going. We answered that the object of our voyage was his own land.

"You lie, he said. It was not in our land that you intended to disembark. It is only that the winds have driven you thither in spite of yourselves.

"When we had admitted that he spoke the truth, he said: Disembark your goods. Sell and buy, you have nothing to fear.

"We brought all our packages to the land and began to trade, a trade which was excellent for us, without any obstacles or customs dues. We made the king a number of presents to which he replied with gifts of equal worth or ones even more valuable. When the time to depart came, we asked his permission to go, and he agreed immediately. The goods we had bought were loaded and business was wound up. When everything was in order, and the king knew of our intention to set sail, he accompanied us to the shore with several of his people, got into one of the boats and came out to the ship with us. He even came on board with seven of his companions.

"When I saw them there, I said to myself: In the Oman market this young king would certainly fetch thirty dinars, and his seven companions sixty dinars. Their clothes alone are not worth less than twenty dinars. One way and another this would give us a profit of at least 3,000 dirhams, and without any trouble. Reflecting thus, I gave the crew their orders. They raised the sails and weighed anchor.

"In the meantime the king was most agreeable to us, making us promise to come back again and promising us a good welcome when we did. When he saw the sails fill with the wind and the ship begin to move, his face changed. You are off, he said. Well, I must say good-bye. And he wished to embark in the canoes which were tied up to the side. But we cut the ropes, and said to him: You will remain with us, we shall take you to our own land. There we shall reward you for all the kindnesses you have shown us.

"Strangers, he said, when you fell upon our beaches, my people wished to eat you and pillage your goods, as they have already done to others like you. But I protected you, and asked nothing from you. As a token of my goodwill I even came down to bid you farewell in your own ship. Treat me then as justice demands, and let me return to my own land.

"But no one paid any heed to his words; no notice was taken of them. As the wind got up, the coast was not slow to disappear from sight. Then night enfolded us in its shrouds and we reached the open sea.

"When the day came, the king and his companions were put with the other slaves whose number reached about 200 head. He was not treated differently from his companions in captivity. The king said not a word and did not even open his mouth. He behaved as if we were unknown to him and as if we did not know him. When he got to Oman, the slaves were sold, and the king with them.

"Now, several years after, sailing from Oman towards Kanbalu, the wind again drove us towards the coasts of Sofala on the Zanj coast, and we arrived at precisely the same place. The negroes saw us, and their canoes surrounded us, and we recognized each other. Fully certain we should perish this time, terror struck us dumb. We made the ritual ablutions in silence, repeated the prayer of death, and said farewell to each other. The negroes seized us, and took us to the king's dwelling and made us go in. Imagine our surprise; it was the same king that we had known, seated on his throne, just as if we had left him there. We prostrated ourselves before him, overcome, and had not the strength to raise ourselves up.

"Ah! said he, here are my old friends! Not one of us was capable of replying. He went on: Come, raise your heads, I give you safe conduct for yourselves and for your goods. Some raised their heads, others had not the strength, and were overcome with shame. But he showed himself gentle and gracious until we had all raised our heads, but without daring to look him in the face, so much were we moved to remorse and fear. But when we had been reassured by his safe conduct, we finally came to our senses, and he said: Ah! Traitors! How you have treated me after all I did for you! And each one of us called out: Mercy, oh King! be merciful to us!

"I will be merciful to you, he said. Go on, as you did last time, with your business of selling and buying. You may trade in full liberty. We could not believe our ears; we feared it was nothing but a trick to make us bring our goods on shore. None the less we disembarked them, and came and brought him a present of enormous value. But he refused it and said: You are not worthy for me to accept a present from you. I will not sully my property with anything that comes from you.

"After that we did our business in peace. When the time to go came, we asked permission to embark. He gave it. At the moment of departure, I went to tell him so. Go, he said, and may God protect you! Oh King, I replied, you have showered your bounty upon us, and we have been ungrateful and traitorous to you. But how did you escape and return to your country?

"He answered: After you had sold me in Oman, my purchaser took me to a town called Basrah,—and he described it. There I learnt to pray and to fast, and certain parts of the Koran. My master sold me to another man who took me to the country of the king of the Arabs, called Baghdad—and he described Baghdad. In this town I learnt to speak correctly. I completed my knowledge of the Koran and prayed with the men in the mosques. I saw the Caliph, who is called al-Muqtadir. I was in Baghdad for a year and more, when there came a party of men from Khorasan mounted on camels. Seeing a large crowd, I asked where all these people were going. I was told: To Mecca. What is Mecca? I asked. There, I was answered, is the House of God to which Muslims make the Pilgrimage. And I was told the history of the temple. I said to myself that I should do well to follow the caravan. My master, to whom I told all this, did not wish to go with them or to let me go. But I found a way to escape his watchfulness and to mix in the crowd of pilgrims. On the road I became a servant to them. They gave me food to

eat and got for me the two cloths needed for the *ihram* [the ritual garments used for the pilgrimage]. Finally, they instructing me, I performed all the ceremonies of the pilgrimage.

"Not daring to go back to Baghdad, for fear that my master would take away my life, I joined up with another caravan which was going to Cairo. I offered my services to the travellers, who carried me on their camels and shared their provisions with me. When I got to Cairo I saw the great river which is called the Nile. I asked: Where does it come from? They answered: Its source is in the land of the Zanj. On which side? On the side of a large town called Aswan, which is on the frontier of the land of the blacks.

"With this information, I followed the banks of the Nile, going from one town to another, asking alms, which was not refused me. I fell, however, among a company of blacks who gave me a bad welcome. They seized on me, and put me among the servants with a load which was too heavy for me to carry. I fled and fell into the hands of another company which seized me and sold me. I escaped again, and went on in this manner, until, after a series of similar adventures, I found myself in the country which adjoins the land of the Zanj. There I put on a disguise. Of all the terrors I had experienced since I left Cairo, there was none equal to that which I felt as I approached my own land. For, I said to myself, a new king has no doubt taken my place on the throne and commands the army. To regain power is not an easy thing. If I make myself known or if anyone recognizes me, I shall be seized upon, taken to the new king and killed at once. Or perhaps one of his favourites will cut off my head to gain his favour.

"So, in prey to mortal terror, I went on my way by night, and stayed hid during the day. When I reached the sea, I embarked on a ship; and, after stopping at various places, I disembarked one night on the shore of my country. I asked an old woman: Is the king who rules here a just king? She answered: My son, we have no king but God. And the good woman told me how the king had been carried off. I pretended the greatest astonishment at her story, as if it had not concerned me and events which I knew very well. The people of the kingdom, she said, have agreed not to have another king until they have certain news of the former one. For the diviners have told them that he is alive and in health, and safe in the land of the Arabs.

"When the day came, I went into the town and walked towards my palace. I found my family just as I had left them, but plunged into grief. My people listened to the account of my story, and it surprised them and filled them with joy. Like myself, they embraced the religion of Islam. Thus I returned into possession of my sovereignty, a month before you came. And here I am, happy and satisfied with the grace God has given me and mine, of knowing the precepts of Islam, the true faith, prayers, fasting, the pilgrimage, and what is permitted and what is forbidden: for no man else in the land of the Zanj has obtained a similar favour. And if I have forgiven you, it is because you were the first cause

of the purity of my religion. But there is still one sin on my conscience which I pray God to take away from me.

"What is this thing, oh King? I asked. It is, he said, that I left my master, when I left Baghdad, without asking him his permission, and that I did not return to him. If I were to meet an honest man, I would ask him to take the price of my purchase to my master. If there were among you a really good man, if you were truly upright men, I would give you a sum of money to give him, a sum ten times what he paid as damages for the delay. But you are nothing but traitors and tricksters.

"We said farewell to him. Go, he said, and if you return, I shall not treat you otherwise than I have done. You will receive the best welcome. And the Muslims may know that they may come here to us, as to brothers, Muslims like themselves. As for accompanying you to your ship, I have reasons for not doing so. And on that we parted."

REVIEW QUESTIONS

1. Did the Arab captain seem to have a definite cargo or trade item in mind when he was blown toward Sofala? What in the article leads you to think he may have intended to capture slaves if he could?
2. What parts of this account could have been added for effect? How does this reveal the attitudes and culture of the storyteller?
3. How did the attitude of the Zanj king change between the first visit of the Arab captain and the second? From this account, how would you describe his style of leadership?
4. In what way did the king's enslavement benefit him? Explain fully.

A Muslim Trader Describes His Experiences in East Africa (tenth century)

AL-MAS'UDI, *Muruj al-Dhahab wa Ma'adin al-Jawhar*

Born into a prosperous trading family in the late ninth century, Al-Mas'udi traveled to Persia (Iran), India, China, and East Africa. Before he died in 945, he had written this account of his trade in the region of Pemba and the southeast African coast. This excerpt from that account chronicles the demand for ivory in China. Although he could have acquired ivory in India, Al-Mas'udi's expedition continued to East Africa because the ivory traded by the Zanj people living on the east coast was of superior quality. His narrative is one of the first important descriptions of this region and its trading activities.

The name *Zanj,* from which Zanzibar originates, may be of Persian origin, and thus is strongly associated with Swahili culture. Early Arab writers used the word to refer to people of the "silent" trade with whom they had no spoken communication. In the ninth century the word *Zanj* also designated thousands of slaves from Africa who worked in the marshes of the Euphrates River. By the time the island of Zanzibar had become the center of the East African trade in the twelfth century, however, the Zanj people were no longer those of the silent trade, but had become an ethnic designation of peoples on the Swahili coast.

The pilots of Oman pass by the channel [of Berbera] to reach the island of Kanbalu, which is in the Zanj sea. It has a mixed population of Muslims and Zanj idolaters. . . . The aforesaid Kanbalu is the furthest point of their voyages on the Zanj sea, and the land of Sofala and the Waqwaq, on the edge of the Zanj mainland and at the end of this branch of the sea. The people of Siraf also make this voyage, and I myself have sailed on this sea, setting off from Sanjar, the capital of Oman, in company with a number of Omani shipowners, among whom were Muhammad ibn al-Zaidbud and Jawhar ibn Ahmad surnamed Ibn Sirah, who was later lost at sea with his ship. My last voyage from Kanbalu to Oman was in A.H. 304 [A.D. 916] on the ship belonging to Ahmad and Abd al-Samad, who were the brothers of Abd al-Rahim ibn Ja'far al-Sirafi, a native of Mikan, which is a quarter of Siraf. They were both lost at sea with all their goods later on. The Amir of Oman at the time of my last voyage was Ahmad ibn Hilal, son of a sister of al-Qital. I have sailed much on the seas, those of China, Rum, the Khazar, Qulzum and Yemen, but I do not know of one more dangerous than that of the Zanj, of which I have just spoken. There the whale is found. . . . There are also many other kinds of fish, with all sorts of shapes. . . . Amber is found in great quantities on the Zanj coast and also near Shihr in Arabia. . . . The best amber is that found in the islands and on the shores of the Zanj sea: it is

round and pale blue, sometimes as big as an ostrich egg, sometimes slightly less. The fish called the whale, which I have already mentioned, swallows it: when the sea is very rough it vomits up pieces of amber as large as rocks, and this fish swallows them. It is asphyxiated by them and then swims up to the surface. Then the Zanj, or men from other lands, who have been biding their time in their boats, seize the fish with harpoons and tackle, cut its stomach open, and take the amber out. The pieces found near the bowels have a nauseating smell, and are called *nedd* by the Iraqi and Persian chemists: but the pieces found near the back are purer than those which have been a long time in the inner part of the body. . . .

The land of Zanj produces wild leopard skins. The people wear them as clothes, or export them to Muslim countries. They are the largest leopard skins and the most beautiful for making saddles. The sea of Zanj and that of Abyssinia lie on the right of the sea of India, and join up. They also export tortoise-shell for making combs, for which ivory is likewise used. The most common animal in these countries is the giraffe: it generally lives in Nubia, and is not found in any part of Abyssinia. . . . As we have said, the Zanj and other Abyssinian peoples are spread about on the right bank of the Nile, as far as the end of the Abyssinian sea. The Zanj are the only Abyssinian people to have crossed the branch which flows out of the upper stream of the Nile into the sea of Zanj. They settled in that area, which stretches as far as Sofala, which is the furthest limit of the land and the end of the voyages made from Oman and Siraf on the sea of Zanj. In the same way that the sea of China ends with the land of Japan, the sea of Zanj ends with the land of Sofala and the Waqwaq, which produces gold and many other wonderful things. It has a warm climate and is fertile. The Zanj capital is there and they have a king called the *Mfalme.* This is the ancient name of their kings, and all the other Zanj kings are subject to him: he has 300,000 horsemen. The Zanj use the ox as a beast of burden, for they have no horses, mules or camels in their land, and do not know of their existence. Like all Abyssinians they do not know of snow or hail. Some of their tribes sharpen their teeth and are cannibals. The land of Zanj begins with the branch which leaves the upper Nile and continues to the land of Sofala and the Waqwaq. The villages stretch for 700 parasangs and the same distance inland: the country is cut up into valleys, mountains and stony deserts. There are many wild elephants but no tame ones. The Zanj do not use them for war or anything else, but only hunt and kill them. When they want to catch them, they throw down the leaves, bark and branches of a certain tree which grows in their country: then they wait in ambush until the elephants come to drink. The water burns them and makes them drunk. They fall down and cannot get up: their limbs will not articulate. The Zanj rush upon them armed with very long spears, and kill them for their ivory. It is from this country that come tusks weighing fifty pounds and more. They usually go to Oman, and from there are sent to China and India. This is the chief trade route, and if it were not so, ivory would be common in Muslim lands.

In China the kings and military and civil officers use ivory palanquins: no officer or notable dares to come into the royal presence in an iron palanquin, and ivory alone can be used. Thus they seek after straight tusks in preference to the curved, to make the things we have spoken of. They also burn ivory before their idols and cense their altars with it, just as Christians use the Mary incense and other perfumes. The Chinese make no other use of the elephant, and consider it unlucky to use it for domestic purposes or war. This fear has its origin in a tradition about one of their most ancient military expeditions. In India ivory is much sought after. It is used for the handles of daggers called *harari* or *harri* in the singular: and also for the curved sword-scabbards called *kartal,* in the plural *karatil.* But the chief use of ivory is making chessmen and backgammon pieces. . . .

In the land of the Zanj the elephant lives about 400 years, according to what the people say, and they speak with certainty of having met an elephant so tall that it was impossible to kill it. . . . It is only in the land of Zanj and in India that elephants reproduce. . . .

Now let us return to our subject of the beginning of the chapter, the Zanj, the description of their country and of the other peoples of Abyssinia. The Zanj, although always busied hunting the elephant and collecting its ivory, make no use of it for domestic purposes. They use iron instead of gold and silver, just as they use oxen, as we said before, both for beasts of burden and for war. These oxen are harnessed like a horse and run as fast. . . .

To go back to the Zanj and their kings, these are known as *Wafalme,* which means son of the Great Lord, since he is chosen to govern them justly. If he is tyrannical or strays from the truth, they kill him and exclude his seed from the throne; for they consider that in acting wrongfully he forfeits his position as the son of the Lord, the King of Heaven and Earth. They call God *Maliknajlu,* which means Great Lord.

The Zanj have an elegant language and men who preach in it. One of their holy men will often gather a crowd and exhort his hearers to please God in their lives and to be obedient to him. He explains the punishments that follow upon disobedience, and reminds them of their ancestors and kings of old. These people have no religious law: their kings rule by custom and by political expediency.

The Zanj eat bananas, which are as common

among them as they are in India; but their staple food is millet and a plant called *kalari* which is pulled out of the earth like truffles. It is plentiful in Aden and the neighbouring part of Yemen near to the town. It is like the cucumber of Egypt and Syria. They also eat honey and meat. Every man worships what he pleases, be it a plant, an animal or a mineral. They have many islands where the coconut grows: its nuts are used as fruit by all the Zanj peoples. One of these islands, which is one or two days' sail from the coast, has a Muslim population and a royal family. This is the island of Kanbalu of which we have already spoken.

REVIEW QUESTIONS

1. What commodities, besides ivory, did Al-Mas'udi obtain from the Zanj? Why were they desirable?
2. What was the nature of Al-Mas'udi's relationship with the Zanj merchants? Was the relationship mutually beneficial? How?
3. Did Al-Mas'udi have a favorable opinion of Zanj culture? What evidence supports your answer?
4. Why did anyone want ivory? What does this tell you about their society's values?

A Spanish Muslim Describes Ghana (1067)

AL BAKRI, *Roads and Kingdoms*

Al Bakri, an eleventh-century Spanish Arab from Cordoba, is best known as the author of a celebrated geographical work, *Roads and Kingdoms.* The description of Ghana included in this work is important because it is written at approximately the same time that Ghana's civilization reached its political and economic apogee. Previously, the Vandal migrations throughout North Africa during the eighth century had disrupted trans-Saharan travel from Iberia. Writing in 1067 from Cordoba, however, Al Bakri describes a Ghana that had gained its power because of its geographical position, which allowed it to dominate north-south trade in a number of commodities, especially gold. Ancient Ghana had its center about a thousand miles to the northwest of modern Ghana and controlled a large and isolated oasis, which was essential to trade. Within a generation of the writing of this account, the upper Niger River would become the new center of this trade, and of the Mali empire.

. . . Ghana is also the title given to their kings; the name of the region is Awkar, and their king today, namely in A.H. 460 [i.e., A.D. 1067–68] is *Tankamanin*. . . . The name of the previous king was Basi. . . . He led a praiseworthy life on account of his love of justice and his friendship for the Muslims. At the end of his life he became blind, but he concealed this from his subjects and pretended that he could see. When something was put before him, he said "This is good" or "This is bad." His ministers deceived the people by telling the king what he had to say in cryptic language so that the commoners could not understand. Basi was a maternal uncle to Tankamanin. This is their custom and their usage. The kingdom is inherited only by the son of the king's sister. He has no doubts that his successor is a son of his sister, while he is not certain that his son is in fact his own, and he does not rely on the genuineness of this relationship. This Tankamanin is powerful, rules an enormous kingdom, and possesses great authority.

The city of Ghana consists of two towns lying in a plain. One of these towns is inhabited by Muslims. It is large and possesses twelve mosques in one of which the people assemble for the Friday prayer. There are imams, muezzins, and assistants as well as jurists and learned men. Around the town are wells of sweet water from which they drink and near which they grow vegetables. The town in which the king lives is six miles from the Muslim one and bears the name Al Ghaba.[1] The land between the two towns is covered with houses. The houses of the inhabitants are made of stone and acacia wood. The king has a palace and a number of dome-shaped dwellings, the whole surrounded by an enclosure like the defensive wall of a city. In the town where the king lives, and not far from the hall where he holds his court of justice, is a mosque where pray the Muslims who come on visiting diplomatic missions. Around the king's town are domed buildings, woods, and copses where live the sorcerers of these people, the men in charge of the religious cult. In these also are idols and the tombs of their kings. These woods are guarded and no unauthorized person can enter them, so that it is not known what is within them. In them also are the prisons of the king, and if anyone is imprisoned there, no more is ever heard of him. The king's interpreters, his treasurer, and the majority of his ministers, are Muslims.

Of the people who follow the king's religion, only he and his heir presumptive, who is the son of his sister, may wear sewn clothes. All other people wear cloths of cotton, silk, or brocade,

according to their means. All men shave their beards and women shave their heads. The king adorns himself like a woman, wearing necklaces and bracelets, and when he sits before the people he puts on a high cap decorated with gold and wrapped in turbans of fine cotton. The court of appeal is held in a domed pavilion around which stand ten horses with gold embroidered trappings. Behind the king stand ten pages holding shields and swords decorated with gold, and on his right are the sons of the subordinate kings of his country, all wearing splendid garments and with their hair mixed with gold. The governor of the city sits on the ground before the king, and around him are ministers seated likewise. At the door of the pavilion are dogs, of excellent pedigree which, guarding the king, hardly ever leave the place where he is. Round their necks they wear collars of gold and silver, studded with a number of balls of the same metals. The audience is announced by the beating of a drum which they call *daba,* made from a long hollow log. When the people who profess the same religion as the king approach him, they fall on their knees and sprinkle their heads with dust, for this is their way of showing him their respect. As for the Muslims, they greet him only by clapping their hands.

The religion of the people of Ghana is paganism and the worship of idols. When their king dies they build, over the place where his tomb will be, an enormous dome of *saj* wood. Then they bring him on a bed covered with a few carpets and cushions and put him inside the dome. At his side they place his ornaments, his weapons, and the vessels from which he used to eat and drink, filled with various kinds of food and beverages. They also place there the men who have served his meals. They close the door of the dome and cover it with mats and materials, and then they assemble the people, who heap earth upon it until it becomes like a large mound. Then they dig a ditch around the mound so that it can be reached only at one place. They sacrifice victims for their dead and make offerings of intoxicating drinks.

For every donkey loaded with salt that enters

---

[1]The forest.

the country, the king takes a duty of one golden *dinar,*[2] and two *dinars* from every one that leaves. From a load of copper the duty due to the king is five *mithqals,* and from a load of merchandise ten *mithqals.* The best gold found in this land comes from the town of Ghiyaru, which is eighteen days traveling from the city of the king, over a country inhabited by tribes of the Negroes, their dwelling places being contiguous. The nuggets found in all the mines of this country are reserved for the king, only gold dust being left for the people. Without this precaution, the

people would accumulate gold until it had lost its value. The nuggets may be of any weight from an ounce to a pound. It is said that the king owns a nugget as large as a big stone. The town of Ghiyaru is twelve miles from the Nile [i.e., the Niger] and contains many Muslims.

The countryside of Ghana is unhealthy and not populous, and it is almost impossible to avoid falling ill there at the season when their crops are growing. The mortality among strangers is highest at the time of the harvest. . . . When the king of Ghana calls up his army, he can put 200,000 men in the field, more than 40,000 of whom are bowmen. The horses in Ghana are very small.

[2]About ⅛ oz. of gold.

REVIEW QUESTIONS

1. Do you find the relationship between Muslims and pagans in Ghana to be unusual? Explain why or why not?
2. What were the special privileges of the king of Ghana? What do they tell us about the political system?
3. What conditions of trade and environment probably contributed to the decline in prosperity of Ghana?

A Muslim Depiction of Mansa Musa's Travels in Mali and Egypt (1340s)

IBN FADL ALL'H AL-'UMARI, *Pathway of Vision in the Realms of the Metropolises*

The following account was written before 1349 by the son of a senior Mameluk official in Cairo and Damascus, Ibn Fadl All'h al-'Umari. Compiled from information given him by Egyptian officials who had met and dealt with Mansa Musa, al-'Umari's work is a principal source for the history of the kingdom of Mali in the fourteenth century. The description of Mali's court suggests comparisons with the furnishings and formalities of the court of the Mameluk sultans in Egypt—perhaps because this is al-'Umari's frame of reference.

Like the Songhay and Kanem kingdoms described in another selection in this chapter, Mali emerged under a strong ruler whose mainstays were the Muslim merchants who frequented the king's court. Mansa Musa ruled for only twenty-five years (1312–1337), but during that time he expanded his lands and became perhaps the richest man in the world. An age characterized by peace and trade allowed him to sell vast quantities of gold and amass an incalculable fortune. As a good Muslim, he made a pilgrimage to Mecca, but in keeping with his desire to inspire competition for his goods among traders, he traveled with a lavishly outfitted entourage. The following description of his reception in Cairo and the impression Mansa Musa made there shows how extraordinary wealth from Africa found its way into the Mediterranean region, where it enriched traders in Venice and Genoa.

The king of this realm sits in his palace on a big dais which they call *banbī* (spelt with "b, n, b") on a big seat made of ebony like a throne and of a size for a very heavily-built sitter. Over the dais, on all sides, are elephant tusks one beside the other. He has with him his arms, which are all of gold—sword, javelin, quiver, bow, and arrows. He wears big trousers cut out of about twenty pieces which none but he wears. About 30 slaves stand behind him, Turks and others who are bought for him in Egypt. One of them carries in his hand a parasol of silk surmounted by a dome and a bird of gold in the shape of a falcon. This is borne on the king's left. His emirs sit around and below him in two ranks to right and left. Further away are seated the chief horsemen of his army. In front of him there stands a man to attend him, who is his executioner [or swordbearer], and another, called *shā'ir* "poet" who is his intermediary between him and the people. Around all these are people with drums in their hands, which they beat. Before the kings are people dancing and he is pleased with them and laughs at them. Behind him two flags are unfurled, and before him two horses are tied ready for him to ride whenever he wishes.

Whoever sneezes while the king is holding court is severely beaten and he permits nobody to do so. But if a sneeze comes to anybody he lies down face to ground to sneeze so that nobody may know of it. As for the king, if he sneezes all those present beat their breasts with their hands.

They wear turbans with ends tied under the chin like the Arabs. Their cloth is white and made of cotton which they cultivate and weave in the most excellent fashion. It is called *kamīṣiyā*. Their costume is like that of the people of the Maghrib—*jubba,* and *durrā'a* without slit. Their brave cavaliers wear golden bracelets. Those whose knightly valour is greater wear gold necklets also. If it is greater still they add gold anklets. Whenever a hero adds to the list of his exploits the king gives him a pair of wide trousers, and the greater the number of a knight's exploits the bigger the size of his trousers. These trousers are characterized by narrowness in the leg and ampleness in the seat. The king is distinguished in his costume by the fact that he lets a turban-end dangle down in front of him. His trousers are of twenty pieces and nobody dares to wear the same.

The king of this country imports Arab horses and pays high prices for them. His army numbers about 100,000, of whom about 10,000 are cavalry mounted on horses and the remainder infantry without horses or other mounts. They have camels but do not know how to ride them with saddles.

Barley is quite lacking; it does not grow there at all.

The emirs and soldiers of this king have fiefs and benefices. Among their chiefs are some whose wealth derived from the king reaches 50,000 mithqāls of gold every year, besides which he keeps them in horses and clothes. His whole ambition is to give them fine clothes and to make his towns into cities. Nobody may enter the abode of this king save barefooted, whoever he may be. Anyone who does not remove his shoes, inadvertently or purposely, is put to death without mercy. Whenever one of the emirs or another comes into the presence of this king he keeps him standing before him for a time. Then the newcomer makes a gesture with his right hand like one who beats the drum of honour in the lands of Tūrān and Īrān. If the king bestows a favour upon a person or makes him a fair promise or thanks him for some deed the person who has received the favour grovels before him from one end of the room to the other. When he reaches there the slaves of the recipient of the favour or some of his friends take some of the ashes which are always kept ready at the far end of the king's audience chamber for the purpose and scatter it over the head of the favoured one, who then returns grovelling until he arrives before the king. Then he makes the drumming gesture as before and rises.

As for this gesture likened to beating the *jūk,* it is like this. The man raises his right hand to near his ear. There he places it, it being held up straight, and places it in contact with his left hand upon his thigh. The left hand has the palm extended so as to receive the right elbow. The right hand too has the palm extended with the fingers held close beside each other like a comb and touching the lobe of the ear.

The people of this kingdom ride with Arab saddles and in respect of most features of their horsemanship resemble the Arabs, but they mount their horses with the right foot, contrary to everybody else.

It is their custom not to bury their dead unless they be people of rank and status. Otherwise those without rank and the poor and strangers are thrown into the bush like other dead creatures.

It is a country where provisions go bad quickly, especially [clarified] butter, which is rotten and stinks after two days. This is not to be wondered at, for their sheep go scavenging over the garbage heaps and the country is very hot, which hastens decomposition.

When the king of this kingdom comes in from a journey a parasol and a standard are held over his head as he rides, and drums are beaten and guitars and trumpets well made of horn are played in front of him. And it is a custom of theirs that when one whom the king has charged with a task or assignment returns to him he questions him in detail about everything which has happened to him from the moment of his departure until his return. Complaints and appeals against administrative oppression are placed before this king and he delivers judgement on them himself. As a rule nothing is written down; his commands are given verbally. He has judges, scribes, and government offices. This is what al-Dukkālī related to me.

The emir Abū 'l-Ḥasan 'Alī b. Amīr Ḥājib told me that he was often in the company of sultan Mūsā the king of this country when he came to Egypt on the Pilgrimage. He was staying in [the] Qarāfa [district of Cairo] and Ibn Amīr Ḥājib was governor of Old Cairo and Qarāfa at that time. A friendship grew up between them and this sultan Mūsā told him a great deal about himself and his country and the people of the Sūdān who were his neighbours. One of the things which he told him was that his country was very extensive and contiguous with the Ocean. By his sword and his armies he had conquered 24 cities each with its surrounding district with villages and estates. It is a country rich in livestock—cattle, sheep, goats, horses, mules—and different kinds of poultry—geese, doves, chickens. The inhabitants of his country are numerous, a vast concourse, but compared with the peoples of the Sūdān who are their neighbours and penetrate far to the south they are like a white birth-mark on a black cow. He has a truce with the gold-plant people, who pay him tribute.

Ibn Amīr Ḥājib said that he asked him about the gold-plant, and he said: "It is found in two forms. One is found in the spring and blossoms after the rains in open country. It has leaves like the *najīl* grass and its roots are gold. The other kind is found all the year round at known sites on the banks of the Nīl and is dug up. There are holes there and roots of gold are found like stones or gravel and gathered up. Both kinds are known as *tibr* but the first is of superior fineness and worth more." Sultan Mūsā told Ibn Amīr Ḥājib that gold was his prerogative and he collected the crop as a tribute except for what the people of that country took by theft.

But what al-Dukkālī says is that in fact he is given only a part of it as a present by way of gaining his favour, and he makes a profit on the sale of it, for they have none in their country; and what Dukkālī says is more reliable.

Ibn Amīr Ḥājib said also that the blazon of this king is yellow on a red ground. Standards are unfurled over him wherever he rides on horseback; they are very big flags. The ceremonial for him who presents himself to the king or who receives a favour is that he bares the front of his head and makes the *jūk*-beating gesture towards the ground with his right hand as the Tatars do; if a more profound obeisance is required he grovels before the king. "I have seen this (says Ibn Amīr Ḥājib) with my own eyes." A custom of this sultan is that he does not eat in the presence of anybody, be he who he may, but eats always alone. And it is a custom of his people that if one of them should have reared a beautiful daughter he offers her to the king as a concubine and he possesses her without a marriage ceremony as slaves are possessed, and this in spite of the fact that Islam has triumphed among them and that they follow the Malikite school and that this sultan Mūsā was pious and assiduous in prayer, Koran reading, and mentioning God.

"I said to him (said Ibn Amīr Ḥājib) that this was not permissible for a Muslim, whether in law or reason, and he said: 'Not even for kings?' and I replied: 'No! not even for kings! Ask the scholars!' He said: 'By God, I did not know that. I hearby leave it and abandon it utterly!'

"I saw that this sultan Mūsā loved virtue and people of virtue. He left his kingdom and appointed as his deputy there his son Muḥammad and emigrated to God and His Messenger. He accomplished the obligations of the Pilgrimage, visited [the tomb of] the Prophet [at Medina] (God's blessing and peace be upon him!) and returned to his country with the intention of handing over his sovereignty to his son and abandoning it entirely to him and returning to Mecca the Venerated to remain there as a dweller near the sanctuary; but death overtook him, may God (who is great) have mercy upon him.

"I asked him if he had enemies with whom he fought wars and he said: 'Yes, we have a violent enemy who is to the Sūdān as the Tatars are to

you. They have an analogy with the Tatars in various respects. They are wide in the face and flat-nosed. They shoot well with [bow and] arrows. Their horses are cross-bred with slit noses. Battles take place between us and they are formidable because of their accurate shooting. War between us has its ups and downs.'"

(Ibn Saʿīd, in the *Mughrib,* mentions the Damādim tribe who burst upon various peoples of the Sūdān and destroyed their countries and who resemble the Tatars. The two groups appeared upon the scene at the same moment.)

Ibn Amīr Ḥājib continued: "I asked sultan Mūsā how the kingdom fell to him, and he said: 'We belong to a house which hands on the kingship by inheritance. The king who was my predecessor did not believe that it was impossible to discover the furthest limit of the Atlantic Ocean and wished vehemently to do so. So he equipped 200 ships filled with men and the same number equipped with gold, water, and provisions enough to last them for years, and said to the man deputed to lead them: "Do not return until you reach the end of it or your provisions and water give out." They departed and a long time passed before anyone came back. Then one ship returned and we asked the captain what news they brought. He said: "Yes, O Sultan, we travelled for a long time until there appeared in the open sea [as it were] a river with a powerful current. Mine was the last of those ships. The [other] ships went on ahead but when they reached that place they did not return and no more was seen of them and we do not know what became of them. As for me, I went about at once and did not enter that river." But the sultan disbelieved him.

"'Then that sultan got ready 2,000 ships, 1,000 for himself and the men whom he took with him and 1,000 for water and provisions. He left me to deputize for him and embarked on the Atlantic Ocean with his men. That was the last we saw of him and all those who were with him, and so I became king in my own right.'

"This sultan Mūsā, during his stay in Egypt both before and after his journey to the Noble Ḥijāz, maintained a uniform attitude of worship and turning towards God. It was as though he were standing before Him because of His continual presence in his mind. He and all those with him behaved in the same manner and were well-dressed, grave, and dignified. He was noble and generous and performed many acts of charity and kindness. He had left his country with 100 loads of gold which he spent during his Pilgrimage on the tribes who lay along his route from his country to Egypt, while he was in Egypt, and again from Egypt to the Noble Ḥijāz and back. As a consequence he needed to borrow money in Egypt and pledged his credit with the merchants at a very high rate of gain so that they made 700 dinars profit on 300. Later he paid them back amply. He sent to me 500 mithqals of gold by way of honorarium.

"The currency in the land of Takrūr consists of cowries and the merchants, whose principal import these are, make big profits on them." Here ends what Ibn Amīr Ḥajib said.

From the beginning of my coming to stay in Egypt I heard talk of the arrival of this sultan Mūsā on his Pilgrimage and found the Cairenes eager to recount what they had seen of the Africans' prodigal spending. I asked the emir Abū 'l-'Abbās Aḥmad b. al-Ḥāk the *mihmandar* and he told me of the opulence, manly virtues, and piety of this sultan. "When I went out to meet him (he said), that is, on behalf of the mighty sultan al-Malik al-Nāṣir, he did me extreme honour and treated me with the greatest courtesy. He addressed me, however, only through an interpreter despite his perfect ability to speak in the Arabic tongue. Then he forwarded to the royal treasury many loads of unworked native gold and other valuables. I tried to persuade him to go up to the Citadel to meet the sultan, but he refused persistently, saying: 'I came for the Pilgrimage and nothing else. I do not wish to mix anything else with my Pilgrimage.' He had begun to use this argument but I realized that the audience was repugnant to him because he would be obliged to kiss the ground and the sultan's hand. I continued to cajole him and he continued to make excuses but the sultan's protocol demanded that I should bring

him into the royal presence, so I kept on at him till he agreed.

"When we came in the sultan's presence we said to him: 'Kiss the ground!' but he refused outright saying: 'How may this be?' Then an intelligent man who was with him whispered to him something we could not understand and he said: 'I make obeisance to God who created me!' then he prostrated himself and went forward to the sultan. The sultan half rose to greet him and sat him by his side. They conversed together for a long time, then sultan Mūsā went out. The sultan sent to him several complete suits of honour for himself, his courtiers, and all those who had come with him, and saddled and bridled horses for himself and his chief courtiers. His robe of honour consisted of an Alexandrian open-fronted cloak embellished with *ṭard waḥsh* cloth containing much gold thread and miniver fur, bordered with beaver fur and embroidered with metallic thread, along with golden fastenings, a silken skull-cap with caliphal emblems, a gold-inlaid belt, a damascened sword, a kerchief [embroidered] with pure gold, standards, and two horses saddled and bridled and equipped with decorated mule[-type] saddles. He also furnished him with accommodation and abundant supplies during his stay.

"When the time to leave for the Pilgrimage came round the sultan sent to him a large sum of money with ordinary and thoroughbred camels complete with saddles and equipment to serve as mounts for him, and purchased abundant supplies for his entourage and others who had come with him. He arranged for deposits of fodder to be placed along the road and ordered the caravan commanders to treat him with honour and respect.

"On his return I received him and supervised his accommodation. The sultan continued to supply him with provisions and lodgings and he sent gifts from the Noble Ḥijāz to the sultan as a blessing. The sultan accepted them and sent in exchange complete suits of honour for him and his courtiers together with other gifts, various kinds of Alexandrian cloth, and other precious objects. Then he returned to his country.

"This man flooded Cairo with his benefactions. He left no court emir nor holder of a royal office without the gift of a load of gold. The Cairenes made incalculable profits out of him and his suite in buying and selling and giving and taking. They exchanged gold until they depressed its value in Egypt and caused its price to fall."

The *mihmandār* spoke the truth, for more than one has told this story. When the *mihmandār* died the tax office found among the property which he left thousands of dinars' worth of native gold which he had given to him, still just as it had been in the earth, never having been worked.

Merchants of Miṣr and Cairo have told me of the profits which they made from the Africans, saying that one of them might buy a shirt or cloak or robe or other garment for five dinars when it was not worth one. Such was their simplicity and trustfulness that it was possible to practice any deception on them. They greeted anything that was said to them with credulous acceptance. But later they formed the very poorest opinion of the Egyptians because of the obvious falseness of everything they said to them and their outrageous behaviour in fixing the prices of the provisions and other goods which were sold to them, so much so that were they to encounter today the most learned doctor of religious science and he were to say that he was Egyptian they would be rude to him and view him with disfavour because of the ill treatment which they had experienced at their hands.

Muhanna' b. 'Abd al-Bāqī al-'Ujrumī the guide informed me that he accompanied sultan Mūsā when he made the Pilgrimage and that the sultan was very open-handed towards the pilgrims and the inhabitants of the Holy Places. He and his companions maintained great pomp and dressed magnificently during the journey. He gave away much wealth in alms. "About 200 mithqals of gold fell to me" said Muhanna' "and he gave other sums to my companions." Muhanna' waxed eloquent in describing the sultan's generosity, magnanimity, and opulence.

Gold was at a high price in Egypt until they came in that year. The mithqal did not go below 25 *dirhams* and was generally above, but from that time its value fell and it cheapened in price and has remained cheap till now. The mithqal does not exceed 22 *dirhams* or less. This has been the state of affairs for about twelve years until this day by reason of the large amount of gold which they brought into Egypt and spent there.

A letter came from this sultan to the court of the sultan in Cairo. It was written in the Maghribī style of handwriting on paper with wide lines. In it he follows his own rules of composition although observing the demands of propriety. It was written by the hand of one of his courtiers who had come on the Pilgrimage. Its contents comprised greetings and a recommendation for the bearer. With it he sent 5,000 mithqals of gold by way of a gift.

The countries of Mālī and Ghāna and their neighbours are reached from the west side of Upper Egypt. The route passes by way of the Oases through desert country inhabited by Arab and then Berber communities until cultivated country is reached by way of which the traveller arrives at Mālī and Ghāna. These are on the same meridian as the mountains of the Berbers to the south of Marrakech and are joined to them by long stretches of wilderness and extensive desolate deserts.

The learned faqih Abū 'l-Rūḥ 'Īsā al-Zawāwī informed me that sultan Mūsā Mansā told him that the length of his kingdom was about a year's journey, and Ibn Amīr Ḥājib told me the same. Al-Dukkālī's version, already mentioned, is that it is four months' journey long by the same in breadth. What al-Dukkālī says is more to be relied on, for Mūsā Mansā possibly exaggerated the importance of his realm.

Al-Zawāwī also said: "This sultan Mūsā told me that at a town called ZKRY he has a copper mine from which ingots are brought to BYTY. "There is nothing in my kingdom (he said) on which a duty is levied except this crude copper which is brought in. Duty is collected on this and on nothing else. We send it to the land of the pagan Sūdān and sell it for two-thirds of its weight in gold, so that we sell 100 mithqals of this copper for 66⅔ mithqals of gold." He also stated that there are pagan nations in his kingdom from whom he does not collect the tribute but whom he simply employs in extracting the gold from its deposits. The gold is extracted by digging pits about a man's height in depth and the gold is found embedded in the sides of the pits or sometimes collected at the bottom of them.

"The king of this country wages a permanently Holy War on the pagans of the Sūdān who are his neighbours. They are more numerous than could ever be counted."

REVIEW QUESTIONS

1. How do the references to religious beliefs and practices compare with those of earlier selections in this chapter?
2. What was the impression Mansa Musa made upon the traders in Cairo?
3. What exaggerations and misinformation do you find in this selection? Why do you believe it is included?
4. In what way did Mansa Musa take advantage of the wealth of his kingdom?

Two African Accounts Depict Kano (late fourteenth century) and Kanem (tenth century)

The Kano Chronicle and YAKUT, Quoting from The Lost Work of Al Muhallabi

The two excerpts in this selection present a rare glimpse into the societies located in the interior sub-Saharan regions east of the Niger River and Lake Chad. The first account depicts the introduction of Islam into Kano, a center of Hausaland, on the southeastern border of the Songhay nation in the fourteenth century. According to the Kano Chronicle (a nineteenth-century document based on records no longer extant), about forty Wangarawa brought Islam with them during the reign of Ali Yagi, who ruled Kano from 1349 to 1385. This narrative clearly demonstrates that the introduction of Islam, although eventually successful, was not unopposed at first. Nevertheless, by the reign of Muhammad Rumfa (1453–1499), Islam was so firmly rooted in Kano that some Muslim scholars came from Timbuktu to teach and preach Islam there and the king consulted Muslim scholars on the affairs of government.

The second excerpt provides information about life in Kanem, in the region around Lake Chad (today Kanem forms the northern part of the Republic of Chad). Islam was accepted for the first time by the Kanem ruler, Umme-Jilmi, who ruled from 1085 to 1097. By the thirteenth century, Kanem was the center of Muslim influence in the central Sudan. As this account relates, Kanem was not a wealthy land of gold and ivory, but an agricultural region of goats, cows, camels, wheat, and beans.

THE KANO CHRONICLE

The eleventh Sarki [king] was Yagi, called Ali. . . . In Yagi's time the Wangara came from Mali, bringing Islam. The name of their leader was Abdurahaman Zaite. . . . When they came they commanded the sarki to observe the times of prayer. He complied and made Gurdumus his imam [religious teacher], and Lawal his muezzin. Awta cut the throats of whatever flesh was eaten. Mandawali was imam of all the Wangara and of the chief men of Kano. Zaite was their Qadi. The sarki commanded every town in Kano country to observe times of prayer. So they all did so. A mosque was built beneath the sacred tree facing east, and prayers were made at the five appointed times in it. The Sarkin Garazawa was opposed to prayer, and when the Muslims after praying had gone home, he would come with his men and defile the whole mosque and cover it with filth. Dan Buji was told off to patrol round the mosque with well-armed men from evening until morning. He kept up a constant halloo. For all that, the pagans tried to win him and his men over. Some of his men followed the pagans and went away, but he and the rest refused. The defilement continued till Sheshe said to Fa Mori, "There is no cure for this but prayer." The people assented. They gathered together on a Tuesday in the mosque at the evening hour of prayer and prayed against the pagans until sunrise. They only came away when the sun was well up. Allah received graciously the prayers addressed to him. The chief of the pagans was struck blind that day, and afterward all the pagans who were present at the defilement—they and all their women. After this they were all afraid. Yagi turned the chief of the pagans out of his office and said to him, "Be thou sarki among the blind." In the days of Yagi, it is said, Sarkin Debbi, Sarkin Dab and Sarkin Geno brought horses to Kano, but this story is not worth credence.

THE LOST WORK OF AL MUHALLABI

The Zaghawa have two cities, one called Manan and the other Tarazaki. Both are in the first clime, and their latitude is 21°. The kingdom of the Zaghawa is said to be a great kingdom among the kingdoms of the Sudan. On their eastern boundary is the kingdom of the Nuba who are above Upper Egypt. Between them is a distance of ten days' journey. They are many tribes. The length of their land is fifteen days' journey through habitations and cultivations all the way. Their houses are all of gypsum, and also the castle of their king. They respect and worship him to the neglect of Allah the most High; and they falsely imagine that he does not eat food. His people provide his food secretly, bringing it into his houses without it being known whence they bring it. If anyone of his subjects happens to meet the camels carrying it, he is immediately killed on the spot. But he drinks in the presence of the chiefs among his companions. His drink is made from Dhura strengthened with honey. His costume is full trousers of thin wool, and he is wrapped round with fine robes of unlined wool, of silk from silk worms, and of delicate brocade. He has absolute power over his subjects, and appropriates what he will of their belongings. Their cattle are goats and cows and camels and horses. Dhura chiefly is cultivated in their land, and beans; also wheat. Most of the ordinary people are naked, covering themselves with skins. Their livelihood is in cultivation and breeding cattle; and their religion is the worship of their kings, believing it is they who bring life and death and sickness and health. From the towns of Bilma and Qusba in the land of Kawar it lies southeast.

REVIEW QUESTIONS

1. What similarities and differences do you find in these two excerpts?
2. From these accounts by tenth- and fourteenth-century Muslim travelers, what impression do you receive of the depth of religious conversion? How might the travelers have misunderstood the situation?
3. From other accounts in this chapter, how did the culture of these two groups compare with those on the east and west coasts of Africa?

A Portuguese Explorer Portrays Life in Africa (1497–1499)

VASCO DA GAMA, *A Journal of the First Voyage of Vasco da Gama*

Vasco da Gama (1469–1524) is responsible, more than any other single figure, for initiating the rich trade between Asia and the West when he became the first European to reach India by sea. Even before he won fame as an explorer, Vasco da Gama had been an experienced seaman and was a favorite at the Portuguese court of King Manuel I. So, when the king decided that Portugal needed to establish a sea route to India, he named da Gama as the expedition's commander. For more than half a century Portuguese sailors had ventured down the west coast of Africa, and in 1488 Bartholomew Diaz rounded the southern tip of Africa and sailed a short distance along the eastern coast. In the meantime Spain, Portugal's most important rival, had sent Columbus across the Atlantic. News of Columbus's voyage and subsequent discoveries suddenly made the Portuguese king eager to find a shorter route to the riches of Asia. This, King Manuel believed, could best be done by sailing around Africa and then eastward. He had an expedition fitted out and asked da Gama to command it. Thus, on July 8, 1497, da Gama sailed from Lisbon with four ships and a crew of about 170 men. For almost five months the expedition sailed steadily south. On November 22, da Gama rounded the Cape of Good Hope, then headed north and stopped at such trading centers as Mozambique, Mombasa, and Malindi, Kenya. Arab traders in Mozambique and Mombasa hated the Portuguese and tried to seize da Gama's ships. The people at Malindi, however, were more friendly, and a group of Indian merchants agreed to supply a guide and pilot to lead the fleet to India. On May 20, 1498, da Gama reached Calicut, India. In the following selection, da Gama recounts some of his experiences in the area around Mozambique.

On Friday [December 1], whilst still in the bay of Sam Brás, about ninety men resembling those we had met at St. Helena Bay made their appearance. Some of them walked along the beach, whilst others remained upon the hills. All, or most of us, were at the time in the captain-major's vessel. As soon as we saw them we launched and armed the boats, and started for the land. When close to the shore the captain-major threw them little round bells, which they picked up. They even ventured to approach us, and took some of these bells from the captain-major's hand. This surprised us greatly, for when Bartholomeu Dias* was here the natives fled without taking any of the objects which he offered them. Nay, on one occasion, when Dias was taking in water, close to the beach, they sought to prevent him, and when they pelted him with stones, from a hill, he killed one of them with the arrow of a cross-bow. It appeared to us that they did not fly on this occasion, because they had heard from the people at the bay of St. Helena (only sixty leagues distant by sea) that there was no harm in us, and that we even gave away things which were ours.

The captain-major did not land at this spot, because there was much bush, but proceeded to an open part of the beach, when he made signs to the negroes to approach. This they did. The captain-major and the other captains then landed, being attended by armed men, some of whom carried cross-bows. He then made the negroes understand, by signs, that they were to disperse, and to approach him only singly or in couples. To those who approached he gave small bells and red caps, in return for which they presented him with ivory bracelets, such as they wore on their arms, for it appears that elephants are plentiful in this country. We actually found some of their droppings near the watering place where they had gone to drink.

On Saturday [December 2] about two hundred negroes came, both young and old. They brought with them about a dozen oxen and cows and four or five sheep. As soon as we saw them we sent ashore. They forthwith began to play on four or five flutes,† some producing high notes and others low ones, thus making a pretty harmony for negroes who are not expected to be musicians; and they danced in the style of negroes.

The captain-major then ordered the trumpets to be sounded, and we, in the boats, danced, and the captain-major did so likewise when he rejoined us. This festivity ended, we landed where we had landed before, and bought a black ox for three bracelets. This ox we dined off on Sunday. We found him very fat, and his meat as toothsome as the beef of Portugal.

On Sunday [December 3] many visitors came, and brought with them their women and little boys, the women remaining on the top of a hill near the sea. They had with them many oxen and cows. Having collected in two spots on the beach, they played and danced as they had done on Saturday. It is the custom of this people for the young men to remain in the bush with their weapons. The [older] men came to converse with us. They carried a short stick in the hand, attached to which was a fox's tail, with which they fan the face. Whilst conversing with them, by signs, we observed the young men crouching in the bush, holding their weapons in their hands. The captain-major then ordered Martin Affonso, who had formerly been in Manicongo [Congo] to advance, and to buy an ox, for which purpose he was supplied with bracelets. The natives, having accepted the bracelets, took him by the hand, and, pointing to the watering place, asked him why we took away their water, and simultaneously drove their cattle into the bush. When the captain-major observed this he ordered us to gather together, and called upon Martin Affonso to retreat, for he suspected some treachery. Having drawn together we proceeded [in our boats] to the place where we had been at first. The negroes followed us. The captain-major then ordered us to land, armed with lances, assegais, and strung cross-bows, and wearing our breastplates, for he wanted to show that we had the means of doing them an injury, although we had no desire to employ them. When they observed this they ran away. The captain-major, anxious that none should be killed by mischance, ordered the boats to draw together; but to prove that we were able, although unwilling to hurt them, he ordered two bombards to be fired from the poop of the long boat. They were by that

---

*Bartholomeu Dias, a Portuguese navigator and explorer, led the first European expedition to round the Cape of Good Hope in 1488, opening the sea route to Asia via the Atlantic and Indian oceans.
†The "gora" is the great musical instrument of the Hottentots.

time all seated close to the bush, not far from the beach, but the first discharge caused them to retreat so precipitately that in their flight they dropped the skins with which they were covered and their weapons. When they were in the bush two of them turned back to pick up the articles which had been dropped. They then continued their flight to the top of a hill, driving their cattle before them.

The oxen of this country are as large as those of Alemtejo,* wonderfully fat and very tame. They are geldings, and hornless. Upon the fattest among them the negroes place a packsaddle made of reeds, as is done in Castille, and upon this saddle they place a kind of litter made of sticks, upon which they ride. If they wish to sell an ox they pass a stick through his nostrils, and thus lead him.

There is an island in this bay, three bowshots from the land, where there are many seals. Some of these are as big as bears, very formidable, with large tusks. These attack man, and no spear, whatever the force with which it is thrown, can wound them. There are others much smaller and others quite small. And whilst the big ones roar like lions, the little ones cry like goats. One day, when we approached this island for our amusement, we counted, among large and small ones, three thousand, and we fired among them with our bombards from the sea. On the same island there are birds as big as ducks, but they cannot fly, because they have no feathers on their wings. These birds, of whom we killed as many as we chose, are called Fotylicayos, and they bray like asses.

Whilst taking in water in this bay of Sam Brás, on a Wednesday, we erected a cross and a pillar. The cross was made out of a mizzen-mast, and very high. On the following Thursday [December 7], when about to set sail, we saw about ten or twelve negroes, who demolished both the cross and the pillar before we had left. . . .

On Friday morning [March 2] Nicolau Coelho, when attempting to enter the bay, mistook the channel and came upon a bank. When putting about ship, towards the other ships which followed in his wake, Coelho perceived some sailing boats approaching from a village on this island, in order to welcome the captain-major and his brother. As for ourselves we continued in the direction of our proposed anchorage, these boats following us all the while, and making signs for us to stop. When we had cast anchor in the roadstead of the island from which these boats had come, there approached seven or eight of them, including *almadias,* the people in them playing upon *anafils.* They invited us to proceed further into the bay, offering to take us into port if we desired it. Those among them who boarded our ships ate and drank what we did, and went their way when they were satisfied.

The captain thought that we should enter this bay in order that we might find out what sort of people we had to deal with; that Nicolau Coelho should go first in his vessel, to take soundings at the entrance, and that, if found practicable, we should follow him. As Coelho prepared to enter he struck the point of the island and broke his helm, but he immediately disengaged himself and regained deep water. I was with him at the time. When we were again in deep water we struck our sails and cast anchor at a distance of two bowshots from the village.

The people of this country are of a ruddy complexion and well made. They are Mohammedans, and their language is the same as that of the Moors. Their dresses are of fine linen or cotton stuffs, with variously coloured stripes, and of rich and elaborate workmanship. They all wear *toucas* with borders of silk embroidered in gold. They are merchants, and have transactions with white Moors, four of whose vessels were at the time in port, laden with gold, silver, cloves, pepper, ginger, and silver rings, as also with quantities of pearls, jewels, and rubies, all of which articles are used by the people of this country. We understood them to say that all these things, with the exception of the gold, were brought thither by these Moors; that further on, where we were going to, they abounded, and that precious stones, pearls and spices were so plentiful

---

*Alemtejo is a province in southeastern Portugal.

that there was no need to purchase them as they could be collected in baskets. All this we learned through a sailor the captain-major had with him, and who, having formerly been a prisoner among the Moors, understood their language.

These Moors, moreover, told us that along the route which we were about to follow we should meet with numerous shoals; that there were many cities along the coast, and also an island, one half the population of which consisted of Moors and the other half of Christians, who were at war with each other. This island was said to be very wealthy.

We were told, moreover, that Prester John* resided not far from this place; that he held many cities along the coast, and that the inhabitants of those cities were great merchants and owned big ships. The residence of Prester John was said to be far in the interior, and could be reached only on the back of camels. These Moors had also brought hither two Christian captives from India. This information, and many other things which we heard, rendered us so happy that we cried with joy, and prayed God to grant us health, so that we might behold what we so much desired.

In this place and island of Moncobiquy [Moçambique] there resided a chief [senhor] who had the title of Sultan, and was like a vice-roy. He often came aboard our ships attended by some of his people. The captain-major gave him many good things to eat, and made him a present of hats, *marlotas,* corals and many other articles. He was, however, so proud that he treated all we gave him with contempt, and asked for scarlet cloth, of which we had none. We gave him, however, of all the things we had.

One day the captain-major invited him to a repast, when there was an abundance of figs and comfits, and begged him for two pilots to go with us. He at once granted this request, subject to our coming to terms with them. The captain-major gave each of them thirty mitkals in gold

*"Prester John" was the legendary Christian ruler of the East, popularized in medieval chronicles and traditions as a potential ally against African Muslims.

and two *marlotas,* on condition that from the day on which they received this payment one of them should always remain on board if the other desired to go on land. With these terms they were well satisfied.

On Saturday, March 10, we set sail and anchored one league out at sea, close to an island, where mass was said on Sunday, when those who wished to do so confessed and joined in the communion.

One of our pilots lived on the island, and when we had anchored we armed two boats to go in search of him. The captain-major went in one boat and Nicolau Coelho in the other. They were met by five or six boats (barcas) coming from the island, and crowded with people armed with bows and long arrows and bucklers, who gave them to understand by signs that they were to return to the town. When the captain saw this he secured the pilot whom he had taken with him, and ordered the bombards to fire upon the boats. Paulo da Gama, who had remained with the ships, so as to be prepared to render succour in case of need, no sooner heard the reports of the bombards than he started in the *Berrio.* The Moors, who were already flying, fled still faster, and gained the land before the *Berrio* was able to come up with them. We then returned to our anchorage.

The vessels of this country are of good size and decked. There are no nails, and the planks are held together by cords, as are also those of their boats (barcos). The sails are made of palm-matting. Their mariners have Genoese needles [mariner's compasses], by which they steer, quadrants, and navigating charts.

The palms of this country yield a fruit as large as a melon, of which the kernel is eaten. It has a nutty flavour. There also grow in abundance melons and cucumbers, which were brought to us for barter.

On the day in which Nicolau Coelho entered the port, the Lord of the place came on board with a numerous suite. He was received well, and Coelho presented him with a red hood, in return for which the Lord handed him a black rosary, which he made use of when saying his prayers, to be held as a pledge. He then begged Nicolau Coelho for the use of his boat, to take him ashore. This was granted. And after he had landed he invited those who had accompanied him to his house, where he gave them to eat. He then dismissed them, giving them a jar of bruised dates made into a preserve with cloves and cumin, as a present for Nicolau Coelho. Sub-sequently he sent many things to the captain-major. All this happened at the time when he took us for Turks or for Moors from some for-eign land, for in case we came from Turkey he begged to be shown the bows of our country and our books of the Law. But when they learnt that we were Christians they arranged to seize and kill us by treachery. The pilot, whom we took with us, subsequently revealed to us all they in-tended to do, if they were able.

REVIEW QUESTIONS

1. Compare the reactions of the Europeans to the various native groups they encountered with the reactions of the native to the Europeans. What generalizations would you make about both groups?
2. Compare this account with the one given by Al-Mas'udi on the ivory trade. How are they similar? How are they different?
3. Compare this account with the one given by Buzurg Ibn Shahriyar of Ramhormuz. How are they similar? How are they different?
4. How did the natives that da Gama encountered respond to the gifts and trading goods brought by the Portuguese? What does this tell us about African societies?

A Portuguese Priest Describes Ethiopia (1520) and Axum (sixteenth century)

FRANCISCO ALVARES, *A True Relation of the Lands of the Prester John*

In 1520 a Portuguese expedition searched for the fabled court of Prester John in the East African kingdom of Ethiopia. An ambassador from Portugal, Dom Rodrigo de Lima, and thirteen others also hoped to find Christian allies against the Muslim world in this area of Africa. This large entourage remained in the lands of the Emperor Lebna Dengel for six years. One member of the expedi-tion, Francisco Alvares, wrote the only eye-witness account of Ethiopia dur-ing the late medieval era. The two excerpts that follow present Alvares's description of the Ethiopian court and of Aksum (Axum), the ancient capital of Ethiopia, before the invasions in the second half of the sixteenth century from Somali and Galla, to the south and east.

By the time this Portuguese expedition arrived, the Christian organiza-tion of the region was over one thousand years old, but it was an outpost of Christianity surrounded by Muslim peoples and Islamic governments in nearby states, such as Nubia to the north. Christian and Muslim peoples lived and traded with each other in a very beneficial manner except for such inter-regnums as the crusading era of the eleventh and twelfth centuries. Now, however, the Portuguese were systematically usurping Arab-Muslim trade along the Swahili coast, as seen in other selections in this chapter, especially that of Vasco da Gama. Consequently, the expedition of Rodrigo de Lima may have coincided with the Portugese crown's intention of driving all Islamic traders and influences from East Africa.

On Tuesday we were all summoned—that is to say, the ambassador and those who were with him; we went and stayed before the first gate or entrance a good three hours; it was very cold indeed and quite night. We passed through the enclosures as we had done twice before. There were many more people assembled than on any of the other times, and many with arms, and many more lighted candles before the gates; and they did not detain us there long, but soon bade us enter with the ambassador, nine Portuguese, beyond the curtains. Beyond these first curtains we found others still richer, and they bade us pass through these also. Having passed these last we found a large and rich dais with very splendid carpets. In front of this dais were other curtains of much greater splendor, and while we were standing before them they opened them, for they were drawn together, and there we saw the Prester John sitting on a platform of six steps very richly adorned. He had on his head a high crown of gold and silver—that is to say, one piece of gold and another of silver from the top downward, and a silver cross in his hand; there was a piece of blue taffeta before his face which covered his mouth and beard, and from time to time they lowered it and the whole of his face appeared, and again they raised it. At his right hand he had a page dressed in silk, with a flat silver cross in his hand, with figures carved in it with a burin; from where we stood it was not possible to make out these figures on the cross, but I saw it later, and saw the figures. The Prester was dressed in a rich mantle of gold bro-cade, and silk shirts of wide sleeves which looked like *pelotes*.[1] From his knees downward he had a

rich cloth of silk and gold well spread out like a bishop's apron, and he was sitting in majesty as they paint God the Father on the wall. Besides the page with the cross, there stood on each side of him another, dressed in the same way, each with a drawn sword in his hand. In age, com-plexion, and stature, he is a young man, not very black. His complexion might be chestnut or bay, not very dark in color; he is very much a man of breeding, of middling stature; they said that he was twenty-three years of age, and he looks like that. His face is round, the eyes large, the nose high in the middle, and his beard is be-ginning to grow. In presence and state he fully looks like the great lord that he is. We were about two lances distant from him. Messages came and went all through the *cabeata*.[2] On each side of the platform were four pages richly dressed, each with lighted candles in their hands. When the questions and answers were ended, the am-bassador gave to the *cabeata* the letters and in-structions of the captain major, put into their letters and language; and he gave them to the Prester, who read them very speedily. . . .

Amongst these peaks, between which we were still going, to the west are wonderful lands and very great lordships, among which is a very great town named Aksum, and it is two days' journey from the town of St. Michael, always between these peaks. We stayed in it for eight months by order of the Prester John. This town was the city, court, and residence of the Queen Sheba, who took the camels laden with gold to Solomon, when he was building the temple of Jerusalem. There is in this town a very noble church, in which we found a very long chronicle

---

[1] Jerkins.

[2] The highest court official who arranged the councils.

written in the language of the country, and it stated at the very beginning that it had been written first in Hebrew, and afterward put into Greek, and from Greek into Chaldean, and from Chaldean into Abyssinian, which it now is, and it begins thus:

How the Queen Sheba hearing related the great and rich buildings which Solomon had begun in Jerusalem, determined to go and see them; and she loaded camels with gold to give for these buildings. And on arriving near the city, and being about to cross a lake, which they passed by a bridge of boats, she dismounted and worshipped the beams and said: "Please God my feet shall not touch the timber on which the Saviour of the world has to hang." And she went round the lake, and went to see Solomon, and begged him to take away those beams from there, and she came to the buildings, and offered her gifts and said: "These buildings are not such as they told me in richness and beauty, because their beauty and richness has no equal, so that they are greater than what was related to me, so much so that the tongues of men cannot tell their nobility and richness, and much I grieve for the small gift which I brought. I will return to my countries and lordships, and I will send whatever abounds for the buildings, of gold, and black wood to inlay." While she was at Jerusalem Solomon had intercourse with her, and she became pregnant of a son, and remained at Jerusalem until she gave birth. After she was able to travel she left her son and returned to her country, and sent from it much gold and black wood to inlay the buildings. And her son grew up to the age of seventeen years, and among the many sons that Solomon had, this one was so proud that he affronted the people of Israel, and all the country of Judea. And the people came to Solomon and said to him: "We are not able to maintain so many kings as you have got, for all your sons are kings, especially this one of Queen Sheba; she is a greater lady than you; send him to his mother, for we are not able to maintain him." Then Solomon sent him very honorably, giving him the officers that are usual in a king's household, and besides, he gave him, in order

that he might rest on the road, the country of Gaza, which is in Egypt; and he made his journey to the country of his mother, where he was a great ruler. The chronicle says that he ruled from sea to sea, and that he had sixty ships in the Indian sea. This book of chronicles is very large, and I copied only the beginning.

In this town of Aksum was the principal residence of Queen Candace who was the beginning of the country's being Christian. She was born (as they say) half a league from here, in a very small village, which now is entirely of blacksmiths. The beginning of her being Christian was this. According to what they say in their books, the angel said to Philip: "Rise and go toward the south, by the road which goes from Jerusalem to Gaza, the desert." St. Philip went and met with a man who was a eunuch, and he was majordomo of the Queen Candace, ruler of Ethiopia. In the country of Gaza, which Solomon had given to his son, this man was the keeper of all the riches of the queen, and he had been to Jerusalem and was returning to his house, and he was going on a chariot. St. Philip came up to him, and heard him sing a prophecy of Isaiah, and asked him how he understood what he was singing. He replied that he did not know, unless some other man taught him. St. Philip mounted into the chariot, and went on explaining to him that prophecy, and converted him, and baptized and instructed him in the faith. Then the Spirit snatched away St. Philip, and he was perfectly instructed. They say that here was fulfilled the prophecy which David spoke: "Ethiopia shall arise, and stretch forth her hands to God." So they say they were the first Christians in the world. The eunuch at once set out very joyfully for Ethiopia, where was the house of his mistress, and converted her and all her household, and baptized them in consequence of what he related to them. And the queen caused all her kingdom, beginning with a kingdom which is now called the kingdom of Buno, to be baptized. This Buno is toward the east from the town of Aksum in the kingdom of the Barnagais, and it is now two lordships. In this town of Aksum, where she became Christian, she built a very noble church, the first there was in Ethiopia: it is named St. Mary of Zion. They say that it is so named because its altar stone came from Zion. In this country they have the custom always to name the churches by the altar stone, because on it is written the name of the patron saint. This stone which they have in this church, they say that the Apostles sent it from Mount Zion. This church is very large. It has five aisles of good width and of great length, vaulted above, and all the vaults closed; the ceiling and sides are painted. Below, the body of the church is well worked with handsome cut stones; it has seven chapels, all with their backs to the east, and their altars well ornamented. It has a choir after our fashion, except that it is low, and they reach the vaulted roof with their heads; and the choir is also over the vault, and they do not use it. This church has a very large circuit, paved with flagstones like the lids of tombs. This consists of a very high wall, and it is not covered over like those of the other churches, but it is left open. This church has a large enclosure, and it is also surrounded by another larger enclosure, like the enclosing wall of a large town or city. Within this enclosure are handsome groups of one-story buildings, and all spout out their water by strong figures of lions and dogs of stone. Inside this large enclosure there are two mansions, one on the right hand and the other on the left, which belong to two rectors of the church: and the other houses are of canons and monks. In the large enclosure, at the gate nearest the church, there is a large ruin, built in a square, which in other times was a house, and it has at each corner a big stone pillar, squared and worked. This house is called Ambacabete, which means house of lions. They say that in this house were the captive lions, and there are still some always traveling, and there go before the Prester John four captive lions. Before the gate of this great enclosure there is a large court, and in it a large tree, which they call Pharaoh's fig tree, and at each end of it there are some very new looking pedestals of masonry well worked, laid down. Only where they reach near the foot of the fig tree, they are injured by the roots,

which raise them up. There are, on the top of these pedestals, twelve stone chairs as well made with stone as though they were of wood, with their seats and rests for the feet. They are not made out of a block, but each one from its own stone and separate piece. They say these belong to the twelve judges who at this time serve in the court of the Prester John. Outside this enclosure there is a large town of very good houses, such that there are none like them in the whole of Ethiopia, and very good wells of water, of worked masonry, and also in most of the houses the before-mentioned ancient figures of lions, dogs, and birds, all well made in stone. At the back of this great church is a very handsome tank of masonry, and upon this masonry are as many other chairs of stone, such as those in the enclosure of the church. This town is situated at the head of a beautiful plain, and almost between two hills, and the rest of this plain is almost all full of these old buildings, and among them many of these chairs, and high pillars with inscriptions. Above this town there are many stones standing up, and others on the ground, very large and beautiful, and worked with beautiful designs, among which is one raised upon another, and worked like an altar stone, except that it is of very great size, and it is set in the other as if enchased.

Above this town, on a hill which overlooks much distant country, and which is about a mile, that is the third of a league, from the town, there are two houses under the ground, into which men do not enter without a lamp. These houses are not vaulted, but of very good straight masonry, both the walls and the roof. The blocks are free on the outside; the walls may be twelve *covados* high; the blocks are set in the wall so close one to the other, that it all looks like one stone. One of these houses is much divided into chambers and granaries; in the doorways are holes for the bars and for the sockets of the doors. In one of these chambers are two very large chests, each one four *covados* in length, and one and a half broad, and as much in overall height, and in the upper part on the inner side they are hollowed at the edge, as though they had lids of stone, as the chests also are of stone. (They say they were the treasure chests of Queen Sheba. . . .) There were in our company Genoese and Catalans, who had been prisoners of the Turks, and they affirmed and swore that they had seen Troy, and the granary of Joseph in the kingdom of Egypt, and that their buildings were very large, but that these of this town were and are altogether much larger, and it seemed to us that the Prester John had sent us here, in order that we should see these buildings, and we had rejoiced at seeing them, as they are much greater than what I write. . . .

As they say the church of Aksum is the most ancient, so it is the most revered of all Ethiopia: and the services are well conducted in it. In this church there are one hundred and fifty canons, and as many monks. It has two head men, one is named *nebrete* of the canons, which means teacher, and the other *nebrete* of the monks. These two heads reside in the palaces which are within the great enclosure and circuit of the church: and the *nebrete* of the canons lodges at the right hand, and he is the principal one, and the more respected. He has jurisdiction over the canons and the laity of all this country: and the *nebrete* of the monks only hears and rules the monks. Both use kettle-drums and trumpets. They have very large revenues, and besides their revenues they have every day a collation which they call *maabar* of bread and wine of the country, when mass is finished. The monks have this by themselves, and the canons also, and this *maabar* is such that the monks seldom eat other food than that. They have this every day except Friday of the Passion, because on that day no one eats or drinks. The canons do not take their *maabar* within the circuit of the church, and are seldom there, except at fixed hours, neither is the *nebrete* in his palace, except at some chance time when he goes to hear cases. This is because they are married, and live with their wives and children in their houses, which are very good and which are outside. Neither women nor laymen go into the enclosure of this church, and they do not go in to receive the communion. On account of their being married, and because the women do not enter the circuit, they take their *maabar* outside, so that their wives and children may enjoy it.

REVIEW QUESTIONS

1. Do you believe that Alvares was impressed by what he saw at the Ethiopian court? In Axum? Why or why not?
2. How does the attitude of Alvares toward the Ethiopians differ from that expressed by Vasco da Gama in his logbook?
3. What similarities and differences do you find between the descriptions of people in the court of the emperor of Ethiopia and that of Al-Mas'udi in the land of the Zanj?

12

South and Southwest Asia, 800–1500

For centuries South Asia has been a focal point for religious and cultural conflict, as well as for innovation. In the *New York Times,* February 22, 2002, an article by Celia Dugger quoted an Islamic scholar who noted, "Everybody thinks of Islam as Arab, but you have to pay attention to Islam in South Asia." Indeed, Islamic contact with South Asia goes back to 711, when an eighteen-year-old general was dispatched from Baghdad to punish local rajas in the Sindh area (near the mouth of the Indus) for not intercepting pirates who had kidnapped widows and children of Arab traders from southwest India and Sri Lanka (Ceylon). The Hindu populace did not react with animosity but, on the contrary, seemed to be relieved with the removal of their overlords. Subsequent contacts, in the forms of invasion and conquest, were not as happy. The contacts and clashes, sometimes almost unbelievably violent, have continued into the twenty-first century. Meanwhile, the Portuguese, with the appearance of Vasco da Gama off the southwest coast in 1498 (led, it should be noted, by a Muslim pilot), added yet other ingredients: strident European mercantilism and Christianity.

This chapter includes accounts of India by several sophisticated Muslims. Alberuni, who entered India with invaders, came to appreciate Indian learning—especially in regard to science—but disapproved of the Hindu culture and religion that are at its core. In contrast is another learned Muslim, Ibn Battuta, perhaps the greatest traveler of his era, who became an actual participant in Indian society, albeit among the governing Islamic elite. Amir Khusrau, who is buried in a shrine in Delhi, was the father of Urdu poetry (a true cultural, linguistic, and literary amalgam of the Central Asian Muslim conquerors and the Hindu populace), and he thought of himself as Indian. His amazing attitude allowed him to go beyond his Persian literary heritage and Muslim culture. But he was most certainly not the only Indian Muslim to feel adamantly Indian: among the many Muslim freedom fighters who identified themselves as Indian and not Pakistani were Maulana Azad and Zakir Husain, who later became president of free India (1967–1969). In the *New York Times* article previously cited, a twenty-year-old Muslim, in spite of communal tensions and attacks, "did not hesitate" to declare that "India is our Motherland." This attachment may well be traced back to Amir Khusrau.

The chapter also includes a selection by a missionary. Even before the dramatic arrival of Vasco da Gama, Western Christian missionaries had made their way into India. The apostle Thomas is considered the founder of the Syrian Church—by far the oldest Christian church in India—and was allegedly martyred in south India. Friar Jordanus shows in his selection that he wanted to propagate the faith, but he failed to recognize the differences among Indian religions, thus foreshadowing the general European apathy toward the cultural and ethnic variety within India. Europeans viewed all Indians, indeed, all peoples of South Asia, simply as non-Western and non-Christian. Hindu spirituality was seen as incorrect, and thus irrelevant; this was perhaps the greatest failure and insult of the British Raj.

One selection does not describe a journey from west to east, but from east to west. Cheng-Ho (Zheng He) led an armada of huge ships from China through the Southeast Asian seas to Africa and back, with visits at ports in South Asia. Although the purpose of the venture was to obtain tribute and acknowledgment of Chinese superiority and, at times, suzerainty, the Chinese respected the Asian peoples and their cultures, in sharp contrast to the Europeans who were to arrive just a few decades later. One wonders what might have occurred had the Chinese continued westward and met the Portuguese coming around the Cape of Good Hope.

The chapter concludes with another selection by Vasco da Gama, who succeeded where Columbus had failed. Da Gama followed a general plan going back to Henry the Navigator: go around Africa. He also carried with him the attitude represented by Friar Jordanus (and by Columbus as well): a sense of superiority, with little if any interest in Indian culture. He was a harbinger of the age of imperialism in India, and indeed in Asia. The Portuguese remained in India until they were expelled in December of 1961—over fourteen years after the British had left. Yet, what developed in their territory of Goa was an almost romantic blend of East and West, with Roman Catholic descendants today playing major roles in the government of the secular but largely Hindu India.

A Muslim Scholar from Central Asia Studies Hindu Society (1017)

ALBERUNI, *Alberuni's India*

One of the most respected outside observers of medieval India was Alberuni (Abu Rayhan Biruni), a central Asian in the service of Sultan Mahmud of Ghazni (near Kabul). From about 1000 to his death in 1030 Mahmud made a series of raids into India at harvest time, destroying Hindu temples and carrying golden idols back to Ghazni. In 1017 he employed Alberuni to accompany the raids in order to study Hindus and to "discuss with them questions of religion, science, and literature, in the very basis of their civilization." These studies continued until Mahmud's death, after which nothing more is heard of Alberuni.

In addition to Hindu society and religion, Alberuni was especially interested in Indian science and mathematics. A scientist himself with knowledge of Arabic, Greek, and Sanskrit, his approach to his studies was that of a scholar. To a remarkable degree he overcame cultural and religious barriers. Although Islamic studies in that period tended to view non-Muslim societies and their fields of learning negatively, Muslim scholars and universities helped preserve knowledge from the ancient Greco-Roman world. Similarly, Alberuni made possible the dissemination of ancient Indian scholarship, through the Arabs, to the West.

ON THE HINDUS IN GENERAL, AS AN INTRODUCTION TO OUR ACCOUNT OF THEM

Before entering on our exposition, we must form an adequate idea of that which renders it so particularly difficult to penetrate to the essential nature of any Indian subject. The knowledge of these difficulties will either facilitate the progress of our work, or serve as an apology for any shortcomings of ours. For the reader must always bear in mind that the Hindus entirely differ from us in every respect, many a subject appearing intricate and obscure which would be perfectly clear if there were more connection between us. The barriers which separate Muslims and Hindus rest on different causes.

First, they differ from us in everything which other nations have in common. And here we first mention the language, although the difference of language also exists between other nations. If you want to conquer this difficulty (*i.e.* to learn Sanskrit), you will not find it easy, because the language is of an enormous range, both in words and inflections, something like the Arabic, calling one and the same thing by various names, both original and derived, and using one and the same word for a variety of subjects, which, in order to be properly understood, must be distinguished from each other by various qualifying epithets. For nobody could distinguish between the various meanings of a word unless he understands the context in which it occurs, and its relation both to the following and the preceding parts of the sentence. The Hindus, like other people, boast of this enormous range of their language, whilst in reality it is a defect.

Further, the language is divided into a neglected vernacular one, only in use among the common people, and a classical one, only in use among the upper and educated classes, which is much cultivated, and subject to the rules of grammatical inflection and etymology, and to all the niceties of grammar and rhetoric.

Besides, some of the sounds (consonants) of which the language is composed are neither identical with the sounds of Arabic and Persian, nor resemble them in any way. Our tongue and uvula could scarcely manage to correctly pronounce them, nor our ears in hearing to distinguish them from similar sounds, nor could we transliterate them with our characters. It is very difficult, therefore, to express an Indian word in our writing, for in order to fix the pronunciation we must change our orthographical points and signs, and must pronounce the case-endings either according to the common Arabic rules or according to special rules adapted for the purpose.

Add to this that the Indian scribes are careless, and do not take pains to produce correct and well-collated copies. In consequence, the highest results of the author's mental development are lost by their negligence, and his book becomes already in the first or second copy so full of faults, that the text appears as something entirely new, which neither a scholar nor one familiar with the subject, whether Hindu or Muslim, could any longer understand. It will sufficiently illustrate the matter if we tell the reader that we have sometimes written down a word from the mouth of Hindus, taking the greatest pains to fix its pronunciation, and that afterwards when we repeated it to them, they had great difficulty in recognising it.

As in other foreign tongues, so also in Sanskrit, two or three consonants may follow each other without an intervening vowel—consonants which in our Persian grammatical system are considered as having a *hidden* vowel. Since most Sanskrit words and names begin with such consonants without vowels, we find it very difficult to pronounce them.

Besides, the scientific books of the Hindus are composed in various favourite metres, by which they intend, considering that the books soon become corrupted by additions and omissions, to preserve them exactly as they are, in order to facilitate their being learned by heart, because they consider as canonical only that which is known by heart, not that which exists in writing. Now it is well known that in all metrical compositions there is much misty and constrained phraseology merely intended to fill up the metre and serving as a kind of patchwork, and this necessitates a certain amount of verbosity. This is also one of the reasons why a word has sometimes one meaning and sometimes another.

From all this it will appear that the metrical form of literary composition is one of the causes which make the study of Sanskrit literature so particularly difficult.

Secondly, they totally differ from us in religion, as we believe in nothing in which they believe, and *vice versâ.* On the whole, there is very little disputing about theological topics among themselves; at the utmost, they fight with words, but they will never stake their soul or body or their property on religious controversy. On the contrary, all their fanaticism is directed against those who do not belong to them— against all foreigners. They call them *mleccha, i.e.,* impure, and forbid having any connection with them, be it by intermarriage or any other kind of relationship, or by sitting, eating, and drinking with them, because thereby, they think, they would be polluted. They consider as impure anything which touches the fire and the water of a foreigner; and no household can exist without these two elements. Besides, they never desire that a thing which once has been polluted should be purified and thus recovered, as, under ordinary circumstances, if anybody or anything has become unclean, he or it would strive to regain the state of purity. They are not allowed to receive anybody who does not belong to them, even if he wished it, or was inclined to their religion. This, too, renders any connection with them quite impossible, and constitutes the widest gulf between us and them.

In the third place, in all manners and usages they differ from us to such a degree as to frighten their children with us, with our dress, and our ways and customs, and as to declare us to be devil's breed, and our doings as the very opposite of all that is good and proper. By the bye, we must confess, in order to be just, that a sim-

ilar depreciation of foreigners not only prevails among us and the Hindus, but is common to all nations towards each other. I recollect a Hindu who wreaked his vengeance on us for the following reason:—

Some Hindu king had perished at the hand of an enemy of his who had marched against him from our country. After his death there was born a child to him, which succeeded him, by the name of Sagara. On coming of age, the young man asked his mother about his father, and then she told him what had happened. Now he was inflamed with hatred, marched out of his country into the country of the enemy, and plentifully satiated his thirst of vengeance upon them. After having become tired of slaughtering, he compelled the survivors to dress in our dress, which was meant as an ignominious punishment for them. When I heard of it, I felt thankful that he was gracious enough not to compel us to Indianise ourselves and to adopt Hindu dress and manners.

Another circumstance which increased the already existing antagonism between Hindus and foreigners is that the so-called Shamaniyya (Buddhists), though they cordially hate the Brahmans, still are nearer akin to them than to others. In former times, Khurâsân, Persis, 'Irâḵ, Mosul, the country up to the frontier of Syria, was Buddhistic, but then Zarathustra went forth from Âdharbaijân and preached Magism in Balkh (Baktra). His doctrine came into favour with King Gushtasp, and his son Isfendiyâd spread the new faith both in east and west, both by force and by treaties. He founded fire-temples through his whole empire, from the frontiers of China to those of the Greek empire. The succeeding kings made their religion (*i.e.* Zoroastrianism) the obligatory state-religion for Persis and 'Irâḵ. In consequence, the Buddhists were banished from those countries, and had to emigrate to the countries east of Balkh. There are some Magians up to the present time in India, where they are called *Maga.* From that time dates their aversion towards the countries of Khurâsân. But then came Islam; the Persian empire perished, and the repugnance of the Hindus against foreigners increased more and more when the Muslims began to make their inroads into their country; for Muḥammad Ibn Elk̲âsim Ibn Elmunabbih entered Sindh from the side of Sijistân (Sakastene) and conquered the cities of Bahmanwâ and Mûlasthâna, the former of which he called *Al-manṣûra,* the latter *Al-ma'mûra.* He entered India proper, and penetrated even as far as Kanauj, marched through the country of Grandhâra, and on his way back, through the confines of Kashmîr, sometimes fighting sword in hand, sometimes gaining his ends by treaties, leaving to the people their ancient belief, except in the case of those who wanted to become Muslims. All these events planted a deeply rooted hatred in their hearts.

Now in the following times no Muslim conqueror passed beyond the frontier of Kâbul and the river Sindh until the days of the Turks, when they seized the power in Ghazna under the Sâmânî dynasty, and the supreme power fell to the lot of Nâṣir-addaula Sabuktagîn. This prince chose the holy war as his calling, and therefore called himself *Al-ghâzî* (i.e., *warring on the road of Allah*). In the interest of his successors he constructed, in order to weaken the Indian frontier, those roads on which afterwards his son Yamîn-addaula Maḥmûd marched into India during a period of thirty years and more. God be merciful to both father and son! Maḥmûd utterly ruined the prosperity of the country, and performed there wonderful exploits, by which the Hindus became like atoms of dust scattered in all directions, and like a tale of old in the mouth of the people. Their scattered remains cherish, of course, the most inveterate aversion towards all Muslims. This is the reason, too, why Hindu sciences have retired far away from those parts of the country conquered by us, and have fled to places which our hand cannot yet reach, to Kashmîr, Benares, and other places. And there the antagonism between them and all foreigners receives more and more nourishment both from political and religious sources.

In the fifth place, there are other causes, the mentioning of which sounds like a satire—peculiarities of their national character, deeply rooted in them, but manifest to everybody. We can only say, folly is an illness for which there is no medicine, and the Hindus believe that there is no country but theirs, no nation like theirs, no kings like theirs, no religion like theirs, no science like theirs. They are haughty, foolishly vain, self-conceited, and stolid. They are by nature niggardly in communicating that which they know, and they take the greatest possible care to withhold it from men of another caste among their own people, still much more, of course from any foreigner. According to their belief, there is no other country on earth but theirs, no other race of man but theirs, and no created beings besides them have any knowledge or science whatsoever. Their haughtiness is such that, if you tell them of any science or scholar in Khurâsân and Persis, they will think you to be both an ignoramus and a liar. If they travelled and mixed with other nations, they would soon change their mind, for their ancestors were not as narrow-minded as the present generation is. One of their scholars, Varâhamihira, in a passage where he calls on the people to honour the Brahmans, says: *"The Greeks, though impure, must be honoured, since they were trained in sciences, and therein excelled others. What, then, are we to say of a Brahman, if he combines with his purity the height of science?"* In former times, the Hindus used to acknowledge that the progress of science due to the Greeks is much more important than that which is due to themselves. But from this passage of Varâhamihira alone you see what a self-lauding man he is, whilst he gives himself airs as doing justice to others. At first I stood to their astronomers in the relation of a pupil to his master, being a stranger among them and not acquainted with their peculiar national and traditional methods of science. On having made some progress, I began to show them the elements on which this science rests, to point out to them some rules of logical deduction and the scientific methods of all mathematics, and then they flocked together round me from all parts, wondering, and most eager to learn from me, asking me at the same time from what Hindu master I had learnt those things, whilst in reality I showed them what they were worth, and thought myself a great deal superior to them, disdaining to be put on a level with them. They almost thought me to be a sorcerer, and when speaking of me to their leading men in their native tongue, they spoke of me as *the sea* or as *the water which is so acid that vinegar in comparison is sweet.*

Now such is the state of things in India. I have found it very hard to work my way into the subject, although I have a great liking for it, in which respect I stand quite alone in my time, and although I do not spare either trouble or money in collecting Sanskrit books from places where I supposed they were likely to be found, and in procuring for myself, even from very remote places, Hindu scholars who understand them and are able to teach me. What scholar, however, has the same favourable opportunities of studying this subject as I have? That would be only the case with one to whom the grace of God accords, what it did not accord to me, a perfectly free disposal of his own doings and goings; for it has never fallen to my lot in my own doings and goings to be perfectly independent, nor to be invested with sufficient power to dispose and to order as I thought best. However, I thank God for that which he has bestowed upon me, and which must be considered as sufficient for the purpose.

The heathen Greeks, before the rise of Christianity, held much the same opinions as the Hindus; their educated classes thought much the same as those of the Hindus; their common people held the same idolatrous views as those of the Hindus. Therefore I like to confront the theories of the one nation with those of the other simply on account of their close relationship, not in order to correct them. For that which is not *the truth* (*i.e.* the true belief or monotheism) does not admit of any correction, and all heathenism, whether Greek or Indian, is in its pith and marrow one and the same belief, because it is only a deviation *from the truth*. The Greeks,

however, had philosophers who, living in their country, discovered and worked out for them the elements of science, not of popular superstition, for it is the object of the upper classes to be guided by the results of science, whilst the common crowd will always be inclined to plunge into wrong-headed wrangling, as long as they are not kept down by fear of punishment. Think of Socrates when he opposed the crowd of his nation as to their idolatry and did not want to call the stars gods! At once eleven of the twelve judges of the Athenians agreed on a sentence of death, and Socrates died faithful to the truth.

The Hindus had no men of this stamp both capable and willing to bring sciences to a classical perfection. Therefore you mostly find that even the so-called scientific theorems of the Hindus are in a state of utter confusion, devoid of any logical order, and in the last instance always mixed up with the silly notions of the crowd, *e.g.* immense numbers, enormous spaces of time, and all kinds of religious dogmas, which the vulgar belief does not admit of being called into question. Therefore it is a prevailing practice among the Hindus *jurare in verba magistri;* and I can only compare their mathematical and astronomical literature, as far as I know it, to a mixture of pearl shells and sour dates, or of pearls and dung, or of costly crystals and common pebbles. Both kinds of things are equal in their eyes, since they cannot raise themselves to the methods of a strictly scientific deduction.

In most parts of my work I simply relate without criticising, unless there be a special reason for doing so. I mention the necessary Sanskrit names and technical terms once where the context of our explanation demands it. If the word is an *original* one, the meaning of which can be rendered in Arabic, I only use the corresponding Arabic word; if, however, the Sanskrit word be more practical, we keep this, trying to transliterate it as accurately as possible. If the word is a secondary or *derived* one, but in general use, we also keep it, though there be a corresponding term in Arabic, but before using it we explain its signification.

REVIEW QUESTIONS

1. How would you characterize Alberuni's accounts of Hindu society and religion?
2. How would you describe his opinion of Hindu scholars? Is it favorable or unfavorable?
3. What was his complaint regarding Hindu scientific literature?
4. Alberuni emphasizes Hindu biases; but was he also biased?

A Persian Poet Praises India (1318)

AMIR KHUSRAU, *Praises of India*

Urdu is the official language of Pakistan and one of the eighteen official languages of India. It has over a hundred million speakers, mostly in the northern part of the Indian subcontinent. Structurally it is the same as Hindi, but it has been strongly influenced by Persian, whereas Hindi literature's classical source is Sanskrit. Thus Urdu literature is closely associated with Islamic culture, and written Urdu uses a modified Perso-Arabic script.

Amir Khusrau (1253–1325), one of the pioneers of Urdu, was born in Delhi of mixed Turkic-Rajput heritage. His mother tongue was an early form of Hindi-Urdu, but he was a prolific writer in Persian. He was a musician as well and was fond of mixing Persian and Indian ragas. He carried this experiment into his poetry, producing a new form that was a harmonization of Urdu and Persian couplets. Like much of Urdu poetry, his poems blend the mystical and the romantic.

Khusrau's Persian poetry was pioneering as well. A great deal of it is what today would be called patriotic: he sings the praises of his native land, considering himself Indian long before any nationalist concept had developed. The landscape is panoramic, the flora and fauna wonderful, the people, rivers, weather, everything, is beautiful. It is the best of all lands. This selection from his Persian classic *Nuh-Sipihr, The Nine Firmaments,* is the most famous such example. It was written in 1318.

Khusrau lived during the Delhi sultanate, a period of Muslim rule in north India. The rulers, who were descendants of central Asian conquerors, were a class apart from the general populace, whether Hindu or Muslim. Khusrau was on good social terms with both groups. Indeed, his poetry is famous for its incorporation of popular terms picked up in the bazaar. (The name *Urdu* is cognate with English *horde* and refers to "the language of the camp," starting as a lingua franca between the conquerors and the people.) There is mention of Khusrau's good-natured banter with village women. Little is known about his personal life, but he is reputed to have mixed the mystical and the risqué. He is buried in Delhi in the compound that includes the tomb of the Muslim spiritual figure Nizamuddin Aulia.

ON INDIA: THE PARADISE

Evidence in support of the argument that India is Paradise itself. This argument stands sustained intellectually.

(1) The Indian Continent is Paradise on Earth and you can just find the argument in favour of this statement on its facing page.

(2) This is undoubtedly a substantial argument, in support of which I shall advance, not one, but seven points (to prove India's superiority over other countries).

(3) First is that it was in this Paradise that Ādam found repose after he was banished from Heaven and was tired under the burden of his sin.

(4) He had taken the grain of wheat which was forbidden. Look! how it became the root-cause of his sin.

(5) Unaware, he was thrown down ruthlessly from Heaven to the Earth, as a punishment (of this sin).

(6) As the chastity of God was his guardian, the stones of mountains upon which he fell became soft like silk.

(7) It was to India that Ādam came from Heaven. As he was a flower of Paradise, who was struck by autumnal wind, it was only to a garden that he could be despatched.

(8) Had he been despatched to Khurasan or Arabia or China, he would have availed of the earth only for a short while.

(9) The Summers and Winters of Khurasan and Arabia, as also of Ray and China, are singularly tortuous (and unbearable).

(10) As Ādam was brought up in Paradise, it was necessary to send him to a similar climate.

(11) Because India had the climate where he could have lived, it is amply proved that it is like the greatest Paradise.

(12) As India was just like Heaven, Ādam could descend here and find repose.

(13) Otherwise, as he was so mild and tender, had he fallen in some other country, he would have been harmed.

(14) Now I put up the second argument by citing the example of Peacock, the Bird of Paradise. This

intelligent argument would be thoroughly convincing.

(15) Peacock is the Bird of Paradise and it can live only in Paradise. If India is not Paradise, why was it made the abode of Peacock, the Bird of Paradise?

(16) Had India not been the Paradise, Peacock, the Bird of Paradise (would not have been found here and it) would have adopted some other garden as its Home.

(17) Had Paradise been in some other country, Peacock would have definitely gone there.

(18) As India was similar to Paradise, Peacock (the Bird of Paradise could live here and it) did not go anywhere else.

(19) If you are still in doubt, my third argument is that the serpent also belonged to the Heavenly Garden (Paradise).

(20) Mythologically, it is said that Serpent accompanied Peacock into Heaven.

(21) But Serpent did not belong to India because it had an un-Indian habit of stinging.

(22) In fact, Serpent did not belong to Heaven (as it had forced its entry into it by strategem) and, hence, it does not belong to India.

(23) As Serpent was a habitual offender, it, deservedly, got a place into the ground (i.e. underneath it).

(24) On the surface of this country, viz. India, where a hundred things originated for the comforts of life, this harmful serpent does not fit in (Hence it has been allotted a place into the ground).

(25) Although here are a large number of snakes in this land, they live inside the ground and do not love to remain outside.

(26) My fourth point of argument is related to Ādam's journey outside India.

(27) (No doubt, he put his foot outside India but) he did this because of his extreme longing for Eve and because no remedy was available for the agony of separation which tormented him.

(28) He travelled for two or three days but he could not find anything to eat until he reached the borders of Sham (Syria).

(29) The delicacies of Paradise which he had in his stomach gradually melted down.

(30) The seas and mountains were formed out of his easements.

(31) The town Ghotah in the desert of Damascus came into being from it, and people know it as such since those times.

(32) Although it was something Heavenly, it was not allowed to fall in India.

(33) So it happened because India is another Paradise (and such acts are not allowed in Paradise) and it would have been bad if it had fallen here.

(34) Were India not Paradise, how that burden was considered an impropriety within the bounds of India?

(35) My fifth point of argument is well-known and everybody is conscious of it.

(36) Pleasures, enjoyments and good climate are also available in the city of Damascus and it also looks like a Paradise.

(37) Wisemen, however, observe that, in view of this factor, Paradise is situated somewhere near it, either below or above it (and it is not Paradise itself).

(38) As Ādam came from India, the pleasant breezes which have given Damascus the appearance of Paradise also come from India, which is a Paradise.

(39) (If somebody raises the doubt, why then Ādam did not settle in India, I would say) Ādam did not like to settle in India without Eve.

(40) The men of wisdom have ultimately found the source of pleasures of the new land (viz. Damascus) which is India.

(41) It was the effect of Ghotah that Ādam chose to shed those delicacies of Paradise there.

(42) I urge upon you also to follow this Heavenly procedure.

(43) It was only this way that Ghotah became a pleasant and enjoyable place and looked like Paradise.

(44) [W]hen Ādam descended from Paradise, the fragrance of Heavenly wine and fruits was fresh upon his lips.

(45) He came to India fresh with the Pleasures and delicacies of Heaven and yet he found this country and its climate perfectly enjoyable (without any difference).

(46) The scent of Paradise which came with him was fresh, pleasant and envigorating.

(47) How stimulating were the soil and flowers of this land for physical pleasure and mental solace!

(48) The special feature of India's beauty is that its flowers blossom the year round and they are all fragrant.

(49) India is not like Ray or Rum where fragrant flowers do not grow except for two or three months.

(50) Even during that period (i.e. during the spring season) roses and poppies which grow there have no fragrance. Otherwise it is all dull due to snowfall and hailstorms.

(51) My sixth argument is based on the Saying of the Prophet (Hadith) which has been fully authenticated.

(52) The Prophet (Muḥammad) said that we do not believe in the worldly pleasures. We shall get reward of our good deeds in the Heaven. Worldly pleasures are meant for infidels only.

(53) India was a Paradise for the unbeliever since the advent of Ādam (on earth) till the inception of Islam.

(54) Even in recent times, these atheists have every pleasure of Heaven such as wine and honey.

(55) If people suffer with hardships, sorrows and privations, it is because they have faith in the blessings of Heaven.

(56) Those who are at present enjoying worldly pleasures, because of their idol-worship they will go to hell and these pleasures would turn into hardships.

(57) Thus, in my humble opinion it is proved in all respects that India on account of its beauties and excellences is Paradise.

(58) Now I put up my seventh argument which is strong and meaningful, and beset like a pearl.

(59) A Musalman who adheres to Truth as long as there is life in him,

(60) For him, this world is like a prison even though, on account of his good deeds, he belongs to Heaven inherently.

(61) But India has such a different atmosphere that here he feels the pleasant effect of Paradise (and it is not a Prison for Musalman).

(62) Because of this special feature, India is deemed to be a Paradise.

(63) That pleasant breeze and enjoyable atmospheric effect are not due to the Garden of Heaven but it is due to the graciousness of our Khalīfah.

(64) It is all due to the graciousness of the Pole of the World, viz. the King, Quṭbu'd-Dīn Mubārak Shāh, that such a beautiful greenery is spread under the sky.

(65) The world became as beautiful as was the face of Shāh Mubārak. In other words, the world owes its graceful appearance to the personality of this King.

(66) May God bless Sultān Quṭbu'd-Dīn Mubārak Shāh to Immortality because the world has become an eternal Paradise owing to his just and benevolent reign.

ON CULTURAL EXCELLENCE OF INDIA

(34) How exhilerating is the climate of this country (India) where so many birds sing melodiously.

(35) Poets, composers and singers rise from this land as abundantly and as naturally as grass.

(36) Most of them are good poets and singers. They know the innermost secrets of their art and their compositions are full of subtle meanings.

(37) The things which have now been revealed to me, were rarely known to me previously.

(38) Each poet and singer (of India) has his unique way of expression and among them, Khusrau is the humblest.

(39) How great is this land which produces men who deserve to be called men.

(40) Intelligence is the natural gift of this land (which no other country possesses) so much so that illiterate persons of this country are also scholars.

(41) There cannot be a better teacher than the way of life of the people and it is this which enlightens the illiterate masses of India. This is a gift of God.

(42) This is very rare in other countries. It is the effect of the cultural environment of this land upon the common people.

(43) The people of India have such an accurate insight, intelligence and understanding that only rarely they miss the point.

(44) Like a shepherd who is well acquainted with his sheep, they are thoroughly conversant with the moods and temperaments of the people.

(45) If, perchance, some Khurāsānī, Rūmī or Arab comes here, he will not have to ask for anything.

(46) Because they will treat him as their own. They will play an excellent host to him and win his heart.

(47) Even if they indulge in humour with him, they also know to smile like flower (and entertain their guest).

REVIEW QUESTIONS

1. Why do you think Khushrau used the story of Adam and Eve in his "Evidence in support of the argument that India is Paradise itself"?
2. How did he compare other central and western Asian regions to India?
3. How would you describe his arguments for the "cultural excellence of India"? Do you agree with it? Why or why not?

A Dominican Friar Observes Hindu Society (c. 1330)

FRIAR JORDANUS, *The Wonders of the East*

Jordanus, a Dominican friar, arrived by way of Persia on the southwest coast of India in about 1320, almost two hundred years before the Portuguese and about thirteen hundred years after St. Thomas. He dismissed the descendants of the first converts as not being true Christians, and he tried to convert the St. Thomas Christians to Roman Catholicism. Jordanus himself has been characterized as "the first resident Catholic missionary" in India.

Jordanus confined his interests to the south, from the Bombay (Mumbai) area to modern Kerala. He had been preceded by Giovanni de Montecorvino, who in 1291 stopped in India on his way to China and stayed thirteen months, trying to convert Nestorian Christians to Roman Catholicism. He reported, "There are very few Christians, and Jews, and they are of little weight." He also noted persecution against Christians "and all who bear Christian names." Jordanus drew considerable hostility from those Nestorians whom he did not convert, and presumably from the general Hindu populations as well. Although Hindus have been generally tolerant of other faiths, they are concerned about influences that upset the fabric of society. If religious figures were persecuted (such as were some Jain monks about this time), it was often because of a perceived challenge to the social structure, not because of spiritual doctrine. In recent time, for instance, affirmative action programs aimed at helping untouchables have on occasion resulted in violence from caste Hindus. Of course, the nature of reality in Hindu thought was (and is) alien to Christianity, and vice versa. In addition, Jordanus's vision of an opportunity to reap a "great harvest" of souls would not have registered with Hindus, whose religion is decidedly nonproselytizing (with the exception of a few modern fringe movements).

In 1328, having returned to Italy, Jordanus was named bishop of Columbum (Quilon, in Kerala) by the Pope. His charge was to convert Muslims and to bring Nestorians into the Roman fold. Probably nothing much was known of Hinduism, Buddhism, and Jainism, and it is doubtful that they would have been distinguished from one another in the European mind. Jordanus, however, never returned to India to undertake his charge, and was lost to history.

CONCERNING INDIA THE LESS*

1. In the entrance to India the Less are [date] palms, giving a very great quantity of the sweetest fruit; but further on in India they are not found.

2. In this lesser India are many things worthy to be noted with wonder; for there are no springs, no rivers, no ponds; nor does it ever rain, except during three months, viz., between the middle of May and the middle of August; and (wonderful!) notwithstanding this, the soil is most kindly and fertile, and during the nine months of the year in which it does not rain, so much dew is found every day upon the ground that it is not

---

*This section refers to northwest India and southwest Pakistan.

dried up by the sun's rays till the middle of the third hour of the day.

3. Here be many and boundless marvels; and in this First India beginneth, as it were, another world; for the men and women be all black, and they have for covering nothing but a strip of cotton tied round the loins, and the end of it flung over the naked back. Wheaten bread is there not eaten by the natives, although wheat they have in plenty; but rice is eaten with its seasoning, only boiled in water. And they have milk and butter and oil, which they often eat uncooked. In this India there be no horses, nor mules, nor camels, nor elephants; but only kine, with which they do all their doings that they have to do, whether it be riding, or carrying, or field labour. The asses are few in number and very small, and not much worth.

4. The days and nights do not vary there more than by two hours at the most.

5. There be always fruits and flowers there, divers trees, and fruits of divers kinds; for (example) there are some trees which bear very big fruit, called *Chaqui* [jack plant]; and the fruit is of such size that one is enough for five persons.

6. There is another tree which has fruit like that just named, and it is called *Bloqui,* quite as big and as sweet, but not of the same species. These fruits never grow upon the twigs, for these are not able to bear their weight, but only from the main branches, and even from the trunk of the tree itself, down to the very roots.

7. There is another tree which has fruit like a plum, but a very big one, which is called *Aniba* [mango]. This is a fruit so sweet and delicious as it is impossible to utter in words.

8. There be many other fruit trees of divers kinds, which it would be tedious to describe in detail.

9. I will only say this much, that this India, as regards fruit and other things, is entirely different from Christendom; except, indeed, that there be lemons there, in some places, as sweet as sugar, whilst there be other lemons sour like ours. There be also pomegranates, but very poor and small. There be but few vines, and they make from them no wine, but eat the fresh grapes; albeit

there are a number of other trees whose sap they collect, and it standeth in place of wine to them.

10. First of these is a certain tree called *Nargil* [coconut]; which tree every month in the year sends out a beautiful frond like [that of] a [date] palm-tree, which frond or branch produces very large fruit, as big as a man's head. There often grow on one such stem thirty of those fruits as big as I have said. And both flowers and fruits are produced at the same time, beginning with the first month and going up gradually to the twelfth; so that there are flowers and fruit in eleven stages of growth to be seen together. A wonder! and a thing which cannot be well understood without being witnessed. From these branches and fruits is drawn a very sweet water. The kernel [at first] is very tender and pleasant to eat; afterwards it waxeth harder, and a milk is drawn from it as good as milk of almonds; and when the kernel waxeth harder still, an oil is made from it of great medicinal virtue. And if any one careth not to have fruit, when the fruit-bearing stem is one or two months old he maketh a cut in it, and bindeth a pot to this incision; and so the sap, which would have been converted into fruit, drops in; and it is white like milk, and sweet like must, and maketh drunk like wine, so that the natives do drink it for wine; and those who wish not to drink it so, boil it down to one-third of its bulk, and then it becometh thick, like honey; and 'tis sweet, and fit for making preserves, like honey and the honeycomb [toddy]. One branch gives one potful in the day and one in the night, on the average throughout the year: thus five or six pots may be found hung upon the same tree at once. With the leaves of this tree they cover their houses during the rainy season. The fruit is that which we call *nuts of India;* and from the rind of that fruit is made the twine with which they stitch their boats together in those parts.

11. There is another tree of a different species, which like that gives all the year round a white liquor pleasant to drink, which tree is called *Tari.* There is also another, called *Belluri,* giving a liquor of the same kind, but better. There be also many other trees, and wonderful ones;

among which is one which sendeth forth roots from high up, which gradually grow down to the ground and enter it, and then wax into trunks like the main trunk, forming as it were an arch; and by this kind of multiplication one tree will have at once as many as twenty or thirty trunks beside one another, and all connected together [banyan]. 'Tis marvellous! And truly this which I have seen with mine eyes, 'tis hard to utter with my tongue. The fruit of this tree is not useful, but poisonous and deadly. There is [also] a tree harder than all, which the strongest arrows can scarcely pierce.

12. The trees in this India, and also in India the Greater, never shed their leaves till the new ones come.

13. To write about the other trees would be too long a business, and tedious beyond measure; seeing that they are many and divers, and beyond the comprehension of man.

14. But about wild beasts of the forest I say this: there be lions, leopards, ounces, and another kind something like a greyhound, having only the ears black and the whole body perfectly white, which among those people is called *Siagois* [perhaps a type of lynx]. This animal, whatever it catches, never lets go, even to death. There is also another animal, which is called *Rhinoceros,* as big as a horse, having one horn long and twisted; but it is not the *unicorn.*

15. There be also venomous animals, such as many serpents, big beyond bounds, and of divers colours, black, red, white, and green, and parti-coloured; two-headed also, three-headed, and five-headed. Admirable marvels!

16. There be also coquodriles, which are vulgarly called *Calcatix,* some of them be so big that they be bigger than the biggest horse. These animals be like lizards, and have a tail stretched over all, like unto a lizard's; and have a head like unto a swine's, and rows of teeth so powerful and horrible that no animal can escape their force, particularly in the water. This animal has, as it were, a coat of mail; and there is no sword, nor lance, nor arrow, which can anyhow hurt him, on account of the hardness of his scales. In the water, in short, there is nothing so strong, noth-

ing so evil, as this wonderful animal. There be also many other reptiles, whose names, to speak plainly, I know not.

17. As for birds, I say plainly that they are of quite different kinds from what are found on this side of the world; except, indeed, crows and sparrows; for there be parrots and popinjays in very great numbers, so that a thousand or more may be seen in a flock. These birds, when tamed and kept in cages, speak so that you would take them for rational beings. There be also bats really and truly as big as kites. These birds fly nowhither by day, but only when the sun sets. Wonderful! By day they hang themselves up on trees by the feet, with their bodies downwards, and in the daytime they look just like big fruit on the tree.[*]

18. There are also other birds, such as peacocks, quails, Indian fowls, and others, divers in kind; some white as white can be, some green as green can be, some parti-coloured, of such beauty as is past telling.

19. In this India, when men go to the wars, and when they act as guards to their lords, they go naked, with a round target,—a frail and paltry affair,—and holding a kind of a spit in their hands; and, truly, their fighting seems like child's play.

20. In this India are many and divers precious stones, among which are the best diamonds under heaven. These stones never can be dressed or shaped by any art, except what nature has given. But I omit the properties of these stones, not to be prolix.

21. In this India are many other precious stones, endowed with excellent virtues, which may be gathered by anybody; nor is anyone hindered.

22. In this India, on the death of a noble, or of any people of substance, their bodies are burned: and eke their wives follow them alive to the fire, and, for the sake of worldly glory, and for the love of their husbands, and for eternal life, burn along with them, with as much joy as if they were going to be wedded; and those who do

---

[*]The reference is to flying foxes, large fruit-eating bats.

this have the higher repute for virtue and perfection among the rest. Wonderful! I have sometimes seen, for one dead man who was burnt, five living women take their places on the fire with him, and die with their dead.

23. There be also other pagan-folk [Parsis, or Zoroastrians] in this India who worship fire; they bury not their dead, neither do they burn them, but cast them into the midst of a certain roofless tower, and there expose them totally uncovered to the fowls of heaven. These believe in two First Principles, to wit, of Evil and of Good, of Darkness and of Light, matters which at present I do not purpose to discuss.

24. There be also certain others which be called *Dumbri,** who eat carrion and carcases; who have absolutely no object of worship; and who have to do the drudgeries of other people, and carry loads.

25. In this India there is green ginger, and it grows there in great abundance. . . .

26. The people of this India are very clean in their feeding; true in speech, and eminent in justice, maintaining carefully the privileges of every man according to his degree, as they have come down from old times.

27. The heat there is perfectly horrible, and more intolerable to strangers than it is possible to say.

28. In this India there exists not, nor is found, any metal but what comes from abroad, except gold, iron, and electrum. There is no pepper there, nor any kind of spice except ginger.

29. In this India the greater part of the people worship idols, although a great share of the sovereignty is in the hands of the Turkish Saracens, who came forth from Multan, and conquered and usurped dominion to themselves not long since, and destroyed an infinity of idol temples, and likewise many churches, of which they made mosques for Mahomet, taking possession of their endowments and property. 'Tis grief to hear, and woe to see!

30. The Pagans of this India have prophecies

of their own that we Latins are to subjugate the whole world.

31. In this India there is a scattered people, one here, another there, who call themselves Christians, but are not so, nor have they baptism, nor do they know anything else about the faith. Nay, they believe St. Thomas the Great to be Christ!

32. There, in the India I speak of, I baptized and brought into the faith about three hundred souls, of whom many were idolaters and Saracens [Muslims].

33. And let me tell you that among the idolaters a man may with safety expound the Word of the Lord; nor is anyone from among the idolaters hindered from being baptized throughout all the East, whether they be Tartars, or Indians, or what not.

34. These idolaters sacrifice to their gods in this manner; to wit, there is one man who is priest to the idol, and he wears a long shirt, down to the ground almost, and above this a white surplice in our fashion; and he has a clerk with a shirt who goes after him, and carries a hassock, which he sets before the priest. And upon this the priest kneels, and so begins to advance from a distance, like one performing his stations; and he carries upon his bent arms a tray of two cubits [long], all full of eatables of different sorts, with lighted tapers at top; and thus praying he comes up to the altar where the idol is, and deposits the offering before it after their manner; and he pours a libation, and places part [of the offering] in the hands of the idol, and then divides the residue, and himself eats a part of it.

35. They make idols after the likeness of almost all living things of the idolaters; and they have besides their god according to his likeness. It is true that over all gods they place One God, the Almighty Creator of all those. They hold also that the world has existed now xxviii thousand years.

The Indians, both of this India and of the other Indies, never kill an ox, but rather honour him like a father; and some, even perhaps the majority, worship him. They will more readily spare him who has slain five men than him who

---

*A subgroup of untouchables or dalits.

has slain one ox, saying that it is no more lawful to kill an ox than to kill one's father. This is because oxen do all their services, and moreover furnish them with milk and butter, and all sorts of good things. The great lords among the idolaters, every morning when they rise, and before they go anywhither, make the fattest cows come before them, and lay their hands upon them, and then rub their own faces, believing that after this they can have no ailment.

36. Let this be enough about Lesser India; for were I to set forth particulars of everything down to worms and the like, a year would not suffice for the description.

37. But [I may say in conclusion] as for the women and men, the blacker they be, the more beautiful they be [held].

HERE FOLLOWETH CONCERNING INDIA THE GREATER

1. Of India the Greater I say this; that it is like unto Lesser India as regards all the folk being black. The animals also are all similar, neither more nor less [in number], except elephants, which they have [in the former] in very great plenty. These animals are marvellous; for they exceed in size and bulk and strength, and also in understanding, all the animals of the world. This animal hath a big head; small eyes, smaller than a horse's; ears like the wings of owls or bats; a nose reaching quite to the ground, extending right down from the top of his head; and two tusks standing out of remarkable magnitude [both in] bulk and length, which are [in fact] teeth rooted in the upper jaw. This animal doth everything by word of command; so that his driver hath nothing to do but say once, "Do this," and he doeth it; nor doth he seem in other respects a brute, but rather a rational creature. They have very big feet, with six hoofs like those of an ox, or rather of a camel. This animal carrieth easily upon him, with a certain structure of timber, more than thirty men; and he is a most gentle beast, and trained for war, so that a single animal counteth by himself equal in war to 1,500 men and more; for they bind to his tusks

blades or maces of iron wherewith he smiteth. Most horrible are the powers of this beast, and specially in war.

2. Two things there be which cannot be withstood by arms: one is the bolt of heaven; the second is a stone from an artillery engine; this is a third! For there is nothing that either can or dare stand against the assault of an elephant in any manner. A marvellous thing! He kneeleth, lieth, sitteth, goeth and cometh, merely at his master's word. In short, it is impossible to write in words the peculiarities of this animal!

3. In this India there are pepper and ginger, cinnamon, brazil, and all other spices.

4. Ginger is the root of a plant which hath leaves like a reed. Pepper is the fruit of a plant something like ivy, which climbs trees, and forms grape-like fruit like that of the wild vine. This fruit is at first green, then when it comes to maturity it becomes all black and corrugated as you see it. 'Tis thus that long pepper is produced, nor are you to believe that fire is placed under the pepper, nor that it is roasted, as some will lyingly maintain. Cinnamon is the bark of a large tree which has fruit and flowers like cloves.

5. In this India be many islands, and more than 10,000 of them inhabited, as I have heard; wherein are many world's wonders. For there is one called Silem [Ceylon], where are found the best precious stones in the whole world, and in the greatest quantity and number, and of all kinds.

6. Between that island and the main are taken pearls or marguerites, in such quantity as to be quite wonderful. So indeed that there are sometimes more than 8,000 boats or vessels, for three months continuously, [engaged in this fishery]. It is astounding, and almost incredible, to those who have not seen it, how many are taken.

7. Of birds I say this: that there be many different from those of Lesser India, and of different colours; for there be some white all over as snow; some red as scarlet of the grain; some green as grass; some parti-coloured; in such quantity and delectability as cannot be uttered. Parrots also, or popinjays, after their kind, of every possible colour except black, for black ones are never

found; but white all over, and green, and red, and also of mixed colours. The birds of this India seem really like creatures of Paradise.

8. There is also a marvellous thing of the islands aforesaid, to wit that there is one of them in which there is a water, and a certain tree in the middle of it. Every metal which is washed with that water becomes gold; every wound on which are placed the bruised leaves of that tree is incontinently healed.

9. In this India, whilst I was at Columbum, were found two cats [flying squirrels] having wings like the wings of bats; and in Lesser India there be some rats [bandicoots] as big as foxes, and venomous exceedingly.

REVIEW QUESTIONS

1. Friar Jordanus has been described as having great "credulity," or gullibility. How do you see that in this selection? How would you describe his attitude toward what he saw?
2. What does his fascination with animals tell you about him?
3. What does his use of words like *pagans* and *idolaters* tell you about him?

A Muslim Pilgrim Depicts Society in Bengal (1346–1347)

IBN BATTUTA, *The Travels of Ibn Battuta*

After thirteen years in Delhi, during which he served as a judge, Ibn Battuta was sent as an ambassador to China by the sultan. On his way (1346–1347) he traveled through Bengal. He got there by way of the Maldives, a series of 1,200 atolls southwest of India that today constitute the Republic of Maldives and for millennia have been a port of call. The explorer and archaeologist Thor Heyrdahl posited that they were a trading center during the time of the Indus civilization (third millennium B.C.E.). When Ibn Battuta was traveling, Muslims ruled the Maldives and Bengal. However, pre-Islamic culture still existed beneath the imposed religion and culture.

THE TRAVELS OF IBN BATTUTA IN BENGAL

Having sailed at last (from the Maldives) we were at sea for forty-three days, and then we arrived in Bengal. This is a country of great extent, and one in which rice is extremely abundant. Indeed I have seen no region of the earth in which provisions are so plentiful, but the climate is muggy, and people from Khorásán call it *Dúza-khast búr ni'amat,* which is as much as to say, *A Hell full of good things!*

He then proceeds to give a number of details as to the cheapness of various commodities, from which we select a few:

Mahomed al Masmúdí the Moor, a worthy man who died in my house at Delhi, had once resided in Bengal. He told me that when he was there with his family, consisting of himself, his wife and a servant, he used to buy a twelve-month's supply of food for the three of them for eight dirhems. For he bought rice in the husk at the rate of eight dirhems for eighty rothl, Delhi weight; and when he had husked it he still had fifty rothl of rice or ten kantárs.

I have seen a milch cow sold in Bengal for three silver dínárs (the cattle of that country are buffaloes). As for fat fowls, I have seen eight sold for a dirhem, whilst small pigeons were to be had at fifteen for a dirhem. . . . A piece of fine cotton cloth of excellent quality, thirty cubits in length, has been sold in my presence for two dínárs (of silver). A beautiful girl of marriageable age I have also seen sold for a dínár of gold, worth two and a half gold dínárs of Barbary. For about the same money I myself bought a young slave girl called Ashura, who was endowed with the most exquisite beauty. And one of my comrades bought a pretty little slave, called Lúlú (*Pearl*), for two golden dínárs.

The first city of Bengal which we entered was called Sadkáwán, a big place on the shore of the Great Sea. The river Ganges, to which the Hindus go on pilgrimage, and the river Jun [Jumna] unite in that neighbourhood before falling into the sea. The people of Bengal maintain a number of vessels on the river, with which they engage in war against the inhabitants of Lakhnaoti [a section of Bengal]. The King of Bengal was the Sultan Fakhruddín, surnamed Fakhrah, a prince of distinction who was fond of foreigners, especially of *Fakirs* and *Súfis* [mystics].

The traveller then recapitulates the hands through which the sceptre of Bengal had passed from the time of the Sultan Nasiruddín (the Bakarra Khan of Elphinstone's *History*), son of Balaban King of Delhi. After it had been held successively by two sons of Nasiruddín, the latter of these was attacked and killed by Mahomed Tughlak [sultan of Delhi].

Mahomed then named as governor of Bengal a brother-in-law of his own, who was murdered by the troops. Upon this Ali Sháh, who was then at Lakhnaoti, seized the kingdom of Bengal. When Fakhruddín saw that the royal authority had thus passed from the family of the Sultan Nasiruddín, whose descendant he was, he raised a revolt in Sadkáwán and Bengal, and declared himself independent. The hostility between him and Ali Sháh was very bitter. When the winter came, bringing rain and mud, Fakhruddín would make an attack upon the Lakhnaoti country by the river, on which he could muster great strength. But when the dry season returned, Ali Sháh would come down upon Bengal by land, his force that way being predominant.

When I entered Sadkáwán I did not visit the Sultan, nor did I hold any personal communication with him, because he was in revolt against the Emperor of India, and I feared the consequences if I acted otherwise. Quitting Sadkáwán I went to the mountains of Kamru, which are at the distance of a month's journey. They form an extensive range, bordering on China and also on the country of Tibet, where the musk-antelopes are found. The inhabitants of those regions resemble the Turks [*i.e.* the Tartars] and are capital people to work, so that as a slave one of them is as good as two or three of another race.

My object in going to the hill country of Kamrú was to see a holy personage who lives there, the Shaikh Jalaluddín of Tabriz. This was one of the most eminent of saints, and one of the most singular of men, who had achieved most worthy deeds, and wrought miracles of great note. He was (when I saw him) a very old man, and told me that he had seen the Khalif Mosta'sim Billah the Abasside at Baghdad, and was in that city at the time of his murder. At a later date I heard from the shaikh's disciples of his death at the age of one hundred and fifty years. I was also told that he had fasted for some forty years, breaking his fast only at intervals of ten days, and this only with the milk of a cow that he kept. He used also to remain on his legs all night. The shaikh was a tall thin man, with little hair on his face. The inhabitants of those mountains embraced Islam at his hands, and this was his motive for living among them.

Some of his disciples told me that the day before his death he called them together, and after exhorting them to live in the fear of God, went on to say: "I am assured that, God willing, I shall leave you to-morrow, and as regards you (my disciples) God Himself, the One and Only, will be my successor." Next day, just as he was finishing the noontide prayer, God took his soul during the last prostration. At one side of the cave in which he dwelt they found a grave ready dug, and beside it a winding sheet with spices. They washed his body, wound it in the sheet, prayed over him, and buried him there.

When I was on my way to visit the shaikh, four of his disciples met me at a distance of two days' journey from his place of abode. They told me that the shaikh had said to the fakirs who were with him: "The Traveller from the West is coming; go and meet him," and that they had come to meet me in consequence of this command. Now he knew nothing whatever about me, but the thing had been revealed to him.

I set out with these people to go and see the shaikh, and arrived at the hermitage outside his cave. There was no cultivation near the hermitage, but the people of the country, both Musulman and heathen, used to pay him visits, bringing presents with them, and on these the fakirs and the travellers [who came to see the shaikh] were supported. As for the shaikh himself he had only his cow, with whose milk he broke his fast every ten days, as I have told you. When I went in, he got up, embraced me, and made inquiries about my country and my travels. I told him about these, and then he said: "Thou art indeed the Traveller of the Arabs!" His disciples who were present here added: "And of the Persians also, Master!"—"Of the Persians also," replied he; "treat him then with consideration." So they led me to the hermitage and entertained me for three days.

The day that I entered the shaikh's presence he was wearing an ample mantle of goat's hair which greatly took my fancy, so that I could not help saying to myself "I wish to God that he would give it to me!" When I went to take my leave of him he got up, went into a corner of his cave, took off this mantle and made me put it on, as well as a high cap which he took from his head, and then himself put on a coat all covered with patches. The fakirs told me that the shaikh

was not in the habit of wearing the dress in question, and that he only put it on at the time of my arrival, saying to them: "The man of the West will ask for this dress; a Pagan king will take it from him, and give it to our Brother Burhán-uddín of Ságharj to whom it belongs, and for whom it was made!" When the fakirs told me this, my answer was: "I've got the shaikh's blessing now he has put his mantle on me, and I'll take care not to wear it in visiting any king whatever, be he idolater or be he Islamite." So I quitted the shaikh, and a good while afterwards it came to pass that when I was travelling in China I got to the city of Khansá. The crowd about us was so great that my companions got separated from me. Now it so happened that I had on this very dress of which we are speaking, and that in a certain street of the city the wazir was passing with a great following, and his eye lighted on me. He called me to him, took my hand, asked questions about my journey, and did not let me go till we had reached the residence of the sultan. I then wanted to quit him; however he would not let me go, but took me in and introduced me to the prince, who began to ask me questions about the various Musulman sovereigns. Whilst I was answering his questions, his eyes were fixed with admiration on my mantle. "Take it off," said the wazir; and there was no possibility of disobeying. So the sultan took the dress, and ordered them to give me ten robes of honour, a horse saddled and bridled, and a sum of money. I was vexed about it; but then came to my mind the shaikh's saying that a Pagan king would take this dress from me, and I was greatly astonished at its being thus fulfilled. The year following I came to the residence of the King of China at Khánbáliq, and betook myself to the Hermitage of the Shaikh Burhánuddín of Ságharj. I found him engaged in reading, and lo! he had on that very dress! So I began to feel the stuff with my hand. "Why dost thou handle it? Didst ever see it before?" "Yes," quoth I, "'tis the mantle the Sultan of Khansá took from me." "This mantle," replied the shaikh, "was made for me by my brother Jalaluddín, and he wrote to me that it would reach me by the hands of such an one." So he showed me Jalaluddín's letter, which I read, marvelling at the shaikh's prophetic powers. On my telling Burhán-uddín the first part of the story, he observed: "My brother Jalaluddín is above all these prodigies now; he had, indeed, supernatural resources at his disposal, but now he hath past to the mercies of God." "They tell me," he added, "that he used every day to say his morning prayers at Mecca, and that every year he used to accomplish the pilgrimage. For he always disappeared on the two days of Arafat and the feast of the Sacrifices, and no one knew whither."

REVIEW QUESTIONS

1. How would you describe the condition of slaves as described in this selection?
2. What do you think of the incident of the mysterious mantle? Explain.
3. What is your opinion of Ibn Battuta as a reporter? Explain.

Chinese Sailors Describe the Nicobar Islands and Sri Lanka (1414)

Stone Tablet Erected by Cheng Ho
FEI-HSIN, *Description of the Starry Raft*
MA HUAN, *Cheng Ho's Naval Expeditions*

China has not been noted much for maritime expeditions, largely because it has had to protect its vast inland frontiers. Nevertheless, overseas contacts go back well before the beginning of the common era, particularly in regard to Southeast Asia (Indochina). During the Southern Song (Sung) period (1127–1279), the Chinese replaced Arabs as the dominant power in the commerce of the Indian Ocean, and they traded with Malabar and Gujarat in western India. Indeed, the first historical reference to the use of the mariner's compass is by the Chinese, about 1100, well before Arab or European use.

Before 1400 the Chinese had had indirect commercial contact with the east coast of Africa, and from Arab and Indian merchants they had learned something about Africa's culture and people. In the early fifteenth century direct contact was achieved. To increase his prestige and obtain homage, the emperor sent at least seven expeditions from 1405 to 1433 through the islands of Southeast Asia, through the Indian Ocean, into the Persian Gulf, and to the east coast of Africa. The fleets consisted of as many as 62 ships and 37,000 soldiers. The chief treasure ship was 400 feet long; by contrast, the *Santa Maria,* Columbus's ship later in the century, was probably only 85 feet long.

The leader of the expedition was a Muslim court eunuch, Cheng Ho (Zheng He). Besides establishing political and commercial contacts, he brought back exotic gifts for the ladies of the harem and is said to have facetiously referred to one expedition as a shopping trip. Most remarkable perhaps was the inclusion of a giraffe, taken by some as an embodiment of a Chinese mythical beast—although apparently not so by the emperor, who was impressed with the show.

Cheng Ho's official reports were destroyed by later court eunuchs opposed to further maritime expeditions. Other accounts, including a dedicatory stone tablet, survive. For the fourth expedition (1414) Cheng Ho recruited Ma Huan, a twenty-five-year-old Muslim who knew Arabic and who became the principal chronicler of the voyages. His accounts show some gullibility, but also some careful observations of social customs. The first three paragraphs of the following selections are from the tablet and from geographical accounts by individuals who accompanied the expeditions. The second, longer selection is the account of Ma Huan regarding the Nicobar Islands and Ceylon (Sri Lanka).

STONE TABLET ERECTED BY CHENG HO

In the unification of seas and continents the imperial Ming Dynasty has surpassed the three dynasties and even excels the Han and T'ang. The countries beyond the horizon and from the ends of the earth have all become subjects, and distances and routes can be calculated to the uttermost parts of the west and farthest bounds of the north, however distant they may be. Thus the barbarians from beyond the seas, though their countries are exceeding far off, with double translation have come to audience, bearing precious objects and presents.

The Emperor, approving of their loyalty and sincerity, has ordered us [Cheng-Ho] and others, at the head of several tens of thousands of officers and flag-troops, to embark on more than a hundred large ships, and to go to confer presents [on the barbarians] in order to manifest the transforming power of the [imperial] virtue and to treat these distant people with kindness. From the third year of Yung-lo (1405) until now we have on seven occasions been commissioned as ambassadors to the countries of the Western Ocean. The barbarian countries which we have visited are: by way of *Chan-ch'eng (Campā) Chao-wa* (Java), *San-fo-ch'i* (Jambi) in Sumatra and *Hsien-lo* (Siam), crossing straight over to *Hsi-lan-shan* (Ceylon) in South India, *Ku-li* (Calicut) and *K'o-chih* (Cochin), we have gone to the western regions, *Hu-lu-mo-ssŭ* (Hormuz), *A-tan* (Aden), *Mu-ku-tu-shu* (Mogadishu), altogether more than thirty countries large and small. We have traversed more than 100,000 *li* of the immense ocean and have beheld on the main huge waves rising mountain-like to the sky; we have seen barbarian regions far away hidden in a blue transparency of light vapours, while by day and night our lofty sails, unfurled like clouds, continued their star-like course, traversing the savage waves as if they were a public thoroughfare. . . .

DESCRIPTION OF THE STARRY RAFT

Pahang

This place is to the west of *Hsien-lo* (Siam). It is encircled by rocky cliffs, rugged and precipitous. From afar the mountains appear like a level rampart. The soil is fertile and grain adequate. The climate is warm. The people are addicted to magic. They cut slips of aromatic wood with which to bring about peoples' deaths, sacrifice with human blood and pray for good fortune to avert calamity. Both men and women tie their hair in a knot and wrap round them a skirt. The women of wealthy families wear four or five gold rings on the tops of their heads, but the common people wear rings of coloured beads. They boil sea-water to obtain salt and ferment syrup to make spirits. The products are *huang-shou* and *shen* [varieties of] gharuwood, flake camphor, tin and lakawood. The goods used [in trading] are gold, silver, coloured silk, *Chao-wa* (Javanese) cottons, ironware and musical instruments. . . .

Keppel Harbour

This place is to the north-west of *San-fo-ch'i (Śri Vijaya)*. There is here a passage-way between hills which face each other and look like "dragons' teeth." Through this ships must pass. The soil is barren, the crops very poor. The climate is constantly hot, with heavy rains in the fourth and fifth moons. Men and women tie their hair in a knot. They wear short bajus and wrap sarongs around them. They are very daring pirates. If a foreign ship happens to pass that way they attack it in hundreds of little boats. If wind and fortune are favourable [the ship] may escape; otherwise [the pirates] will plunder the ship and put both passengers and crew to death.

CHENG HO'S NAVAL EXPEDITIONS

. . . These islands are three or four in number, and one of them, the largest, has the name Sambelong [?]. Its inhabitants live in the hollows of trees and caves. Both men and women there go about stark naked, like wild beasts, without a stitch of clothing on them. No rice grows there. The people subsist solely on wild yams, jack fruit, and plantains, or upon the fish which they catch. There is a legend current among them that, if they were to wear the smallest scrap of clothing, their bodies would break out into sores and ulcers, owing to their ancestors having been cursed by Sakyamuni [Buddha] for having stolen and hidden his clothes while he was bathing, at the time when he passed over from Ceylon and stopped at these islands. Continuing your voyage and sailing westward from here for ten days, the Hawk's Beak Hill is sighted, and in another two or three days the Buddhist Temple Hill is reached near [Dondere Head?] which is the anchorage of the port of Ceylon. On landing, there is to be seen on the shining rock, at the base of the cliff, an impress of a foot, two or more feet in length. The legend attached to it is, that it is the imprint of Sakyamuni's foot, made when he landed at this place. There is a little water in the hollow of the imprint of this foot which never evaporates. People dip their hands in it and wash their faces, and rub their eyes with it, saying, "This is Buddha's water, which will make us pure and clean."

Buddhist temples abound there. In one of them there is to be seen a full length recumbent figure of Sakyamuni, still in a very good state of preservation.

The dais on which the figure reposes is inlaid with all kinds of precious stones. It is made of sandalwood and is very handsome. The temple contains a Buddha's tooth and other relics. This must certainly be the place where Sakyamuni entered nirvana. Four or five *li* distant from here, in a northerly direction, is the capital of the kingdom. The king is a most earnest believer in the Buddhist religion, and one who treats elephants and cows with a feeling of veneration. The people of this country are in the habit of taking cow dung and burning it, which when reduced to ashes they rub over their whole bodies.

They do not venture to eat cow's flesh, they merely drink the milk. When a cow dies they bury it. It is capital punishment for anyone to secretly kill a cow; he who does so can however escape punishment by paying a ransom of a cow's head made of solid gold. Every morning, all those, of whatever degree, residing in the king's palace, take cow dung and mix it with water, which they smear everywhere over the floor of their houses, and upon which they afterwards prostrate themselves, and perform their religious rites.

Near to the king's residence there is a lofty mountain reaching to the skies. On the top of this mountain there is the impress of a man's foot, which is sunk two feet deep in the rock, and is some eight or more feet long. This is said to be the impress of the foot of the ancestor of mankind, a holy man called A-tan [Adam], or P'an Ku.

This mountain abounds with rubies of all kinds and other precious stones. These gems are being continually washed out of the ground by heavy rains, and are sought for and found in the sand carried down the hill by the torrents. It is currently reported among the people that these precious stones are the congealed tears of Buddha.

In the sea off the island there is a bank of snowy white sand, which, with the sun or moon shining on it, sparkles with dazzling brightness. Pearl oysters are continually collecting on this bank.

The king has had an [artificial] pearl pond dug, into which every two or three years he orders pearl oysters to be thrown, and he appoints men to keep watch over it. Those who fish for these oysters, and take them to the authorities for the king's use, sometimes steal and fraudulently sell them.

The kingdom of Ceylon is extensive, and thickly populated and somewhat resembles Java. The people are abundantly supplied with all the necessaries of life. They go about naked, except that they wear a green handkerchief around their loins, fastened with a waistband. Their bodies are clean-shaven and only the hair of their heads is left. They wear a white cloth twisted around their heads. When either of their parents die they allow their beards to grow. This is how they show their filial respect. The women twist their hair up into a knot at the back of the head, and wear a white cloth around their middles. Newly born male children have their heads shaven; the head of a female child is not shaven; the hair is done up into a tuft and is left so until she is grown up. They take no meal without butter and milk; if they have none and wish to eat, they do so unobserved and in private. The betel nut is never out of their mouths. They have no wheat, but have rice, sesame, and peas. The coconut, which they have in abundance, supplies them with oil, wine, sugar, and food. They burn their dead and bury the ashes. It is the custom in a family in which a death has occurred for the relatives' and neighbors' wives to assemble together and smite their breasts with their hands, and at the same time make loud lamentation and weeping.

Among their fruits, they number the plantain and the jack fruit; they have also the sugar cane, melons, herbs, and garden plants. Cows, sheep, fowls, and ducks are not wanting. The king has a gold coin in circulation weighing one candareen six cash. Chinese musk, colored taffetas, blue porcelain basins and cups, copper cash and camphor are much esteemed by them, against which they barter pearls and precious stones. Chinese vessels on their homeward voyages are constantly bringing envoys from their king, who are bearers of presents of precious stones as tribute to the imperial court.

REVIEW QUESTIONS

1. Compare the description here with the one in Chapter 14 by Amerigo Vespucci. How are they different? Are there notable similarities?
2. Compare the Chinese motives for exploration by sea with those of the Europeans (See Chapter 14). How are they different? Are there similarities?
3. What might have happened had China not ceased the expeditions and run into the Portuguese coming the other way?
4. Considering that the Chinese allegedly thought themselves superior to other cultures, how would you characterize Ma Huan's attitude in his observations?

A Portuguese Explorer Describes Calecut (1497–1499)

VASCO DA GAMA, *A Journal of the First Voyage*

One only need to look at a map of the Eastern Hemisphere to see why the Portuguese were interested in a maritime journey around Africa to India. Prince Henry the Navigator (1394–1460) started these efforts, which continued until 1497, when Vasco da Gama (c. 1460–1524), a nobleman with a reputation as an excellent navigator, was commissioned to sail around Africa to India. A fleet of four ships was built for the occasion. Because Columbus discovered, in a sense, the Western Hemisphere, he overshadows da Gama—at least in American textbooks. Nevertheless, da Gama did reach India, accomplishing what Columbus mistakenly thought he had done (hence, the confusion over "Indians" from India and "Indians" from America).

Da Gama left Lisbon harbor on July 8, 1497, and arrived at Calicut on the Malabar coast May 21, 1498, guided by either a Gujarati or an Arab pilot (the sources are contradictory; perhaps he may have been a Gujarati Muslim). The meeting between the Indians and these Europeans was the first such encounter since Alexander's Macedonians had confronted Indians in the Panjab almost two millennia earlier. Both meetings were violent. Just as surely as the meeting of Vikings with Skraelings in North America in the year 1000, this cultural encounter was to become an ironically symbolic conflict for the pattern that was to follow.

Scholars are unsure, or at least not in agreement, as to which of da Gama's officers kept the journal from which this excerpt is taken. Da Gama returned and that is when the atrocities occurred. They were perpetrated by the Portuguese, who, while certainly antagonized by the local ruler, were nonetheless uninvited. This is one facet of imperialism that the Europeans never understood: that resentment toward their behaviors was due to the fact that they were uninvited visitors.

The town of Malindi [Kenya] lies in a bay and extends along the shore. It may be likened to Al-couchette [near Lisbon]. Its houses are lofty and well white-washed, and have many windows; on the landside are palm-groves, and all around it maize and vegetables are being cultivated.

We remained in front of this town during nine days [April 15–23, 1498], and all this time we had fêtes, sham-fights, and musical performances ("fanfares").

[ACROSS THE GULF—THE ARABIAN SEA]

We left Malindi on Tuesday, the 24th of the month [of April] for a city called Qualecut [Calecut] [in modern Kerala], with the pilot whom the king had given us. The coast there runs north and south, and the land encloses a huge bay with a strait. In this bay, we were told, were to be found many large cities of Christians and Moors, including one called Quambay [Cambay], as also six-hundred known islands, and within it the Red Sea and the "house" [Kaabah] of Mecca.

On the following Sunday [April 29] we once more saw the North Star, which we had not seen for a long time.

On Friday, the 18th of May, after having seen no land for twenty-three days, we sighted lofty mountains, and having all this time sailed before the wind we could not have made less than 600 leagues. The land, when first sighted, was at a distance of eight leagues, and our lead reached bottom at forty-five fathoms. That same night we took a course to the S.S.W., so as to get away from the coast. On the following day [May 19] we again approached the land, but owing to the heavy rain and a thunderstorm, which prevailed whilst we were sailing along the coast, our pilot was unable to identify the exact locality. On Sunday [May 20] we found ourselves close to some mountains, and when we were near enough for the pilot to recognise them he told us that they were above Calecut, and that this was the country we desired to go to.

[CALECUT]

{Arrival}

That night [May 20] we anchored two leagues from the city of Calecut, and we did so because our pilot mistook *Capua,* a town at that place, for Calecut. Still further there is another town called *Pandarani.* We anchored about a league and a half from the shore. After we were at anchor, four boats (*almadias*) approached us from the land, who asked of what nation we were. We told them, and they then pointed out Calecut to us.

On the following day [May 21] these same boats came again alongside, when the captain-major sent one of the convicts to Calecut, and those with whom he went took him to two Moors from Tunis, who could speak Castilian and Genoese. The first greeting that he received was in these words: "May the Devil take thee! What brought you hither?" They asked what he sought so far away from home, and he told them that we came in search of Christians and of spices. They said: "Why does not the King of Castile, the King of France, or the Signoria of Venice send hither?" He said that the King of Portugal would not consent to their doing so, and they said he did the right thing. After this conversation they took him to their lodgings and gave him wheaten bread and honey. When he had eaten he returned to the ships, accompanied by one of the Moors, who was no sooner on board, than he said these words: "A lucky venture, a lucky venture! Plenty of rubies, plenty of emeralds! You owe great thanks to God, for having brought you to a country holding such riches!" We were greatly astonished to hear his talk, for we never expected to hear our language spoken so far away from Portugal.

{A Description of Calecut}

The city of Calecut is inhabited by Christians [actually, Hindus]. They are of a tawny complexion. Some of them have big beards and long hair, whilst others clip their hair short or shave the head, merely allowing a tuft to remain on the crown as a sign that they are Christians.

They also wear moustaches. They pierce the ears and wear much gold in them. They go naked down to the waist, covering their lower extremities with very fine cotton stuffs. But it is only the most respectable who do this, for the others manage as best they are able.

The women of this country, as a rule, are ugly and of small stature. They wear many jewels of gold round the neck, numerous bracelets on their arms, and rings set with precious stones on their toes. All these people are well-disposed and apparently of mild temper. At first sight they seem covetous and ignorant.

{A Messenger Sent to the King}

When we arrived at Calecut the king was fifteen leagues [28 miles] away. The captain-major sent two men to him with a message, informing him that an ambassador had arrived from the King of Portugal with letters, and that if he desired it he would take them to where the king then was.

The king presented the bearers of this message with much fine cloth. He sent word to the captain bidding him welcome, saying that he was about to proceed to Qualecut (Calecut). As a matter of fact, he started at once with a large retinue.

{At Anchor at Pandarani, May 27}

A pilot accompanied our two men, with orders to take us to a place called Pandarani, below the place [Capua] where we anchored at first. At this time we were actually in front of the city of Calecut. We were told that the anchorage at the place to which we were to go was good, whilst at the place we were then it was bad, with a stony bottom, which was quite true; and, moreover, that it was customary for the ships which came to this country to anchor there for the sake of safety. We ourselves did not feel comfortable, and the captain-major had no sooner received this royal message than he ordered the sails to be set, and we departed. We did not, however, anchor as near the shore as the king's pilot desired.

When we were at anchor, a message arrived informing the captain-major that the king was already in the city. At the same time the king sent a *bale* [high official], with other men of distinction, to Pandarani, to conduct the captain-major to where the king awaited him. This *bale* is like an *alcaide* [governor] and is always attended by two hundred men armed with swords and bucklers. As it was late when this message arrived, the captain-major deferred going.

{Gama Goes to Calecut}

On the following morning, which was Monday, May 28th, the captain-major set out to speak to the king, and took with him thirteen men, of whom I was one. We put on our best attire, placed bombards in our boats, and took with us trumpets and many flags. On landing, the captain-major was received by the *alcaide,* with whom were many men, armed and unarmed. The reception was friendly, as if the people were pleased to see us, though at first appearances looked threatening, for they carried naked swords in their hands. A palanquin was provided for the captain-major, such as is used by men of distinction in that country, as also by some of the merchants, who pay something to the king for this privilege. The captain-major entered the palanquin, which was carried by six men by turns. Attended by all these people we took the road of Qualecut, and came first to another town, called Capua. The captain-major was there deposited at the house of a man of rank, whilst we others were provided with food, consisting of rice, with much butter, and excellent boiled fish. The captain-major did not wish to eat, and when we had done so, we embarked on a river close by, which flows between the sea and the mainland, close to the coast. The two boats in which we embarked were lashed together, so that we were not separated. There were numerous other boats, all crowded with people. As to those who were on the banks I say nothing; their number was infinite, and they had all come to see us. We went up that river for about a league, and saw many large ships drawn up high and dry on its banks, for there is no port here.

When we disembarked, the captain-major once more entered his palanquin. The road was crowded with a countless multitude anxious to see us. Even the women came out of their houses with children in their arms and followed us.

{A Christian Church}

When we arrived [at Calecut] they took us to a large church, and this is what we saw:—

The body of the church is as large as a monastery, all built of hewn stone and covered with tiles. At the main entrance rises a pillar of bronze as high as a mast, on the top of which was perched a bird, apparently a cock. In addition to this, there was another pillar as high as a man, and very stout. In the centre of the body of the church rose a chapel, all built of hewn stone, with a bronze door sufficiently wide for a man to pass, and stone steps leading up to it. Within this sanctuary stood a small image which they said represented Our Lady. Along the walls, by the main entrance, hung seven small bells. In this church, the captain-major said his prayers, and we with him.

We did not go within the chapel, for it is the custom that only certain servants of the church, called *quafees,* should enter. These *quafees* wore some threads passing over the left shoulder and under the right arm, in the same manner as our deacons wear the stole. They threw holy water over us, and gave us some white earth, which the Christians of this country are in the habit of putting on their foreheads, breasts, around the neck, and on the forearms. They threw holy water upon the captain-major and gave him some of the earth, which he gave in charge of someone, giving them to understand that he would put it on later.

Many other saints were painted on the walls of the church, wearing crowns. They were painted variously, with teeth protruding an inch from the mouth, and four or five arms.

Below this church there was a large masonry tank, similar to many others which we had seen along the road.

{Progress Through the Town}

After we had left that place, and had arrived at the entrance to the city [of Calecut] we were shown another church, where we saw things like those described above. Here the crowd grew so dense that progress along the street became next to impossible, and for this reason they put the captain into a house, and us with him.

The king sent a brother of the *bale,* who was a lord of this country, to accompany the captain, and he was attended by men beating drums, blowing *anafils* and bagpipes, and firing off matchlocks. In conducting the captain they showed us much respect, more than is shown in Spain to a king. The number of people was countless, for in addition to those who surrounded us, and among whom there were two thousand armed men, they crowded the roofs and houses.

{The King's Palace}

The further we advanced in the direction of the king's palace, the more did they increase in number. And when we arrived there, men of much distinction and great lords came out to meet the captain, and joined those who were already in attendance upon him. It was then an hour before sunset. When we reached the palace we passed through a gate into a courtyard of great size, and before we arrived at where the king was, we passed four doors, through which we had to force our way, giving many blows to the people. When, at last, we reached the door where the king was, there came forth from it a little old man, who holds a position resembling that of a bishop, and whose advice the king acts upon in all affairs of the church. This man embraced the captain when he entered the door. Several men were wounded at this door, and we only got in by the use of much force.

{A Royal Audience, May 28}

The king was in a small court, reclining upon a couch covered with a cloth of green velvet, above which was a good mattress, and upon this again a sheet of cotton stuff, very white and fine, more so than any linen. The cushions were after the same fashion. In his left hand the king held a very large golden cup [spittoon], having a capacity of half an almude [8 pints]. At its mouth this cup was two palmas [16 inches] wide, and apparently it was massive. Into this cup the king threw the husks of a certain herb which is chewed by the people of this country because of its soothing effects, and which they call *atambor* [betel nut]. On the right side of the king stood a basin of gold, so large that a man might just encircle it with his arms: this contained the herbs. There were likewise many silver jugs. The canopy above the couch was all gilt.

The captain, on entering, saluted in the manner of the country: by putting the hands together, then raising them towards Heaven, as is done by Christians when addressing God, and immediately afterwards opening them and shutting the fists quickly. The king beckoned to the captain with his right hand to come nearer, but the captain did not approach him, for it is the custom of the country for no man to approach the king except only the servant who hands him the herbs, and when anyone addresses the king he holds his hand before the mouth, and remains at a distance. When the king beckoned to the captain he looked at us others, and ordered us to be seated on a stone bench near him, where he could see us. He ordered that water for our hands should be given us, as also some fruit, one kind of which resembled a melon, except that its outside was rough and the inside sweet, whilst another kind of fruit resembled a fig, and tasted very nice. There were men who prepared these fruits for us; and the king looked at us eating, and smiled; and talked to the servant who stood near him supplying him with the herbs referred to.

Then, throwing his eyes on the captain, who sat facing him, he invited him to address himself to the courtiers present, saying they were men of much distinction, that he could tell them whatever he desired to say, and they would repeat it to him (the king). The captain-major replied that he was the ambassador of the King of Portugal, and the bearer of a message which he could only deliver to him personally. The king said this was good, and immediately asked him to be conducted to a chamber. When the captain-major had entered, the king, too, rose and joined him, whilst we remained where we were. All this

happened about sunset. An old man who was in the court took away the couch as soon as the king rose, but allowed the plate to remain. The king, when he joined the captain, threw himself upon another couch, covered with various stuffs embroidered in gold, and asked the captain what he wanted.

And the captain told him he was the ambassador of a King of Portugal, who was Lord of many countries and the possessor of great wealth of every description, exceeding that of any king of these parts; that for a period of sixty years his ancestors had annually sent out vessels to make discoveries in the direction of India, as they knew that there were Christian kings there like themselves. This, he said, was the reason which induced them to order this country to be discovered, not because they sought for gold or silver, for of this they had such abundance that they needed not what was to be found in this country. He further stated that the captains sent out travelled for a year or two, until their provisions were exhausted, and then returned to Portugal, without having succeeded in making the desired discovery. There reigned a king now whose name was Dom Manuel, who had ordered him to build three vessels, of which he had been appointed captain-major, and who had ordered him not to return to Portugal until he should have discovered this King of the Christians, on pain of having his head cut off. That two letters had been intrusted to him to be presented in case he succeeded in discovering him, and that he would do so on the ensuing day; and, finally, he had been instructed to say by word of mouth that he [the King of Portugal] desired to be his friend and brother.

In reply to this the king said that he was welcome; that, on his part, he held him as a friend and brother, and would send ambassadors with him to Portugal. This latter had been asked as a favour, the captain pretending that he would not dare to present himself before his king and master unless he was able to present, at the same time, some men of this country.

These and many other things passed between the two in this chamber, and as it was already late in the night, the king asked the captain with whom he desired to lodge, with Christians or with Moors? And the captain replied, neither with Christians nor with Moors, and begged as a favour that he be given a lodging by himself. The king said he would order it thus, upon which the captain took leave of the king and came to where we were, that is, to a veranda lit up by a huge candlestick. By that time four hours of the night had already gone.

REVIEW QUESTIONS

1. How would you describe this initial contact between a representative of a European power and a regional king in south India? Were their relations friendly or hostile? Were the two groups equal in power?

2. What aspects of Indian society did Vasco da Gama admire? Which ones did he dislike? What does this tell you about his own values?

3. Compare the description given here by Vasco da Gama with that given by him in Chapter 11. How are they similar? How are they different?

13

East and Southeast Asia, 800–1500

There was considerably more contact among premodern peoples than we generally think. Curiosity overcame ignorance, and it even overcame the sense of superiority that many cultures, both European and Asian, had about themselves. For the most part, contacts were made with some trepidation and with dogged determination. In the early ninth century a Japanese Buddhist monk spent years in China. This foreigner in the Middle Kingdom seemed to receive a mixture of acceptance and rejection, but he persevered. Arab writers showed an interest in Southeast Asia, an area far from their home. A rabbi with a clear focus on Jewish communities east of Europe found that acceptance was not a problem. In contrast, the friar whose account is included here failed to effect mass conversion, but his efforts helped to arouse European interest in Asia. This interest was seldom reciprocated. In the long run, the unrequited European interest in Asian empires paid off handsomely for the Europeans. They became the seekers, then the intruders, and finally the conquerors.

Also included in this chapter are two internal sets of observations: a Chinese man's "practical advice to women" and two remarkable Heian women's observations on their own culture. Both represent a culture that probably was the most sophisticated (albeit isolated) in the world at that time and that produced a golden age of literature by women.

A Japanese Monk Describes His Pilgrimage to China (838–847)

ENNIN, *The Record of a Pilgrimage to China in Search of the Law*

Ennin (794–864) was a monk of the Tendai sect, which is based upon the *Lotus Sutra,* an early popular work preaching multiple Buddhas and multiple worlds. Originating in China, Tendai was brought to Japan in the early ninth century, where it became an immediate sensation. As an early member of Tendai, Ennin went to China to study and travel. He accompanied a Japanese embassy that arrived near the mouth of the Yangtze after two aborted attempts. He was not the first Japanese to visit China, but the lengthy and meticulous diary of his extensive travels (838–847) is the oldest account available by a foreigner in China. He was present during a period in the T'ang dynasty (618–907) that was marked by rich cultural and economic development, beginnings of political decay, and a pervasive bureaucracy.

The following selection is representative of Ennin's frequent contacts—

sometimes clashes—with the Chinese bureaucracy. He came as a member of
the Japanese embassy and as a student or pilgrim. Toward the end of his stay,
imperial persecution of foreign religions (Buddhism had originated in India)
dealt Buddhism a severe blow. This recurring Chinese xenophobia also wiped
out Nestorian Christianity in China.

Later biographies of Ennin, who was important in the development of
Tendai in Japan, provide a chronology and focus on his religious role, but they
offer little on his personality. Their approach toward him, as the twentieth-
century historian and translator of Ennin has put it, is one of "pious awe." Although Ennin's diary is not as introspective as a modern diary, his journal
does reveal his high character, leadership, and sense of responsibility. In spite
of his discouraging dealings with the Chinese bureaucracy, he expresses no
doubt in his faith or his pursuit of the Dharma, or Buddhist doctrine.

Tenth Moon: 3rd day {Oct. 24, 838}

In the evening we two, the Scholar Monk and
the Student Monk, went to the P'ing-ch'iao Inn
and took leave of the Ambassador and Administrative Officers, since they were going to the
capital, and consulted with them. The Administrative Officer Naga-[mine] said that, if he had
statements of our sincere desires, he would take
them to the capital, petition the throne and
quickly obtain permits [for us].

4th day

After the forenoon meal we two monks wrote
out on separate sheets statements of our sincere
desires and sent them to the Administrative
Officer. These documents are as separately [re-
corded].

The officials going to the capital are the Ambassador, the Administrative Officer Nagamine,
the Administrative Officer Sugawara, the Secretary Takaoka, The Secretary Ōmiwa, and the
Interpreter Ōyake. In addition, there are the
Scholar, Tomo no Sugao, The Shingon Scholar
[Monk], Engyō, and thirty-five minor officers
and subordinates. There are five official boats.

The Administrative Officer Naga[mine] has
entrusted me with the record of rank of the Vice-
Ambassador to China of the Enryaku period and
with a memorial essay and also with ten packages of silk floss. I have received a statement
from the Administrative Officer saying:

The Vice-Ambassador to China of the Enryaku period, Ishikawa no Ason Michimasu,
died in Ming-chou. Now, there has been an
Imperial order promoting him to the fourth
rank, which has been entrusted to this embassy to present before his [grave] mound.
You should make inquiries regarding the
route to T'ai-chou and, if you should reach
the borders of Ming-chou, you should then
read the memorial essay and with fire burn
up the record of rank.

The Sanron Student [Monk], Jōgyō, will still
stay at the Kuang-ling Inn and will not be able
to go to the capital.

5th day

At 7 A.M., the Ambassador and the others
boarded the boats and set out for the capital. It
rained all day and all night.

6th day

It was cold for the first time.

7th day

There was a light freeze. . . .

13th day

At noon the Scholar [Monk's] attendant, Igyō,
and the Student [Monk's] attendant, Ninkō,
both shaved their heads.

14th day

I had two large ounces of gold dust changed at the market. The market determined the weight to be one large ounce and seven *ch'ien* and let the seven *ch'ien* be counted as three-quarters [of an ounce]. It was worth nine strings and 400 cash. I also bought two bolts of white silk for two strings of cash and had two Buddhist scarves, a *shichijō* and a *gojō,* made. Again I had the monk Chen-shun attend to this.

After the forenoon meal thirteen Zen and other monks came to see us. [They were] Hui-yün of the Tendai Sect from the Ch'ien-fu-ssu of Ch'ang-an and the Zen Scholar Monks: Hung-chien, Fa-tuan, Shih-shih, Hsing-ch'üan, Ch'ang-mi, Fa-chi, Fa-chen, Hui-shen, Ch'üan-ku, Ts'ung-shih, Chung-ch'üan, and T'an-yu. They wrote by brush.

Together, quite idly and without attachments, like clouds floating about the landscape, we descended from Wu-feng and wandered to Ch'u and Ssu. Now, having reached this region, we are particularly happy to pay you our respects. It is most extraordinary, and great is our rejoicing. We now intend to go to [Mt.] T'ien-t'ai, and so we take leave of you and depart.

Our great esteem.

Writing by brush, we then replied:

We Japanese monks now meet with you monks because in the past we had important affinities with you. We know for certain that one must dwell in the emptiness which is the nature of the Law [Buddhist doctrine]. [Our meeting] is most fortunate. If we reach [Mt.] T'ien-t'ai, we shall certainly see you.

Our great esteem.

19th day

In order to have Ishō and Igyō ordained, I wrote a letter to the Administrative Officer and Secretary [still in Yang-chou]. Because there had been many secret ordinations in the prefectures,

since the second year of T'ai-ho (828) in China orders had been issued to the prefectures forbidding the people to shave their heads and become monks. There are only the ordination platform of Mt. Wu-t'ai and the lapis lazuli ordination platform of Chung-shan in Lo-yang. Aside from these two, all have been banned. Because of this, I asked that the matter be reported and appropriate action taken. . . .

18th day

The Minister of State came to the monastery and worshiped the "auspicious images" in the balcony and inspected the newly made image. Presently, his military aide, the *Ta-fu* Shen Pien, rushed up to us and said that the Minister of State invited us monks [to join him]. On hearing this, we climbed up to the balcony with the messenger. The Minister of State and the Military Inspector, together with Senior Secretaries, Deputy Secretaries, and Administrative Officers of the prefecture, all were seated on chairs drinking tea. When they saw us monks coming, they all arose and paid us respect by joining their hands and standing. They called out to us to sit down, and we all seated ourselves on the chairs and sipped tea. There were the Minister of State and his attendants from the Senior Secretaries down to the Administrative Officers, eight men in all. The Minister of State wore purple, the three Senior Secretaries and Deputy Secretaries wore dark red, and the four Administrative Officers wore green. The police guards, foot soldiers, cavalry, and honor guards were just as before.

The Minister of State, who sat directly in front of us, asked if it were ever cold in our country, and the Student Monk replied that the summers were hot and the winters cold, at which the Minister of State remarked that this was the same as hereabouts. The Minister of State then asked whether or not we had monasteries, and we replied that there were many, and he further asked how many monasteries there were, and we replied that there were about 3,700. He also asked whether or not we had convents, and we replied that there were many. He further asked whether or not we had Taoist priests, and we replied that there were no Taoist priests. The Minister of State also asked how many *li* in area was the capital of our country, and we replied that it was fifteen *li* [about 5½ miles] from east to west and fifteen *li* from south to north. He also asked if we observed summer retirement [from wandering], and we replied that we did. The Minister of State then conversed with us a little longer, and, in consoling us, communicated to us his sympathy. After that, we bowed to each other and descended from the balcony. He also went to the Kuan-yin-yüan ("Kannon Cloister") to inspect the repair work. . . .

Fourth Moon: 1st day

At the morning audience I received our official credentials, and the President of the Ministry gave us three lengths [50 feet] of cloth and six pounds of tea. At the time for the forenoon meal, they had a maigre feast* in this monastery. Today is the birthday of the son of the President of the Ministry, and accordingly a "long life" maigre feast was held.

2nd day

Early in the morning I ate gruel at the house of Hsiao, the Administrative Officer, and then went to the prefectural [offices] to present a letter thanking the President of the Ministry for his gifts and to take leave of him.

The Japanese monk in search of the Law, Ennin, has humbly received from the President of the Ministry in his benevolence a gift of three lengths of cloth and six pounds of tea. Unworthy that he is, he is overwhelmed with gratitude and respectfully presents this letter to express his thanks. Respectfully written in brief.

Presented on the second day of the fourth moon of the fifty year of K'ai-ch'eng by the Japanese monk in search of the Law, Ennin.

---

*A meatless meal eaten on religious occasions.

The President of the Ministry summoned me to his offices and sent word to me that what he had given was trifling and did not merit mention and that he thanked me for coming and I might now go. I next went to the offices of the Assistant Regional Commander, the auxiliary official Chang, to take leave of him. He summoned me into his office and gave me tea and cakes to eat. We sipped our tea, and then I bade farewell to the auxiliary official and went to the monastery. I was invited for the forenoon meal to the home of Chao Te-chi. At sunset the Administrative Officer of the Military Headquarters gave me two tou [pecks] of grain as provisions and two tou of small beans as fodder for the donkey. At dusk I went to the home of the Administrative Officer of the Military Headquarters and thanked him for giving us provisions for the road and took leave of him.

3rd day

At dawn we started. The Administrative Officer of the Military Headquarters sent an official courier to accompany us past the city gate. Ever since we first met, [the Administrative Officer of] the Military Headquarters has been extremely courteous, and while we were at the monastery, daily bestowed gifts on us and inquired kindly after us all the time. Now that we were starting, he sent a man to accompany us and show us the road.

Today the President of the Ministry, the Military Inspector, and the various shrines are praying for rain. From the monastery northwest past the city wall and ten *li* [3.3 miles] out in the country is Mt. Yao, on top of which stands the Shrine of King Yao. When long ago King Yao passed through this area, he built this shrine. I am told that, whenever they pray for rain [here], the rains fall in response.

We went out of the walled city and went north for twenty *li* to the Ch'en household in Shih-yang-ts'un in I-tu-hsien and ate. Our host was a quiet man. After the forenoon meal we went northwest fifteen *li* to Tzu-shui-i in Lin-tzu-hsien and then twenty-five *li* west to the Wang household east of Chin-ling-i and spent the night. Our host was a good and upright man, and when he saw guests, he was courteous. Far to the west we could see Mt. Ch'ang-pai.

4th day

We started at dawn, going sixteen *li* southwest, where we entered a small road from which we could see Mt. Ch'ang-pai in the distance, and then we went five *li* westward to the Chao household in Chang-chao-ts'un in Tzu-ch'uan-hsien in Tzu-chou and ate. Our host was extremely poor and had no food for us to eat, but he was not a bad man at heart. After the forenoon meal we went northwest for thirty *li* to the . . . household in Ku-hsien-ts'un in Ch'ang-shan-hsien and spent the night. Our host was a metal-worker, originally from P'ei-chou. He was a quiet and religious man.

5th day

We started early, going ten *li* northwest to Ch'ang-shan-hsien, and from the subprefecture we went ten *li* west to Chang-li and took our midday rest. Our host was courteous. After the forenoon meal we went fifteen *li* west to the east side of Mt. Ch'ang-pai. It was almost 4 P.M. when we drank tea at the Shih household at Pu-ts'un in front of the Hermit's Terrace and asked for the Li-ch'üan-ssu. Our host replied that, if we went fifteen *li* due west of Pu-ts'un, we would reach it, so we went straight west into the mountains. We went over ten *li* on the wrong road. There were many different roads, and we did not know where they led. Since night was falling, we returned to the Shih household in Pu-ts'un and spent the night. All night long the dogs barked, and we were afraid and could not sleep.

6th day

Early in the morning our host gave us gruel, and he also sent a man to accompany us and point out the road. We went due west into a valley, passing a high ridge, and then, going west down a slope, came on the fruit gardens of the Li-ch'üan-ssu and drank tea there. Then we went south another two *li* and came to the Li-ch'üan-ssu, where we took our midday rest. . . .

9th day

It was raining in the morning, and we could not start. After the forenoon meal the rain stopped, so we started, going fifteen *li* due west to the old subprefecture, that is, the old walled town of Lin-i-hsien. It was going to pieces and had not a single official building. The monasteries of former ages were in ruins, with the images of the Buddhas exposed to the elements, and [the city] had reverted to cultivated fields. It was most melancholy. We went due west for fifteen *li* to the ferry across the Yüan-ho and, crossing the river, went ten *li* to the Li Fu household in Yen-t'ang-ts'un in Yü-ch'eng-hsien and spent the night. Our host was a religious man.

10th day

We started at dawn, going forty *li* due west, and at 2 P.M. reached Yü-ch'eng-hsien. In the market place of the subprefecture millet [costs] forty-five cash for one *tou*, non-glutinous rice one hundred cash for one *tou*, "small beans" fifteen cash per *tou*, and flour seventy or eighty cash. We passed the walled town and went west for ten *li* to the Chao household in Hsien-kung-ts'un and spent the night. All night long there was thunder and lightning, and hail and rain fell. At dawn the thunderstorm stopped. Our host was not a religious man.

11th day

We started at 6 A.M., went due west for thirty *li*, and at noon reached the ferry across the Yellow River. The people nowadays call [this place] Yüeh-chia-k'ou. The water is yellow and muddy in color and flows swift as an arrow. The river is about one *chō* and five *tan* [about 500 feet] wide and flows east. The Yellow River originates in the K'un-lun Mountains and has nine bends, six of which are in the land of the Tibetans and three in China. There are ferry stations on both banks on the north and south, each with walled enclosures more than four *chō* from north to south and about one *chō* from east to west. This Yüeh-chia-k'ou has many boats which are anxious to carry travelers. It costs five cash for each person and fifteen for a donkey. [The area] south of the river is under Yü-ch'eng-hsien in Ch'i-chou and north of the river belongs to the southern part of Te-chou.

After crossing the river we took our midday rest on the north bank. Each one of the four of us ate four bowls of porridge. Our host was astonished and was afraid that if we ate so much cold stuff we would not digest it. Then we went thirty-five *li* due west and at 4 P.M. reached the Chao household in Chao-kuan-ts'un in P'ing-yüan-hsien in Te-chou and spent the night. Our host was not a religious man.

12th day

We started early and went due west for forty *li* to the Chao household in Hsing-k'ai-ts'un in Hsia-ching-hsien in P'ei-chou and took our midday rest. Our host was a religious man and gave us a maigre feast, and we ate our fill of vegetables. After the forenoon meal we started out and went thirty *li* west to the Sun household in Meng-chia-chuang in Hsia-ching-hsien and spent the night. Our host was a religious man.

13th day

We started out and went thirty-five *li* west to the Wang household in Wang-yen-ts'un and took our midday rest. Our host was quite a religious man and gave us a maigre feast. After our forenoon meal we went thirty-five *li* west and at 4 P.M. reached the K'ai-yüan-ssu within the walled city of T'ang-chou and spent the night.

REVIEW QUESTIONS

1. How would you characterize the Chinese bureaucracy Ennin had to deal with? Why?
2. Why do you suppose the Chinese government restricted monastic ordination?
3. What do you think is the most surprising item in this account? Why?

Arab Writers Describe Zabag (851, 916)

SULAIMAN and ABU ZAID HASAN

Zabag (or the empire of Majaraja) was the name given both to a vast Indian empire in the Malay peninsula and archipelago (including Sumatra and Java) and to its capital city. The ruling dynasty was known as the Sailendra, which had contacts with India. Founded about 775, Zabag thrived for three hundred years. Merchants from Arabia and Baghdad frequently placed the Maharaja of Zabag among the powerful rulers who prospered from the wealthy maritime trade routes that existed at that time. Defeated by a Chola (south

India) king in 1025, Zabag then rallied, continuing for three more centuries. In the middle of the thirteenth century, another attack by a south Indian king brought on its decline. In 1349 a Chinese work refers to its king as a local ruler.

The following excerpts are from an account written by an Arab merchant, known as Sulaiman, who traveled in the Persian Gulf, India, and China. His account, written in 851, was published in 916 by a later writer, Abu Zaid Hasan, who amplified Sulaiman's narrative. Although Abu Zaid never visited China or India, he obtained information by questioning other travelers, including Al-Mas'udi (see Chapter 11). Abu Zaid's work is the most detailed existing account of Zabag for this period. He concluded his work with the following remark: "Such is the most interesting matter that I have heard, among the many accounts to which maritime adventure has given birth. I have refrained from recording the false stories which sailors tell, and which the narrators themselves do not believe. A faithful account although short, is preferable to all."

The distance between Zabag and China is one month's journey by sea-route. It may be even less if the winds are favourable.

The king of this town has got the title Mahārāja. The area of the kingdom is about nine-hundred (square) Parsangs. The king is also overlord of a large number of islands extending over a length of one thousand Parsangs or more. Among the kingdoms over which he rules are the island called Sribuza (Śrī Vijaya) with an area of about four-hundred (square) Parsangs, and the island called Rami with an area of about Eight-hundred (square) Parsangs. The maritime country of Kalah, midway between Arabia and China, is also included among the territories of Maharaja. The area of Kalah is about eighty (square) Parsangs. The town of Kalah is the most important commercial centre for trade also, in camphor, sandalwood, ivory, tin, ebony, spices and various other articles. There was a regular maritime intercourse between this port and Oman.

The Mahārāja exercises his sovereignty on all these islands. The island in which he lives is very thickly populated and there is a continuous line of villages there, so that when the cocks crow in the morning, the cry is taken up by those in the next village, and in this way the sound is taken up for nearly a distance of hundred Parsangs.

There is one very extraordinary custom in Zabag. The palace of the king is connected with the sea by a shallow lake. Into this the king throws every morning a brick made of solid gold. These bricks are covered by water during tide, but are visible during ebb. When the king dies, all these bricks are collected, counted and weighed and these are entered in official records. The gold is then distributed among the members of the royal family, generals and royal slaves according to their rank and the remnant is distributed among the poor.

It is said, in the annals of the country of Zābag, that in years gone by the country of Khmer came into the hands of a young prince of very hasty temper. One day he was seated with the Vizier when the conversation turned upon the empire of the Mahārāja, of its splendour, the number of its subjects and of the islands subordinate to it. All at once the king said to the Vizier, "I have taken a fancy into my head which I should much like to gratify. . . . I should like to see before me the head of the king of Zābag in a dish. . . . These words passed from mouth to mouth and so spread that they at length reached the ears of the Mahārāja. That king ordered his Vizier to have a thousand vessels of medium size prepared with their engines of war, and to put on board of each vessel as many arms and soldiers as it could carry. When the preparations were ended, and everything was ready, the king went on board his fleet and proceeded with his troops to Khmer. . . . the king of Khmer knew nothing of the impending danger until the fleet had entered the river which led to his capital, and the troops of the Mahārāja had landed. The Mahārāja thus took the king of Khmer unawares and seized upon his palace. He had the king brought forth and had his head cut off. . . . The Mahārāja returned immediately to his country and neither he nor any of his men touched anything belonging to the king of Khmer. . . . Afterwards the Mahārāja had the head washed and embalmed, then putting it in a vase, he sent it to the prince who then occupied the throne of Khmer.

REVIEW QUESTIONS

1. What is the significance of throwing gold bricks into a lake?
2. Zabag is often depicted as a wealthy state. Do you think this is an accurate portrayal? Why or why not?
3. How would you characterize the motives for war that are described here? How do they compare with motives for war in the early twenty-first century?

Two Japanese Women Depict Their Social World (tenth to eleventh century)

Murasaki Shikibu, *Diary*
Sarashina, *As I Crossed a Bridge of Dreams*

In his study *Japanese Poetic Diaries* (1969), Earl Miner noted that "the Western diarist is aware of time as events, the Japanese of time as process." In that regard, what is usually translated as "diary" (*nikki*) is more of a memoir or sophisticated notebook. It is a type of literature imbued with a poetic nostalgia, a strong sense of karma, and what has been termed "the evanescence of existence." Factual accuracy, although not irrelevant, is not stressed, whereas subjective awareness of the nature of human experience is. A further characteristic, as in Japanese art and poetry, is the tendency to express perception and feeling in the fewest words possible.

In the tenth century, during the Heian period (794–1185), the genre of the diary reached its pinnacle and became the most important form of literature of this culturally rich period. The writers were a small collection of upper-class women attached to the imperial court. This affected "minisociety" was a minority within the upper class, which itself was a minute portion of the entire population. The elite were not involved in the arduous toil of day-to-day existence, and most courtiers had a great deal of time on their hands; the women involved themselves in frivolous affairs and frivolous gossip and snobbery. If the colors of one's sleeves and robe clashed, one's reputation was ruined. Poetry was the medium for expressing oneself and one's emotions, and some of the very brightest became expert at such expression and its extension, the diary.

The author of the first selection is Lady Murasaki, author of *The Tale of Genji,* a masterpiece that is perhaps Japan's finest literary prose work and the world's first psychological novel. The second selection is from *Sarashina Nikki.* The author's name is not known, so she is generally referred to as Lady Sarashina. Whereas Lady Murasaki was attached to the court, Lady Sarashina was the daughter of a provincial governor who, in keeping with custom and edict, spent considerable time in the capital. Murasaki was about thirty years senior to Sarashina, who was born about 1008.

Murasaki's comments have historical as well as literary value. In this selection she refers to Izumi Shikibu as having a genius for writing but "a rather unsavory side to her character." Izumi Shikibu has such a reputation, and her diary tends to confirm both descriptions. Sei Shonagon, author of *The Pillow Book,* does indeed reveal herself in her work as "clever" and "dreadfully conceited."

I heard there was a Lady Chūjō serving in the household of the High Priestess of the Kamo Shrines. By chance someone happened to show me in secret a letter which this Lady Chūjō had written. It was dreadfully affected. She seemed to think there was no one in the world as intelligent or discerning as her; everyone else was judged to be insensitive and lacking in discrimination. When I saw what she had written, I could hardly contain myself and felt very angry, quite "worked up" as the saying goes. I know it was a personal letter but she had actually written: "When it comes to judging poetry, is there anyone who can rival our Princess? She is the only one who could recognize a promising talent nowadays!" There may be some point in what she says, but while she makes such claims for her circle of friends, in fact there are not many poems that her group produces that are of any real merit. Admittedly, it seems to be a very elegant and sophisticated kind of place, but were you to make a comparison, I doubt they would necessarily prove any better than the women I see around me.

They keep themselves very much to themselves. Whenever I have visited them, for it is famous for beautiful moonlit nights, marvellous dawn skies, cherries, and the song of the cuckoo, the High Priestess has always seemed most sensitive. The place has an aura of seclusion and mystery about it, and they have very little to distract them. Rarely are they ever in the rush that we are in whenever Her Majesty visits the Emperor, or when His Excellency decides to come and stay the night. Indeed, the place naturally lends itself to such pleasures, so how could one possibly produce an exchange that offended good taste in the midst of such a striving for the best effects?

If a retiring old fossil like myself were to take service with the High Priestess, I am sure that I would also be able to relax my guard, secure in the knowledge that if I exchanged poems with a man I had not met before I would not automatically be branded a loose woman. I am sure I would absorb the elegance of the place. How much more so if one of our younger women, who have absolutely no drawbacks when it comes to beauty or age, were to put her mind to act seductively and converse by means of poetry; I am convinced that she would compare most favourably.

But here in the Palace there are no other imperial consorts or empresses to keep Her Majesty on her mettle, and there are no ladies-in-waiting in any of the other households who can really challenge us; the result is that all of us, men and women alike, are lacking in any sense of rivalry and simply rest on our laurels. Her Majesty frowns on the slightest hint of seductive behaviour as being the height of frivolity, so anyone who wants to be thought well of takes care never to seem too forward. Of course that is not to say we do not have women among us of quite a different persuasion, women who care nothing for being thought flirtatious and light-hearted and getting a bad name for themselves. The men strike up relationships with this kind of woman because they are such easy game. So they must consider Her Majesty's women either dull or feckless. And as for the upper- and middle-ranking women, they are far too self-satisfied and far too full of themselves. They do nothing to enhance Her Majesty's reputation; in fact they are a disgrace.

Now it may seem that I pretend to know all there is to know about these women, but each one has her own personality and no one is particularly better or worse than anyone else. If they are good in one aspect, they are bad in another, it seems. Mind you, it would, of course, be most improper for the older women to act foolishly at a time when the younger ones themselves are apparently trying to appear serious and dignified; it is just that as a general rule I do wish that they were not quite so stiff.

Her Majesty, although she is so refined, so graceful in all she does, is by nature a little too diffident and will not take the matter up with them. Even were she to do so, she is convinced that there are very few people in this world who can be relied upon with complete confidence. She is right, of course; to do something foolish on an important occasion is worse than just doing things half-heartedly. Once, when she was much younger, Her Majesty heard a lady-in-waiting, who tended to be careless and who thought rather too much of herself on occasions, blurt out some ridiculous things at an important event; it was so dreadfully out of place that she felt deeply shocked. So now she seems to think that the safest policy is to get by in life without a major scandal. I am sure that it is precisely because her women, naïve creatures that they are, have all fitted in so well with her designs that things have turned out as they are.

Her Majesty has gradually matured of late and now understands the ways of the world: that people have their good points and their bad, that they sometimes go to excess and sometimes make mistakes. She is also well aware of the fact that the senior courtiers seem to have become bored with her household, pronouncing it lacking in sparkle.

And yet such reticence is not taken to extremes by all; some women can let themselves go and come out with quite risqué verses. But, although Her Majesty wants the stiff and formal ones to be more lively, and indeed tells them so, their habits are too ingrained. What is more, the young nobles these days are too compliant and act very seriously as long as they are with us. But when they are somewhere like the High Priestess's household they naturally seek to compose all sorts of elegant phrases in praise of the moon or the blossoms, and they say what they think. Here in the Palace, where people traipse in and out day and night and there is little mystery, women who can make the most ordinary conversation sound intriguing or who can compose a passable reply to an interesting poem have become very scarce indeed, or so the men seem to be saying. I have never heard them say this in so many words, however, so I do not know the truth of the matter.

It is ridiculous to respond to someone's overtures with something that causes offence because it has simply been tossed off without due thought. One should take care to give an appropriate response. This is what is meant by the saying "sensitivity is a precious gift." Why should self-satisfied smugness be seen as a sign of wisdom? And there again, why should one continually interfere with other people's lives? To be able to adapt to a situation to the correct degree and then to act accordingly seems to be extremely difficult for most people.

For example, whenever the Master of Her Majesty's Household arrives with a message for Her Majesty, the senior women are so helpless and childish that they hardly ever come out to greet him; and when they do, what happens? They seem unable to say anything in the least bit appropriate. It is not that they are at a loss for words, and it is not that they are lacking in intelligence; it is just that they feel so self-conscious and embarrassed that they are afraid of saying something silly, so they refuse to say anything at all and try to make themselves as invisible as possible. Women in other households cannot possibly act in such a manner! Once one has entered this kind of service, even the highest born of ladies learns how to adapt; but our women still act as though they were little girls who had never left home. And as the Master of the Household has made it plain that he objects to being greeted by a woman of a lower rank, there are times when he leaves without seeing anyone; either because the right woman has gone home or because those women who are in their rooms refuse to come out. Other nobles, the kind who often visit Her Majesty with messages, seem to have secret understandings with particular women of their choice and when that woman is absent they simply retire in disappointment. It is hardly surprising that they take every opportunity to complain the place is moribund.

It must be because of all this that the women in the High Priestess's household look down on us. But even so, it makes little sense to ridicule everyone else and claim: "We are the only ones of note. Everyone else is as good as blind and deaf when it comes to matters of taste." It is very easy to criticize others but far more difficult to put one's own principles into practice, and it is when one forgets this truth, lauds oneself to the skies, treats everyone else as worthless and generally despises others that one's own character is clearly revealed.

It was a letter I would have loved you to have seen for yourself, but the woman who secretly stole it from its hiding place to show me took it back, I remember—such a pity!

Now someone who did carry on a fascinating correspondence was Izumi Shikibu. She does have a rather unsavoury side to her character but has a talent for tossing off letters with ease and seems to make the most banal statement sound special. Her poems are most interesting.

Although her knowledge of the canon and her judgements of other people's poetry leaves something to be desired, she can produce poems at will and always manages to include some clever phrase that catches the attention. Yet when it comes to criticizing or judging the work of others, well, she never really comes up to scratch—the sort of person who relies on a talent for extemporization, one feels. I cannot think of her as a poet of the highest rank.

The wife of the Governor of Tanba is known to everyone in the service of Her Majesty and His Excellency as Masahira Emon. She may not be a genius but she has great poise and does not feel that she has to compose a poem on everything she sees, merely because she is a poet. From what I have seen, her work is most accomplished, even her occasional verse. People who think so much of themselves that they will, at the drop of a hat, compose lame verses that only just hang together, or produce the most pretentious compositions imaginable, are quite odious and rather pathetic.

Sei Shōnagon, for instance, was dreadfully conceited.[1] She thought herself so clever and littered her writings with Chinese characters; but if you examined them closely, they left a great deal to be desired. Those who think of themselves as being superior to everyone else in this way will inevitably suffer and come to a bad end, and people who have become so precious that they go out of their way to try and be sensitive in the most unpromising situations, trying to capture every moment of interest, however slight, are bound to look ridiculous and superficial. How can the future turn out well for them?

Thus do I criticize others from various angles—but here is one who has survived this far without having achieved anything of note. I have nothing in particular to look forward to in the future that might afford me the slightest

---

[1]Sei Shōnagon is the well-known author of the *Pillow Book,* who served Empress Teishi until her mistress died in childbirth in 1000. If she were still alive at this time, and there is no way of telling, she would have been about forty-five.

consolation, but I am not the kind of person to abandon herself completely to despair. And yet, by the same token, I cannot entirely rid myself of such feelings. On autumn evenings, which positively encourage nostalgia, when I go out to sit on the veranda and gaze, I seem to be always conjuring up visions of the past—"and did they praise the beauty of this moon of yore?" Knowing full well that I am inviting the kind of misfortune one should avoid, I become uneasy and move inside a little, while still, of course, continuing to recall the past.[2]

And when I play my *koto* rather badly to myself in the cool breeze of the evening, I worry lest someone might hear me and recognize how I am just "adding to the sadness of it all"; how vain and sad of me. So now both my instruments, the one with thirteen strings and the one with six, stand in a miserable, sooty little closet still ready-strung. Through neglect—I forgot, for example, to ask that the bridges be removed on rainy days—they have accumulated dust and lean against a cupboard. Two *biwa* stand on either side, their necks jammed between the cupboard and a pillar.

There is also a pair of larger cupboards crammed to bursting point. One is full of old poems and tales that have become the home for countless insects which scatter in such an unpleasant manner that no one cares to look at them any more; the other is full of Chinese books that have lain unattended ever since he who carefully collected them passed away. Whenever my loneliness threatens to overwhelm me, I take out one or two of them to look at; but my women gather together behind my back. "It's because she goes on like this that she is so miserable. What kind of lady is it who reads Chinese books?" they whisper. "In the past it was not even the done thing to read *sūtras*!" "Yes," I feel like replying, "but I've never met anyone who lived longer just because they believed in superstitions!" But that would be thoughtless of me. There is some truth in what they say.

Each one of us is quite different. Some are confident, open and forthcoming. Others are born pessimists, amused by nothing, the kind who search through old letters, carry out penances, intone *sūtras* without end, and clack their beads, all of which makes one feel uncomfortable. So I hesitate to do even those things I should be able to do quite freely, only too aware of my own servants' prying eyes. How much more so at court, where I have many things I would like to say but always think the better of it, because there would be no point in explaining to people who would never understand. I cannot be bothered to discuss matters in front of those women who continually carp and are so full of themselves: it would only cause trouble. It is so rare to find someone of true understanding; for the most part they judge purely by their own standards and ignore everyone else.

So all they see of me is a façade. There are times when I am forced to sit with them and on such occasions I simply ignore their petty criticisms, not because I am particularly shy but because I consider it pointless. As a result, they now look upon me as a dullard.

"Well, we never expected this!" they all say. "No one liked her. They all said she was pretentious, awkward, difficult to approach, prickly, too fond of her tales, haughty, prone to versifying, disdainful, cantankerous and scornful; but when you meet her, she is strangely meek, a completely different person altogether!"

How embarrasing! Do they really look upon me as such a dull thing, I wonder? But I am what I am. Her Majesty has also remarked more than once that she had thought I was not the kind of person with whom she could ever relax, but that I have now become closer to her than any of the others. I am so perverse and standoffish. If only I can avoid putting off those for whom I have a genuine regard.

To be pleasant, gentle, calm and self-possessed: this is the basis of good taste and charm in a woman. No matter how amorous or passionate

---

[2]The rhythm here suggests a direct quote from a poem, but no satisfactory source has been identified. Misfortune will come from looking too long and too often at the moon and hence identifying with it; this was said to promote nostalgia, grief and premature ageing.

you may be, as long as you are straightforward and refrain from causing others embarrassment, no one will mind. But women who are too vain and act pretentiously, to the extent that they make others feel uncomfortable, will themselves become the object of attention; and once that happens, people will always find fault with whatever they say or do: whether it be how they enter a room, how they sit down, how they stand up or how they take their leave. Those who end up contradicting themselves and those who disparage their companions are also carefully watched and listened to all the more. As long as you are free from such faults, people will surely refrain from listening to tittle-tattle and will want to show you sympathy, if only for the sake of politeness.

I am of the opinion that when you intentionally cause hurt to another, or indeed if you do ill through mere thoughtless behaviour, you fully deserve to be censured in public. Some people are so good-natured that they can still care for those who despise them, but I myself find it very difficult. Did the Buddha himself in all his compassion ever preach that one should simply ignore those who slander the Three Treasures?[3] How in this sullied world of ours can those who are hard done by be expected not to reciprocate in kind? And yet people react in very different ways. Some glare at each other face to face and fling abuse in an attempt to gain the upper hand; others hide their true intent and appear quite friendly on the surface—thus are true natures revealed.

There is a woman called Saemon no Naishi who, for some strange reason, took a dislike to me. I heard all sorts of malicious, unfounded rumours about myself. His Majesty was listening to someone reading the *Tale of Genji* aloud. "She must have read the *Chronicles of Japan!*" he said. "She seems very learned." Saemon no Naishi suddenly jumped to conclusions and spread it abroad among the senior courtiers that I was flaunting

my learning. She gave me the nickname Lady Chronicle. How very comical! Would I, who hesitate to show my learning even in front of my own servants at home, ever dream of doing so at court?

When my brother, Secretary at the Ministry of Ceremonial, was a young boy learning the Chinese classics, I was in the habit of listening with him and I became unusually proficient at understanding those passages that he found too difficult to grasp and memorize. Father, a most learned man, was always regretting the fact: "Just my luck!" he would say. "What a pity she was not born a man!" But then I gradually realized that people were saying "It's bad enough when a man flaunts his Chinese learning; she will come to no good," and since then I have avoided writing the simplest character. My handwriting is appalling. And as for those "classics" or whatever they are that I used to read, I gave them up entirely. Yet still I kept on hearing these remarks; so in the end, worried what people would think if they heard such rumours, I pretended to be incapable of reading even the inscriptions on the screens. Then Her Majesty asked me to read with her here and there from the *Collected Works* of Po Chü-i,[4] and, because she evinced a desire to know more about such things, to keep it secret we carefully chose times when the other women would not be present, and, from the summer before last, I started giving her informal lessons on the two volumes of "New Ballads." I hid this fact from others, as did Her Majesty, but somehow both His Excellency and His Majesty got wind of it and they had some beautiful copies made of various Chinese books, which His Excellency then presented to her. That gossip Saemon no Naishi could never have found out that Her Majesty had actually asked me to study with her, for had she done so, I would never have heard the last of it. Ah, what a prattling, tiresome world it is!

---

[3] The Three Treasures without which the teachings would not survive were the Buddha himself, the Buddhist Law, and the community of monks who preserved that law. Slander of these three treasures was one of the gravest of offences.

---

[4] Po Chü-i (772–846) was a T'ang dynasty Chinese poet who had the distinction of being well-known and read in Japan during his own lifetime. In Murasaki's time his work still formed the foundation of a courtier's knowledge of Chinese poetry.

Why should I hesitate to say what I want to? Whatever others might say, I intend to immerse myself in reading sūtras for Amida Buddha. Since I have lost what little attachment I ever had for the pains that life has to offer, you might expect me to become a nun without delay. But even supposing I were to commit myself and turn my back on the world, I am certain there would be moments of irresolution before Amida came for me riding on his clouds. And thus I hesitate. I know the time is opportune. If I get much older my eyesight will surely weaken, I shall be unable to read sūtras, and my spirits will fail. It may seem that I am merely going through the motions of being a true believer, but I assure you that now I think of little else. But then someone with as much to atone for as myself may not qualify for salvation; there are so many things that serve to remind one of the transgressions of a former existence.[5] Everything conspires to make me unhappy.

---

[5]Murasaki may be thinking of the fact that she was born a woman and so might well have to go through at least one further rebirth as a man. In Early Buddhism the female state was a major handicap to enlightenment, although by Murasaki's time in Japan textual 'proof' was available, particularly in the *Lotus Sūtra,* that enlightenment was more or less attainable by women.

I want to reveal all to you, the good and the bad, worldly matters and private sorrows, things that I cannot really go on discussing in this letter. But, even though one may be thinking about and describing someone objectionable, should one really go on like this, I wonder? But you must find life irksome at times. I know I do, as you can see. Write to me with your own thoughts—no matter if you have less to say than all my useless prattle, I would love to hear from you. Mind you, if this letter ever got into the wrong hands it would be a disaster—there are ears everywhere.

I have recently torn up and burned most of my old letters and papers. I used the rest to make dolls' houses this last spring and since then no one has written. I feel I should not use new paper, so I am afraid this will look very shabby. It is not through lack of care; quite the opposite.

Please return this as soon as you have read it. There may be parts that are difficult to read and places where I have left out a word or two, but just disregard them and read it through. So you see—I still fret over what others think of me, and, if I had to sum up my position, I would have to admit that I still retain a deep sense of attachment to this world. But what can I do about it?

AS I CROSSED A BRIDGE OF DREAMS

4

Late one Spring night, while immersed in a Tale, I heard a prolonged miaow. I looked up with a start and saw an extremely pretty cat. Where on earth was it from, I wondered. Just then my sister came behind the curtain. "Hush!" she said. "Not a word to anyone! It's a darling cat. Let's keep it!"

The cat was very friendly and lay down beside us. Since we were afraid that people might come looking for her, we kept her hidden in our part of the house. There she stayed faithfully, cuddled up between us; she never went near the servants' quarters and would eat only the daintiest food. We looked after her with great care until one day my sister fell ill and in the confusion I decided to keep our cat in the northern wing of the house. She miaowed loudly at not being allowed into our rooms, but I had expected this and, pitiful though her cries were, I thought it better to keep her away during my sister's illness.

One day my sister suddenly said, "What's happened? Where's our cat? Bring her here!"

"Why?" I asked.

"I've had a dream," she explained. "Our cat

came to me and said, 'I am the daughter of the Chamberlain Major Counsellor, and it is in this form that I have been reborn. Because of some karma between us, your sister grew very fond of me and so I have stayed in this house for a time. But recently she has put me in the servants' quarters, which I find terrible.' She cried and cried, and I thought she looked like a very beautiful and elegant woman. When I awoke, I realized that the words in my dream were the miaowing of our cat. This dream has moved me deeply." I too was moved by my sister's story and thereafter never sent the cat to the northern wing, but looked after her carefully in my own room.

Once when I was alone she came and sat beside me. I stroked her for a long time. "So you are the Major Counsellor's daughter!" I said. "If only I could let His Excellency know that you are here!" Hearing this, she gazed at me intently and gave a long miaow. It may have been my imagination but that moment her eyes were not those of an ordinary cat; they seemed to understand exactly what I was saying.

I heard of a family that owned a copy of *The Song of Everlasting Regret* rewritten as a Tale. I longed to see it, but could not bring myself to ask them. On the seventh day of the Seventh Month I found a suitable opportunity and sent them the poem,

Long ago the Herdsman and the Weaver
    made their vow.
Today my fond thoughts go to them, and
    yearning waves of Heaven's River surge
    within my heart.

This was their reply:

Fondly indeed one views the river where
    those lovers meet,
And forgets the sadness of their ill-starred love.

On the thirteenth night of that month the moon shone brightly, lighting every corner of the earth. At about midnight, when the rest of our household was asleep, my sister and I sat on the veranda. "If I flew away now all of a sudden

and disappeared without a trace," she said, gazing at the sky, "what would you think?" Then, seeing the anxious look on my face, she changed the subject and soon she was laughing and chatting merrily. Presently a carriage approached with a forerunner and stopped by our house. The passenger ordered his attendant to call for someone, "Oginoha, Oginoha!" cried the man, but there was no reply from inside the house and presently he gave up. The gentleman played his flute for a while in a beautiful, clear tone; then the carriage moved away. After it had left I said,

That flute was like the Autumn wind.
Why did the Reed Leaf make no gentle
    answering sound?

My sister nodded and replied,

It was the flute's fault, for it passed too soon
And did not wait for Reed Leaf to reply.

We sat there all night, looking at the sky; at dawn we went to bed.

In the Fourth Month of the following year there was a fire in our house and the cat whom we had tended so carefully as the daughter of His Excellency the Major Counsellor was burnt to death. Whenever I used to call out "Counsellor's daughter!" this cat had miaowed and come to me with a look of understanding on her face. "It really is extraordinary," Father used to say. "I must tell His Excellency about it." How pathetic that she should have died like this!

5

We now had to move into a new house. The old one had been a spacious place that gave one the feeling of being deep in the mountains; and our garden with its Spring blossoms and Autumn leaves had far outshone the surrounding hills. The present house, which had a tiny garden and no trees at all, was smaller than anything I had seen, and the move saddened me greatly. The garden opposite was full of plum trees, which blossomed in a profusion of red and white; when there was a breeze, their scent wafted towards me. One day, overcome with memories of the old house to which I had grown so accustomed, I composed the poem,

> From the neighbouring garden comes a
>   scented breeze.
> Deeply I breathe it in, though longing all
>   the while
> For the plum tree by our ancient eaves.

On the first day of the Fifth Month my sister died while giving birth to her baby. Ever since I was a child the news of people's death, even that of strangers, had disturbed me greatly, and it used to take a long time to recover from the shock. How shattering then was the death of my own sister! I simply cannot describe it. While Mother and the others were gathered in the room where she had died, I took the two little children she had left behind and lay down in my own room, putting one child on my left side, the other on my right. As we lay there, the moon shone through the cracks of the broken shingle roof and lit up the face of one of the children. This seemed a bad omen, so I covered the child's face with the sleeve of my robe and drew the other child close to me. It was distressing to think of what the future would bring.

Some days later I received a letter from a relation: "Your sister asked me to get a copy of this book for her, but I simply could not find out. Just now someone happened to send me a copy. How very sad!" With her letter came a Tale entitled *The Princess Who Sought a Corpse.* Sad indeed! I sent this poem in reply,

> Why should she wish to read of an unburied
>   corpse—
> She who now lies beneath the moss?

My sister's old nurse decided there was nothing to keep her in our house any longer and with much weeping she prepared to leave us and go home. I sent her the farewell poem,

> As she went, so you are leaving too.
> Ah, sorrowful indeed these partings!

"If only I could keep you here as a memory of her!" I added. "I can write no more; for the water in my inkstone has frozen, and my heart too is blocked with grief."

> My brush's strokes that used to flow so free
> Have frozen stiff as icicles.
> What can I write that will remain
> A lasting memory of her who has gone?

Nurse sent this reply,

> There is no comfort left for me.
> Why should the plover now remain
> On the strand of this sad world?

After visiting my sister's grave, Nurse returned in tears and I wrote a further poem,

> There in Toribe Field
> Even the smoke that rose above the pyre
> Has vanished in the sky.
> What traces still remained
> To lead her to my sister's grave?

My stepmother heard about this and sent the following verse,

> There was no trace to lead her to the burial
>   place.
> The only guides were tears
> That fell before her as she walked.

Our relation who had sent a copy of *The Princess Who Sought a Corpse* wrote the poem,

> Ah, what cruel grief was hers
> As she wandered weeping in that desolate
>   bamboo plain,
> Searching for an unmarked grave!

My brother, who had accompanied the funeral procession on that sad night, read this poem and wrote,

> That smoke we watched above her pyre
> Has vanished utterly.

How can she have hoped to find the grave
Among the bamboo grasses of the plain?

6

At a time when it had been snowing for many days I thought of the nun on Mount Yoshino and wrote the poem,

Few travellers pass that way at any time.
Now that the snow has come,
Whom can she hope to see
On Yoshino's steep mountain path?

7

Father had been expecting to celebrate a new appointment after the announcement of the New Year's List, but his hopes were dashed. On the following morning came a letter from someone who had been awaiting the List with the same feelings as ours: "I stayed up all night waiting impatiently for dawn, and confident that my hopes would be realized in spite of everything."

When the tolling of the temple bell
Told me that dawn and my vigil's end had
    come at last,
I felt as though I'd passed a hundred Au-
    tumn nights.

I sent this reply poem,

Why wait the tolling of the temple bell
On a day that took such heavy toll of all
    our hopes?

REVIEW QUESTIONS

1. From Murasaki's description and remarks, what sort of life was it for court women?
2. What is your perception of Murasaki? Explain.
3. The popular translation of Sarashina's diary is entitled *As I Crossed a Bridge of Dreams.* Why do you think the translator picked that title?
4. How is the concept of karma expressed in Sarashina's work?
5. What are some examples of "the evanescence of existence" in either work?

A Rabbi Observes Jewish Communities in East Asia (1160–1173)

RABBI BENJAMIN, *The Travels of Rabbi Benjamin of Tudela*

Rabbi Benjamin of Tudela was born in Tudela, in Navarre, about 1127. Sometime between 1159 and 1163 he embarked on an extensive journey that lasted until 1172 or 1173, when he returned to Navarre. He died in 1173. For about a decade he traveled to or through Italy, Greece, Syria, Palestine, Mesopotamia, Persia, the western borders of China, Egypt, and Sicily. Altogether he visited more than three hundred cities. Rabbi Benjamin's travels are important because they are so extensive and because he kept a meticulous journal of his experiences. Here he described the conditions of the Jewish population of each of the areas he visited, including living conditions, geography, commerce, and politics.

Upon his return to Navarre, Rabbi Benjamin published an account of his travels in Hebrew, *Massaoth Schel Rabbi Benjamin (The Itinerary of Rabbi Benjamin of Tudela).* The importance of this work can be measured by the fact that it was translated into Latin and almost every other European language and became one of the most important travel narratives of the twelfth century. It is especially significant for its account of the Mediterranean world and the Middle East. Moreover, Rabbi Benjamin is considered to be the first European to approach the borders of China.

. . . I returned to the country of Khuzistan, which lies on the Tigris. This river runs downward and falls into the Indian Sea [Persian Gulf], in the vicinity of an island called Kish. The extent of this island is six miles, and the inhabitants do not carry on any agriculture, for they have no rivers, nor more than one spring in the whole island, and are consequently obliged to drink rain water. It is, however, a considerable market, being the spot to which the Indian merchants and those of the islands bring their commodities. While the traders of Mesopotamia, Yemen, and Persia import all silk and purple cloths, flax, cotton, hemp, mash, wheat, barley, millet, rye, and all other sorts of comestibles and pulse, which articles form objects of exchange, those from India import great quantities of spices, and the inhabitants of the island live by what they gain in their capacity of brokers to both parties. The island contains about five hundred Jews.

It is ten days' passage by sea to El-Katif, a city with about five thousand Israelites. In this vicinity the pearls are found. About the twenty-fourth of the month of Nisan [April], large drops of rain are observed upon the surface of the water, which are swallowed by the reptiles, which then close their shells and fall to the bottom of the sea; about the middle of the month of Thishri [October], people dive with the assistance of ropes, collect these reptiles from the bottom, and bring them up, after which they are opened and the pearls taken out.

Seven days distant is Chulam [Marco Polo's Koulam], on the confines of the country of the sun-worshippers, who are descendants of Kush, are addicted to astrology, and are all black. This nation is very trustworthy in matters of trade; and whenever foreign merchants enter their port, three secretaries of the king immediately repair

on board their vessels, write down their names, and report them to him. The king grants them security for their property, which they may even leave in the open fields without any guard. One of the king's officers sits in the market, and receives goods that may have been found anywhere, and which he returns to those applicants who can minutely describe them. This custom is observed in the whole empire of the king.

From Easter to new year [October], during the whole of the summer, the heat is extreme. From the third hour of the day [9:00 A.M.], people shut themselves up in their houses until the evening, at which time everybody goes out. The streets and markets are lighted up, and the inhabitants employ all the night upon their business, which they are prevented from doing in the daytime by the excessive heat.

Pepper grows in this country; the trees which bear this fruit are planted in the fields, which surround the towns, and every one knows his plantation. The trees are small, and the pepper is originally white, but when they collect it they put it into basins and pour hot water upon it; it is then exposed to the heat of the sun, and dried, in order to make it hard and more substantial, in the course of which process it becomes of a black colour. Cinnamon, ginger, and many other kinds of spices also grow in this country.

The inhabitants do not bury their dead, but embalm them with certain spices, put them upon stools, and cover them with cloths, every family keeping apart. The flesh dries upon the bones; and as these corpses resemble living beings, everybody recognizes his parents and all the members of his family for many years to come. These people worship the sun. About half a mile from every town they have large places of worship, and every morning they run towards the rising sun; every place of worship contains a representation of that luminary, so constructed by enchantment that upon the rising of the sun it turns round with a great noise, at which moment both men and women take up their censers and burn incense in honour of this their deity. "This their way is their folly."

All the cities and countries inhabited by these people contain only about one hundred Jews, who are of black colour, as well as the other inhabitants. The Jews are good men, observers of the law, and possess the Pentateuch, the prophets, and some little knowledge of the Talmud and its decisions.

The island of Khandy [Ceylon], is distant twenty-two days' journey. The inhabitants are fire worshippers called Druses, and twenty-three thousand Jews live among them. These Druses have priests everywhere in the houses consecrated to their idols, and these priests are expert necromancers, the like of whom are to be met with nowhere. In front of the altar of their house of prayer is a deep ditch, in which a large fire is continually kept burning; this they call Elahuta, Deity. They pass their children through it, and into this ditch they also throw their dead.

Some of the great of this country take a vow to burn themselves alive; and if any such devotee declares to his children and kindred his intention to do so, they all applaud him and say, "Happy shalt thou be, and it shall be well with thee." When the appointed day arrives, they prepare a sumptuous feast, place the devotee upon his horse, if he be rich, or lead him on foot, if he be poor, to the brink of the ditch. He then throws himself into the fire, and all his kindred manifest their joy by the playing of instruments until he is entirely consumed. Within three days of this ceremony two of the principal priests repair to his house, and thus address his children: "Prepare the house, for to-day you will be visited by your father, who will manifest his wishes unto you." Witnesses are selected among the inhabitants of the town, and lo! the devil appears in the image of the dead. The wife and children inquire after his state in the other world, and he answers: "I have met my companions, but they will not admit me into their company, before I have discharged my debts to my friends and neighbours." He then makes a will, divides his goods among his children, and commands them to discharge all debts he owes and to receive what people owe him; this will is written down by the witnesses. In consequence of this falsehood and deceit, which the priests pass off by magic, they retain a strong hold upon the people, and make them believe that their equal is not to be met with upon earth.

From here the passage to China is effected in forty days. This country lies eastward, and some say that the star Orion predominates in the sea which bounds it, and which is called the Sea of Nikpha. Sometimes this sea is so stormy that no mariner can conduct his vessel; and whenever a storm throws a ship into this sea, it is impossible to govern it; the crew and the passengers consume their provisions, and then die miserably. Many vessels have been lost in this way; but people have learned how to save themselves from this fate by the following contrivance: they take bullocks' hides along with them, and whenever this storm arises and throws them into the Sea of Nikpha, they sew themselves up in the hides, taking care to have a knife in their hand, and being secured against the sea-water, they throw themselves into the ocean. Here they are soon perceived by a large eagle called a griffin, which takes them for cattle, darts down, seizes them in his grip, and carries them upon dry land, where he deposits his burden on a hill or in a dale, there to consume his prey. The man, however, now makes use of his knife to kill the bird, creeps forth from the hide, and tries to reach an inhabited country. Many people have been saved by this stratagem.

Gingaleh is but three days distant by land, although it requires a journey of fifteen days to reach it by sea; this place contains about one thousand Israelites. To Khulan, seven days by sea; no Jews live there. Twelve days to Sebid, which contains but few Jews.

Eight days away is Middle India, which is called Aden, and in Scripture Eden in Thelasar. This country is very mountainous, and contains many independent Jews, who are not subject to the power of the Gentiles, but possess cities and fortresses on the summits of the mountains; from whence they descend into the country of Maatum, with which they are at war. Maatum, also called Nubia, is a Christian kingdom, and the inhabitants are called Nubians. The Jews generally take spoil and plunder from them, which they carry into their mountain fastnesses, the possession of which makes them almost unconquerable. Many of the Jews of Aden visit Egypt and Persia.

REVIEW QUESTIONS

1. From this excerpt, what do you think is the importance of the rabbi's journal?
2. What are some examples of what could be hearsay, rather than firsthand observance?
3. How would you assess the account of Ceylon in regard to credulity and credibility?

A Chinese Scholar Offers Advice to Women (1178)

YÜAN TSAI, *Family and Property in Sung China*

Yüan Tsai, who lived in twelfth-century China, wrote a book of short essays of advice to women. At this time in Japanese society, women themselves seldom wrote; if they did write, very little—with the exception of some outstanding poetry—has survived. The tone of the advice suggests that the author was concerned with women's institutional or societal problems, such as how they fit into the family. He was not interested in problems that women confronted as individuals. This attitude was common in traditional societies, where everybody, men included, had rigidly fixed roles (father/husband, mother/wife). Men's roles, however, were considered of greater import than those of women. Although life was hard in many ways, it could be made more comfortable and pleasant if everybody knew and followed their appropriate roles.

WOMEN SHOULD NOT TAKE PART IN AFFAIRS OUTSIDE THE HOME

Women do not take part in extra-familial affairs. The reason is that worthy husbands and sons take care of everything for them, while unworthy ones can always find ways to hide their deeds from the women.

Many men today indulge in pleasure and gambling; some end up mortgaging their lands, and even go so far as to mortgage their houses without their wives' knowledge. Therefore, when husbands are bad, even if wives try to handle outside matters, it is of no use. Sons must have their mothers' signatures to mortgage their family properties, but there are sons who falsify papers and forge signatures, sometimes borrowing money at high interest from people who would not hesitate to bring their claim to court. Other sons sell illicit tea and salt to get money, which, if discovered by the authorities, results in fines. Mothers have no control in such matters. Therefore, when sons are bad, it is useless for mothers to try to handle matters relating to the outside world.

For women, these are grave misfortunes, but

what can they do? If husbands and sons could only remember that their wives and mothers are helpless and suddenly repent, would that not be best?

WOMEN'S SYMPATHIES SHOULD BE INDULGED

Without going overboard, people should marry their daughters with dowries appropriate to their family's wealth. Rich families should not consider their daughters outsiders but should give them a share of the property. Sometimes people have incapable sons and so have to entrust their affairs to their daughters' families; even after their deaths, their burials and sacrifices are performed by their daughters. So how can people say that daughters are not as good as sons?

Generally speaking, a woman's heart is very sympathetic. If her parents' family is wealthy and her husband's family is poor, she wants to take her parents' wealth to help her husband's family prosper. If her husband's family is wealthy but her parents' family is poor, then she wants to take from her husband's family to enable her parents to prosper. Her parents and husband should be sympathetic toward her feelings and indulge some of her wishes. When her own sons and daughters are grown and married, if either her son's family or her daughter's family is wealthy while the other is poor, she wishes to take from the wealthy one to give to the poor one. Her sons and daughters should understand her feelings and be somewhat indulgent. But taking from the poor to make the rich richer is unacceptable, and no one should ever go along with it.

ORPHANED GIRLS SHOULD HAVE THEIR MARRIAGES ARRANGED EARLY

When a widow remarries she sometimes has an orphaned daughter not yet engaged. In such cases she should try to get a respectable relative to arrange a marriage for her daughter. She should also seek to have her daughter reared in the house of her future in-laws, with the mar-

riage to take place after the girl has grown up. If the girl were to go along with the mother to her step-father's house, she would not be able to clear herself if she were subjected to any humiliations.

FOR WOMEN OLD AGE IS PARTICULARLY HARD TO BEAR

People say that, though there may be a hundred years allotted to a person's life, only a few reach seventy, for time quickly runs out. But for those destined to be poor, old age is hard to endure. For them, until about the age of fifty, the passage of twenty years seems like only ten; but after that age, ten years can feel as long as twenty. For women who live a long life, old age is especially hard to bear, because most women must rely on others for their existence. Before a woman's marriage, a good father is even more important than a good grandfather; a good brother is even more important than a good father; a good nephew is even more important than a good brother. After her marriage, a good husband is even more important than a good father-in-law; a good son is even more important than a good husband; and a good grandson is even more important than a good son. For this reason women often enjoy comfort in their youth but find their old age difficult to endure. It would be well for their relatives to keep this in mind.

IT IS DIFFICULT FOR WIDOWS TO ENTRUST THEIR FINANCIAL AFFAIRS TO OTHERS

Some wives with stupid husbands are able to manage the family's finances, calculating the outlays and receipts of money and grain, without being cheated by anyone. Of those with degenerate husbands, there are also some who are able to manage the finances with the help of their sons without ending in bankruptcy. Even among those whose husbands have died and whose sons are young, there are occasionally women able to raise and educate their sons, keep the affection of all their relatives, manage the family business, and even prosper. All of these are wise and worthy women. But the most remarkable are the women who manage a household after their husbands have died leaving them with young children. Such women could entrust their finances to their husbands' kinsmen or their own kinsmen, but not all relatives are honorable, and the honorable ones are not necessarily willing to look after other people's business.

When wives themselves can read and do arithmetic, and those they entrust with their affairs have some sense of fairness and duty with regard to food, clothing, and support, then things will usually work out all right. But in most of the rest of the cases, bankruptcy is what happens.

BEWARE OF FUTURE DIFFICULTIES IN TAKING IN FEMALE RELATIVES

You should take into your own house old aunts, sisters, or other female relatives whose children and grandchildren are unfilial and do not support them. However, take precautions. After a woman dies, her unfilial sons or grandsons might make outrageous accusations to the authorities, claiming that the woman died from hunger or cold or left valuables in trunks. When the authorities receive such complaints, they have to investigate and trouble is unavoidable. Thus, while the woman is alive, make it clear to the public and to the government that the woman is bringing nothing with her but herself. Generally, in performing charitable acts, it is best to make certain that they will entail no subsequent difficulties.

BEFORE BUYING A SERVANT GIRL OR CONCUBINE, MAKE SURE OF THE LEGALITY

When buying a female servant or concubine, inquire whether it is legal for her to be indentured or sold before closing the deal.[1] If the girl is impoverished and has no one to rely on, then she should be brought before the authorities to give an account of her past. After guarantors have been secured and an investigation conducted, the transaction can be completed. But if she is not able to give an account of her past, then the agent who offered her for sale should be questioned. Temporarily she may be hired on a salaried basis. If she is ever recognized by her relatives, she should be returned to them.

HIRED WOMEN SHOULD BE SENT BACK WHEN THEIR PERIOD OF SERVICE IS OVER

If you hire a man's wife or daughter as a servant, you should return her to her husband or father on completion of her period of service. If she comes from another district, you should send her back to it after her term is over. These practices are the most humane and are widely carried out by the gentry in the Southeast. Yet there are people who do not return their hired women to their husbands but wed them to others instead; others do not return them to their parents but marry them off themselves. Such actions are the source of many lawsuits.

How can one not have sympathy for those separated from their relatives, removed from their hometowns, who stay in service for their entire lives with neither husbands nor sons? Even in death these women's spirits are left to wander all alone. How pitiful they are!

---

[1]In other words, do not buy a girl who was kidnapped, only one whose parents consented to her sale.

REVIEW QUESTIONS

1. Do you discern a "double standard" in regard to men's and women's responsibilities? Explain.
2. How does the question of "rights" apply to this selection? Explain.

3. What is the writer's attitude toward women?
4. Does this reading reflect any fear of women?

A Friar Recounts His Journey to the Mongols (1245)

FRIAR GIOVANNI DA PIAN DEL CARPINI, *The Journey of Friar Giovanni da Pian del Carpini*

Born about 1182, Giovanni da Pian del Carpini (John of Pian de Carpini) at an early age joined the order of Franciscan Friars. He had been an associate of Francis of Assisi and was one of the order's earliest leaders. In 1245 he was put in charge of a papal mission to the Mongols, the first noteworthy journey of a European into the Mongol Empire. This task took him along the famed Silk Road, and despite his age and the hardships involved, the asceticism of his Franciscan training had prepared him well for the arduous journey. The Mongol leader Carpini sought was Kuyuk Khan, a grandson of the great Genghis (Chingiz) Khan. Although Carpini's mission was ostensibly political, he tried to convert Kuyuk, who responded by giving Carpini a letter for the pope demanding his subservience.

Carpini was an astute observer of the Mongol lifestyle, as the following selection shows. Though he understandably disapproved of some Mongol practices, he was rather restrained in his judgment. He seems to have had basic respect for the Mongols, perhaps excusing their more unsavory habits because he understood their nomadic existence and knew that they had not been exposed to Christian doctrine. Much of what is known about Mongol diet and cooking is due to his observations.

OF THE SITUATION, CLIMATE, EMPEROR, AND NATURE OF THE TARTAR'S LAND

There is towards the east a land which is called Mongol, or Tartary, lying in that part of the world which is thought to be most north-easterly. On the east part it has the country of Cathay: on the south part the country of the Saracens: on the south-east the land of the Huins: and on the west the province of Naimans: but on the north side it is bounded by the ocean sea. In some parts it is full of mountains, and in other places plain and smooth ground, but everywhere sandy and barren, neither is the hundredth part of it fruit-

ful. For it cannot bear fruit unless it be moistened with river waters, which are very rare in this country. Therefore they have neither villages nor cities among them, except one which is called Caracarum [the Karakorum of Marco Polo] and is said to be a proper town. We ourselves did not see this town, but were almost within half a day's journey, when we remained at *Syra orda,* which is the great court of their emperor, Kuyuk Khan.

Though this land is unfruitful, yet it is very commodious for the raising of cattle. In certain places there are some small groves of trees growing, but otherwise it is altogether destitute of woods. Therefore the emperor, and his noble men and all others warm themselves, and cook their meat, with fires made of the dung of oxen and horses. The air also in this country is very intemperate; in the midst of summer there are great thunders and lightnings, by the which many men are slain, and at the same time there falls a great abundance of snow. There are also such mighty tempests of cold winds, that sometimes men are not able to sit on horseback. So great is the great wind that we were often constrained to lie grovelling on the earth, and could not see by reason of the dust.

There is never any rain in winter, but only in summer, and so little that sometimes it is scarcely sufficient to down the dust, or to moisten the roots of the grass. There is often times great quantities of hail also. When the emperor-elect was to be placed on his imperial throne, myself being then present, there fell such abundance of hail, that, upon its sudden melting, more than one hundred and sixty persons were drowned. Many tents and other things were also carried away. In the summer season there are sudden waves of extreme heat, and suddenly again waves of intolerable cold.

OF THEIR FORM, HABIT, AND MANNER OF LIVING

The Mongols or Tartars, in outward shape, are unlike to all other people. For they are broader between the eyes, and the balls of their cheeks, than men of other nations. They have flat and small noses, little eyes, and eyelids standing straight upright; they are shaven on the crowns like priests. They wear their hair somewhat longer about their ears, than upon their foreheads; but behind they let it grow long like woman's hair, which they braid into two locks, binding each of them behind either ear. They have short feet also.

The garments, of their men as well as of their women, are all of one fashion. They use neither cloaks, hats, nor capes. But they wear jackets framed after a strange manner, of buckram, scarlet, or brocade. Their gowns are hairy on the outside, and open behind, with tails hanging down

to their hams. They do not wash their garments, neither will they allow them to be washed, especially at the time of thundering.

Their habitations are round and cunningly made with wickers and staves in manner of a tent. But in the middle of the tops, they have an opening to convey the light in and the smoke out. For their fire is always in the midst. Their walls are covered with felt. Their doors are made of felt also. Some of these tabernacles may quickly be taken apart, and set together again, and are carried upon beasts' backs. Others cannot be taken apart, but are moved upon carts. And wherever they go, be it either to war or to any other place, they transport their tabernacles with them.

They are very rich in cattle, such as camels, oxen, sheep, and goats. And I think they have more horses and mares than all the rest of the world. But they have no cows nor other beasts. Their emperors, chiefs, and other of their nobles have much silk, gold, silver, and precious stones.

Their victuals are all things that may be eaten; for we even saw some of them eat lice. They drink milk in great quantity, but especially mares' milk, if they have it. They cook a flour in water, making it so thin, that they may drink thereof. Every one of them drinks off a cupful, or two, in the morning, and sometimes they eat nothing else all the day long. But in the evening each man hath a little flesh given him to eat, and they drink the broth of the meat. In summertime, when they have mares' milk enough, they seldom eat flesh, unless perhaps it be given them, or they take some beast or bird in hunting.

OF THEIR MANNERS, BOTH GOOD AND BAD

Their manners are partly praiseworthy, and partly detestable; for they are more obedient to their lords and masters, than any other either clergy or lay-people in the whole world. They highly reverence them, and will deceive them neither in words nor deeds. They seldom or never fall out among themselves, and, as for fightings or brawlings, wounds or manslaughters, they never happen among them. Neither thieves nor robbers of great riches are to be found, and therefore the tabernacles and carts that have any treasures are not secured with locks or bars.

If any beast should go astray, the finder either lets it go, or drives it to those who are put in office for the purpose, at whose hands the owner of the beast may demand it, and without any difficulty receive it again. They honour one another greatly, and bestow banquets very liberally, notwithstanding that good victuals are dainty and scarce among them. They are also very hardy, and when they have fasted a day or two, they sing and are merry as if they had eaten their bellies full. In riding, they endure much cold and extreme heat. There are, in a manner, no disputes among them, and although they often are drunk, yet they do not quarrel in their drunkenness. No one of them despises another but helps him as much as he conveniently can.

Their women are chaste, neither is there so much as a word uttered concerning dishonesty. Some of them will, however, speak filthy and immodest words. But towards other people, the Tartars are most insolent, and they scorn other persons, noble and ignoble. We saw in the emperor's court the great Duke of Russia, the king's son of Georgia, and many great sultans receiving no due honour. Even the very Tartars assigned to serve them, would always go before them, and take the upper hand of them, and sometimes would even compel them to sit behind their backs. Moreover they are angry and of a disdainful nature unto other people, and beyond all measure deceitful, and treacherous towards them. While they speak fair in the beginning, in conclusion, they sting like scorpions. For crafty they are, and full of falsehood, circumventing all men whom they are able, by their sleights. Whatsoever mischief they intend to practise against a man, they keep it wonderfully secret, so that he may by no means provide for himself, nor find a remedy against their conspiracies.

They are unmannerly also and unclean in taking their meat and their drink, and in other actions. Drunkenness is honourable among them, and when any of them has taken more drink than his stomach can well bear, he calls it up and falls to drinking again. They are most intolerable exactors, most covetous possessors, and most niggardly givers. The slaughter of other people is accounted a matter of nothing with them.

OF THEIR LAWS AND CUSTOMS

Moreover, they have this law or custom, that whatever man and woman are taken in adultery, they are punished with death. A virgin likewise who has committed carnal sin, they slay together with her mate. Whosoever is taken in robbery or theft, is put to death without pity. Also, if any man disclose their secrets, especially in time of war, he receives an hundred blows on the back with a bastinado, laid on by a tall fellow. In like sort when any inferiors offend, they find no favour at their superiors' hands, but are punished with grievous stripes.

They join in matrimony to all in general, even to their near kinsfolks except their mother, daughter and sister by the mother's side. They marry their sister by the father's side only, and also the wife of their father after his decease. The younger brother also, or some other of his kindred, is bound to marry the wife of his elder brother deceased. At the time of our abode in this country, a certain duke of Russia, named Andreas, was accused before Chief Batu for conveying the Tartars' horses out of the land, and for selling them to others; and although it could not be proved, yet he was put to death. His younger brother and the wife of the party deceased, hearing this, came and made their petition to the chief, that the dukedom of Russia might not be taken from them. But he commanded the youth to marry his deceased brother's wife, and the woman also to take him as her husband, according to the custom of the Tartars. She answered that she had rather die, than to so transgress the law. However, he delivered her unto him, although they both refused as much as they could. Carrying them to bed, they compelled the youth, who was lamenting and weeping, to lie down and commit incest with his brother's wife. To be short, after the death of their husbands, the Tartars' wives very seldom marry the second time, unless perhaps some man takes his brother's wife, or his step-mother, in marriage.

They make no difference between the son of their wife and of their concubine, but the father gives what he pleases unto each one. The late king of Georgia having two sons—one lawfully begotten called Melich; but the other, David, born in adultery—at his death left part of his land to his unlawful son. Hereupon Melich, unto whom the kingdom fell by right of his mother because it was governed before-time by women, went unto the Emperor of the Tartars, David also having taken his journey unto him. Now both of them came to the court and brought large gifts. The son of the harlot made suit, that he might have justice, according to the custom of the Tartars. Well, sentence passed against Melich, that David, being his elder brother, should have superiority over him, and should quietly and peaceably possess the portion of land granted unto him by his father.

Whensoever a Tartar has many wives, each one of them has her family and dwelling-place by herself. And sometime the Tartar eats, drinks and lies with one, and sometime with another. One is accounted chief among the rest, with whom he is oftener conversant than with the other. Though they are many, yet do they seldom fall out among themselves.

OF THEIR SUPERSTITIOUS TRADITIONS

By reason of certain traditions, which either they or their predecessors have devised, they believe some things to be faults. One is to thrust a knife into the fire, or any way to touch the fire with a knife, or with their knife to take flesh out of the boiling vessel, or to hew with a hatchet near the fire. For they think by these means one takes away the head or force from the fire. Another is to lean upon a whip with which they beat their horses: for they ride not with spurs. Also to touch arrows with a whip, to take or kill young birds, to strike a horse with the rein of

their bridle, and to break one bone against another. Also to pour out milk, meat, or any kind of drink upon the ground or to make water within their tabernacle: which whosoever does willingly, he is slain, but otherwise he must pay a great sum of money to the enchanter to be purified. Who likewise must cause the tabernacle, with all things therein, to pass between two fires. Before it is in this way purified no man dare enter into it, nor take out anything.

Besides this, if any man has a morsel given him, which he is not able to swallow, and for that cause casts it out of his mouth, there is an hole made under his tabernacle, by which he is drawn forth and slain without compassion. Likewise, whosoever treads upon the threshold of any of their chief's tabernacles, is put to death.

Many other things there are like these, which they take for heinous offences. But to slay men, to invade the dominion of other people, and to rifle their goods, to transgress the commandments and prohibitions of God, are with them no offences at all. They know nothing concerning eternal life and everlasting damnation, and yet they think that after death they shall live in another world; that they shall multiply their cattle, that they shall eat and drink and do other things which living men perform here upon earth.

At a new moon, or a full moon, they begin all new enterprises and they call the moon the Great Emperor, and worship it upon their knees. All men that abide in their tabernacles must be purified with fire: which purification is done in this way. They kindle two fires, and pitch two javelins into the ground near the fires, tying a cord to the tops of the javelins. About the cord they tie certain bits of buckram. Then under the cord, and between the fires, men, beasts, and tabernacles do pass. There stand two women also, one on the right side, and another on the left, casting water, and repeating certain charms. If any man be slain by lightning, all that dwell in the same tabernacle with him must pass by fire in the manner described. Their tabernacles, beds, and carts, they themselves and their garments, and whatever things they have, are touched by no man, but are abandoned by all men as things unclean. In short, they think that all things are to be purged by fire. Therefore, when any ambassadors, princes, or other personages whatsoever come to them, they and their gifts must pass between two fires to be purified, lest they have practised some witchcraft, or have brought some poison or other mischief with them.

REVIEW QUESTIONS

1. What did Carpini like about the Mongols? Why? What did he dislike about the Mongols? Why?
2. How would you compare the marital customs of the Mongols to those of contemporary Americans?
3. How would you evaluate the Mongols' method of punishment?

A Spanish Ambassador Describes the Mongol Court (1403–1406)

RUY GONZALEZ DE CLAVIJO, *The Narrative of the Embassy of Ruy Gonzalez de Clavijo to the Court of Timur*

During his peaceful reign, Enrique III (r. 1379–1406) made a number of attempts to extend diplomatic relations to remote parts of the world. From 1403 to 1406, Ruy Gonzalez de Clavijo led one such expedition to Samarkand, the splendid capital of Timur (Timour, or Tamerlane). A nobleman who kept very meticulous and observant records, he made careful note of the fast horsemen who were the communications and intelligence network of Timur. Since Clavijo did not drink wine, he was able to recount the extraordinary and often drunken feasts popular with Timur and his people. This account, one of the earliest detailed descriptions of Samarkand, is the oldest major Spanish travel narrative still extant.

Europe was in awe of Timur and his conquering army. Indeed, Enrique III had wanted Clavijo to obtain a treaty with Timur, which he didn't get. Although Timur compares with Alexander the Great and Genghis Khan in Central Asian folklore, he failed to build an imperial infrastructure. He is perhaps most noted for his destruction of other states and cities. After Timur's death in 1405 the Timurid Empire withered away, contracting into a kingdom that disappeared a century later.

On Monday, the 8th of September [1404], the ambassadors departed from the garden where they had been lodged, and went to the city of Samarcand. The road went over a plain covered with gardens, and houses, and markets where they sold many things; and at three in the afternoon they came to a large garden and palace, outside the city, where the lord then was. When they arrived, they dismounted, and entered a building outside; where two knights came to them, and said that they were to give up those presents, which they brought for the lord, to certain men who would lay them before him, for such were the orders of the private Meerzas [princes] of the lord; so the ambassadors gave the presents to the two knights. They placed the presents in the arms of men who were to carry them respectfully before the lord, and the ambassador from the Sultan did the same with the presents which he brought.

The entrance to this garden was very broad and high, and beautifully adorned with glazed tiles, in blue and gold. At this gate there were many porters, who guarded it, with maces in their hands. When the ambassadors entered, they came to six elephants, with wooden castles on their backs, each of which had two banners, and there were men on the top of them. The ambassadors went forward, and found the men, who had the presents well arranged on their arms, and they advanced with them in company with the two knights, who held them by the arm pits, and the ambassador whom Timour Beg had sent to the king of Castille was with them; and those who saw him, laughed at him, because he was dressed in the costume and fashion of Castille.

They conducted them to an aged knight, who was seated in an ante-room. He was a son of the sister of Timour Beg, and they bowed reverentially before him. They were then brought before some small boys, grandsons of the lord, who were seated in a chamber, and they also bowed before them. Here the letter, which they brought from the King to Timour Beg, was demanded, and they presented it to one of these boys, who took it. He was a son of Miran Meerza, the eldest son of the lord. The three boys then got up, and carried the letter to the lord; who desired that the ambassadors should be brought before him.

Timour Beg was seated in a portal, in front of the entrance of a beautiful palace; and he was sitting on the ground. Before him there was a fountain, which threw up the water very high, and in it there were some red apples. The lord was seated cross-legged, on silken embroidered carpets, amongst round pillows. He was dressed in a robe of silk, with a high white hat on his head, on the top of which there was a spinal ruby, with pearls and precious stones round it.

As soon as the ambassadors saw the lord, they made a reverential bow, placing the knee on the ground, and crossing the arms on the breast; then they went forward and made another; and then a third, remaining with their knees on the ground. The lord ordered them to rise and come forward; and the knights, who had held them until then, let them go. Three Meerzas, who stood before the lord, and were his most intimate councillors, . . . then came and took the ambassadors by the arms, and led them forward until they stood together before the lord. This was done that the lord might see them better; for his eyesight was bad, being so old that the eyelids had fallen down entirely. He did not give them his hand to kiss, for it was not the custom for any great lord to kiss his hand; but he asked after the king, saying, "How is my son the king? is he in good health?" When the ambassadors had answered, Timour Beg turned to the knights who were seated around him, amongst whom were one of the sons of Tokatmish, the former emperor of Tartary, several chiefs of the blood of the late emperor of Samarcand, and others of the family of the lord himself, and said, "Behold! here are the ambassadors sent by my son the king of Spain, who is the greatest king of the Franks, and lives at the end of the world. These Franks are truly a great people, and I will give my benediction to the king of Spain, my son. It would have sufficed if he had sent you to me with the letter, and without the presents, so well satisfied am I to hear of his health and prosperous state."

The letter which the king had sent was held before the lord, in the hand of his grandson; and the master of theology said, through his interpreter, that no one understood how to read the letter except himself, and that when his highness wished to hear it, he would read it. The lord then took the letter from the hand of his grandson and opened it, saying that he would hear it presently, and that he would send for the master, and see him in private, when he might read it, and say what he desired.

The ambassadors were then taken to a room, on the right hand side of the place where the lord sat; and the Meerzas, who held them by the arms, made them sit below an ambassador, whom the emperor Chayscan, lord of Cathay, had sent to Timour Beg to demand the yearly tribute which was formerly paid. When the lord saw the ambassadors seated below the ambassador from the lord of Cathay, he sent to order that they should sit above him, and he below them. As soon as they were seated, one of the Meerzas of the lord came and said to the ambassador of Cathay, that the lord had ordered that those who were ambassadors from the king of Spain, his son and friend, should sit above him; and that he who was the ambassador from a thief and a bad man, his enemy, should sit below them; and from that time, at the feasts and entertainments given by the lord, they always sat in that order. The Meerza then ordered the interpreter to tell the ambassadors what the lord had done for them.

This emperor of Cathay is called Chuyscan, which means nine empires; but the Zagatays called him Tangus, which means "pig emperor." He is the lord of a great country, and Timour Beg used to pay him tribute, but he refuses to do so now. As soon as these ambassadors, and many others, who had come from distant countries, were seated in order, they brought much meat, boiled, roasted, and dressed in other ways, and roasted horses; and they placed these sheep and horses on very large round pieces of stamped leather. When the lord called for meat, the people dragged it to him on these pieces of leather, so great was its weight; and as soon as it was within twenty paces of him, the carvers came, who cut it up, kneeling on the leather. They cut it in pieces, and put the pieces in basins of gold and silver, earthenware and glass, and porcelain, which is very scarce and precious. The most honorable piece was a haunch of the horse, with the loin, but without the leg, and they placed parts of it in ten cups of gold and silver. They also cut up the haunches of the sheep. They then put pieces of the tripes of the horses, about the size of a man's fist, into the cups, and entire sheep's heads, and in this way they made many dishes. When they had made sufficient, they placed them in rows. Then some men came with soup, and they sprinkled salt over it, and put a little into each dish, as sauce; and they took some very thin cakes of corn, doubled them four times, and placed one over each cup or basin of meat.

As soon as this was done, the Meerzas and courtiers of the lord took these basins, one holding each side, and one helping behind (for a single man could not lift them), and placed them before the lord, and the ambassadors, and the knights who were there; and the lord sent the ambassadors two basins, from those which were placed before him, as a mark of favour. When this food was taken away, more was brought; and it is the custom to take this food, which is given to them, to their lodgings, and if they do not do so, it is taken as an affront; and so much of this food was brought, that it was quite wonderful.

Another custom is, that when they take any food from before any of the ambassadors, they give it to their retinue; and so much food was placed before them, that, if they had taken it away, it would have lasted them for half a year. When the roast and boiled meats were done with, they brought meats dressed in various other ways, and balls of forced meat; and after that, there came fruit, melons, grapes, and nectarines; and they gave them drink out of silver and golden jugs, particularly sugar and cream, a pleasant beverage, which they make in the summer time.

When dinner was finished, the men who bore the presents on their arms passed before the lord, and the same was done with the presents sent by the Sultan of Babylon; and three hundred horses were also brought before the lord, which had been presented that day. After this was done the ambassadors rose, and a knight was appointed to attend upon them, and to see that they were provided with all that they required. This knight, who was the chief porter of the lord, conducted the ambassadors, and the ambassador from the Sultan of Babylon, to a lodging near the place where the lord abode, in which there was a garden, and plenty of water.

When the ambassadors took leave of the lord, he caused the presents which the king had sent, to be brought, and received them with much complacency. He divided the scarlet cloth amongst his women, giving the largest share to his chief wife, named Caño, who was in this garden with him. The other presents, brought by the ambassador from the Sultan, were not received, but returned to the men who had charge of them, who received them, and kept them for three days, when the lord ordered them to be brought again; because it is the custom not to receive a present until the third day. This house and garden, where the lord received the ambassadors, was called Dilkoosha, and in it there were many silken tents, and the lord remained there until the following Friday, when he went to another garden, where there was a very rich palace, which he had lately ordered to be built, called Bayginar. . . .

Now that I have related those things which befell the ambassadors in this city of Samarcand, I will give an account of that city and its territory, and of the things which the lord has done to ennoble it.

The city of Samarcand is situated in a plain, and surrounded by an earthen wall. It is a little larger than the city of Seville, but, outside the city, there are a great number of houses, joined together in many parts, so as to form suburbs. The city is surrounded on all sides by many gardens and vineyards, which extend in some directions a league and a half, in others two leagues, the city being in the middle. In these houses and gardens there is a large population, and there are people selling bread, meat, and many other things; so that the suburbs are much more thickly inhabited than the city within the walls. Amongst these gardens, which are outside the city, there are great and noble houses, and here the lord has several palaces. The nobles of the city have their houses amongst these gardens, and they are so extensive that, when a man approaches the city, he sees nothing but a mass of very high trees. Many streams of water flow through the city, and through these gardens, and among these gardens there are many cotton plantations, and melon grounds, and the melons of this land are good and plentiful; and at Christmas time there is a wonderful quantity of melons and grapes. Every day so many camels come in, laden with melons, that it is a wonder how the people can eat them all. They preserve them from year to year in the villages, in the same way as figs, taking off their skins, cutting them in large slices, and then drying them in the sun.

Outside the city there are great plains, which are covered with populous villages, peopled by the captives which the lord caused to be taken from the countries which he conquered. The land is very plentiful in all things, as well bread as wine, fruit, meat, and birds; and the sheep are very large, and have long tails, some weighing twenty pounds, and they are as much as a man can hold in his hand. . . .

The city is so large, and so abundantly supplied, that it is wonderful; and the name of Samarcand or Cimes-quinte is derived from the two words *cimes* great, and *quinte* a town. The supplies of this city do not consist of food alone, but of silks, satins, gauzes, tafetas, velvets, and other things. The lord had so strong a desire to ennoble this city, that he brought captives to increase its population, from every land which he conquered, especially all those who were skilful in any art. From Damascus he brought weavers of silk, and men who made bows, glass, and earthenware, so that, of those articles, Samarcand produces the best in the world. From Turkey he brought archers, masons, and silversmiths. He also brought men skilled in making engines of war: and he sowed hemp and flax, which had never before been seen in the land.

There was so great a number of people brought to this city, from all parts, both men and women, that they are said to have amounted to one hundred and fifty thousand persons, of many nations, Turks, Arabs, and Moors, Christian Armenians, Greek Catholics, and Jacobites, and those who baptize with fire in the face, who are Christians with peculiar opinions. There was such a multitude of these people that the city was not large enough to hold them, and it was wonderful what a number lived under trees, and in caves outside.

REVIEW QUESTIONS

1. What do you make of the manner in which the Castilian ambassadors are introduced to Timur? What does this tell you about relations between the hosts and their guests?
2. What is your impression of the city?
3. How would you characterize Timur?

Chinese Travelers Describe Malacca (1451, 1436)

MA-HUAN, *Ying-Yai Sheng-Lan* (1451)
FEI-HSIN, *Hsing-Ch'a Sheng-Lan* (1436)

Historically, China's long-standing objective in Southeast Asia has been to gain political and economic hegemony in the area. This policy was the logical culmination of the Chinese view of themselves as inhabitants of the Middle Kingdom, which they considered the cultural and political center of the world. Whenever strong enough to do so, the Chinese demanded tribute from neighboring states and even from those at considerable distances (see accounts of Chinese delegations to Rome and Parthia in Chapters 4 and 5). Because of its geographical location and commercial importance, Malacca would have been a target of special interest. These two accounts in particular reveal the degree of interest China had in states it considered tributary—their people, customs, lands, and even the flora and fauna.

The Chinese could confer a particular status upon regional kingdoms, as related toward the end of the second selection, when Cheng Ho, formally representing the imperial Chinese government, presented prestigious symbols and raised Malacca to the rank of a kingdom. Cheng Ho (Zeng-He) was the famous admiral who in a series of expeditions (1405–1433) traversed the Indian Ocean as far as the east coast of Africa. Some of his adventures are also related in Chapter 12 of this volume.

YING-YAI SHENG-LAN

Formerly [Malacca] was not styled a kingdom but was known as the Five Isles, because there were that number of islands off that part of the coast. It had no king, but only a chieftain. The country was under the rule of *Hsien-lo* (Siam), to which it paid an annual [tribute] of 40 taels of gold. Default [in this matter] would have provoked an attack. In the seventh year of the ssŭ-ch'ou [period] of the Yung-lo [Emperor] the eunuch Cheng-Ho, [in his capacity as] an imperial envoy, conveyed [to Malacca] the commands of the Emperor, [in token of which] he bestowed on the chieftain of that country a pair of silver seals, a head-dress, a girdle and a long robe. He raised the place to the status of a city, since when it has been known as the Kingdom of Malacca. Henceforth the Siamese dared not venture to attack it, and the ruler, now by the imperial favour [styled] king, proceeded in company with his consort to the capital [of China], where he expressed his gratitude and offered products of his country as tribute. The Emperor then assigned him a ship in which to return home so that he might [continue to] govern his land. To the south-east [of this country] is the ocean, to the north-west the mainland, which is continued as a chain of mountains. The soil is sandy and saline. Temperatures are hot during the day, but cool at night. The infertile fields yield little rice, so that the people are not greatly concerned with agriculture. A sizeable stream flows by the royal palace before entering the sea. Over this the King has built a bridge, on which he has constructed some twenty booths for the sale of all kinds of commodities. Both the King and his subjects revere the laws of Islam, and observe its fasts and penances. The King wears a white turban of fine local cloth, a long floral robe of fine green calico, and leather shoes. He fares abroad in a palanquin. Among the [common] people the men wear square, cotton kerchiefs round their heads, and the women dress their hair in chignons. The bodies [of the people] are rather dark [in colour]. They wrap a length of white cotton round their loins and wear short bajus of cotton print. Their customs and usages are pure and simple. Their houses are raised on one-storey platforms and lack a layer of planks [against the ground], but a floor of split coconut-palms is erected and lashed with rattan—exactly as if it were a sheep-pen—at a height of about four feet. On this floor [the people] spread their beds and mats, on which they sit cross-legged, and [on this floor] they also eat, sleep and cook. Most of the inhabitants [of Malacca] are occupied in fishing, for which they venture out to sea in boats hollowed from a single tree [-trunk].

Local products include *Coptis teeta* (rhizomes), ebony, damar, tin and suchlike. Damar in its original state is the sap of a tree which flows into the ground and is then dug up. It oozes from the tree in gouts in the same way as the resin of the pine does. When lit, it continues to burn, and the native people use it for lighting purposes. When they have finished building a boat, they smear this substance along the seams to render them waterproof. The people gather a great deal [of damar] for sale to other countries. A superior variety, which is clear, transparent and resembles amber, is called *sun-tu-lu-ssŭ*. The local people make it into beads for *těngkolok*. These beads, which they sell, are known as water amber. Tin occurs in two localities in the mountains, and the King [of Malacca] has appointed officials to control [these districts]. Men wash [the tin] in sieves, smelt it and cast it into ingots of disk-like shape, the standard weight of which is either 1 kati 8 taels or 1 kati 4 taels. Ten ingots bound together with rattan constitute a small bundle, forty ingots a large bundle. In all their trade transactions [the people] use [these ingots of] tin. The language, the books and the marriage ceremonies [of Malacca] closely resemble those of *Chao-wa* (Java). In the mountainous wilderness [of the interior] is a palm known as the sago. The country folk pound the bark [of this palm], which resembles the root of the Chinese bean, soak it in water, [allow it] to settle and strain it. The flour obtained in this way is moulded into pellets of the size of green peas, which are dried in the sun and sold as food. On the low ground bordering the sea there grows a palm whose fronds are as long as those of the kajang. When its sword-like leaves first appear they are [as pliable as] young bamboo shoots. The fruits have the appearance of lichees, and are of the size of hen's eggs. The people use them to ferment a liquor, which they call kajang wine and which has the power of intoxication. The local folk interweave the leaves of this plant with bamboo to make fine quality mats which, although only two feet wide, exceed ten feet in length. These they offer for sale. There are sugar-cane, plantains, jack-fruit, wild lichees and suchlike.

The vegetables include onions, ginger, leeks, mustard, gourds, watermelons and so forth. Cattle, goats, fowls and ducks are few, and therefore costly, a head of buffalo being priced at a kati of silver. There are neither donkeys nor horses [in the land]. The shores of the sea are inhabited by turtles and by dragons which [are capable of] wounding men. This dragon is three or four feet high, has four legs and a body which is completely encased in scales. It has a ridge of spines along its back, a dragon's head and teeth well adapted to grasping prey. It will devour any man whom it chances to encounter. In the mountains there is a yellow tiger, which is rather smaller than the yellow tiger of China. There is also a black species and a yellow one with dark spots. Some species of tigers, which can assume human form, frequent the capital and mix with the populace. If anyone recognizes one [of these creatures] he seizes and kills it. They are similar to the corpse-headed barbarians of *Chan-ch'eng*

(Campā). When this place (Malacca) is visited by Chinese merchant vessels [the inhabitants] erect a barrier [for the collection of duties]. There are four gates in the city wall, each furnished with watch- and drum-towers. At night men with hand-bells patrol [the precincts]. Inside the walls a second small enclosure of palisades has been built where godowns have been constructed for the storage of specie and provisions. When the government ships were returning homewards, they visited this place in order both to repair [their vessels] and to load local products. Here they waited for a favourable wind from the south, and in the middle of the fifth month they put out to sea on their return voyage. The King [of Malacca], accompanied by his consort, his son and some of his headmen, laid in products of his country and followed [our] fleet [to China], where he came to court and presented tribute.

HSING-CH'A SHENG-LAN

This place did not formerly rank as a kingdom. It can be reached from Palembang on the monsoon in eight days. The coast is rocky and desolate, the population sparse. The country [used to] pay an annual tax of 40 taels of gold to Siam. The soil is infertile and yields low. In the interior there is a mountain from [the slopes of] which a river takes its rise. The [local] folk pan the sands [of this river] to obtain tin, which they smelt into ingots called *tou*. These weigh 1 kati 4 taels standard weight. [The inhabitants] also weave banana fibre into mats. Apart from tin, no other product enters into [foreign] trade. The climate is hot during the day but cool at night. [Both] sexes coil there hair into a knot. Their skin resembles black lacquer, but there are [some] white-complexioned folk among them

who are of Chinese descent. The people esteem sincerity and honesty. They make a living by panning tin and catching fish. Their houses are raised above the ground. [When constructing them] they refrain from joining planks and restrict the building to the length of a [single] piece of timber. When they wish to retire, they spread their bedding side by side. They squat on their haunches when taking their meals. The kitchen and all its appurtenances is [also] raised [on the stilts]. The goods [used in trading at Malacca] are blue and white porcelain, coloured beads, coloured taffetas, gold and silver. In the seventh year of Yung-lo (1409), the imperial envoy, the eunuch Cheng-Ho, and his lieutenants conferred [on the ruler], by Imperial command, a pair of silver seals, and a head-dress, girdle and robe. They also set up a tablet [stating that] Malacca has been raised to the rank of a kingdom, but at first Siam refused to recognize it. In the thirteenth year [of Yung-lo] (1415), the ruler [of Malacca, desirous of] showing his gratitude for the Imperial bounty, crossed the ocean and, accompanied by his consort and son, came to court with tribute. The Emperor rewarded him [appropriately], whereupon [the ruler of Malacca] returned to his [own] country.

REVIEW QUESTIONS

1. Why would the king of Malacca himself have taken the tribute to the Chinese court? Why do you think he had his wife and son accompany him?
2. What are the most important similarities and/or differences between the first account (1451) and the second (1436)?
3. Would you characterize the descriptions given in these accounts as positive or negative? Why? What does this tell you about the authors' values?

14

The Americas, 800–1550

European adventurers, explorers, priests, missionaries, and conquerors have left the first records of travel in the Americas. Although Native Americans also traveled extensively, most writings that would reveal their experiences with each other and various Europeans have been lost or destroyed or have remained untranslated. Consequently, European encounters with Native Americans provide the framework of what is known about the Americas before 1550, and they offer some of the most interesting descriptions of a given society by foreigners in all of world history. All of the accounts in this section were written by Europeans of Norse, Italian, French, German, Spanish, and Portuguese nationalities. The few native accounts that still exist are fragmentary and most of those have not been translated into modern languages. Even the sources that purport to speak from the natives' point of view come to us through the filter of the European mentality. For example, the narrative of Diego de Landa presents his impressions of Mayan histories as told by natives.

The accounts in this chapter record the impressions of the first Europeans who reported their discoveries from their national perspective and usually emphasized cultural criteria that were important in their homelands and occupations. The Norse encounters with the Skraelings of Newfoundland and Pigafetta's account of meetings with Native Americans in Patagonia and islanders in the South Pacific create windows into extraordinary occurrences while they reveal what these explorers believed to be the most important characteristics of civilizations. Belief in a unified Christian religion and close association with nationalistic ties provided the rationalization for their intrusion into native cultures.

The meeting of peoples from the Eastern and Western Hemispheres set a precedent unlike any other before or after. Peoples without writing systems and nations with inferior military technology were unable to tell their stories of the encounters. Even nations without advanced military technology and sophisticated writing systems were disregarded and deemed barbarian and incomprehensible. The existence of a "New World," and an inhabited one at that, shocked Europeans and upset their centuries-old conceptions of the size, shape, and characteristics of their world. Indeed, one wonders if modern people would be more objective in describing life on other planets, should it ever be discovered.

A Norse Epic Recounts Early Voyages in the North Atlantic (late twelfth century)

The Vinland Sagas

In 985 or 986, a merchant ship captained by Bjarni Herjolfsson, carrying colonists from Norway to the Norse colony on the western coast of Greenland, passed its destination in a storm and was blown southwest across the north Atlantic, probably onto the coast of Labrador. Herjolfsson's account is probably the first by a European regarding lands now considered to be American. Fifteen years later, Leif the Lucky followed the route of Herjolfsson's voyage to return to Labrador and attempted to locate usable resources. There he found many natural foods and attributes that were of interest to the Greenland colony, including rivers that teemed with giant salmon and fields of wild wheat. Leif named the country Vinland, or Wineland, because of the abundance of grapes. Although these voyagers may not represent the first European contacts with the New World, they are the first to return to Europe and write about what they found.

The Norsemen who followed Leif the Lucky a few years later had different priorities. They were more interested in establishing permanent settlements than in merely harvesting salmon. Bringing colonists and cattle, Thorfinn Karlsefni, an Icelandic merchant and Leif's brother-in-law, established the first permanent European settlement in the New World about 1015. Recent excavations of a Norse-type village that dates from about 1000 indicate that this colony may have been near the mouth of the St. Lawrence Seaway, at L'Anse aux Meadows, on a bay on the northeast coast of Newfoundland.

Virtually everything we know about the settlers' lives and their relationships with Native Americans comes from the *Vinland Sagas,* from which the following excerpts were taken. About sixty years after Thorfinn Karlsefni's voyage, the first references to the Vinland colony began to be included in these Norse writings. The *Vinland Sagas* comprise two sagas: the *Graenlendinga Saga,* written about 150 years after the events it describes, and *Eirik's Saga,* probably compiled around the mid-1200s. These have been accepted as the most accurate narratives of the experiences of the colony, superseding an earlier account of Vinlandia in 1075 that appeared in a monumental Latin history written by Adam of Bremen.

GRAENLENDINGA SAGA

Leif Explores Vinland

Some time later, Bjarni Herjolfsson sailed from Greenland to Norway and visited Earl Eirik,[1] who received him well. Bjarni told the earl about

---

[1]Earl Eirik Hakonarson ruled over Norway from 1000 to 1014.

his voyage and the lands he had sighted. People thought he had shown great lack of curiosity, since he could tell them nothing about these countries, and he was criticized for this. Bjarni was made a retainer at the earl's court, and went back to Greenland the following summer.

There was now great talk of discovering new countries. Leif, the son of Eirik the Red of Brattahlid, went to see Bjarni Herjolfsson and bought his ship from him, and engaged a crew of thirty-five.

Leif asked his father Eirik to lead this expedition too, but Eirik was rather reluctant: he said he was getting old, and could endure hardships less easily than he used to. Leif replied that Eirik would still command more luck[2] than any of his kinsmen. And in the end, Eirik let Leif have his way.

As soon as they were ready, Eirik rode off to the ship which was only a short distance away. But the horse he was riding stumbled and he was thrown, injuring his leg.

"I am not meant to discover more countries than this one we now live in," said Eirik. "This is as far as we go together."[3]

Eirik returned to Brattahlid, but Leif went aboard the ship with his crew of thirty-five. Among them was a Southerner called Tyrkir.[4]

They made their ship ready and put out to sea. The first landfall they made was the country that Bjarni had sighted last. They sailed right up to the shore and cast anchor, then lowered a boat and landed. There was no grass to be seen, and the hinterland was covered with great glaciers, and between glaciers and shore the land was one great slab of rock. It seemed to them a worthless country.

Then Leif said, "Now we have done better than Bjarni where this country is concerned—we at least have set foot on it. I shall give this country a name and call it *Helluland.*"[5]

They returned to their ship and put to sea, and sighted a second land. Once again they sailed right up to it and cast anchor, lowered a boat and went ashore. This country was flat and wooded, with white sandy beaches wherever they went; and the land sloped gently down to the sea.

Leif said, "This country shall be named after its natural resources: it shall be called *Markland.*"[6]

They hurried back to their ship as quickly as possible and sailed away to sea in a north-east wind for two days until they sighted land again. They sailed towards it and came to an island which lay to the north of it.

They went ashore and looked about them. The weather was fine. There was dew on the grass, and the first thing they did was to get some of it on their hands and put it to their lips, and to them it seemed the sweetest thing they had ever tasted. . . .

Thorvald Explores Vinland

Thorvald prepared his expedition with his brother Leif's guidance and engaged a crew of thirty. When the ship was ready they put out to sea and there are no reports of their voyage until they reached Leif's Houses in Vinland. There they laid up the ship and settled down for the winter, catching fish for their food.

In the spring Thorvald said they should get the ship ready, and that meanwhile a small party of men should take the ship's boat and sail west along the coast and explore that region during the summer.

They found the country there very attractive, with woods stretching almost down to the shore and white sandy beaches. There were numerous islands there, and extensive shallows. They found no traces of human habitation or animals except on one westerly island, where they found a wooden stack-cover. That was the only man-made thing they found; and in the autumn they returned to Leif's Houses.

Next summer Thorvald sailed east with his ship and then north along the coast. They ran into a fierce gale off a headland and were driven ashore; the keel was shattered and they had to stay there for a long time while they repaired the ship.

Thorvald said to his companions, "I want to erect the old keel here on the headland, and call the place *Kjalarness.*"

---

[2]"Luck" had a greater significance in pagan Iceland than the word implies now. Good luck or ill luck were innate qualities, part of the complex pattern of Fate. Leif inherited the good luck associated with his father. . . .
[3]A fall from a horse was considered a very bad omen for a journey. Such a fall clinched Gunnar of Hildarend's decision not to leave Iceland when he was outlawed. . . .
[4]*Southerner* refers to someone from central or southern Europe; Tyrkir appears to have been a German.
[5]Literally, "Slab-land"; probably Baffin Island. . . .

---

[6]Literally, "Forest-land"; probably Labrador. . . .

They did this and then sailed away eastward along the coast. Soon they found themselves at the mouth of two fjords, and sailed up to the promontory that jutted out between them; it was heavily wooded. They moored the ship alongside and put out the gangway, and Thorvald went ashore with all his men.

"It is beautiful here," he said. "Here I should like to make my home."

On their way back to the ship they noticed three humps on the sandy beach just in from the headland. When they went closer they found that these were three skin-boats,[7] with three men under each of them. Thorvald and his men divided forces and captured all of them except one, who escaped in his boat.[*] They killed the other eight and returned to the headland, from which they scanned the surrounding country. They could make out a number of humps farther up the fjord and concluded that these were settlements.

Then they were overwhelmed by such a heavy drowsiness that they could not stay awake, and they all fell asleep—until they were awakened by a voice that shouted, "Wake up, Thorvald, and all your men, if you want to stay alive! Get to your ship with all your company and get away as fast as you can!"

A great swarm of skin-boats was then heading towards them down the fjord.

Thorvald said, "We shall set up breastworks on the gunwales and defend ourselves as best we can, but fight back as little as possible."

They did this. The Skraelings shot at them for a while, and then turned and fled as fast as they could.

Thorvald asked his men if any of them were wounded; they all replied that they were unhurt.

"I have a wound in the armpit," said Thorvald. "An arrow flew up between the gunwale and my shield, under my arm—here it is. This will lead to my death.

"I advise you now to go back as soon as you can. But first I want you to take me to the headland I thought so suitable for a home. I seem to have hit on the truth when I said that I would settle there for a while. Bury me there and put crosses at my head and feet, and let the place be called *Krossaness* for ever afterwards." . . .

Karlsefni in Vinland

That same summer a ship arrived in Greenland from Norway. Her captain was a man called Thorfinn Karlsefni. He was a man of considerable wealth. He spent the winter with Leif Eiriksson at Brattahlid.

Karlsefni quickly fell in love with Gudrid and proposed to her, but she asked Leif to answer on her behalf. She was betrothed to Karlsefni, and the wedding took place that same winter.

There was still the same talk about Vinland voyages as before, and everyone, including Gudrid, kept urging Karlsefni to make the voyage. In the end he decided to sail and gathered a company of sixty men and five women. He made an agreement with his crew that everyone should share equally in whatever profits the expedition might yield. They took livestock of all kinds, for they intended to make a permanent settlement there if possible.

Karlsefni asked Leif if he could have the houses in Vinland; Leif said that he was willing to lend them, but not to give them away.

They put to sea and arrived safe and sound at Leif's Houses and carried their hammocks ashore. Soon they had plenty of good supplies, for a fine big rorqual was driven ashore; they went down and cut it up, and so there was no shortage of food.

The livestock were put out to grass, and soon the male beasts became very frisky and difficult to manage. They had brought a bull with them.

Karlsefni ordered timber to be felled and cut into lengths for a cargo for the ship, and it was left out on a rock to season. They made use of all the natural resources of the country that were available, grapes and game of all kinds and other produce.

The first winter passed into summer, and then

---

[7]Certain Red Indian tribes of the New England area used canoes made of moose-hide instead of the more usual birchbark.

[*]This was the first contact with natives.

they had their first encounter with Skraelings, when a great number of them came out of the wood one day. The cattle were grazing near by and the bull began to bellow and roar with great vehemence. This terrified the Skraelings and they fled, carrying their packs which contained furs and sables and pelts of all kinds. They made for Karlsefni's houses and tried to get inside, but Karlsefni had the doors barred against them. Neither side could understand the other's language.

Then the Skraelings put down their packs and opened them up and offered their contents, preferably in exchange for weapons; but Karlsefni forbade his men to sell arms. Then he hit on the idea of telling the women to carry milk out to the Skraelings, and when the Skraelings saw the milk they wanted to buy nothing else. And so the outcome of their trading expedition was that the Skraelings carried their purchases away in their bellies, and left their packs and furs with Karlsefni and his men.

After that, Karlsefni ordered a strong wooden palisade to be erected round the houses, and they settled in.

About this time Karlsefni's wife, Gudrid, gave birth to a son, and he was named Snorri.

Early next winter the Skraelings returned, in much greater numbers this time, bringing with them the same kind of wares as before. Karlsefni told the women, "You must carry out to them the same produce that was most in demand last time, and nothing else."

As soon as the Skraelings saw it they threw their packs in over the palasade.

Gudrid was sitting in the doorway beside the cradle of her son Snorri when a shadow fell across the door and a woman entered wearing a black, close-fitting tunic; she was rather short and had a band round her chestnut-coloured hair. She was pale, and had the largest eyes that have ever been seen in any human head. She walked up to Gudrid and said, "What is your name?"

"My name is Gudrid. What is yours?"

"My name is Gudrid," the woman replied.

Then Gudrid, Karlsefni's wife, motioned to the woman to come and sit beside her; but at that very moment she heard a great crash and the woman vanished, and in the same instant a Skraeling was killed by one of Karlsefni's men for trying to steal some weapons. The Skraelings fled as fast as they could, leaving their clothing and wares behind. No one had seen the woman except Gudrid.

"Now we must devise a plan," said Karlsefni, "for I expect they will pay us a third visit, and this time with hostility and in greater numbers. This is what we must do: ten men are to go out on the headland here and make themselves conspicuous, and the rest of us are to go into the wood and make a clearing there, where we can keep our cattle when the Skraelings come out of the forest. We shall take our bull and keep him to the fore."

The place where they intended to have their encounter with the Skraelings had the lake on one side and the woods on the other.

Karlsefni's plan was put into effect, and the Skraelings came right to the place that Karlsefni had chosen for the battle. The fighting began, and many of the Skraelings were killed. There was one tall and handsome man among the Skraelings and Karlsefni reckoned that he must be their leader. One of the Skraelings had picked up an axe, and after examining it for a moment he swung it at a man standing beside him, who fell dead at once. The tall man then took hold of the axe, looked at it for a moment, and then threw it as far as he could out into the water. Then the Skraelings fled into the forest as fast as they could, and that was the end of the encounter.

Karlsefni and his men spent the whole winter there, but in the spring he announced that he had no wish to stay there any longer and wanted to return to Greenland. They made ready for the voyage and took with them much valuable produce, vines and grapes and pelts. They put to sea and reached Eiriksfjord safely and spent the winter there. . . .

One day, Freydis Eirik's-daughter travelled from her home at Gardar to visit the brothers Helgi and Finnbogi. She asked them if they would join her with their ship on an expedition to Vinland, sharing equally with her all the profits that might be made from it. They agreed to this. Then she went to see her brother Leif and asked him to give her the houses he had built in Vinland; but Leif gave the same answer as before—that he was willing to lend them but not to give them away.

The two brothers and Freydis had an agreement that each party should have thirty able-bodied men on board, besides women. But Freydis broke the agreement at once by taking five more men, whom she concealed; and the brothers were unaware of this until they reached Vinland.

So they put to sea, and before they left they agreed to sail in convoy if possible. There was not much distance between them, but the brothers arrived in Vinland shortly before Freydis and had moved their cargo up to Leif's Houses by the time Freydis landed. Her crew unloaded her ship and carried the cargo up to the houses.

"Why have you put your stuff in here?" asked Freydis.

"Because," the brothers replied, "we had thought that the whole of our agreement would be honoured."

"Leif lent these houses to me, not to you," she said.

Then Helgi said, "We brothers could never be a match for you in wickedness."

They moved their possessions out and built themselves a house farther inland on the bank of a lake, and made themselves comfortable there. Meanwhile Freydis was having timber felled for her cargo.

When winter set in, the brothers suggested that they should start holding games and other entertainments. This was done for a while until trouble broke out and ill-feeling arose between the two parties. The games were abandoned and all visiting between the houses ceased; and this state of affairs continued for most of the winter.

Early one morning Freydis got up and dressed, but did not put on her shoes. There was heavy dew outside. She put on her husband's cloak and then walked to the door of the brothers' house. Someone had just gone outside, leaving the door ajar. She opened it and stood in the doorway for a while without a word. Finnbogi was lying in the bed farthest from the doorway; he was awake, and now he said, "What do you want here, Freydis?"

"I want you to get up and come outside with me," she replied. "I want to talk to you."

He did so, and they walked over to a tree-trunk that lay beside the wall of the house, and sat down on it.

"How are you getting on?" she asked.

"I like this good country," he replied, "but I dislike the ill-feeling that has arisen between us, for I can see no reason for it."

"You are quite right," she said, "and I feel the same about it as you do. But the reason I came to see you is that I want to exchange ships with you and your brother, for your ship is larger than mine and I want to go away from here."

"I shall agree to that," he said, "if that will make you happy."

With that they parted. Finnbogi went back to his bed and Freydis walked home. When she climbed into bed her feet were cold and her husband Thorvard woke up and asked why she was so cold and wet. She answered with great indignation, "I went over to see the brothers to offer to buy their ship, because I want a larger one; and this made them so angry that they struck me and handled me very roughly. But you, you wretch, would never avenge either my humiliation or your own. I realize now how far I am away from my home in Greenland! And unless you avenge this, I am going to divorce you."[8]

He could bear her taunts no longer and told his men to get up at once and take their weapons. They did so, and went straight over to the brothers' house; they broke in while all the men were asleep, seized them and tied them up, and dragged them outside one by one. Freydis had each of them put to death as soon as he came out.

---

[8]Under Icelandic law of this period, a woman had equal rights in marriage and could obtain a divorce by declaration. If she were judged to have valid grounds she could claim half of the husband's estate.

All the men were killed in this way, and soon only the women were left; but no one was willing to kill them.

Freydis said, "Give me an axe."

This was done, and she herself killed the women, all five of them.

After this monstrous deed they went back to their house, and it was obvious that Freydis thought she had been very clever about it. She said to her companions, "If we ever manage to get back to Greenland I shall have anyone killed who breathes a word about what has just happened. Our story will be that these people stayed on here when we left."

Early in the spring they prepared the ship that had belonged to the brothers and loaded it with all the produce they could get and the ship could carry. Then they put to sea. They had a good voyage and reached Eiriksfjord early in the summer.

Karlsefni was still there when they arrived. His ship was all ready to sail and he was only waiting for a favourable wind. It is said that no ship has ever sailed from Greenland more richly laden than the one Karlsefni commanded.

EIRIK'S SAGA

Karlsefni Goes South

Karlsefni sailed south along the coast, accompanied by Snorri and Bjarni and the rest of the expedition. They sailed for a long time and eventually came to a river that flowed down into a lake and from the lake into the sea. There were extensive sandbars outside the river mouth, and ships could only enter it at high tide.

Karlsefni and his men sailed into the estuary and named the place *Hope* (Tidal Lake). Here they found wild wheat growing in fields on all the low ground and grape vines on all the higher ground. Every stream was teeming with fish. They dug trenches at the high-tide mark, and when the tide went out there were halibut trapped in the trenches. In the woods there was a great number of animals of all kinds.

They stayed there for a fortnight, enjoying

themselves and noticing nothing untoward. They had their livestock with them. But early one morning as they looked around they caught sight of nine skin-boats; the men in them were waving sticks which made a noise like flails, and the motion was sunwise.[9]

Karlsefni said, "What can this signify?"

"It could well be a token of peace," said Snorri. "Let us take a white shield and go to meet them with it."

They did so. The newcomers rowed towards them and stared at them in amazement as they came ashore. They were small and evil-looking, and their hair was coarse; they had large eyes and broad cheekbones. They stayed there for a while, marveling, and then rowed away south round the headland.

Karlsefni and his men had built their settlement on a slope by the lakeside; some of the houses were close to the lake, and others were farther away. They stayed there that winter. There was no snow at all, and all the livestock were able to fend for themselves.

The Skraelings Attack

Then, early one morning in spring, they saw a great horde of skin-boats approaching from the south round the headland, so dense that it looked as if the estuary were strewn with charcoal; and sticks were being waved from every boat. Karlsefni's men raised their shields and the two parties began to trade.

What the natives wanted most to buy was red cloth; they also wanted to buy swords and spears, but Karlsefni and Snorri forbade that. In exchange for the cloth they traded grey pelts. The natives took a span[10] of red cloth for each pelt, and tied the cloth round their heads. The trading went on like this for a while until the cloth began to run short; then Karlsefni and his men cut it up into pieces which were no more

---

[9]Red Indians are known to have used rattle-sticks during various rituals, which may well be the explanation of this threshing sound the Norsemen could hear.
[10]About nine inches.

than a finger's breadth wide; but the Skraelings paid just as much or even more for it.

Then it so happened that a bull belonging to Karlsefni and his men came running out of the woods, bellowing furiously. The Skraelings were terrified and ran to their skin-boats and rowed away south round the headland.

After that there was no sign of the natives for three whole weeks. But then Karlsefni's men saw a huge number of boats coming from the south, pouring in like a torrent. This time all the sticks were being waved anti-clockwise and all the Skraelings were howling loudly. Karlsefni and his men now hoisted red shields and advanced towards them.

When they clashed there was a fierce battle and a hail of missiles came flying over, for the Skraelings were using catapults. Karlsefni and Snorri saw them hoist a large sphere on a pole; it was dark blue in colour. It came flying in over the heads of Karlsefni's men and made an ugly din when it struck the ground.[11] This terrified Karlsefni and his men so much that their only thought was to flee, and they retreated farther up the river. They did not halt until they reached some cliffs, where they prepared to make a resolute stand.

Freydis came out and saw the retreat. She shouted, "Why do you flee from such pitiful wretches, brave men like you? You should be able to slaughter them like cattle. If I had weapons, I am sure I could fight better than any of you."

The men paid no attention to what she was saying. Freydis tried to join them but she could not keep up with them because she was pregnant. She was following them into the woods when the Skraelings closed in on her. In front of her lay a dead man, Thorbrand Snorrason, with a flintstone buried in his head, and his sword beside him. She snatched up the sword and prepared to defend herself. When the Skraelings came rushing towards her she pulled one of her

breasts out of her bodice and slapped it with the sword. The Skraelings were terrified at the sight of this and fled back to their boats and hastened away.

Karlsefni and his men came over to her and praised her courage. Two of their men had been killed, and four of the Skraelings, even though Karlsefni and his men had been fighting against heavy odds.

They returned to their houses and pondered what force it was that had attacked them from inland; they then realized that the only attackers had been those who had come in the boats, and that the other force had just been a delusion.

The Skraelings found the other dead Norseman, with his axe lying beside him. One of them hacked at a rock with the axe, and the axe broke; and thinking it worthless now because it could not withstand stone, they threw it away.

Karlsefni and his men had realized by now that although the land was excellent they could never live there in safety or freedom from fear, because of the native inhabitants. So they made ready to leave the place and return home. They sailed off north along the coast. They came upon five Skraelings clad in skins, asleep; beside them were containers full of deer-marrow mixed with blood. Karlsefni's men reckoned that these five must be outlaws, and killed them.

Then they came to a headland on which there were numerous deer; the headland looked like a huge cake of dung, for the animals used to spend the winters there.

Soon afterwards Karlsefni and his men arrived at Straumfjord, where they found plenty of everything.

According to some people, Bjarni Grimolfsson and Freydis had stayed behind there with a hundred people and gone no farther while Karlsefni and Snorri had sailed south with forty men and, after spending barely two months at Hope, had returned that same summer.

Karlsefni set out with one ship in search of Thorhall the Hunter, while the rest of the company stayed behind. He sailed north past Kjalarness and then bore west, with the land on the

---

[11]This device has been compared with the ballista which ancient traditions of the Algonquin Indians describe.

port beam. It was a region of wild and desolate woodland; and when they had travelled a long way they came to a river which flowed from east to west into the sea. They steered into the river mouth and lay to by its southern bank.

REVIEW QUESTIONS

1. What resources seemed most desirable or essential for the establishment of the colony? Explain your choices.
2. How would you describe the Norse encounters with the Skraelings? Did they change over time? (Compare the two accounts given here.)
3. What were the most serious problems that arose in the colony, other than the colonists' conflicts with Native Americans? Did the colonists solve these problems? How or why not?
4. What does the account of Freydis tell us about the role and power of women in this Norse community?

An Italian Explorer Describes the "New World" (1504)

AMERIGO VESPUCCI, *Letters from a New World*

Amerigo Vespucci is one of the most controversial characters in the history of European exploration. Some historians believe he was a charlatan who never even saw the New World, while others have considered him a great navigator and discoverer after whom America is appropriately named. He first went to sea in 1499, when he explored Brazil, and again in 1501, when he explored the east coast of South America. He seems to have had a good reputation among his peers until he began publishing an account of a voyage in 1497 that never took place. His false claim was first challenged by another noted story-teller, Sebastian Cabot, and later by Bartolomé de Las Casas. Nevertheless, the misunderstanding that Vespucci, not Columbus, discovered the mainland of Central America endured. By the time that most scholars had agreed that Columbus had reached the American mainland first, Vespucci's first name, in the form "America," was too well established to be changed to anything else.

The letter by Amerigo Vespucci included here is one of the most fascinating and important European descriptions of the New World. Unlike the reports of Columbus, who wrote for a queen (Isabel) whom he did not wish to offend, Vespucci wrote a detailed account of native sexual customs and other matters that appealed to the sixteenth-century reading public and that made his work a best-seller. Within a few years, some forty editions of the letter had been published in Latin, Italian, French, German, Flemish, and even Czech. Among those interested in and influenced by Vespucci's work was Martin Waldseemüller, a young professor of geography at Saint-Dié in

Lorraine. Waldseemüller was preparing a new edition of Ptolemy and printed a Latin translation of Vespucci's letter as an appendix to the work. He also placed the word *America* on South America in his 1507 map because he believed that the "fourth part of the world" had been discovered by "Americua" (Amerigo Vespucci). Thus the name *America* gradually worked itself onto sixteenth-century maps and, by midcentury, included North America. Spanish map-makers and writers, however, held out against the name for centuries, continuing to call the new World "Las Indias" (the Indies).

Not everything Vespucci wrote was false, however, or without value. He contributed much to the European understanding of Brazil. He was the first explorer of Central or South America to show any interest in or appreciation of native scenery, flora, and fauna. Most importantly, he carefully observed the human beings he encountered. In this selection, it is easy to see why European readers were fascinated by the vivid descriptions of Native Americans that Vespucci provided.

And the next day, at the crack of dawn, we saw countless people standing on the beach, and they had brought with them their women and children. We went ashore and found that all these women were laden with their provisions, which will be described in due course in this letter. And before we had reached land, many of them threw themselves into the sea and came swimming the distance of a crossbow shot to greet us, for they are quite excellent swimmers, and this trust of theirs was most gratifying.

What we came to know of their life and ways was that they go about completely naked, the men and as well as the women, without covering any shame, exactly as they emerged from their mothers' wombs. They are of medium stature, very well proportioned; their skin is a color that tends toward red like lion's fur, and I believe that if they went about clothed, they would be white like us. They have no hair on their body but for long black hair on their heads, the women especially, which makes them beautiful. They are not very fair of countenance, for they have broad faces somewhat reminiscent of the Tartars, they do not allow any hair to grow on their brows or eyelids, nor in any other part, except the head, because they consider bodily hair an ugly thing. They are very nimble in their walking and running, the men as well as the women, so that a women thinks nothing of running a league or two, for many times we saw them do just that,

and in this they have a very great advantage over us Christians. They swim unbelievably, and the women are better than the men, for many times we encountered and saw them swimming about two leagues out to sea without any support.

Their weapons are very well made bows and arrows, but for the fact that they do not have iron or any other sort of hard metal, and in place of iron they use the teeth of animals or fish, or a scorched twig of hard wood; they are sure bowsmen, striking where they aim, and in some parts the women also use these bows. They have other weapons, such as fire-hardened spears and other extremely well crafted clubs with heads. They make war with people who speak another language, and do so very cruelly, without sparing anyone's life, unless they keep them alive to inflict still greater suffering upon them. When they go to war, they take their women with them, not to make them fight but to carry the provisions, for a women carries a load upon her that a man could not bear, thirty or forty leagues, as we saw many times. They are not accustomed to having any captain, nor do they march in battle order, for each man is his own master. And the cause of their wars is not the desire to rule, or to extend their boundaries, or any inordinate greed, but merely an ancient enmity which has existed among them since olden times; and when we asked them why they warred, they could give no other reason than that they did it to avenge the death of their ancestors and their fathers. These people have neither king nor lord, nor do they obey anyone, for they live in their own liberty; and they are moved to go to war when the enemies have killed or captured one of them, and his eldest relative rises up and goes preaching through the streets that they should follow after him to avenge the death of that relative of his: and in this way they are moved to compassion.

They do not practice justice nor do they punish the wrongdoer, nor do father and mother punish their children, and rarely or never did we observe a quarrel take place among them. They appear to speak simply, and are very cunning and clever in the matters that concern them. They speak tersely, in a low voice; they have the same accentuation as we do, for they form their words either with the palate or with the teeth or the tongue, but they use other names for things. There are many different languages, for every hundred leagues we found the language change, each one mutually incomprehensible to the other.

Their way of life is very barbarous, for they do not eat at specific hours, but when and however often they want, and it matters little to them if their appetite comes at midnight rather than during the day, since they eat at all hours. And they eat on the ground without tablecloth or any other sort of napkin, for they have no such things; they keep their food in earthen bowls of their own manufacture, or in halves of gourds. They sleep in certain nets made of heavy cotton, very big and suspended in the air; and although this way of sleeping of theirs may seem bad, I can tell you that it is a good way to sleep, for countless times we happened to sleep in these nets, and we all slept better than on mattresses. They are clean and neat in their persons, for they are continually washing themselves. When they evacuate (with all respect) their bowels, they do their utmost not to be seen; and as neat and fastidious as they are in this, in making water they are filthy and shameless, the men as well as the women, for while standing and talking with us,

without turning away or showing shame they would release that foulness, since in this they have no shame whatsoever.

There are no marriages among them; each man takes as many women as he wants, and when he wishes to repudiate them, he does so, without it being deemed an injustice to him or a disgrace to the woman, for in this matter the woman has as much liberty as the man. They are not very jealous, and are inordinately lustful, the women much more than the men, though decency bids us pass over the wiles they employ to satisfy their inordinate lust. These women are very fertile women and their pregnancies do not exempt them from any work whatsoever; and their deliveries are so easy that a day after giving birth, they go out as usual, and especially to wash themselves in the river, and are fit as fish. They are so unmoved by love and so cruel that, if they grow angry with their husbands, they immediately make a potion with which to kill the child in their wombs and abort; and on this account they kill innumerable children. They are women of noble body, very well proportioned, for one does not find on their bodies any ill-formed member or thing; and although they go about completely naked, they are fleshy women, and one does not see that part of their shame which he who has not seen these women can imagine, for they cover everything with their thighs, except for that part for which nature did not provide, which is, to speak discreetly, the pubis: in conclusion, they are no more shamed by their shameful parts than we are in showing our nose or mouth. Seldom will you see sagging breasts on a woman, or a womb sagging from repeated childbirths, or other wrinkles, for they all seem as though they never gave birth. They showed themselves to be very desirous to copulate with us Christians.

We do not encounter among these peoples any who had a religion, nor can they be called Moors or Jews, and are worse than heathens, because we never saw them perform any sacrifice, nor did they have any house of prayer. I judge their life to be Epicurean.

Their dwellings are communal, and their houses are built like huts, but sturdily made and constructed out of very big trees and covered with palm leaves, safe from storms and winds, and in some places so wide and long that we found six hundred souls in a single house; and a village we saw had only thirteen houses in which dwelt four thousand souls. Every eight or ten years they change their villages, and asked why they put themselves to so much effort, they gave a natural answer: they said that they did this because of the soil, which, from too much filth, became infected and corrupted and caused illness in their bodies; which seemed to us a good reason.

Their wealth consists of birds' feathers of many colors, and strands of beads they make out of fish bones or white and green stones, which they hang from their cheeks and from their lips and ears, and many other things which we do not value at all. They do not engage in commerce, neither buying nor selling: in short, they live and content themselves with whatever nature gives them. The wealth to which we are accustomed in this Europe of ours and in other parts, such as gold, jewels, pearls, and other riches, are of no interest to them, although they have them in their lands, they neither labor to procure them, nor prize them. They are liberal in giving, and rarely deny you anything, and conversely are liberal in asking, once they have demonstrated that they are your friends; for the great token of friendship they will show you is to give you their women and their young daughters, and a father or mother who has brought you a daughter, even when she is a young virgin, deems it a great honor that you sleep with her; and in this they make the highest show of friendship.

When they die, they observe various forms of obsequies, and some are buried with water or food laid by their heads, since they think they will need to eat: they do not have or perform ceremonies with candles or lamentations. In some other areas they have the most barbarous and inhuman form of burial: which is that when one who is suffering or sick is almost at death's door, his relatives take him into a big forest, and set up between two trees one of those nets of theirs for sleeping, and they place him in it and dance around him for a whole day; and when night comes, they set water and various foods by his bedside, enough for him to maintain himself for four to six days, and then they leave him all alone and return to the village. And if the sick man helps himself and eats and drinks and survives, he returns to the village, and his relatives receive him with ceremony; but few survive in this fashion: without being further visited they die, and that is their burial. And they have many other customs which to avoid prolixity will not be mentioned.

In their sickness they use various types of medicine, so different from ours that we marvelled that anyone survived; for, many times I saw that they bathe a man sick with a rising fever from head to toe, after which they made a big fire around him, and turned him over again and again for two hours more, until, having tired him out they let him sleep; and thus many were cured. Along with this, they frequently practice fasting, for they go three days without eating, and also bloodletting, but not from the arm, rather from the thighs, the haunches, and the calves. Likewise they induce vomiting with herbs which they put in their mouth. And they use many other remedies it would take much time to relate.

They are far too phlegmatic and sanguine because of their food, which largely consists of roots, herbs, fruit, and fish. They do not have seeds for wheat or other grains, and for their usual eating fare they use the root a tree from which they make flour, rather good, which they call yucca, and other roots called cassava, and still others yams. They eat little meat, except for human flesh: for Your Magnificence must know that in this they are so inhuman that they surpass all bestial ways, since they eat all the enemies that they kill or capture, female as well as male, with such ferocity that merely to speak of it seems a brute thing—how much more to see it, as befell me countless times, in many places. And they marvelled to hear us say that we do not eat our enemies, and this Your Magnificence should believe for certain: their other barbarous customs are so many that speech fails to describe such facts.

REVIEW QUESTIONS

1. Is Vespucci's description of Native Americans a flattering one? Why or why not?
2. What aspects of Native American society seemed to interest Vespucci the most? What does this tell us about his values?
3. What were relations like between Native American men and women, according to Vespucci?
4. Using Vespucci as an example, how do you think Europeans defined the word *civilized*? Did Native Americans meet these criteria?

An Italian Voyager Describes South American Natives (1519–1522)

ANTONIO PIGAFETTA, *The First Voyage Around the World*

Historians usually date the beginnings of the European Age of Discovery from the Portuguese capture of Ceuta, on the North African coast opposite Gibraltar, in 1415. For the remainder of the fifteenth century, Portuguese explorers, initially inspired by Prince Henry the Navigator, slowly made their way down the west coast of Africa as they searched for a route to the Indies. In 1498 Bartolomeu Diaz rounded the Cape of Good Hope at the southern tip of the African continent, and a decade later Vasco da Gama traveled all the way to Calicut, in India. By 1513 the Portuguese had reached Canton. Moreover, under the leadership of Alfonso d'Albuquerque, the Portuguese established bases at Goa in India (1510), Malacca on the west coast of the Malay Peninsula (1511), and Ormuz in the Persian Gulf (1515). For most of the next century they dominated the sea routes in the South China Sea and Indian Ocean and between Asia and Europe.

Meanwhile, in 1492 Christopher Columbus, sailing for Spain, crossed the Atlantic to the Caribbean. In three subsequent voyages (1493–1504) he encountered most of the major Caribbean islands and part of the east coast of Central America. The Portuguese were concerned by Spain's entry into a field they considered their own, but a compromise was worked out. By the Treaty of Tordesillas (1494), Spain and Portugal divided the world by running an imaginary line north and south 370 leagues west of the Cape Verde Islands off the west coast of Africa. All new lands to the west of this line were to be Spain's; everything east of the line was to be Portugal's.

In 1517 the Portuguese explorer Ferdinand Magellan sold his services to the Spanish government, and in 1519 he set out to give practical proof to Spain's claim that the Spice Islands lay west of the line of demarcation established by the Treaty of Tordesillas—within the Spanish, not the Portuguese, hemisphere. After a dangerous journey around the southern tip of South America, through the straits that now bear his name, Magellan entered the Pacific Ocean and sailed west until he reached the Philippines. There, Magellan was killed, but his navigator took command and completed the first circumnavigation of the globe.

One important foreigner who joined Magellan's expedition as a volunteer was Antonio Pigafetta of Vicenza, in Lombardy (he appears on the crew list as "Antonio Lombardo"). Although he wrote one of the most famous and important exploration narratives of the sixteenth century, we have little knowledge of Pigafetta's life. He came to Spain with a papal ambassador and no doubt heard about the forthcoming expedition at court. He applied for and received permission from King Charles and the ambassador to sign up with Magellan. Pigafetta says he wanted experience and glory. In the following passage, he describes the "giants" that the expedition encountered. Because the natives' feet looked enormous, Magellan named them *patagóni* (big-foot), and his country, Patagonia.

The men and women are proportioned as we. They eat the human flesh of their enemies, not because it is good, but because it is a certain established custom. That custom, which is mutual, was begun by an old woman, who had but one son who was killed by his enemies. In return some days later, that old woman's friends captured one of the company who had killed her son, and brought him to the place of her abode. She seeing him, and remembering her son, she ran upon him like an infuriated bitch, and bit him on the shoulder. Shortly afterward he escaped to his own people, whom he told that they had tried to eat him, showing them [in proof] the marks on his shoulder. Whomever the latter captured afterward at any time from the former they ate, and the former did the same to the latter, so that such a custom has sprung up in this way. They do not eat the bodies all at once, but every one cuts off a piece, and carries it to his house, where he smokes it. Then every eight days, he cuts off a small bit, which he eats thus smoked with his other food to remind him of his enemies. The above was told me by the pilot, João Carvalho, who was with us, and who had lived in that land for four years.

Those people paint the whole body and the face in a wonderful manner with fire in various fashions, as do the women also. The men are smooth shaven and have no beard, for they pull it out. They clothe themselves in a dress made of parrot feathers, with large round arrangements at their buttocks made from the largest feathers, and it is a ridiculous sight. Almost all the people, except the women and children, have three holes pierced in the lower lip, where they carry round stones, one finger or thereabouts in length and hanging down outside. Those people are not entirely black, but olive-skinned. They keep the privies uncovered, and the body is without hair, while both men and women always go naked. Their king is called *cacich*. They have an infinite number of parrots, and gave us eight or ten for one mirror; and little monkeys that look like lions, only [they are] yellow, and very beautiful. They make round white [loaves of] bread from the marrowy substance of trees, which is not very good, and is found between the wood and the bark and resembles ricotta. They have swine which have their navels on their backs, and large birds with beaks like spoons and no tongues.

The men gave us one or two of their young daughters as slaves for one hatchet or one large knife, but they would not give us their wives in exchange for anything at all. The women will not shame their husbands under any considerations whatever, and according to what was told us, refuse to consent to their husbands by day, but only by night. The women cultivate the fields, and carry all their food from the mountains in panniers or baskets on the head or fastened to the head. But they are always accompanied by their husbands, who are armed only with a bow of brazil-wood or of black palmwood, and a bundle of cane arrows, doing this because they are jealous [of their wives]. The women carry their children hanging [in] a cotton net from their necks. . . .

At first those people thought that the small boats were the children of the ships, and that the latter gave birth to them when they were lowered into the sea from the ships, and when they were lying so alongside the ships (as is the custom), they believed that the ships were nursing them. One day a beautiful young woman came to the flagship, where I was, for no other purpose than to seek what chance might offer. While there and waiting, she cast her eyes upon the master's room, and saw a nail longer than one's finger. Picking it up most gracefully and gallantly, she trust it through the lips of her vagina, and bending down low immediately departed; the capital-general and I witnessed that action. . . .

We remained in that land for thirteen days. Then proceeding on our way, we went as far as 34 and ⅓ degrees toward the Antarctic Pole, where we found people at a freshwater river, called Cannibals, who eat human flesh. One of them, in stature almost a giant, came to the flagship in order to assure [the safety of] the others his friends. He had a voice like a bull. While he was in the ship, the others carried away their possessions from the place where they were living into the interior, for fear of us. Seeing that, we landed one hundred men in order to find an interpreter and converse with them, or to capture one of them by force. They fled, and in fleeing they took such large strides that we, although running, could not gain on them. There are seven islands in that river, in the largest of

which precious gems are found. That place is called the "Cape Santa Maria." It was formerly thought that one passed from there to the sea of *Sur,* that is to say the South Sea, but it was never further explored. Now the name is not [given to] a cape, but [to] a river, with a mouth seventeen leagues in width. A Spanish captain, named Juan de Solis, was eaten by these Cannibals because he trusted them too much, together with sixty men who were going to discover lands like us. . . .

Leaving that place, we finally reached 49 and ½ degrees toward the Antarctic Pole. As it was winter, the ships entered a safe port to winter [Port St. Julian]. We passed two months in that place without seeing anyone. One day we suddenly saw a naked man of giant stature on the shore of the port, dancing, singing, and throwing dust on his head. The captain-general sent one of our men to the giant so that he might perform the same actions as a sign of peace. Having done that, the man led the giant to an islet where the captain-general was waiting. When the giant was in the captain-general's and our presence he marveled greatly, and made signs with one finger raised upward, believing that we had come from the sky. He was so tall that we reached only to his waist, and he was well proportioned. His face was large and painted red all over, while about his eyes he was painted yellow; and he had two hearts painted on the middle of his cheeks. His scanty hair was painted white. He was dressed in the skins of animals skillfully sewn together. That animal has a head and ears as large as those of a mule, a neck and body like those of a camel, the legs of a deer, and the tail of a horse, like which it neighs, and that land has very many of them [the guanaco, a species of llama]. His feet were shod with the same kind of skins, and covered his feet in the manner of shoes. In his hand he carried a short, heavy bow, with a cord somewhat thicker than those of the lute, and made from the intestines of the same animal, and a bundle of rather short cane arrows feathered like ours, and with points of white and black flint stones in the manner of Turkish arrows, instead of iron. Those points were fashioned by means of another stone.

The captain-general had the giant given something to eat and drink, and among other things which were shown to him was a large steel mirror. When he saw his reflection, he was greatly terrified, and jumped back throwing three or four of our men to the ground. After that the captain-general gave him some bells, a mirror, a comb, and some beads and sent him ashore with four armed men. When one of his companions, who would never come to the ships, saw him coming with our men, he ran to the place where the others were, who came [down to the shore] all naked one after the other. When our men reached them, they began to dance and to sing, lifting one finger to the sky, and showing our men some white powder made from the roots of an herb, which they kept in earthen pots, and which they offered our men to eat because they had nothing else. Our men made signs inviting them to the ships, and that they would help them carry their possessions. Thereupon, those men quickly took only their bows, while their women laden like asses carried everything.

The latter are not so tall as the men but are very much fatter. When we saw them we were greatly surprised. Their breasts are one-half cubit long,* and they are painted and clothed like their husbands, except that before their privies they have a small skin which covers them. They led four of those young animals [the guanaco], fastened with thongs like a halter. When those people wish to catch some of those animals, they tie one of these young ones to a thornbush. Thereupon, the large ones come to play with the little ones; and those people kill them with their arrows from their place of concealment. Our men led eighteen of those people, counting men and women, to the ships, and they were distributed on both sides of the port so that they might catch some of those animals.

Six days later, a giant painted and clothed in the same manner was seen by some [of our men]

who were cutting wood. He had in his hand a bow and arrow. When he approached our men, he first touched his head, face, and body, and then did the same to our men, afterward lifting his hands toward the sky. When the captain-general was informed of it, he ordered him to be brought in the small boat, and he was taken to that island in the port where our men had built a house for the smiths and for the storage of some things from the ships. That man was even taller and better built than the others and as tractable and amiable. Jumping up and down, he danced, and when he danced, at every leap, his feet sank a palm's depth into the earth. He remained with us for many days, so long that we baptized him, calling him John. He pronounced the name *Jesus,* the *Pater Noster, Ave Maria* and his own name as distinctly as we, but with an exceedingly loud voice. Then the captain-general gave him a shirt, a woolen jerkin, cloth breeches, a cap, a mirror, a comb, bells, and other things, and sent him away to his companions. He left us very joyous and happy. The following day he brought one of those large animals to the captain-general, in return for which many things were given to him, so that he might bring some more to us; but we did not see him again. We thought that his companions had killed him because he had conversed with us.

After fifteen days we saw four of those giants without their weapons for they had hidden them in certain bushes, as the two whom we captured showed us. Each one was painted differently. The captain-general detained two of them, the youngest and best proportioned, by means of a very cunning trick, in order to take them to Spain. Had he used any other means [than those he employed], they could easily have killed some of us. The trick that he employed to capture them was as follows. He gave them many knives, scissors, mirrors, bells, and glass beads; and those two having their hands filled with those articles, the captain-general had two pairs of iron manacles brought, such as are fastened on the feet, and made motions as if to make a gift of them, at which they were very pleased, since those manacles were of iron, but they did not know

---

*A cubit is between 18 and 21 inches.

how to carry them. They were grieved at leaving them behind, but they had no place to put those gifts; for they had to hold the skin wrapped about them with their hands. The other two giants wished to help them, but the captain refused. Seeing that they were loath to leave those manacles behind, the captain made them a sign that he would put them on their feet, and that they could carry them away. They nodded assent with the head. Immediately, the captain had the manacles put on both of them at the same time. When our men were driving home the cross bolt, the giants began to suspect something, but the captain assuring them they nevertheless stood still. When they saw later that they were tricked, they raged like bulls, calling loudly for *Setebos* to aid them. Only with difficulty were we able to bind the hands of the other two, whom we sent ashore with nine of our men, so that the giants might guide them to the place where the wife of one of the two whom we had captured was; for the latter expressed his great grief at leaving her by signs so that we understood [that he meant] her. While they were on their way, one of the giants freed his hands, and took to his heels with such swiftness that our men lost sight of him. He went to the place where his associates were, but he did not find [there] one of his companions, who had remained behind with the women, and who had gone hunting. He immediately went in search of the latter, and told him all that had happened. The other giant endeavored so hard to free himself from his bonds, that our men struck him, wounding him slightly on the head, whereat he, snorting with rage, led them to where the women were. João Carvalho, the pilot and commander of those men, refused to bring back the woman that evening, but determined to sleep there, for night was approaching. The other two giants came, and seeing their companion wounded, hesitated, but said nothing then. But with the dawn, they spoke to the women; [whereupon] they immediately ran away (and the smaller ones ran faster than the taller), leaving all their possessions behind them. Two of them turned aside to shoot their arrows at our men. The other was leading away those small

animals of theirs in order to hunt. Thus fighting, one of them pierced the thigh of one of our men with an arrow, and he died immediately. When the giants saw that, they ran away quickly. Our men had muskets and cross-bows, but they could never wound any of the giants, [for] when the latter fought, they never stood still, but leaped here and there. Our men buried their dead companion, and burned all the possessions left behind by the giants. Truly those giants run swifter than horses and are exceedingly jealous of their wives.

When those people feel sick to their the stomachs, instead of purging themselves, they thrust an arrow down their throat for two span or more and vomit [a substance of a] green color mixed with blood, for they eat a certain kind of thistle. When they have a headache, they cut themselves across the forehead; and they do the same on the arms or on the legs and in any part of the body, letting a quantity of blood. One of those whom we had captured, and whom we kept in our ship, said that the blood refused to stay there [in the place of the pain], and consequently causes them suffering. They wear their hair cut with the tonsure, like friars, but it is left longer; and they have a cotton cord wrapped about the head, in which they stick their arrows when they go hunting. They bind their privies close to their bodies because of the exceeding great cold. When one of those people die, ten or twelve demons all painted appear to them and dance very joyfully about the corpse. They see that one of those demons is much taller than the others, and he cries out and rejoices more. They paint themselves exactly in the same manner as the demon appears to them painted. They call the larger demon *Setebos* and the others *Cheleulle.* The giant also told us by signs that he had seen the demons with two horns on their heads, and long hair which hung to the feet belching forth fire from mouth and buttocks. The captain-general called those people *Patagoni.* They all clothe themselves in the skins of that animal above mentioned; and they have no houses except those made from the skin of the same animal, and they wander here and there with those houses just as the gypsies do. They live on raw flesh and on a sweet root which they call *chapae.* Each of the two whom we captured ate a basketful of biscuit, and drank half a pail of water at a gulp. They also ate rats without skinning them. . . .

Each one of those people lives according to his own will, for they have no lords. They go naked, and some are bearded and have tangled black hair that reaches to the waist. They wear small palm-leaf hats, as do the Albanians. They are as tall as we, and well built. They worship nothing. They are olive-skinned, but are born white. Their teeth are red and black, for they think that is most beautiful. The women go naked except that they cover their privies with a narrow strip of bark as thin as paper, which grows between the tree and the bark of the palm. They are beautiful, delicately formed, and whiter than the men; they wear their hair which is exceedingly black, loose and hanging down to the ground. The women do not work in the fields but stay in the house, weaving mats, baskets, and other things needed in their houses, from palm leaves. They eat coconuts, potatoes, birds, figs one span in length [bananas], sugarcane, and flying fish, besides other things. They anoint the body and the hair with coconut and beneseed oil.

Their houses are all built of wood covered with planks and thatched with leaves of the fig-tree [banana-tree] two fathoms long; and they have wooden-beam floors and windows. The rooms and the beds are all furnished with the most beautiful palmleaf mats. They sleep on palm straw which is very soft and fine. They use no weapons, except a kind of spear pointed with a fishbone at the end. Those people are poor, but ingenious and very thievish, on account of which we called those three islands "the islands of Thieves." Their amusement is to go with their women upon the seas with those small boats of theirs. Those boats resemble *fucelere,* but are narrower, and some are black, [some] white, and others red. At the side opposite the sail, they have a large piece of wood pointed at the top, with poles laid across it and resting on the water, in order that the boats may sail more safely.

The sail is made from palmleaves sewn together and is shaped like a lateen sail. For rudders they use a certain blade like a baker's peel which has a piece of wood at the end. The stern can serve as the bow and the bow as stern, and those boats resemble the dolphins which leap in the water from wave to wave. Those thieves thought, according to the signs which they made, that there were no other people in the world but themselves. . . .

The king came with six or eight men in the same boat and entered the ship. He embraced the captain-general to whom he gave three porcelain jars covered with leaves and full of raw rice, two very large giltheads, and other things. The captain-general gave the king a garment of red and yellow cloth made in the Turkish fashion, and a fine red cap; and to the others [the king's men], to some knives and to others mirrors. Then the captain-general had a collation spread for them, and had the king told through the slave that he desired to be *casi casi* with him, that is to say, brother. The king replied that he also wished to enter the same relations with the captain-general. Then the captain showed him cloth of various colors, linen, coral [ornaments], and many other articles of merchandise, and all the artillery, which he had discharged for him, whereat some of the natives were greatly frightened. Then the captain-general had a man armed as a soldier, and placed him in the midst of three men armed with swords and daggers, who struck him on all parts of the body. Thereby was the king rendered almost senseless. The king told him through the slave that one of those armed men was worth one hundred of his own men. The captain-general answered that that was a fact, and that he had two hundred men in each ship who were armed in that manner. He showed the king cuirasses, swords, bucklers, and had a review made for him. Then he led the king to the deck of the ship, that is located above at the stern; and had his sea-chart and compass brought. He told the king through the interpreter how he had found the strait in order to voyage there, and how many moons he had been without seeing land, at which the king was astonished. Lastly, he told the king that he would like, if it were pleasing to him, to send two of his men to the king so that the king might show them some of his things. The king replied that he was agreeable, and I went in company of one other.

When I reached shore, the king raised his hands toward the sky and then turned toward the two of us. We did the same toward him as did all the others. The king took me by the hand; one of his more notable men took my companion: and thus they led us under a bamboo covering, where there was a *balanghai,* as long as eighty of my palm lengths, and resembling a *fusta.* We sat down upon the stern of that *balanghai,* constantly conversing with signs. The king's men stood about us in a circle with swords, daggers, spears, and bucklers. The king had a plate of pork brought in and a large jar filled with wine. At every mouthful, we drank a cup of wine. The wine that was left [in the cup] at any time, although that happened but rarely, was put into a jar by itself. The king's cup was always kept covered and no one else drank from it but he and I. Before the king took the cup to drink, he raised his clasped hands toward the sky, and then toward me; and when he was about to drink, he extended the fist of his left hand toward me (at first I thought that he was about to punch me) and then drank. I did the same toward the king. They all make those signs one toward another when they drink. We ate with such ceremonies and with other signs of friendship. I ate meat on Good Friday, for I could not do otherwise.

Before the supper hour I gave the king many things which I had brought. I wrote down the names of many things in their language. When the king and the others saw me writing, and when I told them their words, they were all astonished. While engaged in that, the supper hour, was announced. Two large porcelain dishes were brought in, one full of rice and the other of pork with its gravy. We ate with the same signs and ceremonies. Afterward we went to the palace of the king which was built like a hayloft and was thatched with fig and palm leaves. It was built up high from the ground on huge posts of wood and it was necessary to ascend to it by means of ladders. The king made us sit down there on a bamboo mat with our feet drawn up like tailors. After a half-hour a platter of roast fish cut in pieces was brought in, and ginger freshly gathered, and wine. The king's eldest son, who was the prince, came over to us, whereupon the king told him to sit down near us, and he accordingly did so. Then two platters were brought in (one with fish and its sauce, and the other with rice), so that we might eat with the prince. My companion became intoxicated as a consequence of so much drinking and eating. They used the gum of a tree called *anime* wrapped in palm or fig leaves for illumination. The king made us a sign that he was going to go to sleep. He left the prince with us, and we slept with the latter on a bamboo mat with pillows made of leaves. When day dawned the king came and took me by the hand, and in that manner we went to where we had had supper, in order to have breakfast, but the boat came to get us. Before we left, the king kissed our hands with great joy, and we his. One of his brothers, the king of another island, and three men came with us. The captain-general kept him to dine with us, and gave him many things.

REVIEW QUESTIONS

1. If you were to describe Pigafetta's description of the natives, what features, other than size, would you emphasize? Why?
2. What does Pigafetta's description of these natives tell you about the author's own values and beliefs?
3. How would you characterize the Europeans' treatment of the natives? What evidence in this selection supports your opinion?

An Italian Traveler Observes Native Society in Hispaniola (1541–1556)

GIROLAMO BENZONI, *History of the New World*

When twenty-one-year-old Girolamo Benzoni departed from his native Milan in 1541, he left a thriving trading city and intended to travel to the New World for adventure and fortune. After visiting the Antilles, Panama, Guatemala, and the west coast of South America, he returned in 1556, without riches but with a much greater knowledge of the American natives and of the Spanish activities in those regions. His *History of the New World,* from which this excerpt was taken, first appeared in Venice in 1565. Full of diatribes against Spain and its treatment of American Indians, the book found an eager audience among Spain's enemies. Several editions were published soon after the original, and it was translated into French and English as well as Latin. Spanish readers, of course, found great fault with the tone and content of the book.

The following passage relates Benzoni's visit to Hispaniola, the early center of Spanish control in the New World. As such, it reveals first of all that non-Spanish persons and traders, at least Catholic ones, did enter the closely held Spanish colonies with relative ease from this early date. Consequently, this account gives us an outsider's view of the Spanish administration of the islands. More important, however, Benzoni's observations of native life and customs seem to be amazingly accurate, and modern experts attest to the existence of the practices he describes. The cultivation and use of tobacco and of maize or corn appeared throughout the Americas in the early sixteenth century. Benzoni's description of the *iucca* root coincides with that of the maniac still eaten extensively in the Caribbean islands; in fact, Benzoni explains the native use of many indigenous foods that have become part of their culture.

Touching the religion, not only of this island, but also of all the other nations of the new world, they worshipped, and still worship, various deities, many painted, others sculptured, some formed of clay, others of wood, or gold, or silver; and in some places I have seen them of the shape of birds, of tigers, of stags, and other sorts of animals, but I have mostly seen them made with a tail and feet, like our Satan. And although our priests and monks have endeavoured, and still daily endeavour, to destroy these idols, yet the ministers of their faith keep a great many of them hidden in caves and underground, sacrificing to them occultly, and asking in what manner they can possibly expel the Christians from their country. They have a name for every one, regarding this as their patron on this subject, and that as their patron on that subject; as the Gentiles used to do in ancient times, assigning victories to Mars on earth, and on the sea to Neptune; medicine to Esculapius; Hercules presiding over temporal benefits, promising him a tenth part of their property, so that he might increase and take care of it. But this people only ask of their gods plenty to eat and drink, and good health, and victory over their enemies. Many times the devil appears to them in various shapes, promising to their ministers some of the things for which they have been entreated. And when he does not keep his promise and they complain, he answers, that he has changed his mind because they have committed some great sin; and thus the father of falsehood excuses himself. When the cacique of *La Española* wished to celebrate a feast in honour of his principal false deity, he commanded all his vassals, both men and women, to come to him on a certain day, and on arrival at the appointed spot, they ranged themselves in order. The cacique then advanced, and entered the temple where the ministers were dressing the idol. There he sat down, playing on a drum, and all the other people followed; first the men, painted black, red, and yellow, with plumes of parrots' and other feathers, with ornaments of sea-shells round their necks, their legs, and their arms. The women were not painted at all; the girls were quite naked; the married women had a covering hanging from their waist, as in the Gulf of *Paria,* and other places on the mainland. Thus they entered the temple, dancing and singing certain of their songs in praise of their idol, while their chief saluted them with his drum. Then, by putting a stick down their throat, they vomited, so that the idol might see they had nothing bad either in their stomach or their breast. After performing these foolish ceremonies, they all sat down on their heels, and, with a melancholy noise, they sang some more songs. Then some other women entered the temple with baskets adorned with roses and various flowers, and filled with bread, and they went round to all those who were singing, and repeated a little prayer to them. The singers jumped up on their feet to answer, and when they had finished these songs, they began others to the honour and glory of their chief; after which they presented the bread to their idol. The ministers now took and blessed it, and shared it with all the people, as if it was a holy thing or good relic. Finally, every man, highly elated and content, returned to his own home.

They thought that the sun and the moon came out of a cavern. They had a pumpkin as a relic, saying, that it had come out of the sea, with all the fish in it. They worshipped two wooden figures as the gods of abundance. And at some periods of the year many Indians went on a pilgrimage to them. They had also another idol made with four feet, like a dog, and they believed that when he was angry he went away to the mountains, where being found, they used to bring him back on their shoulders to the temple.

In this island, as also in other provinces of these new countries, there are some bushes, not very large, like reeds, that produce a leaf in shape like that of the walnut, though rather larger, which (where it is used) is held in great esteem by the natives, and very much prized by the slaves whom the Spaniards have brought from Ethiopia.

When these leaves are in season, they pick them, tie them up in bundles, and suspend them near their fire-place till they are very dry; and when they wish to use them, they take a leaf of their grain (maize) and putting some of the others into it, they roll them round tight together; then they set fire to one end, and putting the other end into the mouth, they draw their breath up through it, wherefore the smoke goes into the mouth, the throat, the head, and they retain it as long as they can, for they find a pleasure in it, and so much do they fill themselves with this cruel smoke, that they lose their reason. And there are some who take so much of it, that they fall down as if they were dead, and remain the greater part of the day or night stupified. Some men are found who are content with imbibing only enough of this smoke to make them giddy, and no more. See what a pestiferous and wicked poison from the devil this must be. It has happened to me several times that, going through the provinces of *Guatemala* and *Nicaragua,* I have entered the house of an Indian who had taken this herb, which in the Mexican language is called *tobacco,* and immediately perceiving the sharp fetid smell of this truly diabolical and stinking smoke, I was obliged to go away in haste, and seek some other place.

In *La Española* and the other islands, when their doctors wanted to cure a sick man, they went to the place where they were to administer the smoke, and when he was thoroughly intoxicated by it, the cure was mostly effected. On returning to his senses he told a thousand stories, of his having been at the council of the gods and other high visions. They then turn the invalid round three or four times, rubbing his back and loins well with their hands, making many grimaces at him, and holding a pebble or bone in their mouth all the time. These things the women keep as holy, believing that they aid child birth. If the sick man asks the doctor what will become of him, he answers that he will soon be free; and if he happens to die, they have many excuses at hand, the best of which is that he was mortal. If any doctor ventured to visit a sick man without the usual ceremonies he was severely punished. In all the provinces where I have been or that I have heard of, the priests are also doctors; so that probably it is the same all through these countries. They call them in their language *bocchiti;* and every where they have very great authority. But they generally doctor only the principal people.

The Indians take as many wives as they like, though one is the principal, and commands all the rest. When a cacique dies without heirs, the sons of his sisters succeed, but not those of his brothers; since they can depend on their being her sons, not so as to a man's supposed sons. The reason is, that in those countries there is very little chastity; and in few places are the girls or sisters attended to. They all sleep together like fowls, some on the ground and some suspended in the air. When the women have an infant, they carry it to the sea shore or to a river to wash it, and without any further ado they suckle their children.

Some say that these people were very great thieves, and that for every little fault their laws inflicted hanging; but what could they steal? They are neither avaricious nor rich, and what they least prized was gold and silver, since whoever wished for any could go to the mine and get as much as they liked, as people do at a spring of water. Respecting clothing, they all go naked;

and as to eatables, every body gives to whoever goes to his house. And whenever they assemble at their festivals, the whole tribe bring eatables, and they sing and dance till they get drunk and are tired; and so they freely pass a happy time. I cannot therefore imagine thieving among them, unless they learned the art from the first, second, and third inroads of the Spaniards, when they began to inhabit that country. Would to the Omnipotent God that temporal riches were respected by us as they are by them; the Christian name would be heavenly if avarice were banished.

The grain of these people is commonly called *maize,* and came from *La Española,* which island was first discovered by the Christians; wine is *chichia;* their boats, *canoue;* swords are *macanne;* their chiefs are *caciques.* They do not prepare the earth for sowing their grain, but making a small hole they put in three or four grains, and covering it over suffices; each stem produces three or four ears, containing about a hundred grains each. The stems of the maize are taller than a man, and in some provinces they harvest twice a year.

The women, *molandaie,* who grind it, wet a quantity of this grain the previous evening with cold water, and in the morning they gradually triturate it between two stones. Some stand up to it, others kneel on the ground; nor do they care if any hairs fall into it, or even some *pidocchi.* When they have made a mass by sprinkling in water with the hand, they shape it into little loaves, either long or round, and putting them into some leaves of reeds, with as little water as possible, they cook them. This is the common people's bread; it lasts two days and then mildews. The chief's bread is made in the following way: after soaking and triturating the corn between two stones, the *molandaie* wash it with hot water and pick out the husk, leaving only the flour, which they grind as much as they can and then shape it into small cakes. These are cooked in a round pipkin, applying fire under them by degrees. There is great trouble in making this bread, and it is not good but when fresh, and not very good then nor when cold; indeed, maize is not good either hot or cold. Travelling in uninhabited districts, and with necessity for my guide, I learned to grind it, in order not to eat it raw or roasted. On account of its great hardness the grinding is very severe work, and when I had but little maize I did not pick out the husks as the chief's people do; nor did grinding it fine suit my arms, that were very thin and weak.

They also make another sort of bread called *cazabi,* from a root named *iucca,* of the thickness of a parsnip. This root produces no seed at all, the stem is a thick knotty reed, its leaves are green and resemble those of hemp. At the proper season they cut these reeds into pieces two feet long, and plant them in heaps of earth called *conuchi,* and at the end of two years they form a large root. Whenever the natives wish to make any of this bread, they take up some of these roots (only a few at a time, as they soon spoil), they peel and cut them with sharp stones that they find on the beach, and putting them into a rag they squeeze out the juice, which would be poison to any one drinking it; then laying them on a great brick, like cakes of paste, they cook them on the fire, leaving them as long as they will hold together. Finally, they are put into the sun to dry. They make some thick and some thin. This to my taste was a wretched article of food, but if put into a dry place it would continue good for three or four years. The accompaniment of some moisture in the throat is requisite, else it is harsh and difficult to swallow. The taste seemed to me like earth in the mouth, but with the broth of meat it was better, though not much. All the ships coming to these countries from Spain (except those that go to Vera Cruz, a port of New Spain), lay in a provision of this bread for their return, as in none of the provinces or islands inhabited by the Spaniards in the Northern Sea is there a single grain of wheat. All flour and biscuit come from Mexico; it is brought thence on mules or in carts, a journey of about two hundred miles.

They have also two other sorts of roots, one called *battata,* the other *haie;* they are similar in form, except that the *haie* are smaller and better flavoured than the others. In six months after they are planted they yield fruit; the taste is rather sweet, but it soon satiates, and there is little substance in them. They generate windiness, and are commonly cooked in the embers. Some say that they taste like almond cakes, or sugared chesnuts; but, in my opinion, chesnuts even without sugar are better.

Since I have treated of the making of bread, I ought also to describe their making of wine, especially that from maize.

The *molandaie,* taking a quantity of grain that seems to them sufficient for the wine (or *chichia*) intended to be made, and having ground it, they put it into water in some large jars, and the women who are charged with this operation, taking a little of the grain, and having rendered it somewhat tender in a pipkin, hand it over to some other women, whose office it is to put it into their mouths and gradually chew it; then with an effort they almost cough it out upon a leaf or platter and throw it into the vase with the other mixture, for otherwise this wine, or rather this beverage, would have no strength. It is then boiled for three or four hours, after which it is taken off the fire and left to cool, when it is poured through a cloth, and is esteemed good in proportion as it intoxicates, in the same way as if people drank real wine.

They also make wines of other kinds, of honey, of fruits, and of roots, but these do not intoxicate as the first does. They have a great many plants that produce a sort of wild grapes, and their berries are like the sloes that grow among thorns, with black skins; but from the stone being large and surrounded by very little pulp, they do not make wine of them. There are some trees that produce olives, but smelling horribly and tasting worse. And they have other fruits in abundance, such as *houi,* plantains, pines, *guaiave* (guavas), *mamei* (*mammée apples*), and *guanavana* (sour-sops); the *houi* are like *scanari* (*Canary*) plums, with a large stone and little fruit; when ripe they are yellow. Its tree is large, the leaves small and taste acid. The plantain is a fruit much longer than it is broad, and the little ones (bananas) are much better than the large ones. The leaves are about a foot and a half broad and four feet long; among the leaves there rises a stem producing a hundred or more small plantains, or twenty-five or upwards of large ones. This is a tender tree; it does not yield fruit more than once, and requires a year; from the roots other plants shoot up; if the fruit is ripe they pluck it, but if not they cut the tree down, and by putting it into a hot place the fruit soon ripens and becomes yellow: the skin is as thick as the blade of a knife, the rest is all pulp; in flavour they incline to sweet. The pines grow in bushes; when ripe they are yellow; they smell well and taste better. They are high coloured, and it has happened to me, as to many others when ill, not to be able to eat anything without this fruit; indeed, in my opinion, it is one of the most relishing fruits in the world. When the skin is peeled off all the rest is eatable; they are generally sweet, with a little acidity. The guava is like a peach tree, with a leaf resembling the laurel, but larger and longer; it soon gets old; its fruit is like the medlar, though much larger; it ripens on the tree, and if not plucked when in season it generates worms. They have many small grains in them, the red are better than the white and are well flavoured. The *mamei* tree is the size of a moderate walnut, with a leaf longer than wide. In the *Española* island its fruit is round, but in general on the mainland it is long, more large, and better

flavoured. They contain three or four stones, the flesh is lion-coloured, the rind is thin, and the taste somewhat sweet. The *guananano* is a small and delicate tree; its fruit is shaped like a heart, with a thin green rind, formed like the scales of a fish. They are white within; but there is also another sort that is round and yellow, which is much better than the former and contains three small dark stones.

In none of these islands did they find any quadrupeds, except some small rabbits like dogs. There are some pestiferous *nigue*, insects like fleas, which live in the dust; unseen they insert themselves between the nail and the flesh; especially in the feet. It often happens that they occasion no pain till they are as large as flat peas or lentils; then they are picked out with a needle or a thorn, and are found full of knits. The wound is healed with hot ashes. And many black slaves, from going barefooted, get such numbers in their feet, that hot irons are the only things to extirpate them; and some people are permanently lamed by them. It also happened to me in Peru, in the province of Porto-Vecchio, after the very great fatigue that I had undergone both by land and sea, to be covered with the itch, body and legs; and in my feet I had so great a quantity of these *nigue* that I was frightened. And if I had not been very diligent in cleaning myself, and washing myself often in the rivers, I should indeed have fared very ill, as many Spaniards did; who, unwilling, from idleness, to wash themselves two or three times a day, became lame for life.

REVIEW QUESTIONS

1. Do you find any examples of Benzoni's prejudices about natives' custom and lives? What do these predetermined opinions, or the lack thereof, tell us about this Italian?
2. What customs and practices found in this passage would you expect to find as part of modern life? Explain.
3. How does Benzoni's description of native religious practices compare with those of earlier accounts in this chapter? How do they differ?
4. What was Benzoni's attitude toward the Spanish he observed in the Islands and in Meso-America?

A Spanish Clergyman Assesses Mayan Culture (c. 1566)

Fray Diego de Landa, *Relacíon de las Cosas de Yucatan*

Fray Diego de Landa's *Relación* is important because it provides the earliest accurate description of Mayan life from a missionary's point of view. Moreover, de Landa is the first Spaniard to recognize that the great architectural monuments found in the Yucatan were built by the Maya, rather than some other group. He came to this conclusion after living among the Maya for about two decades and learning their language. In addition to descriptions of native buildings, de Landa's *Relación* provides important information about the Mayan writing system, astrological number systems, social behavior and rituals, and the interaction between the Maya and the Spaniards.

As early as the 1550s, de Landa was trying to repair the damage he and other Spaniards had done to Mayan civilization by burning the sacred texts and destroying the religious buildings of the Maya people. When native resistence to Christian proselytizing led to the establishment of the Inquisition, resulting in the torture and killing of thousands of Maya, de Landa decided to act. He supervised the reconstruction of Mayan monasteries at Izabal and then began collecting Mayan oral histories and traditions. He combined these accounts with his own firsthand observations of Mayan culture to produce his *Relación.* As bishop of the Yucatan from 1571 until his death in 1579, de Landa played a crucial role in recording various aspects of Mayan life before the European encounter—while simultaneously helping to establish Spanish political rule in the Yucatan.

This excerpt presents de Landa's interpretation of the Mayan writing system using the Latin alphabet. His attempt is the earliest in the Yucatan and at the time was being replicated by other priests in Mexico City. These attempts to understand the Mayan writing system were part of the Spanish Catholic desire to convert the natives. Conversion, the Spaniards believed, would be easier if they understood more about the native civilization. This selection also contains information, including a diagram, about the Mayan temple at Izamal and details about the famous site at Chichen Itza. Finally, this reading includes a descriptive account of Mayan animals and food sources.

These people also made use of certain characters or letters, with which they wrote in their books their ancient matters and their sciences, and by these and by drawings and by certain signs in these drawings, they understood their affairs and made others understand them and taught them. We found a large number of books in these characters and, as they contained nothing in which there were not to be seen superstition and lies of the devil, we burned them all, which they regretted to an amazing degree, and which caused them much affliction. Of their letters I will give here an A, B, C, since their ponderousness does not allow anything more; for they use one character for all the aspirations of their letters and afterwards another for joining the parts together, and thus they go on doing *ad infinitum,* as can be seen in the following example: *Le* means a noose and to hunt with it; in order to write it with their characters, we having made them understand that there are two letters, they wrote it with three, putting as an aspiration of the *l*, the vowel, *e*, which it has before it; and in this way they are not mistaken, even though they should be employed in their skilful device, if they wish to. For example

e   l   e   lé

Then they add at the end, the part which is joined. *Ha* means water, and, because the sound of the letter H has *a h*, in front of it, they write it at the beginning with *a* and at the end in this way,

a   ha

They also wrote it in parts, but in both ways. I should not place it here nor should I treat it, except to give a full account of the affairs of this people. *Mainkati* means "I do not wish"; they write it in parts in this way:

ma   i   n   ka   ti

Here follows their a b c:

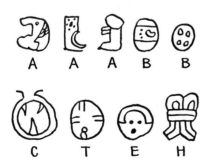

A   A   A   B   B

C   T   E   H

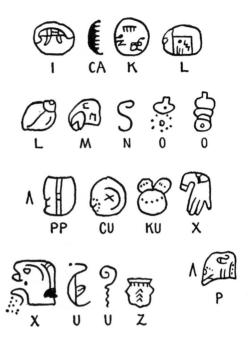

I   CA   K   L

L   M   N   O   O

PP   CU   KU   X

X   U   U   Z   P

This language is without the letters which are not given here, and it has others, which it has added from ours to represent other things of which it has need; but already they do not use at all these characters of theirs, especially the young people who have learned ours.

If Yucatan were to gain a name and reputation from the multitude, the grandeur and the beauty of its buildings, as other regions of the Indies have obtained these by gold, silver and riches, its glory would have spread like that of Peru and New Spain. For it is true that in its buildings and the multitude of them it is the most remarkable of all the things which up to this day have been discovered in the Indies; for they are so many in number and so many are the parts of the country where they are found, and so well built are they of cut stone in their fashion, that it fills one with astonishment. And as this country, although it is a good land, is not at present such as it appears to have been in the prosperous time, when so many and such remarkable buildings were built, without their having any kind of metal with which to build them, I will here give the reasons which I have

Poniente

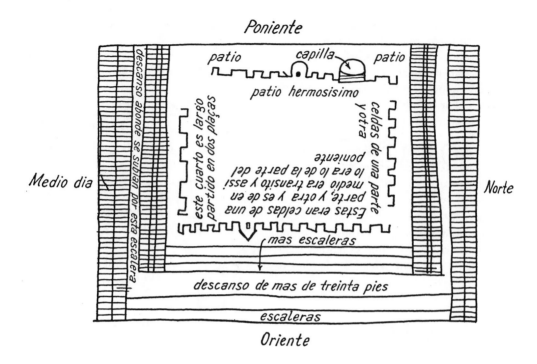

Medio dia

Norte

Oriente

heard advanced by those who have seen them. These reasons are that this nation must have been subject to certain lords, who were desirous of giving them constant occupation and that they occupied them in this work; or that, as they were such worshippers of their idols, they distinguished themselves by joining together in building temples for them. Or else it may be that the (large) towns changed their location for some reason, and so wherever they settled they always built anew their temples, sanctuaries and houses for their lords, according to their custom, and they have always used for themselves wooden houses covered with thatch; or again, it may be that the great abundance of stone and lime and of a white earth, excellent for building, which there is in this country, has given them an opportunity of erecting so many buildings, that except to those who have seen them, it will seem to be jesting to tell about them.

Or else this country hides some secret, which up to this time has not been discovered, nor have the natives of this day discovered it either, for to say that other nations, having subjected the Indians, have built these buildings, is not so, because of the indications that exist that the buildings were erected by a race of Indians and naked, as is seen, on one of the buildings, which in large numbers and of great size are found there on the walls of the bastions of which still remain representations of nude men, having their loins covered with long girdles which they call in their language *ex* and with other decorations which the Indians of these times still wear, all made of an extremely hard cement. . . .

The second buildings, of those which are the chief ones in this country, and so old that there is no memory of their founders, are those of Tihoo. They lie at thirteen leagues from Izamal and eight from the sea, as do the others, and there are signs today of there having been a very beautiful road from one (set of buildings) to the other. Here the Spaniards established a city, which they called Merida, on account of the singularity and size of the buildings; the principal one of which I will show here, as well as I can and as I did that of Izamal, so that what it is like can better be seen.

This is the sketch, which I have been able to make of the edifice. To understand it, it must be understood that it is a square of great size, as it has an extent equal to two runs of a horse. On the eastern side, the staircase starts at once from the ground. It has about seven steps of the same height of those at Izamal. The other faces on the south, west and north sides, are continued with a strong and very broad wall. Then that filling of the whole square is made of stone laid dry, and on its level surface another staircase begins (again) on the same eastern side, in my opinion, setting back toward the centre, twenty-eight or thirty feet, composed of just as many steps and of the same size as the others. It has the same setback on the south side and on the north and not on the west, and two strong walls are carried along until they meet or join the western wall of the square, and so they reach the height of the staircases, making all the filling in between consisting of stone laid dry, so that the height and size fill one with astonishment, as the filling there is artificial. . . .

Chichen Itza, then, is a very fine site, ten leagues from Izamal, and eleven from Vallodolid, in which, as the old men of the Indians say, three lords who were brothers ruled, who as they remember to have heard from their ancestors came to that country from the west, and brought together in those localities a great population of towns and peoples; whom they governed in great peace and justice for some years. They were devoted worshippers of their god; and so they erected many and magnificent buildings, and especially one, which was the largest, of which I will here give a sketch, as I drew it when I was there, so that it can be better understood. These lords lived, they say, without women and in perfect decorum and for all the time that they lived thus, they were held in great esteem and were obeyed by all. Afterwards, as time went on, one of them disappeared, who must have died although, the Indians say, he left the country in the direction of Bakhalal. His absence, however it may have occurred, was such a loss to those who ruled after him, that they at once began to be(come) partisan in the government and so dis-

solute and unbridled in their habits, that the people came to abhor them so greatly that they put them to death. They laid waste and abandoned the land, leaving their buildings, and the site (which is) very beautiful because it is only ten leagues from the sea. It has all around it very fertile lands and provinces. . . .

The Indians have been without many animals and especially have they lacked those which are most necessary for the service of man; but they had others, most of which they made use of for their sustenance and none of them was domesticated except the dogs, who do not know how to bark nor do harm to men, but in hunting it is otherwise for they raise partridges and other birds, follow deer a great deal and some of them are great trackers. They are small and the Indians ate them for their feast and now I think they are ashamed and consider it mean to eat them. They say that they have a good taste. There are tapirs in only one corner in the region which lies back of the mountains of Campeche and there are many of them and the Indians have told me that they are of many colors for there are silver gray, blossom colored, bay and chestnut and very white and black. They go more in that piece of land than in all the rest, since it is an animal very fond of water and in that region there are many lagoons in those woods and mountains. It is an animal of the size of medium sized mules, very fleet, and has a cloven hoof like the ox and a small proboscis on its snout in which it holds water. The Indians considered it an act of great bravery to kill them and the skin or parts of it lasted as a memorial down to the great grandsons as I have seen myself. They call it *tzimin* and from these they have given their name to horses. There are small lions and tigers and the Indians kill them with a bow, climbing up in the trees for this purpose. There is a certain kind of bear or something of the sort. It is wonderfully fond of stripping the hives. It is gray with black spots, long in body and short in legs and round in head. There is a certain kind of little wild goats, small and very active and of darkish color. There are hogs—small animals and very different from ours, for they have their naval on their backs and they stink badly. There are wonderfully many deer, and they are small and their flesh is good to eat. There is an infinite number of rabbits like ours in every respect except for the snout which is long and not at all blunt, but like a sheep. They are large and good to eat. There is a little animal, very sad by nature, which always goes in caverns and hiding places and by night, and for hunting it the Indians set a certain trap in which they catch it. It is like a hare and goes by leaps and is timid. It has very long and thin front teeth, and a little tail even smaller than a hare's, and is of a dark greenish color. It is wonderfully tame and amiable and is called *zub.* There is another little animal like a very small pig lately born, especially in its forefeet and snout, and it is a great rooter. This animal is all covered with pretty shells so that it looks very like a horse covered with armor, with only its ears and fore and hind feet showing and with its neck and forehead covered with the shells. It is very tender and good to eat. There are other animals like small dogs; they have heads of the shape of a hog's and a long tail and are of a smoky color and wonderfully slow, so much so that they often catch them by the tail. They are very gluttonous and go by night into houses, and no hen escapes their slow attack. The females bring forth fourteen and eighteen young like weasels, without any protection of hair and extremely torpid and God provided the mothers with a strange pouch in their abdomen in which they shelter them, since there grows all along the abdomen on each side over the teats a skin and when she joins the sides together the teats remain closed and when she wishes she opens it, and there each of the young receives the nipple of the teat, in its mouth; and when she has them all attached (in this way), she covers them with those flanks or skins and compresses them so closely that none of them falls out and thus loaded with them, she goes about there to search for food. Thus she rears them till they get hair and can walk alone. There are foxes, in everything like those here except that they are not so large nor do they have such a good tail. There is an animal which they call

chic, wonderfully active, as large as a small dog, with a snout like a sucking pig. The Indian women raise them and they leave nothing which they do not root over and turn upside down and it is an incredible thing how wonderfully fond they are of playing with the Indian women and how they clean them from lice and they always go to them and will have nothing to do with a man in their lives. There are many of them and they always go in herds in a row, one after the other, with their snouts thrust in each other's tails, and they destroy to a great extent the field of maize into which they enter. There is a little animal like a white squirrel with dark yellow stripes going around, which they call *pay;* he defends himself from those who follow or harm him by urinating, and that which he throws out is of such a horrible stink that there is no one who can endure it nor can anything on which it falls be worn again. They have told me that it is not urine, but a kind of sweat which he carries in a little bag behind. Be it what it may, its arms defend it so well that it is unusual for the Indians to kill one of them. There are many very pretty squirrels, and moles and weasels and many mice like those of Spain except that they have very long snouts.

The Indians have not lost but rather have gained much by the coming of the Spanish nation, even in matters of small moment, although it is of importance many things have been added to them which as time goes on they must inevitably come to enjoy, and they are already beginning to enjoy and use many of them. There are many good horses and many female and male mules; asses do not do well and I think that making much of them is the reason for it, since without fail they are strong beasts and indulgence harms them. There are many and very beautiful cows, many pigs, sheep, ewes, goats, and such dogs whose usefulness merits it, so that in the Indies they have to reckon it among the useful things. There are cats which are very useful and necessary there and the Indians are very fond of them. Hens, pigeons, oranges, limes, citrons, grapevines, pomegranates, figs, guava trees, date trees, bananas, melons and the rest of the vegetables, and only the melons and gourds are raised from their own seed, since for the others, fresh seed from Mexico is needed. Silk is now raised there and it is very good. Tolls have gone to them and the practical use of mechanical employments and they are adopting the use of them very well. The use of money and of many other things of Spain, which although they had got along and could get along without them, they live incomparably more like men with them and with greater aid in their bodily labors and in the alleviation of them, for according to the remark of the Philosopher (Aristotle?), "Art aids nature."

REVIEW QUESTIONS

1. How does de Landa's description of Native American life compare with that of Benzoni?
2. What generalizations can you make about Mayan civilization based on its architecture?
3. Does de Landa's account demonstrate a bias in favor of, or against, Native Americans? Why do you think so?
4. Did de Landa describe American animals realistically? Explain.

Web Resources

General History Sites

World History Archives

http://www.hartford-hwp.com/archives/index.html   Contains a collection of documents for teaching and understanding world history from a working-class perspective. It is associated with Gateway to World History, which offers general resources for the study of world history.

Internet History Sourcebook Project

http://www.fordham.edu/halsall/   Includes hundreds of excerpts from primary sources sorted by chronological period, area, and topic.

Exploring Ancient World Cultures

http://eawc.evansville.edu/index.htm   Includes an on-line textbook provided by the University of Evansville.

Diotima

http://www.stoa.org/diotima/   Includes materials for the study of women and gender in the ancient world, including images, excerpts from primary sources, on-line course materials, and scholarly articles (accepted only after peer review).

American History

General Site

http://www.academic.marist.edu/history/links/hisamer.htm

From Revolution to Reconstruction

http://odur.let.rug.nl/~usa/   A list of web sites on American history from the colonial period until modern times.

Women's Suffrage

http://www.history.rochester.edu/class/suffrage/home.htm

Cold War Links

http://www.stmartin.edu/~dprice/cold.war.html

The National Civil Rights Museum Web Site

http://www.civilrightsmuseum.org

The Vietnam War

http://www.historicaltextarchive.com

American Women's History

http://www.mtsu.edu/~kmiddlet/history/women/wom-mm.html

Distinguished Women of Past and Present

http://www.DistinguishedWomen.com/

European History

General Site

http://www.academic.marist.edu/history/links/hiseuro.htm

Worlds of Late Antiquity

http://ccat.sas.upenn.edu/jod/wola.html   A home page for miscellaneous materials relating to the culture of the Mediterranean world in late antiquity (roughly 200–700 C.E.).

Classics and Mediterranean Archaeology Home Page

http://rome.classics.lsa.umich.edu/welcome.html

The Ancient City of Athens

http://www.indiana.edu/~kglowack/athens/

Medieval & Renaissance Europe—Primary Historical Documents

http://library.byu.edu/~rdh/eurodocs/medren.html

Discoverer's Web Page

http://www.win.tue.nl/~engels/discovery/

Argos

http://argos.evansville.edu/   Provides a limited area search engine for information on ancient and medieval history and culture.

The Perseus Project

http://www.perseus.tufts.edu/   The best site on the web for Greek History. Also features images related to Roman history, with some Latin texts and their English translations.

The Ancient World Web

http://www.julen.net/ancient/   Provides links to over 1,100 web sites on ancient history.

Romarch

http://acad.depauw.edu/romarch/index.html   Emphasizes Roman art and archaeology. It also features the *Journal of Roman Archaeology*, a large index of maps, and an on-line discussion group.

Russian History

Russian History

http://www.academic.marist.edu/history/links/hisruss.htm   A general site for Russian history.

Russian History

http://www.departments.bucknell.edu/russian/chrono.html   Links major events in Russian history to explanatory and related materials on the web.

African History

General Site

http://www.historicaltextarchive.com

Africa, the Cradle of Civilization

http://library.thinkquest.org/C002739/index2.shtm

History of Africa's Countries-African Cultures

http://africancultures.about.com/culture/africancultures/library/extras/history/blhistory.htm

Internet Sites for the History of Africa

http://personal.ecu.edu/wilburnk/netah.htm

Latin American History

Lords of the Earth

http://www.mayaLords.org/#aztec   Deals with the archeology and anthropology of the Americas.

Asian History

Harappa

http://www.harappa.com/welcome.html

The Ancient Near East

http://eawc.evansville.edu/nepage.htm

Chinese History: To The Qing Dynasty

http://www.usc.edu/isd/locations/ssh/eastasian/toqing.htm

Chinese History

http://www.mrdowling.com/613chinesehistory.html

Other Related Chinese History Links

http://www.freesaves.com/china/related_links.htm

History of India

http://www.historyofindia.com/home.html

Information on India

http://adaniel.tripod.com/history.htm

East and Southeast Asia: An Annotated Directory of Internet Resources

http://newton.uor.edu/Departments&Programs/AsianStudiesDept/japan-history.html
General sources by region or country.

History on Film

Ancient History in the Movies

http:www.fordham.edu/halstall/ancient/asbookmovies.html.   Includes links to movie sites on medieval and modern history.

List of Sources

Chapter 1

P. 5: *Voices from Ancient Egypt: An Anthology of Middle Kingdom Writings,* by R.B. Parkinson. University of Oklahoma Press edition published by special arrangement with British Museum Press, London. Copyright © 1991 by R.B. Parkinson. All rights reserved. P. 7: Miriam Lichtheim, *Ancient Egyptian Literature: A Book of Readings,* Vol. I, pp. 54–55, 223–233. Copyright © 1973–1980 Regents of the University of California. Reprinted with permission of the University of California Press. P. 9: From *Myths of Mesopotamia: Creation, the Flood, Gilgamesh, and Others,* translated by Stephanie Dalley. Copyright © 1989 Stephanie Dalley. Reprinted by permission of Oxford University Press. P. 12: From *The Jerusalem Bible* by Alexander Jones, ed. Copyright © 1996 by Darton, Longman & Todd, ltd. and Doubleday, a division of Random House, Inc. Used by permission of Doubleday, a division of Random House, Inc. P. 18: Rig Veda/Yoga and Beyond: Essays in Indian Philosophy, by Georg Feuerstein and Jeanine Miller, (c) 1971, Ch. 3. P. 19: Birrell, Anne. *Chinese Mythology: An Introduction,* pp. 31–33, 147, 151, 153, 155, 156–157, 158–159. Copyright © 1993 Anne Birrell. Reprinted with permission of The Johns Hopkins University Press. P. 22: From *The Huarochiri Manuscript: A Testament of Ancient and Colonial Andean Religion,* translated and edited by Frank Salomon and George L. Urioste. Copyright © 1991. Reprinted by permission of the University of Texas Press. P. 24: From *The Hero with an African Face* by Clyde W. Ford. Copyright © 1999 by Clyde W. Ford. Used by permission of Bantam Books, a division of Random House, Inc. P. 29: Reprinted with permission from *Myths and Legends of Australia,* by A.W. Reed, Reed New Holland Publishers. P. 31: Reprinted with permission from *Journey to Sunrise: Myths and Legends of the Cherokee.* Copyright © 1977 by Maxine Lowrey.

Chapter 2

P. 35: From Sabatino Mascati, *The Face of the Ancient Orient.* Copyright © 1962, Dover Publications, Inc. P. 37: Reprinted by permission of the publishers and the Trustees of the Loeb Classical library from *Livy, Book I,* translated by B.O. Foster, Cambridge, Mass.: Harvard University Press, 1919. The Loeb Classical Library ® is a registered trademark of the President and Fellows of Harvard College. P. 41: Reprinted by permission of the publishers and the Trustees of the Loeb Classical library from *Dio Cassius,* Vol. VIII, LCL #176, translated by Earnest Carey, Cambridge, Mass.: Harvard University Press, 1925. The Loeb Classical Library ® is a registered trademark of the President and Fellows of Harvard College. P. 45: By Prince Ilango Adigal. Translated by Alain Daniélou, from *Shilappadikaram,* copyright © 1965 by Alain Daniélou. Reprinted by permission of New Directions Publishing Corp. P. 53: Reprinted with the

permission of Simon & Schuster Adult Publishing Group from *Popol Vuh* by Dennis Tedlock. Copyright © 1985, 1996 by Dennis Tedlock. P. 60: Hawaiian runner defeats death. Ahu Ula: The First Feather Cloak, in *Legends of the South Seas* by Antony Alpers, pp. 262–268.

Chapter 3

P. 65: Miriam Lichtheim, *Ancient Egyptian Literature: A Book of Readings.* Copyright © 1973. Reprinted by permission of the University of California Press. P. 72: From *The Jerusalem Bible* by Alexander Jones, ed. Copyright © 1996 by Darton, Longman & Todd, ltd. and Doubleday, a division of Random House, Inc. Used by permission of Doubleday, a division of Random House, Inc. P. 75: From *The Voyage of Argo* (the Argonautica) by Apollonius of Rhodes, translated by E.V. Rieu. Translation copyright © 1950 by E.V. Rieu. Reprinted by permission of Penguin Books, Ltd. P. 78: From Jeannette Mirsky, ed., *The Great Chinese Travelers.* Copyright (c) 1964. P. 81: From *American Indian Mythology,* by Alice Marriott and Carol K. Rachlin. Copyright © 1968. Reprinted by permission of the author. P. 86: From the book *A Treasury of African Folklore* by Harold Courlander. Copyright © 1996 by Harold Courlander. Appears by permission of the publisher, Marlowe & Company.

Chapter 4

P. 94: From *Thucydides: History of the Peloponnesian War,* translated by Rex Warner. Translation copyright © 1954 by Rex Warner. Reprinted by permission of Penguin Books, Ltd. P. 99: Reprinted by permission of the publishers and the Trustees of the Loeb Classical library from *Cornelius Nepos,* LCL #467, translated by J.C. Rolfe, Cambridge, Mass.: Harvard University Press, 1929. The Loeb Classical Library ® is a registered trademark of the President and Fellows of Harvard College. P. 103: From Juvenal, *The Sixteen Satires,* translated by Peter Green. Translation copyright © 1967, 1974 by Peter Green. Reprinted by permission of Penguin Books, Ltd. P. 107: Reprinted by permission of the publishers and the Trustees of the Loeb Classical library from *Polybuis: Vol. II,* LCL #138, translated by W.R. Paton, Cambridge, Mass.: Harvard University Press, 1923. The Loeb Classical Library ® is a registered trademark of the President and Fellows of Harvard College. P. 110: Melinno, "Hymn to Rome," trans. Diane J. Raynor. Copyright © 1991. P. 111: Julius Caesar, *The Gallic War,* trans. H. J. Edwards (London: W. Heinemann; New York: Putnam) Copyright © 1918. pp. 249, 251, 253, 255. P. 113: Fan Yeh, "The Hou-han-shu." *China on the Roman Orient.* Copyright © 1939. pp. 40–43. P. 116: Reprinted by permission of the publishers and the Trustees of the Loeb Classical library from *Tacitus: Vol. I,* LCL #35, translated by M. Hutton, Cambridge, Mass.: Harvard University

Press, 1914. The Loeb Classical Library ® is a registered trademark of the President and Fellows of Harvard College. P. 121: Reprinted by permission of the publishers and the Trustees of the Loeb Classical Library from *Ammianus Marcellinus: Volume III*, Loeb Classical Library, Volume L 331, translated by J.C.Rolfe, pp. 381–387, Cambridge, Mass.: Harvard University Press, 1939. The Loeb Classical Library® is a registered trademark of the President and Fellows of Harvard College.

Chapter 5

P. 126: From *The Jerusalem Bible* by Alexander Jones, ed. Copyright © 1996 by Darton, Longman & Todd, ltd. and Doubleday, a division of Random House, Inc. Used by permission of Doubleday, a division of Random House, Inc. P. 129: The Monolith Inscription of Shalmaneser III (860–824 B.C.) from *Assyrian and Babylonian Literature: Selected Translations* (New York: D. Appleton and Company) Copyright © 1904. pp. 33–36, 38–44. P. 135: From *The Jerusalem Bible* by Alexander Jones, ed. Copyright © 1996 by Darton, Longman & Todd, ltd. and Doubleday, a division of Random House, Inc. Used by permission of Doubleday, a division of Random House, Inc. P. 136: From *The Histories,* by Herodotus, translated by Aubrey de Sélincourt, revised by John Marincola. Translation copyright © 1954 by Aubrey de Sélincourt. Revised edition copyright © John Marincola, 1996. Reprinted by permission of Penguin Books, Ltd. P. 139: From *Persian Expedition,* translated by Rex Warner. Copyright © 1949 by Rex Warner. Reprinted by Permission of Penguin Books Ltd. P. 143: From Jeannette Mirsky, ed., *The Great Chinese Travelers*. Copyright (c) 1964. P. 147: Reprinted from *Egeria's Travels*, trans. John Wilkinson. Copyright © 1971. Reprinted with permission of the Society for Promoting Christian Knowledge.

Chapter 7

P. 162: From *The Histories,* by Herodotus, translated by Aubrey de Sélincourt, revised by John Marincola. Translation copyright © 1954 by Aubrey de Sélincourt. Revised edition copyright © John Marincola, 1996. Reprinted by permission of Penguin Books, Ltd. P. 166: *Egyptian Literature. Volume II: Annals of Nubian Kings* by E. A. Wallis Budge (London: Kegan Paul, Trench, Trübner & Co., Ltd.). Copyright © 1912. pp. 89–104. P. 172: As appeared in *Archaeology and the Bible* by George A. Barton. P. 174: Reprinted by permission of the publishers and the Trustees of the Loeb Classical library from *Aristotle: Vol. XXI, LCL, #264,* trans. H. Rackham, Loeb Classical Library, Cambridge, Mass.: Harvard University Press, 1932. The Loeb Classical Library ® is a registered trademark of the President and Fellows of Harvard College. P. 178: Reprinted by permission of the publishers and the Trustees of the Loeb Classical library from *Pliny: Vol. I, LCL #330,* trans. H. Rackham, Loeb Classical Library, Cambridge, Mass.: Harvard University Press, 1938. The Loeb Classical Library ® is a registered trademark of the President and Fellows of Harvard College. P. 180: From *The Ethiopian Royal Chronicles,* Addis Ababa. Copyright (c) 1967. Published by Oxford University Press, East Africa. P. 183: Reprinted by permission of the publishers and the Trustees of

the Loeb Classical library from *Procopius: Vol. II, LCL #81,* trans. H. B. Dewing, Loeb Classical Library, Cambridge, Mass.: Harvard University Press, 1916. The Loeb Classical Library ® is a registered trademark of the President and Fellows of Harvard College.

Chapter 8

P. 187: From McCrindle's *Ancient India as Described by Megasthenes and Arrian.* Copyright © 1972. P. 189: From *The Mahabharata*, translated by J.A.B. van Buitenen. Copyright (c) 1975 University of Chicago Press. Reprinted with permission of the University of Chicago Press. P. 199: Casson, Lionel, trans., *The Periplus Maris Erythraei.* Copyright © 1989 by Princeton University Press. Reprinted with permission of Princeton University Press. P. 204: From *A Record of Buddhist Kingdoms,* trans. James Legge. Copyright © 1965. Reprinted by permission of Dover Publications, Inc.

Chapter 9

P. 209: Reprinted with the permission of The Free Press, an imprint of Simon & Schuster Adult Publishing Group, from *Chinese Civilization and Society: A Sourcebook,* edited by Patricia Buckley Ebrey. Copyright © 1981 by The Free Press. P. 213: Reprinted with the permission of The Free Press, an imprint of Simon & Schuster Adult Publishing Group, from *Chinese Civilization and Society: A Sourcebook,* edited by Patricia Buckley Ebrey. Copyright © 1981 by The Free Press. P. 216: The Japanese, from *Ch'en Shou: The Japanese in the Essence of Chinese Civilization,* ed. Dun J. Li, (c) 1967, pp. 220–223. P. 223: Reprinted from *The Golden Khersonese* by Paul Wheatley. Copyright © 1961. Reprinted by permission of the University of Malaya Press. P. 226: From Buddhist Records of the Western World, translated by Samuel Beal. P. 229: From *Anthology of Japanese Literature,* edited by Donald Keene. Copyright © 1955 by Grove Press, Inc. Used by permission of Grove/Atlantic, Inc.

Chapter 10

P. 238: From *Journal of English and Germanic Philology.* Copyright © 1923 by the Board of Trustees of the University of Illinois. Used with permission of the University of Illinois Press. P. 242: From *Islam: From the Prophet Muhammad to the Capture of Constantinople, Volume 2: Religion and Society,* edited by Bernard Lewis, translated by Bernard Lewis. Copyright © 1987 by Bernard Lewis. Used by permission of Oxford University Press. P. 246: From *An Arab-Syrian Gentleman and Warrior in the Period of the Crusades: Memoirs of Usamah Ibn-Maunqidh,* translated by Phillip K. Hitti. Copyright © 1929 by Columbia University Press. Reprinted with permission of the publisher. P. 251: From *Other Middle Ages: Witnesses at the Margins of Medieval Society,* edited by Michael Goodrich. Copyright © 1998 University of Pennsylvania. Reprinted with permission. P. 254: *University Records and Life in the Middle Ages,* from Lynn Thorndike, ed. Copyright © 1944 by Columbia University Press. Reproduced with permission of Columbia University Press via Copyright Clearance Center. P. 258: *The Memories of Dona Leonor Lopez de Cordoda,* translated by Kathleen Lacey. Copyright ©